Constructions of Deviance

Social Power, Context, and Interaction

SEVENTH EDITION

PATRICIA A. ADLER
University of Colorado

PETER ADLER
University of Denver

WADSWORTH
CENGAGE Learning

Australia • Brazil • Japan • Korea • Mexico • Singapore • Spain • United Kingdom • United St

WADSWORTH
CENGAGE Learning

Constructions of Deviance: Social Power, Context, and Interaction, Seventh Edition
Patricia A. Adler, Peter Adler

Publisher/Executive Editor: Linda Schreiber-Ganster

Acquisitions Editor: Erin Mitchell

Development Editor: Liana Sarkisian

Editorial Assistant: Mallory Ortberg

Marketing Manager: Andrew Keay

Marketing Communications Manager: Tami Strang

Content Project Management: PreMediaGlobal

Senior Art Director: Caryl Gorska

Manufacturing Buyer: Karen Hunt

RAS, Text: Roberta Broyer

RAS, Image: Roberta Broyer

Production House/Compositor: PreMediaGlobal

Cover Image: Malcolm Tarlofsky

Library of Congress Control Number: 2010937598

Student Edition:

ISBN-13: 978-1-111-18637-1

ISBN-10: 1-111-18637-5

Wadsworth
20 Davis Drive
Belmont, CA 94002
USA

Cengage Learning is a leading provider of customized learning solutions with office locations around the globe, including Singapore, the United Kingdom, Australia, Mexico, Brazil, and Japan. Locate your local office at **www.cengage.com/global**

Cengage Learning products are represented in Canada by Nelson Education, Ltd.

To learn more about Wadsworth Cengage Learning, visit **www.cengage.com/wadsworth**

Purchase any of our products at your local college store or at our preferred online store **www.cengagebrain.com**

Printed in the United States of America
1 2 3 4 5 6 7 15 14 13 12 11

To Diane and Dana
Who remind us that the zest of life lies near the margins

and

To Chuck
Who brings out the deviance in everyone

and

To John
Who showed us the miracle of life and rebirth

and

To Jane
Who lives the ordinary as deviant

and

To Dubs and Linda
Who remind us what friends are for

and

To Lois and David
Who allowed our nephews their independence to be deviant

and

To Marc
Who taught us that dreams can come true

Contents

Preface

Can you remember all the way back to the year 2009? It was the year that the United States inaugurated its first multi-racial president, a seeming impossibility just a few years earlier. That same year, Michael Jackson, pop icon, passed away, and more stories of his bizarre exploits came to light. Tiger Woods, the reigning "athlete of the decade," before then considered a virtual "choir boy" was "outed" as a philanderer and sex addict, despite the appearances of a happy marriage and two children. A couple in Colorado faked the disappearance of their young son in an airborne balloon to get television coverage, while he turned out to be hiding in the basement the whole time. Similarly, an uninvited couple crashed a White House state dinner in their attempt to get on a reality show. Piracy flourished off the Somali coasts, capturing huge cargo ships and obtaining millions in ransom. All-star athletes, such as Alex Rodriguez, admitted to cheating in their sport by using performance-enhancing drugs. The Mexican-American border became a war zone, as rival drug cartels fought for power and control over the multi-billion dollar illicit drug industry. In at least five states and the District of Columbia, same-sex marriages became legal and medical marijuana dispensaries sprang up around the nation. At one of our schools, the University of Denver, cigarette smoking was forbidden *anywhere* on campus, while merely five miles away, the restaurant "Ganga Gourmet," was opened where anyone with a state medical marijuana license could order pot-laced food such as lasagna, hummus, pizza, ice cream, and cheesecake. Yes, it was quite a year!

Deviance is ubiquitous; it is all around us. Turn the pages of your local newspaper, check out your favorite current events Web sites, listen to people talk in your gym locker room, and invariably they will be discussing the latest fads, the newest forms of transgressing the norms, and the ways we continue to push the boundaries of society's expectations. Contrary to what one pundit claimed in the 1990s, deviance is far from dead, but rather flourishing like never before. In the three years since the sixth edition of this book was released, we were able to find more than 75 pertinent scholarly articles related to the sociology of deviant behavior. An embarrassment of riches, they made it difficult to choose among them, to select pieces that you, our readers, would find most interesting, fascinating, and relevant. It is within this context that the seventh edition of *Constructions of Deviance* was born. This book is a labor of love for us as we tweak each edition, remain in touch with the changing nuances in the field, and present to our audience what we feel is the most exciting research in the sociology of deviant behavior today.

As the shifting sands of morality in American society continue to transform our culture, deviance and its changing definitions are at the fore. More than 40 years ago, Gusfield (1967) showed us that with continuous social change, activities that were considered nondeviant a generation ago can take on deviant characteristics (cigarette smoking, distracted driving), whereas activities that were once deviant are now acknowledged as commonplace (tattooing and piercing). For better or worse, rapid social change is occurring in front of our eyes. Against this backdrop, this is a fabulous time to study the varying definitions of deviant behavior and the subsequent consequences for individuals and society. It is our hope that this seventh edition of *Constructions of Deviance* incorporates some of this field's highlights. We want to show the liveliness of the debates, the graphic images that sociologists paint, and the wide array of activities that fall under the domain of deviance.

NEW TO THIS EDITION

In all of this book's editions, we have tried to keep pace with the transformations that have occurred in the research on deviant behavior. Despite the fact that some have decried the theoretical and empirical death of deviance, we had a surfeit of research from which to choose. Our difficulty lay not in finding new pieces, but in winnowing down our selections to the space available. We wanted to keep some basics the same, as they have come to represent the core of the book, while at the same time infusing it with an insurgence of new material. We are pleased to offer you, then, the best of the old and a spate of exciting fresh selections.

New to this volume are chapters on why some issues become "moral panics" and others do not; the unequal and discriminatory treatment that police give young, black men and women in inner cities; the stigma of White Power activists; the relationship between licit (Adderall, Ritalin) and illicit (cocaine, methamphetamine) drugs and eating disorders among college women; the hierarchy of meth-cooking subcultures; a glimpse into the lives of crack whores; the voluntary "enslavement" of men who subject themselves to humiliation, degradation, and impoverishment by Internet dominatrixes in exchange for sexual titillation; new opportunities for white-collar crime (particularly relevant in light of the infamous Madoff $65 billion Ponzi scheme); and people's obstacles to shedding emotional disorder identities.

Further, due to the popular demand of our reviewers and students and their renewed relevance in the world, we have reprised some articles from previous editions of this book, such as on gay male Christian couples and international organized crime. Relatively new pieces that have quickly become students' favorites remain, such as the continuing debates (relativism vs. absolutism) over the definitions of deviance, rationalizations used by shoplifters to neutralize their deviance, the negative connotations faced by male cheerleaders, the stigma management strategies of homeless children, the corrupt complicity between the United States government and Halliburton Corporation, sexual asphyxia, the sexual assault and the party scene on campus, and people's decision to commit burglary. Some of the most popular, now classic, pieces still continue to be relevant, such as the social construction of drug scares, the status battles over smoking, homophobia in women's sport, becoming bisexual, anorexia and bulimia, rapists' rationalizations, women in gangs, pimp-controlled prostitution, and drug dealers and smugglers' attempts to get out of the business.

We have continued to amend the Part Introductions and the synopses that introduce each selection. In fact, we have added a considerable amount of new text to these sections so that this book can be used as either a stand-alone text-reader or easily synthesized with existing standard textbooks. As this book has gone through its various transformations, it has been our intent to convert it into more of a text in its own right, an anthology of empirical works with scholarly commentary from the framing discipline of sociology. We recommend that you take a close look at these new sections.

As from the beginning, the book still proudly represents the social constructionist approach, building upon our own intellectual backgrounds in symbolic interactionism and ethnographic research. As such it retains its vibrant appeal, offering the most contemporary empirical readings that are drawn from qualitative studies rich in experiential descriptions of deviance from the everyday life perspective. At the same time, the book has increasingly incorporated more classical and mainstream theoretical and innovative methodological elements.

We offer this collection as a testimonial to the continuing vibrancy of deviance research. Our sense is that there has never been a better time to study these phenomena and to look at the changes they represent about society. Above all else, we hope that you find the readings enjoyable, enlightening, and thought-provoking.

ACKNOWLEDGMENTS

By now literally thousands of students have been exposed to these readings and have been christened into the sociology of deviance. Many people provided critical feedback that has helped us in fashioning this latest edition. First and foremost are our many students, particularly in Patti's class, "Deviance in U.S. Society," at the University of Colorado, attracting more than 500 each semester, and in Peter's class, "Deviance and Society," at the University of Denver. These intrepid souls continue to brave the material and exams in this course, despite its reputation as among the toughest on each campus. Extra thanks and acknowledgments go to the valiant Assistant Teaching Assistants (ATAs) at the University of Colorado who have dedicated two semesters of their lives to this class to personalize it for other students, to keep the exams hilarious and topical as well as challenging, and to form a cohesive working group. These students have provided us with a template of what contemporary collegians desire, do, and dream about. They remind us of the diversity of sentiments—moral and immoral, normative and deviant, radical and conservative—that exist.

There have been some special people, such as Julia Cantzler, Tim Carpenter, Katherine Coroso, Marci Eads, Marc Eaton, Abby Fagan, Molly George, Tamera Gugelmeyer, Joanna Gregson, Paul Harvey, Tom Hoffman, Katy Irwin, Jennifer Lois, Adina Nack, Patrick O'Brien, Joe Settle, Katie Sirles, Jesse Smith, Jennifer (Skadi) Snook, Sarah Sutherland, John Tribbia, and Zek Valkyrie, who have provided much of the impetus for the changes and amendments we have made throughout. Our friends in the discipline continue to suggest studies, to supply encouragement, and to lend support for our endeavors. Whether through a quick conversation in a hallway or at a convention hotel, an e-mail message, a lengthy letter, or a harangue over the telephone, they remind us that we should keep the edge and continue to search for the latest examples to hold their students' interest.

We have been extremely fortunate to get sets of constructive comments from the reviewers Thomson Wadsworth (now Cengage) has commissioned over the years. For this edition, we are pleased to thank Amanda Burnam, University of Oklahoma; Kate Luther, Pacific Lutheran University; Dr. Patricia H. O'Brien, Elgin Community College; Rebecca Plante, Ithaca College; Donald Stewart, University of Nevada, Las Vegas; Elizabeth Wissinger, Borough of Manhattan Community College. Previous editions received helpful comments from Ken Colburn, Butler University; Kim Davies, Augusta State University; Phil Davis, Georgia State University; Jackie Eller, Middle Tennessee State University; Kerry Ferris, University of California, Los Angeles; Lara Foley, University of Tulsa; Kathryn Fox, University of Vermont; Scott Hunt, University of Kentucky; Phyllis Kitzerow, Westminster College, Teresa Lagrange, Cleveland State University; Matt Lee, University of Delaware; Jay Livingston, Montclair State University; Dorothy Pawluch, McMaster University; Barbara Perry, Northern Arizona University; Paul Price, Pasadena City College; Angus Vail, Willamette University; Aimee van Wagenen, Boston College; James L. Williams, Texas Woman's University; Thomas C. Wilson, Florida Atlantic University; and E. Ernest Wood, Edinboro University of Pennsylvania. The original project received helpful comments from Tom Cook, Wayne State College; William M. Hall, Alfred University; John D. Hewitt, Northern Arizona University; Ruth Horowitz, University of Delaware; Phyllis Kitzerow, Westminster College; and Michael Nusbaumer, Indiana University-Purdue University at Fort Wayne.

The stalwart staff at Thomson Wadsworth (Cengage) has provided unending support during the process of revisions and custom editions. We are fortunate to have worked with such diligent professionals as Matt Ballantyne, Tali Beesley, Paula Begley-Jenkens, Linda deStefano, Halee Dinsey, Jerilyn Emori, Peggy Francomb, Wendy Gordon, Jane Hetherington, Jennifer Jones, Bob Jucha, Bob

Kauser, Ari Levenfeld, Kristin Marrs, Lin Marshall, Andrew Ogus, Reilly O'Neal, Michael Ryder, Erica Silverstein, Denise Simon, Steve Spangler, Jennifer Walsh, Jay Whitney, Staci Wolfram, Matthew Wright, Dee Dee Zobian, and Beth Zuber. Special commendation must go to Eve Howard, our senior editor who worked hand-in-hand with us since the second edition until she left the company this past year, and Serina Beauparlant, the editor who originally conceived the project. More recently, we have had the distinct pleasure to have as part of our team Chris Caldeira, our acquisitions editor, and Michelle Williams, marketing director, shepherding us through the entire production project from reviews to book covers. Our developing friendship with Chris and Michelle made the work on the last couple of editions especially rewarding. They have both moved on to other venues, but their contributions are enduring. For this edition, we are pleased to welcome Erin Mitchell and Liana Sarkisian to our team, and in the short time we have worked with them we can already see that they will have similar impacts as our previous editors and production assistants.

One of the pleasures of editing this book has been sharing it with our friends and relatives. We started a tradition with our first edition, which we have continued throughout all, of dedicating each volume to a different person or couple who has had a meaningful impact on our lives inside and outside the academy. We respectfully dedicated the first edition to our partners in crime, Diane Duffy and Dana Larsen, the second edition to our dear and enduring friend Chuck Gallmeier, the third edition to the implacable John Irwin, the fourth edition to our intimate friend of almost forty years, Jane Horowitz, the fifth edition to neighbors and compadres Linda and Dubs Jacobsen, and the sixth edition to Lois and David Baru, our sister and brother-in-law. For this seventh edition, it is our distinct pleasure to dedicate the book to Marc Taron, architect extraordinaire, brother-in-arms, and the solid foundation of our social network in our new home, Maui. Sadly, this book is also in memory of our dear friend and dedicatee of the third edition, the late John Irwin, who passed away in the first days of 2010, but whose integrity, vitality, professionalism, and honesty will live on forever through the many people he touched in his 80 years on earth. Finally, our children, Jori and Brye, keep us young with their irrepressible energy, enthusiasm, and zest for life. To all our readers of previous editions, thanks for the support; to the new readers of this seventh edition, welcome to the journey. A special note of thanks goes to Divya Divakaran of PreMediaGlobal, who despite some personal turmoil during the production of this book, worked tirelessly and efficiently to make sure that deadlines were met and that the book was uniform and correct. In addition, the copy-editor for PreMediaGlobal was careful and professional every step of the way. Any errors that might appear remain ours, with apologies.

About the Editors

Patricia A. Adler (Ph.D., University of California, San Diego) is Professor of Sociology at the University of Colorado. She has written and taught in the area of deviance, qualitative methods, and the sociology of children. A second edition of her book, *Wheeling and Dealing* (Columbia University Press), a study of upper-level drug traffickers, was published in 1993. She has received many honors, including the Outstanding Teacher in the Faculty of Arts and Sciences, and the Outstanding Researcher Award from the University of Colorado. In addition, Patti was awarded the Mentor Excellence Award in 2004 from the Society for the Study of Symbolic Interaction (SSSI).

Peter Adler (Ph.D., University of California, San Diego) is Professor of Sociology and Criminology at the University of Denver. His research interests include social psychology, drugs and society, and sociology of work, sport, and leisure. His first book, *Momentum*, was published in 1981 by Sage. Peter has been honored with the University Lecturer Award and as the Outstanding Scholar/Teacher at the University of Denver, as well as being named by the Society for the Study of Symbolic Interaction (SSSI) as Mentor of the Year in 2005.

Together the Adlers served as Co-Presidents of the Midwest Sociological Society from 2006-2007. They have edited the *Journal of Contemporary Ethnography* and were the founding editors of *Sociological Studies of Child Development*. In 2010, the third edition of their anthology, *Sociological Odyssey*, was published by Wadsworth Cengage, and in 2001, they released *Encyclopedia of Criminology and Deviant Behavior*, Volume 1, co-edited with Jay Corzine. In addition to publishing over one hundred journal articles, chapters in books, and book reviews, among their many books are *Membership Roles in Field Research*, a treatise on qualitative methods published by Sage in 1987, *Backboards and Blackboards*, a participant-observation study of college athletes that was published by Columbia University Press in 1991, *Peer Power*, a study of the culture of elementary schoolchildren that was published by Rutgers University Press in 1998, and *Paradise Laborers*, a study of hotel workers in Hawai'i, published in 2004 by Cornell University Press. Their current project, *The Tender Cut*, focuses on self-injurers (cutters and burners) and is forthcoming with NYU Press. Peter and Patti divide their time between their homes in Boulder, Colorado, and Maui, Hawai'i.

About the Contributors

Elizabeth A. Armstrong is Associate Professor of Sociology at the University of Michigan. Her research interests include sociology of culture, social movements, sexuality, gender, and higher education. She is the author of *Forging Gay Identities: Organizing Sexuality in San Francisco, 1950–1994* (University of Chicago Press 2002). She is currently working on a book (with Laura Hamilton) exploring the relationship between college peer culture and social inequality.

Howard S. Becker lives and works in San Francisco. He is the author of *Outsiders, Arts Worlds, Writing for Social Scientists*, and *Tricks of the Trade*. He has taught at Northwestern University and the University of Washington. In 1998, the American Sociological Association bestowed upon him the Career of Distinguished Scholarship Award, the association's highest honor.

Michelle Bemiller received her Ph.D. in sociology from the University of Akron in 2005. She is now an Assistant Professor of Sociology at Kansas State University. Her interests include the sociology of deviant behavior, criminology, sociology of gender, and sociology of the family. Currently, she is completing research that examines nontraditional mothers' (e.g., incarcerated mothers, noncustodial mothers) experiences with motherhood. She is also researching sexual assault and domestic violence shelter workers' experiences with occupational burnout.

Douglas J. Besharov, a lawyer, is the Joseph J. and Violet Jacobs Scholar in Social Welfare Studies at the American Enterprise Institute for Public Policy Research and Professor at the University of Maryland School of Public Policy. There, he directs the university's Welfare Reform Academy and teaches courses on family policy, welfare reform, evaluation, and the implementation of social policy. He was the first director of the U.S. National Center on Child Abuse and Neglect. Among his publications is *Recognizing Child Abuse: A Guide for the Concerned* (Free Press).

Joel Best is Professor of Sociology and Criminal Justice at the University Delaware. His books include *Threatened Children* (1990), *Random Violence* (1999), *Damned Lies and Statistics* (2001), *Deviance: Career of a Concept* (2004), and *Social Problems* (2007).

Elaine M. Blinde is Professor and Chair of the Department of Kinesiology at Southern Illinois University–Carbondale. Her research relates to sociological analysis of sport, with a particular focus on gender issues. Recent work and publications relate to disability and sport, gender beliefs of young girls, and women's relationship to baseball.

Rod Brunson is an Associate Professor in the Department of Criminology and Criminal Justice at Southern Illinois University–Carbondale. His research examines youths' experiences in neighborhood contexts, with a specific focus on the interactions of race, class, and gender, and their relationship to criminal justice practices. Dr. Brunson's work appears in the *British Journal of Criminology, Criminology, Criminology & Public Policy, Justice Quarterly, Sociological Quarterly,* and *Urban Affairs Review.* He earned his Ph.D. in Criminal Justice at the University of Illinois–Chicago in 2003.

Robert G. Carlson is a Professor in the Wright State University Boonshoft School of Medicine, Department of Community Health, and Director of the Center for Interventions, Treatment and Addictions Research. He received his Ph.D. in cultural anthropology from the University of Illinois at Urbana–Champaign in 1989 for field research on the production and use of banana beer among the Haya of Northwest Tanzania. Since 1989, Dr. Carlson has conducted ethnographic research on HIV risk behaviors, epidemiologic trends, and health services use among injection drug and other non-medical drug users in Ohio. Currently, he is Principal Investigator of NIH-funded studies on pharmaceutical opioid misuse and a clinical trial comparing a chronic disease model of addiction treatment and outpatient treatment as usual. His research interests include ethnographic methods, the epidemiology of non-medical drug use, natural history research, AIDS prevention, health services research, and political economy.

William J. Chambliss is Professor of Sociology at George Washington University. He is the author and editor of over twenty books, including *Law, Order and Power* (with Robert Seidman); *On the Take: Petty Crooks to Presidents*; *Organizing Crime*; *Exploring Criminology*; *Boxman: A Professional Thief's Journey* (with Harry King); *Crime and the Legal Process*; *Making Law* (with Marjorie S. Zatz); and most recently an introductory text, *Sociology* (with Richard P. Applebaum). He is the past president of the Society for the Study of Social Problems and the American Society of Criminology. He is currently writing a book on the political economy of piracy and smuggling.

Meda Chesney-Lind is Professor of Women's Studies at the University of Hawai'i at Manoa. Nationally recognized for her work on women and crime, her books include *Girls, Delinquency and Juvenile Justice, The Female Offender, Girls, Women, and Crime, Female Gangs in America, Invisible Punishment*, and *Beyond Bad Girls*. She has just finished an edited volume that attempts to make sense of girls' violence entitled *Fighting for Girls: New Perspectives on Gender and Violence*.

Terry Cluse-Tolar received her MSW and Ph.D. in Social Work from Ohio State University. She is currently Associate Professor and Chair of the Social Work Department at the University of Toledo.

Donald R. Cressey was Professor of Sociology at the University of California, Santa Barbara, when he died in 1987. His most well-known publications include *Principles of Criminology* (with Edwin H. Sutherland), *Other People's Money*, and *Theft of the Nation*. Cressey received many honors for his research and teaching, and he cherished none more than the Edwin H. Sutherland Award presented by the American Society of Criminology in 1967.

Paul Cromwell is Professor of Criminal Justice at Wichita State University. He received his Ph.D. in Criminology from Florida State University in 1986. His publications include 16 books and over 50 articles and book chapters. Recent publications include *Breaking and Entering: Burglars on Burglary* (with James Olson), *In Their Own Words: Criminals on Crime*, and *In Her Own Words: Women Offenders Perspectives on Crime and Victimization* (with Leanne Alarid). He has extensive experience in the criminal justice system, including service as Parole Commissioner and Chairman of the Texas Board of Pardons and Paroles.

Scott H. Decker is Professor and Director in the School of Criminology and Criminal Justice at Arizona State University. He received the B.A. in social justice from DePauw University, and the M.A. and Ph.D. in criminology from Florida State University. His main research interests are in the areas of gangs, juvenile justice, criminal justice policy, and the offender's perspective. His books include *European Street Gangs and Troublesome Youth Groups* (winner of the American Society of Criminology, Division of International Criminology Outstanding Distinguished Book Award, 2006) and *The International Handbook of Juvenile Justice* (Springer-Verlag, 2006). His most recent books are *Drug Smugglers on Drug Smuggling: Lessons from the Inside* (Temple University Press 2007) and *Criminology and Public Policy* with Hugh Barlow (Temple University Press 2010).

Douglas Degher is Professor of Sociology at Northern Arizona University. His primary interests are in deviance, theory, and the sociology of sport. Recent work focuses on identity change as well as work on the construction of tragedy as a means of social control. When time permits he travels on his motorcycle, which is becoming more and more often.

Paul J. Draus is an Associate Professor of Sociology and Health Policy Studies in the Department of Behavioral Sciences at the University of Michigan-Dearborn.

He earned his Ph.D. from Loyola University Chicago in 2001. From 1992 until 2000 he was a public health field worker, specializing in tuberculosis control, first in New York City and then in Chicago. He is the author of *Consumed in the City: Observing Tuberculosis at Century's End* (Temple University Press 2004), which was based on his dissertation research. He has also published numerous articles on health issues, behaviors, and social contexts related to substance abuse in rural areas. His current research focuses on social networks and work patterns among daily heroin users, former street sex workers, and returning citizens or ex-offenders in the city of Detroit.

Emile Durkheim (1858–1917) was a French sociologist who is generally considered to be the father of sociology. His major works are *Suicide, The Rules of Sociological Method, The Division of Labor in Society,* and *The Elementary Forms of Religious Life.*

Keith Durkin is Chair of the Department of Psychology and Sociology at Ohio Northern University. His major areas of research interest are cybercrime and deviance. His work has appeared in a variety of journals such as *Deviant Behavior, Federal Probation, Journal of Offender Rehabilitation,* and *Seminars in Integrative Medicine,* as well as a number of edited volumes including *Extreme Deviance, Readings in Deviant Behavior, Theories of Deviance, Deviance and Social Control, Encyclopedia of Criminology and Deviant Behavior,* and *Net.sexxx.*

Oskar Engdahl is Associate Professor and Director for the Master program in Criminology at the Department of Sociology, University of Gothenburg. He received his Ph.D. in sociology in 2003 with a thesis on the development of tax havens and their connections to economic crime. His recent research focuses on the motivation, opportunity, and control of crime in banking and finance.

Kai T. Erikson is Professor Emeritus of Sociology and American Studies at Yale University. He is the author of several books, including *Wayward Puritans; Everything in Its Path;* and *A New Species of Trouble.* He served as President of the American Sociological Association, the Society for the Study of Social Problems, and the Eastern Sociological Society.

Robert Futrell is an Associate Professor of Sociology at the University of Nevada, Las Vegas. He specializes in social movements, environmental sociology, sociology of science and technology, and sustainability. He has published widely on the white power movement, science and technology controversy, and environmental sustainability in the American Southwest. He is coauthor with Pete Simi of the book, *American Swastika: Inside the White Power Movement's Hidden Spaces of Hate.*

John H. Gagnon was Professor of Sociology at the State University of New York, Stony Brook until 1998. He is the author or coauthor of such books as

Sex Offenders; Sexual Conduct, Human Sexualities; and *The Social Organization of Sexuality.* In addition, he has been the coeditor of a number of books, most recently *Conceiving Sexuality* and *Encounter with AIDS: Gay Men and Lesbians Confront the AIDS Epidemic,* as well as the author of many scientific articles.

Roy Godson is Professor of Government at Georgetown University and President of the National Strategy Information Center. He has served as consultant to the president's Foreign Intelligence Advisory Board, the National Security Council, and related agencies of the U.S. government. He has written, coauthored, or edited over sixteen books on intelligence and national security. His most recent books include *Dirty Tricks or Trump Cards: US Covert Action and Counterintelligence; Menace to Society: Political-Criminal Collaboration Around the World; Strategic Denial and Deception: The Twenty-First Century Security Challenge; Organized Crime and Democratic Governability: Mexico and the US-Mexican Borderlands; Security Studies for the Twenty-First Century.*

Laura Hamilton is a doctoral student in Sociology at Indiana University Bloomington. Her dissertation explores how parental financial investment shapes college students' experiences and achievement. She is author of "Adoptive Parents, Adaptive Parents" (*American Sociological Review* 2007, with Simon Cheng and Brian Powell), "Trading on Heterosexuality" (*Gender & Society* 2007), and "Gendered Sexuality" (*Gender & Society* 2009, with Elizabeth Armstrong).

Alex Heckert is Professor of Sociology at Indiana University of Pennsylvania. Most of his published research has been in the areas of family sociology, deviance, and medical sociology. Recent research in the areas of domestic violence has attempted to improve prediction of nonphysical abuse and physical reassault among batterer program participants. He has published in journals such as *Social Forces, Journal of Research in Crime and Delinquency, Journal of Marriage and the Family, Demography, Journal of Family Issues, Rural Sociology, Family Relations, Violence and Victims, Journal of Family Violence, Journal of Interpersonal Violence,* and *The Sociological Quarterly,* among others.

Druann Maria Heckert received her M.A. from the University of Delaware and her Ph.D. from the University of New Hampshire. She teaches at Fayetteville (NC) State University. Her research is in the areas of stigmatized appearance, positive deviance, and deviance theory, and her articles have appeared in journals such as *Deviant Behavior, The Sociological Quarterly, Symbolic Interaction,* and *Free Inquiry in Creative Sociology.*

Anne Hendershott is Head of the Politics, Philosophy, and Economics Program at The King's College, New York City. Dr. Hendershott received her Ph.D. in urban sociology from Kent State University. Her research interests focus on the role of religion and natural law as constraints to engaging in deviant behavior. Her most recent books include *The Politics of Deviance* (Encounter Books), *The Politics of Abortion* (Encounter Books), and *Status Envy* (Transaction).

Travis Hirschi received his Ph.D. in Sociology from the University of California, Berkeley. He is currently Regents Professor Emeritus at the University of Arizona. He served as President of the American Society of Criminology and has received that Society's Edwin H. Sutherland Award. His books include *Delinquency Research* (with Hanan C. Selvin); *Causes of Delinquency*; *Measuring Crime* (with Michael Hindelang and Joseph Weis); and *A General Theory of Crime* (with Michael R. Gottfredson). His most recent book is a coedited volume with Michael Gottfredson, *The Generality of Deviance*.

Malcolm D. Holmes is a Professor of Sociology at the University of Wyoming. His research primarily analyzes the relationships of race/ethnicity to criminal justice outcomes. His recent book, *Race and Police Brutality: Roots of an Urban Dilemma* (with Brad W. Smith), examines the social-psychological dynamics underlying the use of excessive force by the police. Currently he is engaged in empirical and theoretical research projects that investigate the causes of various forms of extra-legal police aggression.

Jenna Howard received her Ph.D. from Rutgers University and was the recipient of the ASA social psychology section award for 2008. She is currently a research analyst with the Department of Family Medicine, University of Medicine and Dentistry of New Jersey-Robert Wood Johnson Medical School. Her research interests revolve around the social psychology of individual and organizational change.

Gerald Hughes is Emeritus Professor of Sociology at the University of Northern Arizona. His primary interests are in identity theory, with the most recent work focusing on the organizational promotion of permanent deviant identities.

Phillip Jenkins was educated at Cambridge University, where he obtained his doctorate in History. Since 1980, he has taught at Penn State University, where he holds the rank of Edwin Erle Sparks Professor of the Humanities. He is also a Distinguished Senior Fellow at Baylor University's Institute for Studies of Religion. He has published 24 books, including *The New Faces of Christianity: Believing the Bible in the Global South* (2006) and *God's Continent: Christianity, Islam and Europe's Religious Crisis* (2007, both from Oxford University Press). His latest book is *The Lost History of Christianity* (HarperOne, 2008)

Robert Jenkot is an Assistant Professor in the Department of Sociology at Coastal Carolina University. He earned his doctorate on the interaction of Illinois University-Carbondale. His research led and deviant behavior. He race, class, and gender as they interact with deviants overcome the is also keenly interested in the way that zation in order to take part moral and ethical boundaries learned through illicit drug use among in non-conforming behavior. Currently allow the concealed carry of college students as well as social firearms on college campuses.

Peter Kaufman is Associate Professor of Sociology at the State University of New York at New Paltz. He received his B.A. from Earlham College and his Ph.D. from Stony Brook University. His teaching and research interests include education, critical pedagogy, symbolic interaction, and the sociology of sport.

Edward O. Laumann is the George Herbert Mead Distinguished Service Professor in the Department of Sociology and the College at the University of Chicago. Previously he has been Editor of the *American Journal of Sociology* and Dean of the Social Sciences Division and Provost at the University of Chicago. Two volumes on sexuality were published in 1994: *The Social Organization of Sexuality* and *Sex in America,* and along with Robert Michael, he has recently published *Sex, Love, and Health: Private Choices and Public Policy* (University of Chicago Press 2001).

Lisa Laumann-Billings completed her doctorate work in developmental and clinical psychology at the University of Virginia. She has worked and published in the areas of divorce, family conflict, and child maltreatment for the past 10 years. She is currently working with Dr. David Olds at the Prevention Research Center in Denver, Colorado on preventative strategies for reducing child maltreatment and family violence in high-risk families.

John Liederbach is Associate Professor of Criminal Justice at Bowling Green State University. His primary research interests are in the areas of white-collar and professional crime, as well as police behavior and the study of community-level influences on officer activities and citizen interactions.

Joseph Marolla is Vice Provost for Instruction, Professor of Sociology, and affiliated with the Sports Management Program at Virginia Commonwealth University. He is conducting research in the sociology of sport and continues to remain interested in the social construction of deviance.

Daniel Martin teaches and conducts research in the areas of community, critical organizational studies, and social movements at the University of Minnesota-Duluth. His present project is on the state suppression of dissent, interviewing police and protesters about their roles in the demonstrations during the 2008 Republican National Convention. He is the recipient of multiple teaching awards, including the Pan Hellenic Award for Outstanding Professor.

Penelope A. McLorg has a Ph.D. in anthropology and is Director of the Gerontology Program at Indiana University–Purdue University Fort Wayne. She specializes in biological and sociocultural aspects of aging, with particular interests in health and of Mexico and in the position, glucose metabolism. Dr. McLorg has conducted research in rural areas and has published on such topics as body composition, bone loss, eating disorders, and physical disability.

Robert T. Michael is the Eliakim Hastings Moore Distinguished Professor and Dean Emeritus of the Harris School of Public Policy at the University of Chicago. From 1984 to 1989 he served as Director of the National Opinion Research Center (NORC).

Stuart Michaels served as Project Manager of the National Health and Social Life Survey (NHLS).

Jody Miller is Professor of Criminology and Criminal Justice at the University of Missouri, St. Louis. Dr. Miller's research focuses on gender, crime, and victimization, particularly in the contexts of urban communities and the commercial sex industry. She has published numerous articles, as well as the monographs *One of the Guys: Girls, Gangs and Gender* (Oxford University Press 2001) and *Getting Played: African American Girls, Urban Inequality, and Gendered* (New York University Press 2008).

William J. Olson is Professor at the Near East and South Asia Center for Strategic Studies at the National Defense University. He has been Staff Director for the Caucus on International Narcotics Control for the U.S. Senate. Previously, he was Deputy Assistant Secretary of State in the Bureau of International Narcotics Matters. He was also Director and served as Acting Deputy Assistant Secretary of Defense for Low Intensity Conflict. His published works include books and articles on U.S. strategic interests in the Persian Gulf, guerilla warfare, counterinsurgency, and the war on drugs.

Devah Pager is Associate Professor of Sociology at Princeton University. Her research focuses on the social and economic consequences of mass incarceration, with a particular emphasis on how our crime policies contribute to enduring racial inequality. Using an experimental field methodology, Pager's research uncovers the hidden world of employment discrimination and illustrates the great barriers faced by both blacks and ex-offenders in their pursuit of economic self-sufficiency. These topics are explored in her recent book, *Marked: Race, Crime, and Finding Work in an Era of Mass Incarceration*.

Douglas W. Pryor is Associate Professor in Sociology of the Department of Sociology, Anthropology and Criminal Justice at Towson University in Maryland. He is coauthor of *Dual Attraction: Understanding Bisexuality* and author of *Unspeakable Acts: Why Men Sexually Abuse Children*. His current research focuses on the varied topics of fear of rape, lifelong friendships, and cheaters and cheating. Recently he has worked in an administrative role as a former department chair and as cochair of his university's reaccreditation self-study committee.

Richard Quinney is Professor of Sociology Emeritus at Northern Illinois University. His books include *The Social Reality of Crime*; *Critique of Legal Order*; *Class, State, and Crime*; *Criminology as Peacemaking* (with Harold E. Pepinsky); and *Criminal Behavior Systems* (with Marshall B. Clinard and John Wildeman). His autobiographical reflections are contained in *Journey to a Far Place* and *For the Time Being*.

Craig Reinarman is Professor of Sociology and Legal Studies at the University of California, Santa Cruz. He has been a visiting professor at Utrecht University and the University of Amsterdam. He has served on the Board of Directors of the College of Problems of Drug Dependence, as a consultant to the Who Health Organization's Programme on Substance Abuse, and a principal investigator on research grants from the National Institute on Drug Abuse. Dr. Reinarman is the author of *States of Mind* (Yale University Press 1987), and coauthor of *Cocaine Changes* (Temple University Press 1991), and *Crack in America* (University of California Press 1997).

Anne R. Roschelle is an Associate Professor of Sociology and an Affiliate in the Women's Studies Program at the State University of New York at New Paltz. She earned her Ph.D. at the State University of New York at Albany and is author of numerous articles on the intersection of race, class, and gender with a focus on extended kinship networks and family poverty. Anne is the author of *No More Kin: Exploring Race, Class, and Gender in Family Networks*, which was a recipient of Choice Magazine's 1997 Outstanding Academic Book Award. Anne has recently published a series of articles on domestic violence, welfare reform, and motherhood among homeless women in San Francisco as well as an article on feminist methodology in Cuba. She is currently writing a book about homeless families in San Francisco. Anne is an avid hiker and plays flute in a local rock band called Questionable Authorities (with coauthor Peter Kaufman).

Dawn Rothe is a Professor at Old Dominion University, Department of Sociology and Criminal Justice. She received her Ph.D. in sociology from Western Michigan University in 2006. She has written, researched, and spoken on state crime and controls (international criminal law, the International Criminal Court) and post-conflict justice. Her current work is centered on post-conflict justice in Africa as well as continued research on cases relevant to the Court including Darfur, the Congo, and Uganda analyzing the etiological and structural factors that led to the atrocities in each area. Rothe is the author of *State Criminality: The Worst of Worst Cases* (2009) and an edited volume, *State Crime: Current Perspectives* (2010), as well as coauthor of *Symbolic Gestures and the Generation of Global Social Control: The International Criminal Court* (2006) and *Blood, Power, and Bedlam: International Criminal Law Violations in Post-Colonial Africa*. She has published over three dozen articles in journals including *Justice Quarterly, Social Justice, Crime, Law and Social Change, International Criminal Law Review, Critical Criminology*, and *Humanity and Society* and has over two dozen book chapters.

Diana Scully is Professor of Sociology and Women's Studies at Virginia Commonwealth University in Richmond, Virginia where she is also Director of the Women's Studies Program. Her books include *Men Who Control Women's Health* (Teachers College Press 1994) and *Understanding Sexual Violence* (Routledge 1994).

Pete Simi is an Associate Professor of Criminology and Criminal Justice at the University of Nebraska, Omaha. His research interests include social psychological approaches to deviance and criminality. He is coauthor with Robert Futrell of *American Swastika: Inside the White Power Movement's Hidden Space of Hate*.

Katherine Anne Sirles received her Ph.D. in sociology from the University of Colorado in 2009. Her research interests include sociology of drugs, deviant behavior, and gender.

Edwin H. Sutherland (1883–1950) received his Ph.D. from the University of Chicago. His major works include his enduring textbook, *Criminology*, which was first published in 1924, and *The Professional Thief* and *White Collar Crime*. He is generally regarded as the founder of differential association theory.

Brian Sweeney received his Ph.D. from Indiana University, Bloomington. He is currently Assistant Professor of Sociology at Long Island University: CW Post Campus. His research focuses on youth and adolescence, peer cultures, gender and sexuality, and education.

Diane E. Taub is Professor of Sociology at Indiana University–Purdue University Fort Wayne. Her research primarily involves the sociology of deviance, with a focus on issues related to identity formation and the management of a deviant identity. Recent publications concern eating disorders and the lived experiences of women with physical disabilities.

Quint Thurman is Professor of Criminal Justice and Department Chairperson at Texas State University–San Marcos. He received a Ph.D. in sociology from the University of Massachusetts (Amherst) in 1987. His publications include seven books and more than 35 refereed articles that have appeared in such journals as the *American Behavioral Scientist, Crime and Delinquency, Criminology and Public Policy, Social Science Quarterly, Justice Quarterly, Police Quarterly*, and the *Journal of Quantitative Criminology*. Recently published books include *Controversies in Policing* (with coauthor Andrew Giacomazzi), an anthology, *Contemporary Policing: Controversies, Challenges, and Solutions* (with Jihong Zhao), and *Police Problem Solving* (with J.D. Jamieson).

Justin L. Tuggle received his B.A. from Humboldt State University and his M.A. from the University of Wyoming. He teaches third grade at Grant Elementary School in Redding, California. He is married with two children.

Brent E. Turvey received a B.S. degree from Portland State University in psychology, with an emphasis on forensic psychology, and an additional B.S. degree in history. He went on to receive his M.S. in forensic science after studying at the University of New Haven. Since graduating in 1996, Brent has consulted with many agencies, attorneys, and police departments in the United States, Australia, China, Canada, Barbados, and Korea on a range of rapes, homicides, and serial/ multiple rape/ death cases, as a forensic scientist and criminal profiler. He has also been court qualified as an expert in the areas of criminal profiling, forensic science, victimology, and crime reconstruction. He is the author of *Criminal Profiling: An Introduction to Behavioral Evidence Analysis*, 2nd edition, and coauthor of the *Rape Investigation Handbook* (2004), and *Crime Reconstruction* (2006)—all with Elsevier Science. He is currently a full partner, Forensic Scientist, Criminal Profiler, and Instructor with Forensic Solutions, LLC, and an Adjunct Professor in Criminology at Oklahoma City University.

Martin S. Weinberg received his Ph.D. at Northwestern University and is Professor of Sociology at Indiana University. He is the coauthor of *Deviance: The Interactionist Perspective*; *The Study of Social Problems*; *Sexual Preference*; *Homosexualities*; *Male Homosexuals*; and *Dual Attraction*, and has contributed articles to such journals as the *American Sociological Review, Social Problems, Journal of Contemporary Ethnography, Archives of Sexual Behavior*, and *Journal of Sex Research*.

Colin J. Williams is Professor of Sociology at Indiana University–Purdue University, Indianapolis. He is coauthor of *Male Homosexuals, Sex and Morality in the U.S.,* and *Dual Attraction*.

Celia Williamson received her B.A. in social work from the University of Toledo, her M.A. in social work from Case Western Reserve University, and her Ph.D. in social work from Indiana University. She is currently Professor in the Department of Social Work at the University of Toledo and Chair of the Second Chance Advisory Board that advocates for services for women in street-level prostitution and children trafficked into the sex trade.

Richard Wright is Curators' Professor and Chair of Criminology and Criminal Justice at the University of Missouri–St. Louis and Editor-in-Chief of the *British Journal of Sociology*. He has been studying active urban street criminals, especially residential burglars, armed robbers, carjackers, and drug dealers for the past two decades. His research has been funded by the National Science Foundation, National Institute of Justice, Harry Frank Guggenheim Foundation, Icelandic Research Council, National Consortium on Violence Research, and Irish Research Council for the Humanities and Social Sciences. Along with Richard Rosenfeld and Scott Jacques, he currently is conducting a major field-based study of respectability and social control among drug sellers in Amsterdam's red light district. His most recent book, coauthored with Bruce Jacobs, is *Street Justice: Retaliation in the Criminal Underworld* (Cambridge University Press 2006).

Andrew Kam-Tuck Yip is Associate Professor and Reader in Sociology at the University of Nottingham (UK). He has published widely in, among others, the area of LGB Christian and Muslim identities and relationships. He is the author of *Gay Male Christian Couples: Life Stories* (1997 Praeger); and coauthor of *Lesbian, Gay and Bisexual Lives Over 50* (2003 York House Publishing), and

Queer Spiritual Spaces: Sexuality and Sacred Places (2010 Ashgate). His articles have appeared in journals such as *Sociology of Religion*, *Journal for the Scientific Study of Religion*, *British Journal of Sociology*, *Sociology*, *Sociological Review*, and *Sexualities*. He is currently involved in two research projects: *Religion, Youth, and Sexuality: A Multi-faith Exploration* (www.nottingham.ac.uk/sociology/rys), and *Citizens in Diversity: A Four-nation Study of Homophobia and Fundamental Rights*.

General Introduction

The topic of deviance has held an enduring fascination for students of sociology, gripping their interest for several reasons. Some people have career plans that include law or law enforcement and want to expand their base of practical knowledge. Others feel a special affinity for the subject of deviance based on personal experience or inclination. A third group is drawn to deviance merely because it is different, offering the promise of excitement or the exotic. Finally, some are interested in how social norms are constructed, in the ways that people and societies decide what is acceptable and what is not. The sociological study of deviance can fulfill all these goals, taking us deep into the criminal underworld, inward to the familiar, outward to the fascinating and bizarre, and finally back to the central core. In the following pages we peer into the deviant realm, looking at both deviants and those who define them as such. In so doing, we look at a range of deviant behaviors, discuss why people engage in these, and analyze how they are sociologically organized. We begin in Part I by defining deviance, in an effort to lay down the parameters of its scope.

STUDYING DEVIANCE

Reasonable theories and social policies pertaining to deviance must be based on a firm foundation of accurate knowledge. Social scientists have an array of different methodologies and sources of data at their disposal, including survey research, experimental design, historical methods, official statistics, and field research (ethnography). All of these methods have obvious strengths and weaknesses, and have been used by sociologists in studying deviance. While some generate statistical portraits about the extensiveness of deviant behaviors, we undertake, in this book, to offer a richer, more experiential understanding of what goes on in deviant worlds, showing *how* things happen and what they *mean* to participant the reports of field researchers, individuals who immerse themselves personally in deviant settings, which yield such depth and descriptive accounts. It is also our belief that, due to the often secretive nature of deviance, methods that objectify or distance researchers from the people being researched will be less likely to accurately portray deviant worlds. Thus, the works in this book are tied together by their descriptive richness and by the belief that researchers must study deviance as it naturally occurs in the real world. The most appropriate methodology for this, field research, advocates that sociologists should get as close as possible to the people they are studying in order to understand their worlds (Adler and Adler 1987). Despite the problems that arise from the secretive and hidden nature of deviant acts, sociologists have devised techniques to penetrate secluded deviant worlds. These methodological ploys often come complete with perils, so it is wise for people who are considering studying deviance to be aware of these issues. Part III discusses field research methods and two of the other common sources of information about deviant behavior.

CONSTRUCTING DEVIANCE

In Parts I, II, and IV we delve into the origins and definitions of deviant behavior. Most sociology courses begin by examining core definitions in the field and leave these ideas behind shortly thereafter. This is not the case with deviance. Definitions of deviance pervade all aspects of the field and are therefore addressed throughout the book. Scholars, politicians, activists, moral entrepreneurs, religious zealots, journalists, and people from all walks of life frequently discuss issues of what is deviant and what is socially acceptable. Those whose definitions come to be reflected in law and social policy gain broad moral and material resources.

There are many approaches to defining and theorizing about deviance, some of which are presented in the chapters in Parts I and II. As our title suggests, we advance a social constructionist view throughout this book. We begin, here, by discussing **three perspectives on defining deviance** and locating these in relation to social constructionism.

Proponents of the **absolutist perspective** have traditionally considered defining deviance as a simple task, implying that a widespread consensus exists about what is deviant and what is not. Emile Durkheim, a functionalist and one of sociology's founding fathers, represents this theoretical approach, arguing that the laws of any given society are objective facts. Laws, he believes, reflect the "collective consciousness" of each society, and thereby reveal its true social nature. They exist before individuals enter the society, and they exist when individuals die; as such, laws represent a level of reality *sui generis* (unique unto themselves), transcending individual lives.

According to this position there is general agreement among citizens that there is something obvious within each deviant act, belief, or condition that makes it different from the conventional norms. At its fundamental core, each embodies the unambiguous, objective "essence" of true or real deviance. This perspective has its roots in both religious and naturalistic assumptions; these people argue that certain acts are contrary to the strictures of God or to the laws of nature. Deviance is thus immoral (possibly evil), sinful, and unnatural. Contemporary religious leaders, especially those of the charismatic and evangelical persuasions, often use these arguments in advancing their moral beliefs in written and verbal oratory. Absolutist views of deviance are eternal and global: if something is judged to have been intrinsically morally wrong in the past (for example, adultery or divorce), it should be recognized as wrong now and always in the future. Similarly, if something is considered to be morally wrong in one place, it should be judged wrong everywhere. Absolutist views on deviance flourish in homogeneous societies, where there is a high degree of universal agreement on social values.

Deviance, then, is not viewed as something that is determined by social norms, customs, or rules, but that is intrinsic to the human condition, standing apart from and existing before the creation of these socially created codes. According to absolutists, deviant attitudes, behavior, or conditions by any name would be recognized and judged similarly. People have backed up this belief system by pointing to the existence of universal taboos surrounding such acts as murder, incest, and lying. These acts, they claim, are deviant in their very essence.

Noteworthy to this perspective is its focus on the deviance itself. Proponents believe that an absolute moral order is a necessary part of reality, enabling all people to know what is right and what is wrong. Normative behavior is inherently good and deviance is inherently bad. Violations of norms, it follows then, should be met with stern reactions. People who question the norms deserve even harsher treatment, as they challenge the moral order. At its core, then, absolutism is an objectivist approach because it relies in its definition on internal, inherent features that stand apart from subjective human judgments. We see contemporary applications of the absolutist perspective in the campaign against gay marriage, with opponents arguing that homosexuality is an abomination and a sin. The morality-based conception of deviance, presented in Hendershott's chapter 4, offers another contemporary illustration of this viewpoint.

Functionalist theories of deviance, as represented in Erikson's chapter 1 and Durkheim's chapter 6, incorporate elements of the absolutist perspective by suggesting that deviance is pathological (diseased) in its substance and negative in its effect. As such, it stands apart from, and in strong contrast to, the "normal." In all ways, the absolutist perspective stands as the foil, or antithesis, to social constructionism.

A group of theories coalesce to form the *social constructionist approach*, grounded in the interactionist theory of deviance. We can draw distinctions between theories, but they all share in common a focus on the norms that bound and define deviance rather than a gaze on the deviance itself. They also share a subjectivist approach to defining deviance, guided by the belief that social meanings, values, and rules, in concrete situations, are often problematic or uncertain. Social meanings, they believe, arise in the situations where they occur, rather than being located within the essences of things, and are heavily influenced by people's perceptions and interpretations. Social constructionists study the way that norms are created, the people who create them, the conditions under which they arise, and their consequences for different groups in society. Fundamentally, they view definitions of deviance as social products and focus on those defining deviance and their definitions, rather than on the acts that generate deviant reactions.

For example, recently there has been greater social awareness about obesity and its deleterious effects. Absolutists would say that the social definition of obesity as deviant was established by doctors as a health issue and that the level of obesity in our society can be objectively measured by a scientific instrument: the scale. They would point to the growth in portion sizes in America (super-sizing), as the average dinner place has expanded from ten to twelve inches. Americans, they would say, are more obese because they are eating more and exercising less. On the other hand, constructionists would suggest that our collective attitudes towards obesity have changed, and that levels of weight that used to raise little attention have become less tolerated now. In addition, they would show that people react to weight differently in various cultures, as citizens in some countries prefer more "full-figured" people, and in other places the image of the skinny (practically anorectic) model is considered the ideal body shape. Clothing companies have subjectively renumbered the sizes of their garments so that size four is the "new" size six (what women should strive for), and size eight is the "new" size 14 (you might as well forget about appearing in public). Crusaders, especially from the medical community, have made campaigns against obesity and raised social awareness about it, making it one of the chief panics in society today. The point is that, although being overweight can lead to numerous physical problems, we have shifted our definitions about how much weight is acceptable. As a result, when we look at people and try to assess if they are slightly overweight, chubby, plump, heavy, fat, or outright obese, our categories have changed. What was previously considered tolerably heavy has now been redefined as obese and labeled deviant.

Falling within social constructionism is the **relativist perspective**, if articulated in Becker's chapter 3. Spurred by the rise of subcultural studies in the 1930s, deviance theorists began to note the existence of norms that differed from, and even conflicted with, those of the larger society. This led them to consider the possibility that groups in society make up rules to fit the practical needs of their situations. The more the relativists examined norms in different places and times, the more they became convinced that definitions of deviance were not universal, but varied to suit the people who hold them. This suggested that definitions of deviance derived, not from absolute, unchanging universals such as God and nature, but from humans. Becker (1963, 9) articulated this position, noting:

> . . . social groups create deviance by making the rules whose infraction constitutes deviance, and by applying these rules to particular people and labeling them as outsiders. From this point of view, deviance is not a quality of the act the person commits, but rather a consequence of the application by others of rules and sanctions to an "offender." (Italics in original)

Deviance, relativists argue, is thus lodged in the eye of the beholder rather than in the act itself, and it may vary in the way it is defined by time and place. Becker (1963, 147–48) further stated,

> Formal rules such as laws require the initiative or enterprise of specific individuals and groups for their reality. They do not exist independently of the actions of moral entrepreneurs to make them real. . . . The prototype of the rule creator is the crusading reformer. He is interested in the content of the rules. The existing rules do not satisfy him because there is some evil which profoundly disturbs him. He feels that nothing can be right in the world unless rules are made to correct it. He operates within an absolute ethic; what he sees is truly and totally evil with no qualification. Any means is justified to do away with it. The crusader is fervent and righteous, often self righteous. . . . [He or she] typically believe[s the] mission is a holy one.

Definitions, this position suggests, are forged by crusading reformers, reforged by them anew in different eras and locations, leading to significant constructions and reconstructions of deviance. When different social contexts frame and give meaning to the perception and interpretation of acts, the same act may be alternately perceived as deviant or normative.

This creates the possibility of multiple definitions of acts, both deviant and nondeviant, simultaneously existing among different groups. We see this clearly in cases of controversial, morally debated acts such as getting an abortion, praying in school, gay marriage, the use of medical marijuana, and illegal immigration. Major campaigns have been assembled to sway public opinion over the morality and appropriateness of these behaviors, with large segments of the country falling into oppositional camps. Groups that are fairly alike in their composition may forge shared agreements about norms that would be differently received among a broader segment of the general public. For example, more widely acceptable behavior, such as dancing, is condemned in some thoroughly conservative environments, such as Bible-Belt religious colleges. At the same time, language that is widely used throughout the country may be condemned as politically incorrect and morally offensive hate crimes on extremely liberal college campuses.

Even some acts that are considered universally taboo can vary in their definitions, as there are conditions under which they would be considered nondeviant. To kill somebody for personal gain, vengeance, freedom, or through negligence might be considered deviant (and, more likely, criminal), but when murder is committed by the state (for executions, war, or covert intelligence), in self-defense, when catching your spouse in bed with someone else (if you are a man, but not if you are a woman), under the influence of insanity, or on one's own property (in states where they have "make my day" laws), it is considered not only non-deviant, but possibly heroic. Similarly, anthropologists have found cultures that condone certain forms of incest to quiet or soothe infants (Henry 1964; Weatherford 1986). Often, too, people differentiate between normal lies and "white" lies, accepting those designed to spare other people's feelings as acceptable. Relativists argue that definitions of deviance are social products that are likely to be situationally invoked under certain circumstances. They represent the social constructionist approach because they focus on the circumstances under which social norms are differentially created and applied.

Paradoxically, extensions of functionalist theory bring it into the social constructionist realm. Despite their belief that deviance is pathological, functionalists overwhelmingly believe that all components of society contribute, somehow, to its existence; they all have positive functions. Since deviance is a universal feature of all societies, they admit that it must offer benefits. Four positive functions of deviance have been outlined. First, when people react against the deviance of others, they bond together into cohesion and social solidarity. We saw this after the terrorist attacks of 9/11. Second, identifying and punishing deviance redefines and reinforces the social boundaries, which are mutable and not fixed, and reinforce the dangers of transgressing those boundaries. When business executives such as Martha Stewart or Kenneth Lay and Jeffrey Skilling of Enron go to prison for insider trading, "creative accounting," and income tax evasion, it clarifies the limits of acceptable behavior. Politicians who get caught abusing their power send an impetus to others to not only avoid such behaviors, but to pass stronger ethics rules. Third, Durkheim noted the seeds of social change in deviance, as new developments are often initially regarded skeptically or fearfully, and have to go through a process of moral passage to become accepted. Although Socrates was considered a political heretic in his time, he paved the way for intellectual freedom. Without deviance, Durkheim suggested, society might stagnate. Fourth, the existence of all the occupations associated with deviance (the criminal justice system, the medical establishment, the media, the scholars, etc.) would be threatened without deviance, so that were crime or deviance to disappear entirely (and we became a "society of saints"), new behaviors would be defined as deviant to fill this void. In sum, functionalists concluded that a certain amount of deviance is good for society. But because too much or too little is not as beneficial as just the right amount, these definitions must be continually socially constructed and adjusted to ensure the smooth functioning of society.

A third position on defining deviance, presented in Quinney's chapter 5, is the **social power perspective.** This builds on the relativist perspective by asserting that views on crime and deviance are not arbitrarily formed by just any group of "others." Closely tied to Marx's conflict theory, the social power approach focuses on the influence that powerful groups and classes have in creating and applying laws. Rather, as Quinney (1970, 43) notes, these laws are a reflection of those with the greatest social power in society:

> Criminal laws support particular interests to the neglect or negation of other interests, thus representing the concerns of only some members of society. Though some criminal laws may involve a compromise of conflicting interests, more likely than not, criminal laws mark the victory of some groups over others. The notion of a compromise of conflicting interests is a myth perpetuated by the pluralistic model of politics. Some interests never find access to the lawmaking process.

Other interests are overwhelmed in it, not compromised. But ultimately some interests succeed in becoming criminal law, and are able to control the conduct of others.

Thus, Quinney believes that laws reflect the interests and concerns of the dominant classes in a society. Dominant classes tend to formulate their definitions of deviance in accord with their own interests, defining things that threaten them as out-of-bounds and things that benefit them as good. All laws reflect power relations, and their existence as well as their enforcement illustrates which groups have the power to control, and which groups are controlled. Dominant groups, then, tend to over-enforce laws against the subordinate classes and under-enforce them against members of their own group.

This approach incorporates social constructionism by challenging the simplistic assumption underlying the absolutist perspective that definitions of deviance are universally shared. According to the social power viewpoint, society is characterized by conflict and struggle between groups whose interests conflict with each other, with the powerful classes dominating the subordinate groups. Members of each group pursue their own needs and desires, but because of the way society is structured, what is good for one class restricts the opportunities of others. This pits groups against each other in active struggles. Those with the greatest social power dominate both the ability to create definitions, rules, and laws, and the way these are negligently or aggressively enforced.

The conflicting interests of the dominant and subordinate groups can fall into the economic realm, as we see some political parties promoting the rights of big businesses to pay fewer taxes, less overtime compensation, and lower health care benefits, while other parties fight for the rights of workers to unionize, to gain job security, and to earn a decent living wage. Other issues along which groups in society may conflict fall into the social realm, including environmental policies, birth control, stem cell research, school prayer, gun control, health care, and drug policies. Pervading all of this, conflict theorists note a systematic differential oppression along the lines of race/ethnicity, social class, and gender.

Feminist theorists share conflict theorists' constructionist orientation, as we find in Chesney-Lind's chapter 10. They focus on the norms, policies, and laws of the patriarchal system that uphold the social, moral, economic, and political order that fosters male privilege. Their approach questions the way men forge and maintain their dominance over women, and the role of deviance definitions in this endeavor. They challenge the bases and benefits of patriarchy, regarding it as a form of socially constructed social control.

Deviance can be defined through the social meanings collectively applied to people's attitudes, behavior, or conditions, which are rooted in the interaction between individuals and social groups. Those who have the power to make and apply rules onto others control the normative order. The politically, socially, and economically dominant groups enforce their definitions onto the downtrodden and powerless. Deviance is thus a representation of unequal power in society.

DEVIANT IDENTITY

The second component of the social constructionist approach lies in the consequences of definitions and applications of deviance. Interactionists have argued that the two sides of constructing deviance, its articulation and its application, are both critical. Society first labels various attitudes, behaviors, and conditions as deviant, and then it labels specific individuals associated with these as deviant. Where definitions of deviance are forged but not applied, they believe, deviance does not really exist. It's as if a tree falls in the forest, but we conclude that it makes no sound because no one is there to hear it. In effect, social constructionists are proposing that the essence of the sound does not lie in the impact of the tree on the ground or in the creation of the sound waves, but in the articulation of those waves against the hearer's eardrum. Specific individuals or groups of people must be labeled by society for deviance to be concretely envisioned.Part V takes up this change of focus away from the construction of deviance definitions to looking at how the application of norms and laws affects people. Now, we move away from macro–societal explanations to focus on microinteraction that occurs in everyday life. Constructionists claim that deviants are people who have undergone some sort of labeling. This section looks at how deviant labels are applied and their subsequent consequences.

Social constructionists emphasize that something profound may occur when the supposed deviants and conventional others interact. In pursuing their actions, individuals may engage in deviance but not think of themselves as deviant actors. Only when they begin to apply the deviant labels "out there" in the world to themselves, do they truly become deviants. This is the process of acquiring a deviant identity. People may become dislodged from their safe identity locations within the "normal" realm through their own observations as well as the actions and remarks of others. The greater the response of others, the stronger their self-conceptions as deviant will be. This may lead to their engaging in further deviance.

Several aspects of this social psychological process are the most critical, and will be addressed most vividly in this section. We begin by looking at how people acquire deviant identities. Many factors are influential, and we consider the ways people creatively use "accounts" or "motive talk" to explain, neutralize, or justify their actions to forestall being labeled as deviant. Although functionalists have suggested that labeling people as deviant has positive results for society, it has negative results for those labeled. They acquire deviant stigma, a stain or pejorative connotation associated with them or their actions. Living with known stigma makes life difficult for people as they may be marked, disparaged, or shunned. People handle their stigma differently, and we examine these variations and their consequences in Part V.

THE SOCIAL ORGANIZATION OF DEVIANCE

We conclude this volume, in Parts VI, VII, and VIII, with a discussion of how deviants, their deviance, and their deviant careers are socially organized. Earlier sections of the book have concentrated on macro and micro levels of addressing deviance by considering the movements and powers that shape deviant definitions at the societal level and by looking at how people's identities are shaped at the interpersonal level. Here, we take a meso (mid-level) focus by looking at how deviants organize their social organization and relationships, activities and acts, and careers, in connection with others. We begin with the study of deviant organization, examining the various ways members of deviant scenes organize their relations with each other. These range from individuals acting on their own, outside of relationships with other deviants, to subcultures, to more tightly connected gangs, to highly committed international cartels, and finally to corporations and the state. We then consider the structure of deviant acts. Some forms of deviance involve cooperation between the participants, where people mutually exchange illicit goods or services. Others are characterized by conflict, where some parties to the act take advantage of others, often against their will. Finally, we look at the phases and contours of deviant careers, beginning with people's entry into the world of deviant behavior and associates, continuing with the way they fashion their involvement in deviance, and concluding with their often problematic, and occasionally inconclusive, retirements from the compelling world of deviance.

PART I

Defining Deviance

In order to study the topic of deviance we must first clarify what we mean by the term. What behaviors or conditions fall into this category, and what is the relation between deviance and other categories such as crime? When we speak of deviance, we refer to violations of social norms. Norms are behavioral codes or prescriptions that guide people into actions and self-presentations conforming to social acceptability. Norms need not be agreed upon by every member of the group doing the defining, but a clear or vocal majority must agree.

One of the founding American sociologists, William Sumner (1907), conceptualized **three types of norms**: *folkways, mores,* and *laws.* He defined folkways as simple everyday norms based on custom, tradition, or etiquette. Violations of folkway norms do not generate serious outrage, but might cause people to think of the violator as odd. Common folkway norms include standards of dress, demeanor, physical closeness to or distance from others, and eating behavior. People who come to class dressed in bathing suits, who never seem to be paying attention when they are spoken to, who sit or stand too close to others, who pick their noses in public or fail to wash their hands in a public washroom, or who eat with their hands instead of silverware (at least in the United States) would be violating a folkway norm. We would not arrest them nor would we impugn their moral character, but we might think that there was something peculiar about them.

Mores (pronounced *mor-ays*) are norms based on broad societal morals whose infraction would generate more serious social condemnation. Interracial marriage, illegitimate childbearing, and drug addiction all constitute moral violations. Upholding these norms is seen as critical to the fabric of society, so that their violation threatens the social order. Interracial marriage threatens racial purity and the stratification hierarchy based on race; illegitimate childbearing threatens the institution of marriage and the transference of money, status, and family responsibility from one generation to the next; drug addiction represents the triumph of hedo-nism over rationality, threatening the responsible behavior necessary to hold society together and to accomplish its necessary tasks. People who violate mores may be considered bad or wicked and potentially harmful to society.

Laws are the strongest norms because they are supported by codified social sanctions. People who violate them are subject to arrest and punishment ranging from fines to imprisonment (and possibly even death). Many laws are directed toward behavior that used to be folkway or, especially, more violations, but became encoded into laws. Others are regarded as necessary for maintaining social order. Although violating a traffic law such as speeding breaks society's rules, it will not usually brand the offender as deviant.

Following closely on Sumner's distinctions, Smith and Pollack (1976) sug-gested that deviance might be conceptualized as violations of the norms associated with *crime, sin,* and *poor taste.* For example, criminal acts, such as murder, rape, assault, robbery, and arson, would be violations of laws. Smith and Pollack view these as generally unacceptable to the large majority of the people in society. Acts of sin tend to be defined in relation to religious proscriptions and often involve such acts as promiscuous, lewd, extramarital, or homosexual sex, gambling, drink-ing, and abortion. While some of these may be subject to criminal sanction, the majority of them are not. Societal responses, rather, tend to fall into the moral category of strong disapproval. Finally, acts of poor taste, like folkways, which challenge existing standards of fashion, manners, or traditions, violate social norms and are unregulated by law.

This discussion returns us to the question about the relationship between *devi-ance* and *crime.* Are they identical terms, is one a subset of the other, or are they overlapping categories? To answer this question, we must consider one facet of it at a time. First, do some acts fall into both categories, crime and deviance? The overlap between these two is extensive, with crimes of violence such as murder and assault and property crimes such as theft, arson, or vandalism considered both deviant and illegal. But are crime and deviance always the same thing? We can see that they are not, because there is much deviance that is not criminal. Non-criminal forms of deviance include obesity, stuttering, physical handicaps, racial intermar-riage, and unwed pregnancy. At the same time, some forms of crime are not con-sidered deviant; they do not violate norms or bring moral censure. Examples of this include some white-collar crimes commonly regarded as merely aggressive business practices, such as income tax evasion, minor traffic offenses, and forms of civil disobedience, where people break laws to protest them. Crime and deviance, then, can best be seen as categories that overlap while at the same time having independent dimensions.

People can be labeled deviant as the result of the **ABCs of deviance**: their *attitudes, behaviors,* or *conditions.* First, they may be branded deviant for alternative sets of *attitudes* or belief systems. These belief systems may fall into the category of religion, with all forms of religious extremism and even moderate forms of non-normative religious beliefs, such as those held by cults, Satanists, and fundamental-ists, regarded askance. Having no religious affiliation is one of the fastest-growing forms of deviant religious belief systems in the United States (those who claimed "no religion" were the only demographic group that grew in all 50 states in the last 18 years), contravening the 85 percent of religious people who claim some reli-gious identity, and the close to 92 percent who report that they believe in the existence of a supernatural or "supreme being." A second category of deviant attitudes consists of people who hold extreme political attitudes (far leftists or right-ists terrorists). Mental illness also falls into the deviant attitudinal category—people with deviant worldviews ("the world is coming to an end") are often considered mentally ill and people with chemical, emotional, or psychological problems may also be considered deviant. These may also be subject to relativity, so that when a poor woman shoplifts a roast people call her a common criminal, but if a rich woman steals a roast, her deviant status is kleptomaniac, a mental illness label.

The *behavioral* category is the most familiar one, with people coming to be regarded as deviant for their outward actions. Deviant behaviors may be intentional or inadvertent, and include such activities as violating dress or speech conventions, engaging in kinky sexual behavior, smoking marijuana, or committing murder. People cast into the deviant realm for their behaviors have an *achieved deviant status:* they have earned the deviant label through something they have done.

Other people regarded as deviant may have an *ascribed deviant status,* based on a *condition* they acquire from birth. This would include having a deviant socioeco-nomic status such as being either extremely poor or ultrarich; a deviant racial status such as being a person of color (in a dominantly Caucasian society); or having a congenital physical disability. Here, there is nothing that such people have done to become deviant and little or nothing they can do to repair their deviant status. Moreover, there may be nothing necessarily inherent in these statuses that make them deviant: they may become deviant through the result of a social definitional process that gives unequal weight to powerful and dom-inant groups in society. Conditional deviant status may be ascribed or achieved. On the one hand, people may be born with conditional deviance due to their personal and/or racial/ethnic characteristics (height, weight, color). On the other hand, a conditional deviant status can also be achieved, such as when people burn or disfigure themselves severely, when they become too fat or too thin, or when they cover their bodies with adornments such as tattoos, piercings, or scarification.

Unlike ascribed statuses, some of these may also be changed, moving the deviant back within the norm.

Finally, it is interesting to consider the way deviance is assessed and categorized, as this varies between different eras, with different behaviors, and to different audiences. Deviance may be perceived and interpreted through the lens of the **three categories of S's**: *sin, sick,* and *selected.* During the Middle Ages and many earlier times when religious paradigms about the world prevailed, deviance from the norm was attributed to religious disorders and viewed as *sinful.* Non-normative attitudes, beliefs, and conditions were attributed to satanic influences, and exorcisms were performed to cure people. Religious leaders were seen as the arbiters of official morality, and called upon to make judgments and administer sanctions. Even today, some religious zealots adhere to this perspective, not only in societies that are officially religious in their governance, but within religious pockets of secular societies. The afflicted, in the eyes of these people, are strongly condemned and often viewed as contagious.

Beginning in the first half of the twentieth century, the medicalization (*sickness*) model emerged as a strong perspective for explaining deviance. Conrad and Schneider (1980) suggested that this process begins when a behavior or condition defined as deviant is "prospected" by people with medical interests to see if they can gain rewards from pulling it under the medical umbrella. Physicians and psychiatrists claimed that homosexuality, alcoholism/drug addiction, sexual misbehavior, mental illness, and other behaviors are rooted in people's psychiatric problems, genetic abnormalities, inherited predispositions, and biochemical characteristics. Psychiatrists sought to claim ownership over the diagnosis of these forms of deviance with their *Diagnostic and Statistical Manual of Mental Disorders* (now in its current edition, the *DSM IV*) so that they could administer outpatient or inpatient therapy and be reimbursed by insurance companies (clinics for specialized medical conditions such as self-injury may charge as much as $1,000 a day and require a thirty-day stay). Turf wars sprang up, with psychiatrists attempting to exert domain claims over a variety of behaviors that were previously conceived as biological or sociological in order to receive research grants for further study, diagnose patients, and then treat them. For example, does your child have "dyspraxia"? Children with this new disorder ("clumsy child syndrome"), affecting two percent of the population (mostly male), will need the support of their families and qualified professionals to succeed in school. Are you boorish, disrespectful of authority, rude, or lacking in etiquette? Perhaps you have "impulse control disorder." Do you spend too many hours on your computer? You should consider having yourself diagnosed with "Internet addiction disorder." Are you an overly aggressive driver? Perhaps you suffer clinically from "road rage." The next edition of the DSM is set to include a new category on "relational disorders" that identifies sickness in groups of individuals and the relationships between them including couples who constantly quarrel, parents and children who clash, and troubled relationships between siblings, defining these as mental illness. This specifically encroaches into sociological behaviors, attempting to psychologize and pathologize them.

The recovery movement, with its coterie of self-help (often twelve-step) programs, educators, and public health organizations, further expanded the reach of this paradigm to include other addictions, eating disorders, self-injury, child abuse, child hyperactivity, compulsive gambling, and interpersonal violence. Doctors and drug companies leapt into the business, manufacturing and prescribing an array of medications to "manage" or "cure" people. As a result, we are now the most legally medicated society in world history. The success of this medicalization movement, fueled by the prestige of science and the lure of the "easy fix" of a pill, drew huge areas of attitudes, behaviors, and conditions into its sphere, so that society no longer tolerates people being too sad, depressed, rebellious, rambunctious, fidgety, eating too much or too little, or having too little or too much sex. One strong allure of the medicalization perspective has been its destigmatization of some deviance, since people who were seen as sick or acting on biological predispositions/inherited "differences" were not seen as making immoral choices, but were doing things "beyond their control." This made them more acceptable to mainstream society, albeit not quite "normal" or "healthy."

At the same time, some thought that the medicalization movement had become too pervasive, absorbing too great a swath of social life within its grasp. Some participants reached out to reclaim the rhetoric of *selection* over their attitudes, behaviors, and conditions, arguing that these were the result of voluntary choice. They, and the researchers who studied them, found groups of people who rejected the medicalized interpretation of such things as homosexuality, gambling, eating disorders, drug use, and self-injury. Participants chaffed at the control that "experts" held over them, their diagnoses, their treatments, and their medicalization. Instead, they cast their behaviors as intentionally selected, as forms of recreation, lifestyle choices, and coping strategies. This demedicalization movement has in some ways empowered and destigmatized people who participated in these forms of behavior. For them, to be seen as ill was to be derogated; to be seen as self-healing or voluntarily deviant is conventional. There is no doubt that these diverse perspectives will continue to compete for the ownership, control, and legitimacy of non-normative forms of expression.

1

On the Sociology of Deviance

KAI T. ERIKSON

This classic selection examines the functions of deviance for society. Erikson asserts that deviance and the social reactions it evokes are key focal concerns of every community. Scrutinized by the mass media, law enforcement, and ordinary citizens, deviance leads us to continually redraw the social boundaries of acceptability. Rather than being a fixed property, norms are subject to shifts and evolution, and the interactions between deviants and agents of social control locate the margins between deviance and respectability.

Erikson notes, ironically, that the very institutions and agencies mandated to manage deviance tend to reinforce it. Once individuals have been identified as deviant they undergo "commitment ceremonies" where they are negatively labeled, experiencing a status change that is hard to reverse. Society's expectations that deviants will not reform foster the "self-fulfilling prophesy," by which norm violators reproduce their deviance, living up to the negative images society holds of them. Erikson suggests several other valuable functions that deviance performs in a society: it fosters boundary maintenance so that people know what is acceptable and unacceptable; it bolsters cohesion, integration, and solidarity, thus preserving the stability of social life; and it promotes full employment, guaranteeing jobs for people working in the deviance- and crime-management sector.

Can you think of any cases where people you know have been pushed into deviance by people's expectations or definitions?

Human actors are sorted into various kinds of collectivity, ranging from relatively small units such as the nuclear family to relatively large ones such as a nation or culture. One of the most stubborn difficulties in the study of deviation is that the problem is defined differently at each one of these levels: behavior that is considered unseemly within the context of a single family may be entirely acceptable to the community in general, while behavior that attracts severe censure from the members of the community may go altogether unnoticed elsewhere in the culture. People in society, then, must learn to deal separately with deviance at each one of these levels and to distinguish among them in his own daily activity. A man may disinherit his son for conduct that violates old family traditions or

From Kai T. Erikson, *Wayward Puritans: A Study in the Sociology of Deviance.* Copyright © 1966 by Pearson Education. Reprinted by permission of the publisher.

ostracize a neighbor for conduct that violates some local custom, but he is not expected to employ either of these standards when he serves as a juror in a court of law. In each of the three situations he is required to use a different set of criteria to decide whether or not the behavior in question exceeds tolerable limits.

In the next few pages we shall be talking about deviant behavior in social units called "communities," but the use of this term does not mean that the argument applies only at that level of organization. In theory, at least, the argument being made here should fit all kinds of human collectivity—families as well as whole cultures, small groups as well as nations—and the term "community" is only being used in this context because it seems particularly convenient.[1]

The people of a community spend most of their lives in close contact with one another, sharing a common sphere of experience which makes them feel that they belong to a special "kind" and live in a special "place." In the formal language of sociology, this means that communities are boundary maintaining: each has a specific territory in the world as a whole, not only in the sense that it occupies a defined region of geographical space but also in the sense that it takes over a particular niche in what might be called cultural space and develops its own "ethos" or "way" within that compass. Both of these dimensions of group space, the geographical and the cultural, set the community apart as a special place and provide an important point of reference for its members.

When one describes any system as boundary maintaining, one is saying that it controls the fluctuation of its consistent parts so that the whole retains a limited range of activity, a given pattern of constancy and stability, within the larger environment. A human community can be said to maintain boundaries, then, in the sense that its members tend to confine themselves to a particular radius of activity and to regard any conduct which drifts outside that radius as somehow inappropriate or immoral. Thus the group retains a kind of cultural integrity, a voluntary restriction on its own potential for expansion, beyond that which is strictly required for accommodation to the environment. Human behavior can vary over an enormous range, but each community draws a symbolic set of parentheses around a certain segment of that range and limits its own activities within that narrower zone. These parentheses, so to speak, are the community's boundaries.

Now people who live together in communities cannot relate to one another in any coherent way or even acquire a sense of their own stature as group members unless they learn something about the boundaries of the territory they occupy in social space, if only because they need to sense what lies beyond the margins of the group before they can appreciate the special quality of the experience which takes place within it. Yet how do people learn about the boundaries of their community? And how do they convey this information to the generations which replace them?

To begin with, the only material found in a society for marking boundaries is the behavior of its members—or rather, the networks of interaction which link these members together in regular social relations. And the interactions which do the most effective job of locating and publicizing the group's outer edges would seem to be those which take place between deviant persons on the one side and official agents of the community on the other. The deviant is a person whose activities have moved outside the margins of the group, and when the community calls him to account for that vagrancy it is making a statement about the nature and placement of its boundaries. It is declaring how much variability and diversity can be tolerated within the group before it begins to lose its distinctive shape, its unique identity. Now there may be other moments in the life of the group which perform a similar service: wars, for instance, can publicize a group's boundaries by drawing attention to the line separating the group from an adversary, and certain kinds of religious ritual, dance ceremony, and other traditional pageantry can dramatize the difference between "we" and "they" by portraying a symbolic encounter between the two. But on the whole, members of a community inform one another about the placement of their boundaries by participating in the confrontations which occur when persons who venture out to the edges of the group are met by policing agents whose special business it is to guard the cultural integrity of the community. Whether these confrontations take the form of criminal trials, excommunication hearings, courts-martial, or even psychiatric case conferences, they act as boundary-maintaining devices in the sense that they demonstrate to whatever audience is concerned where the line is drawn between behavior that belongs in the special universe of the group and behavior that does not. In general, this kind of information is not easily relayed by the straightforward use of language. Most readers of this paragraph, for instance, have a fairly clear idea of the line separating theft from more legitimate forms of commerce, but few of them have ever seen a published statute describing these differences. More likely than not, our information on the subject has been drawn from publicized instances in which the relevant laws were applied—and for that matter, the law itself is largely a collection of past cases and decisions, a synthesis of the various confrontations which have occurred in the life of the legal order.

It may be important to note in this connection that confrontations between deviant offenders and the agents of control have always attracted a good deal of public attention. In our own past, the trial and punishment of offenders were staged in the market place and afforded the crowd a chance to participate in a direct, active way. Today, of course, we no longer parade deviants in the town square or expose them to the carnival atmosphere of a Tyburn, but it is interesting that the "reform" which brought about this change in penal practice coincided almost exactly with the development of newspapers as a medium of mass information. Perhaps this is no more than an accident of history, but it is nonetheless true that newspapers (and now radio and television) offer much the same kind of entertainment as public hangings or a Sunday visit to the local gaol. A considerable portion of what we call "news" is devoted to reports about deviant behavior and its consequences, and it is no simple matter to explain why these items should be considered newsworthy or why they should command the extraordinary attention they do. Perhaps they appeal to a number of psychological perversities among the mass audience, as commentators have suggested, but at the same time they constitute one of our main sources of information about the normative outlines of society. In a figurative sense, at least, morality and immorality meet at the public scaffold, and it is during this meeting that the line between them is drawn.

Boundaries are never a fixed property of any community. They are always shifting as the people of the group find new ways to define the outer limits of their universe, new ways to position themselves on the larger cultural map. Sometimes changes occur within the structure of the group which require its members to make a new survey of their territory—a change of leadership, a shift of mood. Sometimes changes occur in the surrounding environment, altering the background against which the people of the group have measured their own uniqueness. And always, new generations are moving in to take their turn guarding old institutions and need to be informed about the contours of the world they are inheriting. Thus single encounters between the deviant and his community are only fragments of an ongoing social process. Like an article of common law, boundaries remain a meaningful point of reference only so long as they are repeatedly tested by persons on the fringes of the group and repeatedly defended by persons chosen to represent the group's inner morality. Each time the community moves to censure some act of deviation, then, and convenes a formal ceremony to deal with the responsible offender, it sharpens the authority of the violated norm and restates where the boundaries of the group are located.

For these reasons, deviant behavior is not a simple kind of leakage which occurs when the machinery of society is in poor working order, but may be, in controlled quantities, an important condition for preserving the stability of social life. Deviant forms of behavior, by marking the outer edges of group life, give the inner structure its special character and thus supply the framework within which the people of the group develop an orderly sense of their own cultural identity. Perhaps this is what Aldous Huxley had in mind when he wrote:

> Now tidiness is undeniably good—but a good of which it is easily pos-
> sible to have too much and at too high a price…. The good life can
> only be lived in a society in which tidiness is preached and practised, but
> not too fanatically, and where efficiency is always haloed, as it were, by
> a tolerated margin of mess.[2]

This raises a delicate theoretical issue. If we grant that human groups often derive benefit from deviant behavior, can we then assume that they are organized in such a way as to promote this resource? Can we assume, in other words, that forces operate in the social structure to recruit offenders and to commit them to long periods of service in the deviant ranks? This is not a question which can be answered with our present store of empirical data, but one observation can be made which gives the question an interesting perspective—namely, that deviant forms of conduct often seem to derive nourishment from the very agencies devised to inhibit them. Indeed, the agencies built by society for preventing deviance are often so poorly equipped for the task that we might well ask why this is regarded as their "real" function in the first place.

It is by now a thoroughly familiar argument that many of the institutions designed to discourage deviant behavior actually operate in such a way as to perpetuate it. For one thing, prisons, hospitals, and other similar agencies provide aid and shelter to large numbers of deviant persons, sometimes giving them a certain advantage in the competition for social resources. But beyond this, such institutions gather marginal people into tightly segregated groups, give them an opportunity to teach one another the skills and attitudes of a deviant career, and even provoke them into using these skills by reinforcing their sense of alienation from the rest of society.[3] Nor is this observation a modern one:

> The misery suffered in gaols is not half their evil; they are filled with every sort of corruption that poverty and wickedness can generate; with all the shameless and profligate enormities that can be produced by the impudence of ignominy, the range of want, and the malignity of dispair. In a prison the check of the public eye is removed; and the power of the law is spent. There are few fears, there are no blushes. The lewd inflame the more modest; the audacious harden the timid. Everyone fortifies himself as he can against his own remaining sensibility; endeavoring to practise on others the arts that are practised on himself; and to gain the applause of his worst associates by imitating their manners.[4]

These lines, written almost two centuries ago, are a harsh indictment of prisons, but many of the conditions they describe continue to be reported in even the most modern studies of prison life. Looking at the matter from a long-range historical perspective, it is fair to conclude that prisons have done a conspicuously poor job of reforming the convicts placed in their custody; but the very consistency of this failure may have a peculiar logic of its own. Perhaps we find it difficult to change the worst of our penal practices because we *expect* the prison to harden the inmate's commitment to deviant forms of behavior and draw him more deeply into the deviant ranks. On the whole, we are a people who do not really expect deviants to change very much as they are processed through the control agencies we provide for them, and we are often reluctant to devote much of the community's resources to the job of rehabilitation. In this sense, the prison which graduates long rows of accomplished criminals (or, for that matter, the state asylum which stores its most severe cases away in some back ward) may do serious violence to the aims of its founders; but it does very little violence to the expectations of the population it serves.

These expectations, moreover, are found in every corner of society and constitute an important part of the climate in which we deal with deviant forms of behavior.

To begin with, the community's decision to bring deviant sanctions against one of its members is not a simple act of censure. It is an intricate rite of transition, at once moving the individual out of his ordinary place in society and transferring him into a special deviant position.[5] The ceremonies which mark this change of status, generally, have a number of related phases. They supply a formal stage on which the deviant and his community can confront one another (as in the criminal trial); they make an announcement about the nature of his deviancy (a verdict or diagnosis, for example); and they place him in a particular role which is thought to neutralize the harmful effects of his misconduct (like the role of prisoner or patient). These commitment ceremonies tend to be occasions of wide public interest and ordinarily take place in a highly dramatic setting.[6] Perhaps the most obvious example of a commitment ceremony is the criminal trial, with its elaborate formality and exaggerated ritual, but more modest equivalents can be found wherever procedures are set up to judge whether or not someone is legitimately deviant.

Now an important feature of these ceremonies in our own culture is that they are almost irreversible. Most provisional roles conferred by society—those of the student or conscripted soldier, for example—include some kind of terminal ceremony to mark the individual's movement back out of the role once its temporary advantages have been exhausted. But the roles allotted the deviant seldom make allowance for this type of passage. He is ushered into the deviant position by a decisive and often dramatic ceremony, yet is retired from it with scarcely a word of public notice. And as a result, the deviant often returns home with no proper license to resume a normal life in the community. Nothing has happened to cancel out the stigmas imposed upon him by earlier commitment ceremonies; nothing has happened to revoke the verdict or diagnosis pronounced upon him at that time. It should not be surprising, then, that the people of the community are apt to greet the returning deviant with a considerable degree of apprehension and distrust, for in a very real sense they are not at all sure who he is.

A circularity is thus set into motion which has all the earmarks of a "self-fulfilling prophecy," to use Merton's fine phrase. On the one hand, it seems quite obvious that the community's apprehensions help reduce whatever chances the deviant might otherwise have had for a successful return home. Yet at the same time, everyday experience seems to show that these suspicions are wholly reasonable, for it is a well-known and highly publicized fact that many if not most ex-convicts return to crime after leaving prison and that large numbers of mental patients require further treatment after an initial hospitalization. The common feeling that deviant persons never really change, then, may derive from a faulty premise; but the feeling is expressed so frequently and with such conviction that it eventually creates the facts which later "prove" it to be correct. If the returning deviant encounters this circularity often enough, it is quite understandable that he, too, may begin to wonder whether he has fully graduated from the deviant role, and he may respond to the uncertainty by resuming some kind of deviant activity. In many respects, this may be the only way for the individual and his community to agree what kind of person he is.

Moreover this prophecy is found in the official policies of even the most responsible agencies of control. Police departments could not operate with any real effectiveness if they did not regard ex-convicts as a ready pool of suspects to be tapped in the event of trouble, and psychiatric clinics could not do a successful job in the community if they were not always alert to the possibility of former patients suffering relapses. Thus the prophecy gains currency at many levels within the social order, not only in the poorly informed attitudes of the community at large, but in the best informed theories of most control agencies as well.

In one form or another this problem has been recognized in the West for many hundreds of years, and this simple fact has a curious implication. For if our culture has supported a steady flow of deviation throughout long periods of historical change, the rules which apply to any kind of evolutionary thinking would suggest that strong forces must be at work to keep the flow intact—and this because it contributes in some important way to the survival of the culture as a whole. This does not furnish us with sufficient warrant to declare that deviance is "functional" (in any of the many senses of that term), but it should certainly make us wary of the assumption so often made in sociological circles that any well-structured society is somehow designed to prevent deviant behavior from occurring.[7]

It might be then argued that we need new metaphors to carry our thinking about deviance onto a different plane. On the whole, American sociologists have devoted most of their attention to those forces in society which seem to assert a centralizing influence on human behavior, gathering people together into tight clusters called "groups" and bringing them under the jurisdiction of governing principles called "norms" or "standards." The questions which sociologists have traditionally asked of their data, then, are addressed to the uniformities rather than the divergencies of social life: how is it that people learn to think in similar ways, to accept the same group moralities, to move by the same rhythms of behavior, to see life with the same eyes? How is it, in short, that cultures accomplish the incredible alchemy of making unity out of diversity, harmony out of conflict, order out of confusion? Somehow we often act as if the differences between people can be taken for granted, being too natural to require comment, but that the symmetry which human groups manage to achieve must be explained by referring to the molding influence of the social structure.

But variety, too, is a product of the social structure. It is certainly remarkable that members of a culture come to look so much alike; but it is also remarkable that out of all this sameness a people can develop a complex division of labor, move off into diverging career lines, scatter across the surface of the territory they share in common, and create so many differences of temper, ideology, fashion, and mood. Perhaps we can conclude, then, that two separate yet often competing current sare found in any society: those forces which promote a high degree of conformity among the people of the community so that they know what to expect from one another, and those forces which encourage a certain degree of diversity so that people can be deployed across the range of group space to survey its potential, measure its capacity, and, in the case of those we call deviants, patrol its boundaries. In such a scheme, the deviant would appear as a natural product of group differentiation. He is not a bit of debris spun out by faulty social machinery, but a relevant figure in the community's overall division of labor.

NOTES

1. In fact, the first statement of the general notion presented here was concerned with the study of small groups. See Robert A. Dentier and Kai T. Erikson, "The Functions of Deviance in Groups," *Social Problems,* VII (Fall 1959), pp. 98–107.

2. Aldous Huxley, *Prisons: The "Carceri" Etchings by Piranesi* (London: The Trianon Press, 1949), p. 13.

3. For a good description of this process in the modern prison, see Gresham Sykes, *The Society of Captives* (Princeton, N.J.: Princeton University Press, 1958). For discussions of similar problems in two different kinds of mental hospital, see Erving Goffman, *Asylums* (New York: Bobbs-Merrill, 1962) and Kai T. Erikson, "Patient Role and Social Uncertainty: A Dilemma of the Mentally 111," *Psychiatry,* XX (August 1957), pp. 263–274.

4. Written by "a celebrated" but not otherwise identified author (perhaps Henry Fielding) and quoted in John Howard, *The State of the Prisons,* London, 1777 (London: J. M. Dent and Sons, 1929), p. 10.

5. The classic description of this process as it applies to the medical patient is found in Talcott Parsons, *The Social System* (Glencoe, 111.: The Free Press, 1951).

6. See Harold Garfinkel, "Successful Degradation Ceremonies," *American Journal of Sociology,* LXI (January 1956), pp. 420–424.

7. Albert K. Cohen, for example, speaking for a dominant strain in sociological thinking, takes the question quite for granted: "It would seem that the control of deviant behavior is, by definition, a culture goal." See "The Study of Social Disorganization and Deviant Behavior" in Merton et al., *Sociology Today* (New York: Basic Books, 1959), p. 465.

2

An Integrated Typology of Deviance Applied to Ten Middle-Class Norms

ALEX HECKERT AND DRUANN MARIA HECKERT

Deviance has traditionally been regarded as behavior that underconforms to society's norms of acceptability and is negatively received. Deviants were considered anti-social misfits either through their failure to live up to societal standards or through their intentional defiance of norms. In previous works, Heckert and Heckert challenged this view, exploring both of its dimensions: the excessive enactment of pro-social behavior, and people's positive reactions to deviance. They offered a controversial four-fold table interrelating the axis of under/non- and overconformity (how the behavior corresponds to normative expectations) with the suggestion that people do not always react to deviance negatively, but sometimes admire it (their social reactions and collective evaluations). By cross-tabulating the dimension of underconformity and overconformity with that of social evaluation, positive and negative, they yielded four analytic types of deviance: negative deviance, rate-busting, deviance admiration, and positive deviance.

In this chapter they further articulate their typology by applying it to a list of ten middle-class norms developed by Tittle and Paternoster (2000). Addressing such issues as lying, disloyalty, hedonism, irresponsibility, and invasion of privacy, Heckert and Heckert evaluate these forms of "negative deviance" to suggest how such acts might translate into their deviance admiration, positive deviance, and rate-busting counterparts. This creative analysis strengthens their previous typology by fleshing it out with concrete examples that further challenge traditional thinking about definitions of deviance.

What do you think of Heckert and Heckert's typologies? Should we stick with the more conventional definition of deviance as norm violations that are negatively received, or do you buy their assertions about positive deviance? Is too much of a good thing a good thing, or is it really deviant?

A TYPOLOGY OF DEVIANCE INTEGRATING NORMATIVE AND REACTIVIST PERSPECTIVES

An assortment of definitions have clouded the substantive area of deviance, ranging from an absolutist approach to a statistical one to the more ubiquitous normative and reactivist approaches (Goode 2001). Nevertheless, the predominant bifurcation within the discipline is between the normative and reactivist perspectives (Liska 1981). Normative, or objectivist, definitions, on the one hand, primarily focus on the violation of norms (cf., Merton 1966); simply and succinctly, Cohen defined deviance as "behavior that violates normative rules" (1966, p. 12). On the other hand, reactivist or subjectivist definitions focus on the dynamics of the reaction of a social audience (cf., Becker 1963; Erikson 1964; Lemert 1972). As Becker (1963, p. 11) so famously wrote, "Social groups constitute deviance by making rules whose infractions constitute deviance, and by applying those rules to particular people and labeling them as outsiders." Each definition presents a major paradigmatic understanding of deviance. These definitions clearly tend to emphasize behaviors. Most sociologists do, however, extend definitions of deviance to include what Adler and Adler (2000, p. 8) term the "ABCs of deviance: their attitudes, behaviors, or conditions." Although the examples we provide in the current article focus primarily on behaviors, attitudes (or beliefs), and conditions are assuredly essential (since normative expectations and social reactions pertain to both) with regard to deviance and can be fruitfully analyzed using our conceptual framework.

Our typology seeks to integrate the underlying phenomena addressed by each definition (Heckert and Heckert 2002). This typology recognizes the distinction as a false dichotomy and acknowledges the existence of both normative expectations and social reactions. Behavior and conditions can underconform (or nonconform) or overconform to normative expectations, as well as lead to negative or positive reactions. As such, we have cross-classified the significance of both norms and reactions, creating four possible scenarios. As Figure 2.1 shows, negative deviance, on the one hand, is underconformity or nonconformity that results in negative reactions. On the other hand, rate busting is over-conformity that is negatively evaluated. Next, deviance admiration is underconformity or nonconformity that is positively appraised by the collectivity. Finally, positive deviance is overconformity that receives positive reactions. Each type of deviance will be briefly described.

The substantive area of deviance has first and foremost involved the scrutiny of negative deviance. Negative deviance refers to underconformity or nonconformity that is also negatively evaluated; metaphorically, negative deviance is the "Jeffrey Dahmer phenomenon." As Adler and Adler (2000) described this situation, attitudes, behaviors, or conditions can be deviantized. Negative deviants can range from most criminals to the mentally ill to substance abusers to those with unpopular political or religious stances. Essentially, the standard in the field of deviance is the negative reaction to (and sanctioning of) underconformity or nonconformity.

Normative Expectations

Social Reactions and Collective Evaluations	Underconformity or Nonconformity	Overconformity
Negative Evaluations	Negative Deviance	Rate Busting
Positive Evaluations	Deviance Admiration	Positive Deviance

FIGURE 2.1   Deviance Typology

Alternatively, rate busting is negatively appraised overconformity. At the core this cell epitomizes the "geek phenomenon." Various social scientists have noted that norms operate at two levels; the idealized (i.e., that which is believed sublimely better but improbable for most people) and the realistic (i.e., that which is viewed as achievable by typical people) (Homans 1950; Johnson 1978; Heckert 1998). Nevertheless, this overconformity—even if idealized or perhaps because it is idealized—is often subjected to negative evaluations. Rate busting has occurred in various realms of life. For example, Huryn (1986) determined that gifted students are often rejected by their peers; Krebs and Adinolfi (1975) concluded that the attractive are often slighted by members of their same sex; and Heckert (2003) found that blonde women (defined as over-conforming to European standards of beauty) are subjected to epic stereotyping, especially related to their intellectual capacity (or assumed lack thereof).

The third cell is deviance admiration, which focuses on underconformity or nonconformity that is favorably assessed. For all intents and purposes, this condition could be labeled the "John Gotti phenomenon." Although the attribute, behavior, or condition is normatively unacceptable to a collectivity, the response of that group is still assenting. Kooistra (1989) concluded that a fair number of criminals, even brutal ones, have been transformed—by the collective imagination—from thugs to icons. In other words, Robin Hood is not relegated to the realm of myth but has bona fide real-life counterparts, ranging from Billy the Kid to D. B. Cooper to Butch Cassidy. As another example, in a society that castigates those individuals who do not meet culturally dominant and created aesthetic images of appearance, there are also many that admire the stigmatized attribute (e.g., people of size and redheads) and individuals with that attribute.

The final category is positive deviance, which describes overconformity that is responded to in a confirmatory fashion. Essentially, this is the "Mother Theresa phenomenon." Similar to negative deviance, positive deviance has been previously defined from various viewpoints, including from a normative perspective (cf., Wilkins 1965; Winslow 1970), from a labeling point of view (cf., Freedman and Doob 1968; Hawkins and Tiedeman 1975; Scarpitti and McFarlane 1975; Steffensmeier and Terry 1975), and from the perspective that positive deviance is overconformity that is positively evaluated (Dodge 1985; Heckert and Heckert 2002). Examples of positively appraised overconformity include good neighbors and saints (Sorokin 1950), Congressional Medal of Honor winners (Steffensnieier and Terry 1975), and the physically attractive (cf., Berscheid and Walster 1964; Byrne 1971; Reis et al. 1982). Exceeding normative expectations, at times, creates a scenario whereby positive reactions and evaluations flow, often producing all kinds of added advantages; thus, the response transcends even the norm at stake.

All in all, this typology recognizes that the traditional distinction between normative expectations and societal reactions involves a false dichotomy and seeks to integrate normative definitions with reactivist definitions. Thus, attitudes, behaviors, and conditions can become conceptualized as negative deviance, rate busting, deviance admiration, and positive deviance. Clearly, as theorists in the field of deviance have long contended, contexts do have to be considered as audiences can differentially react to the same behavior or conditions. In other words, gifted and overachieving students are rate busters to their peers at the same time they are positive deviants to their teachers. Elite tattoo collectors are simultaneously positive deviants to their subculture and negative deviants to the dominant society (Irwin 2003). As well, many individuals who were admired as extraordinary in a later era were castigated in their own era because they dared not to conform to their time's antiquated or oppressive normative code (Coser 1967; Merton 1968; Dinitz, Dynes, and Clarke 1969). Examples include Galileo, Jesus (to Christians), Socrates, and the French Impressionists. Essentially, for divergent reasons, underconformers or nonconformers are often positively evaluated, and overconformers are often negatively evaluated.

This typology allows sociologists to continue to utilize a traditional notion that deviance is relative and that context is critical (Thio 1983). It is important to analyze why underconformity or nonconformity can result in positive evaluations or negative evaluations, depending on the era, place, or social group involved. The same is true for overconformity (Heckert and Heckert 2002). Power and people's self-interest are critical components. In reference to either underconformity or overconformity, negative reactions are likely to emerge when attitudes, behaviors, or conditions threaten the interests of the social group. . . .

NORMS AND PREDOMINANT MIDDLE-CLASS
NORMS IN THE UNITED STATES

Integral components of any cultural system, norms guide expected behavior and are based directly on values held to be important. For example, based on fourteen common definitions of norms, Gibbs (1981, p. 7) asserted that most commonly a norm has been defined as "a belief shared to some extent by members of a social unit as to what conduct *ought to be* in particular situations or circumstances." Gusfield (1963, p. 65) further suggested that these systems produce "regularities of action."

Other sociologists have indicated that norms could be dually conceptualized between the idealized and the more realistic (Johnson 1960; Johnson 1978) or operative norms. In essence, the more idealized are really values (cf., White 1961; Blake and Davis 1964). Williams (1965) created the seminal and most comprehensive description of the value system of the United States, outlining the following dominant values: achievement and success, individualism, activity and work, efficiency and practicality, science and technology, progress, material comfort, humanitarianism, freedom, democracy, equality, and racism and group superiority. To that list Henslin (1975) added education, religiosity, romantic love, and monogamy. Thus, the American value system has been amply addressed.

Recently, Tittle and Paternoster (2000) have expanded sociological understanding by outlining not the idealized scheme of values but the normative system itself. Their outline is restricted to middle-class values in the United States and includes the following dominant norms: group loyalty, privacy, prudence, conventionality, responsibility, participation, moderation, honesty, peacefulness, and courtesy. Loyalty describes the necessity of the group to survive over individual concerns. Privacy indicates that individuals need to be in command of certain spaces and places. Prudence refers to placing pleasure in perspective and to practicing pleasure with moderation. Conventionality is descriptive of people choosing habits and life scenarios that are similar to those of other people. Responsibility is dependability, especially when others must count on that characteristic. Participation implies personal involvement in both economic and social spheres; alienation constitutes the nonconforming counterpart. Moderation means an avoidance of the extremes in life. Honesty denotes veracity and candor. Peacefulness illustrates a sedate and calm style. Finally, courtesy revolves around refined social etiquette in human interaction. Overall, one set of consequential norms has been thoroughly delineated.

APPLYING THE INTEGRATED NORMATIVE-REACTIVIST TYPOLOGY TO MIDDLE-CLASS NORMS OF THE UNITED STATES

To verify the utility of our integrative typology, we seek to apply this typology to a normative system. In this initial foray, we apply the typology to dominant and current American middle-class norms. Tittle and Paternoster (2000) documented these norms; as well, they highlighted the deviance (or what we will subsequently refer to as, more specifically, negative deviance) forms of each norm. The deviance admiration, rate busting, and positive deviance variety of each norm is specified in Table 2.1 and will be further discussed in the following sections.

TABLE 2.1   A Classification of U.S. Middle-Class Deviance

Norm	Negative Deviance	Deviance Admiration	Rate Busting	Positive Deviance
Group loyalty	Apostasy	Rebellion	Fanaticism	Altruism
Privacy	Intrusion	Investigation	Seclusion	Circumspection
Prudence	Indiscretion	Exhibitionism	Puritanism	Discretion
Conventionality	Bizarreness	Faddishness	Provincialism	Properness
Responsibility	Irresponsibility	Adventurousness	Priggishness	Hyperresponsibility
Participation	Alienation	Independence	Dependence	Cooperation
Moderation	Hedonism	Roguishness	Asceticism	Temperance
Honesty	Deceitfulness	Tactfulness	Tactlessness	Forthrightness
Peacefulness	Disruption	Revelry	Wimpishness	Pacifism
Courtesy	Uncouthness	Irreverence	Obsequiousness	Gentility

Note: Types of negative deviance taken from Tittle and Paternoster 2000, p. 35.

Negative Deviance

To reiterate, negative deviance is underconformity or nonconformity that is negatively evaluated. Tittle and Paternoster (2000) focused on negative deviance and have outlined illuminating examples of each category which are listed in Table 2.2. Again, these examples are quintessentially representative of the traditional nucleus of the substantive area of the sociological study of deviance.

As an example of the valuable work of Tittle and Paternoster (2000), as the survival of the group is viewed as paramount, apostasy becomes deviantized. Consequently, actions and/or actors such as revolution or revolutionaries are deemed deviant. As privacy is critical, intrusion in the form of theft or rape is deviant. Because prudence is valued, indiscretion in the form of prostitution is negatively stigmatized. Because conventionality forms an important normative idea, bizarreness that can include some mentally ill behavior is deviant. For the reason that responsibility is valued, irresponsibility such as family desertion becomes unacceptable to middle-class Americans. Given that participation is normative, alienation—which can include nonparticipatory lifestyles—becomes snubbed. In view of the fact that moderation is critical to middle-class Americans, hedonism in the guise of chiseling or atheism is negatively appraised. Although Tittle and Paternoster (2000) include asceticism as a type of underconformity to the norm of moderation, utilizing this new model we prefer to conceptualize it as over-conformity. Because honesty is appreciated, deceitfulness epitomized by bigamy and price-fixing deviantized. Seeing that peacefulness is valued, disruption in the form of noisy disorganizing behavior or boisterous reveling is not appreciated in the context of this particular normative system. As courtesy is normalized, uncouthness as exemplified by rudeness or uncleanliness is stigmatized. All in all, Tittle and Paternoster (2000) have provided a comprehensive accounting of various deviantized behaviors within the middle class of the United States. This

T A B L E 2.2   A Classification of U.S. Middle-Class Deviance, Negative Deviance

Norm	Negative Deviance	Examples
Group loyalty	Apostasy	Revolution; betraying national secrets; treason; draft dodging; flag defilement; giving up citizenship; advocating contrary government philosophy
Privacy	Intrusion	Theft; burglary; rape; homicide; voyeurism; forgery; record spying
Prudence	Indiscretion	Prostitution; homosexual behavior; incest; bestiality; adultery; swinging; gambling; substance abuse
Conventionality	Bizarreness	"Mentally ill behavior" (handling excrement, nonsense talking, eating human flesh, fetishes); separatist lifestyles
Responsibility	Irresponsibility	Family desertion; reneging on debts; unprofessional conduct; improper role performance; violations of trust; pollution; fraudulent business
Participation	Alienation	Nonparticipatory lifestyles (being a hermit, street living); perpetual unemployment; receiving public assistance; suicide
Moderation	Hedonism	Chiseling; atheism; alcoholism; total deceit; wasting; ignoring children
Honesty	Deceitfulness	Selfish lying; price-fixing; exploitation of the weak and helpless; bigamy; welfare cheating
Peacefulness	Disruption	Noisy disorganizing behavior; boisterous reveling; quarreling; fighting; contentiousness
Courtesy	Uncouthness	Private behavior in public places (picking nose, burping); rudeness (smoking in prohibited places, breaking in line); uncleanliness

Note: Table from Tittle & Paternoster 2000, p. 35.

outline sketches negative deviance, the substance of the long-established and accepted core of the field of deviance.

Rate Busting

Rate busting refers to the negative reaction not to underconformity but to over-conformity and constitutes the "geek phenomenon." In other words, adhering to the idealized level of the norm induces unfavorable evaluations. As Tittle and Paternoster (2000) analyzed a deviant (or negative deviant) form of each norm, we outline a rate busting form of each of the ten norms in Table 2.3. We also provide a nonexhaustive list of examples for each category of rate busting.

Regarding the norm of group loyalty, overconforming to the group can result in negative evaluations. This category is referred to as fanaticism. As examples, NRA participants and hate group members, accepted subculturally, are too responsive to their groups and are deviantized—by various parts of culture in the

TABLE 2.3 **A Classification of U.S. Middle-Class Deviance, Rate Busting**

Norm	Rate Busting	Examples
Group loyalty	Fanaticism	Various religious cults; Ku Klux Klan (who, of course, engage in acts of negative deviance); Aryan Nation; NRA; religious fanatics; superpatriots; "holier than thou"
Privacy	Seclusion	Hermits; loners; Amish and other reclusive religious sects; secretive or reclusive behavior; Howard Hughes
Prudence	Puritanism	Negative attitudes and behavior toward Amish and other conservative religious sects
Conventionality	Provincialism	Stepford wives; Martha Stewart and her followers; keeping up with the Joneses in following every little rule so as to be accepted; individuals who are negatively evaluated for ritualistically following convention
Responsibility	Priggishness	Negative attitude regarding people who are self-righteous; jokes and meanness toward Martha Stewart and her followers; some workaholics; straight-A student
Participation	Dependence	Brownnoser; a person trying so hard to be accepted by every group that they lose their individuality; the concepts of codependency and enabling behavior
Moderation	Asceticism	Negative reactions to not drinking; a person so meek that they never take a stand on anything so as not to offend anyone
Honesty	Tactlessness	Being too honest with friends (e.g., about ugly clothing, unattractive haircut); a person so honest they won't tell a "white lie" or who will say something mean to a child because it is honest rather than to protect child's feelings
Peacefulness	Wimpishness	A person who never parties or "lets their hair down"; a person who will never take a stand or stand up to people; "yes man"
Obsequiousness	Courtesy	The person who is overly polite; making fun of Miss Manners and people who are overly courteous

first case and by the dominant society in the second case—on this basis (and other important ones as well). Religious cult members are also viewed as too immersed in their groups; their individuality is perceived to be lost to the group. Individuals who are "holier than thou" within dominant religious traditions often estrange members of their own group. "Super patriots" who are too enthusiastic in their display of symbolic representations of nation and who will support government under any circumstance often alienate others. Concerning the norm of privacy, the rate busting equivalent is seclusion. Among those who are negatively reacted to in response to what is deemed their seclusive tendencies are the following: hermits, secretive or reclusive individuals such as Howard Hughes in his later years, and reclusive religious groups, such as the Amish. In reference to the normative orientation respecting prudence, Puritanism refers to those who are overly prudent and negatively stigmatized. For example, very conservative religious sects that seem to eschew what dominant Americans view as necessary pleasures—such as the Amish, Hutterites, Shakers (the very few remaining), and Jehovah's Witnesses—are shunned and/or created into exotic humans and not accepted into the dominant cultural fold. With the situation of conventionality, the rate busting scenario is provincialism. Being overly conventional or mindlessly attempting to conform to the habits of others are often negatively appraised. For example, mass media created the Stepford wives, who are fictionally representative of this category. As a flesh-and-blood counterpart, Martha Stewart and her fans have been constant grist for comedians; this stigmatization occurred even prior to her legal troubles. Pertaining to the norm of responsibility, priggishness is the rate busting form. Some workaholics—those motivated by an intense sense of responsibility—have long been subjected to negative treatment by their coworkers, even if praised by their bosses. As well, peers have long taunted overachieving students, who set a high standard in the academic realm.

Concerning participation, dependence is the rate busting counterpart. Among those who overly participate in social and/or economic life are the brownnoser, the codependent and enabling family member of a substance abuser, and the person who wants to be accepted so badly by the group that he or she sacrifices individuality. With regards to moderation, asceticism is overconformity that is negatively appraised. Individuals who drink socially and moderately are conforming; those who do not drink are overconforming and ironically—similarly to pathological drinkers—are negatively evaluated on that basis (even if the stigmatization is not the same type of stigmatization). For example, non-drinkers will often develop explanations (i.e., designated driver) so as to attempt to avoid the almost inevitable questions rooted in disbelief about their choice. In connection with honesty, tactlessness is the overconforming response that will not be positively received. For example, persons so honest that they will never tell a lie, even a socially acceptable lie, are often viewed as tactless. Thus, the following scenario could occur. If a young girl asks an adult if her dress is pretty and the adult replies that it is the ugliest dress ever created, the adult would be veracious and overconforming to honesty. Nevertheless, under middle-class normative conditions, the adult would not be positively received. In respect to peacefulness, the rate busting sort is wimpishness. A meek person who never "lets her or his hair down" or who will never stand up to anybody so as to avoid contentiousness would be looked down upon and labeled with the following appellation: "mousy" or "yes-man." Vis-à-vis courtesy, obsequiousness is the rate busting form. A person who is so very courteous in social interaction that every diminutive rule of etiquette is exactly followed is viewed as overconforming and often spurned. Consequently, Miss Manners becomes almost a comically viewed person, rather than the serious person she professes To be as the arbiter of such matters. Eddie Haskell, a fictionalized character from *Leave It To Beaver,* is also viewed similarly.

All in all, for each of the ten norms, a rate busting form of deviance is listed in Table 2.3. As well, examples readily illuminate each possibility.

Deviance Admiration

To recap, deviance admiration or the "John Gotti phenomenon" occurs in the context of underconformity that is positively evaluated. In other words, people do not view John Gotti as doing right; rather, they accept that he has violated considerably cherished norms and endorse him anyway. Potentially, deviance admiration can surface for each of these norms as shown in Table 2.4. Each of the examples of negative deviance provided by Tittle and Paternoster (2000), then, could be positively evaluated and therefore potentially could serve as examples of deviance admiration.

Rebellion is the deviance admiration form of group loyalty. Among the most historically revered figures in middle-class American life are the American revolutionaries, including George Washington, Thomas Jefferson, John Hancock, Nathan Hale, and Thomas Paine. They are now emblematic of ultimate patriotism because of their rebellion. Investigation constitutes the deviance admiration of the norm of privacy. For example, revelations on the *Jerry Springer Show* constitute a violation of the norm of privacy; though perhaps not universally admired, the enduring tenure of the show suggests that there are many fans. Exhibitionism composes the deviance admiration type of prudence, whereby pleasure is bounded. Famous strippers and entertainers, such as RuPaul, have fashioned abundant economic lives on this premise. Additionally, participants in extreme sports certainly underconform to norms of prudence and are tremendously acclaimed for this imprudence, especially by the young. Faddishness embodies the deviance admiration form of conventionality. Faddishness describes underconformity to the habits of most others in the context of an appreciation of that behavior. For example, Americans are presently charmed by the Osbournes; other than the love that permeates their family bonds, they are not conventional. As well, tattoos (and body piercing) and individuals—such as Dennis Rodman, Allen Iverson, and virtually any rock star—who acquire these accoutrements of a youthful imaginative aesthetic are often appreciated. Adventurousness makes up the deviance admiration form of responsibility. Many adventurers of unconquered terrains, including expeditionary individuals who made early conquests of the Artie, Antarctica, Mount Everest, and outer space, have created a permanent place in history for themselves.

Independence represents the deviance admiration counterpart to participation or involving oneself in the social and economic life of a community. Hoboes or other historical figures viewed to be voluntarily not attached to place or community and keenly uninvolved in community geographical boundaries were almost symbolic of freedom—rather than economic hard times—in another era. As well, those individuals who spend time in settlements in Antarctica, especially those who winter over and thus are effectively cut off from the rest of the planet, fall into this category. Roguishness is illustrative of the deviance admiration component of moderation. Assuredly, dominant middle-class culture has often preferred

TABLE 2.4   A Classification of U.S. Middle-Class Deviance, Deviance Admiration

Norm	Deviance Admiration	Examples
Group loyalty	Rebellion	James Dean (rebel without a cause); American Revolution; Pentagon papers; admiration for men who went to Canada to avoid draft during Vietnam War
Privacy	Investigation	Investigative journalism; private investigators; revelations on *Jerry Springer Show*
Prudence	Exhibitionism	Famous strippers; gay rights movement; famous gamblers; flamboyant entertainers (e.g., Liberace, RuPaul, transvestites, female impersonators); extreme sports; reality television like *The Osbournes* and the *Anna Nicole Smith Show*
Conventionality	Faddishness	*The Osbournes;* tattoos; bizarre subcultures; body-piercing; wiccan and similar subcultures
Responsibility	Adventurousness	Extreme sports (e.g., hang gliding, mountain climbing, free diving, etc.); *Jackass the Movie* humor; explorers
Participation	Independence	Romantic loners; mysterious strangers; drifters; hoboes; explorers
Moderation	Roguishness	Charming rogue; the lovable drunk (e.g., Otis on the *Andy Griffith Show*); Bill Clinton
Honesty	Tactfulness	Honest humor on *The Man Show*, telling "tall tales"; the liar who is admired; telling "white lies"; person who lies to achieve greater goal (e.g., national security, confession from serial killer using "good cop," "bad cop" strategies, an operative who lies to be able to capture an "enemy" such as a terrorist)
Placefulness	Revelry	Mardi Gras; fraternity partying; loud entertainer at a party; Spring Break phenomenon
Courtesy	Irreverence	Class clown; humor on *The Man Show*, rude humor on shows such as *The Simpsons, South Park,* and *Beavis and Butthead*

the enchanting and charming rogue to the earnest, but dull, person. Fictionally, Otis on the *Andy Griffith Show* is representative of this phenomenon; amongst the living, so is Bill Clinton. Tactfulness, particularly as resourcefulness (depending on the context), is the deviance admiration characterization of honesty. In other words, middle-class culture does value lying under certain conditions or for certain reasons. For example, the cop who plays loose with the truth to extract a confession from a serial killer would be positively assessed for his or her resourcefulness in underconforming to the norm of honesty, as would an operative who is dishonest in order to capture a terrorist. On the level of social interaction, those who tactfully tell "white lies" or socially accepted lies—for the purpose of protecting the emotional feelings of another—are usually positively reviewed. Revelry serves as the deviance admiration element of peacefulness. Much vacation behavior falls into this category. Among popular vacation ventures and/or venues that are often adored amongst middle-class Americans are the Mardi Gras, spring break on any warm beach, and Times Square on New Year's Eve. Finally, irreverence is the deviance admiration type of courtesy. Mischievous individuals engage in sly impudence or adopt a mildly mocking stance toward etiquette. The irreverent range from the fictional Dennis the Menace to the real life class clown to virtually any comedian.

Essentially, there is a corresponding deviance admiration form for each of the middle-class norms outlined by Tittle and Paternoster (2000). Various attitudes, behaviors, or conditions (Adler and Adler 2000) exemplify each category.

Positive Deviance

To echo the model, positive deviance denotes overconformity to the norms that is positively evaluated. The "Mother Theresa phenomenon" occurs when positive reactions or labeling follows overconformity to norms. In other words, Mother Theresa overconformed to the norm of altruism; she was almost universally praised as a saintly woman. For each of the norms suggested by Tittle and Paternoster (2000), a corresponding positive deviance category is proffered in Table 2.5.

Altruism is the positive deviance form of loyalty. In this case, the person is extraordinarily loyal to the group, overconforming to that norm, and that which emerges due to that loyalty is positively viewed. For example, historically, religious and political martyrs have fallen into this category. That is, the person is viewed as having sacrificed greatly for his or her group. Examples would be the Sullivan brothers from Iowa in World War II or Joan of Arc. National holidays commemorate this type of positive deviance. Every soldier is honored on Veteran's Day, and soldiers who have died for their society are venerated on Memorial Day. Religious martyrs include figures such as Stephen (from the Christian faith). As well, assassinated political leaders such as Abraham Lincoln, John F. Kennedy, Martin Luther King Jr., and Robert F. Kennedy are greatly admired.

Circumspection constitutes the positive deviance form of privacy. Individuals who have security clearances and honor that code are admired for their circumspection; as well, so are professionals—such as doctors, nurses, and clergy—who deal with confidential aspects of the lives of people and honor those confidences. Discretion composes the positive deviance aspect of prudence. In other words, someone who eschews unnecessary frivolous and pleasurable activities so as to achieve an important goal is often admired. Olympic athletes are often viewed as having to steadfastly deny themselves various pleasures so as to diligently advance toward their goal. Properness is the positive deviance type of conventionality. At times, admiration is granted toward those who over-conform to the expected habits and lifestyles of the middle class. Some admire the Junior Leaguers who engage in exceedingly conventional lifestyles. Hyperresponsibility

T A B L E 2.5   **A Classification of U.S. Middle-Class Deviance, Positive Deviance**

Norm	Positive Deviance	Examples
Group loyalty	Altruism	Kamikaze pilots; martyrs; sharing food or other resources; daring rescues (e.g., at sea, mountains); patriot
Privacy	Circumspection	CIA operatives; FBI/Justice Department agents; loyal company employees (e.g., Oliver North)
Prudence	Discretion	The good friend who practices discretion; a person who denies themselves pleasures to achieve a goal (e.g. Olympians and other athletes)
Conventionality	Properness	Junior League members; Martha Stewart's followers; Boy Scouts, Girl Scouts, and similar groups
Responsibility	Hyperresponsibility	Overachiever; straight-A student (as viewed by parents and teachers); workaholic (as viewed by management); overzealous athlete (e.g. Tiger Woods, Michael Jordan)
Participation	Cooperation	Athletic team where individual talents are deemphasized so the team can win; employees who are positively viewed as team players
Moderation	Temperance	Monks; (nuns); Women's Temperance Movement; Mothers Against Drunk Driving
Honesty	Forthrightness	Honest Abe Lincoln; George Washington cutting down the cherry tree
Peacefulness	Pacifism	Gandhi; Martin Luther King Jr.; Jimmy Carter
Courtesy	Gentility	Miss Manners; the old-fashioned practitioners of southern hospitality who are admired; the gentleman; the "southern belle"

is the positive deviance form of the norm of responsibility. For example, those who overconform on the norm of responsibility are often positively evaluated. Management values the overachieving worker; parents and teachers affirm the overachieving student; and almost everyone acknowledge the overzealous athlete (e.g., Michael Jordan and Tiger Woods).

Cooperation (doing it for the team) represents the positive deviance profile of participation. At times, individuals are so involved in community life that they will diminish their own egos for the good of community involvement. As an example, when individual talents are deemphasized so that an athletic team can win, this process occurs. A long-standing joke in the sports world is that Dean Smith was the only person capable of keeping Michael Jordan under twenty points per game; nevertheless, that team's first and foremost philosophy allowed Michael Jordan and his UNC teammates to defeat Georgetown for the national championship. Temperance illustrates the positive deviance of moderation. When their purpose is a more transcendent one, ascetics or others who overconform to moderation are positively evaluated. Examples include people who choose religion for their life's calling, including priests, monks, nuns, preachers, and rabbis. Specifically, people—from many faith traditions—admire the Dalai Lama for the sublime and spiritual path of his life.

Forthrightness exemplifies positive deviance for the norm of honesty. Virtually every school child in this country is successfully socialized to esteem the importance of honesty through the story of George Washington and the cherry tree and through the honest individual as epitomized by the iconic and, perhaps, most reverentially viewed president—Abraham Lincoln. Pacifism demonstrates the deviance admiration category of peacefulness. Yearly, the Nobel Prize for Peace serves as a formalized positive reward for individuals in this category. Among individuals nearly universally admired in the context of dominant middle-class American values are individuals—such as Gandhi, Martin Luther King Jr., and Jimmy Carter—who practiced peacefulness while working toward social change. Finally, gentility is the positive deviance form of courtesy. Old-world manners (or southern hospitality) are overconforming to norms of courtesy and are often admired.

Certainly, a positive deviance form exists for each of the ten norms assembled by Tittle and Paternoster (2000). Various examples illustrate each of these categories. . . .

CONCLUSION

Long ago Durkheini (1982) pointed out the inevitability or normalcy of deviance; furthermore, Durkheini (1964; 1982) illuminated positive functions of deviance. A variety of social-psychological experiments, such as those by Sherif (1936), Asch (1952), and Schachter (1951), also suggested the fundamental existence of the processes of norms production, conformity, deviance production, and individual and social reactions to (potentially) deviant behaviors, attitudes, and conditions. The importance of power and social context in influencing norms, social reactions, and deviance outcomes cannot be ignored. The behaviors and conditions of more powerful actors are less likely to be deviantized than those of the less powerful. The reactions of powerful actors and social groups, moreover, are more important in determining who and what is successfully labeled deviant. In fact, we have argued that deviant behavior actually serves as a test of power relationships (Heckert and Heckert 2002). When a child lies, for example, she is testing the parent's ability to discern and react to the lie. When the child successfully "gets away" with the lie, a shift in the relative power of the child and parent has occurred.

The central place of norms, social reactions, efforts at social control, and deviance processes, therefore, suggest the importance of an integrated framework for understanding these factors and their interrelationships. Our integrated typology is an initial attempt to eliminate the false dichotomy imposed by previous conceptualizations of deviance.

REFERENCES

Adler, Patricia A., and Peter Adler. 2000. *Constructions of Deviance: Social Power, Context, and Interaction*. 3rd ed. Belmont, CA: Wadsworth.

Asch, Solomon. 1952. *Social Psychology*. Englewood Cliffs, NJ: Prentice Hall.

Becker, Howard. 1963. *Outsiders*. New York: The Free Press of Glencoe.

Berscheid, Ellen, and Elaine Walster. 1964. "Physical Attractiveness." Pp. 157–215 in *Advances in Experimental Social Psychology*. Vol. 7. New York Academic Press.

Blake, Judith, and Kingsley Davis. 1964. "Norms, Values, and Sanctions." Pp. 456–484 in *Handbook of Modern Sociology*, edited by Robert E. L. Faris. Chicago: Rand McNally.

Byrne, Don. 1971. *The Attraction Paradigm*. New York: Academic Press.

Cohen, Albert K. 1966. *Deviance and Control*. Englewood Cliffs, NJ: Prentice Hall.

Coser, Lews A. 1967. *Continuities in the Study of Social Confia*. New York: The Free Press.

Dinitz, Simon, Russell R. Dynes, and Alfred C. Clarke. 1969. *Deviance: Studies in the Process of Stigmatization and Societal Reaction*. New York: Oxford University Press.

Dodge, David L. 1985. "The Over-negativized Conceptualization of Deviance: A Programmatic Exploration." *Deviant Behavior* 6:17–37.

Durkheim, Emile. [1895] 1964. *The Division of Labor in Society*. Trans. J. Solovay and J. Mueller. New York: The Free Press.

———. [1893] 1982. *The Rules of Sociological Method*. Trans. S. Lukes. London: Macmillan

Erikson, Kai T. 1964. "Notes on the Sociology of Deviance." Pp. 9–20 in *The Other Side*, edited by Howard Becker. New York: The Free Press.

Freedman, Jonathan L., and Anthony N. Doob. 1968. *Deviancy: The Psychology of Being Different*. New York: Academic Press.

Gibbs, Jack P. 1981. *Norms, Deviance and Social Control*. New York: Elsevier.

Goode, Erich. 2001. *Deviant Behavior*. 6th ed. Upper Saddle River, NJ: Prentice Hall.

Gusfield, Joseph R. 1963. *Symbolic Crusade*. Urbana, IL: University of Illinois Press.

Hawkins, Richard, and Gary Tiedeman. 1975. *The Creation of Deviance*. Columbus, OH: Charles E. Merrill Publishing Company.

Heckert, Alex, and Druann Maria Heckert. 2002. "A New Typology of Deviance: Integrating Normative and Reactivist Definitions of Deviance." *Deviant Behavior* 23:449–179.

Heckert, Druann. 1998. "Positive Deviance: A Classificatory Model." *Free Inquiry in Creative Sociology* 26:23–30.

———. 2003. "Mixed Blessings: Women and Blonde Hair." *Free Inquiry in Creative Sociology* 31:47–72.

Henslin, James M. 1975. *Introducing Sociology: Toward Understanding Life in Society*. New York: Free Press.

Homans, George C. 1950. *The Human Group*. New York: Harcourt, Brace and Company.

Huryn, Jean Scherz. 1986. "Giftedness as Deviance: A Test of Interaction Theories." *Deviant Behavior* 7: 175–186.

Irwin, Katherine. 2003. "Saints and Sinners: Elite Tattoo Collectors and Tattooists as Positive and Negative Deviants." *Sociological Spectrum* 23:27–58.

Johnson, Elmer Hubert. 1978. *Crime, Correction, and Society*. Homewood, IL: The Dorsey Press.

Johnson, Harry M. 1960. *Sociology*. New York: Harcourt, Brace and World.

Kooistra, Paul. 1989. *Criminals as Heroes: Structure, Power and Identity*. Bowling Green: Bowling Green State University Popular Press.

Krebs, Dennis, and Allen A. Adinolfi. 1975. "Physical Attractiveness, Social Relations, and Personality Style." *Journal of Personality and Social Psychology* 31:245–253.

Lemert, Edwin M. 1972. *Human Deviance, Social Problems, and Social Control*. Englewood Cliffs, NJ: Prentice-Hall.

Liska, Allen W. 1981. *Perspectives on Deviance*. Englewood Cliffs, NJ: Prentice-Hall.

Merton, Robert K. 1966. "Social Problems and Sociological Theory." Pp. 775–827 in *Contemporary Social Problems*, 2nd ed., edited by Robert K. Merton and Robert Nisbet. New York: Harcourt Brace.

____. 1968. *Social Theory and Social Structure*. New York: The Free Press.

Reis, Harry T., Ladd Wheeler, Nancy Spiegel, Michael H. Kerns, John Nezlik, and Michael Perry. 1982. "Physical Attractiveness as Social Interaction II: Why Does Appearance Affect Social Experience?" *Journal Personality and Social Psychology* 43:979–996.

Scarpitti, Frank R., and Paul T. McFarlane. 1975. *Deviance: Action, Reaction, Interaction*. Reading, MA: Addison-Wesley Publishing.

Schachter, Stanley. 1951. "Deviance, Rejection and Communication." *Journal of Abnormal Social Psychology* 46:190–207.

Sherif, Muzifer. 1936. *The Psychology of Social Norms*. New York: Harper.

Sorokin, Pitirim A. 1950. *Altruistic Love*. Boston: The Beacon Press.

Steffensmeier, Darrel J., and Robert M. Terry. 1975. *Examining Deviance Experimentally*. Port Washington, NY: Alfred Publishing.

Thio, Alex. 1983. *Deviant Behavior*. 2nd ed. Boston: Houghton Mifflin.

Tittle, Charles R., and Raymond Paternoster. 2000. *Social Deviance and Crime*. Los Angeles: Roxbury Publishing Company.

White, Winston. 1961. *Beyond Conformity*. Westport, CT: Greenwood Press.

Wilkins, Leslie. 1965. *Social Deviance*. Englewood Cliffs, NJ: Prentice Hall.

Williams, Robin M. Jr. 1965. *American Society*, 2nd ed. New York: Knopf.

Winslow, Robert W. 1970. Society in Transition: A Social Approach to Deviance. New York: The Free Press.

3

Relativism: Labeling Theory

HOWARD S. BECKER

Becker's classic statement of labeling theory advances the relativistic perspective on defining deviance. Here, he argues that the essence of deviance is not contained within individuals' behaviors but in the response others have to these. Deviance, he claims, is a social construction forged by diverse audiences. Becker assesses the level of deviance attached to a behavior by the social reactions to it. He supports this assertion by pointing out that the same behaviors may be received very differently under varying conditions. He notes that variations in the degree of deviance attached to an act may arise due to the temporal or historical contexts framing acts, to the social position and power of those who commit or who have been harmed by acts, and by the consequences that arise from acts. These framing elements, which are sometimes unrelated to the behavior itself, may lead one act to be designated as heinous and relegate another, similar one, to obscurity. Becker thus locates the root of deviance in the response of people rather than the act itself, and in the chain of events that is unleashed once people have labeled acts and their perpetrators as deviant.

The interactionist perspective ... defines deviance as the infraction of some agreed-upon rule. It then goes on to ask who breaks rules, and to search for the factors in their personalities and life situations that might account for the infractions. This assumes that those who have broken a rule constitute a homogeneous category, because they have committed the same deviant act.

Such an assumption seems to me to ignore the central fact about deviance: it is created by society. I do not mean this in the way it is ordinarily understood, in which the causes of deviance are located in the social situation of the deviant or in "social factors" which prompt his action. I mean, rather, that *social groups create deviance by making the rules whose infraction constitutes deviance,* and by applying those rules to particular people and labeling them as outsiders. From this point of view, deviance is *not* a quality of the act the person commits, but rather a consequence of the application by others of rules and sanctions to an "offender." The deviant is one to whom the label has successfully been applied; deviant behavior is behavior that people so label.[1]

Since deviance is, among other things, a consequence of the responses of others to a person's act, students of deviance cannot assume that they are dealing with a homogeneous category when they study people who have been labeled deviant. That is, they cannot assume that those people have actually committed a deviant act or broken some rule, because the process of labeling may not be infallible; some people may be labeled deviant who in fact have not broken a rule. Furthermore, they cannot assume that the category of those labeled deviant will contain all those who actually have broken a rule, for many offenders may escape apprehension and thus fail to be included in the population of "deviants" they study. Insofar as the category lacks homogeneity and fails to include all the cases that belong in it, one cannot reasonably expect to find common factors of personality or life situation that will account for the supposed deviance. What, then, do people who have been labeled deviant have in common? At the least, they share the label and the experience of being labeled as outsiders. I will begin my analysis with this basic similarity and view deviance as the product of a transaction that takes place between some social group and one who is viewed by that group as a rule-breaker. I will be less concerned with the personal and social characteristics of deviants than with the process by which they come to be thought of as outsiders and their reactions to that judgement....

The point is that the response of other people has to be regarded as problematic. Just because one has committed an infraction of a rule does not mean that others will respond as though this had happened. (Conversely, just because one has not violated a rule does not mean that he may not be treated, in some circumstances, as though he had.)

The degree to which other people will respond to a given act as deviant varies greatly. Several kinds of variation seem worth noting. First of all, there is variation over time. A person believed to have committed a given "deviant" act may at one time be responded to much more leniently than he would be at some other time. The occurrence of "drives" against various kinds of deviance illustrates this clearly. At various times, enforcement officials may decide to make an all-out attack on some particular kind of deviance, such as gambling, drug addiction, or homosexuality. It is obviously much more dangerous to engage in one of these activities when a drive is on than at any other time. (In a very interesting study of crime news in Colorado newspapers, Davis found that the amount of crime reported in Colorado newspapers showed very little association with actual changes in the amount of crime taking place in Colorado. And, further, that people's estimate of how much increase there had been in crime in Colorado was associated with the increase in the amount of crime news but not with any increase in the amount of crime.)[2]

The degree to which an act will be treated as deviant depends also on who commits the act and who feels he has been harmed by it. Rules tend to be applied more to some persons than others. Studies of juvenile delinquency make the point clearly. Boys from middle-class areas do not get as far in the legal process when they are apprehended as do boys from slum areas. The middle-class boy is less likely, when picked up by the police, to be taken to the station; less likely when taken to the station to be booked; and it is extremely unlikely that he will be convicted and sentenced.[3] This variation occurs even though the original infraction of the rule is the same in the two cases. Similarly, the law is differentially applied to Negroes and whites. It is well known that a Negro believed to have attacked a white woman is much more likely to be punished than a white man who commits the same offense; it is only slightly less well known that a Negro who murders another Negro is much less likely to be punished than a white man who commits murder[4]. This, of course, is one of the main points of Sutherland's analysis of white-collar crime: crimes committed by corporations are almost always prosecuted as civil cases, but the same crime committed by an individual is ordinarily treated as a criminal offense.[5]

Some rules are enforced only when they result in certain consequences. The unmarried mother furnishes a clear example. Vincent[6] points out that illicit sexual relations seldom result in severe punishment or social censure for the offenders. If, however, a girl becomes pregnant as a result of such activities, the reaction of others is likely to be severe. (The illicit pregnancy is also an interesting example of the differential enforcement of rules on different categories of people. Vincent notes that unmarried fathers escape the severe censure visited on the mother.)

Why repeat these commonplace observations? Because, taken together, they support the proposition that deviance is not a simple quality, present in some kinds of behavior and absent in others. Rather, it is the product of a process which involves responses of other people to the behavior. The same behavior may be an infraction of the rules at one time and not at another or may be an infraction when committed by one person, but not when committed by another; some rules are broken with impunity, others are not. In short, whether a given act is deviant or not depends in part on the nature of the act (that is, whether or not it violates some rule) and in part on what other people do about it.

Some people may object that this is merely a terminological quibble, that one can, after all, define terms any way he wants to and that if some people want to speak of rule-breaking behavior as deviant without reference to the reactions of others they are free to do so. This, of course, is true. Yet it might be worthwhile to refer to such behavior as *rule breaking behavior* and reserve the term *deviant* for those labeled as deviant by some segment of society. I do not insist that this usage be followed. But it should be clear that insofar as a scientist uses "deviant" to refer to any rule-breaking behavior and takes as his subject of study only those who have been *labeled* deviant, he would be hampered by the disparities between the two categories.

If we take as the object of our attention behavior which comes to be labeled as deviant, we must recognize that we cannot know whether a given act will be categorized as deviant until the response of others has occurred. Deviance is not a quality that lies in behavior itself, but in the interaction between the person who commits an act and those who respond to it....

In any case, being branded as deviant has important consequences for one's further social participation and self-image. The most important consequence is a drastic change in the individual's public identity. Committing the improper act and being publicly caught at it place him in a new status. He has been revealed as a different kind of person from the kind he was supposed to be. He is labeled a "fairy," "dope fiend," "nut," or "lunatic," and treated accordingly.

In analyzing the consequences of assuming a deviant identity let us make use of Hughes' distinction between master and auxiliary status traits.[7] Hughes notes that most statuses have one key trait which serves to distinguish those who belong from those who do not. Thus the doctor, whatever else he may be, is a person who has a certificate stating that he has fulfilled certain requirements and is licensed to practice medicine; this is the master trait. As Hughes points out, in our society a doctor is also informally expected to have a number of auxiliary traits: most people expect him to be upper middle-class, white, male, and Protestant. When he is not, there is a sense that he has in some way failed to fill the bill. Similarly, though skin color is the master status trait determining who is Negro and who is white, Negroes are informally expected to have certain status traits and not to have others; people are surprised and find it anomalous if a Negro turns out to be a doctor or a college professor. People often have the master status trait but lack some of the auxiliary, informally expected characteristics; for example, one may be a doctor but be a female or a Negro.

Hughes deals with this phenomenon in regard to statuses that are well thought of, desired, and desirable (noting that one may have the formal qualifications for entry into a status but be denied full entry because of lack of the proper auxiliary traits), but the same process occurs in the case of deviant statuses. Possession of one deviant trait may have a generalized symbolic value, so that people automatically assume that its bearer possesses other undesirable traits allegedly associated with it.

To be labeled a criminal one need only commit a single criminal offense, and this is all the term formally refers to. Yet the word carries a number of connotations specifying auxiliary traits characteristic of anyone bearing the label. A man who has been convicted of housebreaking and thereby labeled criminal is presumed to be a person likely to break into other houses; the police, in rounding up known offenders for investigation after a crime has been committed, operate on this premise. Further, he is considered likely to commit other kinds of crimes as well, because he has shown himself to be a person without "respect for the law." Thus, apprehension for one deviant act exposes a person to the likelihood that he will be regarded as deviant or undesirable in other respects.

There is one other element in Hughes' analysis we can borrow with profit: the distinction between master and subordinate statuses.[8] Some statuses, in our society as in others, override all other statuses and have a certain priority. Race is one of these. Membership in the Negro race, as socially defined, will override most other status considerations in most other situations; the fact that one is a physician or middle-class or female will not protect one from being treated as a Negro first and any of these other things second. The status of deviant (depending on the kind of deviance) is this kind of master status. One receives the status as a result of breaking a rule, and the identification proves to be more important than most others. One will be identified as a deviant first, before other identifications are made....

NOTES

1. The most important earlier statements of this view can be found in Frank Tannenbaum, *Crime and the Community* (New York: Columbia University Press, 1938), and E. M. Lemert, *Social Pathology* (New York: McGraw-Hill Book Co., 1951). A recent article stating a position very similar to mine is John Kitsuse, "Societal Reaction to Deviance: Problems of Theory and Method," *Social Problems* 9 (Winter 1962): 247–256.

2. F. James Davis, "Crime News in Colorado Newspapers," *American Journal of Sociology* LVII (January 1952): 325–330.

3. See Albert K. Cohen and James F. Short, Jr., "Juvenile Delinquency," p. 87 in Robert K. Merton and Robert A. Nisbet, eds., *Contemporary Social Problems* (New York: Harcourt, Brace and World, 1961).

4. See Harold Garfinkel, "Research Notes on Inter-and Intra-Racial Homicides," *Social Forces* 27 (May 1949): 369–381.

5. Edwin Sutherland, "White Collar Criminality," *American Sociological Review* V (February 1940): 1–12.

6. Clark Vincent, *Unmarried Mothers* (New York: The Free Press of Glencoe, 1961), pp. 3–5.

7. Everett C. Hughes, "Dilemmas and Contradictions of Status," *American Journal of Sociology* L (March 1945): 353–359.

8. *Ibid.*

4

The Morality of Deviance

ANNE HENDERSHOTT

Hendershott takes the absolutist perspective on defining deviance, proposing a morally based view. She invokes the concept of morally based, unwritten laws that stretch from community to community over history. She criticizes the medical model of defining deviance as abdicating the responsibilities of judgment, arguing that this glosses over our views of good and evil.

Hendershott suggests that society is founded on consensus, with most people agreeing about right and wrong, urging us to adopt a more sin-based model. She criticizes contemporary sociologists and politicians for failing to speak in this language and condemning the immorality of deviance. Clear boundaries, she argues, protect us from the instability of moral panics. She argues that we should construct the hard principles of the moral order and enforce them. Hendershott's morality-based approach to defining deviance is inherently absolutist because it advances a situationally and temporally consistent universal yardstick for assessing the meaning of behavior that is lodged in the essence of the behavior itself.

What is the point of Hendershott's definitions of "psychological" or "Christian" man? How do these relate to her thoughts about cultural relativism?

In major cultural transitions, words often change their meanings as new norms evolve and old cultural constraints loosen. The process of redefining deviance is a subtle one, and changes in language are so incremental and innocuous that the new meanings appear almost invisibly. Social philosopher Alasdair MacIntyre implores us all examine this process more closely when he writes, "Ours is a culture dominated by experts, experts who profess to assist the rest of us, but who often instead make us their victims." MacIntyre says that we must be able to identify the particular set of precepts that will help us achieve that which contributes to the common good. Most of us know what will contribute to the common good. Most of us know that there are unwritten, morally based "laws" that tell us what kind of behavior is deviant. They have not necessarily been codified within the legal system, but are nonetheless binding.

CULTURAL RELATIVISM

In an age of technology and expertise, we have been convinced that we should listen to the "experts" rather than common sense in determining the norms, values, and attitudes of our families, our churches, and other trusted institutions. Cultural relativists urge us to adapt to the changes of our times, which they define as "progress" rather than mere change whose inevitability is not assured.

The continued attempts to psychologize and "understand" deviance—even in the face of evil such as that which appeared in America on September 11—show the distance some will go to avoid applying moral categories of judgment. Sociologists Peter Conrad and Joseph Schneider cautioned us more than three decades ago that the medicalization of deviance would eventually "shroud conditions, events, and people and prevent them from being confronted as evil." Said's suggestion that the terrorists who tried to blow up America were deranged but not evil demonstrates how prophetic they were. Although medicalizing deviance does not automatically render evil consequences good, the assumption that behavior is the product of a "sick" mind or body gives it a status similar to the of "accidents" removing intent or motive hinders us from comprehending the human element in the decisions we make, the actions we take, and the social structures we create.

MORAL ORDER

The reluctance of sociologists to acknowledge that there are moral judgments to be made when discussing a subject like deviance shows how far this discipline has strayed from its origins. From the earliest days of sociology, scholars were concerned about the question of social order and the common good.

Emerging in the midst of major social, economic, and political transformation sweeping across nineteenth-century Europe as a result of the Industrial Revolution, the discipline of sociology sought to explain how societies maintain stability in the face of dramatic social change. From this time onward, until the upheavals of the 1960s, sociologists continued to assert that social stability is founded on moral order—a common world view that binds people to their families, to their communities, and to the larger economic and political institutions. Integral to this moral order is a shared concept of deviance, and a willingness to identify the boundaries of appropriate behavior.

Today, few sociologists hold these convictions. Yet ironically, the world from which sociology emerged more than a century ago was, in many ways, similar to our own contemporary world of rapid, often overwhelming, social change. Just as the Industrial Revolution brought deplorable living conditions to the industrialized cities, including poverty, sickness, and dramatic changes within the family, so today's technological society presents profound challenges to social order and the common good. Globalization has increased societies based on shared culture rather than on narrow calculations of individual self-interest.

A commitment to a common moral order is much more difficult within a culture of such strong individualism.

The policymakers of the past paid attention when social scientists like Daniel Bell, Edward Banfield, James Coleman, James Q.Wilson, and Daniel Patrich Moynihan spoke out on issues of morality and deviance. But today, compelling pleas for a rational response to deviant behavior are often drowned out by the more emotional appeals—and political cunning—generate by advocacy groups. In 1965, Moynihan tried to warn us of the impending problems in the inner cities when he predicted that chaos would result from single-parent households. Using the language of Durkheim, Moynihan warned that society's mechanisms for social control were breaking down. He was correct—yet for the past thirty years, instead of attacking the problem of fatherless children in the inner cities, social scientists have been more likely to attack Senator Moynihan and any other sociologist who dared to "blame the victims" of poverty.

MORAL BOUNDARIES

For the first sociologists, definitions of deviance marked the outer edges of group life, thus supplying the framework within which the people of the group develop an orderly sense of their own cultural identity and social order. This process allows for some deviation—sociologists have long known that testing the boundaries of established norms can be positive. Indeed, some of the most progressive social change we have experienced in this country has been the result of subtle changes in definitions of deviance—in the direction of common sense and the common good. In the 1950s and 1960s, identifying racism and bigotry as deviance led to positive social change in which discrimination was appropriately stigmatized in our culture and censured in our legal system.

However, this dynamic process of boundary maintenance can also create the kind of social change that is not positive, the kind that Senator Moynihan cautioned us about. His concern was that our refusal to acknowledge as deviant and negatively sanction the increase in out–of–wedlock births would have a detrimental effect upon the black community. He was correct about that. What he did not foresee was that those like himself who challenged the dysfunction in the inner cities would themselves be viewed as deviant for judging the behavior of others.

More than a half–century ago, T. S. Eliot wrote about the sense of alienation that occurs when social regulators begin to splinter and the controlling moral authority of a society is no longer effective. In his play The Cocktail Party, a troubled young protagonist visits a psychiatrist and confides that she feels a "sense of sin" because of her relationship with a married man. She is distressed not so much by the illicit relationship, but rather by the strange feeling of "sinfulness." Eliot writes, "Having a sense of sin seems abnormal" to her–she had never noticed before that such behavior might be seen in those terms. She believed that she had become "ill."

When Eliot speaks of his protagonist's feeling of unease or uncertainty about her behavior, he is really speaking of the sense of *normlessness* that has traditionally been a focus of sociology. In many ways, Eliot's play is about anomie—the state that sociologists identify as resulting when one is caught between the loosening moral norms regulating behavior and one's own moral misgivings. Eliot's play echoes the scholarship of Durkheim. Both men saw that the identification and stigmatization of deviant behavior is functionally for society because it can produce certainty for individuals and solidarity for the group. And both recognized that dramatic social change through rapid redefinition of deviance could be dysfunctional for society. Strong cultural values and clear concepts of good and evil integrate members into the group and provide meaning. When traditional cultural attachments are disrupted, or when behavior is no longer regulated by these common norms and values, individuals are left without a moral compass.

As we have seen, Durkheim knew that social facts like crime statistics and suicide rates can be adequately explained only by analyzing the unique social conditions that evolve when norms break down. The resulting anomic state leads to deviant behavior as the individual's attachment to social bonds is weakened. According to this view, people internalize social norms because of their attachments to others. People care what others think of them and attempt to conform to expectations because they accept what others expect. However, when these same people are unsure about the norms, or when the norms are changing rapidly, there is a growing unwillingness to make moral judgments about all behavior. The door is open to *moral panics*, which flourish in such a climate of anomie.

When a society's moral boundaries are sharp, clear, and secure, and the central norms and values are strongly held, moral panics rarely take hold. When the moral boundaries are fuzzy and shifting, poorly defined by ineffective authority and constant testing, as we see so often now on college campuses, moral panics are far more likely to grow—in an attempt to clarify the moral boundaries.

Reporting on a national study of attitudes and values a few years ago, sociologist Alan Wolfe found that the people he interviewed—whatever their different beliefs—were unified by their increasing reluctance to judge the behavior of others. In interviews with more than two hundred middle-class respondents, Wolfe found that the refusal to judge others was mentioned so often that he identified it as the "Eleventh Commandment for the middle class: Thou Shalt Not Judge." This value-free ideology was predicted thirty years ago by psychologist Philip Rieff, who warned in his now-classic book The Triumph of the Therapeutic that *psychological man* was beginning to replace *Christian man* as the dominant character type in our society. Unlike traditional Christianity, which made moral demands on believers, the secular world of "psychological man" rejected both the idea of sin and the need for salvation.

In an effort to avoid alienating members with diverse lifestyles and values, some religious leaders have become hesitant to speak of morals at all. But in their place, a powerful advocacy community stands ready, willing, and able to define deviance. The only sufficient response to the compelling marketing techniques of these advocacy groups is a renewed willingness to make moral judgments.

In the aftermath of September 11, President George W Bush repeatedly called the terrorist acts "evil" and those who perpetrated them "evildoers:' This language drew only a minor protest from those who on September 10 would have had a field day if the President had used similar terminology. Reassessing the politics and culture after terrorists declared war on America, social critic David Brooks writes.

Life in times of war and recession reminds us of certain hard truths that were easy to ignore during the decades of peace and prosperity. Evil exists. Difficulties, even tragedies are inevitable. Human beings are flawed creatures capable of monstrosity. Not all cultures are compatible. To preserve order, good people must exercise power over destructive people.

MORAL CONSENSUS

Brooks reminds us that in order to cope with the implications of the new reality, we must "construct hard principles" of moral consensus. "When you are faced with the problem of repelling evil, you absolutely must be able to reach a conclusion on serious moral issues."

Perhaps this re–moralization of our public discourse—despite the agitation and murmuring it has caused in certain academic circles—will be the only good to come out of our national tragedy. Perhaps we will begin to recognize that a society that continues to redefine deviance as disease, or refuses to acknowledge and negatively sanction the deviant acts our common sense tells us are destructive, is a society that has lost the capacity to confront evil that has a capacity to dehumanize us all.

5

Social Power: Conflict Theory of Crime

RICHARD QUINNEY

Quinney's conflict theory of crime represents the social power perspective on defining deviance. He builds on Becker's relativist approach by asserting that definitions of deviance are social constructions and not absolute "givens." He, also, rejects the essentialist view of deviance as inherent in specific acts. But while Becker is not specific about the identity of those who formulate the definitions of deviance, Quinney locates the decision-makers in the dominant class. Definitions of deviance, then, stem from the views of those who have the power to make and enforce them. Members of this group formulate the definitions of deviance with the express purpose of advancing themselves by labeling behaviors that threaten their class interests as criminal. They then enforce the definitions unequally: more harshly against their opponents and more leniently against members of their own group. Yet they disguise the self-serving basis of their rule, creating and enforcing through justifications that legitimate their actions and cast these as rational or beneficial to others. In turn, those defined as criminal become more likely to engage in future behavior that will be defined as criminal.

Quinney thus goes beyond Becker to offer a view of society that radically departs from previous perspectives. The conflict perspective envisions two groups in society: the dominant class and those they dominate. Criminals are conceptualized as powerless and oppressed people who threaten the interests of the ruling class. Defining and enforcing crime becomes a means of reproducing the power and socioeconomic inequalities between these groups. Quinney's conflict theory suggests that definitions of deviance represent one of the coercive means through which the elite maintain their dominance over the masses.

How does Quinney's conflict view of society compare or contrast with Erikson's?

A theory that helps us begin to examine the legal order critically is the one I call the *social reality of crime*. Applying this theory, we think of crime as it is affected by the dynamics that mold the society's social, economic, and political

From Richard Quinney, *Criminology* (Boston: Little, Brown, 1975). Reprinted by permission of the author.

structure. First, we recognize how criminal law fits into capitalist society. The legal order gives reality to the crime problem in the United States. Everything that makes up crime's social reality, including the application of criminal law, the behavior patterns of those who are defined as criminal, and the construction of an ideology of crime, is related to the established legal order. The social reality of crime is constructed on conflict in our society.

The theory of the social reality of crime is formulated as follows.

I.   **The Official Definition of Crime:** Crime as a legal definition of human conduct is created by agents of the dominant class in a politically organized society.

The essential starting point is a definition of crime that itself is based on the legal definition. Crime, as *officially* determined, is a *definition* of behavior that is conferred on some people by those in power. Agents of the law (such as legislators, police, prosecutors, and judges) are responsible for formulating and administering criminal law. Upon *formulation and application* of these definitions of crime, persons and behaviors become criminal.

Crime, according to this first proposition, is not inherent in behavior, but is a judgment made by some about the actions and characteristics of others. This proposition allows us to focus on the formulation and administration of the criminal law as it applies to the behaviors that become defined as criminal. Crime is seen as a result of the class-dynamic process that culminates in defining persons and behaviors as criminal. It follows, then, that the greater the number of definitions of crime that are formulated and applied, the greater the amount of crime.

II. **Formulating Definitions of Crime:** Definitions of crime are composed of behaviors that conflict with the interests of the dominant class.

Definitions of crime are formulated according to the interests of those who have the power to translate their interests into public policy. Those definitions are ultimately incorporated into the criminal law. Furthermore, definitions of crime in a society change as the interests of the dominant class change. In other words, those who are able to have their interests represented in public policy regulate the formulation of definitions of crime.

The powerful interests are reflected not only in the definitions of crime and the kinds of penal sanctions attached to them, but also in the *legal policies* on handling those defined as criminals. Procedural rules are created for enforcing and administering the criminal law. Policies are also established on programs for treating and punishing the criminally defined and programs for controlling and preventing crime. From the initial definitions of crime to the subsequent procedures, correctional and penal programs, and policies for controlling and preventing crime, those who have the power regulate the behavior of those without power.

III. **Applying Definitions of Crime:** Definitions of crime are applied by the class that has the power to shape the enforcement and administration of criminal law.

The dominant interests intervene in all the stages at which definitions of crime are created. Because class interests cannot be effectively protected merely by formulating criminal law, the law must be enforced and administered. The interests of the powerful, therefore, also operate where the definitions of crime reach the *application* stage. As Void has argued, crime is "political behavior and the criminal becomes in fact a member of a 'minority group' without sufficient public support to dominate the control of the police power of the state." Those whose interests conflict with the ones represented in the law must either change their behavior or possibly find it defined as criminal.

The probability that definitions of crime will be applied varies according to how much the behaviors of the powerless conflict with the interests of those in power. Law enforcement efforts and judicial activity are likely to increase when the interests of the dominant class are threatened. Fluctuations and variations in applying definitions of crime reflect shifts in class relations.

Obviously, the criminal law is not applied directly by those in power; its enforcement and administration are delegated to authorized *legal agents*. Because the groups responsible for creating the definitions of crime are physically separated from the groups that have the authority to enforce and administer law, local conditions determine how the definitions will be applied. In particular, communities vary in their expectations of law enforcement and the administration of justice. The application of definitions is also influenced by the visibility of offenses in a community and by the public's norms about reporting possible violations. And especially important in enforcing and administering the criminal law are the legal agents' occupational organization and ideology.

The probability that these definitions will be applied depends on the actions of the legal agents who have the authority to enforce and administer the law. A definition of crime is applied depending on their evaluation. Turk has argued that during "criminalization," a criminal label may be affixed to people because of real or fancied attributes: "Indeed, a person is evaluated, either favorably or unfavorably, not because he *does* something, or even because he *is* something, but because others react to their perceptions of him as offensive or inoffensive." Evaluation by the definers is affected by the way in which the suspect handles the situation, but ultimately the legal agents' evaluations and subsequent decisions are the crucial factors in determining the criminality of human acts. As legal agents evaluate more behaviors and persons as worthy of being defined as crimes, the probability that definitions of crime will be applied grows.

IV. How Behavior Patterns Develop in Relation to Definitions of Crime: Behavior patterns are structured in relation to definitions of crime, and within this context people engage in actions that have relative probabilities of being defined as criminal.

Although behavior varies, all behaviors are similar in that they represent patterns within society. All persons—whether they create definitions of crime or are the objects of these definitions—act in reference to *normative systems* learned in relative social and cultural settings. Because it is not the quality of the behavior but the action taken against the behavior that gives it the character of criminality, that which is defined as criminal is relative to the behavior patterns of the class that formulates and applies definitions. Consequently, people whose behavior patterns are not represented when the definitions of crime are formulated and applied are more likely to act in ways that will be defined as criminal than those who formulate and apply the definitions.

Once behavior patterns become established with some regularity within the segments of society, individuals have a framework for creating *personal action patterns*. These continually develop for each person as he moves from one experience to another. Specific action patterns give behavior an individual substance in relation to the definitions of crime.

People construct their own patterns of action in participating with others. It follows, then, that the probability that persons will develop action patterns with a high potential for being defined as criminal depends on (1) structured opportunities, (2) learning experiences, (3) interpersonal associations and identifications, and (4) self-conceptions. Throughout the experiences, each person creates a conception of self as a human social being. Thus prepared, he behaves according to the anticipated consequences of his actions.

In the experiences shared by the definers of crime and the criminally defined, personal-action patterns develop among the latter because they are so defined. After they have had continued experience in being defined as criminal, they learn to manipulate the application of criminal definitions.

Furthermore, those who have been defined as criminal begin to conceive of themselves as criminal. As they adjust to the definitions imposed on them, they learn to play the criminal role. As a result of others' reactions, therefore, people may develop personal-action patterns that increase the likelihood of their being defined as criminal in the future. That is, increased experience with definitions of crime increases the probability of their developing actions that may be subsequently defined as criminal.

Thus, both the definers of crime and the criminally defined are involved in reciprocal action patterns. The personal-action patterns of both the definers and the defined are shaped by their common, continued, and related experiences. The fate of each is bound to that of the other.

V. Constructing an Ideology of Crime: An ideology of crime is constructed and diffused by the dominant class to secure its hegemony.

This ideology is created in the kinds of ideas people are exposed to, the manner in which they select information to fit the world they are shaping, and their way of interpreting this information. People behave in reference to the *social meanings* they attach to their experiences.

Among the conceptions that develop in a society are those relating to what people regard as crime. The concept of crime must of course be accompanied by ideas about the nature of crime. Images develop about the relevance of crime, the offender's characteristics, the appropriate reaction to crime, and the relation of crime to the social order. These conceptions are constructed by communication, and, in fact, an ideology of crime depends on the portrayal of crime in all personal and mass communication. This ideology is thus diffused throughout the society.

One of the most concrete ways by which an ideology of crime is formed and transmitted is the official investigation of crime. The President's Commission on Law Enforcement and Administration of Justice is the best contemporary example of the state's role in shaping an ideology of crime. Not only are we as citizens more aware of crime today because of the President's Commission, but official policy on crime has been established in a crime bill, the Omnibus Crime Control and Safe Streets Act of 1968. The crime bill, itself a reaction to the growing fears of class conflict in American society, creates an image of a severe crime problem and, in so doing, threatens to negate some of our basic constitutional guarantees in the name of controlling crime.

Consequently, the conceptions that are most critical in actually formulating and applying the definitions of crime are those held by the dominant class. These conceptions are certain to be incorporated into the social reality of crime. The more the government acts in reference to crime, the more probable it is that definitions of crime will be created and that behavior patterns will develop in opposition to those definitions. The formulation of definitions of crime, their application, and the development of behavior patterns in relation to the definitions are thus joined in full circle by the construction of an ideological hegemony toward crime.

VI. **Constructing the Social Reality of Crime:** The social reality of crime is constructed by the formulation and application of definitions of crime, the development of behavior patterns in relation to these definitions, and the construction of an ideology of crime.

The first five propositions are collected here into a final composition proposition. The theory of the social reality of crime, accordingly, postulates creating a series of phenomena that increase the probability of crime. The result, holistically, is the social reality of crime.

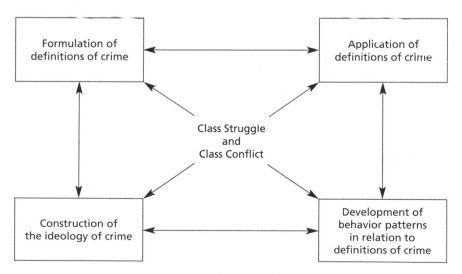

The Social Reality of Crime

Because the first proposition of the theory is a definition and the sixth is a composite, the body of the theory consists of the four middle propositions. These form a model of crime's social reality. The model, as diagrammed, relates the proposition units into a theoretical system (see figure on p. X). Each unit is related to the others. The theory is thus a system of interacting developmental propositions. The phenomena denoted in the propositions and their relationships culminate in what is regarded as the amount and character of crime at any time— that is, in the social reality of crime.

The theory of the social reality of crime as I have formulated it is inspired by a change that is occurring in our view of the world. This change, pervading all levels of society, pertains to the world that we all construct and from which, at the same time, we pretend to separate ourselves in our human experiences. For the study of crime, a revision in thought has directed attention to the criminal process: All relevant phenomena contribute to creating definitions of crime, development of behaviors by those involved in criminal-defining situations, and constructing an ideology of crime. The result is the social reality of crime that is constantly being constructed in society.

PART II

Theories of Deviance

D eviance holds a special intrigue for scholars of theory. Given its pervasive
nature in society, its enigmatic conditions, and its generic appeal, even the
earliest sociologists attempted to explain how and why deviance occurs. Especially considering people's inclination to conformity, the pressing question for
scholars has dealt with why individuals engage in norm-violating behavior.
Explanations for deviant behavior are as divergent as the acts they explain, ranging from acts of delinquency to professional theft, acts of integrity to a search for
kicks, acts of desperation to those of bravado and daring. We next outline some
of the major attempts at understanding deviant behavior.

BIOLOGICAL AND PSYCHOLOGICAL THEORIES

The language of deviance used in everyday life tends to follow biological or psy
chological assumptions about the causes of behavior. Sociology students often
have difficulty thinking in other terms about why people would violate norms.
Reinarman, in Chapter 15, calls this a "vocabulary of attribution," suggesting
that the cultural language of talking about how and why people do things is
individualistic, rather than collective, or sociological. This book aims to remedy
this problem.

In earlier times, scholars of crime approached deviant behavior as rooted
in people's biological abnormalities or predispositions. They tried to find links
between incarcerated criminals and genetic deficiencies. In the 1800s, Cesare
Lombroso and his followers suggested that criminals were more like primitive
human beings, resembling their ape-like ancestors (Lombroso 1876). Women, he
believed, were evolutionarily inferior to men (Lombroso 1920). This approach
viewed criminals as born and not made, therefore unresponsive to rehabilitation

or treatment. People's "defective" criminal tendencies could be classified into distinctive criminal types and inherited from one generation to the next. Other researchers of this era such as Charles Goring (1913) and Earnest Hooton (1939) connected people with physical inferiorities, such as being shorter and lighter, to born criminal types.

At around the same time, body type theorists correlated criminality to three "somatotypes": body builds thought to be related to certain personality characteristics or temperaments. William Sheldon (1949) suggested that neither the slow, soft, and comfort-loving endomorphs nor the lean, fragile ectomorphs were as criminally inclined as the muscular and active mesomorphs, who were more aggressive. Contemporary studies of body type focus on things like Body Mass Index (BMI: a person's weight divided by his or her height squared) or large early muscular development, suggesting that strongly built or well-muscled people are more prone toward violence.

More recent biological approaches have pursued genetic explanations. Some looked for chromosomal patterns in deviants, suggesting that variations on the typical male (XY) and female (XX) configurations could foster abnormal behavior. In particular, criminologists proposed an XYY syndrome creating "double male" or "supermale" individuals who were unusually tall and predisposed to aggressive and violent behavior. An accused murderer in Australia was acquitted on this defense as recently as the 1960s, although it did not work in the trial of Richard Speck, the man charged with killing eight Chicago nurses. Twin studies have been very popular in the nineteenth century as well. The strongest connection between criminally convicted twins, people who would likely be similarly inclined due to their biological imprinting, found only a 35 percent rate of offense for their identical sibling, with an even smaller 12 percent for fraternal siblings.

Brain studies, popular in the 1930s, suggested that some people might cease their deviant ways if their brains were surgically altered. It was believed that chronic deviants, unresponsive to other treatments, might benefit from lobotomies that destroyed the frontal lobe of the brain (as portrayed in the book and film, One Flew Over the Cuckoo's Nest). From the 1930s to the 1950s, approximately 50,000 such operations were performed. These gave way to other forms of psychosurgery involving inserting electric needles into the skull and searing part of the cingulum, the emotional center of the brain. A host of other sociobiological explanations related to diet, learning disorders, endocrine/hormonal imbalance, and allergies thought to influence behavior have since arisen. One example of this can been seen in the "twinkie defense" from the trial of Dan White, charged with killing San Francisco Mayor George Moscone (portrayed in the movie, Milk). Defense attorneys brought in psychiatrists who testified that individuals might become depressed and driven to uncontrollable violence as the result of excessively consuming junk food and sugary soft drinks. They argued that because of these chemicals in his body White exploded, went onto autopilot, and diminished his capacity for rational thought. To some degree jurors bought this argument, rejecting the charge of premeditated murder and instead convicting White of the lesser crime of manslaughter. Brain theories continue to be popular with the public and are being applied to attribute deviant behaviors from rape to spousal and date assault, child abuse and neglect, and cheating, to hormonal functioning (the PMS syndrome defense), cerebral and neuro-allergies to food substances, EEG abnormalities, and a wide range of evolutionary theories.

Although early biological theories focused more on body types, more recent thinking examines how people's inherited characteristics translate into predispositions toward traits such as thrill-seeking, risk-taking, or substance abuse. But biological theories fail to explain why people who share common biological characteristics differ, with some turning to deviance while others remain conventional. It is possible that biological factors may exert some influence on people's behavior, but these theories tend to be limited and offer less convincing explanations than social and cultural factors. Many are now denounced as racist or for condoning genetic research on deviant behavior. They are most commonly used in contemporary society to provide a rationale for conservative ideological principles and support a political climate that blames social ills such as crime and poverty on individuals rather than on social policies.

Psychological theories have their roots in the late eighteenth century, drawing on psychiatric, psychoanalytical, and psychological explanations of how individuals' minds and personalities affect their deviance. Many have tried to articulate a deviant or criminal personality, dating back to Sigmund Freud's model of the id, ego, and superego (Freud 1925). He believed that people with too little ability to resist their impulses had Oedipus/Electra complexes, death wishes, inferiority complexes, frustration–aggression syndromes, castration fears, or penis envy, leading them to commit hostile acts. Freud's early work was succeeded by more contemporary theories about a range of impulse control disorders. Psychologists have also linked personality traits to crime and deviance, especially defiance, hostility, ambivalence towards authority, and emotional psychopathologies. We see the popularity of this approach in criminal profiling, which attempts to construct typical characterizations of certain offenders, although this technique may be more successful in books, movies, and television than in real life.

Other psychological approaches have addressed "operant conditioning," examining the way behavior modification (Skinner 1953) or human conditioning

(Eysenck 1977) can lead individuals to commit crime. Albert Bandura (1973) proposed a social learning theory that suggested exposure to aggressive or aversive behaviors could reinforce people's tendencies to become aggressive.

Many people have tried to link distinct personality types to deviant behavior. This is difficult because deviance comes in so many forms, so that identity thieves are likely to be rather different from robbers, gamblers, or drug users. Samual Yochelson and Stanton Samenow (1976) proposed that criminals have distinctive personalities and thinking patterns, such as being inclined toward chronic lying, unrelenting optimism, manipulativeness, intense anger, fear of being injured or insulted, and an inflexibly high self-image. Although scholars have yet to find evidence of a "criminal mind," Yochelson and Samenow believed criminals were victimizers rather than victims of society.

Finally, intelligence theorists have put forth a range of IQ theories, suggesting that people whose "mental age" lagged behind their chronological age might be predisposed toward criminality, with one (Goddard 1979) even suggesting that criminals were feebleminded morons. Although the connection between IQ and deviance was convincingly refuted by Edwin Sutherland in 1934, people still believe that low intelligence is linked to deviance.

The problem with many of these psychological theories is that they focus almost exclusively on individuals' personalities, ignoring their social conditions or life situations. They tend to blame individuals, rather than the social structure or environmental factors that may have fostered their deviance, a form of victim-blaming. Many of these theorists have approached deviance as intrinsically defined acts, rather than as behavior that is regarded differently by different groups in different times and places. As such, they distinctly overlook the element of social power and its role in defining deviance and implementing such definitions. It is left up to sociology courses to expand students' horizons so that they can better understand the invisible forces of culture and social structure.

THE STRUCTURAL PERSPECTIVE

The dominant theory in sociology for the first half of the twentieth century, structural functionalism, also commanded the greatest amount of sway in explaining deviant behavior. Durkheim advanced the theory that society is a moral phenomenon. He believed that at its root, the morals (norms, values, and laws) that individuals are taught constrain their behavior. Youngsters are taught the "rights" and "wrongs"" of society early in life, with most people conforming to these expectations throughout adulthood. These moral beliefs, in large measure, determine how people behave, what they want, and who they are. Durkheim suggested that societies with high degrees of social integration (bonding, cohesion, community involvement) would increase the conformity of its members. However, and this is what concerned Durkheim, in the modern French society in which he was living, more and more people were becoming distanced from each other, people were partially losing their sense of belonging to their communities, and the norms and expectations of their groups were becoming less clearly defined. He believed that this condition, which he referred to as anomie, was producing a concomitant amount of social disintegration, leading to greater degrees of deviance. Thus, for Durkheim, while norms still existed on the societal level, the lack of social integration created a situation where they were no longer becoming as significant a part of each individual.

Despite his concerns about the increasing rates of deviance that society would produce, Durkheim also subscribed to the idea that deviance was functional for society. As we noted earlier, despite its obvious negative effects, Durkheim felt that deviance produces some positive benefits as well. At a time when people are worrying about the moral breakdown and social disintegration of society, deviance serves to remind us of the moral boundaries in society. Each time a deviant act is committed and publicly announced, society is united in indignation against the perpetrator. This serves to bring people together, rather than tearing them apart. At the same time, society is reminded about what is "right" and "wrong" and, for those who conform, there is greater social integration that ensues. These ideas were perhaps best illustrated by Yale sociologist Kai Erikson who, in his 1966 book, Wayward Puritans (excerpted in Chapter 1), demonstrated the role of deviance in defining morality and bringing people together. Erikson examined Puritan patterns of isolating and treating offenders. He believed that deviance serves as a means to promote a contrast with the rest of the community, thus giving members of the larger society more strength in their moral convictions. Erikson's analysis focused on the transformation of the seventeenth century Bay Colony, as a group of revolutionaries tried to establish a new community in New England. These deviants, the revolutionaries, played an important role in the transformation of norms and values—their behavior elicited societal reaction, which served to clearly define the new community's norms and values. In addition, punishing some people for norm violations reminded others of the rewards for conformity.

Chapter 6, "The Normal and the Pathological," by Durkheim, lays out his theory of the inevitably of deviance in all societies. In his ironic twist, Durkheim argues that deviance is normal rather than pathological, serving a positive function in society. To achieve the maximum benefit, however, a society needs a manageable amount of deviance. When the numbers of people declared deviant by current moral standards rises or falls too much, society alters its moral criteria to maintain the level of deviance in the optimal range. At different times it may "define deviancy down," as Moynihan (1993) has suggested in looking at the way the bar defining acceptable behavior has been lowered. When society lowers the bar of acceptability, fewer acts are viewed as deviant and more become recast as tolerable. Over the years we have normalized violence, divorce, smoking marijuana, homosexuality, premarital sex, tattooing and piercing, and unwed pregnancy. Or society may "define deviancy up," as Krauthammer (1993) has suggested, raising the bar defining normality. When the bar is raised, behavior formerly considered acceptable becomes redefined as deviant. Things now considered deviant (or even criminal) that used to be regarded as tolerable, even if not exactly embraced, include cigarette smoking, spanking, date rape, sexual harassment, panhandling, talking in movie theaters, and hate speech. What deviance does for society is to define the moral boundaries for everyone. Violation of norms serves to remind the masses what is acceptable and what is not; in Durkheim's words, it enforces the "collective conscience" of the group. We saw this in the public outcry over the inadequate governmental response to the Hurricane Katrina victims. Perhaps it is difficult to imagine that behavior that disgusts, reviles, or even nauseates you are not the acts of immoral, sick, or evil people, but are typical and even beneficial parts of all societies. Durkheim's theory suggests that structural needs of the society as a whole, beyond the scope of its individual members, foster the continuing recurrence of deviance.

The structural perspective locates the root cause of crime and deviance outside of individuals, in the invisible social structures that make up any society. Structural explanations for deviance look at features of society that seem to generate higher rates of crime or deviance among some societies or groups within them. In looking for explanations for why some societies are likely to have higher crime rates than others, sociologists have suggested that those with greater degrees of inequality are likely to show more crime than those where people have roughly similar amounts of what the society values. Looking within each society, structuralists locate the cause of crime in two main factors: the differential opportunity structure, and prejudice and discrimination towards certain groups. In a society with inequality, some groups will clearly have greater structural access to certain opportunities than others. Groups with access to greater power, political, and economic opportunity may use these to define their acts as legitimate and the acts of others as deviant, at the same time as they corruptly use their power to their own advantage. Not everyone has equal opportunity to dispense political favors, to manipulate stock prices, or to conduct covert operations.

At the same time, groups with less access to the legitimate opportunity structure due to reduced educational opportunity, diminished access to health, lower class background, and disadvantaged legitimate networks and connections, do not have the same opportunity to succeed normatively. Members of these groups may be propelled by their position in the social structure into alternate pathways.

It was Robert Merton, a mid-twentieth century sociologist from Columbia University, who actually extended Durkheim's ideas and built them into a specific structural strain theory of deviant behavior. He claimed that contradictions are implicit in a stratified system in which the culture dictates success goals for all citizens, while institutional access is limited to just the middle and upper strata. In other words, despite the American Dream of rags-to-riches, some people, most often lower-class individuals, are systematically excluded from the competition. Instead of merely going through the motions while knowing that their legitimate path to success (measured in American society by financial wealth) is blocked, some members of the lower-class retaliate by choosing a deviant alternative. Merton believed that these people have accepted society's goals (to be comfortable, to get rich), but they have insufficient access to the approved means of attaining these goals (deferred gratification, education, hard work). The problem lies in the social structure in society, where even if people follow the approved means, there are "roadblocks" prohibiting them from rising through the stratification system. Deviant behavior occurs when socially sanctioned means are not available for the realization of highly desirable goals. The only way to achieve these goals is to "detour" around them, to bypass the approved means in order to get at the approved goals. For example, for young men raised in urban ghettos with poor housing facilities, dilapidated schools, and inconsistent family lives, their road to "success" is more likely to be through dealing drugs, pimping, or robbing, than it is through the normative route of school and hard work. According to Merton, then, anomie results from the lack of access to culturally prescribed goals and the lack of availability of legitimate means for attaining those goals. Deviance (or, more specifically, crime) is the obvious alternative. Once again, structural opportunities or lack thereof, are seen as the root cause of deviance, rather than some psychological or individual pathology. You can find an articulation of his theory in Chapter 7.

Richard Cloward and Lloyd Ohlin, in *Delinquency and Opportunity* (1960), thought that Merton was correct in directing us toward the notion that members of disadvantaged socioeconomic groups have less opportunity for achieving success in a legitimate manner, but they thought that Merton wrongly assumed that those groups, when confronted with the problem of differential opportunity, could automatically choose deviance and crime. In their differential opportunity theory, Cloward and Ohlin suggested that all disadvantaged people have some lack of opportunity for legitimate pursuits, but they do not have the same opportunity for participating in illegitimate practices. What Cloward and Ohlin believed was that deviant behavior depends on people's access to illegitimate opportunities. They found that three types of deviant opportunities are present: criminal—similar to the type Merton described, these arise from access to deviant subcultures, though not all disadvantaged youth enjoy these avenues; conflict—these attract people who have a propensity for violence and fighting; and retreatist—these attract people who are not inclined toward illegitimate means or violent actions, but who want to withdraw from society, such as drug users. According to Cloward and Ohlin, groups of people may have greater or lesser opportunity to climb the illicit opportunity ladder by virtue of several factors: (1) some neighborhoods are rife with more criminal opportunities, networks, and enterprises than others, and people reared in these grow up amidst these better opportunities; (2) some forms of illicit enterprise are dominated by people of particular racial or ethnic groups, so that members of these groups have an easier time rising to the top of these businesses or organizations; and (3) the upper echelons of crime display a distinct glass ceiling for women, with men dominating the positions of decision-making, earning, and power. Thus, Cloward and Ohlin extended Merton's theory by specifying the existence of differential illegitimate opportunities available to members of disadvantaged groups. It is in this illegitimate opportunity structure, rather than individual motivation, they argue, that the explanation for deviance can be found.

Chapter 5, "Social Power: Conflict Theory of Crime," by Richard Quinney (discussed in connection to the social power perspective in the General Introduction) offers a conflict theory explanation that is not functionalist but is still structural. Conflict theorists see society differently from functionalists in their view of society as pluralistic, heterogeneous, and conflictual rather than unified and consensual. Social conflict arises out of the incompatible interests of diverse groups in society, such as businesses versus their workers, conservatives versus liberals, whites versus people of color, and the rich versus the poor. These groups have a structural conflict of interest with each other that stands above and beyond the individual members, framing the way they come to recognize their interests and act in the world. Not only is conflict a natural outcome of this arrangement, but crime is as well. In a succinct summation of conflict theory's major tenets, Quinney describes how crime exists because some behaviors conflict with the interests of the dominant class. These powerful members of society create legal definitions of human conduct, casting those behaviors that threaten its interests as criminal. Then, the dominant class enforces those laws onto the less powerful groups in society, through the police, the legal, and the criminal justice system, ensuring that their interests are protected. Members of subordinate classes are compelled to commit those actions that have been defined as crimes because their poverty presses them to do so. The dominant group can then create and disseminate their ideology of crime, which is that the most dangerous criminal elements in society can be found in the subordinate classes, and that these groups deserve arrest, prosecution, and imprisonment. Through class struggle and class conflict, crime is constructed, formulated, and applied so that less powerful groups are subdued and more powerful groups are strengthened. These processes are illustrated by the diagram in Quinney's chapter. This approach shows how larger social forces, such as group and class interests, shape the behavior of individual members, leading some to use their advantage to dominate over others, while the others react to their structural subordination by engaging in those behaviors already defined as deviant and deserving of punishment. All of these structural theories place the cause for the incidence of deviance on the structures of society, rather than on individuals and their problems.

Feminist theory, the subject of Chapter 10, takes a structural approach as well, locating the pervasive discrimination and oppression of women in society in the overarching patriarchal system. Through the intertwined effects of major institutions and social structures such as our legal codes, the economy, our political system, social and cultural practices, religion, the family, the educational system, and the media, women are systematically disadvantaged. Women, they argue, are unprotected against verbal, physical, and sexual abuse, and their individual attempts to rise up and protect themselves often subject them to being labeled as offenders. When they flee abusive situations, the patriarchy of the streets oppresses them further, funneling them into acts of survival defined as deviant by the male hegemony. Feminists maintain that theories of deviance are male-centered when they impose stereotyped gender role requirements onto teenage girls and when they problematize women's attempts to survive under oppressive conditions in a system that systematically deprives them of resources.

THE CULTURAL PERSPECTIVE

Whereas structuralist theories had enormous impact on sociologists' thinking about deviance, other authors arose who felt that these were not all-encompassing explanations. These theorists believed that deviance was a collective act, driven and carried out by groups of people. Building on conflict theory's view that multiple groups with different interests exist in society, the subcultural theorists examined the implications of membership in these groups. Groups with conflicting interests include not only dominant and subordinate groups, but a variety of social, religious, political, ethnic, and economic factions. Membership in each of these groups places people in distinct subcultures, each of which contain their own set of distinct norms and values. A pluralistic nation that was once thought of as the world's "melting pot," we have become, in part, a nation of many different groups, each with their own distinct subculture.

Thorsten Sellin, writing about *The Conflict of Conduct Norms* (1938) suggested in his culture conflict theory that to some extent the norms and values of these subcultures incorporated and meshed with the norms and values of the overarching American culture, but to some extent they were different and in conflict. The disparities and different cultural codes between subcultural groups may become apparent in three situations. First, when people from one culture "migrate," or cross over into the territory of another culture, such as when people from a rural area move to the city, they find that their country ways do not mesh with modern urbanity. In these cases, they may find themselves subject to the urban norms and values. Second, cultural conflict may occur during a "takeover" situation, when the laws of one cultural group are extended to apply to another, such as when one group moves into and takes over the territory of another. This may happen when middle-class people gentrify a rundown neighborhood, and the latitude that used to be enjoyed by the former occupants to congregate outdoors, be homeless, do or deal drugs, or solicit prostitution becomes lost. In these cases, the norms of the group that has taken over may apply. Third, cultural codes may clash on the "border" of contiguous cultural areas, such as when people from different cultural groups find themselves in contact. They may be on a national border, a neighborhood border, or they may simply be people encountering members of another subculture. In these cases, no clear set of norms and values necessarily dominates, but individuals have to negotiate their cultural understandings delicately, trying to understand each others' norms and values. This could happen when new first-year students find themselves rooming with someone from a distinctly different background, where neither of their ways necessarily predominates. Sometimes this even happens when college students go home for the holidays, only to find that the norms under which they were living at college are rather different from those in their parents' houses.

In each of these three cases, people may find themselves torn between the norms and values of different group memberships. Following the norms and values of their subcultural group may produce behavior that becomes defined as deviant by the standards of the broader culture. Yet from their subcultural perspective, their behavior may be viewed as representing the acts of good people working to uphold the behaviors they honor. In his writing, Sellin was particularly thinking about the deviance of children belonging to immigrant ethnic or racial groups moving into the United States, caught in the struggle between two cultures, but his theory applies equally well to the large number of diverse subcultural groups in our country. He extended his model to apply to all conflicts between cultural groups that share a close geographic area, especially where there is normative and value domination by one culture over another.

Building on this idea, Albert Cohen, in *Delinquent Boys* (1955), posited a reaction theory, where working-class adolescent males develop a subculture with a different value system from the dominant American culture. These boys, Cohen asserted, have the greatest degree of difficulty in achieving success, since the establishment's standards are so different from their own. They try, at first, to fit in with the cultural expectations, but find that they are unsuccessful. Exposed to middle-class aspirations and judgments they cannot reasonably fulfill, they develop a blockage (or strain) that leads them to experience "status frustration." What results from this frustration is the formation of an oppositionally reactive subculture that allows them to achieve status based on nonutilitarian, malicious, and negativistic behavior. These boys, in reaction against society's perceived unfairness towards them, substitute norms that reverse those of the larger society. Cohen claimed that delinquent boys, due to their societal rejection, turn the society's norms upside down, rejecting middle-class standards and adopting values in direct opposition to those of the majority.

Walter Miller (1958), writing just after Cohen, further delineated the importance of subcultural values for the development of deviant behavior. He believed that the values of the lower-class culture produce deviance for its members because these are "naturally" in discord with middle-class values. Young people who conform to the lower-class culture in which they were born almost automatically become deviant. The culture of the lower-class, by which members attain status in the eyes of their peers, is characterized by several "focal concerns": getting into trouble, showing toughness, maintaining autonomy, demonstrating street-smartness, searching for excitement, and being tied in their lot to the capricious whims of fate. Lower-class culture theory suggests that when these individuals follow the norms of their subculture, they become deviant according to the predominantly middle-class societal norms and values.

The lasting impact of subcultural theories has been to suggest that conflicting values may exist in society. When one part of society can impose its definitions on other parts, the dominant group has the ability to label the minority group's norms and values, and the behavior that results from these, as deviant. Thus, any act can be considered deviant if it is so defined. These theories are suited to illustrating the motivations of people from minority, youth, alternative, or disadvantaged subcultures that are not well-aligned with the dominant culture. They locate the explanation for deviance not in the structures that shape society, but in the flesh of the norms and values that compose different subcultural groups. Through cultural transmission, groups pass their norms and values down from one generation to the next, ensuring their survival and social placement as well as the continuance of cultural conflict.

THE INTERACTIONIST PERSPECTIVE

Although these previous theories produced insight into some explanations for deviance, there are interactional forces that inevitably intervene between the larger causes these sociologists propose and the way deviant behavior takes shape. Many people are exposed to the same structural conditions and the same cultural conflicts and pressures that have been theorized as accounting for deviance, but still resist engaging in deviant behaviors. Left unaddressed is how people from the same structural groups and same subcultures can turn out so differently, how members of some families turn to deviance while others do not, and how members of the same family turn out so differently from each other. Interactionist theories fill this void by looking in a more micro fashion at people's everyday life behavior to try to understand why some people engage in deviance and become so labeled, while others do not. Interactionist theories deal with real flesh and blood people in specific times and places. They look at how people actually encounter specific others, and they look at the influence of these others. They seek to understand not only why deviance occurs, but how it happens. Many of these theories look at specific social-psychological and interactional dynamics, such as family dynamics, the influence of role models, and the role of peer groups. When people confront the problems, pressures, excitements, and allures of the world, they most often do so in conjunction with their peer groups. It is within peer groups that people make decisions about what they will do and how they will do it. Their core feelings about themselves develop and become rooted in such groups. People's actions and reactions are thus guided by the collective perceptions, interpretations, and actions of their peer groups.

Edwin Sutherland and Donald Cressey recognized this point when they proposed their differential association theory of deviance, the subject of Chapter 8. The key feature of this view is the belief that deviant behavior is socially learned, and not from just anyone, but from people's most intimate friends and family members. People may be exposed to a variety of deviant and non-deviant ideas and contacts without that necessarily leading them to engage in deviance. But as their circle of contacts shifts from being primarily composed of people who hold non-deviant ideas to having greater numbers holding deviant ideas and favorable definitions of deviant acts, they become more likely to engage in deviance. The more their friends hold deviant attitudes and engage in deviant behavior, the more likely they are to follow suit.

Sutherland and Cressey further suggested that people learn a variety of elements critical to deviance from their associates: the norms and values of the deviant subculture, the rationalizations for legitimizing deviant behavior, the techniques necessary to commit the deviant acts, and the status system of the subculture, by which members evaluate themselves and others. People, thus, do not decide, at a fixed point in time, to become deviant, but move toward these attitudes and behavior as they shift their circle of associates from more normative friends to more deviant friends. Sutherland argued that people rarely stumble onto deviance through their own devising or by seeing acts of deviance in the mass media (as many would suggest), but rather by having the knowledge, skills, attitudes, values, traditions, and motives passed down to them through interpersonal (not impersonal) means. Influencing this is the age at which they encounter this deviance (earlier in life is likely to be more significant) and the intimacy of the deviant relationships (closer friends and relatives will have greater sway).

Also looking at the interactional level, David Matza (1964) proposed drift theory, noting that this movement into deviant subcultures occurs through a process of drift, as people gradually leave their old crowd and become enmeshed in a circle of deviant associates. In so doing, Matza suggested that rather than just jumping immediately into deviance, they may drift between deviance and legitimacy, keeping one foot in each world. By simultaneously participating in both deviant and legitimate worlds, people can learn about and experience the nuances of the deviant world without having to abandon the advantages of their status within the legitimate world. They may drift indefinitely, without having to make a commitment to either for quite some time.

For example, college students may experiment with a different sexual orientation without revealing this to everyone, and without necessarily giving up their claim to heterosexuality. At some point they may decide to align more firmly with one side, or this may be forced on them by outside events (getting caught, moving away, becoming sick). Being confronted by someone who discovers the deviance may force people to make a choice and get off the fence, or perhaps just leaving college and having to choose which lifestyle and social network to align themselves with may force a choice. An alternate is that individuals choose one path, after a time, and decide to follow it. But Matza suggests that the dual membership condition may precede such a decision, where individuals try out both alternatives for a time without making a commitment. Thus, Matza suggests that it is rare for people to turn to deviance overnight, but more commonly, they take smaller steps, gradually moving to making deviant acquaintances, becoming familiar with deviant ideology, thinking about engaging in deviant acts, trying some out, and then expanding their frequency and range of deviance. Quitting deviance may be a similarly gradual and difficult process, requiring the abandonment of the group of deviant friends and reintegration in conventional circles, perhaps one foot in both worlds again, before normative behavior becomes the mode that is finally chosen.

A third theory under the interactionist perspective is labeling theory, the subject of Chapter 3. This approach suggests that many people dabble to greater or lesser degrees in various forms of deviance. Studies of juvenile delinquency suggest that rates of youthful participation are extremely widespread, nearly universal. How many people can claim to have reached adulthood without experimenting in illicit drinking, drug use, cheating, stealing, or vandalism? Yet do all of these people consider themselves deviants? Most do not. Many people retire out of deviance as they mature, avoiding developing the deviant identity altogether. Others go on to engage in what Becker (1963) has called "secret deviance," conducting their acts of norm violation without ever seriously encountering the deviant label. Yet others, many of them no more experienced in the ways of deviance than the youthful delinquent or the secret deviant, become identified and identify themselves as deviants. What causes this difference? One critical difference, labeling theory suggests, lies in who gets caught. Getting caught sets off a chain reaction of events that leads to profound social and self-conceptual consequences. Frank Tannenbaum (1938) has described how individuals are publicly identified as norm violators and branded with that tag. They may go through official or unofficial social sanctioning where people identify and treat them as deviant. Becker (1963, 9) noted that "the deviant is one to whom that label has successfully been applied; deviant behavior is behavior that people so label." Deviance exists at the macro societal level of social norms and definitions through the collective attitudes we assign to certain acts and conditions. But it also comes into being at the micro everyday life level when the deviant label is applied onto someone. The thrust of labeling theory is twofold, focusing on diverse levels and forces. As Edwin Schur (1979, 160) summarized its complexity:

> The twin emphases in such an approach are on *definition* and *process* at all the levels that are involved in the production of deviant situations and outcomes. Thus, the perspective is concerned not only with what happens to specific individuals when they are branded with deviantness

("labeling," in the narrow sense) but also with the wider domains and processes of social definitions and collective rule-making that frequently lie behind such concrete applications of negative labels (*italics in original*).

In the Chapter 3 on labeling theory, Becker emphasizes that deviance lies in the eye of the beholder. There is nothing inherently deviant in any particular act, he claims, until some powerful group defines the act as deviant. Taking the onus off of the individual, Becker emphasizes the importance of looking at the process by which people are labeled deviant, and understanding that deviance is a consequence of others' reactions. This approach forces us to look, then, at how people are defined as deviant, why some acts are labeled and others ignored, and the circumstances that surround the commission of the act. Thus, deviance only exists when it is created by society. The key emphasis of the labeling theory approach to deviance, then, lies in the importance of human peer interaction in understanding the cause of human behavior.

Rooted at the micro level, but looking less at the specific dynamics of interaction and more at the relationship between individuals and society, is Travis Hirschi's control theory of delinquency, the subject of Chapter 9. Like labeling theory, which took as given that people readily engage in acts of deviance but focused its explanation on the process of identity change that occurs when individuals are caught and labeled, control theory finds it unnecessary to look for the causes of deviant behavior. These are obvious, Hirschi asserts, as deviance and crime may not only be fun, but they offer shortcuts and yield immediate, tangible benefits (albeit, with a risk). What we should be seeking to understand, instead, is what holds people back from committing these acts, what forces constrain and control deviance. Hirschi's answer is that social control lies in the extent to which people develop a stake in conformity, a bond to society. People who have a greater investment in society will be less likely to risk losing this through norm or law violations and will follow the rules more willingly. They may have such a stake through their job, relationships to friends and family, or their reputation in the community. Their stake may be fostered by any of the four components discussed in this chapter: attachment to conventional others; commitment to conventional institutions; involvement in conventional activities, and deep beliefs in conventional norms. The extent to which a society is able to foster greater bonds between itself and its potentially deviant members, by giving them a greater stake in achieving success, will affect the constraint or spread of its deviance, particularly Hirschi notes, of the delinquent variety. It is these ties, interactionally forged and maintained, that influence individuals in their choice between deviant or non-deviant pathways.

Although these overarching perspectives and the theories nested within them differ in the level at which they place their explanations, they all locate them squarely in the social domain. In this they renounce the prevailing tendency towards unidimensional psychological explanation that lodges causation in pathology, compulsion, neurosis, or maladjustment, explanations whose over-simplicity and inadequacy in a modern, complex world cannot be overstated.

The most recent perspective on deviance theory has been advanced by social constructionists, and Joel Best, one of its leading proponents, describes its history and views in Chapter 11, "The Constructionist Stance." Initially coming from a micro-interactionist approach, constructionist theorists sought to revitalize labeling theory by bridging the gap between the way labels are applied to individuals who then internalize them in their everyday life context, and a larger, more macro awareness of the power structure in society that influences the way these labels are defined and enforced. When some citizens have access to greater degrees of social power that enables the dominant groups to rationalize that their ideologies and behavior may be legitimate, they are simultaneously defining the actions of less powerful groups as deviant. In so doing, they use the vehicle of deviance and its enforcement to boost their own power while disempowering those they construct as illegitimate. The definitions they forge are then applied to individuals who lack the power to repel them, and the agents of social control act to carry out their moral edicts. The powerless segments of society become the recipients of the activities of moral entrepreneurs (rule creators and rule enforcers) who lay claims that certain behaviors are menacing and dangerous. Individuals connected to these activities may be defined as deviant, isolated, sought out, labeled, and stigmatized. Social constructionism thus builds on the basic labeling theory foundation of identity construction by integrating conflict theory's sensitivity to inequality, looking at how the power struggle between dominant and subordinate groups is directly tied to interactional and identity consequences.

6

Functionalism: The Normal and the Pathological

EMILE DURKHEIM

One of the founders of the functionalist approach to sociology, Durkheim inte-grates deviance into his overarching view of society. If, as he believes, society can be compared to a living organism, then all of its social institutions, like the parts of a human body, must contribute to its continuing existence. Under this view, deviance, because of its pervasive presence cross-culturally and over the entire course of history, is not an illness or pathology of the system, but rather something that contributes to society's positive functioning. In fact, like Erikson, he notes several positive functions that it provides, including serving as a means of intro-ducing social change, as new behaviors move through criminal and deviant status into respectability. Durkheim argues that deviance is so critical to society that if people stopped engaging in it immediately (if we lived in a "society of saints"), we would have to redefine acts now considered acceptable as deviant. Punishing and curing criminals cannot simply, then, be regarded as the objective of society.

Crime is present not only in the majority of societies of one particular species but in all societies of all types. There is no society that is not confronted with the problem of criminality. Its form changes; the acts thus characterized are not the same everywhere; but, everywhere and always, there have been men who have behaved in such a way as to draw upon themselves penal repression. If, in proportion as societies pass from the lower to the higher types, the rate of crimi-nality, i.e., the relation between the yearly number of crimes and the population, tended to decline, it might be believed that crime, while still normal, is tending to lose this character of normality. But we have no reason to believe that such a regression is substantiated. Many facts would seem rather to indicate a movement in the opposite direction. From the beginning of the [nineteenth] century, statis-tics enable us to follow the course of criminality. It has everywhere increased. In France the increase is nearly 300 percent. There is, then, no phenomenon that presents more indisputably all the symptoms of normality, since it appears closely connected with the conditions of all collective life. To make of crime a form of social morbidity would be to admit that morbidity is not something accidental, but, on the contrary, that in certain cases it grows out of the fundamental constitution of the living organism; it would result in wiping out all distinction between the physiological and the pathological. No doubt it is possible that crime itself will have abnormal forms, as, for example, when its rate is unusually high. This excess is, indeed, undoubtedly morbid in nature. What is normal, simply, is the existence of criminality, provided that it attains and does not exceed, for each social type, a certain level, which it is perhaps not impossible to fix in conformity with the preceding rules.[1]

Here we are, then, in the presence of a conclusion in appearance quite paradoxical. Let us make no mistake. To classify crime among the phenomena of normal sociology is not to say merely that it is an inevitable, although regrettable phenomenon, due to the incorrigible wickedness of men; it is to affirm that it is a factor in public health, an integral part of all healthy societies. This result is, at first glance, surprising enough to have puzzled even ourselves for a long time. Once this first surprise has been overcome, however, it is not difficult to find reasons explaining this normality and at the same time confirming it.

In the first place crime is normal because a society exempt from it is utterly impossible. Crime, we have shown elsewhere, consists of an act that offends certain very strong collective sentiments. In a society in which criminal acts are no longer committed, the sentiments they offend would have to be found without exception in all individual consciousnesses, and they must be found to exist with the same degree as sentiments contrary to them. Assuming that this condition could actually be realized, crime would not thereby disappear; it would only change its form, for the very cause which would thus dry up the sources of criminality would immediately open up new ones.

Indeed, for the collective sentiments which are protected by the penal law of a people at a specified moment of its history to take possession of the public conscience or for them to acquire a stronger hold where they have an insufficient grip, they must acquire an intensity greater than that which they had hitherto had. The community as a whole must experience them more vividly, for it can acquire from no other source the greater force necessary to control these individuals who formerly were the most refractory. For murderers to disappear, the horror of bloodshed must become greater in those social strata from which murderers are recruited; but, first it must become greater throughout the entire society. Moreover, the very absence of crime would directly contribute to produce this horror; because any sentiment seems much more respectable when it is always and uniformly respected.

One easily overlooks the consideration that these strong states of the common consciousness cannot be thus reinforced without reinforcing at the same time the more feeble states, whose violation previously gave birth to mere infraction of convention—since the weaker ones are only the prolongation, the attenuated form, of the stronger. Thus robbery and simple bad taste injure the same single altruistic sentiment, the respect for that which is another's. However, this same sentiment is less grievously offended by bad taste than by robbery; and since, in addition, the average consciousness has not sufficient intensity to react keenly to the bad taste, it is treated with greater tolerance. That is why the person guilty of bad taste is merely blamed, whereas the thief is punished. But, if this sentiment grows stronger, to the point of silencing in all consciousnesses the inclination which disposes man to steal, he will become more sensitive to the offenses which, until then, touched him but lightly. He will react against them, then, with more energy; they will be the object of greater opprobrium, which will transform certain of them from the simple moral faults that they were and give them the quality of crimes. For example, improper contracts, or contracts improperly executed, which only incur public blame or civil damages, will become offenses in law.

Imagine a society of saints, a perfect cloister of exemplary individuals. Crimes, properly so called, will there be unknown; but faults which appear venial to the layman will create there the same scandal that the ordinary offense does in ordinary consciousness. If, then, this society has the power to judge and punish, it will define these acts as criminal and will treat them as such. For the same reason, the perfect and upright man judges his smallest failings with a severity that the majority reserve for acts more truly in the nature of an offense. Formerly, acts of violence against persons were more frequent than they are today, because respect for individual dignity was less strong. As this has increased, these crimes have become more rare; and also, many acts violating this sentiment have been introduced into the penal law which were not included there in primitive times.[2]

In order to exhaust all the hypotheses logically possible, it will perhaps be asked why this unanimity does not extend to all collective sentiments without exception. Why should not even the most feeble sentiment gather enough energy to prevent all dissent? The moral consciousness of the society would be present in its entirety in all the individuals, with a vitality sufficient to prevent all acts offending it—the purely conventional faults as well as the crimes. But a uniformity so universal and absolute is utterly impossible; for the immediate physical milieu in which each one of us is placed, the hereditary antecedents, and the social influences vary from one individual to the next, and consequently diversify consciousnesses. It is impossible for all to be alike, if only because each one has his own organism and that these organisms occupy different areas in space. That is why, even among the lower peoples, where individual originality is very little developed, it nevertheless does exist.

Thus, since there cannot be a society in which the individuals do not differ more or less from the collective type, it is also inevitable that, among these divergences, there are some with a criminal character. What confers this character upon them is not the intrinsic quality of a given act but that definition which the collective conscience lends them. If the collective conscience is stronger, if it has enough authority practically to suppress these divergences, it will also be more sensitive, more exacting; and, reacting against the slightest deviations with the energy it otherwise displays only against more considerable infractions, it will attribute to them the same gravity as formerly to crimes. In other words, it will designate them as criminal.

Crime is, then, necessary; it is bound up with fundamental conditions of all social life, and by that very fact it is useful, because these conditions of which it is part are themselves indispensable to the normal evolution of morality and law.

Indeed, it is no longer possible today to dispute the fact that law and morality vary from one social type to the next, nor that they change within the same type if the conditions of life are modified. But, in order that these transformations may be possible, the collective sentiments at the basis of morality must not be hostile to change, and consequently must have but moderate energy. If they were too strong, they would no longer be plastic. Every pattern is an obstacle to new patterns, to the extent that the first pattern is inflexible. The better a structure is articulated, the more it offers a healthy resistance to all modification; and this is equally true of functional, as of anatomical, organization. If there were no crimes, this condition could not have been fulfilled; for such a hypothesis presupposes that collective sentiments have arrived at a degree of intensity unexampled in history. Nothing is good indefinitely and to an unlimited extent. The authority which the moral conscience enjoys must not be excessive; otherwise no one would dare criticize it, and it would too easily congeal into an immutable form. To make progress, individual originality must be able to express itself. In order that the originality of the idealist whose dreams transcend his century may find expression, it is necessary that the originality of the criminal, who is below the level of his time, shall also be possible. One does not occur without the other.

Nor is this all. Aside from this indirect utility, it happens that crime itself plays a useful role in this evolution. Crime implies not only that the way remains open to necessary changes but that in certain cases it directly prepares these changes. Where crime exists, collective sentiments are sufficiently flexible to take on a new form, and crime sometimes helps to determine the form they will take. How many times, indeed, it is only an anticipation of future morality—a step toward what will be! According to Athenian law, Socrates was a criminal, and his condemnation was no more than just. However, his crime, namely, the independence of his thought, rendered a service not only to humanity but to his country. It served to prepare a new morality and faith which the Athenians needed, since the traditions by which they had lived until then were no longer in harmony with the current conditions of life. Nor is the case of Socrates unique; it is reproduced periodically in history. It would never have been possible to establish the freedom of thought we now enjoy if the regulations prohibiting it had not been violated before being solemnly abrogated. At that time, however, the violation was a crime, since it was an offense against sentiments still very keen in the average conscience. And yet this crime was useful as a prelude to reforms which daily became more necessary. Liberal philosophy had as its precursors the heretics of all kinds who were justly punished by secular authorities during the entire course of the Middle Ages and until the eve of modern times.

From this point of view the fundamental facts of criminality present themselves to us in an entirely new light. Contrary to current ideas, the criminal no longer seems a totally unsociable being, a sort of parasitic element, a strange and unassimilable body, introduced into the midst of society.[3] On the contrary, he plays a definite role in social life. Crime, for its part, must no longer be conceived as an evil that cannot be too much suppressed. There is no occasion for self-congratulation when the crime rate drops noticeably below the average level, for we may be certain that this apparent progress is associated with some social disorder. Thus, the number of assault cases never falls so low as in times of want.[4] With the drop in the crime rate, and as a reaction to it, comes a revision, or the need of a revision in the theory of punishment. If, indeed, crime is a disease, its punishment is its remedy and cannot be otherwise conceived; thus, all the discussions it arouses bear on the point of determining what the punishment must be in order to fulfill this role of remedy. If crime is not pathological at all, the object of punishment cannot be to cure it, and its true function must be sought elsewhere.

NOTES

1. From the fact that crime is a phenomenon of normal sociology, it does not follow that the criminal is an individual normally constituted from the biological and psychological points of view. The two questions are independent of each other. This independence will be better understood when we have shown, later on, the difference between psychological and sociological facts.

2. Calumny, insults, slander, fraud, etc.

3. We have ourselves committed the error of speaking thus of the criminal, because of a failure to apply our rule (*Division du travail social,* pp. 395–96)

4. Although crime is a fact of normal sociology, it does not follow that we must not abhor it. Pain itself has nothing desirable about it; the individual dislikes it as a society does crime, and yet it is a function of normal physiology. Not only is it necessarily derived from the very constitution of every living organism, but it plays a useful role in life, for which reason it cannot be replaced. It would, then, be a singular distortion of our thought to present it as an apology for crime. We would not even think of protesting against such an interpretation, did we not know to what strange accusations and misunderstandings one exposes oneself when one undertakes to study moral facts objectively and to speak of them in a different language from that of the layman.

7

Social Structure and Anomie

ROBERT K. MERTON

Merton's notable contribution to deviance theory locates the root causes of crime in the structure of society, not in the individuals involved in criminal actions. Broader patterns of crime characterize certain groups of people because of the social "strain" they face between the good things society offers and their inability to legitimately attain them. Merton identifies a disjuncture for people between what he calls cultural goals, or the ends toward which we are all socialized to strive (largely conceived by him in a material sense) and institutional norms, or the acceptable means that we use to reach these goals. He refers to this condition, where people cannot attain their goals legitimately, as a "blocked opportunity structure." Societies where goals are more strongly emphasized than the legitimate means of achieving them are likely to see people pursue the innovation adaptation, as when schools make grades more critically important than the learning required to attain them, and when some groups lack the resources to legitimately earn good grades. Merton sketches other ways that groups adapt to their balance of means and ends (conformity, ritualism, retreatism, rebellion) as alternate adaptations to their structural conditions in society.

How can Merton's theory of deviance be seen as the pull of opposing forces in the social structure rather than the decisions of specific individuals?

The framework set out in this essay is designed to provide one systematic approach to the analysis of social and cultural sources of deviant behavior. Our primary aim is to discover how some *social structures exert a definite pressure upon certain persons in the society to engage in nonconforming rather than conforming conduct.* If we can locate groups peculiarly subject to such pressures, we should expect to find fairly high rates of deviant behavior in these groups, not because the human beings comprising them are compounded of distinctive biological tendencies but because they are responding normally to the social situation in which they find themselves. Our perspective is sociological. We look at variations in the *rates* of deviant behavior, not at its incidence. Should our quest be at all successful, some forms of deviant behavior will be found to be as psychologically normal as conformist behavior, and the equation of deviation and psychological abnormality will be put in question.

PATTERNS OF CULTURAL GOALS AND
INSTITUTIONAL NORMS

Among the several elements of social and cultural structures, two are of immediate importance. These are analytically separable although they merge in concrete situations. The first consists of culturally defined goals, purposes, and interests, held out as legitimate objectives for all or for diversely located members of the society. The goals are more or less integrated—the degree is a question of empirical fact—and roughly ordered in some hierarchy of value. Involving various degrees of sentiment and significance, the prevailing goals comprise a frame of aspirational reference. They are the things "worth striving for." They are a basic, though not the exclusive, component of what Linton has called "designs for group living." And though some, not all, of these cultural goals are directly related to the biological drives of man, they are not determined by them.

A second element of the cultural structure defines, regulates, and controls the acceptable modes of reaching out for these goals. Every social group invariably couples its cultural objectives with regulations, rooted in the mores or institutions of allowable procedures for moving toward these objectives. These regulatory norms are not necessarily identical with technical or efficiency norms. Many procedures which from the standpoint of particular individuals would be most efficient in securing desired values—the exercise of force, fraud, power—are ruled out of the institutional area of permitted conduct. At times, the disallowed procedures include some which would be efficient for the group itself—for example, historic taboos on vivisection, on medical experimentation, on the sociological analysis of "sacred" norms—since the criterion of acceptability is not technical efficiency but value-laden sentiments (supported by most members of the group or by those able to promote these sentiments through the composite use of power and propaganda). In all instances, the choice of expedients for striving toward cultural goals is limited by institutionalized norms.

We shall be primarily concerned with the first—a society in which there is an exceptionally strong emphasis upon specific goals without a corresponding emphasis upon institutional procedures. If it is not to be misunderstood, this statement must be elaborated. No society lacks norms governing conduct. But societies do differ in the degree to which the folkways, mores, and institutional controls are effectively integrated with the goals which stand high in the hierarchy of cultural values. The culture may be such as to lead individuals to center their emotional convictions upon the complex of culturally acclaimed ends, with far less emotional support for prescribed methods of reaching out for these ends. With such differential emphases upon goals and institutional procedures, the latter may be so vitiated by the stress on goals as to have the behavior of many individuals limited only by considerations of technical expediency. In this context, the sole significant question becomes: Which of the available procedures is most efficient in netting the culturally approved value?

The technically most effective procedure, whether culturally legitimate or not, becomes typically preferred to institutionally prescribed conduct. As this process of attenuation continues, the society becomes unstable and there develops what Durkheim called "anomie" (or normlessness).

The working of this process eventuating in anomie can be easily glimpsed in a series of familiar and instructive, though perhaps trivial, episodes. Thus, in competitive athletics, when the aim of victory is shorn of its institutional trappings and success becomes construed as "winning the game" rather than "winning under the rules of the game," a premium is implicitly set upon the use of illegitimate but technically efficient means. The star of the opposing football team is surreptitiously slugged; the wrestler incapacitates his opponent through ingenious but illicit techniques; university alumni covertly subsidize "students" whose talents are confined to the athletic field. The emphasis on the goal has so attenuated the satisfactions deriving from sheer participation in the competitive activity that only a successful outcome provides gratification. Through the same process, tension generated by the desire to win in a poker game is relieved by successfully dealing one's self four aces, or when the cult of success has truly flowered, by sagaciously shuffling the cards in a game of solitaire. The faint twinge of uneasiness in the last instance and the surreptitious nature of public delicts indicate clearly that the institutional rules of the game are *known* to those who evade them. But cultural (or idiosyncratic) exaggeration of the success–goal leads men to withdraw emotional support from the rules.

This process is of course not restricted to the realm of competitive sport, which has simply provided us with microcosmic images of the social macrocosm. The process whereby exaltation of the end generates a literal *demoralization,* that is, a deinstitutionalization, of the means occurs in many groups where the two components of the social structure are not highly integrated.

Contemporary American culture appears to approximate the polar type in which great emphasis upon certain success–goals occurs without equivalent emphasis upon institutional means. It would of course be fanciful to assert that accumulated wealth stands alone as a symbol of success just as it would be fanciful to deny that Americans assign it a place high in their scale of values. In some large measure, money has been consecrated as a value in itself, over and above its expenditure for articles of consumption or its use for the enhancement of power. "Money" is peculiarly well adapted to become a symbol of prestige. As Simmel emphasized, money is highly abstract and impersonal. However acquired, fraudulently or institutionally, it can be used to purchase the same goods and services. The anonymity of an urban society, in conjunction with these peculiarities of money, permits wealth, the sources of which may be unknown to the community in which the plutocrat lives or, if known, to become purified in the course of time, to serve as a symbol of high status. Moreover, in the American Dream there is no final stopping point. The measure of "monetary success" is conveniently indefinite and relative. At each income level, as H. F. Clark found,

Americans want just about 25 percent more (but of course this "just a bit more" continues to operate once it is obtained).

In this flux of shifting standards, there is no stable resting point, or rather, it is the point which manages always to be "just ahead." An observer of a community in which annual salaries in six figures are not uncommon reports the anguished words of one victim of the American Dream: "In this town, I'm snubbed socially because I only get a thousand a week. That hurts."

To say that the goal of monetary success is entrenched in American culture is only to say that Americans are bombarded on every side by precepts which affirm the right or, often, the duty of retaining the goal even in the face of repeated frustration. Prestigeful representatives of the society reinforce the cultural emphasis. The family, the school, and the workplace—the major agencies shaping the personality structure and goal formation of Americans—join to provide the intensive disciplining required if an individual is to retain intact a goal that remains elusively beyond reach, if he is to be motivated by the promise of a gratification which is not redeemed. As we shall presently see, parents serve as a transmission belt for the values and goals of the groups of which they are a part— above all, of their social class or of the class with which they identify themselves. And the schools are of course the official agency for the passing on of the prevailing values, with a large proportion of the textbooks used in city schools implying or stating explicitly "that education leads to intelligence and consequently to job and money success." Central to this process of disciplining people to maintain their unfulfilled aspirations are the cultural prototypes of success, the living documents testifying that the American Dream can be realized if one but has the requisite abilities.

Coupled with this positive emphasis upon the obligation to maintain lofty goals is a correlative emphasis upon the penalizing of those who draw in their ambitions. Americans are admonished "not to be a quitter" for in the dictionary of American culture, as in the lexicon of youth, "there is no such word as 'fail.'" The cultural manifesto is clear: one must not quit, must not cease striving, must not lessen his goals, for "not failure, but low aim, is crime."

Thus the culture enjoins the acceptance of three cultural axioms: First, all should strive for the same lofty goals since these are open to all; second, present seeming failure is but a way-station to ultimate success; and third, genuine failure consists only in the lessening or withdrawal of ambition.

In rough psychological paraphrase, these axioms represent, first a symbolic secondary reinforcement of incentive; second, curbing the threatened extinction of a response through an associated stimulus; third, increasing the motive-strength to evoke continued responses despite the continued absence of reward.

In sociological paraphrase, these axioms represent, first, the deflection of criticism of the social structure onto one's self among those so situated in the society that they do not have full and equal access to opportunity; second, the preservation of a structure of social power by having individuals in the lower social strata identify themselves, not with their compeers, but with those at the top (whom they will ultimately join); and third, providing pressures for conformity with the cultural dictates of unslackened ambition by the threat of less than full membership in the society for those who fail to conform.

It is in these terms and through these processes that contemporary American culture continues to be characterized by a heavy emphasis on wealth as a basic symbol of success, without a corresponding emphasis upon the legitimate avenues on which to march toward this goal. How do individuals living in this cultural context respond? And how do our observations bear upon the doctrine that deviant behavior typically derives from biological impulses breaking through the restraints imposed by culture? What, in short, are the consequences for the behavior of people variously situated in a social structure of a culture in which the emphasis on dominant success–goals has become increasingly separated from an equivalent emphasis on institutionalized procedures for seeking these goals?

TYPES OF INDIVIDUAL ADAPTATION

Turning from these culture patterns, we now examine types of adaptation by individuals within the culture-bearing society. Though our focus is still the cultural and social genesis of varying rates and types of deviant behavior, our perspective shifts from the plane of patterns of cultural values to the plane of types of adaptation to these values among those occupying different portions in the social structure.

We here consider five types of adaptation, as these are schematically set out in the following table, where (+) signifies "acceptance," (−) signifies "rejection," and (±) signifies "rejection of prevailing values and substitution of new values."

I. Conformity

To the extent that a society is stable, adaptation type I—conformity to both cultural goals and institutionalized means—is the most common and widely diffused. Were this not so, the stability and continuity of the society could not be maintained....

II. Innovation

Great cultural emphasis upon the success–goal invites this mode of adaptation through the use of institutionally proscribed but often effective means of attaining at least the simulacrum of success—wealth and power. This response occurs when

T A B L E   7.1   A Typology of Modes of Individual Adaptation

Modes of Adaptation	Culture Goals	Institutionalized Means
I. Conformity	+	+
II. Innovation	+	−
III. Ritualism	−	+
IV. Retreatism	−	−
V. Rebellion	±	±

the individual has assimilated the cultural emphasis upon the goal without equally internalizing the institutional norms governing ways and means for its attainment.

It appears from our analysis that the greatest pressures toward deviation are exerted upon the lower strata. Cases in point permit us to detect the sociological mechanisms involved in producing these pressures. Several researchers have shown that specialized areas of vice and crime constitute a "normal" response to a situation where the cultural emphasis upon pecuniary success has been absorbed, but where there is little access to conventional and legitimate means for becoming successful. The occupational opportunities of people in these areas are largely confined to manual labor and the lesser white-collar jobs. Given the American stigmatization of manual labor *which has been found* to hold *rather uniformly in all social classes,* and the absence of realistic opportunities for advancement beyond this level, the result is a marked tendency toward deviant behavior. The status of unskilled labor and the consequent low income cannot readily compete *in terms of established standards of worth* with the promises of power and high income from organized vice, rackets, and crime.

For our purposes, these situations exhibit two salient features. First, incentives for success are provided by the established values of the culture *and* second, the avenues available for moving toward this goal are largely limited by the class structure to those of deviant behavior. It is the *combination* of the cultural emphasis and the social structure which produces intense pressure for deviation....

III. Ritualism

The ritualistic type of adaptation can be readily identified. It involves the abandoning or scaling down of the lofty cultural goals of great pecuniary success and rapid social mobility to the point where one's aspirations can be satisfied. But though one rejects the cultural obligation to attempt "to get ahead in the world," though one draws in one's horizons, one continues to abide almost compulsively by institutional norms....

We should expect this type of adaptation to be fairly frequent in a society which makes one's social status largely dependent upon one's achievements. For, as has so often been observed, this ceaseless competitive struggle produces acute status anxiety. One device for allaying these anxieties is to lower one's level of aspiration—permanently. Fear produces inaction, or, more accurately, routinized action.

The syndrome of the social ritualist is both familiar and instructive. His implicit life-philosophy finds expression in a series of cultural clichés: "I'm not sticking *my* neck out," "I'm playing safe," "I'm satisfied with what I've got," "Don't aim high and you won't be disappointed." The theme threaded through these attitudes is that high ambitions invite frustration and danger whereas lower aspirations produce satisfaction and security. It is the perspective of the frightened employee, the zealously conformist bureaucrat in the teller's cage of the private banking enterprise or in the front office of the public works enterprise.

IV. Retreatism

Just as Adaptation I (conformity) remains the most frequent, Adaptation IV (the rejection of cultural goals and institutional means) is probably the least common. People who adapt (or maladapt) in this fashion are, strictly speaking, *in* the society but not *of* it. Sociologically these constitute the true aliens. Not sharing the common frame of values, they can be included as members of the *society* (in distinction from the *population*) only in a fictional sense.

In this category fall some of the adaptive activities of psychotics, autists, pariahs, outcasts, vagrants, vagabonds, tramps, chronic drunkards, and, drug addicts. They have relinquished culturally prescribed goals and their behavior does not accord with institutional norms. The competitive order is maintained but the frustrated and handicapped individual who cannot cope with this order drops out. Defeatism, quietism, and resignation are manifested in escape mechanisms which ultimately lead him to "escape" from the requirements of the society. It is thus an expedient which arises from continued failure to near the goal by legitimate measures and from an inability to use the illegitimate route because of internalized prohibitions.

V. Rebellion

This adaptation leads men outside the environing social structure to envisage and seek to bring into being a new, that is to say, a greatly modified social structure. It presupposes alienation from reigning goals and standards. These come to be regarded as purely arbitrary. And the arbitrary is precisely that which can neither exact allegiance nor possess legitimacy, for it might as well be otherwise. In our society, organized movements for rebellion apparently aim to introduce a social structure in which the cultural standards of success would be sharply modified and provision would be made for a closer correspondence between merit, effort, and reward.

THE STRAIN TOWARD ANOMIE

The social structure we have examined produces a strain toward anomie and deviant behavior. The pressure of such a social order is upon outdoing one's competitors. So long as the sentiments supporting this competitive system are distributed throughout the entire range of activities and are not confined to the final result of "success," the choice of means will remain largely within the ambit of institutional control. When, however, the cultural emphasis shifts from the satisfactions deriving from competition itself to almost exclusive concern with the outcome, the resultant stress makes for the breakdown of the regulatory structure.

8

Differential Associa...

EDWIN H. SUTHERLAND AND DONALD R. CRESSEY

Like Durkheim, Sutherland and Cressey do not regard crime and deviance as the result of either pathology in society or pathological behavior patterns. Crime, they argue, is learned in much the same way as all ordinary behavior and represents the expression of the same behavioral needs and values as other behavior. Crime is less likely to be learned, in fact, from frightening or suspicious outsiders than from people's own intimate associates. In this way, Sutherland and Cressey cast the learning of crime and deviance as a normal process, and note that it is a likely occurrence as people become surrounded with increasing numbers of deviant friends. Sutherland and Cressey place the learning of deviance within people's most intense and personal relations: families and peer groups. By repeatedly watching others modeling crime, by learning from them how to effectively do it, and by becoming convinced by their rationalizations and neutralizations that such behaviors are acceptable, individuals move into criminal or deviant behavior patterns.

How does Sutherland and Cressey's perspective on the causes of deviance separate the behavior of individuals from members of their subcultural group or broader society?

The following statements refer to the process by which a particular person comes to engage in criminal behavior.

1. *Criminal behavior is learned.* Negatively, this means that criminal behavior is not inherited, as such; also, the person who is not already trained in crime does not invent criminal behavior, just as a person does not make mechanical inventions unless he has had training in mechanics.

2. *Criminal behavior is learned in interaction with other persons in a process of communication.* This communication is verbal in many respects but includes also "the communication of gestures."

3. *The principal part of the learning of criminal behavior occurs within intimate personal groups.* Negatively, this means that the impersonal agencies of communication, such as movies and newspapers, play a relatively unimportant part in the genesis of criminal behavior.

From Edwin H. Sutherland, Donald R. Cressey, and David F. Luckenbill, *Principles of Criminology, 11th Edition* (1992). Reprinted by permission of Alta Mira Press.

hen criminal behavior is learned, the learned includes (a) techniques of committing the crime, which are sometimes very complicated, sometimes very simple; (b) the specific direction of motive, drives, rationalizations, and attitudes.

5.   *The specific direction of motives and drives is learned from definitions of the legal codes as favorable or unfavorable.* In some societies an individual is surrounded by persons who invariably define the legal codes as rules to be observed, while in others he is surrounded by persons whose definitions are favorable to the violation of the legal codes. In our American society these definitions are almost always mixed, with the consequence that we have culture conflict in relation to the legal codes.

6.   *A person becomes delinquent because of an excess of definitions favorable to violation of law over definitions unfavorable to violation of law.* This is the principle of differential association. It refers to both criminal and anticriminal associations and has to do with counteracting forces. When persons become criminal, they do so because of contacts with criminal patterns and also because of isolation from anticriminal patterns. Any person inevitably assimilates the surrounding culture unless other patterns are in conflict; a southerner does not pronounce *r* because other southerners do not pronounce *r*. Negatively, this proposition of differential association means that associations which are neutral so far as crime is concerned have little or no effect on the genesis of criminal behavior. Much of the experience of a person is neutral in this sense, for example, learning to brush one's teeth. This behavior has no negative or positive effect on criminal behavior except as it may be related to associations which are concerned with the legal codes. This neutral behavior is important especially as an occupier of the time of a child so that he is not in contact with criminal behavior during the time he is so engaged in the neutral behavior.

7.   *Differential associations may vary in frequency, duration, priority, and intensity.* This means that associations with criminal behavior and also associations with anticriminal behavior vary in those respects. "Frequency" and "duration" as modalities of associations are obvious and need no explanation. "Priority" is assumed to be important in the sense that lawful behavior developed in early childhood may persist throughout life, and also that delinquent behavior developed in early childhood may persist throughout life. This tendency, however, has not been adequately demonstrated, and priority seems to be important principally through its selective influence. "Intensity" is not precisely defined, but it has to do with such things as the prestige of the source of a criminal or anticriminal pattern and with emotional reactions related to the associations. In a precise description of the criminal behavior of a person, these modalities would be rated in quantitative form and a mathematical ratio reached. A formula in this sense has not been developed, and the development of such a formula would be extremely difficult.

8.   *The process of learning criminal behavior by association with criminal and anticriminal patterns involves all of the mechanisms that are involved in any other*

learning. Negatively, this means that the learning of criminal behavior is not restricted to the process of imitation. A person who is seduced, for instance, learns criminal behavior by association, but this process would not ordinarily be described as imitation.

9. *While criminal behavior is an expression of general needs and values, it is not explained by those general needs and values, since noncriminal behavior is an expression of the same needs and values.* Thieves generally steal in order to secure money, but likewise honest laborers work in order to secure money. The attempts by many scholars to explain criminal behavior by general drives and values, such as the happiness principle, striving for social status, the money motive, or frustration, have been, and must continue to be, futile, since they explain lawful behavior as completely as they explain criminal behavior. They are similar to respiration, which is necessary for any behavior, but which does not differentiate criminal from noncriminal behavior.

It is not necessary, at this level of explanation, to explain why a person has the associations he has; this certainly involves a complex of many things. In an area where the delinquency rate is high, a boy who is sociable, gregarious, active, and athletic is very likely to come in contact with other boys in the neighborhood, learn delinquent behavior patterns from them, and become a criminal; in the same neighborhood the psychopathic boy who is isolated, introverted, and inert may remain at home, not become acquainted with the other boys in the neighborhood, and not become delinquent. In another situation, the sociable, athletic, aggressive boy may become a member of a scout troop and not become involved in delinquent behavior. The person's associations are determined in a general context of social organization. A child is ordinarily reared in a family; the place of residence of the family is determined largely by family income; and the delinquency rate is in many respects related to the rental value of the houses. Many other aspects of social organization affect the kinds of associations a person has.

The preceding explanation of criminal behavior purports to explain the criminal and noncriminal behavior of individual persons. It is possible to state sociological theories of criminal behavior which explain the criminality of a community, nation, or other group. The problem, when thus stated, is to account for variations in crime rates and involves a comparison of the crime rates of various groups or the crime rates of a particular group at different times. The explanation of a crime rate must be consistent with the explanation of the criminal behavior of the person, since the crime rate is a summary statement of the number of persons in the group who commit crimes and the frequency with which they commit crimes. One of the best explanations of crime rates from this point of view is that a high crime rate is due to social disorganization. The term *social disorganization* is not entirely satisfactory, and it seems preferable to substitute for it the term *differential social organization.* The postulate on which this theory is based, regardless of the name, is that crime is rooted in the social organization and is an expression of that social organization. A group may be organized for criminal behavior or organized against criminal behavior. Most communities are organized for both criminal and anticriminal behavior, and in that sense the crime rate is an expression of the differential group organization. Differential group organization as an explanation of variations in crime rates is consistent with the differential association theory of the processes by which persons become criminals.

9

Control Theory

TRAVIS HIRSCHI

Hirschi focuses on youthful delinquency, the age where most deviation from the norms generally occurs. In contrast to previous perspectives, Hirschi's model is a more individualistic one, looking at the bond between each person and society. Conforming behavior is reinforced by individuals' attachment to norm-abiding members of society, the commitment and investment they have made in a legitimate life and identity (educational credentials, respectable reputation), their level of involvement in legitimate activities and organizations, and their subscription to the commonly held beliefs and values characterizing normative society. People who violate norms have a flaw in one or more of these bonds to society, and can be brought back into the normative ranks by strengthening and reinforcing these weak bonds. Hirschi's perspective is thus more social psychological than structural.

How can Hirschi's theory suggest specific types of social policies that could hold people back from entry into deviance?

Control theories assume that delinquent acts result when an individual's bond to society is weak or broken. Since these theories embrace two highly complex concepts, the *bond* of the individual to *society*, it is not surprising that they have at one time or another formed the basis of explanations of most forms of aberrant or unusual behavior. It is also not surprising that control theories have described the elements of the bond to society in many ways, and that they have focused on a variety of units as the point of control....

ELEMENTS OF THE BOND

Attachment

In explaining conforming behavior, sociologists justly emphasize sensitivity to the opinion of others.[1] Unfortunately, ... they tend to suggest that man *is* sensitive to the opinion of others and thus exclude sensitivity from their explanations of deviant behavior. In explaining deviant behavior, psychologists, in contrast,

From Travis Hirschi, *Causes of Deliquency* (Berkeley: University of California Press). Reprinted by permission of the author.

emphasize insensitivity to the opinion of others.[2] Unfortunately, they too tend to ignore variation, and, in addition, they tend to tie sensitivity inextricably to other variables, to make it part of a syndrome or "type," and thus seriously to reduce its value as an explanatory concept. The psychopath is characterized only in part by "deficient attachment to or affection for others, a failure to respond to the ordinary motivations founded in respect or regard for one's fellow";[3] he is also characterized by such things as "excessive aggressiveness," "lack of superego control," and "an infantile level of response."[4] Unfortunately, too, the behavior that psychopathy is used to explain often becomes part of the *definition* of psychopath. As a result, in Barbara Wootton's words: "[The psychopath] is ... *par excellence, and* without shame or qualification, the model of the circular process by which mental abnormality is inferred from anti-social behavior while anti-social behavior is explained by mental abnormality."[5]

The problems of diagnosis, tautology, and name-calling are avoided if the dimensions of psychopathy are treated as causally and therefore problematically interrelated, rather than as logically and therefore necessarily bound to each other. In fact, it can be argued that all of the characteristics attributed to the psychopath follow from, are effects of, his lack of attachment to others. To say that to lack attachment to others is to be free from moral restraints is to use lack of attachment to explain the guiltlessness of the psychopath, the fact that he apparently has no conscience or superego. In this view, lack of attachment to others is not merely a symptom of psychopathy, it *is* psychopathy; lack of conscience is just another way of saying the same thing; and the violation of norms is (or may be) a consequence.

For that matter, given that man is an animal, "impulsivity" and "aggressiveness" can also be seen as natural consequences of freedom from moral restraints. However, since the view of man as endowed with natural propensities and capacities like other animals is peculiarly unpalatable to sociologists, we need not fall back on such a view to explain the amoral man's aggressiveness.[6] The process of becoming alienated from others often involves or is based on active interpersonal conflict. Such conflict could easily supply a reservoir of *socially derived* hostility sufficient to account for the aggressiveness of those whose attachments to others have been weakened.

Durkheim said it many years ago: "We are moral beings to the extent that we are social beings."[7] This may be interpreted to mean that we are moral beings to the extent that we have "internalized the norms" of society. But what does it mean to say that a person has internalized the norms of society? To violate a norm is, therefore, to act contrary to the wishes and expectations of other people. If a person does not care about the wishes and expectations of other people—that is, if he is insensitive to the opinion of others—then he is to that extent not bound by the norms. He is free to deviate.

The essence of internalization of norms, conscience, or superego thus lies in the attachment of the individual to others.[8] This view has several advantages over the concept of internalization. For one, explanations of deviant behavior based on attachment do not beg the question, since the extent to which a person is attached to others can be measured independently of his deviant behavior.

Furthermore, change or variation in behavior is explainable in a way that it is not when notions of internalization or superego are used. For example, the divorced man is more likely after divorce to commit a number of deviant acts, such as suicide or forgery. If we explain these acts by reference to the superego (or internal control), we are forced to say that the man "lost his conscience" when he got a divorce; and, of course, if he remarries, we have to conclude that he gets his conscience back.

This dimension of the bond to conventional society is encountered in most social control-oriented research and theory. F. Ivan Nye's "internal control" and "indirect control" refer to the same element, although we avoid the problem of explaining changes over time by locating the "conscience" in the bond to others rather than making it part of the personality.[9] Attachment to others is just one aspect of Albert J. Reiss's "personal controls"; we avoid his problems of tautological empirical *observations* by making the relationship between attachment and delinquency problematic rather than definitional.[10] Finally, Scott Briar and Irving Piliavin's "commitment" or "stake in conformity" subsumes attachment, as their discussion illustrates, although the terms they use are more closely associated with the next element to be discussed.[11]

Commitment

"Of all passions, that which inclineth men least to break the laws, is fear. Nay, excepting some generous natures, it is the only thing, when there is the appearance of profit or pleasure by breaking the laws, that makes men keep them."[12] Few would deny that men on occasion obey the rules simply from fear of the consequences. This rational component in conformity we label commitment. What does it mean to say that a person is committed to conformity? In Howard S. Becker's formulation it means the following:

> First, the individual is in a position in which his decision with regard to some particular line of action has consequences for other interests and activities not necessarily [directly] related to it. Second, he has placed himself in that position by his own prior actions. A third element is present though so obvious as not to be apparent; the committed person must be aware [of these other interests] and must recognize that his decision in this case will have ramifications beyond it.[13]

The idea, then, is that the person invests time, energy, himself, in a certain line of activity—say, getting an education, building up a business, acquiring a reputation for virtue. When or whenever he considers deviant behavior, he must consider the costs of this deviant behavior, the risk he runs of losing the investment he has made in conventional behavior.

If attachment to others is the sociological counterpart of the superego or conscience, commitment is the counterpart of the ego or common sense. To the person committed to conventional lines of action, risking one to ten years in prison for a ten-dollar holdup is stupidity, because to the committed person the costs and risks obviously exceed ten dollars in value. (To the psychoanalyst, such an act exhibits failure to be governed by the "reality-principle.") In the sociological control theory, it can be and is generally assumed that the decision to commit a criminal act may well be rationally determined—that the actor's decision was not irrational given the risks and costs he faces. Of course, as Becker points out, if the actor is capable of in some sense calculating the costs of a line of action, he is also capable of calculational errors: ignorance and error return, in the control theory, as possible explanations of deviant behavior.

The concept of commitment assumes that the organization of society is such that the interest of most persons would be endangered if they were to engage in criminal acts. Most people, simply by the process of living in an organized society, acquire goods, reputations, prospects that they do not want to risk losing. These accumulations are society's insurance that they will abide by the rules. Many hypotheses about the antecedents of delinquent behavior are based on this premise. For example, Arthur L. Stinchcombe's hypothesis that "high school rebellion ... occurs when future status is not clearly related to present performance"[14] suggests that one is committed to conformity not only by what one has but also by what one hoped to obtain. Thus "ambition" and/or "aspiration" play an important role in producing conformity. The person becomes committed to a conventional line of action, and he is therefore committed to conformity.

Most lines of action in a society are of course conventional. The clearest examples are educational and occupational careers. Actions thought to jeopardize one's chances in these areas are presumably avoided. Interestingly enough, even nonconventional commitments may operate to produce conventional conformity. We are told, at least, that boys aspiring to careers in the rackets or professional thievery are judged by their "honesty" and "reliability"—traits traditionally in demand among seekers of office boys.[15]

Involvement

Many persons undoubtedly owe a life of virtue to a lack of opportunity to do otherwise. Time and energy are inherently limited: "Not that I would not, if I could, be both handsome and fat and well dressed, and a great athlete, and make a million a year, be a wit, a bon vivant, and a lady killer, as well as a philosopher, a philanthropist, a statesman, warrior, and African explorer, as well as a 'tone-poet' and saint. But the thing is simply impossible."[16] The things that William James here says he would like to be or do are all, I suppose, within the realm of conventionality, but if he were to include illicit actions he would still have to eliminate some of them as simply impossible.

Involvement or engrossment in conventional activities is thus often part of a control theory. The assumption, widely shared, is that a person may be simply too busy doing conventional things to find time to engage in deviant behavior. The person involved in conventional activities is tied to appointments, deadlines, working hours, plans, and the like, so the opportunity to commit deviant acts rarely arises. To the extent that he is engrossed in conventional activities, he cannot even think about deviant acts, let alone act out his inclinations.[17]

what about boredom? Lack of opportunity to do

This line of reasoning is responsible for the stress placed on recreational facilities in many programs to reduce delinquency, for much of the concern with the high school dropout, and for the idea that boys should be drafted into the army to keep them out of trouble. So obvious and persuasive is the idea that involvement in conventional activities is a major deterrent to delinquency that it was accepted even by Sutherland: "In the general area of juvenile delinquency it is probable that the most significant difference between juveniles who engage in delinquency and those who do not is that the latter are provided abundant opportunities of a conventional type for satisfying their recreational interests, while the former lack those opportunities or facilities."[18]

The view that "idle hands are the devil's workshop" has received more sophisticated treatment in recent sociological writings on delinquency. David Matza and Gresham M. Sykes, for example, suggest that delinquents have the values of a leisure class, the same values ascribed by Veblen to *the* leisure class: a search for kicks, disdain of work, a desire for the big score, and acceptance of aggressive toughness as proof of masculinity.[19] Matza and Sykes explain delinquency by reference to this system of values, but they note that adolescents at all class levels are "to some extent" members of a leisure class, that they "move in a limbo between earlier parental domination and future integration with the social structure through the bonds of work and marriage."[20] In the end, then, the leisure of the adolescent produces a set of values, which, in turn, leads to delinquency.

Belief

Unlike the cultural deviance theory, the control theory assumes the existence of a common value system within the society or group whose norms are being violated. If the deviant is committed to a value system different from that of conventional society, there is, within the context of the theory, nothing to explain. The question is, "Why does a man violate the rules in which he believes?" It is not, "Why do men differ in their beliefs about what constitutes good and desirable conduct?" The person is assumed to have been socialized (perhaps imperfectly) into the group whose rules he is violating; deviance is not a question of one group imposing its rules on the members of another group. In other words, we not only assume the deviant *has* believed the rules, we assume he believes the rules even as he violates them.

How can a person believe it is wrong to steal at the same time he is stealing? In the strain theory, this is not a difficult problem. (In fact, ... the strain theory was devised specifically to deal with this question.) The motivation to deviance adduced by the strain theorist is so strong that we can well understand the deviant act even assuming the deviator believes strongly that it is wrong.[21] However, given the control theory's assumptions about motivation, if both the deviant and the nondeviant believe the deviant act is wrong, how do we account for the fact that one commits it and the other does not?

Control theories have taken two approaches to this problem. In one approach, beliefs are treated as mere words that mean little or nothing if the other forms of control are missing. "Semantic dementia," the dissociation between rational faculties and emotional control which is said to be characteristic of the psychopath, illustrates this way of handling the problem.[22] In short, beliefs, at least insofar as they are expressed in words, drop out of the picture; since they do not differentiate between deviants and nondeviants, they are in the same class as "language" or any other characteristic common to all members of the group. Since they represent no real obstacle to the commission of delinquent acts, nothing need be said about how they are handled by those committing such acts. The control theories that do not mention beliefs (or values), and many do not, may be assumed to take this approach to the problem.

The second approach argues that the deviant rationalizes his behavior so that he can at once violate the rule and maintain his belief in it. Donald R. Cressey had advanced this argument with respect to embezzlement,[23] and Sykes and Matza have advanced it with respect to delinquency.[24] In both Cressey's and Sykes and Matza's treatments, these rationalizations (Cressey calls them "verbalizations," Sykes and Matza term them "techniques of neutralization") occur prior to the commission of the deviant act. If the neutralization is successful, the person is free to commit the act(s) in question. Both in Cressey and in Sykes and Matza, the strain that prompts the effort at neutralization also provides the motive force that results in the subsequent deviant act. Their theories are thus, in this sense, strain theories. Neutralization is difficult to handle within the context of a theory that adheres closely to control theory assumptions, because in the control theory there is no special motivational force to account for the neutralization. This difficulty is especially noticeable in Matza's later treatment of this topic, where the motivational component, the "will to delinquency," appears *after* the moral vacuum has been created by the techniques of neutralization.[25] The question thus becomes: Why neutralize?

In attempting to solve a strain-theory problem with control-theory tools, the control theorist is thus led into a trap. He cannot answer the crucial question. The concept of neutralization assumes the existence of moral obstacles to the commission of deviant acts. In order plausibly to account for a deviant act, it is necessary to generate motivation to deviance that is at least equivalent in force to the resistance provided by these moral obstacles. However, if the moral obstacles are removed, neutralization and special motivation are no longer required. We therefore follow the implicit logic of control theory and remove these moral obstacles by hypothesis. Many persons do not have an attitude of respect toward the rules of society; many persons feel no moral obligation to conform regardless of personal advantage. Insofar as the values and beliefs of these persons are consistent with their feelings, and there should be tendency toward consistency, neutralization is unnecessary; it has already occurred.

Does this merely push the question back a step and at the same time produce conflict with the assumption of a common value system? I think not. In the first place, we do not assume, as does Cressey, that neutralization occurs in order to make a specific criminal act possible.[26] We do not assume, as do Sykes and Matza, that neutralization occurs to make many delinquent acts possible. We do not assume, in other words, that the person constructs a system of rationalizations in order to justify commission of acts he *wants* to commit. We assume, in contrast, that the beliefs that free a man to commit deviant acts are *unmotivated* in the sense that he does not construct or adopt them in order to facilitate the attainment of illicit ends. In the second place, we do not assume, as does Matza, that "delinquents concur in the conventional assessment of delinquency."[27] We assume, in contrast, that there is *variation* in the extent to which people believe they should obey the rules of society, and, furthermore, that the less a person believes he should obey the rules, the more likely he is to violate them.[28]

In chronological order, then, a person's beliefs in the moral validity of norms are, for no teleological reason, weakened. The probability that he will commit delinquent acts is therefore increased. When and if he commits a delinquent act, we may justifiably use the weakness of his beliefs in explaining it, but no special motivation is required to explain either the weakness of his beliefs or, perhaps, his delinquent act.

The keystone of this argument is of course the assumption that there is variation in belief in the moral validity of social rules. This assumption is amenable to direct empirical test and can thus survive at least until its first confrontation with data. For the present, we must return to the idea of a common value system with which this section was begun.

The idea of a common (or perhaps better, a single) value system is consistent with the fact, or presumption, of variation in the strength of moral beliefs. We have not suggested that delinquency is based on beliefs counter to conventional morality; we have not suggested that delinquents do not believe delinquent acts are wrong. They may well believe these acts are wrong, but the meaning and efficacy of such beliefs are contingent on other beliefs and, indeed, on the strength of other ties to the conventional order.[29]

NOTES

1. Books have been written on the increasing importance of interpersonal sensitivity in modern life. According to this view, controls from within have become less important than controls from without in *producing* conformity. Whether or not this observation is true as a description of historical trends, it is true that interpersonal sensitivity has become more important in *explaining* conformity. Although logically it should also have become more important in explaining nonconformity, the opposite has been the case, once again showing that Cohen's observation that an explanation of conformity should be an explanation of deviance can not be translated as "an explanation of conformity has to be an explanation of deviance." For the view that interpersonal sensitivity currently plays a greater role than formerly in producing conformity, see William J. Goode, "Norm Commitment and Conformity to Role-Status Obligations," *American Journal of Sociology* LXVI (1960): 246–258. And, of course, also see David Riesman, Nathan Glazer, and Reuel Denney, *The Lonely Crowd* (Garden City, New York: Doubleday, 1950), especially Part I.

2. The literature on psychopathy is voluminous. See William McCord and Joan McCord, *The Psychopath* (Princeton: D. Van Nostrand, 1964).

3. John M. Martin and Joseph P. Fitzpatrick, *Delinquent Behavior* (New York: Random House, 1964), p. 130.

4. *Ibid.* For additional properties of the psychopath, see McCord and McCord, *The Psychopath*, pp. 1–22.

5. Barbara Wootton, *Social Science and Social Pathology* (New York: Macmillan, 1959), p. 250.

6. "The logical untenability [of the position that there are forces in man 'resistant to socialization'] was ably demonstrated by Parsons over 30 years ago, and it is widely recognized that the position is empirically unsound because it assumes [!] some universal biological drive system distinctly separate from socialization and social context—a basic and intransigent human nature" (Judith Blake and Kingsley Davis, "Norms, Values, and Sanctions," *Handbook of Modem Sociology*, ed. Robert E. L. Pans [Chicago: Rand McNally, 1964], p. 471).

7. Emile Durkheim, *Moral Education*, trans. Everett K. Wilson and Herman Schnurer (New York: The Free Press, 1961), p. 64.

8. Although attachment alone does not exhaust the meaning of internalization, attachments and beliefs combined would appear to leave only a small residue of "internal control" not susceptible in principle to direct measurement.

9. F. Ivan Nye, *Family Relationships and Delinquent Behavior* (New York: Wiley, 1958), pp. 5–7.

10. Albert J. Reiss, Jr., "Delinquency as the Failure of Personal and Social Controls," *American Sociological Review* XVI (1951): 196–207. For example, "Our observations show ... that delinquent recidivists are less often

persons with mature ego ideals or nondelinquent social roles" (p. 204).

11. Scott Briar and Irving Piliavin, "Delinquency, Situational Inducements, and Commitment to Conformity," *Social Problems* XIII (1965): 41–42. The concept "stake in conformity" was introduced by Jackson Toby in his "Social Disorganization and Stake in Conformity: Complementary Factors in the Predatory Behavior of Hoodlums," *Journal of Criminal Law, Criminology and Police Science* XLVIII (1957): 12–17. See also his "Hoodlum or Business Man: An American Dilemma," in *The Jews*, ed. Marshall Sklare (New York: The Free Press, 1958), pp. 542–550. Throughout the text, I occasionally use "stake in conformity" in speaking in general of the strength of the bond to conventional society. So used, the concept is somewhat broader than is true for either Toby or Briar and Piliavin, where the concept is roughly equivalent to what is here called "commitment."

12. Thomas Hobbes, *Leviathan* (Oxford: Basil Blackwell, 1957), p. 195.

13. Howard S. Becker, "Notes on the Concept of Commitment," *American Journal of Sociology* LXVI (1960): 35–36.

14. Arthur L. Stinchcombe, *Rebellion in a High School* (Chicago: Quadrangle, 1964), p. 5.

15. Richard A. Cloward and Lloyd E. Ohlin, *Delinquency and Opportunity* (New York: The Free Press, 1960), p. 147, quoting Edwin H. Sutherland, ed., The Professional Thief (Chicago: University of Chicago Press, 1937), pp. 211–213.

16. William James. *Psychology* (Cleveland: World Publishing Co., 1948), p. 186.

17. Few activities appear to be so engrossing that they rule out contemplation of alternative lines of behavior, at least if estimates of the amount of

time men spend plotting sexual deviations have any validity.

18. *The Sutherland Papers*, ed. Albert K. Cohen et al. (Bloomington: Indiana University Press, 1956), p. 37.

19. David Matza and Gresham M. Sykes, "Juvenile Delinquency and Subterranean Values," *American Sociological Review XXVI* (1961): 712–719.

20. *Ibid.*, p. 718.

21. The starving man stealing the loaf of bread is the image evoked by most strain theories. In this image, the starving man's belief in the wrongness of his act is clearly not something that must be explained away. It can be assumed to be present without causing embarrassment to the explanation.

22. McCord and McCord, *The Psychopath*, pp. 12–15.

23. Donald R. Cressey, *Other People's Money* (New York: The Free Press, 1953).

24. Gresham M. Sykes and David Matza, "Techniques of Neutralization: A Theory of Delinquency," *American Sociological Review XXII* (1957), 664–670.

25. David Matza, *Delinquency and Drift* (New York: Wiley, 1964), pp. 181–191.

26. In asserting that Cressey's assumption is invalid with respect to delinquency, I do not wish to suggest that it is invalid for the question of embezzlement, where the problem faced by the deviator is fairly specific and he can reasonably be assumed to be an upstanding citizen. (Although even here the fact that the embezzler's nonsharable financial problem often results from some sort of hanky-panky suggests that "verbalizations" may be less necessary than might otherwise be assumed.)

27. *Delinquency and Drift*, p. 43.

28. This assumption is not, I think, contradicted by the evidence presented by Matza against the existence of a delinquent subculture. In comparing the attitudes and actions of delinquents with the picture painted by delinquent subculture theorists, Matza emphasizes— and perhaps exaggerates—the extent to which delinquents are tied to the conventional order. In implicitly comparing delinquents with a supermoral man, I emphasize—and perhaps exaggerate— the extent to which they are not tied to the conventional order.

29. The position taken here is therefore somewhere between the "semantic dementia" and the "neutralization" positions. Assuming variation, the delinquent is, at the extremes, freer than the neutralization argument assumes. Although the possibility of wide discrepancy between what the delinquent professes and what he practices still exists, it is presumably much rarer than is suggested by studies of articulate "psychopaths."

10

Feminist Theory

MEDA CHESNEY-LIND

Chesney-Lind speaks strongly for the feminist perspective in pointing out that most theories of crime and deviance have focused overly on a male model of offending. She points out that girls and women hold a very different structural position in society, and the experience they are likely to encounter along with the opportunities (or lack thereof) they face are often markedly at odds with those of boys and men. Girls grow up in America facing vastly different sets of pressures, encounters, and forms of social control than their male counterparts.

Gender, she notes, is a master status, which means that most of girls' experiences in society are filtered through this lens. From early youth, their role in society is affected by the structure of male domination. When we consider the effect of patriarchy on women, the special pathways that girls take into crime and deviance are illuminated. Girls are more vulnerable to physical and sexual abuse in the home than boys, and lack the resources to rebuff or escape them, not only interpersonally, within the family, but due to the double standard of sexuality and sexual control embedded within the juvenile justice system. Runaways who escape from abusive families are systematically returned right back into them. Girls who stay and remain subjected to further abuse often marry at a young age to get out, but often find themselves domestically abused by their partners. Girls who are strong enough to fight for survival escape abusive family contexts to the street, where their opportunities (both legitimately and within the world of crime) are extremely limited. Once again, then, they find themselves subject to the domination and abuse of male predators. In these situations, girls' background experiences and lack of other survival techniques lead them into adult situations of abuse to which they voluntarily and involuntarily subject themselves in order to stay fed, sheltered, and clothed.

This cycle of victimization to criminalization characterizes the gender-related pathway of girls into deviance and crime, and illustrates the structural disadvantage faced by young and older women in society.

From *Crime & Delinquency*, 35(1), pp. 10–11, pp. 19–27. Copyright © 1989 by Sage Publications. Reprinted by Permission of Sage Publications, Inc.

How should we place Chesney-Lind's feminist theory among the broader perspectives on deviance? Where is she placing the root causes of women's deviance: in society, subcultures, or individuals?

There is considerable question as to whether existing theories that were admittedly developed to explain male delinquency can adequately explain female delinquency. Clearly, these theories were much influenced by the notion that class and protest masculinity were at the core of delinquency. Will the "add women and stir approach" be sufficient? Are these really theories of delinquent behavior as some have argued?

This article will suggest that they are not. The extensive focus on male delinquency and the inattention to the role played by patriarchal arrangements in the generation of adolescent delinquency and conformity has rendered the major delinquency theories fundamentally inadequate to the task of explaining female behavior. There is, in short, an urgent need to rethink current models in light of girls' situation in patriarchal society.

… This discussion will also establish that the proposed overhaul of delinquency theory is not, as some might think, solely an academic exercise. Specifically, it is incorrect to assume that because girls are charged with less serious offenses, they actually have few problems and are treated gently when they are drawn into the juvenile justice system. Indeed, the extensive focus on disadvantaged males in public settings has meant that girls' victimization and the relationship between that experience and girls' crime has been systematically ignored. Also missed has been the central role played by the juvenile justice system in the sexualization of girls' delinquency and the criminalization of girls' survival strategies. Finally, it will be suggested that the official actions of the juvenile justice system should be understood as major forces in girls' oppression as they have historically served to reinforce the obedience of all young women to demands of patriarchal authority no matter how abusive and arbitrary….

TOWARD A FEMINIST THEORY OF DELINQUENCY

To sketch out completely a feminist theory of delinquency is a task beyond the scope of this article. It may be sufficient, at this point, simply to identify a few of the most obvious problems with attempts to adapt male-oriented theory to explain female conformity and deviance. Most significant of these is the fact that all existing theories were developed with no concern about gender stratification.

Note that this is not simply an observation about the power of gender roles (though this power is undeniable). It is increasingly clear that gender stratification in patriarchal society is as powerful a system as is class. A feminist approach to delinquency means construction of explanations of female behavior that are sensitive to its patriarchal context. Feminist analysis of delinquency would also examine ways in which agencies of social control—the police, the courts, and the persons—act in ways to reinforce woman's place in male society. Efforts to construct a feminist model of delinquency must first and foremost be sensitive to the situations of girls. Failure to consider the existing empirical evidence on girls' lives and behavior can quickly lead to stereotypical thinking and theoretical dead ends.

An example of this sort of flawed theory building was the early fascination with the notion that the women's movement was causing an increase in women's crime; a notion that is now more or less discredited. A more recent example of the same sort of thinking can be found in recent work on the "power-control" model of delinquency. Here, the authors speculate that girls commit less delinquency in part because their behavior is more closely controlled by the patriarchal family. The authors' promising beginning quickly gets bogged down in a very limited definition of patriarchal control (focusing on parental supervision and variations in power within the family). Ultimately, the authors' narrow formulation of patriarchal control results in their arguing that mother's work force participation (particularly in high status occupations) leads to increases in daughters' delinquency since these girls find themselves in more "egalitarian" families."

This is essentially a not-too-subtle variation on the earlier "liberation" hypothesis. Now, mother's liberation causes daughter's crime. Aside from the methodological problems with the study (e.g., the authors argue that female-headed households are equivalent to upper-class "egalitarian" families where both parents work, and they measure delinquency using a six-item scale that contains no status offense items), there is a more fundamental problem with the hypothesis. There is no evidence to suggest that as women's labor force participation has increased, girls' delinquency has increased. Indeed, during the last decade when both women's labor force participation accelerated and the number of female-headed households soared, aggregate female delinquency measured both by self-report and official statistics either declined or remained stable.

By contrast, a feminist model of delinquency would focus more extensively on the few pieces of information about girls' actual lives and the role played by girls' problems, including those caused by racism and poverty, in their delinquency behavior. Fortunately, a considerable literature is now developing on girls' lives and much of it bears directly on girls' crime.

CRIMINALIZING GIRLS' SURVIVAL

It has long been understood that a major reason for girls' presence in juvenile courts was the fact that their parents insisted on their arrest. In the early years, conflicts with parents were by far the most significant referral source; in Honolulu 44% of the girls who appeared in court in 1929 through 1930 were referred by parents.

Recent national data, while slightly less explicit, also show that girls are more likely to be referred to court by "sources other than law enforcement agencies" (which would include parents). In 1983, nearly a quarter (23%) of all girls but only 16% of boys charged with delinquent offenses were referred to court by non-law enforcement agencies. The pattern among youth referred for status offenses (for which girls are overrepresented) was even more pronounced. Well over half (56%) of the girls charged with these offenses and 45% of the boys were referred by sources other than law enforcement.

The fact that parents are often committed to two standards of adolescent behavior is one explanation for such a disparity—and one that should not be discounted as a major source of tension even in modern families. Despite expectations to the contrary, gender-specific socialization patterns have not changed very much and this is especially true for parents' relationships with their daughters. It appears that even parents who oppose sexism in general feel "uncomfortable tampering with existing traditions" and "do not want to risk their children becoming misfits." Clearly, parental attempts to adhere to and enforce these traditional notions will continue to be a source of conflict between girls and their elders. Another important explanation for girls' problems with their parents, which has received attention only in more recent years, is the problem of physical and sexual abuse. Looking specifically at the problem of childhood sexual abuse, it is increasingly clear that this form of abuse is a particular problem for girls.

Girls are, for example, much more likely to be the victims of child sexual abuse than are boys. Finkelhor and Baron estimate from a review of community studies that roughly 70% of the victims of sexual abuse are female, they are more likely than boys to be assaulted by a family member (often a stepfather), and, as a consequence, their abuse tends to last longer than male sexual abuse. All of these factors are associated with more severe trauma—causing dramatic short- and long-term effects in victims. The effects noted by researchers in this area move from the more well known "fear, anxiety, depression, anger and hostility, and inappropriate sexual behavior" to behaviors of greater familiarity to criminologists, including running away from home, difficulties in school, truancy, and early marriage. Herman's study of incest survivors in therapy found that they were more likely to have run away from home than a matched sample of women whose fathers were "seductive" (33% compared to 5%). Another study of women patients found that 50% of the victims of child sexual abuse, but only 20% of the nonvictim group, had left home before the age of 18.

Not surprisingly, then, studies of girls on the streets or in court populations are showing high rates of both physical and sexual abuse. Silbert and Pines (1981, p. 409) found, for example, that 60% of the street prostitutes they interviewed had been sexually abused as juveniles. Girls at an Arkansas diagnostic unit and school who had been adjudicated for either status or delinquent offenses reported similarly high-levels of physical abuse; 53% indicated they had been sexually abused, 25% recalled scars, 38% recalled bleeding from abuse, and 51% recalled bruises. A sample survey of girls in the juvenile justice system in Wisconsin revealed that 79% had been subjected to physical abuse that resulted in some form of injury, and 32% had been sexually abused by parents or other persons who were closely connected to their families. Moreover, 50% had been sexually assaulted ("raped" or forced to participate in sexual acts). Even higher figures were reported by McCormack and her associates in their study of youth in a runaway shelter in Toronto. They found that 73% of the females and 38% of the males had been sexually abused. Finally, a study of youth charged with running away, truancy, or listed as missing persons in Arizona found that 55% were incest victims.

Many young women, then, are running away from profound sexual victimization at home, and once on the streets they are forced further into crime in order to survive. Interviews with girls who have run away from home show, very clearly, that they do not have a lot of attachment to their delinquent activities. In fact, they are angry about being labeled as delinquent, yet all engaged in illegal acts. The Wisconsin study found that 54% of the girls who ran away found it necessary to steal money, food, and clothing in order to survive. A few exchanged sexual contact for money, food, and/or shelter. In their study of runaway youth, McCormack, Janus, and Burgess found that sexually abused female runaways were significantly more likely than their nonabused counterparts to engage in delinquent or criminal activities such as substance abuse, petty theft, and prostitution. No such pattern was found among male runaways.

Research on the backgrounds of adult women in prison underscores the important links between women's childhood victimizations and their later criminal careers. The interviews revealed that virtually all of this sample were the victims of physical and/or sexual abuse as youngsters; over 60% had been sexually abused and about half had been raped as young women. This situation promoted these women to run away from home (three-quarters had been arrested for status offenses) where once on the streets they began engaging in prostitution and other forms of petty property crime. They also begin what becomes a lifetime problem with drugs. As adults, the women continue in these activities since they possess truncated educational backgrounds and virtually no marketable occupational skills.

Confirmation of the consequences of childhood sexual and physical abuse on adult female criminal behavior has also recently come from a large quantitative study of 908 individuals with substantiated and validated histories of these victimizations. Widom (1988) found that abused or neglected females were twice as likely as a matched group of controls to have an adult record (16% compared to 7.5). The difference was also found among men, but it was not as dramatic (42% compared to 33%). Men with abuse backgrounds were also more likely to contribute to the "cycle of violence" with more arrests for violent offenses as adult offenders than the control group. In contrast, when women with abuse backgrounds did become involved with the criminal justice system, their arrests tended to involve property and order offenses (such as disorderly conduct, curfew, and loitering violations).

Given this information, a brief example of how a feminist perspective on the causes of female delinquency might look seems appropriate. First, like young men, girls are frequently the recipients of violence and sexual abuse. But unlike boys, girls' victimization and their response to that victimization is specifically shaped by their status as young women. Perhaps because of the gender and sexual scripts found in patriarchal families, girls are much more likely than boys to be victims of family-related sexual abuse. Men, particularly men with traditional attitudes toward women, are likely to define their daughters or stepdaughters as their sexual property. In a society that idealizes inequality in male/female relationships and venerates youth in women, girls are easily defined as sexually attractive by older men. In addition, girls' vulnerability to both physical and sexual abuse is heightened by norms that require that they stay at home where their victimizers have access to them.

Moreover, their victimizers (usually males) have the ability to invoke official agencies of social control in their efforts to keep young women at home and vulnerable. That is to say, abusers have traditionally been able to utilize the uncritical commitment of the juvenile justice system toward parental authority to force girls to obey them. Girls' complaints about abuse were, until recently, routinely ignored. For this reason, statutes that were originally placed in law to "protect" young people have, in the case of girls' delinquency, criminalized their survival strategies. As they run away from abusive homes, parents have been able to employ agencies to enforce their return. If they persisted in their refusal to stay in that home, however intolerable, they were incarcerated.

Young women, a large number of whom are on the run from homes characterized by sexual abuse and parental neglect, are forced by the very statutes designed to protect them into the lives of escaped convicts. Unable to enroll in school or take a job to support themselves because they fear detection, young female runaways are forced into the streets. Here they engage in panhandling, petty theft, and occasional prostitution in order to survive. Young women in conflict with their parents (often for very legitimate reasons) may actually be forced by present laws into petty criminal activity, prostitution, and drug use.

In addition, the fact that young girls (but not necessarily young boys) are defined as sexually desirable and, in fact, more desirable than their older sisters due to the double standard of aging means that their lives on the streets (and their survival strategies) take on unique shape—once again shaped by patriarchal values. It is no accident that girls on the run from abusive homes, or on the streets because of profound poverty, get involved in criminal activities that exploit their sexual object status. American society has defined as desirable youthful, physically perfect women. This means that girls on the streets, who have little else of value to trade, are encouraged to utilize this "resource." It also means that the criminal subculture views them from this perspective.

FEMALE DELINQUENCY, PATRIARCHAL AUTHORITY, AND FAMILY COURTS

The early insights into male delinquency were largely gleaned by intensive field observation of delinquent boys. Very little of this sort of work has been done in the case of girls' delinquency, though it is vital to an understanding of girls' definitions of their own situations, choices, and behavior. Time must be spent listening to girls. Fuller research on the settings, such as families and schools, that girls find themselves in and the impact of variations in those settings should also be undertaken. A more complete understanding of how poverty and racism shape girls' lives is also vital.

Finally, current qualitative research on the reaction of official agencies to girls' delinquency must be conducted. This latter task, admittedly more difficult, is particularly critical to the development of delinquency theory that is as sensitive to gender as it is to race and class.

It is clear that throughout most of the court's history, virtually all female delinquency has been placed within the larger context of girls' sexual behavior. One explanation for this pattern is that familial control over girls' sexual capital has historically been central to the maintenance of patriarchy. The fact that young women have relatively more of this capital has been one reason for the excessive concern that both families and official agencies of social control have expressed about youthful female defiance (otherwise much of the behavior of criminal justice personnel makes virtually no sense). Only if one considers the role of women's control over their sexuality at the point in their lives that their value to patriarchal society is so pronounced, does the historic pattern of jailing of huge numbers of girls guilty of minor misconduct make sense.

This framework also explains the enormous resistance that the movement to curb the juvenile justice system's authority over status offenders encountered. Supporters of this change were not really prepared for the political significance of giving youth the freedom to run. Horror stories told by the opponents of deinstitutionalization about victimized youth, youthful prostitution, and youthful involvement in pornography all neglected the unpleasant reality that most of these behaviors were often in direct response to earlier victimization, frequently by parents, that officials had, for years, routinely ignored. What may be at stake in efforts to roll back deinstitutionalization efforts is not so much "protection" of youth as it is curbing the right of young women to defy patriarchy.

In sum, research in both the dynamics of girls' delinquency and official reactions to that behavior is essential to the development of theories of delinquency that are sensitive to its patriarchal as well as class and racial context.

REFERENCES

Silbert, Mimi. H., and Ayah Pines. 1981. "Sexual Child Abuse as an Antecedent to Prostitution." *International Journal of Child Abuse ana Neglect* 5:407–411.

Widom, Cathy Spatz. 1988. "Sampling Biases and Implications for Child Abuse Research." *American Journal of Orthopsychiatry* 58(2): 260–270.

11

The Constructionist Stance

JOEL BEST

Best, one of the leading practitioners of the social constructionist approach, offers a historical analysis of the way theories of deviance have evolved. He notes the rise and decline in significance of several approaches to deviance theory, showing how social constructionism arose from its early roots in the sociology of deviance and moved into explaining social problems. The constructionist perspective represents a wedding of the views of labeling and conflict theories, as we noted in the General Introduction. It joins the micro analysis of the former by looking at how individuals encounter societal reactions and become labeled as deviants with the broader, more structural, social power contribution of the latter, isolating certain groups as more likely to have social reactions and definitions formed and applied by and against them. It is this social constructionist stance that will frame the organization and selections comprising the remainder of this book, as we examine the process by which groups vie for power in society and try to legislate their views into morality, and then focus on how people develop deviant identities and manage their stigma as a result of those definitions and enforcements.

What parts of Best's analysis of the social construction of social problems can be applied to defining deviance?

What does it mean to say that deviance is "socially constructed?" Some people assume that social construction is the opposite of real, but this is a mistake. Reality, that is everything we understand about the world, is socially constructed. The term calls attention to the processes by which people make sense of the world: we create—or construct—meaning. When we define some behavior as deviant, we are socially constructing deviance. The constructionist approach recognizes that people can only understand the world in terms of words and categories that they create and share with one another.

THE EMERGENCE OF CONSTRUCTIONISM

The constructionist stance had its roots in two developments. The first was the publication of Peter L. Berge and Thomas Luckmann's (1966) *The Social Construction of Reality*. Berger and Luckmann were writing about the sociology of knowledge—how social life shapes everything that people know. Their book introduced the term "social construction" to a wide sociological audience, and soon other sociologists were writing about the construction of science, news, and other sorts of knowledge, including what we think about deviance.

Second, labeling theory, which had become the leading approach to studying deviance during the 1960s, came under attack from several different directions by the mid-1970s. Conflict theorists charged that labeling theory ignored how elites shaped definitions of deviance and social control policies. Feminists complained that labeling ignored the victimization of women at the hands of both male offenders and male-dominated social control agencies. Activists for gay rights and disability rights insisted that homosexuals and the disabled should be viewed as political minorities, rather than deviants. At the same time, mainstream sociologists began challenging labeling theory's claims about the ways social control operated and affected deviants' identities.

THE CONSTRUCTIONIST RESPONSE

In response to these attacks, some sociologists sympathetic to the labeling approach moved away from studying deviance. Led by John I. Kitsuse, a sociologist whose work had helped shape labeling theory, these sociologists of deviance turned to studying the sociology of social problems. With Malcolm Spector, Kitsuse published *Constructing Social Problems* (1977)—a book that would inspire many sociologists to begin studying how and why particular social problems emerged as topics of public concern. They argued that sociologists ought to redefine social problems as claims that various conditions constituted social problems; therefore, the constructionist approach involved studying claims and those who made them—the claimsmakers. In this view, sociologists ought to study how and why particular issues such as date rape or binge drinking on college campuses suddenly became the focus of attention and concern. How were these problems constructed?

There were several advantages to studying social problems. First, constructionists had the field virtually to themselves. Although many sociology departments taught social problems courses, there were no rival well-established, coherent theories of social problems. In contrast, labeling had to struggle against functionalism, conflict theory, and other influential approaches to studying deviance.

The constructionist approach was also flexible. Analysts of social problems construction might concentrate on various actors: some examined the power of political and economic elites in shaping definitions of social problems; others focused on the role of activists in bringing attention to problems; and still others concentrated on how media coverage shaped the public's and policymakers' understandings of problems. This flexibility meant that constructionists might criticize some claims as exaggerated, distorted, or unfounded (the sort of critique found in several studies of claims about the menace of Satanism), but they might also celebrate the efforts of claimsmakers to draw attention to neglected problems (for example, researchers tended to treat claims about domestic violence sympathetically).

Again, it is important to appreciate that "socially constructed" is not a synonym for erroneous or mistaken. All knowledge is socially constructed; to say that a social problem is socially constructed is not to imply that it does not exist, but rather that it is through social interaction that the problem is assigned particular meanings.

THE RETURN TO DEVIANCE

Although constructionists studied the emergence and evolution of many different social problems, ranging from global warming to homelessness, much of their work remained focused on deviance. They studied the construction of rape, child abduction, illicit drugs, family violence, and other forms of deviance.

Closely related to the rise of constructionism were studies of medicalization (Conrad and Schneider 1980). Medicalization—defining deviance as a form of illness requiring medical treatment—was one popular, contemporary way of constructing deviance. By the end of the twentieth century, medical language—"disease," "symptom," "therapy," and so on—was used, not only by medical authorities, but even by amateurs (for example, in the many Twelve-Step programs of the recovery movement).

A large share of constructionist studies traced the rise of social problems to national attention; for example, the construction of the federal War on Drugs was studied by several constructionist researchers. However, other sociologists began studying how deviance was constructed in smaller settings, through interpersonal interaction. In particular, they examined social problems work (Holstein and Miller 1993). Even after claimsmakers have managed to draw attention to some social problem and shape the creation of social policies to deal with it, those claims must be translated into action. Police officers, social workers, and other social problems workers must apply broad constructions to particular cases. Thus, after wife abuse is defined as a social problem, it is still necessary for the police officer investigating a domestic disturbance call to define—or construct—these particular events as an instance of wife abuse (Loseke 1992). Studies of this sort of social problems work are a continuation of earlier research on the labeling process.

CONSTRUCTIONISM'S DOMAIN

Social constructionism, then, has become an influential stance for thinking about deviance, particularly for understanding how concerns about particular forms of deviance emerge and evolve, and for studying how social control agents construct particular acts as deviance and individuals as deviants. Constructionism emphasizes the role of interpretation, of people assigning meaning, or making sense of the behaviors they classify as deviant. This can occur at a societal level, as when the mass media draw attention to a new form of deviance and legislators pass laws against it, but it can also occur in face-to-face interaction, when one individual expresses disapproval of anther's rule breaking. Deviance, like all reality, is constantly being constructed.

REFERENCES

Berger, Peter L., and Thomas Luckmann. 1966. *The Social Construction of Reality.* New York: Doubleday.

Conrad, Peter, and Joseph W. Schneider. 1980. *Deviance and Medicalization.* St. Louis: Mosby.

Holstein, James A ., and Gale Miller. 1993. "Social Constructionist and Social Problems Work." Pp.151–72. *Reconsidering Social Constructionism,* edited by James Holstein and Gale Miller. Hawthorne, NY: Aldine de Gruyter.

Loseke, Donileen R. 1992. *The Battered Woman and Shelters.* Albany: State University of New York Press.

Spector, Malcolm, and John I. Kitsuse. 1977. *Constructing Social Problems.* Menlo Park, CA: Cummings.

PART III

Studying Deviance

Accurate and reliable knowledge about deviance is critically important to many groups in society. First, policy makers are concerned with deviant groups such as the homeless and transient, the chronically mentally ill, high school dropouts, criminal offenders, prostitutes, juvenile delinquents, gang members, runaways, and other members of disadvantaged and disenfranchised populations. These people pose social problems that lawmakers and social welfare agencies want to alleviate. Second, sociologists and other researchers have an interest in deviance based on their goal of understanding human nature, human behavior, and human society. Deviants are a critical group to this enterprise because they reside near the margins of social definition: they help define the boundaries of what is acceptable and unacceptable by given groups.

In this part we will discuss information about deviance coming from three primary data sources: official statistics, survey research, and field research. **Official statistics** are numerical tabulations compiled by government officials and employees of social service agencies (often those receiving financial grants or assistance from the government) in the course of doing their jobs. These people routinely collect information about their clients as they process them and combine them into statistics about deviance. This information includes arrest data that are compiled by the police and published by the FBI (the *Uniform Crime Reports*), census data on various shifting populations (such as the homeless), victim data from helping agencies (such as battered women's shelters), medical data from emergency rooms (such as DAWN, the Drug Abuse Warning Network) or from state public health agencies (such as the coroner or medical examiner offices), and prosecution data on cases that are tried in the courts. These precollected official statistics are then compiled by the various government organizations responsible for collecting them and made available to the public.

Official statistics are connected to the absolutist perspective on defining deviance because they are considered an objective source of measurement.

Another source of statistical data about deviance is **survey research**. Sometimes sociologists want information about behavior that is not routinely collected by the government or official agencies. So, for example, when we wanted to find out how emergency room admissions for self-injury varied over time we were unable to do so, because the only category emergency rooms use to document such cases is "self-inflicted injury." Self-inflicted injury includes self-cutting, burning, and branding, but it also includes (and is mostly made up of) suicide attempts. There is no way to differentiate between these very different types of acts, and therefore there are no official statistics on hospital admissions for self-injury. Rather than being limited to official sources of data or the categories that officials use, many sociologists choose to gather their own data. One very popular way is to use large-scale questionnaire surveys. Prominent ones include the National Youth Survey, a self-report questionnaire about delinquent behavior; the annual survey, "Monitoring the Future," conducted by the Institute for Social Research at the University of Michigan on the drug use of high school seniors (in which many of you reading this book have probably participated); and some of the Kinsey surveys about sexual behavior. Survey research can inquire into instances of various behaviors, but it can also collect information about people's attitudes. Survey research is particularly prevalent in the political domain, where we see opinion polls conducted all the time.

A third kind of information, richly descriptive and analytical rather than numerical, comes from sociologists who conduct **field research** (also called participant observation) on deviance. Much like anthropologists who go out to live among native peoples, sociological fieldworkers live with members of deviant groups and become intimately familiar with their lives. They hang around with people, befriend them, become part of their lives, and learn how and why they do things. They learn what their subjects think about things, how their attitudes and behaviors change over time, and how they resolve the many contradictions people find in life. This type of research yields information more deeply based in the subjects' own perspectives, detailing how they see the world, the allure of deviance for them, the problems they encounter, the ways they resolve these, the significant individuals and groups in their lives, and their role among these others. Unlike other types of research, participant observation is generally a longitudinal method, entailing years of involvement with subjects. Researchers must gain acceptance by group members, develop meaningful relationships with them, and learn about their deepest thoughts and emotions.

There are many differences among these types of data and among the methods used to gather them. Each has its advantages and disadvantages, and each may do a better job than the others of answering certain research questions. Thus, depending on people's particular needs, they may turn to one type of data or use a mixed-method approach. Official statistics have the advantage of being inexpensive to gather and quick to access, since they are already collected and published. They intend to include the entire population of those they address, not some subsample, that is, all criminals, all victims, all emergency room admittees. Records about these occurrences can be accessed back as far as the official statistics have been collected, potentially a rather long time. Yet they have certain validity problems and tend to be inaccurate in patterned and systematic ways.

Official police statistics, the *Uniform Crime Reports,* for example, fail to include a host of crimes for several reasons: crimes may be unrecognized by victims who do not notice their occurrence or lack the power to define them as deviant; crimes may be unreported by individuals who see no gain by, or fear embarrassment, censure, or retaliation from calling police attention to their victimization; or crimes may be unrecorded by police officers who use their broad discretion to handle problems informally. Official statistics on suicide, determined and collected by coroners and medical examiners, also fluctuate (Whitt 2006). They may be unreliable in rural areas because officials know families, making them loathe to render a verdict on the cause of death that would stigmatize a family or impede their collecting an insurance settlement. In urban areas they may rise and fall due to political pressures, personnel turnovers, fluctuating resources, or policy changes, being suppressed under other labels (such as drug overdoses or indeterminate causes) or "found" (such as in single-car accidents).

Other types of official statistics vastly underrepresent criminal activity for similar and other reasons, and may be problematic because the categories used to conceive of them and the way they are assembled and reported changes over time, making comparisons over the years frustrating. In sum, although official statistics yield information about a broad spectrum of people, they may be fairly shallow and unreliable in nature. Besharov and Laumann's chapter on child abuse statistics discusses the dramatic rise in the number of reported cases of child abuse and some of the sociological factors that have accounted for this wild swing in the official statistics. They discuss factors that artificially both inflate and deflate our official estimates of child abuse and their consequences for the protection of abused children.

Survey research lets social scientists collect data on the topics of their choice, but it is a more expensive and time-consuming enterprise. Through careful sampling procedures, researchers can gather data about a smaller population and generalize from it to a much larger group with a high degree of accuracy (external reliability). Strict controls over standardization of procedures and detachment of data-gatherers makes this a relatively objective method. Correlations (although not causal relations) between social factors can be established carefully. But survey research, like official statistics, has internal validity problems: it may not yield an accurate portrait of the sample group it is studying, especially for topics as sensitive as deviance. First, it is unlikely that people, especially deviants, will fill out a questionnaire and readily disclose information about the hidden aspects of their lives. Second, in responding to the questionnaire, subjects may not define their behavior the same way or use the same terms as the researchers who are writing the questions (prostitutes' conceptions of "date" may be different from those of survey researchers', and runaways may mean different things when they refer to their "home" than researchers intend). Researchers are then likely to misinterpret the nature and extent of behavior from the answers they receive. Third, sometimes the correlational connections of survey research, that is, what trends occur together (such as deviance and divorce, or violence in the media and violence in everyday life) are mistakenly assumed to be causal connections. But survey research cannot tell us *why* or *how* people act; it can only tell us *what* people are doing, even if these trends range across a broad spread of the population. A much-heralded study of sexual behavior is featured in Laumann et al.'s description of their survey, a major, highly professionally designed and conducted study, that gives us a glimpse into the problems and creative adaptations that can arise when a comprehensive effort is made to conduct large-scale survey research into Americans' sexual practices.

Field research, in contrast, cannot reach as many people, but yields deeper and more accurate information about the people studied, backed by researchers' own direct observations, to enhance its internal validity. Participant observers spend long amounts of time in the field becoming close to the people they study, and learning how their subjects perceive, interpret, and act upon the complex and often contradictory nature of their social worlds. In contrast to the detached and objective relationships between survey researchers and their subjects, field researchers rely on the subjectivity and strength of the close personal relationships they forge with the people they study to get behind false fronts and to find out what is really going on. Depth understanding is especially important when studying a topic such as deviance, where so much behavior is hidden due to its stigma and illicit status. Also critically important is the ability of field research to study deviance as it occurs in situ, in its natural setting, not via the structural constraints of police reporting or the interpretation and recollection of questionnaire research (Polsky 1967). But although often less costly than survey research to conduct, it is very time-consuming, as rapport and trust with subjects take a long time to develop. Field research also lacks the generalizability of careful survey research, as subjects tend to be gathered through a referral ("snowball") technique or because they are members of a common "scene." The assurance of randomization and objectivity, then, is not as strong as in other methodologies. We share with readers our own experiences with participant-observation in the chapter on field research, where we talk about what it is like to carry out such research with a criminal, and potentially dangerous, group.

Figure 12.1 offers a comparison of the strengths and weakness of these three methods or sources of data.

FIGURE 12.1 Strengths and Weakness of the Three Sources of Data

	Survey Research	Field Research	Official Statistics
Cost	High	Low	Free
Time	Medium	Long	Short
Approach	Objective	Subjective	Clerical
Generalizability	High	Low	High
Accuracy	Medium	High	Low

The empirical chapters that fill the remainder of this book are primarily based on participant-observation studies of deviance for two main reasons. First, as Becker (1973) remarked, participation-observation is the method of the interactionist perspective; it offers direct access to the way definitions and laws are socially constructed, to the way people's actions are influenced by their associates, and to the way people's identities are affected by the deviant labels cast on them. Second, these types of studies offer a deeper view of people's feelings, experiences, motivations, and social psychological states, which give a richer and more vivid portrayal of deviance than charts of numbers.

12

Child Abuse Reporting

DOUGLAS J. BESHAROV WITH LISA A. LAUMANN-BILLINGS

Besharov and Laumann-Billings discuss official statistics in our first chapter on the varieties of ways that deviance is studied. They note the spectacular rise in our official rates of child abuse, with figures increasing by 300 percent over a recent 30-year period. Such a dramatic change cannot be solely attributable to changes in deviant behavior, but must also involve a measurement artifact. They root the increase in child abuse statistics in three factors: mandatory reporting laws, the media campaigns surrounding child abuse, and the changed social definition of what constitutes abuse. Besharov and Laumann-Billings discuss two ironically opposing problems associated with child abuse statistics, the presence of both unreported and unsubstantiated cases. On the one hand, they claim, we are still unaware of many cases of child abuse because it tends to be hidden, defined as a private family matter, and regarded as "normal" childrearing practice.

Yet at the same time, the way we, as a society, tumultuously attacked this "discovered" social problem and deputized numerous social groups to document it, resulted in cases that could not be substantiated. Some of these were unfounded because they were investigated and found to be lacking in substance, but others were unprovable because the families could not be located, the child abuse, when investigated, was able to remain hidden, or the huge increase in the number of cases requiring investigation overburdened the dockets of social service agencies and diminished their ability to resolve all allegations. Some desperate situations are being attended to, but others are slipping through the cracks due to over-reporting problems. These cases signal continued ambiguity over definitions of child abuse.

Together these problems cast light on the work of social welfare agents to gather official statistics and some of the enormous inaccuracies inherent in these kinds of data. Official statistics have the advantage of being inexpensive and quick to gather (they are precollected by people in the course of doing their jobs), going backwards in time over long periods, and bypassing sampling to contain information about the entire population of interest, but they are notoriously inaccurate, relying on the carelessness of disinterested data-gatherers, the personal and political pressures to skew official reports, and the limited resources of public agencies to collect these data.

What do Besharov and Laumann-Billings suggest about the relative strengths and weaknesses of these kinds of official statistics?

For 30 years, advocates, program administrators, and politicians have joined to encourage even more reports of suspected child abuse and neglect. Their efforts have been spectacularly successful, with about three million cases of suspected child abuse having been reported in 1993. Large numbers of endangered children still go unreported, but an equally serious problem has developed: Upon investigation, as many as 65 percent of the reports now being made are determined to be "unsubstantiated," raising serious civil liberties concerns and placing a heavy burden on already overwhelmed investigative staffs.

These two problems—nonreporting and inappropriate reporting—are linked and must be addressed together before further progress can be made in combating child abuse and neglect. To lessen both problems, there must be a shift in priorities—away from simply seeking more reports and toward encouraging better reports.

REPORTING LAWS

Since the early 1960s, all states have passed laws that require designated professionals to report specified types of child maltreatment. Over the years, both the range of designated professionals and the scope of reportable conditions have been steadily expanded.

Initially, mandatory reporting laws applied only to physicians, who were required to report only "serious physical injuries" and "nonaccidental injuries." In the ensuing years, however, increased public and professional attention, sparked in part by the number of abused children revealed by these initial reporting laws, led many states to expand their reporting requirements. Now almost all states have laws that require the reporting of all forms of suspected child maltreatment, including physical abuse, physical neglect, emotional maltreatment, and of course, sexual abuse and exploitation.

Under threat of civil and criminal penalties, these laws require most professionals who serve children to report suspected child abuse and neglect. About twenty states require all citizens to report, but in every state, any citizen is permitted to report.

These reporting laws, associated public awareness campaigns, and professional education programs have been strikingly successful. In 1993, there were about three million reports of children suspected of being abused or neglected. This is a twenty-fold increase since 1963, when about 150,000 cases were reported to the authorities. (As we will see, however, this figure is bloated by reports that later turn out to be unfounded.)

Many people ask whether this vast increase in reporting signals a rise in the incidence of child maltreatment. Recent increases in social problems such as out-of-wedlock births, inner-city poverty, and drug abuse have probably raised the underlying rates of child maltreatment, at least somewhat. Unfortunately, so many maltreated children previously went unreported that earlier reporting statistics do not provide a reliable baseline against which to make comparisons. One thing is clear, however: The great bulk of reports now received by child protective agencies would not be made but for the passage of mandatory reporting laws and the media campaigns that accompanied them.

This increase in reporting was accompanied by a substantial expansion of prevention and treatment programs. Every community, for example, is now served by specialized child protective agencies that receive and investigate reports. Federal and state expenditures for child protective programs and associated foster care services now exceed $6 billion a year. (Federal expenditures for foster care, child welfare, and related services make up less than 50 percent of total state and federal expenditures for these services; in 1992, they amounted to a total of $2,773.7 million. In addition, states may use a portion of the $2.8 billion federal Social Services Block Grant for such services, though detailed data on these expenditures are not available. Beginning in 1994, additional federal appropriations funded family preservation and support services.)

As a result, many thousands of children have been saved from serious injury and even death. The best estimate is that over the past twenty years, child abuse and neglect deaths have fallen from over 3,000 a year—and perhaps as many as 5,000—to about 1,000 a year. In New York State, for example, within five years of the passage of a comprehensive reporting law, which also created specialized investigative staffs, there was a 50 percent reduction in child fatalities, from about two hundred a year to less than one hundred. (This is not meant to minimize the remaining problem. Even at this level, maltreatment is the sixth largest cause of death for children under fourteen.)

UNREPORTED CASES

Most experts agree that reports have increased over the past 30 years because professionals and laypersons have become more likely to report apparently abusive and neglectful situations. But the question remains: How many more cases still go unreported?

Two studies performed for the National Center on Child Abuse and Neglect by Westat, Inc., provide a partial answer. In 1980 and then again in 1986, Westat conducted national studies of the incidence of child abuse and neglect. (A third Westat incidence study is now underway.) Each study used essentially the same methodology: In a stratified sample of counties, a broadly representative sample of professionals who serve children was asked whether, during the study period, the children they had seen in their professional capacities appeared to have been abused or neglected. (Actually, the professionals were not asked the ultimate question of whether the children appeared to be "abused" or "neglected". Instead, they were asked to identify children with certain specified harms or conditions, which were then decoded into a count of various types of child abuse and neglect.)

Because the information these selected professionals provided could be matched against pending cases in the local child protective agency, Westat was able to estimate rates of nonreporting among the surveyed professionals. It could not, of course, estimate the level of unintentional nonreporting, since there is no way to know of the situations in which professionals did not recognize signs of possible maltreatment. There is also no way to know how many children the professionals recognized as being maltreated but chose not to report to the study. Obviously, since the study methodology involved asking professionals about children they had seen in their professional capacities, it also did not allow Westat to estimate the number of children seen by nonprofessionals, let alone their nonreporting rate.

Westat found that professionals failed to report many of the children they saw who had observable signs of child abuse and neglect. Specifically, it found that in 1986, 56 percent of apparently abused or neglected children, or about 500,000 children, were not reported to the authorities. This figure, however, seems more alarming than it is: Basically, the more serious the case, the more likely the report. For example, the surveyed professionals reported over 85 percent of the fatal or serious physical abuse cases they saw, 72 percent of the sexual abuse cases, and 60 percent of the moderate physical abuse cases. In contrast, they only reported 15 percent of the educational neglect cases they saw, 24 percent of the emotional neglect cases, and 25 percent of the moderate physical neglect cases.

Nevertheless, there is no reason for complacency. Translating these raw percentages into actual cases means that in 1986, about 2,000 children with observable physical injuries severe enough to require hospitalization were not reported and that more than 100,000 children with moderate physical injuries went unreported, as did more than 30,000 apparently sexually abused children. And these are the rates of nonreporting among relatively well-trained professionals. One assumes that nonreporting is higher among less-well-trained professionals and higher still among laypersons.

Obtaining and maintaining a high level of reporting requires a continuation of the public education and professional training begun 30 years ago. But, now, such efforts must also address a problem as serious as nonreporting: inappropriate reporting.

At the same time that many seriously abused children go unreported, an equally serious problem further undercuts efforts to prevent child maltreatment: The nation's child protective agencies are being inundated by inappropriate reports. Although rules, procedures, and even terminology vary—some states use the phrase "unfounded," others "unsubstantiated" or not indicated—an "unfounded" report, in essence, is one that is dismissed after an investigation finds insufficient evidence upon which to proceed.

UNSUBSTANTIATED REPORTS

Nationwide, between 60 and 65 percent of all reports are closed after an initial investigation determines that they are "unfounded" or "unsubstantiated." This is in sharp contrast to 1974, when only about 45 percent of all reports were unfounded.

A few advocates, in a misguided effort to shield child protective programs from criticism, have sought to quarrel with estimates that I and others have made that the national unfounded rate is between 60 and 65 percent. They have grasped at various inconsistencies in the data collected by different organizations to claim either that the problem is not so bad or that it has always been this bad.

To help settle this dispute, the American Public Welfare Association (APWA) conducted a special survey of child welfare agencies in 1989. The APWA researchers found that between fiscal year 1986 and fiscal year 1988, the weighted average for the substantiation rates in 31 states declined 6.7 percent—from 41.8 percent in fiscal year 1986 to 39 percent in fiscal year 1988.

Most recently, the existence of this high unfounded rate was reconfirmed by the annual Fifty State Survey of the National Committee to Prevent Child Abuse (NCPCA), which found that in 1993 only about 34 percent of the reports received by child protective agencies were substantiated.

The experience of New York City indicates what these statistics mean in practice. Between 1989 and 1993, as the number of reports received by the city's child welfare agency increased by over 30 percent (from 40,217 to 52,472), the percentage of substantiated reports fell by about 47 percent (from 45 percent to 24 percent). In fact, the number of substantiated cases—a number of families were reported more than once—actually fell by about 41 percent, from 14,026 to 8,326. Thus, 12,255 additional families were investigated, while 5,700 fewer families received child protective help.

The determination that a report is unfounded can only be made after an unavoidably traumatic investigation that is inherently a breach of parental and family privacy. To determine whether a particular child is in danger, caseworkers must inquire into the most intimate personal and family matters. Often it is necessary to question friends, relatives, and neighbors, as well as school teachers, day-care personnel, doctors, clergy, and others who know the family.

Laws against child abuse are an implicit recognition that family privacy must give way to the need to protect helpless children. But in seeking to protect children, it is all too easy to ignore the legitimate rights of parents. Each year, about 700,000 families are put through investigations of unfounded reports. This is a massive and unjustified violation of parental rights.

Few unfounded reports are made maliciously. Studies of sexual abuse reports, for example, suggest that, at most, from 4 to 10 percent of these reports are knowingly false. Many involve situations in which the person reporting, in a well-intentioned effort to protect a child, overreacts to a vague and often misleading possibility that the child may be maltreated. Others involve situations of poor child care that, though of legitimate concern, simply do not amount to child abuse or neglect. In fact, a substantial proportion of unfounded cases are referred to other agencies for them to provide needed services for the family.

Moreover, an unfounded report does not necessarily mean that the child was not actually abused or neglected. Evidence of child maltreatment is hard to obtain and might not be uncovered when agencies lack the time and resources to complete a thorough investigation or when inaccurate information is given to the investigator. Other cases are labeled unfounded when no services are available to help the family. Some cases must be closed because the child or family cannot be located.

A certain proportion of unfounded reports, therefore, is an inherent—and legitimate—aspect of reporting *suspected* child maltreatment and is necessary to ensure adequate child protection. Hundreds of thousands of strangers report their suspicions; they cannot all be right. But unfounded rates of the current magnitude go beyond anything reasonably needed. Worse, they endanger children who are really abused.

The current flood of unfounded reports is overwhelming the limited resources of child protective agencies. For fear of missing even one abused child, workers perform extensive investigations of vague and apparently unsupported reports. Even when a home visit based on an anonymous report turns up no evidence of maltreatment, they usually interview neighbors, school teachers, and day-care personnel to make sure that the child is not abused. And even repeated anonymous and unfounded reports do not prevent a further investigation. But all this takes time.

As a result, children in real danger are getting lost in the press of inappropriate cases. Forced to allocate a substantial portion of their limited resources to unfounded reports, child protective agencies are less able to respond promptly and effectively when children are in serious danger. Some reports are left uninvestigated for a week and even two weeks after they are received. Investigations often miss key facts, as workers rush to clear cases, and dangerous home situations receive inadequate supervision, as workers must ignore pending cases as they investigate the new reports that arrive daily on their desks. Decision making also suffers. With so many cases of unsubstantiated or unproven risk to children, caseworkers are desensitized to the obvious warning signals of immediate and serious danger.

These nationwide conditions help explain why from 25 to 50 percent of child abuse deaths involve children previously known to the authorities. In 1993, the NCPCA reported that of the 1,149 child maltreatment deaths, 42 percent had already been reported to the authorities. Tens of thousands of other children suffer serious injuries short of death while under child protective agency supervision.

In a 1992 New York City case, for example, five-month-old Jeffrey Harden died from burns caused by scalding water and three broken ribs while under the supervision of New York City's Child Welfare Administration. Jeffrey Harden's family had been known to the administration for more than a year and a half. Over this period, the case had been handled by four separate caseworkers, each conducting only partial investigations before resigning or being reassigned to new cases. It is unclear whether Jeffrey's death was caused by his mother or her boyfriend, but because of insufficient time and overburdened caseloads, all four workers failed to pay attention to a whole host of obvious warning signals: Jeffrey's mother had broken her parole for an earlier conviction of child sexual abuse, she had a past record of beating Jeffrey's older sister, and she had a history of crack addiction and past involvement with violent boyfriends.

Here is how two of the Hardens' caseworkers explained what happened: Their first caseworker could not find Ms. Harden at the address she had listed in her files. She commented, "It was an easy case. We couldn't find the mother so we closed it." Their second caseworker stated that he was unable to spend a sufficient amount of time investigating the case, let alone make the minimum monthly visits because he was tied down with an overabundance of cases and paperwork. He stated, "It's impossible to visit these people within a month. They're all over New York City." Just before Jeffrey's death every worker who had been on the case had left the department. Ironically, by weakening the system's ability to respond, unfounded reports actually discourage appropriate ones. The sad fact is that many responsible individuals are not reporting endangered children because they feel that the system's response will be so weak that reporting will do no good or may even make things worse....

13

Survey of Sexual Behavior
of Americans

EDWARD O. LAUMANN, JOHN H. GAGNON, ROBERT T. MICHAEL,
AND STUART MICHAELS

A much-heralded study of sexual behavior is featured in this selection by Laumann et al. This major study, which is highly professionally designed and conducted, gives us a glimpse into the problems and creative adaptations that arise when a comprehensive effort is made to conduct large-scale survey research into Americans' sexual practices. This selection outlines the procedures for conceiving and carrying out the study, from initial conceptualization to sampling, administration, interviewer training, questionnaire design, and issues of privacy and confidentiality. Readers can get some feel for both the generic features of survey research, the specific decisions as to how this project was implemented, and the strengths and weaknesses associated with this mode of gathering data about deviance. Survey research is an objective methodology, scientifically controlled through the standardization of the interview questionnaire and the careful training of interviewers so that they do not lead respondents into or away from particular answers. When careful probability sampling is used, such as we see here, survey research holds the greatest potential for generalizability from the sample population back to the larger population of interest. Political, voting, and public opinion polls, for example, use this kind of methodology and (with careful sampling) have a high degree of accurately predicting the attitudes and behavior of large swaths of people. Yet surveys have their disadvantages as well, especially in their problems of internal validity, or accuracy. People regularly misrepresent themselves on surveys either because they can't understanding the meaning of the questions, because they misremember their past attitudes or behavior, or just plain intentionally. When we look at the cost of survey research, we see that this approach can be rather expensive, making a solid, social-scientific study unaffordable without grant funding. Survey research represents one of the major sources of information about deviance, and is preferred by public policy analysts because of its numbers and use of the rhetoric of science. Its strength lies in gathering moderately shallow levels of information about less sensitive subjects from a broad spectrum of people.

From Edward O. Laumann, et al., *The Social Organization of Sexuality* (1994). Reprinted by permission of the University of Chicago Press and the author.

What kinds of sociological questions can best be answered using the survey research approach? How is it better in some ways that using official statistics or field research? How is it worse in other ways?

Most people with whom we talked when we first broached the idea of a national survey of sexual behavior were skeptical that it could be done. Scientists and laypeople alike had similar reactions: "Nobody will agree to participate in such a study." "Nobody will answer questions like these, and, even if they do, they won't tell the truth." "People don't know enough about sexual practices as they relate to disease transmission or even to pleasure or physical and emotional satisfaction to be able to answer questions accurately." It would be dishonest to say that we did not share these and other concerns. But our experiences over the past seven years, rooted in extensive pilot work, focus-group discussions, and the fielding of the survey itself, resolved these doubts, fully vindicating our growing conviction that a national survey could be conducted according to high standards of scientific rigor and replicability....

The society in which we live treats sex and everything related to sex in a most ambiguous and ambivalent fashion. Sex is at once highly fascinating, attractive, and, for many at certain stages in their lives, preoccupying, but it can also be frightening, disturbing, or guilt inducing. For many, sex is considered to be an extremely private matter, to be discussed only with one's closest friends or intimates, if at all. And, certainly for most if not all of us, there are elements of our sexual lives never acknowledged to others, reserved for our own personal fantasies and self-contemplation. It is thus hardly surprising that the proposal to study sex scientifically, or any other way for that matter, elicits confounding and confusing reactions. Mass advertising, for example, unremittingly inundates the public with explicit and implicit sexual messages, eroticizing products and using sex to sell. At the same time, participants in political discourse are incredibly squeamish when handling sexual themes, as exemplified in the curious combination of horror and fascination displayed in the public discourse about Long Dong Silver and pubic hairs on pop cans during the Senate hearings in September 1991 on the appointment of Clarence Thomas to the Supreme Court. We suspect, in fact, that with respect to discourse on sexuality there is a major discontinuity between the sensibilities of politicians and other self-appointed guardians of the moral order and those of the public at large, who, on the whole, display few hang-ups in discussing sexual issues in appropriately structured circumstances. This work is a testament to that proposition.

The fact remains that, until quite recently, scientific research on sexuality has been taboo and therefore to be avoided or at best marginalized. While there is a visible tradition of (in)famous sex research, what is, in fact, most striking is how little prior research exists on sexuality in the general population. Aside from the research on adolescence, premarital sex, and problems attendant to sex such as fertility, most research attention seems to have been directed toward those believed to be abnormal, deviant, criminal, perverted, rare, or unusual, toward sexual pathology, dysfunction, and sexually transmitted disease—the label used typically reflecting the way in which the behavior or condition in question is to be regarded. "Normal sex" was somehow off limits, perhaps because it was considered too ordinary, trivial, and self-evident to deserve attention. To be fair, then, we cannot blame the public and the politicians entirely for the lack of sustained work on sexuality at large—it also reflects the prejudices and understandings of researchers about what are "interesting" scientific questions. There has simply been a dearth of mainstream scientific thinking and speculation about sexual issues. We have repeatedly encountered this relative lack of systematic thinking about sexuality to guide us in interpreting and understanding the many findings reported in this book.

... In order to understand the results of our survey, the National Health and Social Life Survey (NHSLS), one must understand how these results were generated. To construct a questionnaire and field a large-scale survey, many research design decisions must be made. To understand the decisions made, one needs to understand the multiple purposes that underlie this research project. Research design is never just a theoretical exercise. It is a set of practical solutions to a multitude of problems and considerations that are chosen under the constraints of limited resources of money, time, and prior knowledge.

SAMPLE DESIGN

The sample design for the NHSLS is the most straightforward element of our methodology because nothing about probability sampling is specific to or changes in a survey of sexual behavior....

Probability sampling, that is, sampling where every member of a clearly specified population has a known probability of selection—what lay commentators often somewhat inaccurately call random sampling—is the sine qua non of modern survey research (see Kish 1965, the classic text on the subject). There is no other scientifically acceptable way to construct a representative sample and thereby to be able to generalize from the actual sample on which data are collected to the population that that sample is designed to represent. Probability sampling as practiced in survey research is a highly developed practical application of statistical theory to the problem of selecting a sample. Not only does this type of sampling avoid the problems of bias introduced by the researcher or by subject self-selection bias that come from more casual techniques, but it also allows one to quantify the variability in the estimates derived from the sample.

In order to determine how large a sample size for a given study should be, one must first decide how precise the estimates to be derived need to be. To illustrate this reasoning process, let us take one of the simplest and most commonly used statistics in survey research, the proportion. Many of the most important results reported are proportions. For example, what proportion of the population had more than five sex partners in the last year? What proportion engaged in anal intercourse? With condoms? Estimates based on our sample will differ from the true proportion in the population because of sampling error (i.e., the random fluctuations in our estimates that are due to the fact that they are based on samples rather than on complete enumerations or censuses). If one drew repeated samples using the same methodology, each would produce a slightly different estimate. If one looks at the distribution of these *estimates*, it turns out that they will be normally distributed (i.e., will follow the famous bell-shaped curve known as the Gaussian or normal distribution) and centered around the true proportion in the population. The larger the sample size, the tighter the distribution of estimates will be.

This analysis applies to an estimate of a single proportion based on the whole sample. In deciding the sample size needed for a study, one must consider the subpopulations for which one will want to construct estimates. For example, one almost always wants to know not just a single parameter for the whole population but parameters for subpopulations such as men and women, whites, blacks, and Hispanics, and younger people and older people. Furthermore, one is usually interested in the intersections of these various breakdowns of the population, for example, young black women. The size of the interval estimate for a proportion based on a subpopulation depends on the size of that group in the sample (sometimes called the *base "N,"* i.e., the number in the sample on which the estimate is based). It is actually this kind of number that one needs to consider in determining the sample size for a study.

When we were designing the national survey of sexual behavior in the United States for the NICHD (National Institute of Child Health and Development), we applied just these sorts of considerations to come to the conclusion that we needed a sample size of about 20,000 people....

GAINING COOPERATION: THE RESPONSE RATE

First, let us consider the cooperation or response rate. No survey of any size and complexity is able to get every sampling-designated respondent to complete an interview. Individuals can have many perfectly valid reasons why they cannot participate in the survey: being too ill, too busy, or always absent when an effort to schedule an interview is made or simply being unwilling to grant an interview. While the face-to-face or in-person survey is considerably more expensive than other techniques, such as mail or telephone surveys, it usually gets the highest response rate. Even so, a face-to-face, household-based survey such as the General Social Survey successfully interviews, on the average, only about 75 percent of the target sample (Davis and Smith 1991). The missing 25 percent pose a serious problem for the reliability and validity of a survey: is there some systematic (i.e., nonrandom) process at work that distinguishes respondents from nonrespondents? That is, if the people who refuse to participate or who can never be reached to be interviewed differ systematically in terms of the issues being researched from those who are interviewed, then one will not have a representative sample of the population from which the sample was drawn. If the respondents and nonrespondents do not differ systematically, then the results will not be affected. Unfortunately, one usually has no (or only minimal) information about nonrespondents. It is thus a challenge to devise ways of evaluating the extent of bias in the selection of respondents and nonrespondents. Experience tells us that, in most well-studied fields in which survey research has been applied, such moderately high response rates as 75 percent do not lead to biased results. And it is difficult and expensive to push response rates much higher than that. Experience suggests that a response rate close to 90 percent may well represent a kind of upper limit.

Because of our subject matter and the widespread skepticism that survey methods would be effective, we set a completion rate of 75 percent as the survey organization's goal. In fact, we did much better than this; our final completion rate was close to 80 percent. We have extensively investigated whether there are detectable participation biases in the final sample.... To summarize these investigations, we have compared our sample and our results with other surveys of various sorts and have been unable to detect systematic biases of any substantive significance that would lead us to qualify our findings at least with respect to bias due to sampling.

One might well ask what the secret was of our remarkably high response rate, by far the highest of any national sexual behavior survey conducted so far. There is no secret. Working closely with the NORC (National Opinion Research Center) senior survey and field management team, we proceeded in the same way as one would in any other national area probability survey. We did not scrimp on interviewer training or on securing a highly mobilized field staff that was determined to get respondent participation in a professional and respectful manner. It was an expensive operation: the average cost of a completed interview was approximately $450.

We began with an area probability sample, which is a sample of households, that is, of addresses, not names. Rather than approach a household by knocking on the door without advance warning, we followed NORC's standard practice of sending an advance letter, hand addressed by the interviewer, about a week before the interviewer expected to visit the address. In this case, the letter was signed by the principal investigator, Robert Michael, who was identified as the dean of the Irving B. Harris Graduate School of Public Policy Studies of the University of Chicago. The letter briefly explained the purpose of the survey as helping "doctors, teachers, and counselors better understand and prevent the spread of diseases like AIDS and better understand the nature and extent of harmful and of healthy sexual behavior in our country." The intent was to convince the potential respondent that this was a legitimate scientific study addressing personal and potentially sensitive topics for a socially useful purpose. AIDS was the original impetus for the research, and it certainly seemed to provide a timely justification for the study. But any general purpose approach has drawbacks. One problem that the interviewers frequently encountered was potential respondents who did not think that AIDS affected them and therefore that information about their sex lives would be of little use.

Mode of Administration: Face-to-Face, Telephone, or Self-Administered

Perhaps the most fundamental design decision, one that distinguishes this study from many others, concerned how the interview itself was to be conducted.

In survey research, this is usually called the *mode* of interviewing or of questionnaire administration. We chose face-to-face interviewing, the most costly mode, as the primary vehicle for data collection in the NHSLS. What follows is the reasoning behind this decision.

A number of recent sex surveys have been conducted over the telephone, ... The principal advantage of the telephone survey is its much lower cost. Its major disadvantages are the length and complexity of a questionnaire that can be realistically administered over the telephone and problems of sampling and sample control.... The NHSLS, cut to its absolute minimum length, averaged about ninety minutes. Extensive field experience suggests an upper limit of about forty-five minutes for phone interviews of a cross-sectional survey of the population at large. Another disadvantage of phone surveys is that it is more difficult to find people at home by phone and, even once contact has been made, to get them to participate.... One further consideration in evaluating the phone as a mode of interviewing is its unknown effect on the quality of responses. Are people more likely to answer questions honestly and candidly or to dissemble on the telephone as opposed to face-to-face? Nobody knows for sure.

The other major mode of interviewing is through self-administered forms distributed either face to face or through the mail.[1] When the survey is conducted by mail, the questions must be self-explanatory, and much prodding is typically required to obtain an acceptable response rate.... This procedure has been shown to produce somewhat higher rates of reporting socially undesirable behaviors, such as engaging in criminal acts and substance abuse. We adopted the mixed-mode strategy to a limited extent by using four short, self-administered forms, totaling nine pages altogether, as part of our interview. When filled out, these forms were placed in a "privacy envelope" by the respondent so that the interviewer never saw the answers that were given to these questions....

The fundamental disadvantage of self-administered forms is that the questions must be much simpler in form and language than those that an interviewer can ask. Complex skip patterns must be avoided. Even the simplest skip patterns are usually incorrectly filled out by some respondents on self-administered forms. One has much less control over whether (and therefore much less confidence that) respondents have read and understood the questions on a self-administered form. The NHSLS questionnaire (discussed below) was based on the idea that questions about sexual behavior must be framed as much as possible in the specific contexts of particular patterns and occasions. We found that it is impossible to do this using self-administered questions that are easily and fully comprehensible to people of modest educational attainments.

To summarize, we decided to use face-to-face interviewing as our primary mode of administration of the NHSLS for two principal reasons: it was most likely to yield a substantially higher response rate for a more inclusive cross section of the population at large, and it would permit more complex and detailed questions to be asked. While by far the most expensive approach, such a strategy provides a solid benchmark against which other modes of interviewing can and should be judged. The main unresolved question is whether another mode has an edge over face-to-face interviewing when highly sensitive questions likely to be upsetting or threatening to the respondent are being asked. As a partial control and test of this question, we have asked a number of sensitive questions in both formats so that an individual's responses can be systematically compared.... Suffice it to say at this point that there is a stunning consistency in the responses secured by the different modes of administration.

Recruiting and Training Interviewers

Gaining respondents' cooperation requires mastery of a broad spectrum of techniques that successful interviewers develop with experience, guidance from the research team, and careful field supervision. This project required extensive training before entering the field. While interviewers are generally trained to be neutral toward topics covered in the interview, this was especially important when discussing sex, a topic that seems particularly likely to elicit emotionally freighted sensitivities both in the respondents and in the interviewers. Interviewers needed to be fully persuaded about the legitimacy and importance of the research. Toward this end, almost a full day of training was devoted to presentations and discussions with the principal investigators in addition to the extensive advance study materials to read and comprehend. Sample answers to frequently asked questions by skeptical respondents and brainstorming about strategies to convert reluctant respondents were part of the training exercises. A set of endorsement letters from prominent local and national notables and refusal conversion letters were also provided to interviewers. A hotline to the research office at the University of Chicago was set up to allow potential respondents to call in with their concerns. Concerns ranged from those about the legitimacy of the survey, most fearing that it was a commercial ploy to sell them something, to fears that the interviewers were interested in robbing them. Ironically, the fact that the interviewer initially did not know the name of the respondent (all he or she knew was the address) often led to behavior by the interviewer that appeared suspicious to the respondent. For example, asking neighbors for the name of the family in the selected household and/or questions about when the potential respondent was likely to be home induced worries that had to be assuaged. Another major concern was confidentiality—respondents wanted to know how they had come to be selected and how their answers were going to be kept anonymous.

THE QUESTIONNAIRE

The questionnaire itself is probably the most important element of the study design. It determines the content and quality of the information gathered for analysis. Unlike issues related to sample design, the construction of a questionnaire is driven less by technical precepts and more by the concepts and ideas motivating the research. It demands even more art than applied sampling design requires.

Before turning to the specific forms that this took in the NHSLS, we should first discuss several general problems that any survey questionnaire must address.

The essence of survey research is to ask a large sample of people from a defined population the *same set of questions*. To do this in a relatively short period of time, many interviewers are needed. In our case, about 220 interviewers from all over the country collected the NHSLS data. The field period, beginning on 14 February 1992 and ending in September, was a time in which over 7,800 households were contacted (many of which turned out to be ineligible for the study) and 3,432 interviews were completed. Central to this effort was gathering comparable information on the same attributes from each and every one of these respondents. The attributes measured by the questionnaire become the variables used in the data analysis. They range from demographic characteristics (e.g., gender, age, and race/ethnicity) to sexual experience measures (e.g., numbers of sex partners in given time periods, frequency of particular practices, and timing of various sexual events) to measures of mental states (e.g., attitudes toward premarital sex, the appeal of particular techniques like oral sex, and levels of satisfaction with particular sexual relationships).

Very early in the design of a national sexual behavior survey, in line with our goal of not reducing this research to a simple behavioral risk inventory, we faced the issue of where to draw the boundaries in defining the behavioral domain that would be encompassed by the concept of sex. This was particularly crucial in defining sexual activity that would lead to the enumeration of a set of sex partners. There are a number of activities that commonly serve as markers for sex and the status of sex partner, especially intercourse and orgasm. While we certainly wanted to include these events and their extent in given relationships and events, we also felt that using them to define and ask about sexual activity might exclude transactions or partners that should be included. Since the common meaning and uses of the term *intercourse* involve the idea of the intromission of a penis, intercourse in that sense as a defining act would at the very least exclude a sexual relationship between two women. There are also many events that we would call sexual that may not involve orgasm on the part of either or both partners.

Another major issue is what sort of language is appropriate in asking questions about sex. It seemed obvious that one should avoid highly technical language because it is unlikely to be understood by many people. One tempting alternative is to use colloquial language and even slang since that is the only language that some people ever use in discussing sexual matters. There is even some evidence that one can improve reporting somewhat by allowing respondents to select their own preferred terminology (Blair et al. 1977; Bradburn, Sudman et al. 1979; Bradburn and Sudman 1983). Slang and other forms of colloquial speech, however, are likely to be problematic in several ways. First, the use of slang can produce a tone in the interview that is counterproductive because it downplays the distinctiveness of the interviewing situation itself. An essential goal in survey interviewing, especially on sensitive topics like sex, is to create a neutral, nonjudgmental and confiding atmosphere and to maintain a certain professional distance between the interviewer and the respondent. A key advantage that the interviewer has in initiating a topic for discussion is being a stranger or an outsider who is highly unlikely to come in contact with the respondent again.

It is not intended that a longer-term bond between the interviewer and the respondent be formed, whether as an advice giver or a counselor or as a potential sex partner.[2]

The second major shortcoming of slang is that it is highly variable across class and education levels, ages, regions, and other social groupings. It changes meanings rapidly and is often imprecise. Our solution was to seek the simplest possible language—standard English—that was neither colloquial nor highly technical. For example, we chose to use the term *oral sex* rather than the slang *blow job* and *eating pussy* or the precise technical but unfamiliar *terras, fellatio,* and *cunnilingus.* Whenever possible, we provided definitions when terms were first introduced in a questionnaire—that is, we tried to train our respondents to speak about sex in our terms. Many terms that seemed clear to us may not, of course, be universally understood; for example, terms like *vaginal* or *heterosexual* are not understood very well by substantial portions of the population. Coming up with simple and direct speech was quite a challenge because most of the people working on the questionnaire were highly educated, with strong inclinations toward the circumlocutions and indirections of middle-class discourse on sexual themes. Detailed reactions from field interviewers and managers and extensive pilot testing with a broad cross section of recruited subjects helped minimize these language problems.

ON PRIVACY, CONFIDENTIALITY, AND SECURITY

Issues of respondent confidentiality are at the very heart of survey research. The willingness of respondents to report their views and experiences fully and honestly depends on the rationale offered for why the study is important and on the assurance that the information provided will be treated as confidential. We offered respondents a strong rationale for the study, our interviewers made great efforts to conduct the interview in a manner that protected respondents' privacy, and we went to great lengths to honor the assurances that the information would be treated confidentially. The subject matter of the NHSLS makes the issues of confidentiality especially salient and problematic because there are so many easily imagined ways in which information voluntarily disclosed in an interview might be useful to interested parties in civil and criminal cases involving wrongful harm, divorce proceedings, criminal behavior, or similar matters.

NOTES

1. We ruled out the idea of a mail survey because its response rate is likely to be very much lower than any other mode of interviewing (see Bradburn, Sudman et al. 1979).

2. Interviewers are not there to give information or to correct misinformation. But such information is often requested in the course of an interview. Interviewers are given training

in how to avoid answering such questions (other than clarification of the meaning of particular questions). They are not themselves experts on the topics raised and often do not know the correct answers to questions. For this reason, and also in case emotionally freighted issues for the respondent were raised during the interview process, we provided interviewers with a list of toll-free phone numbers for a variety of professional sex- and health-related referral services (e.g., the National AIDS Hotline, an STD hotline, the National Child Abuse Hotline, a domestic violence hotline, and the phone number of a national rape and sexual assault organization able to provide local referrals).

REFERENCES

Blair, Ellen, Seymour Sudman, Norman M. Bradburn, and Carol Stacking. 1977. "How to Ask Questions About Drinking and Sex: Response Effects in Measuring Consumer Behavior." *Journal of Marketing Research* 14: 316–321.

Bradburn, Norman M., and Seymour Sudman. 1983. *Asking Questions: A Practical Guide to Questionnaire Design.* San Francisco: Jossey-Bass.

Bradburn, Norman M., Seymour Sudman, Ed Blair, and Carol Stacking. 1979. *Improving Interview Method and Design.* San Francisco: Jossey-Bass.

Davis, James Allan, and Tom W. Smith. 1991. *General Social Surveys, 1972–1991: Cumulative Codebook.* Chicago: National Opinion Research Center.

Kish, Leslie. 1965. *Survey Sampling.* New York: Wiley.

14

Researching Dealers and Smugglers

PATRICIA A. ADLER

Adler offers us a glimpse of what it is like to carry out participant observation research with a deviant group in this description of her study of upper-level drug traffickers. This natural history carefully explains the process used in field research, the relationships formed with setting members, and the feelings researchers experience. This stage-by-stage analysis of the activities, pitfalls, mishaps, intimacies, and relationships Adler encountered shows the connection and overlap between the development of research ties and those found in natural, everyday life. Field research, we learn, cannot be carried out by just anyone in every setting, but is dependent on researchers' ability to build a bridge of understanding, rapport, and trust between themselves and their subjects. Adler's experiences vividly show us the dangers posed to fieldworkers in criminal and deviant settings and the intimacy of the connections forged there. These kinds of ties, which form the basis of the data-gathering, make participant observation a subjective, rather than an objective, type of research. The strength of the data rest on the real-world bonds forged in the field as well as on researchers' ability to not only hear what their subjects have to say but to see them in action, and to cross-check their self-presentations against hard facts, the accounts of others, and common sense.

Field research, while costing considerably less than survey research, takes much longer to conduct, requiring years to find deviants, develop trust and relationships, and obtain deeply meaningful information. This approach not only offers us a better idea of the sequential development of causal forces in the field, but gives us the best insight into what is really going on in a deviant scene inhabited by a hidden population. Thus, while field research may not yield the ability to generalize with as much scientific precision as survey research, it is the preferred approach for those who want to deeply and accurately understand the perceptions, interpretations, analyses, life worlds, and unfolding careers of secretive deviants.

What kinds of research questions can best be answered by field research? Do its strengths outweigh its potential ethical and interpersonal dilemmas?

I strongly believe that investigative field research (Douglas 1976), with emphasis on direct personal observation, interaction, and experience, is the only way to acquire accurate knowledge about deviant behavior. Investigative techniques are

From Patricia A. Adler, *Wheeling and Dealing* (New York: Columbia University Press).

especially necessary for studying groups such as drug dealers and smugglers because the highly illegal nature of their occupation makes them secretive, deceitful, mistrustful, and paranoid. To insulate themselves from the straight world, they construct multiple false fronts, offer lies and misinformation, and withdraw into their group. In fact, detailed, scientific information about upper-level drug dealers and smugglers is lacking precisely because of the difficulty sociological researchers have had in penetrating into their midst. As a result, the only way I could possibly get close enough to these individuals to discover what they were doing and to understand their world from their perspectives (Blumer 1969) was to take a membership role in the setting. While my different values and goals precluded my becoming converted to complete membership in the subculture, and my fears prevented my ever becoming "actively" involved in their trafficking activities, I was able to assume a "peripheral" membership role (Adler and Adler 1987). I became a member of the dealers' and smugglers' social world and participated in their daily activities on that basis. In this chapter, I discuss how I gained access to this group, established research relations with members, and how personally involved I became in their activities.

GETTING IN

When I moved to Southwest County [California] in the summer of 1974, I had no idea that I would soon be swept up in a subculture of vast drug trafficking and unending partying, mixed with occasional cloak-and-dagger subterfuge. I had moved to California with my husband, Peter, to attend graduate school in sociology. We rented a condominium town house near the beach and started taking classes in the fall. We had always felt that socializing exclusively with academicians left us nowhere to escape from our work, so we tried to meet people in the nearby community. One of the first friends we made was our closest neighbor, a fellow in his late twenties with a tall, hulking frame and gentle expression. Dave, as he introduced himself, was always dressed rather casually, if not sloppily, in T-shirts and jeans. He spent most of his time hanging out or walking on the beach with a variety of friends who visited his house, and taking care of his two young boys, who lived alternately with him and his estranged wife. He also went out of town a lot. We started spending much of our free time over at his house, talking, playing board games late into the night, and smoking marijuana together. We were glad to find someone from whom we could buy marijuana in this new place, since we did not know too many people. He also began treating us to a fairly regular supply of cocaine, which was a thrill because this was a drug we could rarely afford on our student budgets. We noticed right away, however, that there was something unusual about his use and knowledge of drugs: while he always had a plentiful supply and was fairly expert about marijuana and cocaine, when we tried to buy a small bag of marijuana from him he had little idea of the going price. This incongruity piqued our curiosity and raised suspicion. We wondered if he might be dealing in larger quantities. Keeping our suspicions to ourselves, we began observing Dave's activities a little more closely. Most of his friends were in their late twenties and early thirties and, judging by their lifestyles and automobiles, rather wealthy. They came and left his house at all hours, occasionally extending their parties through the night and the next day into the following night. Yet throughout this time we never saw Dave or any of his friends engage in any activity that resembled a legitimate job. In most places this might have evoked community suspicion, but few of the people we encountered in Southwest County seemed to hold traditionally structured jobs. Dave, in fact, had no visible means of financial support. When we asked him what he did for a living, he said something vague about being a real estate speculator, and we let it go at that. We never voiced our suspicions directly since he chose not to broach the subject with us.

We did discuss the subject with our mentor, Jack Douglas, however. He was excited by the prospect that we might be living among a group of big dealers, and urged us to follow our instincts and develop leads into the group. He knew that the local area was rife with drug trafficking, since he had begun a life history case study of two drug dealers with another graduate student several years previously. That earlier study was aborted when the graduate student quit school, but Jack still had many hours of taped interviews he had conducted with them, as well as an interview that he had done with an undergraduate student who had known the two dealers independently, to serve as a cross-check on their accounts. He therefore encouraged us to become friendlier with Dave and his friends. We decided that if anything did develop out of our observations of Dave, it might make a nice paper for a field methods class or independent study.

Our interests and background made us well suited to study drug dealing. First, we had already done research in the field of drugs. As undergraduates at Washington University we had participated in a nationally funded project on urban heroin use (see Cummins et al. 1972). Our role in the study involved using fieldwork techniques to investigate the extent of heroin use and distribution in St. Louis. In talking with heroin users, dealers, and rehabilitation personnel, we acquired a base of knowledge about the drug world and the subculture of drug trafficking. Second, we had a generally open view toward soft drug use, considering moderate consumption of marijuana and cocaine to be generally nondeviant. This outlook was partially etched by our 1960s-formed attitudes, as we had first been introduced to drug use in an environment of communal friendship, sharing, and counterculture ideology. It also partially reflected the widespread acceptance accorded to marijuana and cocaine use in the surrounding local culture. Third, our age (mid-twenties at the start of the study) and general appearance gave us compatibility with most of the people we were observing.

We thus watched Dave and continued to develop our friendship with him. We also watched his friends and got to know a few of his more regular visitors. We continued to build friendly relations by doing, quite naturally, what Becker (1963), Polsky (1969), and Douglas (1972) had advocated for the early stages of field research: we gave them a chance to know us and form judgments about our trustworthiness by jointly pursuing those interests and activities which we had in common.

Then one day something happened which forced a breakthrough in the research. Dave had two guys visiting him from out of town and, after snorting quite a bit of cocaine, they turned their conversation to a trip they had just made from Mexico, where they piloted a load of marijuana back across the border in a small plane. Dave made a few efforts to shift the conversation to another subject, telling them to "button their lips," but they apparently thought that he was joking. They thought that anybody as close to Dave as we seemed to be undoubtedly knew the nature of his business. They made further allusions to his involvement in the operation and discussed the outcome of the sale. We could feel the wave of tension and awkwardness from Dave when this conversation began, as he looked toward us to see if we understood the implications of what was being said, but then he just shrugged it off as done. Later, after the two guys left, he discussed with us what happened. He admitted to us that he was a member of a smuggling crew and a major marijuana dealer on the side. He said that he knew he could trust us, but that it was his practice to say as little as possible to outsiders about his activities. This inadvertent slip, and Dave's subsequent opening up, were highly significant in forging our entry into Southwest County's drug world. From then on he was open in discussing the nature of his dealing and smuggling activities with us.

He was, it turned out, a member of a smuggling crew that was importing a ton of marijuana weekly and 40 kilos of cocaine every few months. During that first winter and spring, we observed Dave at work and also got to know the other members of his crew, including Ben, the smuggler himself. Ben was also very tall and broad shouldered, but his long black hair, now flecked with gray, bespoke his earlier membership in the hippie subculture. A large physical stature, we observed, was common to most of the male participants involved in this drug community. The women also had a unifying physical trait: they were extremely attractive and stylishly dressed. This included Dave's ex-wife, Jean, with whom he reconciled during the spring. We therefore became friendly with Jean and through her met a number of women ("dope chicks") who hung around the dealers and smugglers. As we continued to gain the friendship of Dave and Jean's associates, we were progressively admitted into their inner circle and apprised of each person's dealing or smuggling role.

Once we realized the scope of Ben's and his associates' activities, we saw the enormous research potential in studying them. This scene was different from any analysis of drug trafficking that we had read in the sociological literature because of the amounts they were dealing and the fact that they were importing it themselves. We decided that, if it was at all possible, we would capitalize on this situation, to "opportunistically" (Riemer 1977) take advantage of our prior expertise and of the knowledge, entrée, and rapport we had already developed with several key people in this setting. We therefore discussed the idea of doing a study of the general subculture with Dave and several of his closest friends (now becoming our friends). We assured them of the anonymity, confidentiality, and innocuousness of our work. They were happy to reciprocate our friendship by being of help to our professional careers. In fact, they basked in the subsequent attention we gave their lives.

We began by turning first Dave, then others, into key informants and collecting their life histories in detail. We conducted a series of taped, in-depth interviews with an unstructured, open-ended format. We questioned them about such topics as their backgrounds, their recruitment into the occupation, the stages of their dealing careers, their relations with others, their motivations, their lifestyle, and their general impressions about the community as a whole.

We continued to do taped interviews with key informants for the next six years until 1980, when we moved away from the area. After that, we occasionally did follow-up interviews when we returned for vacation visits. These later interviews focused on recording the continuing unfolding of events and included detailed probing into specific conceptual areas, such as dealing networks, types of dealers, secrecy, trust, paranoia, reputation, the law, occupational mobility, and occupational stratification. The number of taped interviews we did with each key informant varied, ranging between 10 and 30 hours of discussion.

Our relationship with Dave and the others thus took on an added dimension—the research relationship. As Douglas (1976), Henslin (1972), and Wax (1952) have noted, research relationships involve some form of mutual exchange. In our case, we offered everything that friendship could entail. We did routine favors for them in the course of our everyday lives, offered them insights and advice about their lives from the perspective of our more respectable position, wrote letters on their behalf to the authorities when they got in trouble, testified as character witnesses at their non-drug-related trials, and loaned them money when they were down and out. When Dave was arrested and brought to trial for check-kiting, we helped Jean organize his defense and raise the money to pay his fines. We spelled her in taking care of the children so that she could work on his behalf. When he was eventually sent to the state prison we maintained close ties with her and discussed our mutual efforts to buoy Dave up and secure his release. We also visited him in jail. During Dave's incarceration, however, Jean was courted by an old boyfriend and gave up her reconciliation with Dave. This proved to be another significant turning point in our research because, desperate for money, Jean looked up Dave's old dealing connections and went into the business herself. She did not stay with these marijuana dealers and smugglers for long, but soon moved into the cocaine business. Over the next several years her experiences in the world of cocaine dealing brought us into contact with a different group of people. While these people knew Dave and his associates (this was very common in the Southwest County dealing and smuggling community), they did not deal with them directly. We were thus able to gain access to a much wider and more diverse range of subjects than we would have had she not branched out on her own.

Dave's eventual release from prison three months later brought our involvement in the research to an even deeper level. He was broke and had nowhere to go. When he showed up on our doorstep, we took him in. We offered to let him stay with us until he was back on his feet again and could afford a place of his own. He lived with us for seven months, intimately sharing his daily experiences with us. During this time we witnessed, firsthand, his transformation from a scared ex-con who would never break the law again to a hard-working legitimate employee who only dealt to get money for his children's Christmas presents, to a full-time dealer with no pretensions at legitimate work. Both his process of changing attitudes and the community's gradual reacceptance of him proved very revealing.

We socialized with Dave, Jean, and other members of Southwest County's dealing and smuggling community on a near-daily basis, especially during the first four years of the research (before we had a child). We worked in their legitimate businesses, vacationed together, attended their weddings, and cared for their children. Throughout their relationship with us, several participants became co-opted to the researcher's perspective[1] and actively sought out instances of behavior which filled holes in the conceptualizations we were developing. Dave, for one, became so intrigued by our conceptual dilemmas that he undertook a "natural experiment" entirely on his own, offering an unlimited supply of drugs to a lower-level dealer to see if he could work up to higher levels of dealing, and what factors would enhance or impinge upon his upward mobility.

In addition to helping us directly through their own experiences, our key informants aided us in widening our circle of contacts. For instance, they let us know when someone in whom we might be interested was planning on dropping by, vouching for our trustworthiness and reliability as friends who could be included in business conversations. Several times we were even awakened in the night by phone calls informing us that someone had dropped by for a visit, should we want to "casually" drop over too. We rubbed the sleep from our eyes, dressed, and walked or drove over, feeling like sleuths out of a television series. We thus were able to snowball, through the active efforts of our key informants,[2] into an expanded study population. This was supplemented by our own efforts to cast a research net and befriend other dealers, moving from contact to contact slowly and carefully through the domino effect.

THE COVERT ROLE

The highly illegal nature of dealing in illicit drugs and dealers' and smugglers' general level of suspicion made the adoption of an overt research role highly sensitive and problematic. In discussing this issue with our key informants, they all agreed that we should be extremely discreet (for both our sakes and theirs). We carefully approached new individuals before we admitted that we were studying them. With many of these people, then, we took a covert posture in the research setting. As nonparticipants in the business activities which bound members together into the group, it was difficult to become fully accepted as peers. We therefore tried to establish some sort of peripheral, social membership in the general crowd, where we could be accepted as "wise" (Goffman 1963) individuals and granted a courtesy membership. This seemed an attainable goal, since we had begun our involvement by forming such relationships with our key informants. By being introduced to others in this wise rather than overt role, we were able to interact with people who would otherwise have shied away from us. Adopting a courtesy membership caused us to bear a courtesy stigma,[3] however, and we suffered since we, at times, had to disguise the nature of our research from both lay outsiders and academicians.

In our overt posture we showed interest in dealers' and smugglers' activities, encouraged them to talk about themselves (within limits, so as to avoid acting like narcs), and ran home to write field notes. This role offered us the advantage of gaining access to unapproachable people while avoiding researcher effects, but it prevented us from asking some necessary, probing questions and from tape recording conversations.[4] We therefore sought, at all times, to build toward a conversion to the overt role. We did this by working to develop their trust.

DEVELOPING TRUST

Like achieving entrée, the process of developing trust with members of unorganized deviant groups can be slow and difficult. In the absence of a formal structure separating members from outsiders, each individual must form his or her own judgment about whether new persons can be admitted to their confidence. No gatekeeper existed to smooth our path to being trusted, although our key informants acted in this role whenever they could by providing introductions and references. In addition, the unorganized nature of this group meant that we met people at different times and were constantly at different levels in our developing relationships with them. We were thus trusted more by some people than by others, in part because of their greater familiarity with us. But as Douglas (1976) has noted, just because someone knew us or even liked us did not automatically guarantee that they would trust us.

We actively tried to cultivate the trust of our respondents by tying them to us with favors. Small things, like offering the use of our phone, were followed with bigger favors, like offering the use of our car, and finally really meaningful favors, like offering the use of our home. Here we often trod a thin line, trying to ensure our personal safety while putting ourselves in enough of a risk position, along with our research subjects, so that they would trust us. While we were able to build a "web of trust" (Douglas 1976) with some members, we found that trust, in large part, was not a simple status to attain in the drug world. Johnson (1975) has pointed out that trust is not a one-time phenomenon, but an ongoing developmental process. From my experiences in this research I would add that it cannot be simply assumed to be a one-way process either, for it can be diminished, withdrawn, reinstated to varying degrees, and re-questioned at any point. Carey (1972) and Douglas (1972) have remarked on this waxing and waning process, but it was especially pronounced for us because our subjects used large amounts of cocaine over an extended period of time. This tended to make them alternately warm and cold to us. We thus lived through a series of ups and downs with the people we were trying to cultivate as research informants.

THE OVERT ROLE

After this initial covert phase, we began to feel that some new people trusted us. We tried to intuitively feel when the time was right to approach them and go overt. We used two means of approaching people to inform them that we were involved in a study of dealing and smuggling: direct and indirect. In some cases our key informants approached their friends or connections and, after vouching for our absolute trustworthiness, convinced these associates to talk to us. In other instances, we approached people directly, asking for their help with our project. We worked our way through a progression with these secondary contacts, first discussing the dealing scene overtly and later moving to taped life history interviews. Some people reacted well to us, but others responded skittishly, making appointments to do taped interviews only to break them as the day drew near, and going through fluctuating stages of being honest with us or putting up fronts about their dealing activities. This varied, for some, with their degree of active involvement in the business. During the times when they had quit dealing, they would tell us about their present and past activities, but when they became actively involved again, they would hide it from us.

This progression of covert to overt roles generated a number of tactical difficulties. The first was the problem of *coming on too fast and* blowing it. Early in the research we had a dealer's old lady (we thought) all set up for the direct approach. We knew many dealers in common and had discussed many things tangential to dealing with her without actually mentioning the subject. When we asked her to do a taped interview of her bohemian lifestyle, she agreed without hesitation. When the interview began, though, and she found out why we were interested in her, she balked, gave us a lot of incoherent jumble, and ended the session as quickly as possible. Even though she lived only three houses away we never saw her again. We tried to move more slowly after that.

A second problem involved simultaneously *juggling our overt and covert roles* with different people. This created the danger of getting our cover blown with people who did not know about our research (Henslin 1972). It was very confusing to separate the people who knew about our study from those who did not, especially in the minds of our informants. They would make occasional veiled references in front of people, especially when loosened by intoxicants, that made us extremely uncomfortable. We also frequently worried that our snooping would someday be mistaken for police tactics. Fortunately, this never happened.

CROSS-CHECKING

The hidden and conflictual nature of the drug-dealing world made me feel the need for extreme certainty about the reliability of my data. I therefore based all my conclusions on independent sources and accounts that we carefully verified. First, we tested information against our own common sense and general knowledge of the scene. We adopted a hard-nosed attitude of suspicion, assuming people were up to more than they would originally admit. We kept our attention especially riveted on "reformed" dealers and smugglers who were living better than they could outwardly afford, and were thereby able to penetrate their public fronts.

Second, we checked out information against a variety of reliable sources. Our own observations of the scene formed a primary reliable source, since we were involved with many of the principals on a daily basis and knew exactly what they were doing. Having Dave live with us was a particular advantage because we could contrast his statements to us with what we could clearly see was happening. Even after he moved out, we knew him so well that we could generally tell when he was lying to us or, more commonly, fooling himself with optimistic dreams. We also observed other dealers' and smugglers' evasions and misperceptions about themselves and their activities. These usually occurred when they broke their own rules by selling to people they did not know, or when they commingled other people's money with their own. We also crosschecked our data against independent, alternative accounts. We were lucky, for this purpose, that Jean got reinvolved in the drug world. By interviewing her, we gained additional insight into Dave's past, his early dealing and smuggling activities, and his ongoing involvement from another person's perspective. Jean (and her connections) also talked to us about Dave's associates, thereby helping us to validate or disprove their statements. We even used this pincer effect to verify information about people we had never directly interviewed. This occurred, for instance, with the tapes that Jack Douglas gave us from his earlier study. After doing our first round of taped interviews with Dave, we discovered that he knew the dealers Jack had interviewed. We were excited by the prospect of finding out what had happened to these people and if their earlier stories checked out. We therefore sent Dave to do some investigative work. Through some mutual friends he got back in touch with them and found out what they had been doing for the past several years.

Finally, wherever possible, we checked out accounts against hard facts: newspaper and magazine reports; arrest records; material possessions; and visible evidence. Throughout the research, we used all these cross-checking measures to evaluate the veracity of new information and to prod our respondents to be more accurate (by abandoning both their lies and their self-deceptions).[5]

After about four years of near-daily participant observation, we began to diminish our involvement in the research. This occurred gradually, as first pregnancy and then a child hindered our ability to follow the scene as intensely and spontaneously as we had before. In addition, after having a child, we were less willing to incur as many risks as we had before; we no longer felt free to make decisions based solely on our own welfare. We thus pulled back from what many have referred to as the "difficult hours and dangerous situations" inevitably present in field research on deviants (see Becker 1963; Carey 1972; Douglas 1972). We did, however, actively maintain close ties with research informants (those with whom we had gone overt), seeing them regularly and periodically doing follow-up interviews.

PROBLEMS AND ISSUES

Reflecting on the research process, I have isolated a number of issues which I believe merit additional discussion. These are rooted in experiences which have the potential for greater generic applicability.

The first is the *effect of drugs on the data-gathering process*. Carey (1972) has elaborated on some of the problems he encountered when trying to interview respondents who used amphetamines, while Wax (1952, 1957) has mentioned the difficulty of trying to record field notes while drinking sake. I found that marijuana and cocaine had nearly opposite effects from each other. The latter helped the interview process, while the former hindered it. Our attempts to interview respondents who were stoned on marijuana were unproductive for a number of reasons. The primary obstacle was the effects of the drug. Often, people became confused, sleepy, or involved in eating to varying degrees. This distracted them from our purpose. At times, people even simulated overreactions to marijuana to hide behind the drug's supposed disorienting influence and thereby avoid divulging information. Cocaine, in contrast, proved to be a research aid. The drug's warming and sociable influence opened people up, diminished their inhibitions, and generally increased their enthusiasm for both the interview experience and us.

A second problem I encountered involved *assuming risks while doing research*. As I noted earlier, dangerous situations are often generic to research on deviant behavior. We were most afraid of the people we studied. As Carey (1972), Henslin (1972), and Whyte (1955) have stated, members of deviant groups can become hostile toward a researcher if they think that they are being treated wrongfully. This could have happened at any time from a simple occurrence, such as a misunderstanding, or from something more serious, such as our covert posture being exposed. Because of the inordinate amount of drugs they consumed, drug dealers and smugglers were particularly volatile, capable of becoming malicious toward each other or us with little warning. They were also likely to behave erratically owing to the great risks they faced from the police and other dealers. These factors made them moody, and they vacillated between trusting us and being suspicious of us.

At various times we also had to protect our research tapes. We encountered several threats to our collection of taped interviews from people who had granted us these interviews. This made us anxious, since we had taken great pains to acquire these tapes and felt strongly about maintaining confidences entrusted to us by our informants. When threatened, we became extremely frightened and shifted the tapes between different hiding places. We even ventured forth one rainy night with our tapes packed in a suitcase to meet a person who was uninvolved in the research at a secret rendezvous so that he could guard the tapes for us.

We were fearful, lastly, of the police. We often worried about local police or drug agents discovering the nature of our study and confiscating or subpoenaing our tapes and field notes. Sociologists have no privileged relationship with their subjects that would enable us legally to withhold evidence from the authorities should they subpoena it.[6] For this reason we studiously avoided any publicity about the research, even holding back on publishing articles in scholarly journals until we were nearly ready to move out of the setting. The closest we came to being publicly exposed as drug researchers came when a former sociology graduate student (turned dealer, we had heard from inside sources) was arrested at the scene of a cocaine deal. His lawyer wanted us to testify about the dangers of doing drug-related research, since he was using his research status as his defense. Fortunately, the crisis was averted when his lawyer succeeded in suppressing evidence and had the case dismissed before the trial was to have begun. Had we been exposed, however, our respondents would have acquired guilt by association through their friendship with us.

Our fear of the police went beyond our concern for protecting our research subjects, however. We risked the danger of arrest ourselves through our own violations of the law. Many sociologists (Becker 1963; Carey 1972; Polsky 1969; Whyte 1955) have remarked that field researchers studying deviance must inevitably break the law in order to acquire valid participant observation data. This occurs in its most innocuous form from having "guilty knowledge": information about crimes that are committed. Being aware of major dealing and smuggling operations made us an accessory to their commission, since we failed to notify the police. We broke the law, secondly, through our "guilty observations," by being present at the scene of a crime and witnessing its occurrence (see also Carey 1972). We knew it was possible to get caught in a bust involving others, yet buying and selling was so pervasive that to leave every time it occurred would have been unnatural and highly suspicious. Sometimes drug transactions even occurred in our home, especially when Dave was living there, but we finally had to put a stop to that because we could not handle the anxiety. Lastly, we broke the law through our "guilty actions," by taking part in illegal behavior ourselves. Although we never dealt drugs (we were too scared to be seriously tempted), we consumed drugs and possessed them in small quantities. Quite frankly, it would have been impossible for a nonuser to have gained access to this group to gather the data presented here. This was the minimum involvement necessary to obtain even the courtesy membership we achieved. Some kind of illegal action was also found to be a necessary or helpful component of the research by Becker (1963), Carey (1972), Johnson (1975), Polsky (1969), and Whyte (1955).

Another methodological issue arose from the *cultural clash between our research subjects and ourselves*. While other sociologists have alluded to these kinds of differences (Humphreys 1970; Whyte 1955), few have discussed how the research relationships affected them. Relationships with research subjects are unique because they involve a bond of intimacy between persons who might not ordinarily associate together, or who might otherwise be no more than casual friends. When field-workers undertake a major project, they commit themselves to maintaining a long-term relationship with the people they study. However, as researchers try to get depth involvement, they are apt to come across fundamental differences in character, values, and attitudes between their subjects and themselves. In our case, we were most strongly confronted by differences in present versus future orientations, a desire for risk versus security, and feelings of spontaneity versus self-discipline. These differences often caused us great frustration. We repeatedly saw dealers act irrationally, setting themselves up for failure. We wrestled with our desire to point out their patterns of foolhardy behavior and offer advice, feeling competing pulls between our detached, observer role which advised us not to influence the natural setting, and our involved, participant role which called for us to offer friendly help whenever possible.[7]

Each time these differences struck us anew, we gained deeper insights into our core, existential selves. We suspended our own taken-for-granted feelings and were able to reflect on our culturally formed attitudes, character, and life choices from the perspective of the other. When comparing how we might act in situations faced by our respondents, we realized where our deepest priorities lay. These revelations had the effect of changing our self-conceptions: whereas we, at one time, had thought of ourselves as what Rosenbaum (1981) has called "the hippest of non-addicts" (in this case nondealers), we were suddenly faced with being the straightest members of the crowd. Not only did we not deal, but we had a stable, long-lasting marriage and family life, and needed the security of a reliable monthly paycheck. Self-insights thus emerged as one of the unexpected outcomes of field research with members of a different cultural group.

The final issue I will discuss involved the various *ethical problems* which arose during this research. Many field-workers have encountered ethical dilemmas or pangs of guilt during the course of their research experiences (Carey 1972; Douglas 1976; Humphreys 1970; Johnson 1975; Klockars 1977, 1979; Rochford 1985). The researchers' role in the field makes this necessary because they can never fully align themselves with their subjects while maintaining their identity and personal commitment to the scientific community. Ethical dilemmas, then, are directly related to the amount of deception researchers use in gathering the data, and the degree to which they have accepted such acts as necessary and therefore neutralized them.

Throughout the research, we suffered from the burden of intimacies and confidences. Guarding secrets which had been told to us during taped interviews was not always easy or pleasant. Dealers occasionally revealed things about themselves or others that we had to pretend not to know when interacting with their close associates. This sometimes meant that we had to lie or build elaborate stories to cover for some people. Their fronts therefore became our fronts, and we had to weave our own web of deception to guard their performances. This became especially disturbing during the writing of the research report, as I was torn by conflicts between using details to enrich the data and glossing over description to guard confidences.[8]

Using the covert research role generated feelings of guilt, despite the fact that our key informants deemed it necessary, and thereby condoned it. Their own covert experiences were far more deeply entrenched than ours, being a part of their daily existence with non–drug world members. Despite the universal presence of covert behavior throughout the setting, we still felt a sense of betrayal every time we ran home to write research notes on observations we had made under the guise of innocent participants.

We also felt guilty about our efforts to manipulate people. While these were neither massive nor grave manipulations, they involved courting people to procure information about them. Our aggressively friendly postures were based on hidden ulterior motives: we did favors for people with the clear expectation that they could only pay us back with research assistance. Manipulation bothered us in two ways: immediately after it was done, and over the long run. At first, we felt awkward, phony, almost ashamed of ourselves, although we believed our rationalization that the end justified the means. Over the long run, though, our feelings were different. When friendship became intermingled with research goals, we feared that people would later look back on our actions and feel we were exploiting their friendship merely for the sake of our research project.

The last problem we encountered involved our feelings of whoring for data. At times, we felt that we were being exploited by others, that we were putting more into the relationship than they, that they were taking us for granted or using us. We felt that some people used a double standard in their relationship with us: they were allowed to lie to us, borrow money and not repay it, and take advantage of us, but we were at all times expected to behave honorably. This was undoubtedly an outgrowth of our initial research strategy where we did favors for people and expected little in return. But at times this led to our feeling bad. It made us feel like we were selling ourselves, our sincerity, and usually our true friendship, and not getting treated right in return.

CONCLUSIONS

The aggressive research strategy I employed was vital to this study. I could not just walk up to strangers and start hanging out with them as Liebow (1967) did, or be sponsored to a member of this group by a social service or reform organization as Whyte (1955) was, and expect to be accepted, let alone welcomed. Perhaps such a strategy might have worked with a group that had nothing to hide, but I doubt it. Our modern, pluralistic society is so filled with diverse subcultures whose interests compete or conflict with each other that each subculture has a set of knowledge which is reserved exclusively for insiders. In order to serve and prosper, they do not ordinarily show this side to just anyone. To obtain the kind of depth insight and information I needed, I had to become like the members in certain ways. They dealt only with people they knew and trusted, so I had to become known and trusted before I could reveal my true self and my research interests. Confronted with secrecy, danger, hidden alliances, misrepresentations, and unpredictable changes of intent, I had to use a delicate combination of overt and covert roles. Throughout, my deliberate cultivation of the norm of reciprocal exchange enabled me to trade my friendship for their knowledge, rather than waiting for the highly unlikely event that information would be delivered into my lap. I thus actively built a web of research contacts, used them to obtain highly sensitive data, and carefully checked them out to ensure validity.

Throughout this endeavor I profited greatly from the efforts of my husband, Peter, who served as an equal partner in this team field research project. It would have been impossible for me to examine this social world as an unattached female and not fall prey to sex role stereotyping which excluded women from business dealings. As a couple, our different genders allowed us to relate in different ways to both men and women (see Warren and Rasmussen 1977). We also protected each other when we entered the homes of dangerous characters, buoyed each other's initiative and courage, and kept the conversation going when one of us faltered. Conceptually, we helped each other keep a detached and analytical eye on the setting, provided multiperspectival insights, and corroborated, clarified, or (most revealingly) contradicted each other's observations and conclusions. Finally, I feel strongly that to ensure accuracy, research on deviant groups must be conducted in the settings where it naturally occurs. As Polsky (1969: 115–16) has forcefully asserted:

> This means—there is no getting away from it—the study of career criminals *au natural,* in the field, the study of such criminals as they normally go about their work and play, the study of "uncaught" criminals and the study of others who in the past have been caught but are not caught at the time you study them…. Obviously we can no longer afford the convenient fiction that in studying criminals in their natural habitat, we would discover nothing really important that could not be discovered from criminals behind bars.

By studying criminals in their natural habitat I was able to see them in the full variability and complexity of their surrounding subculture, rather than within the artificial environment of a prison. I was thus able to learn about otherwise inaccessible dimensions of their lives, observing and analyzing firsthand the nature of their social organization, social stratification, lifestyle, and motivation.

NOTES

1. Gold (1958) discouraged this methodological strategy, cautioning against overly close friendship or intimacy with informants, lest they lose their ability to act as informants by becoming too much observers. Whyte (1955), in contrast, recommended the use of informants as research aides, not for helping in conceptualizing the data but for their assistance in locating data which supports, contradicts, or fills in the researcher's analysis of the setting.

2. See also Biernacki and Waldorf 1981; Douglas 1976; Henslin 1972; Hoffman 1980; McCall 1980; and West 1980 for discussions of "snowballing" through key informants.

3. See Kirby and Corzine 1981; Birenbaum 1970; and Henslin 1972 for more detailed discussion of the nature, problems, and strategies for dealing with courtesy stigmas.

4. We never considered secret tapings because, aside from the ethical problems involved, it always struck us as too dangerous.

5. See Douglas (1976) for a more detailed account of these procedures.

6. A recent court decision, where a federal judge ruled that a sociologist did not have to turn over his field notes to a grand jury investigating a suspicious fire at a restaurant where he worked, indicates that this situation may be changing (Fried 1984).

7. See Henslin 1972 and Douglas 1972, 1976 for further discussions of this dilemma and various solutions to it.

8. In some cases I resolved this by altering my descriptions of people and their actions as well as their names so that other members of the dealing and smuggling community would not recognize them. In doing this, however, I had to keep a primary concern for maintaining the sociological integrity of my data so that the generic conclusions I drew from them would be accurate. In places, then, where my attempts to conceal people's identities from people who know them have been inadequate, I hope that I caused them no embarrassment. See also Polsky 1969; Rainwater and Pittman 1967; and Humphreys 1970 for discussions of this problem.

REFERENCES

Adler, Patricia A., and Peter Adler. 1987. *Membership Roles in Field Research.* Beverly Hills, CA: Sage.

Becker, Howard. 1963. *Outsiders.* New York: Free Press.

Biernacki, Patrick, and Dan Waldorf. 1981. "Snowball sampling." *Sociological Methods and Research* 10: 141–63.

Birenbaum, Arnold. 1970. "On managing a courtesy stigma." *Journal of Health and Social Behavior* 11: 196–206.

Blumer, Herbert. 1969. *Symbolic Interadionism.* Engle-wood Cliffs, NJ: Prentice Hall.

Carey, James T. 1972. "Problems of access and risk in observing drug scenes." In Jack D. Douglas, ed., *Research on Deviance*, pp. 71–92. New York: Random House.

Cummins, Marvin, et al. 1972. *Report of the Student Task Force on Heroin Use in Metropolitan Saint Louis.* Saint Louis: Washington University Social Science Institute.

Douglas, Jack D. 1972. "Observing deviance." In Jack D. Douglas, ed., *Research on Deviance,* pp. 3–34. New York: Random House.

————. 1976. *Investigative Social Research.* Beverly Hills, CA: Sage.

Fried, Joseph P. 1984. "Judge protects waiter's notes on fire inquiry." *New York Times*, April 8: 47.

Goffman, Erving. 1963. *Stigma.* Englewood Cliffs, NJ: Prentice Hall.

Gold, Raymond. 1958. "Roles in sociological field observations." *Social Forces* 36: 217–23.

Henslin, James M. 1972. "Studying deviance in four settings: research experiences with cabbies, suicides, drug users and abortionees." In Jack D. Douglas, ed., *Research on Deviance*, pp. 35–70. New York: Random House.

Hoffman, Joan E. 1980. "Problems of access in the study of social elites and boards of directors." In William B. Shaffir, Robert A. Stebbins, and Allan Turowetz, eds., *Fieldwork Experience*, pp. 45–56. New York: St. Martin's.

Humphreys, Laud. 1970. *Tearoom Trade.* Chicago: Aldine.

Johnson, John M. 1975. *Doing Field Research.* New York: Free Press.

Kirby, Richard, and Jay Corzine. 1981. "The contagion of stigma." *Qualitative Sociology* 4: 3–20.

Klockars, Carl B. 1911. "Field ethics for the life history." In Robert Weppner, ed., *Street Ethnography*, pp. 201–26. Beverly Hills, CA: Sage.

———. 1979. "Dirty hands and deviant subjects." In Carl B. Klockars and Finnbarr W. O'Connor, eds., *Deviance and Decency*, pp. 261–82. Beverly Hills, CA: Sage.

Liebow, Elliott. 1967. *Tally's Corner*. Boston: Little, Brown.

McCall, Michal. 1980. "Who and where are the artists?" In William B. Shaffir, Robert A. Stebbins, and Allan Turowetz, eds., *Fieldwork Experience*, pp. 145–58. New York: St. Martin's.

Polsky, Ned. 1969. *Hustlers, Beats, and Others*. New York: Doubleday.

Rainwater, Lee R., and David J. Pittman. 1967. "Ethical problems in studying a politically sensitive and deviant community." *Social Problems* 14: 357–66.

Riemer, Jeffrey W. 1977. "Varieties of opportunistic research." *Urban Life* 5: 467–77.

Rochford, E. Burke, Jr. 1985. *Hare Krishna in America*. New Brunswick, NJ: Rutgers University Press.

Rosenbaum, Marsha. 1981. *Women on Heroin*. New Brunswick, NJ: Rutgers University Press.

Warren, Carol A. B., and Paul K. Rasmussen. 1911. "Sex and gender in field research." *Urban Life* 6: 349–69.

Wax, Rosalie. 1952. "Reciprocity as a field technique." *Human Organization* 11: 34–37.

———. 1957. "Twelve years later: An analysis of a field experience." *American Journal of Sociology* 63: 133–42.

West, W. Gordon. 1980. "Access to adolescent deviants and deviance." In William B. Shaffir, Robert A. Stebbins, and Allan Turowetz, eds., *Fieldwork Experience*, pp. 31–44. New York: St. Martin's.

Whyte, William F. 1955. *Street Corner Society*. Chicago: University of Chicago Press.

PART IV

Constructing Deviance

As we noted in the General Introduction, the social constructionist perspective suggests that deviance should be regarded as lodged in a process of definition, rather than in some objective feature of an object, person, or act. It therefore guides us to look at the process by which a society constructs definitions of deviance and applies them to specific groups of people associated with these objects or acts. The dynamics of these deviance-defining processes may sometimes eclipse the factual grounding on which they rest in their significance for the rise of collective moral sentiments.

MORAL ENTREPRENEURS: CAMPAIGNING

The process of constructing and applying definitions of deviance can be understood as a moral enterprise. That is, it involves the constructions of moral meanings and the association of them with specific acts or conditions. The way people "make" deviance is similar to the way they manufacture anything else, but because deviance is an abstract concept rather than a tangible product, this process involves individuals drawing on the power and resources of organizations, institutions, agencies, symbols, ideas, communication, and audiences. Becker (1963) has suggested that we call the people involved in these activities **moral entrepreneurs**. The deviance-making enterprise has two facets: rule-creating (without which there would be no deviant behavior) and rule-enforcing (applying these rules to specific groups of people). We have two kinds of moral entrepreneurs: rule creators and rule enforcers. Rule creators would include such people as politicians, crusading public figures, teachers, parents, school administrators, and CEOs of business organizations. When we think of rule enforcers we immediately imagine the police/courts/judges, but these can also be dormitory RAs, members of neighborhood associations, the Inter-Fraternity Council, and (here as well) parents.

Rule creating can be done by individuals acting either alone or in groups. Prominent individuals who have been influential in campaigning for definitions of deviance include former First Lady Nancy Reagan for her "Just Say No" and D.A.R.E. antidrug campaigns in the 1980s, actor Charlton Heston for his presidency of the National Rifle Association (NRA), John Walsh for founding the Missing and Exploited Children's Network and the television show, "America's Most Wanted," and filmmaker Michael Moore for his documentaries about General Motors (*Roger and Me*), the gun lobby (*Bowling for Columbine*), the oil industry/Bush administration (*Fahrenheit 9/11*), and the healthcare industry (*Sicko*). More commonly, however, individuals band together to use their collective energy and resources to change social definitions and to create norms and rules. Groups of moral entrepreneurs represent interest groups that can be galvanized and activated into pressure groups, such as Mothers Against Drunk Driving (MADD), the Group Against Smoking Pollution (GASP), the National Organization for the Reform of Marijuana Laws (NORML), and Focus on the Family (a right-wing, Christian pro-family group). Rule creators ensure that our society is supplied with a constant stock of deviance by defining the behavior of others as immoral. They do this because they perceive people as threats and feel fearful, distrustful, and suspicious of their behavior. In so doing, they seek to transform private troubles into public issues and their private morality into the normative order.

Moral entrepreneurs manufacture public morality through a multistage process. Their first goal is to generate broad **awareness** of a problem. They do this through a process of what Spector and Kitsuse (1977) called "claims-making." Claims-makers draw our attention to given issues by asserting "danger messages." Not only do they use these messages to create a sense that certain conditions are problematic and pose a present or future potential danger to society, but they usually have specific solutions that they recommend. Issues about which we have recently seen danger messages raised include secondhand smoke, drunk driving, hate crimes, college binge drinking, illegal immigrants (and their link to terrorists), outsourcing, guns in schools, junk food, politics in the classroom, and obesity. Because no rules exist to deal with the threatening condition, claims-makers construct the impression that these are necessary.

In so doing, they draw on the testimonials of various "experts" in the field, such as scholars, doctors, eyewitnesses, ex-participants (professional -ex's), and others with specific knowledge of the situation. Issues are framed in these testimonials and disseminated to society via the media as "typical" to promote specific examples, orientations, causes, and solutions. We see the Surgeon General warning about the dangers of secondhand smoke, college administrators talking about student drinking and deaths, psychiatrists writing about the dangers of self-injury and eating disorders, sociologists discussing the spread of date and acquaintance rape, national conservative watchdogs such as David Horowitz monitoring liberal bias in the classroom, and ex-FLDS (Fundamentalist Latter Day Saints) members warning about the forced marriage (statutory rape) of young girls, the expulsion of teenage boys, and the isolation and subservience of whole communities to the point of brainwashing.

Several rhetorical techniques are used to package and present these facts in the most compelling way. Statistics may show the rise in incidence of a given behavior, or its correlation with other social problems. For example, suicide statistics may be contrasted with homicide statistics to draw attention to the importance of suicide, which occurs at a rate nearly 50 percent higher than homicide. Growth in the rates of obesity and its relation to diabetes, heart disease, stroke, and worker absenteeism may be documented. We may hear about the rising tide of illegal immigrants and their financial drain on our public schools and medical services. Free trade agreements may be tied to increasing rates of unemployment. Dramatic case examples can paint a picture of horror in the public's mind, inspiring fear and loathing. Particular cases are usually selected because they have no moral ambiguity and feature the dimension of the problem that is being highlighted.

Thus, for missing children we want to see stranger abductors rather than snatchings by noncustodial parents, while for AIDS we want to see innocent children who are sick rather than gay men. New syndromes can be advanced, packaging different issues together into a behavioral pattern portrayed as dangerous, such as "Internet-addiction disorder" (caution: people are abandoning their homes and families to spend all their time and money in chat rooms), "centerfold syndrome" (caution: men who read pornography objectify, commodify, and victimize women, seek unattainable trophy figurines, and are unable to engage in meaningful relationships), "road rage disorder" (caution: traffic induces people to cut us off and give us the finger), "compulsive hoarding" (caution: practitioners have excessive clutter, difficulty categorizing, organizing, making decisions about, and throwing away possessions, and fears about needing items that could be thrown away), "chronic procrastination" (caution: you may be an "arousal procrastinator," where you put things off for the last-minute rush, or an "avoider" and put off dealing with things out of fear of failure or success), and ADHD (caution: you could have this medical problem if you daydream or are slow to complete tasks, fidget, have poor concentration, or are distractible, hyperactive, impulsive, and/or reckless). Finally, rhetoric requires that each side seek the (usually competing) "moral high ground" in their assertions and attacks on each other, disavowing special interests and pursuing only the purest public good. For example, people who are opposed to gay marriage are upholding the Bible, decency, and the sanctity of marriage, while people who support it are upholding individual civil liberties and fighting unjust discrimination.

Second, rule creators must bring about a **moral conversion**, convincing others of their views. With the problem outlined, they have to convert neutral parties and previous opponents into supporting partisans. Their successful conversion of others further legitimates their own beliefs. To effect a moral conversion, rule creators must compete for space in the public arena, often a limited resource. Hilgartner and Bosk (1988) have suggested that only so many issues can claim widespread attention, and they do so at the expense of others. As Durkheim noted for deviance, only a limited number of public concerns can be supported in society at any given time. Moral entrepreneurs must draw on elements of drama, novelty, politics, and deep mythic themes of the culture to gain the visibility they need. To gain visibility, moral entrepreneurs must attract the media attention necessary to spread word of their campaign widely. They may orchestrate this through hunger strikes (students protesting the manufacturing of university-labeled clothing in Third World "sweat shops"), demonstrations (antiwar, pro-immigration), civil disobedience (such as environmentalists tying themselves to trees to prevent deforestation or blocking highways to prevent nuclear waste from being stored in their state), marches (the Gay Pride and Civil Rights movements), and strikes and picketing (against de-unionization).

They must also enlist the support of sponsors, opinion leaders who need not have expert knowledge on any particular subject, but are liked and respected, to provide them with public endorsements. Moral entrepreneurial campaigners often turn to athletes, actors, musicians, religious leaders, and media personalities for such endorsements. Former Democratic Presidential candidate Al Gore is notable for his campaign highlighting the growth of global warming (*An Inconvenient Truth*), actor Tom Cruise has actively promoted the dangers of antidepressants, and actor Michael J. Fox campaigned for Democratic candidates to endorse stem cell research.

Finally, they look to different groups in society to form alliances or coalitions to support their campaigns. Alliances are made up of long-term allies, such the Christian Coalition, Focus on the Family, conservative Republican politicians, and big business. Coalitions, on the other hand, represent groups that do not normally lobby together, but are bonded by their mutual interests in a single issue, such as we see in the strange union when family groups, conservative Republicans, religious leaders, and, ironically, radical feminists come together to campaign against pornography.

At times, the efforts of moral entrepreneurs are so successful that they create a "**moral panic**." The term moral panic was coined by Jock Young, but popularized in the field of deviance by Stanley Cohen's (1972) book on the Mods and the Rockers, making it a widespread and enduring concept. Moral panics arise when a threat to society is depicted, promoting terror and dread with its powerfully persuasive focus on folk devils. Conditions of unsettling social strain make a community ripe for a moral panic to erupt. When it does, expert "claims-makers" (Spector and Kitsuse 1977), or issue entrepreneurs, articulate the scope and specific danger of the problem, identifying social conditions that members of a group perceived to be offensive and undesirable. To make a claim it is necessary to engage in a variety of specific activities: naming the problem, distinguishing it from other similar or more encompassing problems, determining the scientific, technical, moral or legal basis of the claim, and gauging who is responsible for taking ameliorative action. The level of moral anxiety becomes stoked by concerned individuals promoting the problem, legislators who react and heighten the alarm, and sensationalist news media that whip the public into a "feeding frenzy" through highly emotional claims and fear-based appeals. Folk devils become treated as threats to dominant social interests and values. Moral panics, most recently witnessed in cases of school shootings, priesthood pedophilia, child kidnapping, drinking and rioting on college campuses, Internet predators, obesity, Satanic exploitation of children, gangs, drugs, and domestic terrorists, tend to develop a life of their own, irrationally moving in exaggerated propulsion beyond their original impetus. Significant contests may emerge between claims-makers arguing for the stigmatization of various folk devils and those who attempt to reject or even reverse the stigmatization onto the original accusers or some other parties. These stigma contests, central to moral panic theory, tend to play out in the political domain. Their goal is to achieve the dominance of specific moral perceptions and values. Launching a moral panic in a complex and diverse society, where public attention is being sought by many different claims-makers and issues, is difficult, and not all would-be moral panics materialize. Moral panics, at their core, are thus power struggles between various groups in society about which of them can dominate and impose their world views and values on others as legitimate and true.

Erich Goode and Nachman Ben-Yehuda (1994) articulated a stage-by-stage analysis of moral panics. To be successful, they argued, moral panics usually have to occur during a ripe historical *time*, when a combination of social, ecological, ideological, professional, and/or political forces have contributed to some grow-ing cultural anxiety. They are then *triggered* by a specific incident that precipitates awareness of what is going on, and *targets* the public's attention toward a specific folk devil. Folk devils can take the form of specific individuals, groups, or even behavioral trends. The *content* of the moral panic is explored, investigated in detail, repeated innumerably, and possibly blown out of proportion. Awareness of the danger and the ripples of the moral panic may be spread through the mass media, grassroots word-of-mouth communication, Internet warnings, public presentations, government hearings, and the testimony of experts (claims-makers, or what Tuggle and Holmes refer to in chapter 16 as the "knowledge class" and what Reinarman in chapter 15 refers to as "professional interest groups"). But all moral panics fade or *decline* eventually, since they represent inflated fears and cannot be sustained indefinitely. They may founder of their own accord because the problem has been addressed and solved, because the danger has been found to be overexaggerated and the claims-makers grow silent, or because they are replaced by new panics that steal the public's attention. They usually leave in their wake some residual effect, often taking the form of new institutional arrangements or bureaucratic structures. For example, flying in America will never be the same as it was prior to 9/11. The Jenkins article on Internet pornography in chapter 17 offers some additional suggestions about the types of factors that foster or impair the likelihood that a social concern will become elevated to the level of a moral panic.

Once the public viewpoint has been swayed and a majority (or a vocal and powerful enough minority) of people have adopted a social definition, it may remain at the level of a norm or become elevated to the status of law through a legislative effort. For example, although obesity has been defined as disgusting and unhealthy it is not illegal, while antismoking campaigns have been successful in legally banning cigarette use in most public places.

After norms or rules have been enacted, rule enforcers ensure that they are applied. In our society, this process often tends to be selective. Various indivi-duals or groups have greater or lesser power to resist the enforcement of rules against them due to their socioeconomic, racial, religious, gender, political, or other status. Whole battles may begin anew over individuals' or groups' strength to apply or resist the enforcement of norms and laws, with this arena becoming once again a moral entrepreneurial combat zone. President George W. Bush's efforts, after the invasion of Iraq went sour; to rebuff the investigatory efforts of the Democratic Party into charges of manipulated intelligence over his claims about WMDs (weapons of mass destruction) illustrates core issues of social power.

DIFFERENTIAL SOCIAL POWER: LABELING

Specific behavioral acts are not the only things that can be constructed as deviant; this definition can also be applied to a social status, demographic characteristic, or lifestyle. When entire groups of people become relegated to a deviant status through their condition (especially if it is ascribed through birth rather than voluntarily achieved), we see the force of inequality and differential social power in operation. This dynamic has been discussed earlier in reference to both conflict theory and social constructionism, as we noted that those who control the resources in society (politics, social status, gender, wealth, religious beliefs, mobilization of the masses) have the ability to dominate, both materially and ideologically, over the subordinate groups. Thus, certain kinds of laws and enforcement are a product of political action by moral entrepreneurial interest groups that are connected to society's power base. Dominant groups use their strength and position to label and to subjugate the weak.

A range of different factors give certain groups greater **social power** in society to construct definitions of deviance and to apply those labels onto others. Money is one of the clearest elements, with its potential influence being felt at least two ways. Big businesses can use it to make campaign contributions and sway political candidates, to fund research favorable to their products (studies paid for by the soft drink industry were recently found eight time more likely to find no harmful health influences of drinking soda than those otherwise funded), to lobby against unfavorable legislation, and to fight restrictive lawsuits. Money also defines individuals' social class, and while rich people do not have as much cash available to do what businesses can afford, it is much harder to define the practices of the middle and upper classes as deviant than those of the lower, working, and under classes. Second, race and ethnicity influence social power, so that the behaviors of the dominant white population are less likely to be defined and enforced than those of Hispanics and blacks. Gender is a third element of social power, with men dominating over women politically, economically, historically, religiously, occupationally, culturally, and, hence, interpersonally.

Fourth, people's age affects their relative power in society, with young people (up to the age of 30) and older people (65 and older) holding less respect, influence, attention, and command than their middle-aged counterparts. Fifth, greater numbers and organization can empower groups, as positions backed by larger populations often hold sway over smaller ones. Yet at the same time, well-organized groups, even if they are in the minority, may dominate over bigger, unorganized masses. We acknowledge education as a sixth element of social power since, as the chapters in this section argue, well-educated professionals have the ability to speak as experts, to organize moral entrepreneurial campaigns, to advocate for their positions, and to argue from a legitimate base of knowledge. Finally, social status (apart from social class) generates power through the prestige, tradition, and respectability associated with various positions in society. For example, religious people have greater social status in contemporary society than atheists, heterosexual people command greater legitimacy than homosexuals, and married individuals hold greater sway, as a group, than single ones. There are, of course, many more elements of social power that could be articulated as having an influence over labeling individuals, groups, and their characteristics as deviant, but these, to us, represent the key ones.

In a society characterized by striving for social influence, status, and power, one way to attain this is to pass and enforce rules that define others' behavior as deviant. Thus, the deviant labeling of attitudes, behaviors, and conditions such as minority ethnic or racial status, female gender, lower social class, youthful age, homosexual orientation, and a criminal record (as some of the following readings show), if taken in this light, can be seen to reflect the application of differential social power in our society. Individuals in these groups may find themselves discriminated against or blocked from the mainstream of society by virtue of this basic feature of their existence, unrelated to any particular situation or act. This application of the deviant label emphatically illustrates the role of power in the deviance-defining enterprise, as those positioned closer to the center of society, holding the greater social, economic, political, and moral resources, can turn the force of the deviant stigma onto others less fortunately placed. In so doing, they use the definition of deviance to reinforce their own favored position. This politicization of deviance and the power associated with its use serve to remind us that deviance is not a category inhabited only by those on the marginal outskirts of society: the exotics, erotics, and neurotics. Instead, any group can be pushed into this category by the exercise of another group's greater power.

DIFFERENTIAL SOCIAL POWER: RESISTING LABELING

On the other side of the coin, powerful groups may be successful in working to resist the application of definitions of deviance to them. Like better looking people, they are granted a "halo effect" that leads others to think highly of them. Higher-status groups in society are less likely to be perceived as deviant whether they actively work to fight the label or not.

In some cases they undertake proactive collective identity protection as a group. Many organizations such as gun owners, pharmaceutical companies, and the manufacturers of cigarettes or alcoholic beverages work to build and sustain a positive social image. They may hire claims-makers, lobbyists, contribute to politicians' campaigns, or fund research showing that they are upstanding individuals and organizations. As mentioned above, one comparative study recently showed that research funded by the soft drink industry was eight times as likely to find no negative correlation between consuming soft drinks and poor health as those otherwise financed.

But even when they do not become specifically involved in protecting their images, members of more powerful and respected groups in society are less likely to become tainted by deviant labels. Part of the reason for this is that people hold preconceived biases in their favor, and assume that they are responsible and prosocial, whether they are or are not. People also make perceptual biases toward them based on their appearances, occupations, behavior, and/or associations, forming instantaneous judgments about them that are positive. Members of such protected groups are often unaware of their privileged status in society and do not realize the discrimination routinely encountered by underprivileged populations.

This differential social power may be applied either directly or comparatively, as when society judges the behavior of one group against another, or when individuals or a group are judged on their own. Together, these groups of people continue to receive treatment from society as either deviant or non-deviant that reinforces social inequality and the status quo.

15

The Social Construction of Drug Scares

CRAIG REINARMAN

In this overview of America's social policies, Reinarman tackles moral and legal attitudes toward illicit drugs. He briefly offers a history of drug scares, the major players engineering them, and the social contexts that have enhanced their development and growth. He then outlines seven factors common to drug scares. These enable him to dissect the essential processes in the rule creation and enforcement phases of drug scares, despite the contradictory cultural values of temperance and hedonistic consumption. From this selection, we can see how drugs have been sca-pegoated to account for a wide array of social problems and used to keep some groups down by defining their actions as deviant. It is clear that despite our society's views on the negative features associated with all illicit drugs, our moral entrepreneurial and enforcement efforts have been concentrated more stringently against the drugs used by members of the powerless underclass and minority racial groups.

What kind of analysis do you think Reinarman is offering us here of the root causes of drug scares: structural, cultural, or interactionist (or some combination)?

Drug "wars," anti-drug crusades, and other periods of marked public concern about drugs are never merely reactions to the various troubles people can have with drugs. These drug scares are recurring cultural and political phenomena *in their own right and* must, therefore, be understood sociologically on their own terms. It is important to understand why people ingest drugs and why some of them develop problems that have something to do with having ingested them. But the premise of this chapter is that it is equally important to understand patterns of acute societal concern about drug use and drug problems. This seems especially so for U.S. society, which has had *recurring* anti-drug crusades and a *history* of repressive anti-drug laws.

Many well-intentioned drug policy reform efforts in the U.S. have come face to face with staid and stubborn sentiments against consciousness–altering substances. The repeated failures of such reform efforts cannot be explained solely in terms of ill-informed or manipulative leaders. Something deeper is

Reprinted by permission of Craig Reinarman.

involved, something woven into the very fabric of American culture, something which explains why claims that some drug is the cause of much of what is wrong with the world are *believed* so often by so many. The origins and nature of the *appeal* of anti-drug claims must be confronted if we are ever to understand how "drug problems" are constructed in the U.S. such that more enlightened and effective drug policies have been so difficult to achieve.

In this chapter I take a step in this direction. First, I summarize briefly some of the major periods of anti-drug sentiment in the U.S. Second, I draw from them the basic ingredients of which drug scares and drug laws are made. Third, I offer a beginning interpretation of these scares and laws based on those broad features of American culture that make *self-control* continuously problematic.

DRUG SCARES AND DRUG LAWS

What I have called drug scares (Reinarman and Levine, 1989a) have been a recurring feature of U.S. society for 200 years. They are relatively autonomous from whatever drug-related problems exist or are said to exist.[1] I call them "scares" because, like Red Scares, they are a form of moral panic ideologically constructed so as to construe one or another chemical bogeyman, à la "communists," as the core cause of a wide array of preexisting public problems.

The first and most significant drug scare was over drink. Temperance movement leaders constructed this scare beginning in the late 18th and early 19th century. It reached its formal end with the passage of Prohibition in 1919.[2] As Gusfield showed in his classic book *Symbolic Crusade* (1963), there was far more to the battle against booze than long-standing drinking problems. Temperance crusaders tended to be native born, middle-class, non-urban Protestants who felt threatened by the working-class, Catholic immigrants who were filling up America's cities during industrialization.[3] The latter were what Gusfield termed "unrepentant deviants" in that they continued their long-standing drinking practices despite middle-class W.A.S.P. norms against them. The battle over booze was the terrain on which was fought a cornucopia of cultural conflicts, particularly over whose morality would be the dominant morality in America.

In the course of this century-long struggle, the often wild claims of Temperance leaders appealed to millions of middle-class people seeking explanations for the pressing social and economic problems of industrializing America. Many corporate supporters of Prohibition threw their financial and ideological weight behind the Anti-Saloon League and other Temperance and Prohibitionist groups because they felt that traditional working-class drinking practices interfered with the new rhythms of the factory, and thus with productivity and profits (Rumbarger, 1989). To the Temperance crusaders' fear of the bar room as a breeding ground of all sorts of tragic immorality, Prohibitionists added the idea of the saloon as an alien, subversive place where unionists organized and where leftists and anarchists found recruits (Levine, 1984).

This convergence of claims and interests rendered alcohol a scapegoat for most of the nation's poverty, crime, moral degeneracy, "broken" families, illegitimacy, unemployment, and personal and business failure—problems whose sources lay in broader economic and political forces. This scare climaxed in the first two decades of this century, a tumultuous period rife with class, racial, cultural, and political conflict brought on by the wrenching changes of industrialization, immigration, and urbanization (Levine, 1984; Levine and Reinarman, 1991).

America's first real drug law was San Francisco's anti-opium den ordinance of 1875. The context of the campaign for this law shared many features with the context of the Temperance movement. Opiates had long been widely and legally available without a prescription in hundreds of medicines (Brecher, 1972; Musto, 1973; Courtwright, 1982; cf. Baumohl, 1992), so neither opiate use nor addiction was really the issue. This campaign focused almost exclusively on what was called the "Mongolian vice" of opium *smoking* by Chinese immigrants (and white "fellow travelers") in dens (Baumohl, 1992). Chinese immigrants came to California as "coolie" labor to build the railroad and dig the gold mines. A small minority of them brought along the practice of smoking opium—a practice originally brought to China by British and American traders in the 19th century. When the railroad was completed and the gold dried up, a decade-long depression ensued. In a tight labor market, Chinese immigrants were a target. The white Workingman's Party fomented racial hatred of the low-wage "coolies" with whom they now had to compete for work. The first law against opium smoking was only one of many laws enacted to harass and control Chinese workers (Morgan, 1978).

By calling attention to this broader political-economic context I do not wish to slight the specifics of the local political-economic context. In addition to the Workingman's Party, downtown businessmen formed merchant associations and urban families formed improvement associations, both of which fought for more than two decades to reduce the impact of San Francisco's vice districts on the order and health of the central business district and on family neighborhoods (Baumohl, 1992).

In this sense, the anti-opium den ordinance was not the clear and direct result of a sudden drug scare alone. The law was passed against a specific form of drug use engaged in by a disreputable group that had come to be seen as threatening in lean economic times. But it passed easily because this new threat was understood against the broader historical backdrop of long-standing local concerns about various vices as threats to public health, public morals, and public order. Moreover, the focus of attention were dens where it was suspected that whites came into intimate contact with "filthy, idolatrous" Chinese (see Baumohl, 1992). Some local law enforcement leaders, for example, complained that Chinese men were using this vice to seduce white women into sexual slavery (Morgan, 1978). Whatever the hazards of opium smoking, its initial criminalization in San Francisco had to do with both a general context of recession, class conflict, and racism, and with specific local interests in the control of vice and the prevention of miscegenation.

A nationwide scare focusing on opiates and cocaine began in the early 20th century. These drugs had been widely used for years, but were first criminalized when the addict population began to shift from predominantly white, middle-class, middle-aged women to young, working-class males, African Americans in particular. This scare led to the Harrison Narcotics Act of 1914, the first federal anti-drug law (see Duster, 1970).

Many different moral entrepreneurs guided its passage over a six-year campaign: State Department diplomats seeking a drug treaty as a means of expanding trade with China, trade which they felt was crucial for pulling the economy out of recession; the medical and pharmaceutical professions whose interests were threatened by self-medication with unregulated proprietary tonics, many of which contained cocaine or opiates; reformers seeking to control what they saw as the deviance of immigrants and Southern Blacks who were migrating off the farms; and a pliant press which routinely linked drug use with prostitutes, criminals, transient workers (e.g., the Wobblies), and African Americans (Musto, 1973). In order to gain the support of Southern Congressmen for a new federal law that might infringe on "states' rights," State Department officials and other crusaders repeatedly spread unsubstantiated suspicions, repeated in the press, that, e.g., cocaine induced African-American men to rape white women (Musto, 1973: 6–10, 67). In short, there was more to this drug scare, too, than mere drug problems.

In the Great Depression, Harry Anslinger of the Federal Narcotics Bureau pushed Congress for a federal law against marijuana. He claimed it was a "killer weed" and he spread stories to the press suggesting that it induced violence—especially among Mexican Americans. Although there was no evidence that marijuana was widely used, much less that it had any untoward effects, his crusade resulted in its criminalization in 1937—and not incidentally a turnaround in his Bureau's fiscal fortunes (Dickson, 1968). In this case, a new drug law was put in place by a militant moral-bureaucratic entrepreneur who played on racial fears and manipulated a press willing to repeat even his most absurd claims in a context of class conflict during the Depression (Becker, 1963). While there was not a marked scare at the time, Anslinger's claims were never contested in Congress because they played upon racial fears and widely held Victorian values against taking drugs solely for pleasure.

In the drug scare of the 1960s, political and moral leaders somehow reconceptualized this same "killer weed" as the "drop out drug" that was leading America's youth to rebellion and ruin (Himmelstein, 1983). Bio-medical scientists also published uncontrolled, retrospective studies of very small numbers of cases suggesting that, in addition to poisoning the minds and morals of youth, LSD produced broken chromosomes and thus genetic damage (Cohen et al., 1967). These studies were soon shown to be seriously misleading if not meaningless (Tijo et al., 1969), but not before the press, politicians, the medical profession, and the National Institute of Mental Health used them to promote a scare (Weil, 1972: 44–46).

I suggest that the reason even supposedly hard-headed scientists were drawn into such propaganda was that dominant groups felt the country was at war—and not merely with Vietnam. In this scare, there was not so much a "dangerous class" or threatening racial group as multi-faceted political and cultural conflict, particularly between generations, which gave rise to the perception that middle-class youth who rejected conventional values were a dangerous threat.[4] This scare resulted in the Comprehensive Drug Abuse Control Act of 1970, which criminalized more forms of drug use and subjected users to harsher penalties.

Most recently we have seen the crack scare, which began in earnest *not* when the prevalence of cocaine use quadrupled in the late 1970s, nor even when thousands of users began to smoke it in the more potent and dangerous form of free-base. Indeed, when this scare was launched, crack was unknown outside of a few neighborhoods in a handful of major cities (Reinarnian and Levine, 1989a) and the prevalence of illicit drug use had been dropping for several years (National Institute on Drug Use, 1990). Rather, this most recent scare began in 1986 when freebase cocaine was renamed crack (or "rock") and sold in precooked, inexpensive units on ghetto street corners (Reinarnian and Levine, 1989b). Once politicians and the media linked this new form of cocaine use to the inner-city, minority poor, a new drug scare was underway and the solution became more prison cells rather than more treatment slots.

The same sorts of wild claims and Draconian policy proposals of Temperance and Prohibition leaders resurfaced in the crack scare. Politicians have so outdone each other in getting "tough on drugs" that each year since crack came on the scene in 1986 they have passed more repressive laws providing billions more for law enforcement, longer sentences, and more drug offenses punishable by death. One result is that the U.S. now has more people in prison than any industrialized nation in the world—about half of them for drug offenses, the majority of whom are racial minorities.

In each of these periods more repressive drug laws were passed on the grounds that they would reduce drug use and drug problems. I have found no evidence that any scare actually accomplished those ends, but they did greatly expand the quantity and quality of social control, particularly over subordinate groups perceived as dangerous or threatening. Reading across these historical episodes one can abstract a recipe for drug scares and repressive drug laws that contains the following *seven ingredients:*

1. **A Kernel of Truth** Humans have ingested fermented beverages at least since human civilization moved from hunting and gathering to primitive agriculture thousands of years ago. The pharmacopoeia has expanded exponentially since then. So, in virtually all cultures and historical epochs, there has been sufficient ingestion of consciousness-altering chemicals to provide some basis for some people to claim that it is a problem.

2. **Media Magnification** In each of the episodes I have summarized and many others, the mass media has engaged in what I call the *routinization of caricature*—rhetorically recrafting worst cases into typical cases and the episodic into the epidemic. The media dramatize drug problems, as they do other problems, in the course of their routine news-generating and

sales-promoting procedures (see Brecher, 1972: 321–34; Reinarman and Duskin, 1992; and Molotch and Lester, 1974).

3. **Politico–Moral Entrepreneurs** I have added the prefix "politico" to Becker's (1963) seminal concept of moral entrepreneur in order to empha-size the fact that the most prominent and powerful moral entrepreneurs in drug scares are often political elites. Otherwise, I employ the term just as he intended: to denote the *enterprise,* the work, of those who create (or enforce) a rule against what they see as a social evil.[5]

In the history of drug problems in the U.S., these entrepreneurs call attention to drug using behavior and define it as a threat about which "something must be done." They also serve as the media's primary source of sound bites on the dangers of this or that drug. In all the scares I have noted, these entrepreneurs had interests of their own (often financial) which had little to do with drugs. Political elites typically find drugs a functional demon in that (like "outside agitators") drugs allow them to deflect attention from other, more systemic sources of public problems for which they would otherwise have to take some responsibility. Unlike almost every other po-litical issue, however, to be "tough on drugs" in American political culture allows a leader to take a firm stand without risking votes or campaign contributions.

4. **Professional Interest Groups** In each drug scare and during the passage of each drug law, various professional interests contended over what Gusfield (1981: 10–15) calls the "ownership" of drug problems—"the ability to create and influence the public definition of a problem" (1981: 10), and thus to define what should be done about it. These groups have included industrialists, churches, the American Medical Association, the American Pharmaceutical Association, various law enforcement agencies, scientists, and most recently the treatment industry and groups of those former addicts converted to disease ideology.[6] These groups claim for themselves, by virtue of their specialized forms of knowledge, the legitimacy and authority to name what is wrong and to prescribe the solution, usually garnering resources as a result.

5. **Historical Context of Conflict** This trinity of the media, moral entre-preneurs, and professional interests typically interact in such a way as to inflate the extant "kernel of truth" about drug use. But this interaction does not by itself give rise to drug scares or drug laws without underlying conflicts which make drugs into functional villains. Although Temperance crusaders persuaded millions to pledge abstinence, they campaigned for years without achieving alcohol control laws. However, in the tumultuous period leading up to Prohibition, there were revolutions in Russia and Mexico, World War I, massive immigration and impoverishment, and socialist, anarchist, and labor movements, to say nothing of increases in routine problems such as crime. I submit that all this conflict made for a level of cultural anxiety that provided fertile ideological soil for Prohibition. In each of the other scares, similar conflicts—economic, political, cultural, class, racial, or a

combination—provided a context in which claims makers could viably construe certain classes of drug users as a threat.

6. **Linking a Form of Drug Use to a "Dangerous Class"** Drug scares are never about drugs *per se,* because drugs are inanimate objects without social consequence until they are ingested by humans. Rather, drug scares are about the use of a drug by particular groups of people who are, typically, *already* perceived by powerful groups as some kind of threat (see Duster, 1970; Himmelstein, 1978). It was not so much alcohol problems *per se* that most animated the drive for Prohibition but the behavior and morality of what dominant groups saw as the "dangerous class" of urban, immigrant, Catholic, working-class drinkers (Gusfield, 1963; Rumbarger, 1989). It was *Chinese* opium smoking dens, not the more widespread use of other opiates, that prompted California's first drug law in the 1870s. It was only when smokable cocaine found its way to the African-American and Latino underclass that it made headlines and prompted calls for a drug war. In each case, politico-moral entrepreneurs were able to construct a "drug problem" by linking a substance to a group of users perceived by the powerful as disreputable, dangerous, or otherwise threatening.

7. **Scapegoating a Drug for a Wide Array of Public Problems** The final ingredient is scapegoating, i.e., blaming a drug or its alleged effects on a group of its users for a variety of preexisting social ills that are typically only indirectly associated with it. Scapegoating may be the most crucial element because it gives great explanatory power and thus broader resonance to claims about the horrors of drugs (particularly in the conflictual historical contexts in which drug scares tend to occur).

Scapegoating was abundant in each of the cases noted previously. To listen to Temperance crusaders, for example, one might have believed that without alcohol use, America would be a land of infinite economic progress with no poverty, crime, mental illness, or even sex outside marriage. To listen to leaders of organized medicine and the government in the 1960s, one might have surmised that without marijuana and LSD there would have been neither conflict between youth and their parents nor opposition to the Vietnam War. And to believe politicians and the media in the past six years is to believe that without the scourge of crack the inner cities and the so-called underclass would, if not disappear, at least be far less scarred by poverty, violence, and crime. There is no historical evidence supporting any of this.

In short, drugs are richly functional scapegoats. They provide elites with fig leaves to place over unsightly social ills that are endemic to the social system over which they preside. And they provide the public with a restricted aperture of attribution in which only a chemical bogeyman or the lone deviants who ingest it are seen as the cause of a cornucopia of complex problems.

TOWARD A CULTURALLY SPECIFIC
THEORY OF DRUG SCARES

Various forms of drug use have been and are widespread in almost all societies comparable to ours. A few of them have experienced limited drug scares, usually around alcohol decades ago. However, drug scares have been *far* less common in other societies, and never as virulent as they have been in the U.S. (Brecher, 1972; Levine, 1992; MacAndrew and Edgerton, 1969). There has never been a time or place in human history without drunkenness, for example, but in *most* times and places drunkenness has not been nearly as problematic as it has been in the U.S. since the late 18th century. Moreover, in comparable industrial democracies, drug laws are generally less repressive. Why then do claims about the horrors of this or that consciousness-altering chemical have such unusual power in American culture?

Drug scares and other periods of acute public concern about drug use are not just discrete, unrelated episodes. There is a historical pattern in the U.S. that cannot be understood in terms of the moral values and perceptions of individual anti-drug crusaders alone. I have suggested that these crusaders have benefited in various ways from their crusades. For example, making claims about how a drug is damaging society can help elites increase the social control of groups perceived as threatening (Duster, 1970), establish one class's moral code as dominant (Gusfield, 1963), bolster a bureaucracy's sagging fiscal fortunes (Dickson, 1968), or mobilize voter support (Reinarman and Levine, 1989a, b). However, the recurring character of pharmaco-phobia in U.S. history suggests that there is something about our *culture* which makes citizens more vulnerable to anti-drug crusaders' attempts to demonize drugs. Thus, an answer to the question of America's unusual vulnerability to drug scares must address why the scapegoating of consciousness-altering substances regularly *resonates* with or appeals to substantial portions of the population.

There are three basic parts to my answer. The first is that claims about the evils of drugs are especially viable in American culture in part because they provide a welcome *vocabulary of attribution* (cf. Mills, 1940). Armed with "DRUGS" as a generic scapegoat, citizens gain the cognitive satisfaction of having a folk devil on which to blame a range of bizarre behaviors or other conditions they find troubling but difficult to explain in other terms. This much may be true of a number of other societies, but I hypothesize that this is particularly so in the U.S. because in our political culture individualistic explanations for problems are so much more common than social explanations.

Second, claims about the evils of drugs provide an especially serviceable vocabulary of attribution in the U.S. in part because our society developed from a *temperance culture* (Levine, 1992). American society was forged in the fires of ascetic Protestantism and industrial capitalism, both of which demand *self-control*. U.S. society has long been characterized as the land of the individual "self-made man." In such a land, self-control has had extraordinary importance. For the middle-class Protestants who settled, defined, and still dominate the U.S., self-control was both central to religious worldviews and a characterological necessity for economic survival and success in the capitalist market (Weber, 1930 [1985]). With Levine (1992), I hypothesize that in a culture in which self-control is inordinately important, drug-induced altered states of consciousness are especially likely to be experienced as "loss of control," and thus to be inordinately feared.[7]

Drunkenness and other forms of drug use have, of course, been present everywhere in the industrialized world. But temperance cultures tend to arise only when industrial capitalism unfolds upon a cultural terrain deeply imbued with the Protestant ethic.[8] This means that only the U.S., England, Canada, and parts of Scandinavia have Temperance cultures, the U.S. being the most extreme case.

It may be objected that the influence of such a Temperance culture was strongest in the 19th and early 20th century and that its grip on the American *Zeitgeist* has been loosened by the forces of modernity and now, many say, post-modernity. The third part of my answer, however, is that on the foundation of a Temperance culture, advanced capitalism has built a *postmodern, mass consumption culture* that exacerbates the problem of self-control in new ways.

Early in the 20th century, Henry Ford pioneered the idea that by raising wages he could simultaneously quell worker protests and increase market demand for mass-produced goods. This mass consumption strategy became central to modern American society and one of the reasons for our economic success (Marcuse, 1964; Aronowitz, 1973; Ewen, 1976; Bell, 1978). Our economy is now so fundamentally predicated upon mass consumption that theorists as diverse as Daniel Bell and Herbert Marcuse have observed that we live in a mass consumption culture. Bell (1978), for example, notes that while the Protestant work ethic and deferred gratification may still hold sway in the workplace, Madison Avenue, the media, and malls have inculcated a new indulgence ethic in the leisure sphere in which pleasure seeking and immediate gratification reign.

Thus, our economy and society have come to depend upon the constant cultivation of new "needs," the production of new desires. Not only the hardware of social life such as food, clothing, and shelter but also the software of the self—excitement, entertainment, even eroticism—have become mass consumption commodities. This means that our society offers an increasing number of incentives for indulgence—more ways to lose self-control—and a decreasing number of countervailing reasons for retaining it.

In short, drug scares continue to occur in American society in part because people must constantly manage the contradiction between a Temperance culture that insists on self-control and a mass consumption culture which renders self-control continuously problematic. In addition to helping explain the recurrence of drug scares, I think this contradiction helps account for why in the last dozen years millions of Americans have joined 12-Step groups, more than 100 of which have nothing whatsoever to do with ingesting a drug (Reinarman, 1995). "Addiction," or the generalized loss of self-control, has become the meta-metaphor for a staggering array of human troubles. And, of course, we also seem to have a staggering array of politicians and other moral entrepreneurs who take advantage of such cultural contradictions to blame new chemical bogeymen for our society's ills.

NOTES

1. In this regard, for example, Robin Room wisely observes "that we are living at a historic moment when the rate of (alcohol) dependence as a cognitive and existential experience is rising, although the rate of alcohol consumption and of heavy drinking is falling." He draws from this a more general hypothesis about "long waves" of drinking and societal reactions to them: "[I]n periods of increased questioning of drink ing and heavy drinking, the trends in the two forms of dependence, psychological and physical, will tend to run in opposite directions. Conversely, in periods of a "wettening" of sentiments, with the curve of alcohol consumption beginning to rise, we may expect the rate of physical dependence… to rise while the rate of dependence as a cognitive experience falls" (1991: 154).

2. I say "formal end" because Temperance ideology is not merely alive and well in the War on Drugs but is being applied to all manner of human troubles in the burgeoning 12-Step Movement (Reinarman, 1995).

3. From Jim Baumohl I have learned that while the Temperance movement attracted most of its supporters from these groups, it also found supporters among many others (e.g., labor, the Irish, Catholics, former drunkards, women), each of which had its own reading of and folded its own agenda into the movement.

4. This historical sketch of drug scares is obviously not exhaustive. Readers interested in other scares should see, e.g.,

Brecher's encyclopedic work *Licit and Illicit Drugs* (1972), especially the chapter on glue sniffing, which illustrates how the media actually created a new drug problem by writing hysterical stories about it. There was also a PCP scare in the 1970s in which law enforcement officials claimed that the growing use of this horse tranquilizer was a severe threat because it made users so violent and gave them such super-human strength that stun guns were necessary. This, too, turned out to be unfounded and the "angel dust" scare was short-lived (see Feldman et al., 1979). The best analysis of how new drugs themselves can lead to panic reactions among users is Becker (1967).

5. Becker wisely warns against the "one-sided view" that sees such crusaders as merely imposing their morality on others. Moral entrepreneurs, he notes, do operate "with an absolute ethic," are "fervent and righteous," and will use "any means" necessary to "do away with" what they see as "totally evil." However, they also "typically believe that their mission is a holy one," that if people do what they want it "will be good for them." Thus, as in the case of abolitionists, the crusades of moral entrepreneurs often "have strong humanitarian overtones" (1963: 147–8). This is no less true for those whose moral enterprise promotes drug scares. My analysis, however, concerns the character and consequences of their efforts, not their motives.

6. As Gusfield notes, such ownership sometimes shifts over time, e.g., with alcohol problems, from religion to criminal law to medical science. With other drug problems, the shift in ownership has been away from medical science toward criminal law. The most insightful treatment of the medicalization of alcohol/drug problems is Peele (1989).

7. See Baumohrs (1990) important and erudite analysis of how the human will was valorized in the therapeutic temperance thought of 19th-century inebriate homes.

8. The third central feature of Temperance cultures identified by Levine (1992), which I will not dwell on, is predominance of spirits drinking, i.e., more concentrated alcohol than wine or beer and thus greater likelihood of drunkenness.

REFERENCES

Aronowitz, Stanley. 1973. *False Promises: The Shaping of American Working Class Consciousness*. New York: McGraw-Hill.

Baumohl, Jim. 1990. "Inebriate Institutions in North America, 1840–1920." *British Journal of Addidion* 85: 1187–1204.

Baumohl, Jim. 1992. "The 'Dope Fiend's Paradise' Revisited: Notes from Research in Progress on Drug Law Enforcement in San Francisco, 1875–1915." *Drinking and Drug Practices Surveyor* 24: 3–12.

Becker, Howard S. 1963. *Outsiders: Studies in the Sociology of Deviance*. Glencoe, IL: Free Press.

———. 1967. "History, Culture, and Subjective Experience: An Exploration of the Social Bases of Drug-Induced Experiences." *Journal of Health and Social Behavior* 8: 162–176.

Bell, Daniel. 1978. *The Cultural Contradictions of Capitalism*. New York: Basic Books.

Brecher, Edward M. 1972. *Licit and Illicit Drugs*. Boston: Little Brown.

Cohen, M. M., K. Hirshorn, and W. A. Frosch. 1967. "In Vivo and in Vitro Chromosomal Damage Induced by LSD-25." *New England Journal of Medicine* 227: 1043.

Courtwright, David. 1982. *Dark Paradise: Opiate Addiction in America Before 1940*. Cambridge, MA: Harvard University Press.

Dickson, Donald. 1968. "Bureaucracy and Morality." *Social Problems* 16: 143–156.

Duster, Troy. 1970. *The Legislation of Morality: Law, Drugs, and Moral Judgement*. New York: Free Press.

Ewen, Stuart. 1976. *Captains of Consciousness: Advertising and the Social Roots of Consumer Culture*. New York: McGraw-Hill.

Feldman, Harvey W., Michael H. Agar, and George M. Beschner. 1979. *Angel Dust*. Lexington, MA: Lexington Books.

Gusfield, Joseph R. 1963. *Symbolic Crusade: Status Politics and the American Temperance Movement*. Urbana: University of Illinois Press.

———. 1981. *The Culture of Public Problems: Drinking-Driving and the Symbolic Order*. Chicago: University of Chicago Press.

Himmelstein, Jerome. 1978. "Drug Politics Theory." *Journal of Drug Issues* 8.

———. 1983. *The Strange Career of Marihuana*. Westport, CT: Greenwood Press.

Levine, Harry Gene. 1984. "The Alcohol Problem in America: From

Temperance to Alcoholism." *British Journal of Addiction* 84: 109–119.

————. 1992. "Temperance Cultures: Concern About Alcohol Problems in Nordic and English-Speaking Cultures." In G. Edwards et al., eds., *The Nature of Alcohol and Drug Related Problems.* New York: Oxford University Press.

Levine, Harry Gene, and Craig Reinarman. 1991. "From Prohibition to Regulation: Lessons from Alcohol Policy for Drug Policy." *Milbank Quarterly* 69: 461–494.

MacAndrew, Craig, and Robert Edgerton. 1969. *Drunken Comportment.* Chicago: Aldine.

Marcuse, Herbert. 1964. *One-Dimensional Man: Studies in the Ideology of Advanced Industrial Society.* Boston: Beacon Press.

Mills, C. Wright. 1940. "Situated Actions and Vocabularies of Motive." *American Sociological Review* 5: 904–913.

Molotch, Harvey, and Marilyn Lester. 1974. "News as Purposive Behavior: On the Strategic Uses of Routine Events, Accidents, and Scandals." *American Sociological Review* 39: 101–112.

Morgan, Patricia. 1978. "The Legislation of Drug Law: Economic Crisis and Social Control." *Journal of Drug Issues* 8: 53–62.

Musto, David. 1973. *The American Disease: Origins of Narcotic Control.* New Haven, CT: Yale University Press.

National Institute on Drug Abuse. 1990. *National Household Survey on Drug Abuse: Main Findings 1990.* Washington, DC: U.S. Department of Health and Human Services.

Peele, Stanton. 1989. *The Diseasing of America: Addiction Treatment Out of Control.* Lexington, MA: Lexington Books.

Reinarman, Craig. 1995. "The 12-Step Movement and Advanced Capitalist Culture: Notes on the Politics of Self-Control in Postmodernity." In B. Epstein, R. Flacks, and M. Darnovsky, eds., *Contemporary Social Movements and Cultural Politics.* New York: Oxford University Press.

Reinarman, Craig, and Ceres Duskin. 1992. "Dominant Ideology and Drugs in the Media." *International Journal on Drug Policy* 3: 6–15.

Reinarman, Craig, and Harry Gene Levine. 1989a. "Crack in Context: Politics and Media in the Making of a Drug Scare." *Contemporary Drug Problems* 16: 535–577.

————. 1989b. "The Crack Attack: Politics and Media in America's Latest Drug Scare." In Joel Best, ed., *Images of Issues: Typifying Contemporary Social Problems,* pp. 115–137. New York: Aldine de Gruyter.

Room, Robin G. W. 1991. "Cultural Changes in Drinking and Trends in Alcohol Problems Indicators: Recent U.S. Experience." In Walter B. Clark and Michael E. Hilton, eds., *Alcohol in America: Drinking Practices and Problems,* pp. 149–162. Albany: State University of New York Press.

Rumbarger, John J. 1989. *Profits, Power, and Prohibition: Alcohol Reform and the Industrializing of America, 1800–1930.* Albany: State University of New York Press.

Tijo. J. H., W. N. Pahnke, and A. A. Kurland. 1969. "LSD and Chromosomes: A Controlled Experiment." *Journal of the American Medical Association* 210: 849.

Weber, Max. 1985 (1930). *The Protestant Ethic and the Spirit of Capitalism.* London: Unwin.

Weil, Andrew. 1972. *The Natural Mind.* Boston: Houghton Mifflin.

16

Blowing Smoke: Status Politics and the Smoking Ban

JUSTIN L. TUGGLE AND MALCOLM D. HOLMES

Tuggle and Holmes' chapter on the struggle over cigarette smoking in America expands Reinarman's consideration to the licit drug realm, examining the struggle and counter struggle over tobacco between the moral entrepreneurs and the status quo defenders. They note the medical, ethical, and socioeconomic arguments raised to sway public opinion and demonize public consumption of cigarettes. They mention the spate of claims put forward, pitting anti-smoking groups that have argued that secondhand smoke is toxic and that smokers should not be allowed to inflict their pollution onto others, against opponents who have argued that the government should not legislate their morality. These issues illustrate the concern that frequently arises in deviance, where society must balance the right of individual freedoms (the desire to smoke) against the needs of the common good (public health). This reading also shows the relation between claims-making and social power, tracing the status of the social groups on each side of this campaign. Its fundamental message lies in how moral entrepreneurs use their status to attach deviant labels to the behavior of others, and, in so doing, to keep those others in a subordinate status position. They thus show deviance, like Quinney does, as a tool by which higher status groups retain and enforce their interests over subordinate groups.

What features of Reinarman's view of how deviance is socially constructed do we see reinforced by Tuggle and Holmes? How does their thesis explain why some groups of society morally crusade against issues that might, seemingly, have little direct impact on them?

Over the past half century, perceptions of tobacco and its users have changed dramatically. In the 1940s and 1950s, cigarette smoking was socially accepted and commonly presumed to lack deleterious effects (see, e.g., Ram 1941). Survey data from the early 1950s showed that a minority believed cigarette smoking caused lung cancer (Viscusi 1992). By the late 1970s, however, estimates from survey data revealed that more than 90% of the population thought that this link existed (Roper Organization 1978). This and other harms associated with tobacco consumption have provided the impetus for an antismoking crusade that aims to normatively redefine smoking as deviant behavior (Markle and Troyer 1979).

There seems to be little question that tobacco is a damaging psychoactive substance characterized by highly adverse chronic health effects (Steinfeld 1991). In this regard, the social control movement probably makes considerable sense in terms of public policy. At the same time, much as ethnicity and religion played a significant role in the prohibition of alcohol (Gusfield 1963), social status may well play a part in this latest crusade.

Historically, attempts to control psychoactive substances have linked their use to categories of relatively powerless people. Marijuana use was associated with Mexican Americans (Bonnie and Whitebread 1970), cocaine with African Americans (Ashley 1975), opiates with Asians (Ben-Yehuda 1990), and alcohol with immigrant Catholics (Gusfield 1963). During the heyday of cigarette smoking, it was thought that

> Tobacco's the one blessing that nature has left for all humans to enjoy.
> It can be consumed by both the "haves" and "have nots" as a common
> leveler, one that brings all humans together from all walks of life
> regardless of class, race, or creed. (Ram 1941, p. 125)

But in contrast to this earlier view, recent evidence has shown that occupational status (Ferrence 1989; Marcus et al. 1989; Covey et al. 1992), education (Ferrence 1989; Viscusi 1992), and family income (Viscusi 1992), are related negatively to current smoking. Further, the relationships of occupation and education to cigarette smoking have become stronger in later age cohorts (Ferrence 1989). Thus we ask, *is the association of tobacco with lower-status persons a factor in the crusade against smoking in public facilities?* Here we examine that question in a case study of a smoking ban implemented in Shasta County, California.

STATUS POLITICS AND THE
CREATION OF DEVIANCE

Deviance is socially constructed. Complex pluralistic societies have multiple, competing symbolic-moral universes that clash and negotiate (Ben-Yehuda 1990). Deviance is relative, and social morality is continually restructured. Moral, power, and stigma contests are ongoing, with competing symbolic-moral universes striving to legitimize particular lifestyles while making others deviant (Schur 1980; Ben-Yehuda 1990).

The ability to define and construct reality is closely connected to the power structure of society (Gusfield 1963). Inevitably, then, the distribution of deviance is associated with the system of stratification. The higher one's social position, the greater one's moral value (Ben-Yehuda 1990). Differences in lifestyles and moral beliefs are corollaries of social stratification (Gusfield 1963; Zürcher and Kirkpatrick 1976; Luker 1984). Accordingly, even though grounded in the system of stratification, status conflicts need not be instrumental; they may also be symbolic. Social stigma may, for instance, attach to behavior thought indicative of a weak will (Goffman 1963). Such moral anomalies occasion status degradation ceremonies, public denunciations expressing indignation not at a behavior per se, but rather against the individual motivational type that produced it (Garfinkel 1956). The denouncers act as public figures, drawing upon communally shared experience and speaking in the name of ultimate values. In this respect, status degradation involves a reciprocal element: Status conflicts and the resultant condemnation of a behavior characteristic of a particular status category symbolically enhances the status of the abstinent through the degradation of the participatory (Garfinkel 1956; Gusfield 1963).

Deviance creation involves political competition in which moral entrepreneurs originate moral crusades aimed at generating reform (Becker 1963; Schur 1980; Ben-Yehuda 1990). The alleged deficiencies of a specific social group are revealed and reviled by those crusading to define their behavior as deviant. As might be expected, successful moral crusades are generally dominated by those in the upper social strata of society (Becker 1963). Research on the anti-abortion (Luker 1984) and antipornography (Zürcher and Kirkpatrick 1976) crusades has shown that activists in these movements are of lower socioeconomic status than their opponents, helping explain the limited success of efforts to redefine abortion and pornography as deviance.

Moral entrepreneurs' goals may be either assimilative or coercive reform (Gusfield 1963). In the former instance, sympathy to the deviants' plight engenders integrative efforts aimed at lifting the repentant to the superior moral plane allegedly held by those of higher social status. The latter strategy emerges when deviants are viewed as intractably denying the moral and status superiority of the reformers' symbolic-moral universe. Thus, whereas assimilative reform may employ educative strategies, coercive reform turns to law and force for affirmation.

Regardless of aim, the moral entrepreneur cannot succeed alone. Success in establishing a moral crusade is dependent on acquiring broader public support. To that end, the moral entrepreneur must mobilize power, create a perceived threat potential for the moral issue in question, generate public awareness of the issue, propose a clear and acceptable solution to the problem, and overcome resistance to the crusade (Becker 1963; Ben-Yehuda 1990).

THE STATUS POLITICS OF CIGARETTE SMOKING

The political dynamics underlying the definition of deviant behaviors may be seen clearly in efforts to end smoking in public facilities. Cigarettes were an insignificant product of the tobacco industry until the end of the 19th century, after which they evolved into its staple (U.S. Department of Health and Human Services 1992). Around the turn of the century, 14 states banned cigarette smoking and all but one other regulated sales to and possession by minors (Nuehring and Markle 1974). Yet by its heyday in the 1940s and 1950s, cigarette smoking was almost universally accepted, even considered socially desirable (Nuehring and Markle 1974; Steinfeld 1991). Per capita cigarette consumption in the United States peaked at approximately 4,300 cigarettes per year in the early 1960s, after which it declined to about 2,800 per year by the early 1990s (U.S. Department of Health and Human Services 1992). The beginning of the marked decline in cigarette consumption corresponded to the publication of the report to the surgeon general on the health risks of smoking (U.S. Department of Health, Education and Welfare 1964). Two decades later, the hazards of passive smoking were being publicized (e.g., U.S. Department of Health and Human Services 1986).

Increasingly, the recognition of the apparent relationship of smoking to health risks has socially demarcated the lifestyles of the smoker and nonsmoker, from widespread acceptance of the habit to polarized symbolic-moral universes. Attitudes about smoking are informed partly by medical issues, but perhaps even more critical are normative considerations (Nuehring and Markle 1974); more people have come to see smoking as socially reprehensible and deviant, and smokers as social misfits (Markle and Troyer 1979). Psychological assessments have attributed an array of negative evaluative characteristics to smokers (Markle and Troyer 1979). Their habit is increasingly thought unclean and intrusive.

Abstinence and bodily purity are the cornerstones of the nonsmoker's purported moral superiority (Feinhandler 1986). At the center of their symbolic-moral universe, then, is the idea that people have the right to breathe clean air in public spaces (Goodin 1989). Smokers, on the other hand, stake their claim to legitimacy in a precept of Anglo-Saxon political culture—the right to do whatever one wants unless it harms others (Berger 1986). Those sympathetic to smoking deny that environmental tobacco smoke poses a significant health hazard to the nonsmoker (Aviado 1986). Yet such arguments have held little sway in the face of counterclaims from authoritative governmental agencies and high status moral entrepreneurs.

The development of the antismoking movement has targeted a lifestyle particularly characteristic of the working classes (Berger 1986). Not only has there been an overall decline in cigarette smoking, but, as mentioned above, the negative relationships of occupation and education to cigarette smoking have become more pronounced in later age cohorts (Ferrence 1989). Moreover, moral entrepreneurs crusading against smoking are representatives of a relatively powerful "knowledge class," comprising people employed in areas such as education and the therapeutic and counseling agencies (Berger 1986).

Early remedial efforts focused on publicizing the perils of cigarette smokers, reflecting a strategy of assimilative reform (Neuhring and Markle 1974; Markle and Troyer 1979). Even many smokers expressed opposition to cigarettes and a generally repentant attitude. Early educative efforts were thus successful in decreasing cigarette consumption, despite resistance from the tobacco industry. Then, recognition of the adverse effects of smoking on nonusers helped precipitate a turn to coercive reform measures during the mid-1970s (Markle and Troyer 1979). Rather than a repentant friend in need of help, a new definition of the smoker as enemy emerged. Legal abolition of smoking in public facilities became one focus of social control efforts, and smoking bans in public spaces have been widely adopted in recent years (Markle and Troyer 1979; Goodin 1989).

The success of the antismoking crusade has been grounded in moral entrepreneurs' proficiency at mobilizing power, a mobilization made possible by highly visible governmental campaigns, the widely publicized health risks of smoking, and the proposal of workable and generally acceptable policies to ameliorate the problem. The success of this moral crusade has been further facilitated by the association of deviant characteristics with those in lower social strata, whose stigmatization reinforces existing relations of power and prestige. Despite the formidable resources and staunch opposition of the tobacco industry, the tide of public opinion and policy continues to move toward an antismoking stance.

RESEARCH PROBLEM

The study presented below is an exploratory examination of the link between social status and support for a smoking ban in public facilities. Based on theorizing about status politics, as well as evidence about patterns of cigarette use, it was predicted that supporters of the smoking ban would be of higher status than those who opposed it. Further, it was anticipated that supporters of the ban would be more likely to make negative normative claims denouncing the allegedly deviant qualities of smoking, symbolically enhancing their own status while lowering that of their opponents.

The site of this research was Shasta County, California. The population of Shasta County is 147,036, of whom 66,462 reside in its only city, Redding (U.S. Bureau of the Census 1990). This county became the setting for the implementation of a hotly contested ban on smoking in public buildings.

In 1988, California voters passed Proposition 99, increasing cigarette taxes by 25 cents per pack. The purpose of the tax was to fund smoking prevention and treatment programs. Toward that end, Shasta County created the Shasta County Tobacco Education Program. The director of the program formed a coalition with officials of the Shasta County chapters of the American Cancer Society and American Lung Association to propose a smoking ban in all public buildings. The three groups formed an organization to promote that cause, Smoke-Free Air For Everyone (SAFE). Unlike other bans then in effect in California, the proposed ban included restaurants and bars, because its proponents considered these to be places in which people encountered significant amounts of secondhand smoke. They procured sufficient signatures on a petition to place the measure on the county's general ballot in November 1992.

The referendum passed with a 56% majority in an election that saw an 82% turnout. Subsequently, the Shasta County Hospitality and Business Alliance, an antiban coalition, obtained sufficient signatures to force a special election to annul the smoking ban. The special election was held in April 1993. Although the turnout was much lower (48%), again a sizable majority (58.4%) supported the ban. The ordinance went into effect on July 1, 1993.

ANALYTIC STRATEGY

... [D]ata were analyzed in our effort to ascertain the moral and status conflicts underlying the Shasta County smoking ban ... [based on] interviews with five leading moral entrepreneurs and five prominent status quo defenders.[1] These individuals were selected through a snowball sample, with the original respondents identified through interviews with business owners or political advertisements in the local mass media. The selected respondents repeatedly surfaced as the leading figures in their respective coalitions. Semistructured interviews were conducted to determine the reasons underlying their involvement. These data were critical to understanding how the proposed ban was framed by small groups of influential proponents and opponents; it was expected that their concerns would be reflected in the larger public debate about the ban.

FINDINGS

Moral Entrepreneur/Status Quo Defender Interviews

The moral entrepreneurs and status quo defenders interviewed represented clearly different interests. The former group included three high-level administrators in the county's chapters of the American Cancer Society and American Lung Association. A fourth was an administrator for the Shasta County Tobacco Education Project. The last member of this group was a pulmonary physician affiliated with a local hospital. The latter group included four bar and/or restaurant owners and an attorney who had been hired to represent their interests. Thus the status quo defenders were small business owners who might see their economic interests affected adversely by the ban. Importantly, they were representatives of a less prestigious social stratum than the moral entrepreneurs.

The primary concern of the moral entrepreneurs was health. As one stated,

I supported the initiative to get the smoking ban on the ballot because of all the health implications that secondhand smoke can create. Smoking and secondhand smoke are the most preventable causes of death in this nation.

Another offered that

On average, secondhand smoke kills 53,000 Americans each year. And think about those that it kills in other countries! It contains 43 cancer-causing chemical agents that have been verified by the Environmental Protection Agency. It is now listed as a Type A carcinogen, which is the same category as asbestos.

Every one of the moral entrepreneurs expressed concern about health issues during the interviews. This was not the only point they raised, however. Three of the five made negative normative evaluations of smoking, thereby implicitly degrading the status of smokers. They commented that "smoking is no longer an acceptable action," that "smoke stinks," or that "it is just a dirty and annoying habit." Thus, whereas health was their primary concern, such comments revealed the moral entrepreneurs' negative view of smoking irrespective of any medical issues. Smokers were seen as engaging in unclean and objectionable behavior—stigmatized qualities defining their deviant social status.

The stance of the status quo defenders was also grounded in two arguments. All of them expressed concern about individual rights. As one put it,

> I opposed that smoking ban because I personally smoke and feel that it is an infringement of my rights to tell me where I can and cannot smoke. Smoking is a legal activity, and therefore it is unconstitutional to take that right away from me.

Another argued that

> Many people have died for us to have these rights in foreign wars and those also fought on American soil. Hundreds of thousands of people thought that these rights were worth dying for, and now some small group of people believe that they can just vote away these rights.

Such symbolism implies that smoking is virtually a patriotic calling, a venerable habit for which people have been willing to forfeit their lives in time of war. In the status quo defenders' view, smoking is a constitutionally protected right.

At the same time, each of the status quo defenders was concerned about more practical matters, namely business profits. As one stated, "my income was going to be greatly affected." Another argued,

> If these people owned some of the businesses that they are including in this ban, they would not like it either. By taking away the customers that smoke, they are taking away the mainstay of people from a lot of businesses.

The competing viewpoints of the moral entrepreneurs and status quo defenders revealed the moral issues—health versus individual rights—at the heart of political conflict over the smoking ban. Yet it appears that status issues also fueled the conflict. On the one hand, the moral entrepreneurs denigrated smoking, emphasizing the socially unacceptable qualities of the behavior and symbolically degrading smokers' status. On the other hand, status quo defenders were concerned that their livelihood would be affected by the ban. Interestingly, the occupational status of the two groups differed, with the moral entrepreneurs representing the new knowledge class, the status quo defenders a lower stratum of small business owners. Those in the latter group may not have been accorded the prestige and trust granted those in the former (Berger 1986). Moreover, the status quo defenders' concern about business was likely seen as self-aggrandizing.

SUMMARY AND DISCUSSION

This research has examined the moral and status politics underlying the implementation of a smoking ban in Shasta County, California. Moral entrepreneurs crusading for the ban argued that secondhand smoke damages health, implicitly grounding their argument in the principle that people have a right to a smoke-free environment. Status quo defenders countered that smokers have a constitutional right to indulge wherever and whenever they see fit. Public discourse echoed these themes, as seen in the letters to the editor of the local newspaper.

Thus debate about the smoking ban focused especially on health versus smokers' rights; yet evidence of social status differences between the competing symbolic-moral universes also surfaced. Competing symbolic-moral universes are defined not only by different ethical viewpoints on a behavior, but also by differences in social power—disparities inevitably linked to the system of stratification (Ben-Yehuda 1990). Those prevailing in moral and stigma contests typically represent the higher socioeconomic echelons of society.

The moral entrepreneurs who engineered the smoking ban campaign were representatives of the prestigious knowledge class, including among their members officials from the local chapters of respected organizations at the forefront of the national antismoking crusade. In contrast, the small business owners who were at the core of the opposing coalition, of status quo defenders, represented the traditional middle class. Clearly, there was an instrumental quality to the restaurant and bar owners' stance, because they saw the ban as potentially damaging to their business interests. But they were unable to shape the public debate, as demonstrated by the letters to the editor.

In many respects, the status conflicts involved in the passage of the Shasta County smoking ban were symbolic. The moral entrepreneurs focused attention on the normatively undesirable qualities of cigarette smoking, and their negative normative evaluations of smoking were reflected in public debate about the ban. Those who wrote in support of the ban more frequently offered negative normative evaluations than antiban writers; their comments degraded smoking and, implicitly, smokers. Since the advent of the antismoking crusade in the United States, smoking has come to be seen as socially reprehensible, smokers as social misfits characterized by negative psychological characteristics (Markle and Troyer 1979).

Ultimately, a lifestyle associated with the less educated, less affluent, lower occupational strata was stigmatized as a public health hazard and targeted for coercive reform. Its deviant status was codified in the ordinance banning smoking in public facilities, including restaurants and bars. The ban symbolized the deviant status of cigarette smokers, the prohibition visibly demonstrating the community's condemnation of their behavior. Further, the smoking ban symbolically amplified the purported virtues of the abstinent lifestyle. A political victory such as the passage of a law is a prestige-enhancing symbolic triumph that is perhaps even more rewarding than its end result (Gusfield 1963). The symbolic nature of the ban serendipitously surfaced in another way during one author's unstructured observations in 42 restaurants and 21 bars in the area: Whereas smoking was not observed in a single restaurant, it occurred without sanction in all but one of the bars. Although not deterring smoking in one of its traditional bastions, the ban called attention to its deviant quality and, instrumentally, effectively halted it in areas more commonly frequented by the abstemious.

Although more systematic research is needed, the findings of this exploratory case study offer a better understanding of the dynamics underlying opposition to smoking and further support to theorizing about the role of status politics in the creation of deviant types. Denunciation of smoking in Shasta County involved not only legitimate allegations about public health, but negative normative evaluations of those engaged in the behavior. In the latter regard, the ban constituted a status degradation ceremony, symbolically differentiating the pure and abstinent from the unclean and intrusive. Not coincidentally, the stigmatized were more likely found among society's lower socioeconomic strata, their denouncers among its higher echelons.

Certainly the class and ethnic antipathies underlying attacks on cocaine and opiate users earlier in the century were more manifest than those revealed in the crusade against cigarette smoking. But neither are there manifest status conflicts in the present crusades against abortion (Luker 1984) and pornography (Zürcher and Kirkpatrick 1976); yet the underlying differences of status between opponents in those movements are reflected in their markedly different symbolic-moral universes, as was the case in the present study.

This is not to suggest that smoking should be an approved behavior. The medical evidence seems compelling: Cigarette smoking is harmful to the individual smoker and to those exposed to secondhand smoke. However, the objective harms of the psychoactive substance in question are irrelevant to the validity of our analysis, just as they were to Gusfield's (1963) analysis of the temperance movement's crusade against alcohol use. Moreover, it is not our intention to imply that the proban supporters consciously intended to degrade those of lower social status. No doubt they were motivated primarily by a sincere belief that smoking constitutes a public health hazard. In the end, however, moral indignation and social control flowed down the social hierarchy. Thus we must ask: Would cigarette smoking be defined as deviant if there were a positive correlation between smoking and socioeconomic status?

NOTE

1. Although the term moral entrepreneur is well established in the literature on deviance, there seems to be little attention to or consistency in a corresponding term for the interest group (s) opposing them. Those that have been employed such as "forces for the status quo" (Markle and Troyer 1979), tend to be awkward. "Status quo defenders" is used here for lack of a simpler or more common term.

REFERENCES

Ashley, Richard. 1975. *Cocaine: Its History, Uses, and Effects.* New York: St. Martin's Press.

Aviado, Domingo M. 1986. "Health Issues Relating to 'Passive' Smoking." Pp. 137–165 in *Smoking and Society: Toward a More Balanced Assessment,* edited by Robert D. Tollison. Lexington, MA: Lexington Books.

Becker, Howard S. 1963. *Outsiders: Studies in the Sociology of Deviance.* New York: Free Press.

Ben-Yehuda, Nachman. 1990. *The Politics and Morality of Deviance: Moral Panics, Drug Abuse, Deviant Science, and Reversed Stigmatization.* Albany, NY: State University of New York Press.

Berger, Peter L. 1986. "A Sociological View of the Antismoking Phenomenon." Pp. 225–240 in *Smoking and Society: Toward a More Balanced Assessment,* edited by Robert D. Tollison. Lexington, MA: Lexington Books.

Bonnie, Richard J., and Charles H. Whitebread II. 1970. "The Forbidden Fruit and the Tree of Knowledge: An Inquiry into the Legal History of American Marihuana Prohibition." *Virginia Law Review* 56: 971–1203.

Covey, Lirio S., Edith A. Zang, and Ernst L. Wynder. 1992. "Cigarette Smoking and Occupational Status: 1977 to 1990." *American Journal of Public Health* 82: 1230–1234.

Feinhandler, Sherwin J. 1986. *The Social Role of Smoking*. Pp. 167–187 in *Smoking and Society: Toward a More Balanced Assessment,* edited by Robert D. Tollison. Lexington, MA: Lexington Books.

Ferrence, Roberta G. 1989. *Deadly Fashion: The Rise and Fall of Cigarette Smoking in North America*. New York: Garland.

Garfinkel, Harold. 1956. "Conditions of Successful Degradation Ceremonies." *American Journal of Sociology* 61: 402–424.

Goffman, Erving. 1963. *Stigma: Notes on the Management of Spoiled Identity*. Englewood Cliffs, NJ: Prentice Hall.

Goodin, Robert E. 1989. *No Smoking: The Ethical Issues*. Chicago: University of Chicago Press.

Gusfield, Joseph R. 1963. *Symbolic Crusade: Status Politics and the American Temperance Movement*. Urbana, IL: University of Illinois Press.

Luker, Kristin. 1984. *Abortion and the Politics of Motherhood*. Berkeley, CA: University of California.

Marcus, Alfred C, Donald R. Shopland, Lori A. Crane, and William R. Lynn. 1989. "Prevalence of Cigarette Smoking in United States: Estimates from the 1985 Current Population Survey." *Journal of the National Cancer Institute* 81: 409–114.

Markle, Gerald E., and Ronald J. Troyer. 1979. "Smoke Gets in Your Eyes: Cigarette Smoking as Deviant Behavior." *Social Problems* 26: 611–625.

Neuhring, Elane, and Gerald E. Markle. 1974. "Nicotine and Norms: The Re-Emergence of a Deviant Behavior." *Social Problems* 21: 513–526.

Ram, Sidney P. 1941. *How to Get More Fun Out of Smoking*. Chicago: Cuneo.

Roper Organization. 1978, May. *A Study of Public Attitudes Toward Cigarette Smoking and the Tobacco Industry in 1978, Volume 1*. New York: Roper.

Schur, Edwin M. 1980. *The Politics of Deviance: Stigma Contests and the Uses of Power*. New York: Random House.

Steinfeld, Jesse. 1991. "Combating Smoking in the United States: Progress Through Science and Social Action." *Journal of the National Cancer Institute* 83: 1126–1127.

U.S. Bureau of the Census. 1990. *General Population Characteristics*. Washington, DC: U.S. Government Printing Office.

U.S. Department of Health, Education and Welfare. 1964. *Smoking and Health: Report of the Advisory Committee to the Surgeon General of the Public Health Service*. Washington, DC: U.S. Government Printing Office.

U.S. Department of Health and Human Services. 1986. *The Health Consequences of Involuntary Smoking. A Report of the Surgeon General*. Washington, DC: U.S. Government Printing Office.

U.S. Department of Health and Human Services. 1992. *Smoking and Health in the Americas. A 1992 Report of the Surgeon General, in Collaboration with the Pan American Health Organization*. Washington, DC: U.S. Government Printing Office.

Viscusi, W. Kip. 1992. *Smoking: Making the Risky Decision*. New York: Oxford University Press.

Zürcher, Louis A. Jr., and R. George Kirkpatrick. 1976. *Citizens for Decency: Antipornography Crusades as Status Defense*. Austin, TX: University of Texas Press.

17

Failure to Launch

Why Do Some Social Issues
Fail to Detonate Moral Panics?

PHILIP JENKINS

As we saw in the Part Introduction, moral panics are irrational overreactions to fears about deviance. Like moral entrepreneurial campaigns, we see here that moral panics can be analytically broken down into core, essential components. By considering a negative case, Jenkins sheds further light on what features of potential forms of deviance are likely to bloom into full-fledged panics. We are a society that is somewhat conflicted about fears of Internet sexuality. Conventional wisdom suggests that parents worry greatly about the sexual dangers of the Internet, yet Jenkins argues for the opposite view: there's more out there than meets the eye. What do you think of his argument that society lacks the technological expertise or depth understanding of Internet sexuality to adequately become scared about it?

How does the Reinarman chapter suggest that we are prone to moral panics, and how do his causes compare to the ideas suggested by Jenkins? How does his model of drug scares fit into Jenkins' theory of issues that are likely or unlikely to generate panics?

If only through frequent repetition, certain passages from sociological works acquire something like canonical status. One example would be Stan Cohen's famous declaration in 1972 that:

> Societies appear to be subject, every now and then, to periods of moral panic. A condition, episode, person, or group of persons emerges to become defined as a *threat to societal values* and interests; its nature is presented in a stylized and *stereotypical fashion* by the mass media; the moral barricades are manned by editors, bishops, politicians, and other right thinking people; socially accredited experts pronounce then diagnoses and solutions; ways of coping are evolved or (more often) resorted

to; the condition then *disappears, submerges or deteriorates* and becomes more visible. Sometimes the object of the panic is quite novel, and at other times it is something which has been in existence long enough, but suddenly appears in the limelight. (Cohen 2002:1)

Later studies have described such common themes as the novelty of a particular menace (real or imagined); its association with emerging social or scientific trends; its sudden explosive growth; and the menace it poses both to accepted moral standards, and to vulnerable groups and individuals. In the words of Stuart Hall *et al.*:

When the official reaction to a person, groups, of persons, or series of events is *out of all proportion* to the actual threat offered, when *'experts'*, in the form of police chiefs the judiciary, politicians, and editors perceive the threat in all but identical terms, and appear to talk 'with one voice' of rates, diagnoses, prognoses, and solutions, when the *media representations* universally stress 'sudden and dramatic' increases (in numbers involved or events) and 'novelty', above and beyond that which a sober, realistic appraisal could sustain, then we believe it is appropriate to speak of the beginning of a moral panic. (Hall et al. 1978, all emphases in the original)

After 35 years, we have become quite adept at tracing the emergence of panics, their later metastasis and their eventual fate. We spend far less time, though, on the non-construction of problems, of understanding why issues fail to generate panics, when they appear to fulfill all the classic criteria. Of course, we can understand how problems might be prioritized: society cannot panic about everything at once, and some issues must therefore take a subordinate role to others. But some issues just seem just so naturally tempting that it is difficult to understand their absence from centre-stage. By understanding why some issues do not generate panics, we are better able to predict which problems might or might not achieve prominence.

Throughout this process, too, we see some limitations of the original moral panic model, which was so exceptionally useful in its day in sparking novel approaches to social issues. Yet, for all its virtues, moral panic theory was always founded on a set of implicit value judgments, which assumed that the subject of analysis must, by definition, be somehow bogus or exaggerated—the result of hysterical exaggeration and ill-placed fears. Whoever heard of a *legitimate* panic, or of a *well founded* hysteria? There is something suspect about any form of analysis that begins by applying such a pejorative label. Moreover, case studies of moral panics tend to explore topics to which the researcher and his/her presumed audience often have an ideological vested interest in debunking or exposing. Given the left-liberal leanings prevailing in the academic world, whether in Europe or North America, one is not likely to see concern over "progressive" issues analyzed in terms of moral panic. "It seems virtually inconceivable that concern expressed about racial attacks, rape, or police misconduct would be described as a moral panic."

This inherit ideological bias explains why so much of the effort once de-voted to moral panic theory has subsequently evolved into what aspires to be the more objective realm of social constructionism. Using this approach, scholars examining a given social problem may or may not accept that the phenomenon exists, or, if it does, whether it is indeed harmful. The central question is how the condition comes to be viewed as a problem in the first place. For a constructionist, "our sense of what is or what is not a social problem is a product, something that has been produced or constructed through social activities" (Best 1995: 6). A con-structionist approach thus makes no initial assumptions about the legitimacy of the subject matter such as are implied by the word "panic." And, from a constructionist perspective, we can ideally understand the means by which problems are built and marketed, without assuming that their success or failure depends on irrational pub-lic terror. The understanding of social problems must rely primarily on analyzing the rhetorical work of claims-makers and their ability (or lack of it) to appeal to public tastes and prejudices, which may or may not be well founded

The issue of Internet child pornography offers one puzzling instance of the surprising lack of panic response. In 2001, I published the book *Beyond Tolerance*, which was based on an unusual kind of first-hand evidence, growing as it did out of several months' observation of the bulletin board traffic of sites used by major manufacturers and dealers. It thus involved a snapshot of major criminal activity as it was occurring, rather than as it might be reconstructed through the retroac-tive interpretations of incarcerated offenders. My book argued that the popular construction of child pornography was factually incorrect in more or less every detail. My skepticism applied to the conclusions presented by police agencies, whose evidence mainly derived from profiles of individuals arrested, but I also rejected the critical analysis of social theorists, who suggested that police and media had exaggerated the child-porn menace (Jenkins 2001).

Briefly, I argued that the online child-pornography trade was (and is) vastly larger in volume than claimed by either law enforcement, media, or critics, and that its scale swelled enormously during the 1990s. The material traded is also more current, in the sense of recent manufacture, and is not just recycled images from decades past. Also, a remarkable amount of the traffic is very hard-core in its nature, and does not just constitute harmless photos from nudist beaches. The process of manufacture involves actual abusive behavior in the present, not in the distant past.

We can illustrate this fact from the so-called KG and KX series—the "kindergarten" photos—which, as of 2000, represented perhaps the most prized collections available on the Internet. KG is a series of hundreds (maybe thousands) of nude images of very young girls, mainly aged between three and six years old, with each item including the girl's name, like Helga, Inga, and so on. The photo-graphs date from the mid-nineties, and they likely derive from either Germany or Scandinavia. In the words of one fan of the series, "Once upon a time, there was a chemist that had earned his Ph.D. Well, he got married and along with his wife opened up a day care center. Well, as the story goes, he managed to take pictures of lots and lots of things. Eventually he got busted." The KG collection exists in parallel with a still more sought-after version—KX—which depicts the same children in hard-core sexual situations with one or more men. Put simply, most are pictures of four and five-year-old girls performing oral sex and masturbation on adult men. The immense popularity of the KG images ensured an enthusiastic market for KX. Although such materials would now be very dated, presumably, their present-day successors still enjoy a comparably fanatical following. True aficionados own collections of images running into the hundreds of thousands, and the largest collection reported by police included 1.5 million.

Although the size of the trade is very difficult to estimate, we can make some plausible guesses. Putting the different trafficker/dealer bulletin boards together, I suggested that the core population as of 2000 should be counted somewhere in the range of perhaps 50,000 to 100,000 individuals, though that is a very loose figure. Within this number, we can find some figures who fit the folk-demon stereotype quite well, including serial molesters and powerful international dealers.

Matters have changed a little since I undertook my work, but not, I think, in any substantial way. Rather, the subculture has retreated from the absolutely open character it enjoyed in around 2000 and has now retreated behind quite tight security walls. Like every other aspect of the Internet, the subculture has also become much more technically sophisticated. The biggest single change has been in the growth of real-time action, where sexually explicit behavior involving minors can be witnessed live via webcams.

In many ways, then, I would suggest that Internet child porn has every qualification to become the basis of a moral panic. The underlying situation is large-scale, and can easily be portrayed as threatening, particularly as it affects children. It is also undergoing rapid expansion, as the Internet further extends its hegemony over global commerce and communication. Several other potent elements come to mind: the issue brings in the harmful effects of globalization, the undermining of national laws and sovereignty, while it offers all kinds of bonuses in terms of popular fears of technology. The issue also has obvious political implications, in exposing the exploitation of vulnerable children by sinister men—a theme that could appeal equally to feminists or to conservative law and order adherents. And the demon figures are ready and waiting.

Yet, the social response has been virtually nil. No bishops occupy the barricades and we have not heard much recently from any socially accredited experts. In the United States, congressional and legislative hearings come and go, but generate little media attention. Beyond the obvious point that Internet child porn is a bad thing, the U.S. media in particular pay little attention to the topic. Arrests are reported from time to time, sometimes involving hundreds of suspects, but rarely with any contextualization. The subject only attracts headlines when suspects are either celebrities or highly placed individuals. Although they are reported in duly horrifying terms, these potentially sensational cases provide no springboard for wider rhetoric. Most available books on the topic—and there are not many—tend to be sober works of academic criminology or psychology, usually from scholarly and professional-oriented presses. No genre of true crime accounts exists, and I can think of just a couple of passing fictional references in the past decade. No genre of films depicts heroic investigators hunting down child-porn rings or criminal overlords while rescuing pathetic victims. While I hesitate to suggest that nobody cares, at least we see nothing constituting moral panic.

Why? One major reason is technological. Most law-enforcement agencies work at a technological level that is simply too low to comprehend the trade as it actually existed a decade ago, and still less today. They have little idea of the nature of the trade, its complex world of concealment and deception through proxies and anonymizers, to say nothing of the more recent shift into P2P networks.

Popular accounts of child-porn arrests tend to give the impression that sophisticated law-enforcement agencies have somehow observed a person or group involved in child-porn activity, presumably by tracing or intercepting Internet traffic. That is wholly inaccurate, and such electronic interception is very rare indeed. Although police have broken some significant networks, most arrests in this area—especially in the United States—involve a person who has committed acts of molestation or abuse, leading to a search of his computer and the discovery of child-porn images. It is, in other words, quite difficult to be arrested for child-porn activity except insofar as this represents collateral activity arising from other crime. By far the largest breakthroughs in the campaign against child-porn networks have resulted from offenders committing flagrantly stupid acts, notably using their own credit cards to subscribe to online child-porn sites. When police do break such a major public operation, they thus have access to tens of thousands of suspects. This is what happened in the celebrated Operation Ore, when the investigation of a Texas-based business produced the names of thousands of customers around the world who had used their cards to access child-porn sites.

With this experience in mind, we may suggest some reasons that might cause an apparent social problem to abort before becoming a moral panic—a failure to launch. In this particular instance, reasons include:

1. *Lack of technological understanding.* The underlying problem involves a kind of technological activity that is beyond the capacity of law enforcement, legislators, or media. The technological shortcomings of law-enforcement agencies force them to interpret available data according to familiar forms of knowledge, rather than comprehending or publicizing new forms of deviant organization. Instead of representing a new form of deviant activity and organization, child pornography thus becomes an annex to the already known problem of child abuse, which has its own stereotypical features. Agencies thus fail to represent the distinctively new features of the nascent problem, and can provide no enlightenment or guidance to media or legislators.

2. *Comprehensive official control of an issue.* Within the U.S. especially, the child-porn issue is strictly within the hands of federal law-enforcement agencies who face no pressures, external or internal, to deliver a response more effective than what they are already offering. In fact, the institutional culture of these agencies actively discourages any effort at greater technological sophistication, as that would reveal the shortcomings of existing programs. Agents active in this field operate according to traditional paradigms of

hierarchical criminal organizations, and place the highest value on their ability to unravel such networks through intelligence gathering and skillful interrogation. None of these abilities has any particular relevance to the child-porn subculture.

This chasm between official expectations and the actual problem faced survives in consequence of:

1. *Lack of media access.* Child porn represents an unusual legal area, in which journalistic access to original material is entirely forbidden: within the United States, no journalistic exemption applies to very stringent federal laws, and "just looking" is not possible. Other countries enforce somewhat less strict rules, granting researchers some access under police supervision, but such licensing is granted very sparingly. It is not therefore possible for media to check independently on the nature or scale of illegal material, access to which is entirely controlled through law-enforcement gate-keepers. The kind of study that I was able to do in 1999–2000 is now impossible, as the bulletin boards are now strictly password-protected. The media exert no pressure to change this situation because of

2. *The invisibility of the problem.* Child-porn material exists within a relatively self-contained universe that the ordinary user cannot simply "stumble across." While accidental contact may occur, it does not suggest the real scale of the issue

3. *Preemption by other causes and interest groups.* Given the lack of appreciation of the child-porn world, the topic can be appropriated in symbolic forms by various pressure groups. Anti-pornography activists, for instance, use generalized concerns about children and the Internet to focus on the issue of children being exposed to pornographic materials online. Particularly given the lack of possible media activism in this area, no pressure can be generated to expose or combat the actual trade. Federal agencies speak mainly in terms of online seduction or pedophiles stalking victims via computers—an area in which police can hope to achieve results. In consequence, the larger problem is merged with other issues, including *cyberstalking,* or predatory individuals who seek to contact and seduce children online; *cyberporn,* or children gaining electronic access to adult pornographic materials; and *child pornography,* or the distribution of obscene or indecent images of under-aged subjects. Serious child-pornography trafficking is thus ignored and the problem left unconstructed.

If, then, we are seeking the reasons whey the child-porn panic never occurred, we would need primarily to understand the legal and bureaucratic environment, and the means by which news is gathered, processed, and interpreted. If *claims-makers* are absent or few in number, if their understanding of the issue is flawed or limited, then even such a tempting topic will largely escape public gaze.

The Ideal Panic

A particular sensational episode might make the headlines for a few days but, in order to achieve the status of fully fledged moral panic, it must gain the kind of traction that is only possible when mass media collaborate with agencies or political interests. And, even then, the panic can only move forward if it meets certain criteria. Several factors are conductive to the creation of panic conditions:

- A diversity of *agencies and interest groups* must exist, from which the media can draw and which can make rival claims. Ideally, each should have some degree of public prestige and media access. Panics are most likely to flourish and escalate when their subject matter is contested between competing forces.

- The *story must be comprehensible* to agencies and journalists themselves before it can be repackaged for the general public.

- The issue must be sufficiently *overt and accessible* that ordinary consumers will have some chance of encountering what they believe to be its manifestations.

- The panic should offer a *narrative*, with characters who are easily understood: heroes and villains must have identifiable faces.

- The story should lend itself to *visual portrayal*. There should be some standard faces or settings that can be used as stereotypical points of reference. Examples might include the scene of gang fights, drug supermarkets, and the faces of serial killers.

- The narrative must also have an *outcome*, in that solutions, plausible or otherwise, must be identified.

- For consumers, the narrative will have maximum impact if it meshes with *previous expectations and knowledge*, often because earlier movements and controversies have laid the foundations for later explosions.

But, as we have seen, certain limitations constrain the free development of panic conditions: these limitations might involve either the supply of official information and interpretation designed to promote concern or an absence of demand from the likely consumers:

- If the problem is the preserve of one particular agency, the ensuing lack of competition restricts the opportunities for a panic response.

- Agencies might be unable themselves to understand the issue, to fit it into their intellectual framework. This might involve gaps in technological understanding or inability to understand forms of deviant organization.

- If agency experts do not themselves understand the issue, they are unable to put it in terms that lend themselves to discussion in briefing papers or executive summaries. Over-complex narratives do not lend themselves to successful panic building.

- The likely trajectory of an issue might be politically embarrassing, with for an agency or powerful interest groups that could bring pressure to bear upon it.

- In the absence of official stimulus to concern, a panic is unlikely to result over issues that ordinary consumers have little change of encountering directly or that they do not perceive as an immediate threat.

- If some or all of these limiting factors are present, then such public responses as do occur fall short of a full-scale panic. Media responses will commonly ignore the meaty core issues, while exploiting fringe or marginal aspects of the problem.

In summary, small villains are much more fertile sources of moral panics than large or well-connected ones.

I have stressed the capacity to understand and summarize social issues as a limiting factor in shaping panics. If that is correct, we should over the coming years see an ever-greater disconnect between the most significant social issues and those that attract the most public attention. As social issues focus more on scientific areas that demand substantial background—in information technology and biotechnology, to name just two—it will be interesting to see how interest groups create problems that touch on public fears but, in the most tangential ways, rarely touch on the substantive issues. The gap between scientific reality and panic image seems destined to grow dramatically.

REFERENCES

Hall, S., C. Gritcher, T. Jefferson, J. Clarke, and Roberts. (1978). *Policing the Crisis: Mugging, the State and Law and Order.* London: Macmillan.

Jenkins, P. (1999), "Fighting Terrorism as if Women Mattered: Anti-Abortion Violence as Unconstructed Terrorism"

in J. Ferrell and N. Websdale, eds. *Making Trouble: Cultural Constructions of Crime, Deviance and Control*, 319–46. Hawthorne, NY: Aldine Dc Gruyter.

Beyond Tolerance: Child Pornography Online, New York: University Press.

18

Gender, Race, and Urban Policing

ROD K. BRUNSON AND JODY MILLER

Beyond moral entrepreneurial campaigns, a range of social factors affect the like-lihood of different groups in society being defined as deviant and having defini-tions of deviance enforced against them. Brunson and Miller look at three demographic variables, race, sex, and age, to see the way groups of people are treated differently by agents of social control. If you've not lived in poor neigh-borhoods of color, you may not be aware of the routine ways police interact with and harass young men and women there. Drawing on conflict theory, we see here how deviant status is used by the police to subordinate less powerful groups.

How valid do you find the complaints of these young men and women? How do you think the way police officers treat them affects their communities? Their behavior? How does it affect men and women differently?

Law enforcement strategies in poor urban communities produce a range of harms to African American residents. These include disproportionate experiences with surveillance and stops, disrespectful treatment, excessive force, police deviance, and fewer police protections. Attempts to explain these patterns examine how young Black men come to symbolize the stereotypical offender and have drawn from minority group threat theories and social ecological models. However, few studies have considered how gender intersects with race and neighborhood context in determining how police behaviors are experienced. It is taken for granted that young minority *men* are the primary targets of negative police experiences.

Feminist scholars suggest that young Black women are far from immune from negative experiences with the justice system. Girls are more likely than boys to experience juvenile justice interventions for relatively minor offenses, and African American women and girls receive more punitive treatment than their white counterparts. Moreover, research suggests that Black women crime victims are less likely than white women to receive police assistance.

From Rod K. Brunson and Jody Miller, "Gender, Race, and Urban Policing," *Gender and Society*. Copyright © 2006. Reprinted by permission of Sage Publications.

While feminist research has illuminated how formal aspects of the justice system adversely affect Black women and girls, we know less about their experiences with the police, including discretionary police activities in their neighborhoods. Officers' ability to use discretion is a low-visibility but defining feature of policing, and the process through which many racially biased practices emerge. In general, criminological investigations of minority citizens' experiences with the police have focused on adults rather than adolescents, and this work is based largely on survey research or official data on citizen complaints. Few studies have drawn from in-depth interviews, which allow a deeper understanding of the context of events and their meanings for the individuals involved.

We analyze in-depth interviews with African American youths in a poor urban community to investigate how gender shapes their interactions with and perceptions of the police. We compare young women's and young men's accounts of their personal experiences with the police, their understanding of neighborhood policing, and their knowledge of police misconduct in their communities. Our comparative analysis allows us to examine how gender intersects with race and place in shaping youths' expectations of law enforcement and the nature of police/youth interactions.

METHOD

This investigation is based on survey and in-depth interviews with 75 African American youths living in St. Louis, Missouri. The sample includes 35 young women and 40 young men. They range in age from 12 to 19, with a mean age of approximately 16 for both genders. Interviewing began in spring 1999 and was completed in the spring of 2000. Interviews were voluntary and typically lasted about one and a half hours. Youths were paid $20 for their participation and promised strict confidentiality. Pseudonyms are used throughout for research participants and the streets they occasionally reference.

Youths were recruited into the project with the cooperation of several organizations working with "at-risk" and delinquent youths, including a local community agency and two alternative public high schools. Approximately equal numbers of young men and women were drawn from each location. The community agency was a neighborhood drop-in center for adolescents in north St. Louis. The second author volunteered at the center the summer prior to data collection. The two alternative schools served youths expelled from St. Louis public schools for a variety of infractions. The counselor at each school identified youths for study participation when they were known to reside in disadvantaged neighborhoods in the city. Interviews were conducted in a private office or empty classroom at each of the research sites.

We narrow our focus to urban Black adolescents because they are the group for whom involuntary police contacts are most frequent and salient. Sampling was purposive in nature. Our inclusion of young women and young men permits us to examine how gender shapes youths' experiences with and perceptions of the police. In addition, we sought to compare youths involved in serious delinquency—whom we would reasonably expect to have more involuntary police contact—with those who were not.

In all, 16 of the 40 young men and 15 of the 35 young women reported participating in serious delinquency in the past six months. Serious delinquency included the following self-report items: stealing more than $50, stealing a motor vehicle, attacking someone with a weapon or with the intent to seriously hurt them, committing a robbery, and selling marijuana, crack-cocaine, or other drugs. On the other hand, all of the youths reported having engaged in minor forms of delinquency, including skipping classes, being loud or rowdy in public, avoiding paying for things, stealing $5 or less, lying about their age to get into someplace or buy something, or running away. Research suggests that girls are more likely than boys to face juvenile justice interventions for such minor offenses. Thus, our sample captured variations in delinquent involvement.

STUDY SETTING

St. Louis is a highly distressed U.S. city with large concentrations of extreme poverty that result in social isolation, limited resources, and high crime rates. Table 18.1 compares youths' neighborhoods, St. Louis city and county. Study participants were drawn from neighborhoods characterized by racial segregation and high rates of poverty, unemployment, and female-headed families.

Youths provided a stark account of how these statistics translate into lived experience. Asked to describe her neighborhood, Cleshay explained,

> [It's terrible. Every man for theyself. Ghetto, in the sense of raggedy, people uncool to people, just outside, street light never come on, police don't come in after four o'clock.... Heavy drug dealing. They loud, they don't care about, you know, the old people in the neighborhood or nuttin'.

Likewise, Maurice explained,

> [There's] a lot of gangs, lot of drugs, dirt. Dirty, like the streets are polluted. A lot of abandoned houses, lot of burned up houses. 'Cause of the drugs and the gangs I guess Vandalism. They get into a lot of fights.

TABLE 18.1   Select Neighborhood Characteristics (in Percentages)

	Youths' Neighborhoods	St. Louis City	St. Louis County
African American	82.6	51.2	18.9
Poverty	33.8	24.6	6.9
Unemployment	18.0	11.3	4.6
Female-Headed Families with Children	43.1	28.8	10.7

SOURCE: U.S. Census (2000; see http://www.census.gov/).

Bring property value down, you know, people don't take care of they houses. And you know, don't nobody really wanna live there.

Many youths said their neighborhoods were physically run-down, and most described drug dealing, street gangs, and associated violence as commonplace. Moreover, youths saw their own neighborhoods as typical of the surrounding community. Asked how her neighborhood compared to others nearby, Tisha surmised, "It's not different at all. They all do the same thing." Raymond noted, "In every neighborhood there's drug activity and gang activity." And Tami explained, "It's mostly every neighborhood got drug dealers in they neighborhood. Or people that be shootin' and stuff".

These descriptions are consistent with scholarly research, which demonstrates that poor African American neighborhoods tend to be ecologically clustered and lacking in institutional resources necessary to insulate them from crime. In fact, even when youths described their immediate blocks as relatively problem free (which they attributed to having primarily older adults or young children present), they nonetheless described gangs, drugs, and violence nearby.

These are precisely the ecological contexts associated with aggressive policing, police deviance, and underpolicing. Policing strategies in respondents' neighborhoods relied heavily on proactive encounters to address problems such as drugs and gangs. This involved frequent pedestrian and vehicle stops by patrol officers, detectives, and members of specialized units. To examine these issues further, we now turn to youths' narrative accounts of their experiences with the police, focusing on similarities and differences across gender.

THE EXPERIENCE OF AFRICAN-AMERICAN YOUTH

The survey reports offer evidence of the gendered nature of policing in urban Black neighborhoods. Table 18.2 shows that most youths knew someone who had been harassed by the police, including 37 young men and 33 young women.

T A B L E 18.2 Perceptions of Neighborhood Policing

	Young Men (n = 40)	Young Women (n = 35)
Harassed or mistreated by the police	33	16
Knows someone who has been harassed or mistreated by the police	37	30
"The police are often easy to talk to"	5	5
"The police are almost never easy to talk to"	26	19
"The police are often polite to people in the neighborhood"	4	2
"The police often harass or mistreat people in the neighborhood"	19	18

However, young men more often reported being mistreated themselves. In all, 33 young men, versus 16 young women, described experiencing police harassment. In addition, young men reported harassment regardless of their participation in delinquency, while more of the young women we interviewed reported harassment when they were involved in delinquency. Specifically, 19 of the 24 young men who did not engage in serious delinquency nonetheless said they had been harassed by the police, compared to 6 of 20 young women. The majority of young men (14 of 16) and young women (10 of 15) who reported participation in serious delinquency also noted experiences with police harassment.

Youths' responses to survey items about how the police behave in their neighborhoods were consistent across gender. As Table 18.2 shows, similar numbers of young men and women described the police as impolite and difficult to talk to, and about half said the police often harass and mistreat people in their neighborhoods. In fact, only about one in five youths said this almost never occurs. These survey findings corroborate youths' in-depth interview accounts of their treatment by the police, the extent and nature of police harassment in their neighborhoods, and their beliefs about how gender shapes police/youth interactions.

Youths described frequent pedestrian and vehicle stops as the primary policing strategy in their neighborhoods. Their accounts of police harassment emphasized how the police behaved during such stops. Cherise explained, "I don't like police 'cause they mean. They don't know how to talk to people right, they disrespectful. They treat people like they ain't nothing, and especially Black people. They act like Black people are worthless." However, many youth suggested that severe police behaviors were typically reserved for young men. Destiny remarked, "It's little stuff they be sayin' to us [girls], but like with the dudes, they'll try to lock them up and try to take them to jail." Tommie noted,

> The police will mess with the males quicker than the females. If it's a group of girls standing across the street and it's a group of dudes standing across the street, [the police] fina [getting ready to] shine they lights on the dudes and they ain't fina mess with the girls.

Tommie also suggested that the police were somewhat less aggressive when young men were stopped in the company of women: "You alright if you with your momma, your girlfriend, then that's a different story, [with] your kids or something.... They'll still bother you, but they won't look at you like that. [Their behavior] wouldn't be different [but] they'd hesitate.' Wayne believed that the police posed one of the primary dangers for young men in his neighborhood: "I would say males are in more danger [than females]' cause you gotta deal with police. All police ain't good police. You ain't even gotta be doing nothing. If they think you doing something, they get out [of their cars. If] they can't catch you, next time they see you, they put something on you." Nonetheless, young women were not immune from negative encounters. Janelle clarified, "The police harass the guys a little bit more than the girls, but there's always certain females that they'll pick to harass." Next we examine these patterns in detail.

Young Men and the Police

Young men's discussions focused on their frequent involuntary contact with the police. They believed that the police besieged their neighborhoods because officers believed that many of the people living there, particularly young Black men, were criminals. Ricky described how hanging out on the street attracted police attention, regardless of whether anyone was involved in crime:

> Two blocks up from me it's like a lil' heroin area. The police is *real* hot on this area now.... One day I was walkin' from over there and the police.... seen me standing out over there. I mean, they know I don't sell dope, they know I go to school every day.... Everybody don't got to be doing the same thing. This what I tried to explain to them: "Just 'cause I'm out here don't mean I sell dope, man. I mean, every time you check me [I'm clean]." I mean I don't even carry money no more.... How am I sellin' dope and I don't never have no money in my pocket? Check my shoes, make me take my socks off. Man it's cold outside. "Pull your pants down."... All types of stuff, man, and it's freezin' outside. Make you lay on the ground. To me, that's police brutality.

Such searches were also described as **physically intrusive,** with numerous complaints about the police "trying to put they hands all in your mouth."

Young men believed the police sought to **limit their use of public space** by designating neighborhood locations as crime hot spots. Shaun noted, "They a trip, we be sitting on the front [porch] or something, they'll pull up just' cause we sitting there. Or we be chillin' in front of the store, [they] get out checking everybody.' Terence observed,

> On certain days, [police] might do a sweep through the neighborhood. They'll come in like, three or four cars deep, two paddy wagons, and they'll just roll down every block that they think mainly sellin' drugs or whatever. And anybody outside, if they think you got something, they gon' check you. Just everybody that happen to be on the block. If you look like you got something or look like you fina do something—so they say—then they just come up to you, tell you to assume the position or whatever. Put your hands on the hood, check you ... talk bad to you for a lil' minute and then tell you to go on about your business.

Young men believed officers failed to consider that designated crime hot spots might also be places where law-abiding youths gather. Because pedestrian stops seemed arbitrary, they questioned whether the police were really concerned with addressing neighborhood crime or were merely interested in harassing them. Darnell commented, "Police over there by me, they stop you just to mess with you for real.... Sometimes they'll pull up and be like, 'get that damn crack out your mouth boy!' and keep going."

While they understood that certain contexts might subject them to increased suspicion, young men nonetheless found it **prejudicial**. They believed officers viewed them as criminals because they were young Black men living in poor neighborhoods. Jamal commented, "[Police] feel that if you have fancy clothes or you have a lot [of] money, you selling drugs. They can't see a Black male these days having a good job. They always want to pull you over or search you.'

Young men were especially frustrated when stops occurred in situations they believed warranted no suspicion. Several described being stopped on their way to school. Eugene explained,

> I was going to school one time and a cop just swerved, pulled up on me. I'm like, "Whoa, what's up?" He said I fit a description of some dude that robbed a store. So I'm like, "Robbed a store where?" He's like, "Way on the southside." I am like, "I'm on the northside so that don't got nothin' to do with me." And then they ... put my hands on the car, you know, frisked me, asked me did I have any weapons or narcotics. I was like, "No." He said, "Where you going?" I'm like, "I'm going to school" and stuff, you know. And then people across the street lookin'. They like, "Dang, why they stop you?" I'm like, "I don't know."

An additional frustration was officers' refusal to acknowledge young men's innocence, even when no evidence was found. Instead, they were described as expressing that young men merely "got lucky this time."

Finally, young men were critical of officers' routine use of *antagonistic language,* derogatory remarks, and racial epithets. Cooper commented, "They need to change the way they talk to people.... They show us no respect ... [call us] niggers and all that." Ricky concurred: "They'll talk bad, call you all types of punks and sissies, and say you don't wanna be nothing and you ain't gon' be nothing.' Tony described whistling to a friend when a passing officer "told me, 'Shut up whistling, you Black monkey!" Thus, young men's complaints about police harassment were not just about routinely being stopped and treated as suspects but were tied to their sense that officers refused to treat them with dignity and respect.

Young Women and the Police

Young women's descriptions of police harassment differed from young men's. Their most common complaint, particularly when alone or in the company of other girls, was being stopped for *curfew violations.* Katie explained:

> On weekends we can be out 'til twelve, but long as you sittin' on your front or close by your house. But if you like outside our gate or in the street or something the police, they be like, ... If we ride past again then we're gonna lock you all up ... or whatever... We just sittin' outside the house there, I don't know why they always messin' with us.

Kristy observed, "Police be harassing you constantly. I mean, if they not trying to get you for truancy, [they] trying to get you for curfew." She described a recent encounter:

> It was like eleven o'clock at night. I was getting off the Lake Street bus. I walked down the street, police put their high beams on me, they was

like, Where you going?' And I'm like, Man, I'm going home, leave me alone.' They was like, Don't talk to us like that, we the police, we deserve respect, we here to protect y'all.' [I'm] like, 'Man, y'all ain't doin nuttin' but bothering me.

Once Kristy challenged the officers, the situation escalated:

They was like, 'I heard you fit a description, assume the position.' Like hands on the wall, hands behind your head. I'm like, 'I ain't doin' nuttin'.' They like, You must want us to put your little black ass in jail.' ... [I was like], 'Just let me go home, that's all I'm trying to do, I got school in the morning.' ... They was like, 'Well fuck her, we got better things to do.' So they let me go. I walked home mad as a dog.

After Kristy challenged the police, they **treated her as a criminal suspect.** Up until that point, however, they appeared to be concerned that she was out past curfew. This differed from young men's accounts: They described being treated as suspects from the onset of their encounters with the police. In addition, whereas young men described being stopped throughout the day, young women described being stopped mostly at night. That they were stopped for curfew violations confirms research suggesting that the police intervene on girls for minor or status offenses. Despite the police's initially telling Kristy that they were "there to protect y' all," young women believed such stops had little to do with genuine concern about their well-being.

LaSondra, who had been sexually assaulted in her neighborhood, illustrates the tension for young women between concern over how the police treat people and the **desire for protection** from neighborhood dangers:

[The police] just pull people over for no reason at all. Sometimes they just check people, see if they got sonic drugs. It could be the innocent person on the block they just pull 'em over and just start checking 'em.... It's messed up. They'll yell at 'em too for no reason you know.... Sometimes the police, they just sit on the block and they just watch the block and stuff.... But over there you have to watch. Especially when you walking or something 'cause you never know who might be behind you.

Although the police came to the hospital after LaSondra's sexual assault, she felt they were not responsive. Asked why, she explained, "Police don't do nothing. Some of 'em just give up. They could care less."

In the survey, only four girls (vs. nine boys) described the police as responding quickly to calls for service. Several girls described calling the police when a woman was victimized but reported they did not come. Jamellah saw a woman robbed and beaten near her home and brought the victim in her house to call the police: "[They] ain't never come.... We waited like 30 minutes and they ain't never show. So I waited at the bus stop with her ... and she caught the bus home.' Rennesha's parents called the police after a neighboring child asked for help because her stepfather was beating her mother. Rennesha explained, "The lil' girl looked so sorry. But the police never did come."

Complaints about police responsiveness emerged primarily in interviews with young women and centered on incidents of *violence against women.* This may be because such events are more likely to result in calls for service; thus, negative outcomes are more apparent. Or it may be that the police are less responsive to such calls because they do not fit neatly into the urban crime-fighting mission. Either way, the young women who were interviewed expected the police to come to the aid of crime victims, particularly women. Their frustration with the police in their neighborhoods stemmed both from negative interactions and from the lack of responsiveness toward crime victims. Jamelle surmised, "I feel the police are there to protect and serve you, not to harass you for no reason."

Young women reported being *treated as suspects* in two contexts: when they were in the company of young men and when they were involved in offending. Most often, they described being stopped while passengers in vehicles driven by young Black men. In the company of young men, girls became suspects as well. Youths believed that vehicle stops occurred under the guise of enforcing traffic laws, but their true purpose was to search for weapons and drugs. Felicia's example is illustrative:

> We was coming from the riverfront and we went to Taco Bell to get something to eat, and [the police] had followed us … and they pulled us over…. [The officer] was like, "Do you have any warrants? Is there any illegal substances or any drugs in the car?" and we was like, "No, not that we know of." He was like, "Well, can everybody step out of the car?" So we asked him, why did we need to step out the car? He said, "Don't worry about it, just get out of the car."… There was two male police officers. They searched everybody, even us girls.

When the search failed to produce contraband, Felicia said the officer issued a series of tickets for minor infractions, including not wearing their seatbelts, having windows that were "too tinted:' and playing the radio too loud. Felicia noted, "Everything came out clear [the driver's] insurance, his registration, his license, no warrants so [the officer] got mad. He got to going off, he got to writing up tickets, just writing 'em up:' She continued:

> I felt they was wrong. In one sense they was wrong 'cause they searched us and we women. They should've called a female officer to search us if they felt that we needed to be searched. I felt there wasn't no need for everybody to get out of the car. Wasn't no need for him slamming they heads into the car. Wasn't no need for all that. The boy gave you everything you asked for. He didn't talk back, he didn't get loud, he wasn't disrespectful. You got mad 'cause all his stuff was legit so you feel like if you can't get him on nothing in his car then you can write tickets on whatever come into your mind and that's what he did…. [Even for] not using his blinker to pull over when he flagged 'im.

Although the surveys indicated that most of the young women stopped by the police were involved in serious delinquency, Destiny and Janelle provided the only accounts that connected police behaviors to their delinquency. Perhaps delinquent girls spend more time on the streets than other girls, and this presence accounts for their greater likelihood of being stopped. However, their descriptions suggest that they tend to be stopped for minor offenses like curfew and truancy rather than for their participation in crime.

Destiny's and Janelle's descriptions parallel those provided by young men. Although atypical for girls, such incidents were routine for young men, regardless of their criminal activities. For boys, simply being in public spaces was sufficient to warrant suspicion. In addition, through shifts in pronoun usage, Destiny distinguished between her treatment and that received by the young men: The police talked poorly to "us:' but beat on and arrested "them." This also resonates with Felicia's complaints: She was upset about being searched by male officers but described the officers slamming the young men's heads into the car.

DISCUSSION

Research on race and policing is often inattentive to gender and rarely considers the perspectives of minority citizens. Feminist scholars insist, however, that minority standpoints are a vital aspect of sociological knowledge building and that discriminatory practices can best be understood by examining the cross cutting nature of gender and racial inequalities (Collins 1990). With these insights in mind, we described urban African American youths' accounts of their interactions with the police, comparing young women's and young men's experiences with and perceptions of policing in their neighborhoods. Our research offers compelling evidence that the aggressive policing strategies used in urban poor neighborhoods pose harms to their adolescent residents and that these harms are shaped by gender.

In keeping with previous research, we found that young men were the disproportionate recipients of aggressive policing tactics such as stops and searches. Youths characterized such incidents as harassment because of their intrusive and antagonistic nature. While both young men and young women said such incidents were routine in their neighborhoods, they also distinguished them as gendered. They believed young Black men were burdened by a presumption of guilt that served as justification for aggressive police behavior.

Girls' accounts most closely paralleled those of boys when they were in young men's company and thus tainted by the suspicion applied to young men. In addition, girls who reported participating in serious delinquency described being stopped by the police. Ironically, though, they were typically stopped for curfew or truancy violations rather than for their involvement in criminal offenses. There were also notable temporal differences across gender. Young women often described being stopped at night. Young men, however, were treated as "out of place" in public spaces, regardless of the time of day.

The presence of young Black men in neighborhoods seemed to symbolize criminal wrongdoing, while definitions of femininity deny young women access to public spaces after dark.

Finally, youths' experiences with police violence were deeply gendered as well. With few exceptions, young men faced more severe violence at the hands of the police, and youths were deeply troubled by the frequency of such incidents in their neighborhoods. Perhaps as a consequence, young women often challenged officers who they believed were conducting themselves improperly. Our findings suggest that young women may do so more than men because they believe such challenges will not be met with physical aggression. In fact, Mastrofski, Snipes, and Supina (1996, 276) argue that women may be "more likely to resist compliance ... in anticipation of greater police tolerance."

African American youths provide vital knowledge about how they experience policing in their neighborhoods and its effects on police/community relations. In addition, they reveal police practices as deeply gendered. Our study contributes to research on race, gender, and policing by offering further evidence of the differential harms experienced by African American girls and boys within the juvenile justice system—in this case, with a focus on events beyond the scope of formal intervention. Future research on discriminatory policing will benefit from more systematic attention to the intersections of race, place, and gender.

REFERENCES

Ferguson, A. A. 2001. *Bad boys: Public schools in the making of Black masculinity.* Ann Arbor: University of Michigan Press.

Fine, M., N. Freudenberg, Y. Payne, T. Perkins, K. Smith, and K. Wanzer. 2003. "Anything can happen with police around: Urban youth evaluate strategies of surveillance in public places." *Journal of Social Issues* 59:141–58.

Mastrofski, S. D., J. B. Snipes, and A. E. Supina. 1996. "Compliance on demand." *Journal of Research in Crime and Delinquency* 33:269–305.

19

Homophobia and Women's Sport

ELAINE M. BLINDE AND DIANE E. TAUB

Blinde and Taub explore the role of attributed sexual orientation in disempowering women who violate gender norms: varsity female collegiate athletes. By challenging the gender order and opposing male domination, these women intrude into a traditional male sanctum and threaten the male domain of physicality and strength. By casting the lesbian label on women athletes, society stigmatizes them as masculine and as sexual perverts. While the homosexual label is routinely used to degrade male athletes who fail to live up to the hypermasculine ideal, the lesbian label is used to divide and silence female athletes. They may adopt the perspective of their oppressors and demean their teammates as lesbians, thus destroying team solidarity, and/or shun the label, but be forced to acknowledge its demeaning power as they attempt to escape it. The forceful effect of the lesbian label applied to women athletes shows the dominance not only of heterosexuals over homosexuals, but of men over women.

Why do you think the women athletes in this article passively accept the stigma cast onto them? What factors lead some stigmatized groups to fight their social labels, while others accept these and hide their deviance?

Central to the preservation of a patriarchal and heterosexist society is a well-established gender order with clearly defined norms and sanctions governing the behavior of men and women. This normative gender system is relayed to and installed in members of society through a pervasive socialization network that is evident in both everyday social interaction and social institutions (Schur 1984). Conformity to established gender norms contributes to the reproduction of male dominance and heterosexual privilege (Lenskyj 1991; Stockard and Johnson 1980).

Despite gender role socialization, not all individuals engage in behavior consistent with gender expectations. Recognizing the potential threat of such aberrations, various mechanisms exist that encourage compliance with the normative gender order. Significant in such processes are the stigmatization and devaluation of those whose behavior deviates from the norm (Schur 1984).

From Elaine M. Blinde and Diane E. Taub, "Homophobia and Women's Sport: The Disempowerment of Athletes." *Sociological Focus, the Journal of the North Central Sociological Association*, Vol. 25, No. 2, May 1992. Reprinted by permission of the North Central Sociological Association.

Women's violation of traditional gender role norms represents a particularly serious threat to the patriarchal and heterosexist society because this deviant behavior resists women's subordinate status (Schur 1984). When women engage in behavior that challenges the established gender order, and thus opposes male domination, attempts are often made by those most threatened to devalue these women and ultimately control their actions. One means of discrediting women who violate gender norms and thereby questioning their "womanhood" is to label them lesbian (Griffin 1987).

The accusation of lesbianism is a powerful controlling mechanism given the homophobia that exists within American society. Homophobia, representing a fear of or negative reaction to homosexuality (Pharr 1988), results in stigmatization directed at those assumed to violate sexuality norms. Lesbianism, in particular, is viewed as threatening to the established patriarchal order and heterosexual family structure since lesbians reject their "natural" gender role, as well as resist economic, emotional, and sexual dependence on men (Gartrell 1984; Lenskyj 1991).

As a means for both discouraging homosexuality and maintaining a patriarchal and heterosexist gender order (Pharr 1988), homophobia controls behavior through contempt for purported norm violators (Koedt, Levine, and Rapone 1973). One method of control is the frequent application of the lesbian label to women who move into traditional male-dominated fields such as politics, business, or the military (Lenskyj 1991). This "lesbian baiting" (Pharr 1988:19) suggests that women's advancement into these arenas is inappropriate. Such messages are particularly potent since they are lodged in a society that condemns, devalues, oppresses, and victimizes individuals labeled as homosexuals (Lenskyj 1990).

Another male arena in which women have made significant strides, and thus risk damaging accusation and innuendo, is that of sport (Blinde and Taub 1992; Lenskyj 1990). Sport is a particularly susceptible arena for lesbian labeling due to the historical linkage of masculinity with athleticism (Birrell 1988). When women enter the domain of sport they are viewed as violating the docile female gender role and therefore extending culturally constructed boundaries of femininity (Cobban 1982; Lenskyj 1986; Watson 1987). The attribution of masculine qualities to women who participate in sport leads to a questioning of their sexuality and subsequently makes athletes targets of homophobic accusations (Lenskyj 1986)....

Therefore, the present study explores the stereotyping of women athletes as lesbians and the accompanying homophobia fostering this label. General themes and processes which inform us of how these individuals handle the lesbian issue are identified. These dynamics are grounded in the contextual experiences of women athletes and relayed through their voices.

Athletic directors at seven large Division I universities were contacted by telephone and asked to participate in a study examining various aspects of the sport experience of female college athletes. These administrators were requested to provide a list of the names and addresses of all varsity women athletes for the purpose of contacting them for telephone interviews.... Interested athletes were encouraged to return an informed consent form indicating their willingness to participate in a tape-recorded telephone interview. Based on this initial contact, a total of 16 athletes agreed to be in the study.

In order to increase the sample size to the desired 20 to 30 respondents, the names of 30 additional athletes were randomly and proportionately selected from the three lists. Eight of these athletes agreed to be interviewed, resulting in a final sample size of 24. Athletes in the sample were currently participating in a variety of women's intercollegiate varsity sports—basketball (n = 5), track and field (n = 4), volleyball (n = 3), swimming (n = 3), softball (n = 3), tennis (n = 2), diving (n = 2), and gymnastics (n = 2). With an average age of 20.2 years and overwhelmingly Caucasian (92%), the sample contained 2 freshmen, 9 sophomores, 5 juniors, and 8 seniors. A majority of the athletes (n = 22) were recipients of an athletic scholarship....

Semistructured telephone interviews were conducted by two trained female interviewers. All interviews were tape-recorded and lasted from 50 to 90 minutes. Questions were open-ended in nature so that athletes would not feel constrained in discussing those issues most relevant to their experiences. Follow-up questions were utilized to probe how societal perceptions of women athletes impact their behavior and experiences.

RESULTS

Examination of the responses of athletes revealed two prevailing themes related to the presence of the lesbian stereotype in women's sport—(a) a silence surrounding the issue of lesbianism in women's sport, and (b) athletes' internalization of societal stereotypes concerning lesbians and women athletes. It is suggested that these two processes disempower women athletes and thus are counterproductive to the self-actualizing capability of sport participation (Theberge 1987).

Silence Surrounding Lesbianism in Women's Sport

One of the most pervasive themes throughout the interviews related to the general silence associated with the lesbian stereotype in women's sport. Although a topic of which athletes are cognizant, reluctance to discuss and address lesbianism in women's sport was evident. Based on the responses of athletes, this silence was manifested in several ways: (a) athletes' difficulty in discussing lesbian topic, (b) viewing lesbianism as a personal and irrelevant issue, (c) disguising athletic identity to avoid lesbian label, (d) team difficulty in addressing lesbian issue, and (e) administrative difficulty in addressing lesbian issue.

Athletes' Difficulty in Discussing Lesbian Topic

Initial indication of silencing was illustrated by the difficulty and uneasiness many athletes experienced in discussing the lesbian stereotype. Some respondents were initially reluctant to mention the topic of lesbianism; discussion of the issue was frequently preceded by awkward or long pauses suggesting feelings of uneasiness or discomfort. Athletes were most likely to introduce this topic when questions were asked about societal perceptions of women's sport and female athletes, as well as inquiries about the existence of stereotypes associated with women athletes. Moreover, the lesbian issue was sometimes discussed without specifically using the term lesbian. For example, some athletes evaded the issue by making indirect references to lesbianism (e.g., using the word "it" rather than a more descriptive term)....

Respondents' approach to the topic of lesbianism indicates the degree to which women athletes have been socialized into a cycle of silence. Such silence highlights the suppressing effects of homophobia. Moreover, athletes' reluctance to discuss topics openly related to lesbianism may be to avoid what Goffman (1963) has termed "courtesy stigma," a stigma conferred despite the absence of usual qualifying behavior.

Viewing Lesbianism as a Personal and Irrelevant Issue

A second indicator of the silence surrounding the lesbian stereotype was reflected in athletes' general comments about lesbianism. Many respondents indicated that sexual orientation was a very personal issue and thus represented a private and extraneous aspect of an individual's life. These athletes felt it was inappropriate for others to be concerned about the sexual orientation of women athletes.

Although such a manifestation of silence might reflect the path of least resistance by relieving athletes of the need to discuss or disclose their sexual orientation (Lenskyj 1991), it does not eliminate the stigma and stress experienced by women athletes. Also, making lesbianism a private issue does not confront or challenge the underlying homophobia that allows the label to carry such significance. The strategy of making sexual orientation a personal issue depoliticizes lesbianism and ignores broader societal issues.

Disguising Athletic Identity to Avoid Lesbian Label

A third form of silence surrounding the lesbian stereotype was the tendency for athletes to hide their athletic identities. Nearly all respondents indicated that despite feeling pride in being an athlete, there were situations where they preferred that others not know their athletic identity. Although not all athletes indicated that this concealment was to prevent being labeled a lesbian, it was obvious that there was a perceived stigma associated with athletics that many women wanted to avoid (e.g., masculine women, women trying to be men, jock image). In most cases, respondents indicated that disguising their athletic identity was either directly or indirectly related to the lesbian stereotype....

Athletes also stated that they (or other athletes they knew) accentuated certain behaviors in order to reduce the possibility of being labeled a lesbian. Being seen with men, having a boyfriend, or even being sexually promiscuous with men were commonly identified strategies to reaffirm an athlete's heterosexuality. As one athlete commented. "If you are a female athlete and do not have a boyfriend, you are labeled [lesbian]."

As reflected in the responses of athletes, the role of sport participant was often intentionally de-emphasized in order to reduce the risk of being labeled lesbian. Modification of athletes' behavior, even to the point of denying critical aspects of self, was deemed necessary for protection from the negativism attached to the lesbian label. This disguising of athletic identity exemplifies what Kitzinger (1987:92) termed "role inversion." In such a situation individuals attempt to demonstrate that their group stereotype is inaccurate by accentuating traits that are in opposition to those commonly associated with the group (in the case of women athletes, stressing femininity and heterosexuality).

Team Difficulty in Addressing Lesbian Issue

Not only did the silence surrounding lesbianism impact certain aspects of the lives of individual athletes, but it also affected interpersonal relationships among team members. This silence was often counterproductive to the development of positive group dynamics (e.g., team cohesion, open lines of communication).

As was often true at the individual level, women's sport teams were unable collectively to discuss, confront, or challenge the labeling of women athletes as lesbians. One factor complicating the ability of women athletes to confront the lesbian stereotype was the divisive nature of the label itself (Gentile 1982); the lesbian issue sometimes split teams into factions or served as the basis for clique formation.

Heterosexual and lesbian athletes often had limited interaction with each other outside the sport arena. Moreover, athletes established distance between themselves and those athletes most likely to be labeled lesbian (i.e., those possessing "masculine" physical or personality characteristics)....

From the interviews, there was little evidence that lesbian and nonlesbian athletes collectively pooled their efforts to confront or challenge the lesbian stereotype so prevalent in women's sport. The silence surrounding lesbianism creates divisions among women athletes; this dissension has the effect of preventing female bonding and camaraderie (Lenskyj 1986). Rather than recognizing their shared interests, women athletes focus on their differences and thus deny the formation of "alliance" (Pheterson 1986:149). This difficulty in attaining team cohesion is unfortunate since women's sport is an activity where women as a group can strive for common goals (Lenskyj 1990). The lesbian stereotype not only limits female solidarity, but also minimizes women's ability to challenge collectively the patriarchal and heterosexist system in which they reside (Bennett et al. 1987).

Administrative Difficulty in Addressing Lesbian Issue

Another manifestation of silence relayed in the responses of athletes was the apparent unwillingness of coaches and athletic directors to confront openly the lesbian stereotype. As was found with individual athletes and teams, those in leadership positions in women's sport refused to address or challenge this stereotype. Reluctance to confront the lesbian issue at the administrative level undoubtedly influenced the manner in which athletes handled the stereotype....

Because the women's intercollegiate sport system is homophobic and predominately male-controlled (i.e., over half of coaches and four-fifths of administrators are men) (Acosta and Carpenter 1992), it is assumed that survival in women's sport requires collusion in a collective strategy of silence about and denial of lesbianism (Griffin 1987). Coaches and administrators fear that openly addressing the lesbian issue may result in women's sport losing the recent gains made in such areas as fan support, budgets, sponsorship, and credibility (Griffin 1987). Therefore, leaders yield to this fear as they strive to achieve acceptability for women's sport. Such accommodation to the patriarchal, heterosexist sport structure not only contributes to isolation as coaches and administrators are afraid to discuss lesbianism, but also limits their identification with feminist and women's issues (Duquin 1981; Hargreaves 1990; Pharr 1988; Zipter 1988).

CONCLUSIONS

Based on athletes' responses, it was evident that the silence surrounding the lesbian issue in women's sport was deeply ingrained at all levels of the women's intercollegiate sport structure. Such widespread silencing reflects the negativism and fear associated with lesbianism that are so prevalent in a homophobic society. This strategy of silence or avoidance, however, is counterproductive to efforts to dispel or minimize the impact of the lesbian stereotype. Not only does silence disallow a direct confrontation with those who label athletes lesbian, but it also perpetuates the power of the label by leaving unchallenged rumors and insinuations. Moreover, the fear, ignorance, and negative images that are frequently associated with women athletes are reinforced by this silence (Zipter 1988).

Numerous aspects of women's experience in sport are ignored due to the silence surrounding the subject of lesbianism. For example, refusing to address this issue has limited understanding of the dimensionality and complexity of women's sport participation. Moreover, since the stigma associated with the lesbian label inhibits athletes from discussing this topic with each other, these women frequently do not realize that they possess shared experiences that would provide the foundation for female bonding. Without an "alliance" among athletes, little progress is made in improving their plight (Pheterson 1986). Finally, as a result of this preoccupation with silence, women athletes often engage in self-denial as they hide their athletic identity.

Athletes' Internalization of Societal Stereotypes

A second major theme reflected in the responses of athletes was a general internalization of Stereotypie representations of lesbians and women athletes. As argued by Kitzinger (1987) and Pheterson (1986), members of oppressed and socially marginalized groups often find themselves accepting the stereotypes and prejudices held by the dominant society. Representing "internalized oppression" (Pheterson 1986:148), the responses of athletes revealed an identification with the aggressor, self-concealment, and dependence on others for self-definition

(Kitzinger 1987; Pheterson 1986). Acceptance of these societal representations by a disadvantaged group (in this case women athletes) grants legitimacy to the position of those who oppress and contributes to the continued subordination of the oppressed (Wolf 1986). Based on our interviews, athletes' internalization of stereotypes and prejudices were reflected by three categories of responses: (1) acceptance of lesbian stereotypes, (2) acceptance of women's sport team stereotypes, and (3) acceptance of negative images of lesbianism.

Acceptance of Lesbian Stereotypes

In response to various open-ended questions, it was apparent that athletes were able to identify a variety of factors that they felt led others to label women athletes as lesbians (e.g., physical appearance, dress, personality characteristics, nature of sport activity). Given that the attribution of homosexuality is most likely to be associated with traits and behaviors judged to be more appropriate for members of the opposite sex (Dunbar, Brown, and Amoroso 1973; Dunkle and Francis 1990), it was not surprising that athletes' rationale for the lesbian label included such attributes as muscularity, short hair, masculine clothing, etc.

When athletes were asked about the validity of the lesbian label in women's sport, affirmative replies were frequently based on conjecture. For example, to provide support for why they felt there was a basis for labeling women athletes as lesbians, respondents made such comments as "there are masculine girls on some teams," "it is really obvious," or "you can just tell that some athletes are lesbians."

These explanations tend to reflect an acceptance of societal definitions of lesbianism—beliefs that are largely male-centered and supportive of a patriarchal, heterosexist system (e.g., "girls who look like guys"). Indeed, previous research has shown that people associate physical appearance with homosexuality (Levitt and Klassen 1974; McArthur 1982; Unger, Hilderbrand, and Madar 1982). For example, attractiveness is equated with heterosexuality and a larger, muscular body build is identified with lesbianism.

Moreover, the remarks of athletes demonstrate that the very group that is oppressed (in this case women athletes) accepts societal stereotypes about lesbians and has incorporated these images into their managing of the situation. As suggested by Gartrell (1984) and certainly evident in this sample of women athletes, cultural myths about lesbianism perpetuated in a homophobic society are often firmly ingrained in the thinking of affected individuals.

Acceptance of Women's Sport Team Stereotypes

Relative to providing a rationale for why the lesbian label was more likely to be associated with athletes in certain sports, respondents again demonstrated an understanding and internalization of societal stereotypes. The sports most commonly identified with the lesbian label were softball, field hockey, and basketball. In attempting to explain why these team sports were singled out, athletes mentioned such factors as the nature of bodily contact or amount of aggression in the sport, as well as the body build, muscularity, or athleticism needed to play the sport.

Respondents often relied on the "masculine" and "feminine" stereotypes to differentiate sports in which participating women were more or less likely to be subjected to the lesbian label. Although participants in team sports were more likely than individual sports (e.g., gymnastics, swimming, tennis, golf) to be associated with the lesbian label, it was interesting to note that volleyball was often exempt from the connotations of lesbianism.

The higher incidence of lesbian labeling found in team sports (as opposed to individual sports) may also be related to the potential that team sports provide for interpersonal interactions. As previously mentioned, emphasizing teamwork and togetherness, team sports allow women rare opportunities to bond collectively in pursuit of a group goal (Lenskyj 1990). Recognition of this power of female bonding is often reflected by male opposition to women-only activities (Lenskyj 1990).

Acceptance of Negative Images of Lesbianism

During the course of the interviews, a large majority of athletes made comments about lesbians which reflected an internalization of the negativism associated with lesbianism. Respondents also demonstrated a similar acceptance when they relayed conversations they had had with both teammates and outsiders.

One form of negativism was reflected by statements that specifically "put down" lesbians. Athletes' negative comments about lesbians were included in conversations with outsiders so others would not associate the lesbian label with them. Representing a form of projection (Gross 1978), some athletes attempted to disassociate from traits that they saw in themselves (e.g., strength, muscularity, aggressiveness)....

It is ironic that athletes rarely directed their anger or condemnations at the homophobic society that restricts the actions of women athletes, including the nonlesbian athlete. Rather, by focusing on athletes as lesbians, a blame-the-victim approach diverts attention from the cause of the oppression (Pharr 1988). As is often true of oppressed groups, a blame-the-victim philosophy results in an acceptance of the belief system of the oppressor (in this case a patriarchal, heterosexist society) (Pharr 1988). Like other marginalized groups, women athletes accept the normative definitions of their deviance (Kitzinger 1987); in effect, such responses represent a form of collusion with the oppressive forces (Pheterson 1986). Interestingly, no mention was made by respondents about attempts to engage the assistance or support of units on campus sympathetic to gay and lesbian issues (e.g., feminist groups, gay and lesbian organization, affirmative action offices).

SUMMARY

From the interview responses, it was evidence that athletes had internalized societal stereotypes related to lesbians and women athletes, as well as the negativism directed toward lesbianism. This acceptance was so ingrained in these athletes that they were generally unaware of the political ramifications of both lesbianism and the accompanying lesbian stereotype as applied to women athletes. Despite their gender norm violation as athletes, these women often had a superficial understanding of gender issues. Such a lack of awareness may be due in part to the absence of a feminist consciousness in athletes (Boutilier and San Giovanni 1983; Kaplan 1979) and their open disavowal of being a "feminist," "activist," or "preacher of women's liberation." Accepting societal definitions of their deviance, as well as the inability to see their personal experiences as political in nature, attests to this limited consciousness (Boutilier and SanGiovanni 1983). Athletes' responses are indicative of the degree to which they exhibit internal homophobia so common in American society.

Only a few athletes possessed deeper insight into factors that may underlie the labeling of women athletes as lesbians. For example, one respondent felt women athletes were a "threat to men since they can stand on their own feet." Or, in another situation, an athlete viewed lesbian labeling as a means to devalue women athletes or successful women in general. Still another respondent suggested the label stemmed from jealousy and thus was used as a means to "get back" at women athletes. These rare remarks by respondents transcend the blame-the-victim view held by the majority of athletes. Such commitments indicate a deeper understanding of how homophobia and patriarchal ideology limit or control women's activities and their bodies.

Disempowerment

Given the silence surrounding the lesbian issue and the degree to which athletes have internalized societal images of lesbians and women athletes, the presence of the lesbian stereotype has negative ramifications for women athletes. Although sport participation possesses the potential for creativity and physical excellence (Theberge 1987), women modify their behavior so they will not be viewed as "stepping out of line." Women athletes become disempowered (Pharr 1988) through processes that detract from or reduce the self-actualizing potential of the sport experience.

Attaching the label of lesbian to women who engage in sport diminishes the sporting accomplishments of athletes. Women athletes are seen as something less than "real women" because they do not exemplify traditional female qualities (e.g., dependency, weakness, passivity); thus their accomplishments are not viewed as threatening to men (Birrell 1988). Interestingly, the athletes interviewed believed that the specific group most likely to engage in lesbian labeling was male athletes.

Discrediting women with the label of lesbian works further to control the number of females in sport, particularly in a homophobic society where prejudice against lesbians is intense (Birrell 1988; Zipter 1988). Keeping women out of sport, in turn, prevents females from discovering the power and joy of their own physicality (Birrell 1988) and experiencing the potential of their body. Moreover, discouraging women from participating in sport disempowers them by removing an arena where women can bond together (Birrell 1988; Cobban 1982)....

Another form of disempowerment occurs for those athletes who are lesbians. Intense homophobia often forces lesbians to deny their very essence, thus making the lesbian athlete invisible. Concealment, although protecting thsse lesbian athletes' identity, imposes psychological strain and can undermine positive self-conceptions (Schur 1984). Misrepresenting their sexuality, lesbian athletes are not in a position to confront the homophobia so prevalent in women's sport. Consequently, this ideology not only remains intact, but also is strengthened (Ettore 1980).

REFERENCES

Acosta, R. Vivian and Linda Jean Carpenter. 1992. "Women in Intercollegiate Sport: A Longitudinal Study—Fifteen Year Update 1977–1992." Unpublished manuscript, Brooklyn College, Department of Physical Education, Brooklyn.

Bennett, Roberts S., K. Gail Whitaker, Nina Jo Woolley Smith, and Anne Sablove. 1987. "Changing the Rules of the Game: Reflections Toward a Feminist Analysis of Sport." *Women's Studies International Forum* 10: 369–386.

Birrell, Susan. 1988. "Discourses on The Gender/Sport Relationship: From Women in Sport to Gender Relations." Pp. 459–502 in *Exercise and Sport Science Reviews,* vol. 16, edited by K. B. Pandolf New York: MacMillan.

Blinde, Elaine M. and Diane E. Taub. 1992. "Women Athletes as Falsely Accused Deviants: Managing the Lesbian Stigma." *The Sociological Quarterly* 33: 521–533.

Boutilier, Mary A. and Lucinda, SanGiovanni. 1983. *The Sporting Woman.* Champaign, IL: Human Kinetics.

Cobban, Linn Ni. 1982. "Lesbians in Physical Education and Sport." Pp. 179–186 in *Lesbian Studies: Present and Future,* edited by M. Cruikshank. New York: Feminist Press.

Dunbar, John, Marvin Brown, and Donald M. Amoroso. 1973. "Some Correlates of Attitudes Toward Homosexuality." *Journal of Social Psychology* 89: 271–279.

Dunkle, John H. and Patricia L. Francis. 1990. "The Role of Facial Masculinity/Feminity in The Attribution of Homosexuality." *Sex Roles* 23: 157–167.

Duquin, Mary E. 1981. "Feminism and Patriarchy in Physical Education." Paper presented at the annual meetings of the North American Society for the Sociology of Sport, Fort Worth, TX.

Ettore, E. M. 1980. *Lesbians, Women and Society.* London: Routledge and Kegan Paul.

Gartrell, Nanette. 1984. "Combatting Homophobia in the Psychotherapy of Lesbians." *Women and Therapy* 3: 13–29.

Gentile, S. 1982. "Out of The Kitchen." *City Sports Monthly* 8: 27.

Goffman, Erving. 1963. *Stigma: Notes on the Management of Spoiled Identity.* Englewood Cliffs, NJ: Prentice Hall.

Griffin, Patricia S. 1987. "Homophobia, Lesbians, and Women's Sports: An Exploratory Analysis." Paper presented at the annual meetings of the American Psychological Association, New York.

Gross, Martin L. 1978. *The Psychological Society.* New York: Simon & Schuster.

Hargreaves, Jennifer A. 1990. "Gender on the Sports Agenda." *International Review for Sociology of Sport* 25: 287–308.

Kaplan, Janice. 1979. *Women and Sports.* New York: Viking.

Kitzinger, Celia. 1987. The Social Construction of Lesbianism. London: Sage.

Koedt, Anne, Ellen Levine, and Anita Rapone. 1973. *Radical Feminism.* NewYork: Quadrangle.

Lenskyj, Helen. 1986. *Out of Bounds: Women, Sport and Sexuality.* Toronto: Women's Press.

———. 1990. "Power and Play: Gender and Sexuality Issues in Sport and Physical Activity." *International Review for Sociology of Sport* 25: 235–245.

———. 1991. "Combatting Homophobia in Sport and Physical Education." *Sociology of Sport Journal* 8: 61–69.

Levitt, Eugene E., and Albert D. Klassen, Jr. 1974. "Public Attitudes toward Homosexuality: Part of the 1970 National Survey by the Institute for Sex Research." *Journal of Homosexuality* 1: 29–43.

McArthur, Leslie Z. 1982. "Judging a Book by Its Cover: A Cognitive Analysis of the Relationship between Physical Appearance and Stereotyping." Pp.149–211 in *Cognitive Social Psychology,* edited by Albert H. Hastorf and Alice M. Isen. New York: Elsevier/North-Holland.

Pharr, Suzanne. 1988. *Homophobia: A Weapon of Sexism.* Inverness, CA: Clurdon.

Pheterson, Gail. 1986. "Alliances between Women: Overcoming Internalized Oppression and Internalized Domination." *Signs: Journal of Women in Culture and Society* 12: 146–160.

Schur, Edwin M. 1984. *Labeling Women Deviant: Gender, Stigma, and Social Control.* New York: McGraw-Hill.

Stockard, Jean and Miriam M. Johnson. 1980. *Sex Roles: Sex Inequality and Sex Role Development.* Englewood Cliffs, NJ: Prentice Hall.

Theberge, Nancy. 1987. "Sport and Women's Empowerment." *Women's Studies International Forum* 10: 387–393.

Unger, Rhoda K., Marcia Hilderbrand, and Theresa, Madar. 1982. "Physical Attractiveness and Assumptions about Social Deviance: Some Sex-by-Sex Comparisons." *Personality and Social Psychology Bulletin* 8: 293–301.

Watson, Tracey. 1987. "Women Athletes and Athletic Women: The Dilemmas and Contradictions of Managing Incongruent Identities." *Sociological Inquiry* 57: 431–446.

Wolf, Charlotte. 1986. "Legitimation of Oppression: Response and Reflexivity." *Symbolic Interaction* 9: 217–234.

Zipter, Yvonne. 1988. Diamonds Are a Dyke's Best Friend: Reflections, Reminiscences, and Reports from the Field on the Lesbian National Pastime. Ithaca, NY: Firebrand Books.

20

The Mark of a Criminal Record

DEVAH PAGER

To measure concretely the interactive effects of race and a criminal record, Pager devised an experimental design where she constructed a fabricated pair of job applicants who were matched on all features except their criminal history. She then sent out these matched pairs, white pairs and black pairs, to apply for real jobs in Milwaukee, and noted how far the candidates got in the interview process. Along the way she recorded the employer's likelihood of dismissing the applicants right away, checking their references, calling them back for further interviews, and offering them the job. In a real demonstration of the effects of race and criminal record on employment opportunities, Pager found that while whites were offered more jobs than blacks and applicants with no criminal history were offered more jobs than those who had served time, even whites with criminal pasts were more likely to be hired than blacks who had led law-abiding lives. She found that employers were more likely to hold stereotypes suspecting blacks, especially young black men, of being prone to crime and of being unreliable employees.

While stratification researchers typically focus on schools, labor markets, and the family as primary institutions affecting inequality, a new institution has emerged as central to the sorting and stratifying of young and disadvantaged men: the criminal justice system. With over 2 million individuals currently incarcerated, and over half a million prisoners released each year, the large and growing numbers of men being processed through the criminal justice system raises important questions about the consequences of this massive institutional intervention.

This article focuses on the consequences of incarceration for the employment outcomes of black and white men. While previous survey research has demonstrated a strong *association* between incarceration and employment, there remains little understanding of the mechanisms by which these outcomes are produced. In the present study, I adopt an experimental audit approach to test formally the degree to which a criminal record affects subsequent employment opportunities. By using matched pairs of individuals to apply for real entry-level

From Devah Pager, "The Mark of a Criminal Record." *American Journal of Sociology* 108(5). Copyright © 2003 by the University of Chicago Press. Reprinted with permission of the publisher and author.

jobs, it becomes possible to directly measure the extent to which a criminal record—in the absence of other disqualifying characteristics—serves as a barrier to employment among equally qualified applicants. Further, by varying the race of the tester pairs, we can assess the ways in which the effects of race and criminal record interact to produce new forms of labor market inequalities.

TRENDS IN INCARCERATION

Over the past three decades, the number of prison inmates in the United States has increased by more than 600%, leaving it the country with the highest incarceration rate in the world (Bureau of Justice Statistics 2002; Barclay, Tavares, and Siddique 2001). During this time, incarceration has changed from a punishment reserved primarily for the most heinous offenders to one extended to a much greater range of crimes and a much larger segment of the population. Recent trends in crime policy have led to the imposition of harsher sentences for a wider range of offenses, thus casting an ever-widening net of penal intervention.[1]

While the recent "tough on crime" policies may be effective in getting criminals off the streets, little provision has been made for when they get back out. Of the nearly 2 million individuals currently incarcerated, roughly 95% will be released, with more than half a million being released each year (Slevin 2000). According to one estimate, there are currently over 12 million exfelons in the United States, representing roughly 8% of the working-age population (Uggen, Thompson, and Manza 2000). Of those recently released, nearly two-thirds will be charged with new crimes and over 40% will return to prison within three years (Bureau of Justice Statistics 2000). Certainly some of these outcomes are the result of desolate opportunities or deeply ingrained dispositions, grown out of broken families, poor neighborhoods, and little social control (Sampson and Laub 1993; Wilson 1997). Besides these contributing factors, there is evidence that experience with the criminal justice system in itself has adverse consequences for subsequent opportunities. In particular, incarceration is associated with limited future employment opportunities and earnings potential (Freeman 1987; Western 2002), which themselves are among the strongest predictors of recidivism (Shover 1996; Sampson and Laub 1993; Uggen 2000).

The expansion of the prison population has been particularly consequential for blacks. The incarceration rate for young black men in the year 2000 was nearly 10%, compared to just over 1% for white men in the same age group (Bureau of Justice Statistics 2001). Young black men today have a 28% likelihood of incarceration during their lifetime (Bureau of Justice Statistics 1997), a figure that rises above 50% among young black high school dropouts (Pettit and Western 2001). These vast numbers of inmates translate into a large and increasing population of black ex-offenders returning to communities and searching for work. The barriers these men face in reaching economic self-sufficiency are compounded by the stigma of minority status and criminal record. The consequences of such trends for widening racial disparities are potentially profound (see Western and Pettit 1999; Freeman and Hölzer 1986).

The objective of this study is to assess whether the effect of a criminal record differs for black and white applicants. Most research investigating the differential impact of incarceration on blacks has focused on the differential *rates* of incarceration and how those rates translate into widening racial disparities. In addition to disparities in the rate of incarceration, however, it is also important to consider possible racial differences in the *effects* of incarceration. Almost none of the existing literature to date has explored this issue, and the theoretical arguments remain divided as to what we might expect.

On one hand, there is reason to believe that the signal of a criminal record should be less consequential for blacks. Research on racial stereotypes tells us that Americans hold strong and persistent negative stereotypes about blacks, with one of the most readily invoked contemporary stereotypes relating to perceptions of violent and criminal dispositions (Smith 1991; Sniderman and Piazza 1993; Devine and Elliott 1995). If it is the case that employers view all blacks as potential criminals, they are likely to differentiate less among those with official criminal records and those without. Actual confirmation of criminal involvement then will provide only redundant information, while evidence against it will be discounted. In this case, the outcomes for all blacks should be worse, with less differentiation between those with criminal records and those without.

On the other hand, the effect of a criminal record may be worse for blacks if employers, already wary of black applicants, are more hesitant when it comes to taking risks on blacks with proven criminal tendencies. The literature on racial stereotypes also tells us that stereotypes are most likely to be activated and reinforced when a target matches on more than one dimension of the stereotype (Quillian and Pager 2002; Darley and Gross 1983; Fiske and Neuberg 1990). While employers may have learned to keep their racial attributions in check through years of heightened sensitivity around employment discrimination, when combined with knowledge of a criminal history, negative attributions are likely to intensify.

A third possibility, of course, is that a criminal record affects black and white applicants equally. The results of this audit study will help to adjudicate between these competing predictions.

STUDY DESIGN

The basic design of this study involves the use of four male auditors (also called testers), two blacks and two whites. The testers were 23-year-old college students from Milwaukee who were matched on the basis of physical appearance and general style of self-presentation. Objective characteristics that were not already identical between pairs—such as educational attainment and work experience—were made similar for the purpose of the applications. Within each team, one auditor was randomly assigned a "criminal record" for the first week; the pair then rotated which member presented himself as the ex-offender for each successive week of employment searches, such that each tester served in the criminal record condition for an equal number of cases. By varying which member of the pair presented himself as having a criminal record, unobserved differences within the pairs of applicants were effectively controlled. No significant differences were found for the outcomes of individual testers or by month of testing.

Job openings for entry-level positions (defined as jobs requiring no previous experience and no education greater than high school) were identified from the Sunday classified advertisement section of the *Milwaukee Journal Sentinel*.[2] In addition, a supplemental sample was drawn *from Jobnet,* a state-sponsored Web site for employment listings, which was developed in connection with the W-2 Welfare-to-Work initiatives.[3]

The audit pairs were randomly assigned 15 job openings each week. The white pair and the black pair were assigned separate sets of jobs, with the same-race testers applying to the same jobs. One member of the pair applied first, with the second applying one day later (randomly varying whether the ex-offender was first or second). A total of 350 employers were audited during the course of this study: 150 by the white pair and 200 by the black pair. Additional tests were performed by the black pair because black testers received fewer callbacks on average, and there were thus fewer data points with which to draw comparisons. A larger sample size enabled me to calculate more precise estimates of the effects under investigation.

Immediately following the completion of each job application, testers filled out a six-page response form that coded relevant information from the test. Important variables included type of occupation, metropolitan status, wage, size of establishment, and race and sex of employer.[4] Additionally, testers wrote narratives describing the overall interaction and any comments made by employers (or included on applications) specifically related to race or criminal records.

TESTER PROFILES

In developing the tester profiles, emphasis was placed on adopting characteristics that were both numerically representative and substantively important. In the present study, the criminal record consisted of a felony drug conviction (possession with intent to distribute, cocaine) and 18 months of (served) prison time. A drug crime (as opposed to a violent or property crime) was chosen because of its prevalence, its policy salience, and its connection to racial disparities in incarceration.[5] It is important to acknowledge that the effects reported here may differ depending on the type of offense.

THE EFFECT OF A CRIMINAL RECORD FOR WHITES

I begin with an analysis of the effect of a criminal record among whites. White noncriminals can serve as our baseline in the following comparisons, representing the presumptively nonstigmatized group relative to blacks and those with

FIGURE 20.1 The effect of a criminal record on employment opportunities for whites. The effect of a criminal record is statistically significant (P < .01).

criminal records. Given that all testers presented roughly identical credentials, the differences experienced among groups of testers can be attributed fully to the effects of race or criminal status.

Figure 20.1 shows the percentage of applications submitted by white testers that elicited callbacks from employers, by criminal status. As illustrated below, there is a large and significant effect of a criminal record, with 34% of whites without criminal records receiving callbacks, relative to only 17% of whites with criminal records. A criminal record thereby reduces the likelihood of a callback by 50%.

There were some fairly obvious examples documented by testers that illustrate the strong reaction among employers to the signal of a criminal record. In one case, a white tester in the criminal record condition went to a trucking service to apply for a job as a dispatcher. The tester was given a long application, including a complex math test, which took nearly 45 minutes to fill out. During the course of this process, there were several details about the application and the job that needed clarification, some of which involved checking with the supervisor about how to proceed. No concerns were raised about his candidacy at this stage. When the tester turned the application in, the secretary brought it into a back office for the supervisor to look over, so that an interview could perhaps be conducted. When the secretary came back out, presumably after the supervisor had a chance to look over the application more thoroughly, he was told the position had already been filled. While, of course, isolated incidents like this are not conclusive, this was not an infrequent occurrence. Often testers reported seeing employers' levels of responsiveness change dramatically once they had glanced down at the criminal record question.

Clearly, the results here demonstrate that criminal records close doors in employment situations. Many employers seem to use the information as a

screening mechanism, without attempting to probe deeper into the possible context or complexities of the situation. As we can see here, in 50% of cases, employers
were unwilling to consider equally qualified applicants on the basis of their criminal
record.

Of course, this trend is not true among all employers, in all situations. There
were, in fact, some employers who seemed to prefer workers who had been
recently released from prison. One owner told a white tester in the criminal
record condition that he "like[d] hiring people who ha[d] just come out of prison
because they tend to be more motivated, and are more likely to be hard workers
[not wanting to return to prison]." Another employer for a cleaning company
attempted to dissuade the white noncriminal tester from applying because the job
involved "a great deal of dirty work." The tester with the criminal record, on the
other hand, was offered the job on the spot. A criminal record is thus not an
obstacle in all cases, but on average, as we see above, it reduces employment
opportunities substantially.

THE EFFECT OF RACE

A second major focus of this study concerns the effect of race. African Americans
continue to suffer from lower rates of employment relative to whites, but there is
tremendous disagreement over the source of these disparities. The idea that race
itself—apart from other correlated characteristics—continues to play a major role
in shaping employment opportunities has come under question in recent years
(e.g., D'Souza 1995; Steele 1991). The audit methodology is uniquely suited
to address this question. While the present study design does not provide the
kind of cross-race matched-pair tests that earlier audit studies of racial discrimination have used, the between-group comparisons (white pair vs. black pair)
can nevertheless offer an unbiased estimate of the effect of race on employment
opportunities.

Figure 20.2 presents the percentage of callbacks received for both categories
of black testers relative to those for whites. The effect of race in these findings
is strikingly large. Among blacks without criminal records, only 14% received
callbacks, relative to 34% of white noncriminals (P < .01). In fact, even whites
with criminal records received more favorable treatment (17%) than blacks *without*
criminal records (14%). The rank ordering of groups in this graph is painfully
revealing of employer preferences: race continues to play a dominant role in
shaping employment opportunities, equal to or greater than the impact of a
criminal record.

The magnitude of the race effect found here corresponds closely to those
found in previous audit studies directly measuring racial discrimination. Bendick
et al. (1994), for example, found that blacks were 24 percentage points less likely
to receive a job offer relative to their white counterparts, a finding very close to
the 20 percentage point difference (between white and black nonoffenders)
found here. Thus in the eight years since the last major employment audit of

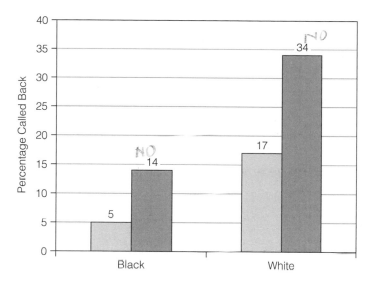

F I G U R E 20.2   The effect of a criminal record for black and white job applicants. The main effects of race and criminal record are statistically significant (P < .01). The interaction between the two is not significant in the full sample. Light bars represent criminal record; dark bars represent no criminal record.

race was conducted, very little has changed in the reaction of employers to minority applicants. Despite the many rhetorical arguments used to suggest that direct racial discrimination is no longer a major barrier to opportunity (e.g., D'Souza 1995; Steele 1991), as we can see here, employers, at least in Milwaukee, continue to use race as a major factor in hiring decisions.

RACIAL DIFFERENCES IN THE EFFECTS
OF A CRIMINAL RECORD

The final question this study sought to answer was the degree to which the effect of a criminal record differs depending on the race of the applicant. Based on the results presented in Figure 20.2, the effect of a criminal record appears more pronounced for blacks than it is for whites. While this interaction term is not statistically significant, the magnitude of the difference is nontrivial. While the ratio of callbacks for nonoffenders relative to ex-offenders for whites is 2:1, this same ratio for blacks is nearly 3:1. The effect of a criminal record is thus 40% larger for blacks than for whites.

This evidence is suggestive of the way in which associations between race and crime affect interpersonal evaluations. Employers, already reluctant to hire blacks, appear even more wary of blacks with proven criminal involvement. Despite the face that these testers were bright articulate college students with effective styles of self-presentation, the cursory review of entry-level applicants leaves little room for these qualities to be noticed. Instead, the employment barriers of minority status and criminal record are compounded, intensifying the stigma toward this group.

The salience of employers' sensitivity toward criminal involvement among blacks was highlighted in several interactions documented by testers. On three separate occasions, for example, black testers were asked in person (before submitting their applications) whether they had a prior criminal history. None of the white testers were asked about their criminal histories up front.

DISCUSSION

There is serious disagreement among academics, policy makers, and practitioners over the extent to which contact with the criminal justice system—in itself—leads to harmful consequences for employment. The present study takes a strong stand in this debate by offering direct evidence of the causal relationship between a criminal record and employment outcomes. While survey research has produced noisy and indirect estimates of this effect, the current research design offers a direct measure of a criminal record as a mechanism producing employment disparities. Using matched pairs and an experimentally assigned criminal record, this estimate is unaffected by the problems of selection, which plague observational data. While certainly there are additional ways in which incarceration may affect employment outcomes, this finding provides conclusive evidence that mere contact with the criminal justice system, in the absence of any transformative or selective effects, severely limits subsequent employment opportunities. And while the audit study investigates employment barriers to ex-offenders from a microperspective, the implications are far-reaching. The finding that ex-offenders are only one-half to one-third as likely as nonoffenders to be considered by employers suggests that a criminal record indeed presents a major barrier to employment. With over 2 million people currently behind bars and over 12 million people with prior felony convictions, the consequences for labor market inequalities are potentially profound.

Second, the persistent effect of race on employment opportunities is painfully clear in these results. Blacks are less than half as likely to receive consideration by employers, relative to their white counterparts, and black nonoffenders fall behind even whites with prior felony convictions. The powerful effects of race thus continue to direct employment decisions in ways that contribute to persisting racial inequality. In light of these findings, current public opinion seems largely misinformed. According to a recent survey of residents in Los Angeles, Boston, Detroit, and Atlanta, researchers found that just over a quarter of whites believe there to be "a lot" of discrimination against blacks, compared to nearly two-thirds of black respondents (Kluegel and Bobo 2001). Over the past decade, affirmative action has come under attack across the country based on the argument that direct racial discrimination is no longer a major barrier to opportunity. According to this study, however, employers, at least in Milwaukee, continue to use race as a major factor in their hiring decisions. When we combine the effects of race and criminal record, the problem grows more intense. Not only are blacks much more likely to be incarcerated than whites; based on the findings presented here, they may also be more strongly affected by the impact of a criminal record. Previous estimates of the aggregate consequences of incarceration may therefore underestimate the impact on racial disparities.

Finally, in terms of policy implications, this research has troubling conclusions. In our frenzy of locking people up, our "crime control" policies may in fact exacerbate the very conditions that lead to crime in the first place. Research consistently shows that finding quality steady employment is one of the strongest predictors of desistance from crime (Shover 1996; Sampson and Laub 1993; Uggen 2000). The fact that a criminal record severely limits employment opportunities—particularly among blacks—suggests that these individuals are left with few viable alternatives.[6]

As more and more young men enter the labor force from prison, it becomes increasingly important to consider the impact of incarceration on the job prospects of those coming out. No longer a peripheral institution, the criminal justice system has become a dominant presence in the lives of young disadvantaged men, playing a key role in the sorting and stratifying of labor market opportunities. This article represents an initial attempt to specify one of the important mechanisms by which incarceration leads to poor employment outcomes. Future research is needed to expand this emphasis to other mechanisms (e.g., the transformative effects of prison on human and social capital), as well as to include other social domains affected by incarceration (e.g., housing, family formation, political participation, etc.); in this way, we can move toward a more complete understanding of the collateral consequences of incarceration for social inequality.

At this point in history, it is impossible to tell whether the massive presence of incarceration in today's stratification system represents a unique anomaly of the late 20th century, or part of a larger movement toward a system of stratification based on the official certification of individual character and competence. Whether this process of negative credentialing will continue to form the basis of emerging social cleavages remains to be seen.

NOTES

1. For example, the recent adoption of mandatory sentencing laws, most often used for drug offenses, removes discretion from the sentencing judge to consider the range of factors pertaining to the individual and the offense that would normally be taken into account. As a result, the chances of receiving a state prison term after being arrested for a drug offense rose by 547% between 1980 and 1992 (Bureau of Justice Statistics 1995).

2. Occupations with legal restrictions on ex-offenders were excluded from the sample. These include jobs in the health care industry, work with children and the elderly, jobs requiring the handling of firearms (i.e., security

guards), and jobs in the public sector. An estimate of the collateral consequences of incarceration would also need to take account of the wide range of employment formally off-limits to individuals with prior felony convictions.

3. Employment services like *Jobnet* have become a much more common method of finding employment in recent years, particularly for difficult-to-employ populations such as welfare recipients and ex-offenders. Likewise, a recent survey by Hölzer and Stoll (2001) found that nearly half of Milwaukee employers (46%) *use Jobnet* to advertise vacancies in their companies.

4. See Pager (2002) for a discussion of the variation across each of these dimensions.

5. Over the past two decades, drug crimes were the fastest growing class of offenses. In 1980, roughly one out of every sixteen state inmates was incarcerated for a drug crime; by 1999, this figure had jumped to one out of every five (Bureau of Justice Statistics 2000). In federal prisons, nearly three out of every five inmates are incarcerated for a drug crime (Bureau of justice Statistics 2001). A significant portion of this increase can be attributed to changing policies concerning drug enforcement. By 2000, every state in the country had adopted some form of truth-in-sentencing laws, which impose mandatory sentencing minimums for a range of offenses. These laws have been applied most frequently to drug crimes, leading to more than a fivefold rise in the number of drug arrests that result in incarceration and a doubling of the average length of sentences for drug convictions (Mauer 1999; Blumstein and Beck 1999). While the steep rise in drug enforcement has been felt across the population, this "war on drugs" has had a dispropor-

tionate impact on African Americans. Between 1990 and 1997, the number of black inmates serving time for drug offenses increased by 60%, compared to a 46% increase in the number of whites (Bureau of justice Statistics 1995). In 1999, 26% of all black state inmates were incarcerated for drug offenses, relative to less than half that proportion of whites (Bureau of justice Statistics 2001).

6. There are two primary policy recommendations implied by these results. First and foremost, the widespread use of incarceration, particularly for non-violent drug crimes, has serious, long-term consequences for the employment problems of young men. The substitution of alternatives to incarceration, therefore, such as drug treatment programs or community supervision, may serve to better promote the well-being of individual offenders as well as to improve public safety more generally through the potential reduction of recidivism. Second, additional thought should be given to the widespread availability of criminal background information. As criminal record databases become increasingly easy to access, this information may be more often used as the basis for rejecting otherwise qualified applicants. If instead criminal history information were suppressed—except in cases that were clearly relevant to a particular kind of job assignment—ex-offenders with appropriate credentials might be better able to secure legitimate employment. While there is some indication that the absence of official criminal background information may lead to a greater incidence of statistical discrimination against blacks (see Bushway 1997; Hölzer et al. 2001), the net benefits of this policy change may in fact outweigh the potential drawbacks.

REFERENCES

Barclay, Gordon, Cynthia Tavares, and Siddique Arsalaan. 2001. "International Comparisons of Criminal Justice Statistics, 1999." London: U.K. Home Office for Statistical Research.

Bendick, Marc, Jr., Charles Jackson, and Victor Reinoso. 1994, "Measuring Employment Discrimination through Controlled Experiments." *Review of Black Political Economy* 23:25–48.

Blumstein, Alfred, and Allen J. Beck. 1999. "Population Growth in U.S. Prisons, 1980–1996." Pp. 17–62 in *Prisons: Crime and Justice: A Review of Research,* vol. 26. Edited by Michael Tonry and J. Petersilia. Chicago: University of Chicago Press.

Bureau of Justice Statistics. 1995. *Prisoners in 1994,* by Allen J. Beck and Darrell K. Gilliard. Special report. Washington, DC: Government Printing Office.

———. 1997. *Lifetime Likelihood of Going to State or Federal Prison,* by Thomas P. Bonczar and Allen J. Beck. Special report, March.

———. 2000. Bulletin. *Key Facts at a Glance: Number of Persons in Custody of State Correctional Authorities by Most Serious Offense 1980–99.* Washington, DC: Government Printing Office.

———. 2001. *Prisoners in 2000,* by Allen J. Beck and Paige M. Harrison. August. Bulletin. Washington, DC: NCJ 188207.

———. 2002. *Sourcebook of Criminal Justice Statistics.* (Last accessed March 1, 2003.) Available www.albany.edu/sourcebook.

Bushway, Shawn D. 1997. "Labor Market Effects of Permitting Employer Access to Criminal History Records." Working paper. University of Maryland, Department of Criminology.

Darley, J. M., and P. H., Gross. 1983. "A Hypothesis-Confirming Bias in Labeling Effects." *Journal of Personality and Social Psychology* 44:20–33.

Devine, P. G., and A. J., Elliot. 1995. "Are Racial Stereotypes Really Fading? The Princeton Trilogy Revisited." *Personality and Social Psychology Bulletin* 21 (11): 1139–50.

D'Souza, Dinesh. 1995. *The End of Racism. Principles for a Multiracial Society.* New York: Free Press.

Fiske, Susan, and Steven Neuberg. 1990. "A Continuum of Impression Formation, from Category-Based to Individuating Processes." Pp. 1–63 in *Advances in Experimental Social Psychology,* vol. 23. Edited by Mark Zanna. New York: Academic Press.

Freeman, Richard B. 1987. "The Relation of Criminal Activity to Black Youth Employment." *Review of Black Political Economy* 16 (1–2): 99–107.

Freeman, Richard B., and Harry J. Holzer, eds. 1986. *The Black Youth Employment Crisis.* Chicago: University of Chicago Press for National Bureau of Economic Research.

Hölzer, Harry, Steven Raphael, and Michael Stoll. 2001. "Perceived Criminality, Criminal Background Checks, and the Racial Hiring Practices of Employers." Discussion Paper no. 1254—02. University of Wisconsin—Madison, Institute for Research on Poverty.

Hölzer, Harry, and Michael Stoll. 2001. *Employers and Welfare Recipients: The Effects of Welfare Reform in the Workplace.* San Francisco: Public Policy Institute of California.

Kluegel, James, and Lawrence Bobo. 2001. "Perceived Group Discrimination and Policy Attitudes: The Sources and Consequences of the Race and Gender Gaps." Pp. 163–216 in *Urban Inequality: Evidence from*

Four Cities, edited by Alice O'Connor, Chris Tilly, and Lawrence D. Bobo. New York: Russell Sage Foundation.

Mauer, Marc. 1999. *Race to Incarcerate*. New York: New Press.

Pager, Devah. 2002. "The Mark of a Criminal Record." *Doctoral dissertation*. Department of Sociology, University of Wisconsin-Madison.

Pettit, Becky, and Bruce, Western. 2001. "Inequality in Lifetime Risks of Imprisonment." Paper presented at the annual meetings of the American Sociological Association. Anaheim, August.

Quillian, Lincoln, and Devah, Pager. 2002. "Black Neighbors, Higher Crime? The Role of Racial Stereotypes in Evaluations of Neighborhood Crime." *American Journal of Sociology* 107 (3): 717–67

Sampson, Robert J., and John H. Laub. 1993. *Crime in the Making: Pathways and Turning Points through Life*. Cambridge, Mass: Harvard University Press.

Shover, Neil. 1996. *Great Pretenders: Pursuits and Careers of Persistent Thieves*. Boulder, Colo: Westview.

Slevin, Peter. 2000. "Life after Prison: Lack of Services Has High Price." *Washington Post*, April 24.

Smith, Tom W. 1991. *What Americans Say about Jews*. New York: American Jewish Committee.

Sniderman, Paul M., and Thomas, Piazza. 1993. *The Scar of Race*. Cambridge, Mass: Harvard University Press.

Steele, Shelby. 1991. *The Content of Our Character: A New Vision of Race in America*. New York: Harper Perennial.

Uggen, Christopher. 2000. "Work as a Turning Point in the Life Course of Criminals: A Duration Model of Age, Employment, and Recidivism." *American Sociological Review* 65 (4): 529–46.

Uggen, Christopher, Melissa Thompson, and Jeff, Manza. 2000. "Crime, Class, and Reintegration: The Socioeconomic, Familial, and Civic Lives of Offenders." Paper presented at the American Society of Criminology meetings, San Francisco, November 18.

Western, Bruce. 2002. "The Impact of Incarceration on Wage Mobility and Inequality." *American Sociological Review* 67 (4): 526–46.

Western, Bruce, and Becky Pettit. 1999. "Black-White Earnings Inequality, Employment Rates, and Incarceration." Working Paper no. 150. New York: Russell Sage Foundation.

Wilson, William Julius. 1997. When Work Disappears : The World of the New Urban Poor. New York: Vintage Books.

21

The Saints and the Roughnecks

WILLIAM J. CHAMBLISS

Chambliss' description of the Saints and the Roughnecks shows how the power of social class can operate to facilitate groups' resistance of deviant labels. In this classic selection from the sociological literature, Chambliss describes how the Saints engage in as many or more delinquent acts than the Roughnecks, yet are perceived as "good boys" merely engaging in typical adolescent hijinks. The greater social power contained in their higher class background enables the definition of their behavior as socially normative, allowing the police, teachers, community members, and parents to look the other way. On the other hand, the Roughnecks, who come from the "wrong side of the tracks," are perceived to be troublemakers, rabble-rousers, and delinquents. We see conflict and labeling theories in effect here since social class is the determinant of society's reactions. Behavior done by teenagers from upstanding, middle-class families is tolerated, while similar behavior engaged in by lower-class youth is reinforced as deviant. Once again, labels are applied based on status, not on patterns of behavior.

How does Chambliss' concept of reinforcement compare to Erikson's use of the self-fulfilling prophecy? How does it affect the Saints and the Roughnecks differently?

Eight promising young men—children of good, stable, white, upper-middle-class families, active in school affairs, good pre-college students—were some of the most delinquent boys at Hanibal High School. While community residents and parents knew that these boys occasionally sowed a few wild oats, they were totally unaware that sowing wild oats completely occupied the daily routine of these young men. The Saints were constantly occupied with truancy, drinking, wild driving, petty theft, and vandalism. Yet not one was officially arrested for any misdeed during the two years I observed them.

This record was particularly surprising in light of my observations during the same two years of another gang of Hanibal High School students, six lower-class white boys known as the Roughnecks. The Roughnecks were constantly in

Reprinted by permission of Springer and Transaction Publishers. "The Saints and the Roughnecks" by William J. Chambliss, from *Society*, Vol. 11, No. 1, 1973. Copyright © 1973 by Transaction Publishers.

trouble with police and community even though their rate of delinquency was about equal with that of the Saints. What was the cause of this disparity? The result? The following consideration of the activities, social class, and community perceptions of both gangs may provide some answers.

THE SAINTS FROM MONDAY TO FRIDAY

The Saints' principal daily concern was with getting out of school as early as possible. The boys managed to get out of school with minimum danger that they would be accused of playing hookey through an elaborate procedure for obtaining "legitimate" release from class. The most common procedure was for one boy to obtain the release of another by fabricating a meeting of some committee, program, or recognized club. Charles might raise his hand in his 9:00 chemistry class and ask to be excused—a euphemism for going to the bathroom. Charles would go to Ed's math class and inform the teacher that Ed was needed for a 9:30 rehearsal of the drama club play. The math teacher would recognize Ed and Charles as "good students" involved in numerous school activities and would permit Ed to leave at 9:30. Charles would return to his class, and Ed would go to Tom's English class to obtain his release. Tom would engineer Charles's escape. The strategy would continue until as many of the Saints as possible were freed. After a stealthy trip to the car (which had been parked in a strategic spot), the boys were off for a day of fun.

Over the two years I observed the Saints, this pattern was repeated nearly every day. There were variations on the theme, but in one form or another, the boys used this procedure for getting out of class and then off the school grounds. Rarely did all eight of the Saints manage to leave school at the same time. The average number avoiding school on the days I observed them was five.

Having escaped from the concrete corridors the boys usually went either to a pool hall on the other (lower-class) side of town or to a cafe in the suburbs. Both places were out of the way of people the boys were likely to know (family or school officials), and both provided a source of entertainment. The pool hall entertainment was the generally rough atmosphere, the occasional hustler, the sometimes drunk proprietor, and, of course, the game of pool. The cafe's entertainment was provided by the owner. The boys would "accidentally" knock a glass on the floor or spill cola on the counter—not all the time, but enough to be sporting. They would also bend spoons, put salt in sugar bowls, and generally tease whoever was working in the cafe. The owner had opened the cafe recently and was dependent on the boys' business which was, in fact, substantial since between the horsing around and the teasing they bought food and drinks.

THE SAINTS ON WEEKENDS

On weekends the automobile was even more critical than during the week, for on weekends the Saints went to Big Town—a large city with a population of over a million 25 miles from Hanibal. Every Friday and Saturday night most of the Saints would meet between 8:00 and 8:30 and would go into Big Town. Big Town activities included drinking heavily in taverns or nightclubs, driving drunkenly through the streets, and committing acts of vandalism and playing pranks.

By midnight on Fridays and Saturdays the Saints were usually thoroughly high, and one or two of them were often so drunk they had to be carried to the cars. Then the boys drove around town, calling obscenities to women and girls; occasionally trying (unsuccessfully so far as I could tell) to pick girls up; and driving recklessly through red lights and at high speeds with their lights out. Occasionally they played "chicken." One boy would climb out the back window of the car and across the roof to the driver's side of the car while the car was moving at high speed (between 40 and 50 miles an hour); then the driver would move over and the boy who had just crawled across the car roof would take the driver's seat.

Searching for "fair game" for a prank was the boys' principal activity after they left the tavern. The boys would drive alongside a foot patrolman and ask directions to some street. If the policeman leaned on the car in the course of answering the question, the driver would speed away, causing him to lose his balance. The Saints were careful to play this prank only in an area where they were not going to spend much time and where they could quickly disappear around a corner to avoid having their license plate number taken.

Construction sites and road repair areas were the special province of the Saints' mischief. A soon-to-be-repaired hole in the road inevitably invited the Saints to remove lanterns and wooden barricades and put them in the car, leaving the hole unprotected. The boys would find a safe vantage point and wait for an unsuspecting motorist to drive into the hole. Often, though not always, the boys would go up to the motorist and commiserate with him about the dreadful way the city protected its citizenry.

Leaving the scene of the open hole and the motorist, the boys would then go searching for an appropriate place to erect the stolen barricade. An "appropriate place" was often a spot on a highway near a curve in the road where the barricade would not be seen by an oncoming motorist. The boys would wait to watch an unsuspecting motorist attempt to stop and (usually) crash into the wooden barricade. With saintly bearing the boys might offer help and understanding.

A stolen lantern might well find its way onto the back of a police car or hang from a street lamp. Once a lantern served as a prop for a reenactment of the "midnight ride of Paul Revere" until the "play," which was taking place at 2:00 A.M. in the center of a main street of Big Town, was interrupted by a police car several blocks away. The boys ran, leaving the lanterns on the street, and managed to avoid being apprehended.

Abandoned houses, especially if they were located in out-of-the-way places, were fair game for destruction and spontaneous vandalism. The boys would break windows, remove furniture to the yard and tear it apart, urinate on the walls, and scrawl obscenities inside.

Through all the pranks, drinking, and reckless driving the boys managed miraculously to avoid being stopped by police. Only twice in two years was

I aware that they had been stopped by a Big City policeman. Once was for speeding (which they did every time they drove whether they were drunk or sober), and the driver managed to convince the policeman that it was simply an error. The second time they were stopped they had just left a nightclub and were walking through an alley. Aaron stopped to urinate and the boys began making obscene remarks. A foot patrolman came into the alley, lectured the boys, and sent them home. Before the boys got to the car one began talking in a loud voice again. The policeman, who had followed them down the alley, arrested this boy for disturbing the peace and took him to the police station where the other Saints gathered. After paying a $5.00 fine, and with the assurance that there would be no permanent record of the arrest, the boy was released.

The boys had a spirit of frivolity and fun about their escapades. They did not view what they were engaged in as "delinquency," though it surely was by any reasonable definition of that word. They simply viewed themselves as having a little fun and who, they would ask, was really hurt by it? The answer had to be no one, although this fact remains one of the most difficult things to explain about the gang's behavior. Unlikely though it seems, in two years of drinking, driving, carousing, and vandalism no one was seriously injured as a result of the Saints' activities.

THE SAINTS IN SCHOOL

The Saints were highly successful in school. The average grade for the group was "B," with two of the boys having close to a straight "A" average. Almost all of the boys were popular and many of them held offices in the school. One of the boys was vice-president of the student body one year. Six of the boys played on athletic teams.

At the end of their senior year, the student body selected ten seniors for special recognition as the "school wheels"; four of the ten were Saints. Teachers and school officials saw no problem with any of these boys and anticipated that they would all "make something of themselves."

How the boys managed to maintain this impression is surprising in view of their actual behavior while in school. Their technique for covering truancy was so successful that teachers did not even realize that the boys were absent from school much of the time. Occasionally, of course, the system would backfire and then the boy was on his own. A boy who was caught would be most contrite, would plead guilty and ask for mercy. He inevitably got the mercy he sought.

Cheating on examinations was rampant, even to the point of orally communicating answers to exams as well as looking at one another's papers. Since none of the group studied, and since they were primarily dependent on one another for help, it is surprising that grades were so high. Teachers contributed to the deception in their admitted inclination to give these boys (and presumably others like them) the benefit of the doubt. When asked how the boys did in school, and when pressed on specific examinations, teachers might admit that they were disappointed in John's performance, but would quickly add that they "knew that he was capable of doing better," so John was given a higher grade than he had actually earned. How often this happened is impossible to know. During the time that I observed the group, I never saw any of the boys take homework home. Teachers may have been "understanding" very regularly.

One exception to the gang's generally good performance was Jerry, who had a "C" average in his junior year, experienced disaster the next year, and failed to graduate. Jerry had always been a little more nonchalant than the others about the liberties he took in school. Rather than wait for someone to come get him from class, he would offer his own excuse and leave. Although he probably did not miss any more classes than most of the others in the group, he did not take the requisite pains to cover his absences. Jerry was the only Saint whom I ever heard talk back to a teacher. Although teachers often called him a "cut up" or a "smart kid," they never referred to him as a troublemaker or as a kid headed for trouble. It seems likely, then, that Jerry's failure his senior year and his mediocre performance his junior year were consequences of his not playing the game the proper way (possibly because he was disturbed by his parents' divorce). His teachers regarded him as "immature" and not quite ready to get out of high school.

THE POLICE AND THE SAINTS

The local police saw the Saints as good boys who were among the leaders of the youth in the community. Rarely, the boys might be stopped in town for speeding or for running a stop sign. When this happened the boys were always polite, contrite, and pled for mercy. As in school, they received the mercy they asked for. None ever received a ticket or was taken into the precinct by the local police.

The situation in Big City, where the boys engaged in most of their delinquency, was only slightly different. The police there did not know the boys at all, although occasionally the boys were stopped by a patrolman. Once they were caught taking a lantern from a construction site. Another time they were stopped for running a stop sign, and on several occasions they were stopped for speeding. Their behavior was as before: contrite, polite, and penitent. The urban police, like the local police, accepted their demeanor as sincere. More important, the urban police were convinced that these were good boys just out for a lark.

THE ROUGHNECKS

Hanibal townspeople never perceived the Saints' high level of delinquency. The Saints were good boys who just went in for an occasional prank. After all, they were well dressed, well mannered, and had nice cars. The Roughnecks were a different story. Although the two gangs of boys were the same age, and both groups engaged in an equal amount of wild-oat sowing, everyone agreed that the not-so-well-dressed, not-so-well-mannered, not-so-rich boys were heading for trouble. Townspeople would say, "You can see the gang members at the drugstore, night after night, leaning against the storefront (sometimes drunk) or slouching around inside buying cokes, reading magazines, and probably stealing old Mr. Wall blind. When they are outside and girls walk by, even respectable girls, these boys make suggestive remarks. Sometimes their remarks are downright lewd."

From the community's viewpoint, the real indication that these kids were in for trouble was that they were constantly involved with the police. Some of them had been picked up for stealing, mostly small stuff, of course, "but still it's stealing small stuff that leads to big time crimes." "Too bad," people said. "Too bad that these boys couldn't behave like the other kids in town: stay out of trouble, be polite to adults, and look to their future."

The community's impression of the degree to which this group of six boys (ranging in age from 16 to 19) engaged in delinquency was somewhat distorted. In some ways the gang was more delinquent than the community thought; in other ways they were less.

The fighting activities of the group were fairly readily and accurately perceived by almost everyone. At least once a month, the boys would get into some sort of fight, although most fights were scraps between members of the group or involved only one member of the group and some peripheral hanger-on. Only three times in the period of observation did the group fight together: once against a gang from across town, once against two blacks, and once against a group of boys from another school. For the first two fights the group went out "looking for trouble"—and they found it both times. The third fight followed a football game and began spontaneously with an argument on the football field between one of the Roughnecks and a member of the opposition's football team.

Jack had a particular propensity for fighting and was involved in most of the brawls. He was a prime mover of the escalation of arguments into fights.

More serious than fighting, had the community been aware of it, was theft. Although almost everyone was aware that the boys occasionally stole things, they did not realize the extent of the activity. Petty stealing was a frequent event for the Roughnecks. Sometimes they stole as a group and coordinated their efforts; other times they stole in pairs. Rarely did they steal alone.

The thefts ranged from very small things like paperback books, comics, and ballpoint pens to expensive items like watches. The nature of the thefts varied from time to time. The gang would go through a period of systematically shoplifting items from automobiles or school lockers. Types of thievery varied with the whim of the gang. Some forms of thievery were more profitable than others, but all thefts were for profit, not just thrills.

Roughnecks siphoned gasoline from cars as often as they had access to an automobile, which was not very often. Unlike the Saints, who owned their own cars, the Roughnecks would have to borrow their parents' cars, an event which occurred only eight or nine times a year. The boys claimed to have stolen cars for joy rides from time to time.

Ron committed the most serious of the group's offenses. With an unidentified associate the boy attempted to burglarize a gasoline station. Although this station had been robbed twice previously in the same month, Ron denied any involvement in either of the other thefts. When Ron and his accomplice approached the station, the owner was hiding in the bushes beside the station. He fired both barrels of a double-barreled shotgun at the boys. Ron was severely injured; the other boy ran away and was never caught. Though he remained in critical condition for several months, Ron finally recovered and served six months of the following year in reform school. Upon release from reform school, Ron was put back a grade in school, and began running around with a different gang of boys. The Roughnecks considered the new gang less delinquent than themselves, and during the following year Ron had no more trouble with the police.

The Roughnecks, then, engaged mainly in three types of delinquency: theft, drinking, and fighting. Although community members perceived that this gang of kids was delinquent, they mistakenly believed that their illegal activities were primarily drinking, fighting, and being a nuisance to passersby. Drinking was limited among the gang members, although it did occur, and theft was much more prevalent than anyone realized.

Drinking would doubtless have been more prevalent had the boys had ready access to liquor. Since they rarely had automobiles at their disposal, they could not travel very far, and the bars in town would not serve them. Most of the boys had little money, and this, too, inhibited their purchase of alcohol. Their major source of liquor was a local drunk who would buy them a fifth if they would give him enough extra to buy himself a pint of whiskey or a bottle of wine.

The community's perception of drinking as prevalent stemmed from the fact that it was the most obvious delinquency the boys engaged in. When one of the boys had been drinking, even a casual observer seeing him on the corner would suspect that he was high.

There was a high level of mutual distrust and dislike between the Roughnecks and the police. The boys felt very strongly that the police were unfair and corrupt. Some evidence existed that the boys were correct in their perception.

The main source of the boys' dislike for the police undoubtedly stemmed from the fact that the police would sporadically harass the group. From the standpoint of the boys, these acts of occasional enforcement of the law were whimsical and uncalled-for. It made no sense to them, for example, that the police would come to the corner occasionally and threaten them with arrest for loitering when the night before the boys had been out siphoning gasoline from cars and the police had been nowhere in sight. To the boys, the police were stupid on the one hand, for not being where they should have been and catching the boys in a serious offense, and unfair on the other hand, for trumping up "loitering" charges against them.

From the viewpoint of the police, the situation was quite different. They knew, with all the confidence necessary to be a policeman, that these boys were engaged in criminal activities. They knew this partly from occasionally catching them, mostly from circumstantial evidence ("the boys were around when those tires were slashed"), and partly because the police shared the view of the community in general that this was a bad bunch of boys. The best the police could hope to do was to be sensitive to the fact that these boys were engaged in illegal acts and arrest them whenever there was some evidence that they had been involved. Whether or not the boys had in fact committed a particular act in a particular way was not especially important. The police had a broader view: their job was to stamp out these kids' crimes; the tactics were not as important as the end result.

Over the period that the group was under observation, each member was arrested at least once. Several of the boys were arrested a number of times and spent at least one night in jail. While most were never taken to court, two of the boys were sentenced to six months' incarceration in boys' schools.

THE ROUGHNECKS IN SCHOOL

The Roughnecks' behavior in school was not particularly disruptive. During school hours they did not all hang around together, but tended instead to spend most of their time with one or two other members of the gang who were their special buddies. Although every member of the gang attempted to avoid school as much as possible, they were not particularly successful and most of them attended school with surprising regularity. They considered school a burden— something to be gotten through with a minimum of conflict. If they were "bugged" by a particular teacher, it could lead to trouble. One of the boys, Al, once threatened to beat up a teacher and, according to the other boys, the teacher hid under a desk to escape him.

Teachers saw the boys the way the general community did, as heading for trouble, as being uninterested in making something of themselves. Some were also seen as being incapable of meeting the academic standards of the school. Most of the teachers expressed concern for this group of boys and were willing to pass them despite poor performance, in the belief that failing them would only aggravate the problem.

The group of boys had a grade point average just slightly above "C." No one in the group failed a grade, and no one had better than a "C" average. They were very consistent in their achievement or, at least, the teachers were consistent in their perception of the boys' achievement.

Two of the boys were good football players. Herb was acknowledged to be the best player in the school and Jack was almost as good. Both boys were criticized for their failure to abide by training rules, for refusing to come to practice as often as they should, and for not playing their best during practice. What they lacked in sportsmanship they made up for in skill, apparently, and played every game no matter how poorly they had performed in practice or how many practice sessions they had missed.

TWO QUESTIONS

Why did the community, the school, and the police react to the Saints as though they were good, upstanding, nondeliquent youths with bright futures but to the Roughnecks as though they were tough, young criminals who were headed for trouble? Why did the Roughnecks and the Saints in fact have quite different careers after high school—careers which, by and large, lived up to the expectations of the community?

The most obvious explanation for the differences in the community's and law enforcement agencies' reactions to the two gangs is that one group of boys was "more delinquent" than the other. Which group *was* more delinquent? The answer to this question will determine in part how we explain the differential responses to these groups by the members of the community and, particularly, by law enforcement and school officials.

In sheer number of illegal acts, the Saints were the more delinquent. They were truant from school for at least part of the day almost every day of the week. In addition, their drinking and vandalism occurred with surprising regularity. The Roughnecks, in contrast, engaged sporadically in delinquent episodes. While these episodes were frequent, they certainly did not occur on a daily or even a weekly basis.

The difference in frequency of offenses was probably caused by the Roughnecks' inability to obtain liquor and to manipulate legitimate excuses from school. Since the Roughnecks had less money than the Saints, and teachers carefully supervised their school activities, the Roughnecks' hearts may have been as black as the Saints', but their misdeeds were not nearly as frequent.

There are really no clear-cut criteria by which to measure qualitative differences in antisocial behavior. The most important dimension of the difference is generally referred to as the "seriousness" of the offenses.

If seriousness encompasses the relative economic costs of delinquent acts, then some assessment can be made. The Roughnecks probably stole an average of about $5.00 worth of goods a week. Some weeks the figure was considerably higher, but these times must be balanced against long periods when almost nothing was stolen.

The Saints were more continuously engaged in delinquency but their acts were not for the most part costly to property. Only their vandalism and occasional theft of gasoline would so qualify. Perhaps once or twice a month they would siphon a tankful of gas. The other costly items were street signs, construction lanterns, and the like. All of these acts combined probably did not quite average $5.00 a week, partly because much of the stolen equipment was abandoned and presumably could be recovered. The difference in cost of stolen property between the two groups was trivial, but the Roughnecks probably had a slightly more expensive set of activities than did the Saints.

Another meaning of seriousness is the potential threat of physical harm to members of the community and to the boys themselves. The Roughnecks were more prone to physical violence; they not only welcomed an opportunity to fight; they went seeking it. In addition, they fought among themselves frequently. Although the fighting never included deadly weapons, it was still a menace, however minor, to the physical safety of those involved.

The Saints never fought. They avoided physical conflict both inside and outside the group. At the same time, though, the Saints frequently endangered their own and other people's lives. They did so almost every time they drove a car, especially if they had been drinking. Sober, their driving was risky; under the influence of alcohol it was horrendous. In addition, the Saints endangered the lives of others with their pranks. Street excavations left unmarked were a very serious hazard.

Evaluating the relative seriousness of the two gangs' activities is difficult. The community reacted as though the behavior of the Roughnecks was a problem, and they reacted as though the behavior of the Saints was not. But the members of the community were ignorant of the array of delinquent acts that character-ized the Saints' behavior. Although concerned citizens were unaware of much of the Roughnecks' behavior as well, they were much better informed about the Roughnecks' involvement in delinquency than they were about the Saints'.

Visibility

Differential treatment of the two gangs resulted in part because one gang was infinitely more visible than the other. This differential visibility was a direct func-tion of the economic standing of the families. The Saints had access to automo-biles and were able to remove themselves from the sight of the community. In as routine a decision as to where to go to have a milkshake after school, the Saints stayed away from the mainstream of community life. Lacking transportation, the Roughnecks could not make it to the edge of town. The center of town was the only practical place for them to meet since their homes were scattered throughout the town and any noncentral meeting place put an undue hardship on some mem-bers. Through necessity the Roughnecks congregated in a crowded area where everyone in the community passed frequently, including teachers and law enforce-ment officers. They could easily see the Roughnecks hanging around the drugstore.

The Roughnecks, of course, made themselves even more visible by making remarks to passersby and by occasionally getting into fights on the corner. Mean-while, just as regularly, the Saints were either at the cafe on one edge of town or in the pool hall at the other edge of town. Without any particular realization that they were making themselves inconspicuous, the Saints were able to hide their time-wasting. Not only were they removed from the mainstream of traffic, but they were almost always inside a building.

On their escapades the Saints were also relatively invisible, since they left Hanibal and travelled to Big City. Here, too, they were mobile, roaming the city, rarely going to the same area twice.

Demeanor

To the notion of visibility must be added the difference in the responses of group members to outside intervention with their activities. If one of the Saints was confronted with an accusing policeman, even if he felt he was truly innocent of a wrongdoing, his demeanor was apologetic and penitent. A Roughneck's attitude was almost the polar opposite. When confronted with a threatening adult authority, even one who tried to be pleasant, the Roughneck's hostility and disdain were clearly observable. Sometimes he might attempt to put up a veneer of respect, but it was thin and was not accepted as sincere by the authority.

School was no different from the community at large. The Saints could manipulate the system by feigning compliance with the school norms. The availability of cars at school meant that once free from the immediate sight of the teacher, the boys could disappear rapidly. And this escape was well enough planned that no administrator or teacher was nearby when the boys left. A Roughneck who wished to escape for a few hours was in a bind. If it were possible to get free from class, downtown was still a mile away, and even if he arrived there, he was still very visible. Truancy for the Roughnecks meant almost certain detection, while the Saints enjoyed almost complete immunity from sanctions.

Bias

Community members were not aware of the transgressions of the Saints. Even if the Saints had been less discreet, their favorite delinquencies would have been perceived as less serious than those of the Roughnecks.

In the eyes of the police and school officials, a boy who drinks in an alley and stands intoxicated on the street corner is committing a more serious offense than is a boy who drinks to inebriation in a nightclub or a tavern and drives around afterwards in a car. Similarly, a boy who steals a wallet from a store will be viewed as having committed a more serious offense than a boy who steals a lantern from a construction site.

Perceptual bias also operates with respect to the demeanor of the boys in the two groups when they are confronted by adults. It is not simply that adults dislike the posture affected by boys of the Roughneck ilk; more important is the conviction that the posture adopted by the Roughnecks is an indication of their devotion and commitment to deviance as a way of life. The posture becomes a cue, just as the type of the offense is a cue, to the degree to which the known transgressions are indicators of the youths' potential for other problems.

Visibility, demeanor, and bias are surface variables that explain the day-to-day operations of the police. Why do these surface variables operate as they do? Why did the police choose to disregard the Saints' delinquencies while breathing down the backs of the Roughnecks?

The answer lies in the class structure of American society and the control of legal institutions by those at the top of the class structure. Obviously, no representative of the upper class drew up the operational chart for the police which led them to look in the ghettoes and on street corners—which led them to see the demeanor of lower-class youth as troublesome and that of upper-middle-class youth as tolerable. Rather, the procedure simply developed from experience—experience with irate and influential upper-middle-class parents insisting that their son's vandalism was simply a prank and his drunkenness only a momentary "sowing of wild oats"—experience with cooperative or indifferent, powerless, lower-class parents who acquiesced to the law's definition of their son's behavior.

ADULT CAREERS OF THE SAINTS
AND THE ROUGHNECKS

The community's confidence in the potential of the Saints and the Roughnecks apparently was justified. If anything the community members underestimated the degree to which these youngsters would turn out "good" or "bad."

Seven of the eight members of the Saints went on to college immediately after high school. Five of the boys graduated from college in four years. The sixth one finished college after two years in the army, and the seventh spent four years in the air force before returning to college and receiving a B.A. degree. Of these seven college graduates, three went on for advanced degrees. One finished law school and is now active in state politics, one finished medical school and is practicing near Hanibal, and one boy is now working for a Ph.D. The other four college graduates entered submanagerial, managerial, or executive training positions with larger firms.

The only Saint who did not complete college was Jerry. Jerry had failed to graduate from high school with the other Saints. During his second senior year, after the other Saints had gone on to college, Jerry began to hang around with what several teachers described as a "rough crowd"—the gang that was heir apparent to the Roughnecks. At the end of his second senior year, when he did graduate from high school, Jerry took a job as a used car salesman, got married, and quickly had a child. Although he made several abortive attempts to go to college by attending night school, when I last saw him (ten years after high school) Jerry was unemployed and had been living on unemployment for almost a year. His wife worked as a waitress.

Some of the Roughnecks have lived up to community expectations. A number of them were headed for trouble. A few were not.

Jack and Herb were the athletes among the Roughnecks and their athletic prowess paid off handsomely. Both boys received unsolicited athletic scholarships to college. After Herb received his scholarship (near the end of his senior year), he apparently did an about-face. His demeanor became very similar to that of the Saints. Although he remained a member in good standing of the Roughnecks, he stopped participating in most activities and did not hang on the corner as often.

Jack did not change. If anything, he became more prone to fighting. He even made excuses for accepting the scholarship. He told the other gang members that the school had guaranteed him a "C" average if he would come to play football—an idea that seems far-fetched, even in this day of highly competitive recruiting.

During the summer after graduation from high school, Jack attempted suicide by jumping from a tall building. The jump would certainly have killed most people trying it, but Jack survived. He entered college in the fall and played four years of football. He and Herb graduated in four years, and both are teaching and coaching in high schools. They are married and have stable families. If anything, Jack appears to have a more prestigious position in the community than does Herb, though both are well respected and secure in their positions.

Two of the boys never finished high school. Tommy left at the end of his junior year and went to another state. That summer he was arrested and placed on probation on a manslaughter charge. Three years later he was arrested for murder; he pleaded guilty to second degree murder and is serving a 30-year sentence in the state penitentiary.

Al, the other boy who did not finish high school, also left the state in his senior year. He is serving a life sentence in a state penitentiary for first-degree murder.

Wes is a small-time gambler. He finished high school and "bummed around." After several years he made contact with a bookmaker who employed him as a runner. Later he acquired his own area and has been working it ever since. His position among the bookmakers is almost identical to the position he had in the gang; he is always around but no one is really aware of him. He makes no trouble and he does not get into any. Steady, reliable, capable of keeping his mouth closed, he plays the game by the rules, even though the game is an illegal one.

That leaves only Ron. Some of his former friends reported that they had heard he was "driving a truck up north," but no one could provide any concrete information.

REINFORCEMENT

The community responded to the Roughnecks as boys in trouble, and the boys agreed with that perception. Their pattern of deviancy was reinforced, and breaking away from it became increasingly unlikely. Once the boys acquired an image of themselves as deviants, they selected new friends who affirmed that self-image. As that self-conception became more firmly entrenched, they also became willing to try new and more extreme deviances. With their growing alienation came freer expression of disrespect and hostility for representatives of the legitimate society. This disrespect increased the community's negativism, perpetuating the entire process of commitment to deviance. Lack of a commitment to deviance works the same way. In either case, the process will perpetuate itself unless some event (like a scholarship to college or a sudden failure) external to the established relationship intervenes. For two of the Roughnecks (Herb and Jack), receiving college athletic scholarships created new relations and culminated in a break with the established pattern of deviance. In the case of one of the Saints (Jerry), his parents' divorce and his failing to graduate from high school changed some of his other relations. Being held back in school for a year and losing his place among the Saints had sufficient impact on Jerry to alter his self-image and virtually to assure that he would not go on to college as his peers did. Although the experiments of life can rarely be reversed, it seems likely in view of the behavior of the other boys who did not enjoy this special treatment by the school that Jerry, too, would have "become something" had he graduated as anticipated. For Herb and Jack outside intervention worked to their advantage; for Jerry it was his undoing.

Selective perception and labeling—finding, processing, and punishing some kinds of criminality and not others—means that visible, poor, nonmobile, outspoken, undiplomatic "tough" kids will be noticed, whether their actions are seriously delinquent or not. Other kids, who have established a reputation for being bright (even though underachieving), disciplined and involved in respectable activities, who are mobile and monied, will be invisible when they deviate from sanctioned activities. They'll sow their wild oats—perhaps even wider and thicker than their lower-class cohorts—but they won't be noticed. When it's time to leave adolescence most will follow the expected path, settling into the ways of the middle class, remembering fondly the delinquent but unnoticed fling of their youth. The Roughnecks and others like them may turn around, too. It is more likely that their noticeable deviance will have been so reinforced by police and community that their lives will be effectively channeled into careers consistent with their adolescent background.

22

Doctors' Autonomy and Power

JOHN LIEDERBACH

Doctors are another group with the social status and power to rise above the deviant acts they commit and maintain a prestigious reputation. Malfeasance and misconduct are rampant in the medical professions, as we constantly read in the newspaper, yet we are less likely to suspect doctors of wrongdoing, Liederbach suggests, due to their positive reputation and role as altruistic healers. They are, nonetheless, as subject to the temptations for fraud and abuse as any other individuals. Liederbach describes such common practices as fee splitting, self-referrals, prescription violations, unnecessary treatments, and sexual misconduct that have led insurers and health maintenance organizations (HMOs) to tighten up their scrutiny of the medical industry. Regulation by the government is less conscientious, it appears, and the presence of overpayment, fraud, and abuse of the Medicaid and Medicare systems are more widespread. Liederbach notes that occupational crimes such as these, where people engage in deviance for their own benefit, not that of their organizations, will occur wherever opportunities can be found. This chapter is especially relevant to today's political debates about universal health care, the precarious financial footing of Medicaid and Medicare, and the loss of governmental resources (for example, in Hurricane Katrina) due to lack of oversight, carelessness, and fraud.

What sources of social power are discussed in this chapter that give doctors the ability to refute their potential labeling as deviant?

Over time, health care has grown into a trillion dollar a year enterprise. The delivery of patient services involves not only physicians, but also large-scale insurance companies, government-financed benefit programs, and Health Maintenance Organizations (HMOs). Estimates of the cost of health-care fraud range from fifty to eighty billion dollars annually (Witkin, Friedman, and Doran 1992). In the Medicare program alone, some seventeen billion dollars a year is lost (Shogren 1995). The financial cost of medical crime has led one observer to characterize the situation as "white-collar wilding" (Witkin, Friedman, and Doran 1992).

The consequences of medical crime are not merely financial. Unnecessary medical procedures, negligent care, prescription violations, and the sexual abuse of patients exact an enormous physical toll as well. Each year some 400,000 patients become victims of negligent mistakes or misdiagnoses. One Harvard researcher estimates that 180,000 patients die every year, due at least in part to negligent care ("Patients, Doctors, Lawyers" 1990). Up to two million patients are needlessly subjected to physical risks through unnecessary operations each year; the resulting price tag approaches four billion dollars (Jesilow, Pontell, and Geis 1993).

THE "PROTECTIVE CLOAK": STATUS, ALTRUISM, AND AUTONOMY

Physicians are recognized as a special group in society—a privileged caste able to decipher puzzling ailments and able to fix broken-down bodies. The privilege is hard won through years of education and exhaustive training. The physician's honored rank, however, sponsors opportunities for doctors to commit crimes within their profession. Attributes synonymous with medical practice, such as high social status, trustworthiness, and professional autonomy, have provided doctors with what some have termed a "protective cloak" that has shielded doctors from scrutiny and legal accountability (Jesilow, Pontell, and Geis 1993; Parsons 1951).

One element of the "cloak," high social status, has helped to afford doctors the protections necessary to commit medical crimes. Doctors' traditional high status derives from two related elements, namely, lucrative salaries and occupational prestige. Physicians remain one of the most highly compensated occupational groups, with median annual incomes exceeding $120,000 (Ruffenach 1988). Aided by the prestige that typically accompanies high salaries in American culture, physicians have been able to retain an elite social position.

Historically, there has also been a general reluctance in American society to use the criminal law against high-status offenders, and criminologists have long recognized the important role that status plays in shaping the criminal opportunities afforded to professional groups. Professionals possess the financial and political wherewithal to influence the manner in which criminal statutes are written and enforced, and they are more apt to "escape arrest and conviction ... than those who lack such power" (Sutherland 1949). While scholars debate whether this reluctance stems from public apathy and/or ignorance concerning the costs connected to elite crimes (Cullen, Maakestad, and Cavender 1987; Evans, Cullen, and Dubeck 1993; Wilson 1975), the typically lenient sanctions currently imposed on doctors who pillage government benefit programs, provide negligent care, or otherwise physically abuse their patients points to a historical reluctance to treat as criminal even the most egregious forms of physician malfeasance (Jesilow, Pontell, and Geis 1993; Rosoffi Pontell, and Tillman 1998; Tillman and Pontell 1992; Wolfe et al. 1998).

A second protective element is the altruistic and trustworthy image projected by doctors. This image is cemented in the physician's code of ethics. The oath serves to define doctors as selfless professionals who perform an invaluable service without regard to personal financial gain (Jesilow, Pontell, and Geis 1993). The image structures criminal opportunities in several ways: the image creates an assumption of good will on the part of doctors that makes charges of intentional wrongdoing difficult to justify. Prosecutors may find it too challenging to prove intentionally fraudulent or harmful behavior in cases against highly respected and trusted doctors. Also, the physician's altruistic image has traditionally engendered a certain level of trust from patients (McKinlay and Stoeckle 1988; Stoeckle 1989). Trusting patients who are victims of fraudulent medical schemes or negligent care may fail to hold doctors accountable for their crimes. One observer has defined the impact of these factors more generally as a "pattern of deference" to doctors—a prevailing unwillingness to question their presumed trustworthiness (Bucy 1989).

Third, doctors have been relatively immune from legal scrutiny because of the medical professions' historical preference for self-regulation. State medical review boards, whose members are predominantly physicians themselves, are supposed to provide a "first line of defense" against doctors who violate legal or ethical codes (Wolfe et al. 1998). These boards can revoke medical licenses or otherwise discipline doctors who fail to meet professional or legal standards. Doctors argue that self-regulation and autonomy characterize any profession— that is, doctors alone possess the specialized expertise and unique qualifications to judge the actions of other physicians. The medical community regards the imposition of civil and/or criminal penalties as both unwarranted and unnecessary, especially in cases that involve errors in clinical judgment (Abramovsky 1995). The profession's reliance on self-regulation, however, may facilitate criminal opportunities by shielding its members from more effective punishments. State medical boards, for example, have continually failed to identify doctors who are chronically incompetent, and often punish them with "slaps on the wrist" (Wolfe et al. 1998). The case of one New York doctor illustrates the dangers of relying solely on professional controls:

> During the mid-1980s [Dr. Benjamin] was investigated by the Department of Health in connection with numerous medical irregularities. In 1986, after a medical review board convicted him on 38 counts of gross negligence and incompetence, the New York State Health Commissioner asked the Board to revoke his license.... The doctor's punishment was reduced, to a three-month suspension and three years' probation. In June 1993 ... the Department revoked Dr. Benjamin's license for five botched abortions performed in one year. However, Dr. Benjamin was allowed to continue performing abortions pending appeal. Less than a month later (patient) Gaudalupe Negron met her death from another of Dr. Benjamin's botched procedures. (Abramovsky 1995)

The lax enforcement typically provided by state medical boards has created an inviting opportunity structure for doctors to commit fraud and abuse within their profession. The problems related to professional control are exacerbated by the well-documented "code of silence" that exists among medical professionals (Rosoff, Pontell, and Tillman 1998). Doctors are often hesitant to report fraud and abuse for fear of professional recriminations (Karlin 1995; Levy 1995). Still, some in the medical community recognize the extent of the problem: "The profession has done a lousy job of policing its own," acknowledges Arthur Caplan, chairman of the Center for Bioethics at the University of Pennsylvania (Grey 1995).

SELECTED MEDICAL OFFENSES

Medical "Kickbacks": Fee Splitting and Self-Referrals

"Kickbacks" are generally defined as payments from one party to another in exchange for referred business or other income-producing deals. Their acceptance by doctors is considered unethical, and in most cases illegal, because they create a conflict of interest between the physicians' commitment to quality patient care and their own financial self-interest. Doctors who are primarily concerned with financial gain compromise their loyalty to patients, as well as their independent professional judgment. Two well-recognized types of medical kickbacks include fee splitting and self-referrals.

Fee splitting occurs when one physician (usually a general practitioner) receives payment from a surgeon or other specialists in exchange for patient referrals. Fee splitting artificially inflates medical costs, provides incentives for unnecessary tests and specialized treatment, and can also endanger the quality of patient care (Stevens 1971). As Sutherland (1949) explained, the fee-splitting doctor "tends to send his patients to the surgeon who will split the largest fee rather than to the surgeon who will do the best work." Early observers regarded fee splitting as an "almost universal" practice, and estimated that 50 to 90% of physicians split fees (MacEachern 1948; Williams 1948). Despite the advent of more secure payment sources provided by the spread of health insurance coverage in the post-World War II years, congressional investigations in the 1970s continued to recognize fee splitting as a problem (Rodwin 1992; U.S. Congress 1976). While it remains difficult to determine whether the prevalence of fee splitting has increased or decreased over time, it clearly has persisted (Rodwin 1992).

Alternatives to fee splitting have developed more recently, including self-referrals. Self-referrals involve sending patients to specialized medical facilities in which the physician has a financial interest. Between 50,000 and 75,000 doctors have a financial stake in ancillary medical services (quoted in Rosoff, Pontell, and Tillman 1998). Recent research identifies the problems associated with self-referrals, including higher utilization costs and unnecessary services (Hillman et al. 1990; Mitchell and Scott 1992; Rodwin 1992). Self-referring doctors refer patients for laboratory testing at a 45% higher rate than noninvesting physicians (U.S. Department of Health and Human Services 1989). Physicians' utilization of clinical laboratories, diagnostic imaging centers, and rehabilitation facilities was found to be significantly higher when physicians owned these facilities (Hillman et al. 1990).

The medical profession's traditional response to financial conflicts of interest has been less than overwhelming. While most states had declared fee splitting illegal by the mid-1950s, the medical profession did not explicitly address financial conflicts in ethical codes until the 1980s (Rodwin 1992). One newspaper characterized the profession's response with embarrassing clarity: "Fee splitting has been like a venereal disease ... it exist(s), but nice people do not talk about it" (quoted in Rodwin 1992). The legal and professional response to self-referrals has been more ambivalent. Despite recent legislative attempts to prohibit self-referrals, the practice remains legal. Likewise, professional standards have not been effective in curtailing abuses:

> Unlike other professionals who are subject to extensive conflict of interest regulation ... physicians have addressed these issues largely on their own, and have been subject to minimal regulation by state and federal laws or even professional codes ... The American Medical Association addresses these issues primarily by relying on professional norms, individual discretion and subjective standards ... (the profession) lacks an effective means to hold physicians accountable. (Rodwin 1992, 734)

Prescription Violations

Only doctors possess the education and specialized expertise required to safely prescribe dangerous and often addictive drugs, including narcotics, amphetamines, tranquilizers, and other controlled substances. The privilege is entrusted with the legal responsibility to limit access to these drugs on the basis of medical need. While the vast majority of physicians uphold these responsibilities, an alarming number of doctors violate this trust. Between 1988 and 1996, 1,521 doctors were disciplined for misprescribing or overprescribing drugs (Wolfe et al. 1998). Numerous doctors were caught selling blank prescriptions to known addicts. One physician dispensed expired drugs from old, unlabeled spice jars. Another doctor prescribed dangerous weight loss pills to a patient for four years without even examining her—eventually resulting in the patient having a stroke (Wolfe et al. 1998). Some prescription violations are coupled with fraudulent billing schemes designed to maximize profits from illegal prescriptions. Jesilow, Pontell, and Geis (1993) relate one of the most appalling cases:

> In Los Angeles, one investigator reported a Medicaid doctor who saw so many patients daily that red, blue, and yellow lines had been painted on his office floor to expedite traffic. Each color represented a different kind of pill. (22)

Similar to the case of medical kickbacks, the medical profession has also largely failed to adequately discipline doctors who violate prescription laws. At least 69% of the doctors cited between 1988 and 1996 were not even temporarily suspended from practicing medicine (Wolfe et al. 1998).

Unnecessary Treatments

Doctors who intentionally subject patients to medically unnecessary treatments violate the law in two ways. First, unnecessary treatments are fraudulent because they result in compensation that is deceptively gained. More important, unnecessary procedures that are invasive, such as surgery, may be considered a form of assault because they needlessly expose patients to physical risks (Lanza-Kaduce 1980). The highly publicized case of one California ophthalmologist dearly illustrates how unnecessary treatments can result in serious physical harm to patients. The doctor performed unneeded cataract surgery on patients solely to collect a $584 operation fee. In the process, the doctor admitted needlessly "blinding a lot of people" (Pontell, Geis, and Jesilow 1984).

Determining the prevalence of "unnecessary" treatments is often difficult given the inherent uncertainties involved in diagnosing and treating patients. Green (1997) has outlined several methods used by researchers to estimate the extent of unnecessary surgeries: (1) geographical variations in surgical rates, (2) studies of second surgical opinions, (3) variations in surgical rates between payment plans, and (4) expert opinions based on predetermined criteria. Although these studies present mixed findings, wide geographical variations in surgical rates can be used to suggest that unnecessary surgeries occur with some frequency. For example, hysterectomies are performed at an 80% higher rate in Southern states, and 1,000% rate variations in pacemaker operations have been identified in Massachusetts (quoted in Green 1997). Similarly, one government-sponsored study found a 120% higher surgical rate for patients enrolled in fee-for-service plans versus patients enrolled in HMOs (U.S. Department of Health, Education, and Welfare 1971).

Sexual Misconduct

Sexual misconduct by doctors can take a variety of forms (Jacobs 1994). Doctors may engage in sexual misconduct in exchange for professional services. Alternatively, doctors may allow relationships with patients to escalate beyond what is ethically acceptable. Finally, doctors may sexually assault patients while they are under the control of anesthesia or otherwise incapable of consenting to a sexual act (Green 1997). These offenses are especially abhorrent, because they represent an abuse of power by the doctor in situations where the patient is particularly vulnerable. From 1987 to 1996, 393 doctors were disciplined by state medical boards for sexual misconduct with patients. At least 34% of those doctors were not forced to even temporarily stop practicing (Wolfe et al. 1998).

MEDICAID FRAUD AND ABUSE

Medicaid began in 1965 as one of the "Great Society" programs initiated during the Lyndon B. Johnson administration. The program extended health coverage to needy Americans who could not otherwise afford it. Perhaps overshadowed by the nobility of this goal, the program's costs were not considered a primary concern (Jesilow, Pontell, and Geis 1993). Since its inception, fraud and abuse has been endemic to the program. Jesilow, Pontell, and Geis (1993), in their exposé on Medicaid crime, identify several reasons why the introduction of Medicaid has surreptitiously expanded the scope of the medical crime problem.

The medical profession opposed the initial Medicaid legislation. Doctors perceived Medicaid as a threat to their professional autonomy, because the program dictated the price of their professional medical services (Jesilow, Pontell, and Geis 1993). The Medicaid program introduced an unwelcome influence— the government—into decisions that were traditionally left to the independent professional discretion of doctors. This intrusion into the professional autonomy of doctors created widespread dissatisfaction within the medical community, and served to facilitate fraud and abuse within the program in at least two important ways (Jesilow, Pontell, and Geis 1993). First, the medical community's initial opposition led to certain flaws in the program's design that created easy opportunities to violate the law. For example, the original Medicaid legislation did not include provisions for punishing doctors who violated program rules (Jesilow, Pontell, and Geis 1993). The omission was not an accident, but an attempt to placate doctors, without whose cooperation the program could not be launched. As a result, the program lacked the effective sanctions necessary to police an additional design flaw, the program's fee-for-service payment structure. The fee-for-service plan reimbursed doctors a fixed amount for each procedure, but the doctor could earn additional income by double-billing for the same patient, billing for more expensive procedures than those performed, or even charging the program for services that were never done (Jesilow, Pontell, and Geis 1993). A significant number of Medicaid providers could not resist the combination of easy opportunities and lenient sanctions.

Second, the government's intrusion on the professional autonomy of doctors gave rise to an aggressively defiant attitude among some practitioners against the rules that governed Medicaid work. As Jesilow, Pontell, and Geis (1993) explain, this militant defiance "dramatically reduced one of the most powerful deterrents to crime, especially for middle and upper class perpetrators: the sense of guilt and the force of conscience associated with depredations against known human victims." Because they believed Medicaid to be an illegitimate intrusion on their professional autonomy, some Medicaid violators "redefined" their criminal behavior in a positive light. As a result, many of these doctors did not view their actions as wrong (Jesilow, Pontell, and Geis 1993).

This combination of opportunities, motivations, and lax sanctions has produced a dizzying array of violations related to the Medicaid program. Perhaps the most striking example of Medicaid fraud, however, is the discovery of Medicaid "mills" by fraud investigators (Jesilow, Pontell, and Geis 1993).

> Located in dilapidated areas, often in storefronts, and catering almost exclusively to patients on Medicaid rolls, the mills resemble clinics in that doctors with different specialties are gathered under one roof. But the mill's providers often rent space in the building and bill Medicaid individually.... Criminal activities flourished in the Medicaid mills.

Some employed "hawkers" to round up customers. Several catered to
drug traffic. Various government agents, all claiming to be suffering
from nothing more than the common cold, had been seen by eighty-five
doctors in Medicaid mills. They underwent eighteen electrocardiograms,
eight tuberculosis tests, four allergy tests, as well as a hearing, glaucoma,
and electroencephalogram tests. (50)

The inception of the Medicaid program posed one of the first significant
challenges to the professional autonomy of physicians. Although this challenge
did serve to extend health benefits to many of the nation's most indigent citizens,
the program also altered the traditional opportunity structure for medical crime,
and created new and unique avenues for physicians to commit offenses relating
to their medical practice....

One indication of increasing physician vulnerability is the recent spate of
criminal prosecutions against doctors who have killed or maimed patients
through negligent or reckless medical care. Because of the protections traditionally afforded to doctors, errors in clinical judgment—even if they resulted in the
death of patient—have traditionally been sanctioned exclusively through civil actions or peer-oriented sanctions. The filing of *violent* criminal charges, such as
manslaughter, assault, reckless homicide, or murder, against doctors who victimize patients in the course of their medical practice had been an exceedingly rare
occurrence (Abramovsky 1995; Crane 1994; Green 1997). However, at least
seven doctors have been criminally prosecuted for their violent victimization
of patients over the last ten years (Liederbach, Cullen, Sundt, and Geis 1998).
The case against Dr. Joseph Verbrugge is indicative not only because of the
gravity of his mistakes, but also because he is believed to be the first doctor
to stand trial in Colorado accused of a violent crime related to a medical
procedure:

Verbrugge was charged with reckless manslaughter in connection
with the death of eight-year-old Richard Leonard during ear surgery.
The normally routine procedure went awry when the boy's heart
rate jumped significantly after Verbrugge administered the anesthetic.
During the surgery, the patient's breathing became irregular and
his temperature soared to 107 degrees. Prosecutors contended that
Verbrugge failed to react to those danger signs because he had fallen
asleep during the operation. The patient died after three hours in
surgery. His reaction to the anesthesia had increased the level of carbon
monoxide in his blood to four times the normal level. (Liederbach,
Cullen, Sundt, and Geis 1998)

It remains to be seen how prevalent criminal prosecutions against doctors
for medical "mistakes" will become. However, the recent cluster of these cases
may suggest the beginning of a trend toward increasing physician vulnerability. These
cases may be a signpost indicating that the traditional protections afforded to doctors
have eroded. In particular, as long-term doctor-patient relationships wane and as
HMOs increasingly influence the delivery of medical services, patient trust in

doctors—especially when things go badly in a medical procedure—will decline, and the ability to see reckless doctors as *criminals* may increase (Liederbach, Cullen, Sundt, and Geis 1998).

REFERENCES

Abramovsky, A. 1995. "Depraved Indifference and the Incompetent Doctor." *New York Law Journal* November 8, pp. 3–10.

Bucy, P. H. 1989. "Fraud by Fright: White Collar Crime by Health Care Providers." *North Carolina Law Review* 67: 855–937.

Crane, M. 1994. "Could Clinical Mistakes Land You in Jail? The Case of Gerald Einaugler." *Medical Economics* 71: 46–52.

Cullen, F. T., W. J. Maakestad, and G. Cavender. 1987. *Corporate Crime under Attack: The Ford Pinto Case and Beyond.* Cincinnati: Anderson.

Evans, D. T., F. T. Cullen, and P. J. Dubeck. 1993. "Public Perceptions of White Collar Crime." Pp. 85–114 in *Understanding Corporate Criminality,* edited by M. B. Blankenship. New York: Garland.

Green, G. S. 1997. *Occupational Crime,* 2nd ed. Chicago: Nelson Hall.

Grey, B. 1995. "Medical Scandal." *Baltimore Sun,* August 21.

Hillman, B. J., V. A. Joseph, M. R. Mabry, J. H. Sunshine, S. D. Kennedy, and M. Noether. 1990. "Frequency and Costs of Diagnostic Imaging in Office Practice—A Comparison of Self-Referring and Radiologist Referring Physicians." *New England Journal of Medicine* 323: 1604–8.

Jacobs, S. 1994. "Social Control of Sexual Assault by Physicians and Lawyers within the Professional Relationship: Criminal and Disciplinary Actions." *American Journal of Criminal Justice* 19(1): 43–60.

Jesilow, P., H. N. Pontell, and G. Geis. 1993. *Prescription for Profit: How Doctors Defraud Medicaid.* Berkeley: University of California Press.

Karlin, R. 1995. "Selective Silence Is under Scrutiny." *The Time Union* (Albany, NY), August 28, p. Bl.

Lanza-Kaduce, L. 1980. "Deviance among Professionals: The Case of Unnecessary Surgery." *Deviant Behavior* 1: 333–59.

Levy, D. 1995. "Physicians Can Run, Hide from Deadly Errors." *USA Today,* September 11, p. ID.

Liederbach, J., F. T. Cullen, J. Sundt, and G. Geis. 1998. "The Criminalization of Physician Violence: Social Control in Transformation?" Paper presented at the annual meeting of the American Society of Criminology, Washington, DC.

MacEachern, M. 1948. "College Continues Militant Stance against Fee-Splitting and Rebates." *Bulletin of the American College of Surgeons* 33: 65–67.

McKinlay, J. B., and J. D. Stoeckle. 1988. "Corporatization and the Social Transformation of Medicine." *International Journal of Health Services* 18: 191–200.

Mitchell, J. M., and E. Scott. 1992. "New Evidence on the Prevalence and Scope of Physician Joint Ventures." *Journal of the American Medical Association* 268: 80–84.

Parsons, T. 1951. *The Social System,* Glencoe, IL: Free Press.

"Patients, Doctors, Lawyers: Medical Injury, Malpractice Litigation, and Patient Compensation." 1990. *Harvard*

Medical Practices Study. Boston: President and Fellows of Harvard University.

Pontell, H. N., G. Geis, and P. D. Jesilow. 1984. "Practitioner Fraud and Abuse in Government Medical Benefit Programs." Washington, DC: U.S. Department of Justice.

Rodwin, M. A. 1992. "The Organized American Medical Profession's Response to Financial Conflicts of Interest: 1890–1992." *Milbank Quarterly* 70(4): 703–41.

Rosoff, S. M., H. N. Pontell, and R. Tillman. 1998. *Profit without Honor: White Collar Crime and the Looting of America.* Upper Saddle River, NJ: Prentice Hall.

Ruffenach, G. 1988. "No Need to Worry, Doctors Do Just Fine." *Wall Street Journal,* October 10.

Shogren, G. 1995. "Rampant Fraud Complicates Medicare Cures." *Los Angeles Times,* October 8, p. 1.

Stevens, R. 1971. *American Medicine and the Public Interest.* New Haven: Yale University Press.

Stoeckle, J. D. 1989. "Reflections on Modern Doctoring." *Milbank Quarterly* 66: 76–89.

Sutherland, E. H. 1949. *White-Collar Crime,* New Haven: Yale University Press.

Tillman, R., and H. N. Pontell. 1992. "Is Justice Color Blind?: Punishing Medicaid Provider Fraud." *Criminology* 30(4): 547–74.

U.S. Congress. Senate Subcommittee on Long-Term Care, Special Committee on Aging. 1976. *Fraud and Abuse among Practitioners Participating in the Medicaid Program.* Washington, DC.

U.S. Department of Health, Education, and Welfare. 1971. *The Federal Employees Health Benefit Program— Enrollment and Utilization of Health Services 1961–1968.* Washington, DC: U.S. Government Printing Office.

U.S. Department of Health and Human Services. 1989. *Financial Arrangements between Physicians and Health Care Businesses.* Washington, DC: U.S. Government Printing Office.

Williams, G. 1948. "The Truth About Fee-Splitting." *Modern Hospital* 70: 43–48 (reprinted in *Reader's Digest,* July 1948).

Wilson, J. Q. 1975. *Thinking about Crime.* New York: Basic Books.

Witkm, G., D. Friedman, and G. Doran. 1992. "Health Care Fraud." *US News and WorldReport,* February 24, pp. 34–13.

Wolfe, S., K. M. Franklin, P. McCarthy, P. Bame, and B. M. Adler. 1998. *16,638 Questionable Doctors Disciplined by State and Federal Governments.* Washington, DC: Public Citizens Health Research Group.

PART V

Deviant Identity

We have just looked at how some categories of people and behavior become defined as deviant. Yet social constructionism suggests that a deviant classification floating around abstractly in society is not meaningful unless it gets attached to people. Groups in society not only work to create definitions of deviance, but also to create situations where deviance occurs and is labeled. In this section we will examine the way deviance is evoked and shaped. Becoming deviant does not only entail having a definition of deviance and an environment in which it can occur; it also requires that people accept the identity and make it their own. Identities refer to the way people think of themselves. The study of deviant identities has focused on how people develop and manage non-normative self-conceptions. In Part V we will examine this process: how the concept of deviance becomes applied to individuals and how it affects their self-conception.

IDENTITY DEVELOPMENT

We mentioned earlier that although many people engage in deviance, the label is applied to only a small percentage of them. Such labeling is tied to their formerly "secret deviance" (Becker 1963) becoming exposed, or to an abstract status coming to bear on their personal experience. Thus, Jews may not feel stigmatized unless they experience anti-Semitism, and embezzlers may not think of themselves as thieves until they are caught. When this happens, they enter the pathway to the deviant identity, a pathway that follows a certain trajectory. The process of acquiring a deviant identity unfolds in stages as a "deviant" (Becker 1963) or "moral" (Goffman 1961) career, with people passing through stages that move them out of their innocent identities towards one labeled as "different" by society. In our own work (Adler and Adler 2007), we proposed a model of the seven stages of the **deviant identity career**.

Stage one begins once people are *caught and publicly identified* as deviant; their lives change in several ways. Others start to think of them differently. For example, suppose there has been a rash of thefts in a college dormitory, and Jessica, a first-year student, is finally caught and identified as the culprit. She may or may not be reported to authorities and charged with theft, but regardless, she will experience an informal labeling process. Once she is caught, the news about her is likely to spread. In stage two, people will probably change their attitudes toward her, as they find themselves talking about her behind her back. They may look at her behavior and engage in *"retrospective interpretation"* (Schur 1971) as they think about her differently, reflecting back onto the past to see if her current and earlier behavior can be recast differently in light of their new information. Where did she say she was when the last theft occurred? Where did she say she got the money to buy that new sweater?

In stage three, as this news spreads, either informally or through official agencies of social control, Jessica may develop what Goffman (1963) has called a *"spoiled identity,"* one with a tarnished reputation. Erikson (chapter one) noted that news about deviance is of high interest in a community, commanding intense focus from a wide audience. Deviant labeling is hard to reverse, he suggested, and once people's identities are spoiled they are hard to socially rehabilitate. He discussed "commitment ceremonies," such as trials or psychiatric hearings, where individuals are officially labeled as deviant. Few corresponding ceremonies exist, he remarked, to mark the cleansing of people's identities and welcome them back into the normative fold. Individuals may thus find it hard to recover from the lasting effect of such identity labeling, and despite their best efforts, they often find that society expects them to commit further deviance. Merton (1938) referred to this as the "self-fulfilling prophesy," where people tend to enact the labels placed upon them, despite possible intentions otherwise.

Jessica's dormmates and former friends may then engage in what Lemert (1951), in stage four, has called *"the dynamics of exclusion,"* deriding and ostracizing her from their social group. When she enters the room she may notice that a sudden hush falls over the conversation. People may not feel comfortable leaving her alone in their room. They may exclude her from their meal plans and study groups. She may become progressively shut out from non-deviant activities and circles such as honors societies, professional associations, relationships, or jobs. At the same time, in stage five, others may welcome or *include* her in their deviant les or activities. She may find that she has developed a reputation that, though repelling to some groups, is attractive to others. They may welcome her as "cool" and invite her into their circles. Thus, individuals may find that as they move down the pathway of their deviant careers, they shift friendship circles, being pushed away from the company of some, while being simultaneously welcomed into the company of others.

Sixth, others usually begin to *treat differently* those defined as deviant, indicating through their actions that their feelings and attitudes towards the newly deviant have shifted, often in a negative sense. They may not accord Jessica the same level of credibility they previously had, and they may tighten the margin of social allowance they allot her. Seventh, and finally, people react to this treatment using what Charles Horton Cooley referred to as their "looking glass selves." In the culminating stage of the identity career, they *internalize the deviant label* and come to think of themselves differently. This is likely to affect their future behavior. Although not all people who get caught in deviance progress completely through this full set of stages, Becker (1963) described this process as the effects of labeling.

Once people are labeled as deviant and accept that label into their self-conceptions, a variety of outcomes may ensue. We all juggle a range of identities and social selves through which we relate to people including those of sibling, child, friend, student, neighbor, and customer. Identities also derive from some of our demographic or occupational features, such as race, gender, age, religion, or social class. Hughes (1945) has suggested that some statuses are very dominant, overpowering others and coloring the way people are viewed. Having a known deviant identity may become one of these "**master statuses**," rising to the top of the hierarchy, infusing people's self-concept and others' reactions, and taking precedence over all others. Many social statuses fade in and out of relevance as people move through various situations, but a master status accompanies them into all their contexts, forming the key identity through which others see them. Deviant attributes such as a minority race, heroin addiction, and homosexuality are prime examples of such master statuses. Others, then, may think of an actor, for example, as a Hispanic person, a heroin addict, or as gay, with the individual's occupation or hobbies being seen as secondary to his or her deviant attribute. Hughes noted that master statuses are linked in society to **auxiliary traits**, the common social preconceptions that people associate with these. Self-injurers, for example, may be widely assumed to be adolescent white women from either middle-class backgrounds or disadvantaged youth whose lives are unhappy. They may be thought of as lacking impulse control, seeking attention, abuse survivors, mentally unstable, or as people who seek to cry for help or inject control into their lives. Heroin addicts may be suspected of being prostitutes or thieves and homosexuals may be suspected of being sexually promiscuous or AIDS infected. This type of identification spreads the image of deviance to cover the person as a whole and not just one part of him or her.

The relationship between master statuses and their auxiliary traits in society is reciprocal. When people learn that others have a certain deviant master status, they may impute the associated auxiliary traits onto them. Inversely, when people begin to recognize a few traits that they can put together to form the pattern of auxiliary traits associated with a particular deviant master status, they are likely to attribute that master status to others. For example, if parents notice that their children are staying out late with their friends, wearing "alternative" clothing styles, growing dreadlocks in their hair, dropping out of after-school activities, and hanging out with the "wrong" crowd of friends, they may suspect them of using drugs or committing crimes.

Lemert (1967) asserted another processual depiction of the deviant identity career with his concepts of **primary** and **secondary deviance**. Primary deviance refers to a stage when people commit deviant acts, but their deviance goes unrecognized. As a result, others do not cast the deviant label onto them, and they neither assume it nor perform a deviant role. Their self-conceptions are free of this image. Some people remain at the primary deviance stage throughout the time they are committing deviance, never advancing further. Yet a percentage of them do progress to secondary deviance. The seven stages of the identity career, described above, move people from primary to secondary deviance; their infractions become discovered, others identify them as deviant, and the labeling process ensues with all of its identity consequences. Others come to regard them as deviant, and they do as well. As they move into secondary deviance, individuals initially deny the label, but eventually come to accept it reluctantly as it becomes increasingly pressed upon them. They recognize their own deviance as they are forced to interact through this stigma with others. Sometimes this internalization comes as a justification or social defense to the problems associated with their deviant label, as individuals use it to take the offensive. At any rate, it becomes an identity that significantly affects their role performance. Some people may compartmentalize their deviant identity, but others exhibit "role engulfment" (Schur 1971), becoming totally caught up in this master status.

Most individuals who progress to secondary deviance advance no further, but a subset of them moves on to what Kitsuse (1980) called **tertiary deviance**. In contrast to primary deviants who engage in deviance denial, and secondary deviants who accept their deviant identities, Kitsuse sees tertiary deviants as those who engage in deviance embracement. These are people who decide that their deviance is not a bad thing. They may adopt a relativist perspective and decide that their deviant label is socially constructed by society, not intrinsic to their behavior, such as individuals with learning differences who consider themselves more creative than "typical" people. Or they may hold to an absolutist perspective and embrace their deviant category as intrinsically real, such as gays who "discover" their underlying homosexuality and accept it as natural. They therefore strongly identify with their deviance and fight, usually with the organized help of like others, to combat the deviant label that is applied to them. They may engage in "identity politics" and speak publicly, protest, rally, pursue civil disobedience, educate, raise funds, lobby, and practice various other forms of political advocacy to change society's view of their deviance. Examples of this include people who fight to destigmatize labels such as obesity, prostitution, and race/ethnicity.

All of these identity career concepts encompass a progression through several stages. They begin with the commission of the deviance and lead to individuals' apprehension and public identification. They move through the changing expectations of others towards them, marked by shifting social acceptance or rejection by their friends and acquaintances. The breadth, seriousness, and longevity of the deviant identity label are significantly more profound when individuals undergo official labeling processes than when they are merely informally labeled. With their internalization of the deviant label, adoption of the self-identity, and public interaction through it, they ultimately move into groups of differential deviant associates and commit further acts of deviance.

ACCOUNTS

When people say or do things that appear odd to others, they risk being labeled as deviant. We all engage in instances of deviant behavior, but at the same time we desire to maintain a positive self-image in both our own eyes and the eyes of others. In order to avoid the negative consequences of being labeled as deviant and to preserve their untarnished identities, individuals may engage in a variety of interactional strategies designed to normalize their behavior. Mills (1940) suggested that people use "vocabularies of motive" in conversation, where they present legitimate reasons to others around them that explain the meaning of their actions. This motive talk restores a sense of normalcy to interactions that are disrupted by questionable events.

Sykes and Matza (1957, 666) suggested that people commonly make "justifications for deviance that are seen as valid by the delinquent but not by the legal system or society at large." Individuals using these were attempting to resolve the contradictions between what people say and what they do. They offered five **"techniques of neutralization"** through which people rationalize their behavior, either prospectively or retrospectively. Through *denials of responsibility*, individuals suggest that their deviance was due to acts beyond their control ("I couldn't help myself," "it was not my fault"). In *denying injury*, they mitigate their offense by alluding to the lack of consequences, arguing that no one was hurt ("no harm, no foul"). When they make a *denial of the victim*, they legitimate their behavior by suggesting that either no specific victim can be identified ("it's a huge corporation; nobody will notice it"), or that the persons hurt do not deserve victim status ("gays deserve to be beaten up"). Some people *appeal to higher loyalties* by casting their behavior as serving a greater good (loyalty to a friend, to higher principles, to God). Finally, in *condemning the condemners*, people turn the table on the accusers, throwing attention away from themselves by focusing on things their accusers have done wrong ("oh, you think you're so easy to live with?" "police are nothing but pigs").

Scott and Lyman (1968) further refined our conception of accounts by suggesting that all accounts can be seen as either **excuses** or **justifications**. In offering excuses, individuals admit the wrongfulness of their actions but distance themselves from the blame. These excuses are often fairly standard phrases or ideas designed to soften the deviance and relieve individuals of their accountability. These may include *appeals to accidents* ("my computer malfunctioned and lost my file"), *appeals to defeasibility* or misinformation ("I thought my roommate turned my paper in"), *appeals to biological drives* ("men will be men") and *scapegoating* ("she borrowed my notes and I couldn't get them back in time to study for the test").

With justifications, individuals accept responsibility for their actions but seek to have specific instances excused. In so doing, they try to legitimate the acts or its consequences. In drawing on justifications, individuals may invoke *sad tales* ("I am a prostitute so that I can afford to put food on the table to feed my kids" or "I turn tricks because I was sexually abused as a child") or the need for *self-fulfillment* ("taking hallucinogenic drugs expands my consciousness and makes me a more caring person").

Hewitt and Stokes (1975) added to our understanding of accounts by presenting a set of verbal explanations specifically designed to precede the deviant acts that people saw as imminent in their future. They suggested that Lyman and Scott's accounts were primarily retrospective in nature, and that their **"disclaimers"** were fundamentally prospective. People *hedge*, they suggested, in prefacing their remarks to indicate a measure of uncertainty about what they are going to do ("I'm not sure this is going to work but …"). They use *credentializing* when they know their act will be discredited but they are attempting to give a purpose or legitimacy to it ("I'm not prejudiced, in fact some of my best friends are XXX, but ..."). Sometimes people invoke *sin licenses* when they know their behavior will be poorly received but they want to suggest that this is a time where the ordinary rules might be suspended ("I realize you might think this is wrong but ..."). *Cognitive disclaimers* try to make sense out of something that looks like it might not be well understood ("This may seem strange to you ..."). Finally, *appeals for the suspension of judgment* aim to deflect the negative consequences of acts or remarks that may be offensive or angering ("Hear me out before you explode ..."). Disclaimers, then, are specifically conversational tactics that people invoke before they launch ahead into something commonly judged as inappropriate.

STIGMA MANAGEMENT

When people are labeled as deviant, it marks them with a stigma in the eyes of society. As we have seen, this label may lead to devaluation and exclusion. Consequently, people with deviant features learn how to "manage" their stigma so that they are not shamed or ostracized. This effort requires considerable social skills.

Goffman (1963) has suggested that people with potential deviant stigma fall into two categories: **"the discreditable"** and **"the discredited."** The former are those with easily concealable deviant traits (ex-convicts, secret homosexuals) who may manage themselves so as to avoid the deviant stigma. The latter are either members of the former category who have revealed their deviance or those who cannot hide their deviance (the obese, racial minorities, the physically disabled). These people's lives are characterized by a constant focus on secrecy and information control. Goffman observed that most discreditables engage in **"passing"** as "normals" in their everyday lives, concealing their deviance and fitting in with regular people. They may do this by avoiding contacts with "stigma symbols," those objects or behaviors that would tip people off to their deviant condition (an anorectic avoiding family meals, mental patients surreptitiously taking their medications). Another technique for passing includes using "disidentifiers" such as props, actions, or verbal expressions to distract and fool people into thinking that they do not have the deviant stigma (homosexuals bragging about heterosexual conquests or taking a date to the company picnic, members of ethnic minorities who laugh at ethnic slurs about their group). Finally, they may "lead a double life," maintaining two different lifestyles with two distinct groups of people, one that knows about their deviance and one that does not.

In this endeavor, people may employ the aid of others to help conceal their deviance by "**covering**" for them. In these team performances, friends and family members may assist the deviants by concealing their identities, their whereabouts, their deficiencies, or their pasts. They may even coach the deviants on how to construct stories designed to hide their deviance.

Another form of stigma management, sometimes adopted when concealment fails, involves disclosing the deviance. People may do this for cathartic reasons (alleviating their burden of secrecy), therapeutic reasons (casting it in a positive light), or preventive reasons (so others don't find out in negative ways later). Although many people find that their disclosures lead to rejection, others are more fortunate when people may even sympathize with their condition, such as people with sexually transmitted diseases.

Disclosures of deviance can follow two courses. In observing the interactions between discredited deviants and normals, Davis (1961) noted that non-deviants often interact with people who possess recognizably apparent deviant traits in patterned ways. He proposed a normalization process that begins with "**deviance disavowal**": the non-deviants ignore the others' deviance and act as if it does not exist. After this conspicuous and stilted ignoring of the individual's deviance, if they spend more time in the company of the deviants, non-deviants progresses to a stage of limited engagement where more relaxed interaction begins and interaction is directed at features of the people other than their deviant stigma. The relationship can only achieve full normalization, the point where the deviant stigma is overlooked and almost forgotten, when the deviance is broached by someone (usually the deviants) and discussed enough so that all questions are answered and set to rest. He illustrated this by discussing the case of physically disabled people who, at first, are shunned by their coworkers or fellow students, but who gradually fit into the crowd when others realize that there is more to them than their disability (they root for the same teams, listen to the same music, share the same major).

In contrast, deviant people can strive to normalize their relationships with non-deviants through "**deviance avowal**" (Turner 1972), in which they openly acknowledge their stigma and try to present themselves in a positive light. This avowal often takes the form of humor, "breaking the ice" by joking about their deviant attribute. In this way they show others that they can take the perspective of the normal and see themselves as deviant too, thus forming a bridge to others. This action further asserts that they have non-deviant aspects and that they can see the world as others do. This can be the case when members of ethnic minority groups make self-deprecating comments about themselves based on stereotypes.

Thus far we have considered individual modes of adaptation to deviant stigma. Yet these stigma can also be managed through a group or collective effort. Many voluntary associations of stigmatized individuals exist, from the early organizations of prostitutes (COYOTE—Call Off Your Old Tired Ethics), to more recent ones such as the Gay Liberation Front, the Little People of America, the National Stuttering Project, and the Gray Panthers. Most well known are the 12-step programs modeled after the tremendous success of Alcoholics Anonymous (AA), including such groups as Overeaters Anonymous, Narcotics Anonymous, and Gamblers Anonymous.

These groups vary in character. Some groups are organized as what Lyman (1970) calls an **expressive** dimension, whose primary function is to provide support for their members. This support can take the form of organizing social and recreational activities, dispersing legal or medical information, or offering services such as shopping, meals, or transportation. Expressive groups tend to be apolitical, helping their members adapt to their social stigma rather than evade it. They also serve as places where members can come together in the company of other deviants, avoid the censure of non-stigmatized normals, and seek collective solutions to their common problems. It is here that they can make disclosures to others without fear of rejection. For instance, the Little People of America have an annual conference which not only provides a social gathering for people of similar height but also offers support and advice for practical problems (setting up one's house) and social concerns (dating).

Lyman has also described groups with an **instrumental** dimension, where members gather together not only to accomplish the expressive functions, but also to organize for political activism. This embodies Kitsuse's tertiary deviation, where individuals reject the societal conception and treatment of their stigma and organize to change social definitions. They fight to get others to modify their views of the status or behavior in question so that society, like they, will no longer regard it as deviant. Examples of such groups include ACT UP, an AIDS organization whose members have tried to change social attitudes toward AIDS patients, the National Organization for Women (NOW), and the Disabled in Action.

On another continuum, Lyman noted that groups may vary between **conformity** and **alienation**. Conformative groups fundamentally adhere to the norms and values of society. They accept most conventional views, with the occasional exception of their own deviance. They generally use their back-stage arenas to counsel members on how to fit in with others who may neither accept nor understand them. Thus, support groups for bipolar people may offer advice to members on how to find the right doctor, various benefits and side effects of different drugs, and the risks and benefits of going drug free. But they do not generally glorify either mania or depression. Where groups do break with society in the way they regard their own deviance and members instrumentally try to fight for the legitimation of their deviance, they use conventional means to attain their goals.

Groups may be alienative for one of two reasons: they are willing to step outside of conventional means to fight for changed definitions of their single form of deviance, or they have multiple conflicting values with society. Activists, such as the Black Panthers, a single-issue group, were willing to break the law to fight for improved social opportunities and status for African Americans. Radical feminists might not resort to violating laws, but their dissatisfaction with the social structures that disempower women are grounded in multiple dimensions of society. Modern-day descendants of the Ku Klux Klan such as the skinheads, Aryan Nation, and various militia groups may incorporate both elements, rejecting social attitudes of acceptance towards Blacks, Jews, immigrants, gays, and others. At the same time, they have resorted to violence to attain their ends, such as blowing up the Murrah Federal Building in Oklahoma City to avenge the Waco siege where members of the Branch Davidian cult and their leader, David Koresh, perished during an FBI assault. Members of other alienative groups, such as the Amish, nudists, and hippie communes, simply want to take their radically different values and form communities removed from conventional society.

23

The Adoption and Management of a "Fat" Identity

DOUGLAS DEGHER AND GERALD HUGHES

Degher and Hughes' selection on the way people come to think of themselves as fat is a study in identity transformation. They posit a model where individuals align their self-conception with cues that they derive from their external environment. Although the subjects in this study originally do not hold a view of themselves as obese, they receive active status cues (people say things) and passive status cues (their clothes no longer fit) that jar them away from their former self-conceptions. They follow a process of recognizing that they can no longer be considered to have a normal build, and placing themselves with the new category that fits them more appropriately. This leads to their reconceptualizing themselves as fat. The fat status has a new, negative identity that they adopt, devaluing them and locating them within the deviant realm.

Do you accept their suggestion that people change their identities by going through this sequential process or do you think it is something that happens in other ways: more suddenly, or through another process? How important do you consider the role of others versus the individuals themselves in shifting to a identity?

The interactionist perspective has come to play an important part in contemporary criminological and deviance theory. Within this approach, deviance is viewed as a subjectively problematic identity rather than an objective condition of behavior. At the core is the emphasis on "process" rather than on viewing deviance as a static entity. To paraphrase vintage Howard Becker, "... social groups create deviance by making the rules whose infraction constitutes deviance. Consequently, deviance is not a quality of the act... but rather a consequence of the application by others of rules and sanctions to an offender" (Becker, 1963, p. 9). Attention is focused upon the *interaction* between those

From Douglas Degher and Gerald Hughes, "The Identity Change Process: A Field Study of Obesity." *Deviant Behavior*, 12(4). Copyright © 1991. Reproduced by permission of Taylor & Francis, LLC, http://www.taylorandfrancis.com.

being labeled deviant and those promoting the deviant label. In the interactionist literature, emphases are in two major areas: (a) the conditions under which the label "deviant" comes to be applied to an individual and the consequences for the individual of having adopted that label (Tannenbaum, 1939; Lemert, 1951; Kitsuse, 1962, p. 247; Goffman, 1963; Baum, 1987, p. 96; Greenberg, 1989, p. 79), and/or (b) the role of social control agents[1] in contributing to the application of deviant labels (Becker, 1963; Piliavm & Briar, 1964, p. 206; Cicourel, 1968; Schur, 1971; Conrad, 1975, p. 12).

Much of this literature frequently assumes that once an individual has been labeled, the promoted label and attendant identity is either internalized or rejected. As Lemert proposes, the shift from primary to secondary deviance is a categorical one, and is primarily a response to problems created by the societal reaction (Lemert, 1951, p. 40).

What is most often neglected is an examination of the mechanistic features of this identity shift. Our focus is on this "identity change process," which is what we have chosen to call this identity shift. Of interest is how individuals come to make some personal sense out of proffered labels and their attendant identities.

METHODOLOGY

The primary methodological tool employed to construct our identity change process model comes from "grounded" analysis.... The model presented in this paper emerged from comments and codes appearing in interviews with obese members of a weight reduction organization that had weekly meetings. The frequency of attendance allowed us to consider the members typical, and allowed us to suggest that major issues of obesity are transsituational and temporally durable. If obesity disappeared tomorrow, we would still be able to apply the generic concepts generated from our data to make statements about the process of "identity change." As suggested by Hadden, Degher, and Fernandez, our focus is on process rather than on unit characteristics of social phenomena (Hadden, Degher, & Fernandez, 1989, p. 9). This provides us with insights that have import for major issues in sociological theory.

SITE SELECTION

Because obese individuals suffer both internally (negative self-concepts) and externally (discrimination), they possess what Goffman refers to as a "spoiled identity" (Goffman, 1963). This seems to be the case particularly in contemporary America with what may be described as an almost pathological emphasis on fitness. The boom in health clubs, sales of videotapes on fitness, diet books, and so forth promote a definition of the "healthy" physical presence. As Kelly (1990) sees it, the boom in physical fitness in the mid-1980s is an attempt by many people to create a specific image of an ideal body. Thus, body build becomes a crucial element in self-appraisal. Consequently, fat people are an ideal strategic group within which to study the "identity change process."

Obese people are not only the subject of negative stereotypes, they are also actively discriminated against in college admissions (Canning & Mayers, 1966, p. 1172), pay more for goods and services (Petit, 1974), receive prejudicial medical treatment (Maddox, Back, & Liederman, 1968, p. 287; Maddox & Liederman, 1969, p. 214), are treated less promptly by salespersons (Pauley, 1989, p. 713), have higher rates of unemployment (Laslett & Warren, 1975, p. 69), and receive lower wages (Register, 1990, p. 130). The obese label is one that seems to clearly fit Becker's description of a "master status," that is,

> Some statuses in our society, as in others, override all other statuses and have a certain priority... the status deviant (depending on the kind of deviance) is this kind of master status ... one will be identified as a deviant first, before other identifications are made. (Becker, 1963, p. 33)

Obese people are "fat" first, and only secondarily are seen as possessing ancillary characteristics.

The site for the field observations had to meet two requirements: (a) it had to contain a high proportion of obese, or formerly obese individuals; and (b) these individuals had to be identifiable by the observer. The existence of a large number of national weight control organizations (a) whose membership is composed of individuals who have internalized an obese identity, and (b) who emphasize a radical program of identity change, make these organizations an excellent choice as strategic sites for study and analysis. The local franchise chapter of one of these national weight loss organizations satisfied both of our requirements, and was selected as the site for our study.

Attendance at the weekly meetings of this national weight control group is restricted to individuals who are current members of the organization. Since one requirement for membership is that the individual be at least 10 pounds over the maximum weight for his or her sex and height (according to New York Life tables), all of the people attending the meetings are, or were, overweight, and a high proportion of them are, or were, sufficiently overweight to be classified as obese."[2]

During the period of the initial field observations, the weekly membership of the group varied from 30 to 100 members, with an average attendance of around 60 members. Although there was a considerable turnover in membership, the greatest part of this turnover consisted of "rejoins" (individuals who had been members previously, and were joining again).

Although we have no quantitative data from which to generalize, the group membership appeared to represent a cross section of the larger community. The group included both male and female members, although females did constitute about three-fourths of the membership. Although the membership was predominantly white, a range of ethnicities, notably Hispanic and Native American, existed within the group. The majority of the members appeared to fall within the 30 to 50 age range, although there was a member as young as 11, and one over 70.

DATA COLLECTION

Two types of data were gathered for this study: field observations and in-depth interviews. The field observations were performed while attending meetings of a local weight control organization. The insights gained from these observations were used primarily to develop interview guides. There were two major sources of observation during this period: premeeting conversations; and exchanges during the meeting itself.[3] The observations were recorded in note form and served to provide an orientation for the subsequent interviews. The goal during this period of observation was to gain insight into the basic processes of obesity and the obese career.

The in-depth interviews were carried out with 29 members from the local group. The interviews were solicited on a voluntary basis, and each individual was assured anonymity. The interviewees were representative of the group membership. Although most were middle-aged, middle-income white females, various age groups, ethnicities, marital statuses, genders, and social classes were represented.

These interviews lasted in length from ½ to 2½ hours, with the average interview being about 1 hour and 15 minutes in duration. The interviews produced almost 40 hours of taped discussion, which yielded more than 600 pages of typed transcript for coding.

THE IDENTITY CHANGE PROCESS

In conceptualizing the "identity changes" process, the concept of "career" was employed. As Goffman notes, "career" refers "... to any social strand of any person's course through life" (Goffman, 1961, p. 127). In the present paper, our concern is the change process that takes place as individuals come to see definitions of self in light of specific transmitted information.

An important aspect of this career model is what Becker referred to as "career contingencies," or "... those factors on which mobility from one position to another depends. Career contingencies include both the objective facts of social structure, and changes in the perspectives, motivations, and desires of the individual" (Becker, 1963, p. 24).

Thus, the "identity change" process must be viewed on two levels: a public (external) and a private (internal) level. As Goffman has stated, "One value of the concept of career is its two-sidedness. One side is linked to internal matters held dearly and closely, such as image of self and felt identity; the other publicly acceptable institutional complex" (Goffman, 1961, p. 127).

On the public level, social status exists as part of the public domain; social status is socially defined and promoted. The social environment not only contains definitions and attendant stereotypes for each status, it also contains information, in the form of *status cues*, about the applicability of that status for the individual.

On the internal level, two distinct cognitive processes must take place for the identity change process to occur: first, the individual must come to recognize

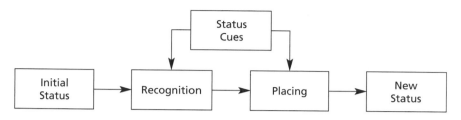

FIGURE 23.1   Visualization of the identity Change Process (ICP)

that the current status is inappropriate; and second, the individual must locate a new, more appropriate status. Thus, in response to the external status cues, the individual comes to recognize internally that the initial status is inappropriate; and then he or she uses the cues to locate a new, more appropriate status. The identity change occurs in response to, and is mediated through, the status cues that exist in the social environment (see Figure 23.1).

STATUS CUES: THE EXTERNAL COMPONENT

Status cues make up the public or external component of the identity change process. A status cue is some feature of the social environment that contains information about a particular status or status dimension. Because this paper is about obesity, the cues of interest are about "fatness." Such status cues provide information about whether or not the individual is "fat," and if so, how "fat."

"Recognizing" and "placing" comprise the internal component of the identity change process and occur in response to, and are mediated through, the status cues that exist in the social environment. In order to understand fully the identity change process, it is necessary to explain the interaction between outer and inner processes (Scheff, 1988, p. 396), or in our case, external and internal components of the process.

Status cues are transmitted in two ways: actively and passively. Active cues are communicated through interaction. For example, people are informed by peers, friends, spouses, etc., that they are overweight. The following are some typical comments that occurred repeatedly in the interviews in response to the question, "How did you know that you were fat?"

> I was starting to be called chubby, and being teased in school.
> When my mother would take me shopping, she'd get angry because the clothes that were supposed to be in my age group wouldn't fit me. She would yell at me.
> Well, people would say, "When did you put on all your weight, Bob?" You know, something like that. You know, you kind of get the message, that, you know, I did put on weight.

A second category of cues might accurately be described as passive in form. The information in these cues exists within the environment, but the individual must be sensitized in some way to that information. For example, standing on a scale will provide an individual with information about weight. It is up to the individual to get on the scale, look at the numbers, and then make some sense out of them. Other passive cues might involve seeing one's reflection in a mirror, standing next to others, fitting in chairs, or, as frequently mentioned by respondents, the sizing of clothes. The comments below, all made in response to the question, "How did you know that you were fat?" are representative of passive cue statements.

> I think that it was not being able to wear the clothes that the other kids wore.
> How did I know? Because when we went to get weighed, I weighed more than my, uh, a girl my height should have weighed, according to the chart, according to all the charts that I used to read. That's when I first noticed that I was overweight.
> I would see all these ladies come in and they could wear size 11 and 12, and I thought, Why can't I do that? I should be able to do that.

Both active and passive cues serve as mechanisms for communicating information about a specific status. As can be seen from the data, events occur that force the individual to evaluate his or her conceptions of self.

RECOGNIZING

The term "recognizing" refers to the cognitive process by which an individual becomes aware that a particular status is no longer appropriate. As shown in the figure, the process assumes the individual's acceptance of some initial status. For obese individuals, the initial status is that of "normal body build.[4] "This assumption is based on the observation that none of our interviewees assumed that they were "always fat." Even those who were fat as children could identify when they became aware that they were "fat." Through the perception of discrepant status cues, the individual comes to recognize that the initial status is inappropriate. It is possible that the person will perceive the discrepant cues and will either ignore or reject them, in which case the initial status is retained. The factors regulating such a failure to recognize are important, but are not dealt with in this paper. Further research on this point is called for.

Status cues are the external mechanisms through which the recognizing takes place, but it is paying attention to the information contained in these cues that triggers the internal cognitive process of recognizing.

An important point is that the acceptance (or rejection) of a particular status does not occur simply because the individual possesses a set of objective characteristics. For example, two people may have similar body builds, but one may have a self-definition of "fat" whereas the other may not. There appears to be a rather tenuous connection between objective condition and subjective definition. The following comments are supportive of this disjunction.

> I was really, as far as pounds go, very thin, but I had a feeling about myself that I was huge.
>
> Well, I don't remember ever thinking about it until I was about in eighth grade. But I was looking back at pictures when I was little. I was always chunky, chubby.

This lack of necessary connection between objective condition and subjective definition points up an important and frequently overlooked feature of social statuses: the extent to which they are *self-evident*. Self-evidentiality refers to the degree to which a person who possesses certain objective status characteristics is *aware* that a particular status label applies to them.[5]

Some statuses possess a high degree of evidentiality: gender identification is one of these.[6] On the other hand, being beautiful or intelligent is somewhat non-self-evident. This is not to imply that individuals are either ignorant of these statuses or of the characteristics upon which they are assigned. People may know that other people are intelligent, but they may be unaware that the label is equally applicable to them.

One idea that emerged quite early from the interviews was that being "fat" is a relatively non-self-evident status. Individuals do not recognize that "fat" is a description that applies to them.[7] The objective condition of being overweight is not sufficient, in itself, to promote the adoption of a "fat" identity. This non-self-evidentiality is demonstrated in the following excerpts.

> I think that I just thought that it was a little bit here and there. I didn't think of it, and I didn't think of myself as looking bad. But you know, I must have.
>
> I have pictures of me right after the baby was born. I had no idea that I was that fat.

The self-evidentiality of a status is important in the discussion of the identity change process. The less self-evident a status, the more difficult the recognizing process becomes. Further, because recognition occurs in response to status cues, the self-evidentiality of a status will influence the type of cues that play the most prominent role in identity change.

A somewhat speculative observation should be made about status cues in the recognizing process. For our subjects, recognizing occurred primarily through active cues. When passive cues were involved, they typically were highly visible and unambiguous. In general, active cues appear to be more potent in forcing the individual's attention to the information that the current status is inappropriate. The predominance of these active cues is possibly a consequence of the relatively non-self-evident character of the "fat" status. It is probable that the less self-evident a status, the more likely that the recognizing process will occur through active rather than passive cues.

Once the individual comes to recognize the inappropriateness of the initial status, it becomes necessary to locate a new, more appropriate status. This search for a more appropriate status is referred to as the "placing" process.[8]

PLACING

Placing refers to a cognitive process whereby an individual comes to identify an appropriate status from among those available. The number of status categories along a status dimension influences the placing process. A status dimension may contain any number of status categories. If there are only two status dimensional categories, such as in the case of gender, the placement process is more or less automatic. When individuals recognize that they do not belong in one category, the remaining category becomes the obvious alternative. The greater the number of status categories, the more difficult the placing process becomes.

The body build dimension contains an extremely large number of categories. When an individual recognizes that he or she does not possess a "normal" body build, there are innumerable alternatives open. The knowledge that one's status lies toward the "fat" rather than the "thin" end of the continuum still presents a wide range of choices. In everyday conversation, we hear terms that describe these alternatives: chubby, porky, plump, hefty, full-figured, beer belly, etc. All are informal descriptions reflecting the myriad categories along the body build dimension.

> I wasn't real fat in my eyes. I don't think. I was just chunky.
>
> Not fat. I didn't exactly classify it as fat. I just thought, I'm, you know, I am a pudgy lady.
>
> I don't think that I have ever called myself fat. I have called myself heavy.

Even when individuals adopt a "fat" identity, they attempt to make distinctions about how fat they are. Because being fat is a devalued status, individuals attempt to escape the full weight of its negative attributes while still acknowledging the nonnormal status. The following responses exemplify this attempt to neutralize the pejorative connotations of having a "fat" status. The practice of differentiating one's status from others becomes vital in managing a fat identity.

> Q. How did you know that you weren't that fat?
>
> A. Well, comparing myself to others at the time, I didn't really feel that I was that fat. But I knew maybe because they didn't treat me the same way they treated people who were heavier than me. You know, I got teased lightly, but I was still liked by a lot of people, and the people that were heavy weren't.

As is apparent from this excerpt, the individual neutralized self-image by linking "fatness" with the level of teasing done by peers.

NEW STATUS

The final phase of the identity change process involves the acceptance of a new status. For our informants, it was the acceptance of a "fat" status, along with its previously mentioned pejorative characterizations.[9]

I hate to look in mirrors. I hate that. It makes me feel so self-conscious. If I walk into a store, and I see my reflection in the glass, I just look away.

We'd go somewhere and I would think, "I never look as good as everybody else." You know everybody always looks better. I'd cry before we'd go bowling because I'd think, "Oh, I just look awful."

As is clear, the final phase of the identity change process involves the internalization of a negative (deviant) definition of self. For many fat people accepting a new status means starting on the merry-go-round of weight reduction programs.[10] Many of these programs or organizations attempt to get members to accept a devalued status fully, and then work to change it. Consequently, individuals are forced to "admit" that they are fat and to "witness" in front of others.[11] The new identity becomes that of a "fat" person, which the weight reduction programs then attempt to transform. A further analysis of the impact of informal organizations on the identity change process will be attempted in another paper.

CONCLUSION

In this paper, we have attempted to fill a void within the interactionist literature by presenting an inductively generated model of the identity change process. The proposed model treats the change process from a career focus, and thus addresses both the external (public) and the internal (cognitive) features of the identity change.

We have suggested that the adoption of a new status takes place through two sequential cognitive processes, "recognizing" and "placing." First, the individual must come to recognize that a current status is no longer appropriate. Second, the individual must locate a new, more appropriate status from among those available. We have further suggested that these internal or cognitive processes are triggered by and mediated through status cues, which exist in the external environment. These cues can be either active or passive. Active cues are transmitted through interaction, whereas passive cues must be sought out by the individual.

We also found a relationship between the evidentiality of the status, that is, how obvious that status is to the individual, and the role of the different types of cues in the identity change process. Finally, we have suggested that the adoption of a new status is a trigger for further career changes.

Although the model presented in this paper was generated inductively from field data on obese individuals, we are confident that it may be fruitfully applied to the study of other deviant careers. It seems particularly appropriate where the identity involved has a low degree of self-evidentiality.

In addition, we feel that the focus upon the different types of status cues and their differing roles in the recognizing and placing processes can lead to a better understanding of how institutionally promoted identity change occur.

NOTES

1. Included here is research on both rule creators and rule enforcers. We have not made an attempt to analytically separate the two types of investigation.

2. Some of the members had successfully lost their excess weight. When these people were present at a meeting, a leader was careful to introduce them to the other members of the class and to tell how much weight they had lost. This was done to uphold their claim to acceptance by the other group members.

3. Access to this information was gained from an "insider" perspective because one of the researchers was well known among the membership, being an "off and on" member of the organization for three years. Thus, he was not confronted with the problem of gaining entry into a semiclosed social setting. Similarly, because the observer had "been an ongoing participant of the group," he did not have to desensitize the other members of the group to his presence.

4. It is important to note that this process can operate generically. That is, it is not only applicable to the "identity change" from a "normal" to a "deviant" identity, but can encompass the reverse process as well. In a forthcoming project, we will use the process to analyze how various rehabilitation programs attempt to get individuals back to the initial status.

5. This concept is different in an important way from what Goffman calls "visibility." He uses the term to refer to "... how well or how badly the stigma is adapted to provide means of communicating that the individual possesses it" (Goffman, 1963, p. 48). The focus of the concept is on how readily the social environment can identify that the individual possesses a stigmatized trait. The concept of self-evidentiality deals with how readily the individual can internalize possession of the stigmatized trait. The focus is upon the actor's perceptions, not on the audience.

6. We are referring here to the physiological description of being male or female. We realize that sex roles are much less self-evident.

7. Conversely, a number of individuals thought of themselves as "fat" or "obese," and were objectively "normal." In this case, the existence of objective indicators was insufficient to prevent the individual from adopting a "fat" identity.

8. In some instances, recognizing and placing occur simultaneously. This is especially true when the cue involved is an active one, and contains information about both the initial and new statuses. For example, if peers call a child "fatty," this interaction informs the child that the "normal" status is inappropriate. At the same time, it informs the child that being "fat" is the appropriate status. Even here however, the individual must recognize before it is possible to place.

9. This phase corresponds closely to that presented in much of the "subcultural" research. (See Schur, 1971; Becker, 1963; Sykes & Matza, 1957, p. 664.)

10. Weight Watchers, TOPS, Overeaters Anonymous, Diet Center, and OptiFast are typical examples of this type of program.

11. By witnessing, we are referring to the process whereby individuals come to renounce, in front of others, a former self and former behaviors associated with that self. Some religious groups, Synanon, Alcoholics Anonymous, etc., seem to encourage this type of degradation of self.

REFERENCES

Baum, L. 1987, August 3. Extra pounds can weigh down your career. *Business Week* p. 96.

Becker, H. S. 1963. *Outsiders: Studies in the sociology of deviance.* New York: Free Press.

Canning, H., and J. Mayers, 1966. Obesity: Its possible effects on college acceptance. *New England Journal of Medicine* 275(24) 1172–1174.

Cicourel, A. 1968. *The social organization of juvenile justice.* New York: Wiley.

Conrad, P. 1975. The discovery of hyperkinesis: Notes on the medicalization of deviant behavior. *Social Problems,* 23(1), 12–21.

Goffman, E. 1961. *Asylums.* Garden City, NY: Anchor.

———. 1963. *Stigma: Notes on the management of spoiled identity.* Englewood Cliffs, NJ: Prentice Hall.

Greenberg, D. 1989. The antifat conspiracy. *New Scientist* 22 (April 22): 79.

Hadden, S. O, D. Degher, and R. Fernandez. 1989. Sports as a strategic ethnographic arena. *Arena Review* 13(1), 9–19.

Kelly, J. R. 1990. *Leisure* 2nd ed. Englewood Cliffs, NJ: Prentice Hall.

Kitsuse, J. 1962. Societal reactions to deviant behavior: Problems of theory and method. *Social Problems 9* (Winter): 247–256.

Laslett, B., and C. A. B. Warren. 1975. Losing weight: The organizational promotion of behavior change. *Social Problems* 23(1), 69–80.

Lemert, E. 1951. *Social Pathology.* New York: McGraw-Hill.

Maddox, G. L., K. W. Back, and V. Liederman. 1968. Overweight as social deviance and disability. *Journal of Health and Social Behavior,* 9(4): 287–298.

Maddox, G. L., V. Liederman. 1969. Overweight as a social disability with medical implications. *Journal of Medical Education,* 9(4): 287–298.

Pauley, L. L. 1989. Customer weights as a variable in salespersons' response time. *Journal of Social Psychology* 129: 713–714.

Petit, D. W. 1974. The ills of the obese. In G. A. Gray and J. E. Bethunee *Treatment and management of obesity.* New York: Harper & Row.

Piliavin, I., & Briar, S. 1964. Police encounters with juveniles. *American Journal of Sociology* (September): 206–214.

Register, C. A. 1990. Wage effects of obesity among young workers. *Social Science Quarterly* 71 (March): 130–141.

Scheff, T. 1988. Shame and conformity: The deference emotion system. *American Journal of Sociology* 53 (June): 395–406.

Schur, E. M. 1971. *Labeling deviant behavior: Its sociological implications.* New York: Harper & Row.

Sykes, G., & D. Matza, 1957. Techniques of neutralization: A theory of delinquency. *American Sociological Review* (December): 664–670.

Tannenbaum, F. 1939. *Crime and the community.* New York: Columbia University Press.

24

Becoming Bisexual

MARTIN S. WEINBERG, COLIN J. WILLIAMS, AND DOUGLAS W. PRYOR

Weinberg, Williams, and Pryor's study of the identity career followed by individuals who become bisexual illustrates a much more complex identity trajectory than Degher and Hughes' portrayal of their fat subjects. The attraction of individuals in this selection to members of the same gender leads them to question and reject their affiliation with the heterosexual identity. But their continuing attraction to members of the other gender leads them to question the appropriateness, for them, of the homosexual designation. Aware that they do not fit comfortably into either of these common sexual identity labels, they are confused and troubled. After struggling with their ambivalence about their dual sexual orientations, they discover the bisexual option and begin the process of reconceptualizing themselves. Although finding this label and discovering established bisexual others aids their process of self-acceptance, problems remain for people trying to establish identities outside of the more common sexual norms. They remain doubly stigmatized due to their rejection by both the heterosexual and homosexual communities, and never feel completely comfortable with this liminal identity.

How important do you consider the role of individuals, people they encounter, their subculture, and/or society in affecting deviant identities? How likely do you think it is for people to form and reform their identity over time?

Becoming bisexual involves the rejection of not one but two recognized categories of sexual identity: heterosexual and homosexual. Most people settle into the status of heterosexual without any struggle over the identity. There is not much concern with explaining how this occurs; that people are heterosexual is simply taken for granted. For those who find heterosexuality unfulfilling, however, developing a sexual identity is more difficult.

How is it then that some people come to identify themselves as "bisexuals"? As a point of departure we take the process through which people come to identify themselves as "homosexual." A number of models have been formulated that chart the development of a homosexual identity through a series of stages. While each model involves a different number of stages, the models all share three elements.

The process begins with the person in a state of identity confusion—feeling different from others, struggling with the acknowledgment of same-sex attractions. Then there is a period of thinking about possibly being homosexual—involving associating with self-identified homosexuals, sexual experimentation, forays into the homosexual subculture. Last is the attempt to integrate one's self-concept and social identity as homosexual—acceptance of the label, disclosure about being homosexual, acculturation to a homosexual way of life, and the development of love relationships. Not every person follows through each stage. Some remain locked in at a certain point. Others move back and forth between stages.

To our knowledge, no previous model of *bisexual* identity formation exists. In this chapter we present such a model based on the following questions: To what extent is there overlap with the process involved in becoming homosexual? How far is the label "bisexual" clearly recognized, understood, and available to people as an identity? Does the absence of a bisexual subculture in most locales affect the information and support needed for sustaining a commitment to the identity? For our subjects, then, what are the problems in finding the "bisexual" label, understanding what the label means, dealing with social disapproval from two directions, and continuing to use the label once it is adopted? From our fieldwork and interviews, we found that four stages captured our respondents' most common experiences when dealing with questions of identity: initial confusion, finding and applying the label, settling into the identity, and continued uncertainty.

THE STAGES

Initial Confusion

Many of the people interviewed said that they had experienced a period of considerable confusion, doubt, and struggle regarding their sexual identity before defining themselves as bisexual. This was ordinarily the first step in the process of becoming bisexual.

They described a number of major sources of early confusion about their sexual identity. For some, it was the experience of having strong sexual feelings for both sexes that was unsettling, disorienting, and sometimes frightening. Often these were sexual feelings that they said they did not know how to easily handle or resolve.

> In the past, I couldn't reconcile different desires I had. I didn't understand them. I didn't know what I was. And I ended up feeling really mixed up, unsure, and kind of frightened. (F)
>
> I thought I was gay, and yet I was having these intense fantasies and feelings about fucking women. I went through a long period of confusion. (M)

Others were confused because they thought strong sexual feelings for, or sexual behavior with, the same sex meant an end to their long-standing heterosexuality.

> I was afraid of my sexual feelings for men and … that if I acted on
> them, that would negate my sexual feelings for women. I knew
> absolutely no one else -who had… sexual feelings for both men
> and -women, and didn't realize that -was an option. (M)
>
> When I first had sexual feelings for females, I had the sense I should
> give up my feelings for men. I think it would have been easier to give
> up men. (F)

A third source of confusion in this initial stage stemmed from attempts by
respondents trying to categorize their feelings for, and/or behaviors with, both
sexes, yet not being able to do so. Unaware of the term "bisexual," some tried
to organize their sexuality by using readily available labels of "heterosexual" or
"homosexual"—but these did not seem to fit. No sense of sexual identity jelled;
an aspect of themselves remained unclassifiable.

> When I was young, I didn't know what I was. I knew there were
> people like Mom and Dad—heterosexual and married—and that there
> were "queens." I knew I wasn't like either one. (M)
>
> I thought I had to be either gay or straight. That was the big lie. It
> was confusing…. That all began to change in the late 60s. It was a long
> and slow process….(F)

Finally, others suggested they experienced a great deal of confusion because
of their "homophobia"—their difficulty in facing up to the same-sex component
of their sexuality. The consequence was often long-term denial. This was more
common among the men than the women, but not exclusively so.

> At age seventeen, I became close to a woman who was gay. She had
> sexual feelings for me. I had some… for her but I didn't respond.
> Between the ages of seventeen and twenty-six I met another gay
> woman. She also had sexual feelings towards me. I had the same for her
> but I didn't act on… or acknowledge them…. I was scared…. I was also
> attracted to men at the same time…. I denied that I was sexually
> attracted to women. I was afraid that if they knew the feelings were
> mutual they would act on them … and put pressure on me. (F)
>
> I thought I might be able to get rid of my homosexual tendencies
> through religious means—prayer, belief, counseling—before I came to
> accept it as part of me. (M)

The intensity of the confusion and the extent to which it existed in the lives
of the people we met at the Bisexual Center, whatever its particular source, was
summed up by two men who spoke with us informally. As paraphrased in our
field notes:

> The identity issue for him was a very confusing one. At one point, he
> almost had a nervous breakdown, and when he finally entered college,
> he sought psychiatric help.
>
> Bill said he thinks this sort of thing happens a lot at the Bi Center.
> People come in "very confused" and experience some really painful stress.

Finding and Applying the Label

Following this initial period of confusion, which often spanned years, was the experience of finding and applying the label. We asked the people we interviewed for specific factors or events in their lives that led them to define themselves as bisexual. There were a number of common experiences.

For many who were unfamiliar with the term bisexual, the discovery that the category in fact existed was a turning point. This happened by simply hearing the word, reading about it somewhere, or learning of a place called the Bisexual Center. The discovery provided a means of making sense of long-standing feelings for both sexes.

> Early on I thought I was just gay, because I was not aware there was another category, bisexual. I always knew I was interested in men and women. But I did not realize there was a name for these feelings and behaviors until I took Psychology 101 and read about it, heard about it there. That was in college. (F)
>
> The first time I heard the word, which was not until I was twenty six, I realized that was what fit for me. What it fit was that I had sexual feelings for both men and women. Up until that point, the only way that I could define my sexual feelings was that I was either a latent homosexual or a confused heterosexual. (M)
>
> Going to a party at someone's house, and finding out there that the party was to benefit the Bisexual Center. I guess at that point I began to define myself as bisexual. I never knew there was such a word. If I had heard the word earlier on, for example as a kid, I might have been bisexual then. My feelings had always been bisexual. I just did not know how to define them. (F)
>
> Reading *The Bisexual Option* … I realized then that bisexuality really existed and that's what I was. (M)

In the case of others the turning point was their first homosexual or heterosexual experience coupled with the recognition that sex was pleasurable with both sexes. These were people who already seemed to have knowledge of the label "bisexual," yet without experiences with both men and women, could not label themselves accordingly.

> The first time I had actual intercourse, an orgasm with a woman, it led me to realize I was bisexual, because I enjoyed it as much as I did with a man, although the former occurred much later on in my sexual experiences.... I didn't have an orgasm with a woman until twenty-two, while with males, that had been going on since the age of thirteen. (M)
>
> Having homosexual fantasies and acting those out.... I would not identify as bi if I only had fantasies and they were mild. But since my fantasies were intensely erotic, and I acted them out, these two things led me to believe I was really bisexual.... (M)
>
> After my first involved sexual affair with a woman, I also had feelings for a man, and I knew I did not fit the category dyke. I was also

dating gay-identified males. So I began looking at gay/lesbian and heterosexual labels as not fitting my situation. (F)

Still others reported not so much a specific experience as a turning point, but emphasized the recognition that their sexual feelings for both sexes were simply too strong to deny. They eventually came to the conclusion that it was unnecessary to choose between them.

I found myself with men but couldn't completely ignore my feelings for women. When involved with a man I always had a close female relationship. When one or the other didn't exist at any given time, I felt I was really lacking something. I seem to like both. (F)

The last factor that was instrumental in leading people to initially adopt the label bisexual was the encouragement and support of others. Encouragement sometimes came from a partner who already defined himself or herself as bisexual.

Encouragement from a man I was in a relationship with. We had been together two or three years at the time—he began to define as bisexual.... [He] encouraged me to do so as well. He engineered a couple of threesomes with another woman. Seeing one other person who had bisexuality as an identity that fit them seemed to be a real encouragement. (F)

Encouragement from a partner seemed to matter more for women. Occasionally the "encouragement" bordered on coercion as the men in their lives wanted to engage in a *ménage à trois* or group sex.

I had a male lover for a year and a half who was familiar with bisexuality and pushed me towards it. My relationship with him brought it up in me. He wanted me to be bisexual because he wanted to be in a threesome. He was also insanely jealous of my attractions to men, and did everything in his power to suppress my opposite-sex attractions. He showed me a lot of pictures of naked women and played on my reactions. He could tell that I was aroused by pictures of women and would talk about my attractions while we were having sex.... He was twenty years older than me. He was very manipulative in a way. My feelings for females were there and [he was] almost forcing me to act on my attractions.... (F)

Encouragement also came from sex-positive organizations, primarily the Bisexual Center, but also places like San Francisco Sex Information (SFSI), the Pacific Center, and the Institute for Advanced Study of Human Sexuality, ...

At the gay pride parade I had seen the brochures for the Bisexual Center. Two years later I went to a Tuesday night meeting. I immediately felt that I belonged and that if I had to define myself that this was what I would use. (M)

Through SFSI and the Bi Center, I found a community of people ... [who] were more comfortable for me than were the exclusive gay or heterosexual communities.… [It was] beneficial for myself to be … in a sex-positive community. I got more strokes and came to understand myself better.… I felt it was necessary to express my feelings for males and females without having to censor them, which is what the gay and straight communities pressured me to do. (F)

Thus our respondents became familiar with and came to the point of adopting the label bisexual in a variety of ways: through reading about it on their own, being in therapy, talking to friends, having experiences with sex partners, learning about the Bi Center, visiting SFSI or the Pacific Center, and coming to accept their sexual feelings.

Settling into the Identity

Usually it took years from the time of first sexual attractions to, or behaviors with, both sexes before people came to think of themselves as bisexual. The next stage then was one of settling into the identity, which was characterized by a more complete transition in self-labeling.

Most reported that this settling-in stage was the consequence of becoming more self-accepting. They became less concerned with the negative attitudes of others about their sexual preferences.

I realized that the problem of bisexuality isn't mine. It's society's. They are having problems dealing with my bisexuality So I was then thinking if they had a problem dealing with it, so should I. But I don't. (F)

I learned to accept the fact that there are a lot of people out there who aren't accepting. They can be intolerant, selfish, shortsighted and so on. Finally, in growing up, I learned to say "So what, I don't care what others think." (M)

I just decided I was bi. I trusted my own sense of self. I stopped listening to others tell me what I could or couldn't be. (F)

The increase in self-acceptance was often attributed to the continuing support from friends, counselors, and the Bi Center, through reading, and just being in San Francisco.

Fred Klein's *The Bisexual Option* book and meeting more and more bisexual people … helped me feel more normal.… There were other human beings who felt like I did on a consistent basis. (M)

I think going to the Bi Center really helped a lot. I think going to the gay baths and realizing there were a lot of men who sought the same outlet I did really helped. Talking about it with friends has been helpful and being validated by female lovers that approve of my bisexuality. Also the reaction of people who I've told, many of whom weren't even surprised. (M)

The most important thing -was counseling. Having the support of a bisexual counselor. Someone who acted as somewhat of a mentor. [He] validated my frustration …, helped me do problem solving, and guide

[d] me to other supportive experiences like SFSI. Just engaging myself in a supportive social community. (M)

The majority of the people we came to know through the interviews seemed settled in their sexual identity. We tapped this through a variety of questions.... Ninety percent said that they did not think they were currently in transition from being homosexual to being heterosexual or from being heterosexual to being homosexual. However, when we probed further by asking this group "Is it possible, though, that someday you could define yourself as either lesbian/gay or heterosexual?" about 40 percent answered yes. About two-thirds of these indicated that the change could be in either direction, though almost 70 percent said that such a change was not probable.

We asked those who thought a change was possible what it might take to bring it about. The most common responses referred to becoming involved in a meaningful relationship that was monogamous or very intense. Often the sex of the hypothetical partner was not specified, underscoring that the overall quality of the relationship was what really mattered.

Love. I think if I feel insanely in love with some person, it could possibly happen. (M)

If I should meet a woman and want to get married, and if she was not open to my relating to men, I might become heterosexual again. (M)

Getting involved in a longer-term relationship like marriage where I wouldn't need a sexual involvement with anyone else. The sex of the ... partner wouldn't matter. It would have to be someone who I could commit my whole life to exclusively, a lifelong relationship. (F)

A few mentioned the breaking up of a relationship and how this would incline them to look toward the other sex.

Steve is one of the few men I feel completely comfortable with. If anything happened to him, I don't know if I'd want to try and build up a similar relationship with another man. I'd be more inclined to look towards women for support. (F)

Changes in sexual behavior seemed more likely for the people we interviewed ... than changes in how they defined themselves. We asked "Is it possible that someday you could behave either exclusively homosexual or exclusively heterosexual?" Over 80 percent answered yes. This is over twice as many as those who saw a possible change in how they defined themselves, again showing that a wide range of behaviors can be subsumed under the same label. Of this particular group, the majority (almost 60 percent) felt that there was nothing inevitable about how they might change, indicating that it could be in either a homosexual or a heterosexual direction. Around a quarter, though, said the change would be to exclusive heterosexual behavior and 15 percent to exclusive homosexual behavior. (Twice as many women noted the homosexual direction, while many more men than women said the heterosexual direction.) Just over 40 percent responded that a change to exclusive heterosexuality or homosexuality was not very probable, about a third somewhat probable, and about a quarter very probable.

Again, we asked what it would take to bring about such a change in behavior. Once more the answers centered on achieving long-term monogamous and involved relationship, often with no reference to a specific sex.

> For me to behave exclusively heterosexual or homosexual would
> require that I find a lifetime commitment from another person
> with a damn good argument of why I should not go to bed with
> somebody else. (F)
>   I am a romantic. If I fell in love with a man, and our relationship
> was developing that way, I might become strictly homosexual. The
> same possibility exists with a woman. (M)

Thus "settling into the identity" must be seen in relative terms. Some of the people we interviewed did seem to accept the identity completely. When we compared our subjects' experiences with those characteristic of homosexuals, however, we were struck by the absence of closure that characterized our bisexual respondents—even those who appeared most committed to the identity. This led us to posit a final stage in the formation of sexual identity, one that seems unique to bisexuals.

Continued Uncertainty

The belief that bisexuals are confused about their sexual identity is quite common. The conception has been promoted especially by those lesbians and gays who see bisexuality as being in and of itself a pathological state. From their point of view, "confusion" is literally a built-in feature of "being" bisexual. As expressed in one study:

> While appearing to encompass a wider choice of love objects ... [the
> bisexual] actually becomes a product of abject confusion; his self-image is
> that of an overgrown young adolescent whose ability to differentiate one
> form of sexuality from another has never developed. He lacks above all a
> sense of identity.... [He] cannot answer the question: What am I?

One evening a facilitator at a Bisexual Center rap group put this belief in a slightly different and more contemporary form:

> One of the myths about bisexuality is that you can't be bisexual without
> somehow being "schizoid." The lesbian and gay communities do not
> see being bisexual as a crystallized or complete sexual identity. The
> homosexual community believes there is no such thing as bisexuality.
> They think that bisexuals are people who are in transition [to becoming
> homosexual] or that they are people afraid of being stigmatized
> [as homosexual] by the heterosexual majority.

We addressed the issue directly in the interviews with two questions: "Do you *presently* feel confused about your bisexuality?" and "Have you ever felt confused...?" ... For the men, a quarter and 84 percent answered "yes," respectively. For the women, it was about a quarter and 56 percent.

When asked to provide details about this uncertainty, the primary response was that *even after having discovered and applied the label "bisexual" to themselves, and having come to the point of apparent self-acceptance, they still experienced continued intermittent periods of doubt and uncertainty regarding their sexual identity.* One reason was the lack of social validation and support that came with being a self-identified bisexual. The social reaction people received made it difficult to sustain the identity over the long haul.

While the heterosexual world was said to be completely intolerant of any degree of homosexuality, the reaction of the homosexual world mattered more. Many bisexuals referred to the persistent pressures they experienced to relabel themselves "gay" or "lesbian" and to engage in sexual activity exclusively with the same sex. It was asserted that no one was *really* bisexual, and that calling oneself "bisexual" was a politically incorrect and unauthentic identity. Given that our respondents were living in San Francisco (which has such a large homosexual population) and that they frequently moved in and out of the homosexual world (to whom they often looked for support) this could be particularly distressing.

> Sometimes the repeated denial the gay community directs at us. Their negation of the concept and the term bisexual has sometimes made me wonder whether I was just imagining the whole thing. (M)
>
> My involvement with the gay community. There was extreme political pressure. The lesbians said bisexuals didn't exist. To them, I had to make up my mind and identify as lesbian.... I was really questioning my identity, that is, about defining myself as bisexual....(F)

For the women, the invalidation carried over to their feminist identity (which most had). They sometimes felt that being with men meant they were selling out the world of women.

> I was involved with a woman for several years. She was straight when I met her but became a lesbian. She tried to "win me back" to lesbianism. She tried to tell me that if I really loved her, I would leave Bill. I did love her, but I could not deny how I felt about him either. So she left me and that hurt. I wondered if I was selling out my woman identity and if it [being bisexual] was worth it. (F)

A few wondered whether they were lying to themselves about their heterosexual side. One woman questioned whether her heterosexual desires were a result of "acculturation" rather than being her own choice. Another woman suggested a similar social dimension to her homosexual component:

> There was one period when I was trying to be gay because of the political thing of being totally woman-identified rather than being with men. The Women's Culture Center in college had a women's studies minor, so I was totally immersed in women's culture.... (F)

Lack of support also came from the absence of bisexual role models, no real bisexual community aside from the Bisexual Center, and nothing in the way of public recognition of bisexuality which bred uncertainty and confusion.

I went through a period of dissociation, of being very alone and isolated. That was due to my bisexuality. People would ask, well, what was I? I wasn't gay and I wasn't straight. So I didn't fit. (F)

I don't feel like I belong in a lot of situations because society is so polarized as heterosexual or homosexual. There are not enough bi organizations or public places to go to like bars, restaurants, clubs.... (F)

For some, continuing uncertainty about their sexual identity was related to their inability to translate their sexual feelings into sexual behaviors. (Some of the women had *never* engaged in homosexual sex.)

Should I try to have a sexual relationship with a woman? ... Should I just back off and keep my distance, just try to maintain a friendship? I question whether I am really bisexual because I don't know if I will ever act on my physical attractions for females. (F)

I know I have strong sexual feelings towards men, but then I don't know how to get close to or be sexual with a man. I guess that what happens is I start wondering how genuine my feelings are.... (M)

For the men, confusion stemmed more from the practical concerns of implementing and managing multiple partners or from questions about how to find an involved homosexual relationship and what that might mean on a social and personal level.

I felt very confused about how I was going to manage my life in terms of developing relationships with both men and women. I still see it as a difficult lifestyle to create for myself because it involves a lot of hard work and understanding on my part and that of the men and women I'm involved with. (M)

I've thought about trying to have an actual relationship with a man. Some of my confusion revolves around how to find a satisfactory sexual relationship. I do not particularly like gay bars. I have stopped having anonymous sex.... (M)

Many men and women felt doubts about their bisexual identity because of being in an exclusive sexual relationship. After being exclusively involved with an opposite-sex partner for a period to time, some of the respondents questioned the homosexual side of their sexuality. Conversely, after being exclusively involved with a partner of the same sex, other respondents called into question the heterosexual component of their sexuality.

When I'm with a man or a woman sexually for a period of time, then I begin to wonder how attracted I really am to the other sex. (M)

In the last relationship I had with a woman, my heterosexual feelings were very diminished. Being involved in a lesbian lifestyle put stress on my self-identification as a bisexual. It seems confusing to me because I am monogamous for the most part, monogamy determines my lifestyle to the extremes of being heterosexual or homosexual. (F)

Others made reference to a lack of sexual activity with weaker sexual feelings and affections for one sex. Such learning did not fit with the perception that bisexuals should have balanced desires and behaviors. The consequence was doubt about "really" being bisexual.

On the level of sexual arousal and deep romantic feelings, I feel them much more strongly for women than for men. I've gone so far as questioning myself when this is involved. (M)

I definitely am attracted to and it is much easier to deal with males. Also, guilt for my attraction to females has led me to wonder if I am just really toying with the idea. Is the sexual attraction I have for females something I constructed to pass time or what? (F)

Just as "settling into the identity" is a relative phenomenon, so too is "continued uncertainty," which can involve a lack of closure as part and parcel of what it means to be bisexual.

We do not wish to claim too much for our model of bisexual identity formation. There are limits to its general application. The people we interviewed were unique in that not only did *all* the respondents define themselves as bisexual (a consequence of our selection criteria), but they were also all members of a bisexual social organization in a city that perhaps more than any other in the United States could be said to provide a bisexual subculture of some sort. Bisexuals in places other than San Francisco surely must move through the early phases of the identity process with a great deal more difficulty. Many probably never reach the later stages.

Finally, the phases of the model we present are very broad and somewhat simplified. While the particular problems we detail within different phases may be restricted to the type of bisexuals in this study, the broader phases can form the basis for the development of more sophisticated models of bisexual identity formation.

Still, not all bisexuals will follow these patterns. Indeed, given the relative weakness of the bisexual subculture compared with the social pressures toward conformity exhibited in the gay subculture, there may be more varied ways of acquiring a bisexual identity. Also, the involvement of bisexuals in the heterosexual world means that various changes in heterosexual lifestyles (e.g., a decrease in open marriages or swinging) will be a continuing, and as yet unexplored, influence on bisexual identity. Finally, wider societal changes, notably the existence of AIDS, may make for changes in the overall identity process. Being used to choice and being open to both sexes can give bisexuals a range of adaptations in their sexual life that are not available to others.

25

Anorexia Nervosa and Bulimia

PENELOPE A. McLorg and DIANE E. TAUB

McLorg and Taub's study of eating disorders describes and analyzes women's progression along an identity career from their initial stage of hyper-conformity through Lemert's stages of primary and secondary deviance. They illustrate how the intense societal preoccupation about weight leads women to the kind of deviant behavior that maintains (initially) their positive external status while they are deteriorating internally. Along the way, these women move through a progression of more common fixations about dieting to frustration with dieting and movement toward more radical solutions such as bingeing, purging, compulsive exercising, and lack of eating. These behaviors stand apart from their identities, McLorg and Taub argue, since they can avoid the deviant label and self-conception, remaining in the primary deviance stage until they get caught and labeled as having an eating disorder. Once this occurs they move to secondary deviance, reconceptualized by others as anorectic or bulimic. With this label cast on them, they are forced to interact with others through the vehicle of their deviance, thus reinforcing their eating disorders

How might you relate this article to the typology of deviance proposed by Heckert and Heckert?

Current appearance norms stipulate thinness for women and muscularity for men; these expectations, like any norms, entail rewards for compliance and negative sanctions for violations. Fear of being overweight—of being visually deviant—has led to a striving for thinness, especially among women. In the extreme, this avoidance of overweight engenders eating disorders, which themselves constitute deviance. Anorexia nervosa, or purposeful starvation, embodies visual as well as behavioral deviation; bulimia, binge-eating followed by vomiting, and/or laxative abuse, is primarily behaviorally deviant.

Besides a fear of fatness, anorexics and bulimics exhibit distorted body images. In anorexia nervosa, a 20 to 25 percent loss of initial body weight occurs, resulting from self-starvation alone or in combination with excessive exercising, occasional binge-eating, vomiting and/or laxative abuse. Bulimia denotes cyclical (daily, weekly, for example) binge-eating followed by vomiting or laxative abuse;

weight is normal or close to normal (Humphries et al., 1982). Common physical manifestations of these eating disorders include menstrual cessation or irregularities and electrolyte imbalances; among behavioral traits are depression, obsessions/compulsions, and anxiety (Russell, 1979; Thompson and Schwartz, 1982).

Increasingly prevalent in the past two decades, anorexia nervosa and bulimia have emerged as major health and social problems. Termed an epidemic on college campuses (Brody, as quoted in Schur, 1984: 76), bulimia affects 13 percent of college students (Halmi et al., 1981). Less prevalent, anorexia nervosa was diagnosed in 0.6 percent of students utilizing a university health center (Stangler and Printz, 1980). However, the overall mortality rate of anorexia nervosa is 6 percent (Schwartz and Thompson, 1981) to 20 percent (Humphries et al., 1982); bulimia appears to be less life-threatening (Russell, 1979).

Particularly affecting certain demographic groups, eating disorders are most prevalent among young, white, affluent (upper-middle to upper class) women in modern, industrialized countries (Crisp, 1977; Willi and Grossman, 1983). Combining all of these risk factors (female sex, youth, high socioeconomic status, and residence in an industrialized country), prevalence of anorexia nervosa in upper class English girls' schools is reported at 1 in 100 (Crisp et al., 1976). The age of onset for anorexia nervosa is bimodal at 14.5 and 18 years (Humphries et al., 1982); the most frequent age of onset for bulimia is 18 (Russell, 1979).

Eating disorders have primarily been studied from psychological and medical perspectives.[1] Theories of etiology have generally fallen into three categories: the ego psychological (involving an impaired child-maternal environment); the family systems (implicating enmeshed, rigid families); and the endocrinological (involving a precipitating hormonal defect). Although relatively ignored in previous studies, the sociocultural components of anorexia nervosa and bulimia (the slimness norm and its agents of reinforcement, such as role models) have been postulated as accounting for the recent, dramatic increases in these disorders (Schwartz et al., 1982; Boskmd-White, 1985).[2]

Medical and psychological approaches to anorexia nervosa and bulimia obscure the social facets of the disorders and neglect the individuals' own definitions of their situations. Among the social processes involved in the development of an eating disorder is the sequence of conforming behavior, primary deviance, and secondary deviance. Societal reaction is the critical mediator affecting the movement through the deviant career (Becker, 1963). Within a framework of labeling theory, this study focuses on the emergence of anorexic and bulimic identities, as well as on the consequences of being career deviants.

METHODOLOGY

Sampling and Procedures

Most research on eating disorders has utilized clinical subjects or nonclinical respondents completing questionnaires. Such studies can be criticized for simply counting and describing behaviors and/or neglecting the social construction of the disorders. Moreover, the work of clinicians is often limited by therapeutic orientation. Previous research may also have included individuals who were not in therapy on their own volition and who resisted admitting that they had an eating disorder.

Past studies thus disregard the intersubjective meanings respondents attach to their behavior and emphasize researchers' criteria for definition as anorexic or bulimic. In order to supplement these sampling and procedural designs, the present study utilizes participant observation of a group of self-defined anorexics and bulimics[3] As the individuals had acknowledged their eating disorders, frank discussion and disclosure were facilitated.

Data are derived from a self-help group, BANISH, Bulimics/Anorexics In Self-Help, which met at a university in an urban center of the mid-South. Founded by one of the researchers (D.E.T.), BANISH was advertised in local newspapers as offering a group experience for individuals who were anorexic or bulimic. Despite the local advertisements, the campus location of the meetings may have selectively encouraged university students to attend. Nonetheless, in view of the modal age of onset and socioeconomic status of individuals with eating disorders, college students have been considered target populations (Crisp et al., 1976; Halmi et al., 1981).

The group's weekly two-hour meetings were observed for two years. During the course of this study, 30 individuals attended at least one of the meetings. Attendance at meetings was varied: 10 individuals came nearly every Sunday; 5 attended approximately twice a month; and the remaining 15 participated once a month or less frequently, often when their eating problems were "more severe" or "bizarre." The modal number of members at meetings was 12. The diversity in attendance was to be expected in self-help groups of anorexics and bulimics.

> [Most] people's involvement will not be forever or even a long time. Most people get the support they need and drop out. Some take the time to help others after they themselves have been helped but even they may withdraw after a time. It is a natural and in many cases *necessary* process. (Emphasis in original.) (American Anorexia/Bulimia Association, 1983)

Modeled after Alcoholics Anonymous, BANISH allowed participants to discuss their backgrounds and experiences with others who empathized. For many members, the group constituted their only source of help; these respondents were reluctant to contact health professionals because of shame, embarrassment, or financial difficulties.

In addition to field notes from group meetings, records of other encounters with all members were maintained. Participants visited the office of one of the researchers (D.E.T.), called both researchers by phone, and invited them to their homes or out for a cup of coffee. Such interaction facilitated genuine communication and mutual trust. Even among the 15 individuals who did not attend the meetings regularly, contact was maintained with 10 members on a monthly basis.

Supplementing field notes were informal interviews with 15 group members, lasting from two to four hours. Because they appeared to represent more extensive experience with eating disorders, these interviewees were chosen to amplify their comments about the labeling process, made during group meetings. Conducted near the end of the two-year observation period, the interviews focused on what the respondents thought antedated and maintained their eating disorders. In addition, participants described others' reactions to their behaviors as well as their own interpretations of these reactions. To protect the confidentiality of individuals quoted in the study, pseudonyms are employed.

Description of Members

The demographic composite of the sample typifies what has been found in other studies (Fox and James, 1976; Crisp, 1977; Herzog, 1982; Schlesier-Stropp, 1984). Group members' ages ranged from 19 to 36, with the modal age being 21. The respondents were white, and all but one were female. The sole male and three of the females were anorexic; the remaining females were bulimic.[4]

Primarily composed of college students, the group included four non-students, three of whom had college degrees. Nearly all members derived from upper-middle or lower-upper class households. Eighteen students and two non-students were never-marrieds and uninvolved in serious relationships; two non-students were married (one with two children); two students were divorced (one with two children); and six students were involved in serious relationships. The duration of eating disorders ranged from 3 to 15 years.

CONFORMING BEHAVIOR

In the backgrounds of most anorexics and bulimics, dieting figures prominently, beginning in the teen years (Crisp, 1977; Johnson et al., 1982; Lacey et al., 1986). As dieters, these individuals are conformist in their adherence to the cultural norms emphasizing thinness (Garner et al., 1980; Schwartz et al., 1982). In our society, slim bodies are regarded as the most worthy and attractive; overweight is viewed as physically and morally unhealthy—"obscene," "lazy," "slothful," and "gluttonous" (Dejong, 1980; Ritenbaugh, 1982; Schwartz et al., 1982).

Among the agents of socialization promoting the slimness norm is advertising. Female models in newspaper, magazine, and television advertisements are uniformly slender. In addition, product names and slogans exploit the thin orientation; examples include "Ultra Slim Lipstick," "Miller Lite," and "Virginia Slims." While retaining pressures toward thinness, an Ayds commercial attempts a compromise for those wanting to savor food: "Ayds… so you can taste, chew, and enjoy, while you lose weight." Appealing particularly to women, a nationwide fast-food restaurant chain offers low-calorie selections, so individuals can have a "license to eat." In the latter two examples, the notion of enjoying food is combined with the message to be slim. Food and restaurant advertisements overall convey the pleasures of eating, whereas advertisements for other products, such as fashions and diet aids, reinforce the idea that fatness is undesirable.

Emphasis on being slim affects everyone in our culture, but it influences women especially because of society's traditional emphasis on women's appearance. The slimness norm and its concomitant narrow beauty standards exacerbate the objectification of women (Schur, 1984). Women view themselves as visual entities and recognize that conforming to appearance expectations and "becoming attractive object[s] [are] role obligation[s]" (Laws, as quoted in Schur, 1984: 66). Demonstrating the beauty motivation behind dieting, a recent Nielsen survey indicated that of the 56 percent of all women aged 24 to 54 who dieted during the previous year, 76 percent did so for cosmetic, rather than health, reasons (Schwartz et al., 1982). For most female group members, dieting was viewed as a means of gaining attractiveness and appeal to the opposite sex. The male respondent, as well, indicated that "when I was fat, girls didn't look at me, but when I got thinner, I was suddenly popular."

In addition to responding to the specter of obesity, individuals who develop anorexia nervosa and bulimia are conformist in their strong commitment to other conventional norms and goals. They consistently excel at school and work (Russell, 1979; Bruch, 1981; Humphries et al., 1982), maintaining high aspirations in both areas (Theander, 1970; Lacey et al., 1986). Group members generally completed college-preparatory courses in high school, aware from an early age that they would strive for a college degree. Also, in college as well as high school, respondents joined honor societies and academic clubs.

Moreover, pre-anorexics and -bulimics display notable conventionality as "model children" (Humphries et al., 1982: 199), "the pride and joy" of their parents (Bruch, 1981: 215), accommodating themselves to the wishes of others. Parents of these individuals emphasize conformity and value achievement (Bruch, 1981). Respondents felt that perfect or near-perfect grades were expected of them; however, good grades were not rewarded by parents, because "A's" were common for these children. In addition, their parents suppressed conflicts, to preserve the image of the "all-American family" (Humphries et al., 1982). Group members reported that they seldom, if ever, heard their parents argue or raise their voices.

Also conformist in their affective ties, individuals who develop anorexia nervosa and bulimia are strongly, even excessively, attached to their parents. Respondents' families appeared close-knit, demonstrating palpable emotional ties. Several group members, for example, reported habitually calling home at prescribed times, whether or not they had any news. Such families have been termed "enmeshed" and "overprotective," displaying intense interaction and concern for members' welfare (Minuchin et al., 1978; Selvini-Palazzoli, 1978). These qualities could be viewed as marked conformity to the norm of familial closeness.[5]

Another element of notable conformity in the family milieu of pre-anorexics and -bulimics concerns eating, body weight/shape, and exercising (Kalucy et al., 1977; Humphries et al., 1982). Respondents reported their fathers' preoccupation with exercising and their mothers' engrossment in food preparation. When group members dieted and lost weight, they received an extraordinary amount of approval. Among the family, body size became a matter of "friendly rivalry." One bulimic informant recalled that she, her mother, and her coed sister all strived to wear a size five, regardless of their heights and body frames. Subsequent to this study, the researchers learned that both the mother and sister had become bulimic.

As preanorexics and -bulimics, group members thus exhibited marked conformity to cultural norms of thinness, achievement, compliance, and parental attachment. Their families reinforced their conformity by adherence to norms of family closeness and weight/body shape consciousness.

PRIMARY DEVIANCE

Even with familial encouragement, respondents, like nearly all dieters (Chemin, 1981), failed to maintain their lowered weights. Many cited their lack of will-power to eat only restricted foods. For the emerging anorexics and bulimics, extremes such as purposeful starvation or binging accompanied by vomiting and/or laxative abuse appeared as "obvious solutions" to the problem of retaining weight loss. Associated with these behaviors was a regained feeling of control in lives that had been disrupted by a major crisis. Group members' extreme weight-loss efforts operated as coping mechanisms for entering college, leaving home, or feeling rejected by the opposite sex.

The primary inducement for both eating adaptations was the drive for slimness: with slimness came more self-respect and a feeling of superiority over "unsuccessful dieters." Brian, for example, experienced a "power trip" upon consistent weight loss through starvation. Binges allowed the purging respondents to cope with stress through eating while maintaining a slim appearance. As former strict dieters, Teresa and Jennifer used binging/purging as an alternative to the constant self-denial of starvation. Acknowledging their parents' desires for them to be slim, most respondents still felt it was a conscious choice on their part to continue extreme weight-loss efforts. Being thin became the "most important thing" in their lives—their "greatest ambition."

In explaining the development of an anorexic or bulimic identity, Lemert's (1951; 1967) concept of primary deviance is salient. Primary deviance refers to a transitory period of norm violations which do not affect an individual's self-concept or performance of social roles. Although respondents were exhibiting anorexic or bulimic behavior, they did not consider themselves to be anorexic or bulimic.

At first, anorexics' significant others complimented their weight loss, expounding on their new "sleekness" and "good looks." Branch and Eurman (1980: 631) also found anorexics' families and friends describing them as "well-groomed," "neat," "fashionable," and "victorious." Not until the respondents approached emaciation did some parents or friends become concerned and withdraw their praise. Significant others also became increasingly aware of the anorexics' compulsive exercising, preoccupation with food preparation (but not consumption), and ritualistic eating patterns (such as cutting food into minute pieces and eating only certain foods at prescribed times).

For bulimics, friends or family members began to question how the respondents could eat such large amounts of food (often in excess of 10,000 calories a day) and stay slim. Significant others also noticed calluses across the bulimics' hands, which were caused by repeated inducement of vomiting. Several bulimics were "caught in the act," bent over commodes. Generally, friends and family required substantial evidence before believing that the respondents' binging or purging was no longer sporadic.

SECONDARY DEVIANCE

Heightened awareness of group members' eating behavior ultimately led others to label the respondents "anorexic" or "bulimic." Respondents differed in their histories of being labeled and accepting the labels. Generally first termed anorexic by friends, family, or medical personnel, the anorexics initially vigorously denied the label. They felt they were not "anorexic enough," not skinny enough; Robin did not regard herself as having the "skeletal" appearance she associated with anorexia nervosa. These group members found it difficult to differentiate between socially approved modes of weight loss—eating less and exercising more—and the extremes of those behaviors. In fact, many of their activities—cheerleading, modeling, gymnastics, aerobics—reinforced their pursuit of thinness. Like other anorexics, Chris felt she was being "ultra-healthy" with "total control" over her body.

For several respondents, admitting they were anorexic followed the realization that their lives were disrupted by their eating disorder. Anorexics' inflexible eating patterns unsettled family meals and holiday gatherings. Their regimented lifestyle of compulsively scheduled activities—exercising, school, and meals—precluded any spontaneous social interactions. Realization of their adverse behaviors preceded the anorexics' acknowledgment of their subnormal body weight and size.

Contrasting with anorexics, the binge/purgers, when confronted, more readily admitted that they were bulimic and that their means of weight loss was "abnormal." Teresa, for example, knew "very well" that her bulimic behavior was "wrong and unhealthy," although "worth the physical risks." While the bulimics initially maintained that their purging was only a temporary weight-loss method, they eventually realized that their disorder represented a "loss of control." Although these respondents regretted the self-indulgence, "shame," and "wasted time," they acknowledged their growing dependence on binging/purging for weight management and stress regulation.

The application of anorexic or bulimic labels precipitated secondary deviance, wherein group members internalized these identities. Secondary deviance refers to norm violations which are a response to society's labeling: "secondary deviation … becomes a means of social defense, attack or adaptation to the overt and covert problems created by the societal reaction to primary deviance" (Lemert, 1967: 17). In contrast to primary deviance, secondary deviance is generally prolonged, alters the individual's self-concept, and affects the performance of his/her social roles.

As secondary deviants, respondents felt that their disorders "gave a purpose" to their lives. Nicole resisted attaining a normal weight because it was not "her"—she accepted her anorexic weight as her "true" weight. For Teresa, bulimia became a "companion"; and Julie felt "every aspect of her life," including time management and social activities, was affected by her bulimia. Group members' eating disorders became the salient element of their self-concepts, so that they related to familiar people and new acquaintances as anorexics or bulimics. For example, respondents regularly compared their body shapes and sizes with those of others. They also became sensitized to comments about their appearance, whether or not the remarks were made by someone aware of their eating disorder.

With their behavior increasingly attuned to their eating disorders, group members exhibited role engulfment (Schur, 1971). Through accepting anorexic or bulimic identities, individuals centered activities around their deviant role, downgrading other social roles. Their obligations as students, family members, and friends became subordinate to their eating and exercising rituals. Socializing, for example, was gradually curtailed because it interfered with compulsive exercising, binging, or purging.

Labeled anorexic or bulimic, respondents were ascribed a new status with a different set of role expectations. Regardless of other positions the individuals occupied, their deviant status, or master status (Hughes, 1958; Becker, 1963), was identified before all others. Among group members, Nicole, who was known as the "school's brain," became known as the "school's anorexic." No longer viewed as conforming model individuals, some respondents were termed "starving waifs" or "pigs."

Because of their identities as deviants, anorexics' and bulimics' interactions with others were altered. Group members' eating habits were scrutinized by friends and family and used as a "catchall" for everything negative that happened to them. Respondents felt self-conscious around individuals who knew of their disorders; for example, Robin imagined people "watching and whispering" behind her. In addition, group members believed others expected them to "act" anorexic or bulimic. Friends of some anorexic group members never offered them food or drink, assuming continued disinterest on the respondents' part. While being hospitalized, Denise felt she had to prove to others she was not still vomiting, by keeping her bathroom door open. Other bulimics, who lived in dormitories, were hesitant to use the restroom for normal purposes lest several friends be huddling at the door, listening for vomiting. In general, individuals interacted with the respondents largely on the basis of their eating disorder; in doing so, they reinforced anorexic and bulimic behaviors.

Bulimic respondents, whose weight-loss behavior was not generally detectable from their appearance, tried earnestly to hide their bulimia by binging and purging in secret. Their main purpose in concealment was to avoid the negative consequences of being known as a bulimic. For these individuals, bulimia connoted a "cop-out": like "weak anorexics," bulimics pursued thinness but yielded to urges to eat. Respondents felt other people regarded bulimia as "gross" and had little sympathy for the sufferer. To avoid these stigmas or "spoiled identities," the bulimics shrouded their behaviors.

Distinguishing types of stigma, Goffman (1963) describes discredited (visible) stigmas and discreditable (invisible) stigmas. Bulimics, whose weight was approximately normal or even slightly elevated, harbored discreditable stigmas. Anorexics, on the other hand, suffered both discreditable and discredited stigmas—the latter due to their emaciated appearance. Certain anorexics were more reconciled than the bulimics to their stigmas: for Brian, the "stigma of anorexia was better than the stigma of being fat." Common to the stigmatized individuals was an inability to interact spontaneously with others. Respondents were constantly on guard against topics of eating and body size.

Both anorexics and bulimics were held responsible by others for their behavior and presumed able to "get out of it if they tried." Many anorexics reported being told to "just eat more," while bulimics were enjoined to simply "stop eating so much." Such appeals were made without regard for the complexities of the problem. Ostracized by certain friends and family members, anorexics and bulimics felt increasingly isolated. For respondents, the self-help group presented a nonthreatening forum for discussing their disorders. Here, they found mutual understanding, empathy, and support. Many participants viewed BANISH as a haven from stigmatization by "others."

Group members, as secondary deviants, thus endured negative consequences, such as stigmatization, from being labeled. As they internalized the labels anorexic or bulimic, individuals' self-concepts were significantly influenced. When others interacted with the respondents on the basis of their eating disorders, anorexic or bulimic identities were encouraged. Moreover, group members' efforts to counteract the deviant labels were thwarted by their master statuses.

DISCUSSION

Previous research on eating disorders has dwelt almost exclusively on medical and psychological facets. Although necessary for a comprehensive understanding of anorexia nervosa and bulimia, these approaches neglect the social processes involved. The phenomena of eating disorders transcend concrete disease entities and clinical diagnoses. Multifaceted and complex, anorexia nervosa and bulimia require a holistic research design, in which sociological insights must be included.

A limitation of medical/psychiatric studies, in particular, is researchers' use of a priori criteria in establishing salient variables. Rather than utilizing predetermined standards of inclusion, the present study allows respondents to construct their own reality. Concomitant to this innovative approach to eating disorders is the selection of a sample of self-admitted anorexics and bulimics. Individuals' perceptions of what it means to become anorexic or bulimic are explored. Although based on a small sample, findings can be used to guide researchers in other settings.

With only 5 to 10 percent of reported cases appearing in males (Crisp, 1977; Stangler and Printz, 1980), eating disorders are primarily a women's aberrance. The deviance of anorexia nervosa and bulimia is rooted in the visual objectification of women and attendant slimness norm. Indeed, purposeful starvation and bingeing/purging reinforce the notion that "a society gets the deviance it deserves" (Schur, 1979: 71). As recently noted (Schur, 1984), the sociology of deviance has generally bypassed systematic studies of women's norm violations. Like male deviants, females endure label applications, internalizations, and fulfillments.

The social processes involved in developing anorexic or bulimic identities comprise the sequence of conforming behavior, primary deviance, and secondary deviance. With a background of exceptional adherence to conventional norms, especially the striving for thinness, respondents subsequently exhibit the primary deviance of starving or binging/purging. Societal reaction to these behaviors leads to secondary deviance, wherein respondents' self-concepts and master statuses become anorexic or bulimic. Within this framework of labeling theory, the persistence of eating disorders, as well as the effects of stigmatization, is elucidated.

Although during the course of this research some respondents alleviated their symptoms through psychiatric help or hospital treatment programs, no one was labeled "cured." An anorexic is considered recovered when weight is normal for two years; a bulimic is termed recovered after being symptom-free for one and one-half years (American Anorexia/Bulimia Association Newsletter, 1985). Thus deviance disavowal (Schur, 1971), or efforts after normalization to counteract the deviant labels, remains a topic for future exploration.

NOTES

1. Although instructive, an integration of the medical, psychological, and socio-cultural perspectives on eating disorders is beyond the scope of this paper.

2. Exceptions to the neglect of socio-cultural factors are discussions of sex-role socialization in the development of eating disorders. Anorexics' girlish appearance has been interpreted as a rejection of femininity and womanhood (Orbach, 1979; Bruch, 1981; Orbach, 1985). In contrast, bulimics have been characterized as over-conforming to traditional female sex roles (Boskmd-Lodahl, 1976).

3. Although a group experience for self-defined bulimics has been reported (Boskind-Lodahl, 1976), the researcher, from the outset, focused on Gestalt and behaviorist techniques within a feminist orientation.

4. One explanation for fewer anorexics than bulimics in the sample is that, in the general population, anorexics are outnumbered by bulimics at 8 or 10 to

1 (Lawson, as reprinted in American Anorexia/Bulimia Association Newsletter, 1985: 1). The proportion of bulimics to anorexics in the sample is 6.5 to 1. In addition, compared to bulimics, anorexics may be less likely to attend a self-help group as they have a greater tendency to deny the existence of an eating problem (Humphries et al., 1982). However, the four anorexics in the present study were among the members who attended the meetings most often.

5. Interactions in the families of anorexics and bulimics might seem deviant in being inordinately close. However, in the larger societal context, the family members epitomize the norms of family cohesiveness. Perhaps unusual in their occurrence, these families are still within the realm of conformity. Humphries and colleagues (1982: 202) refer to the "highly enmeshed and protective" family as part of the "idealized family myth."

REFERENCES

American Anorexia/Bulimia Association. 1983. Correspondence. April.

American Anorexia/Bulimia Association Newsletter. 1985. 8(3).

Becker, Howard S. 1963. *Outsiders*. New York: Free Press.

Boskind-Lodahl, Marlene. 1976. Cinderella s stepsisters: A feminist perspective on anorexia nervosa and bulimia." *Signs, Journal of Women in Culture and Society* 2: 342–56.

Boskind-White, Marlene. 1985. "Bulimarexia: A socio-cultural perspective." In S. W. Emmett (ed.), *Theory and Treatment of Anorexia Nervosa and Bulimia: Biomédical, Sociocultural and Psychological Perspective*, pp. 113–26. New York: Brunner/Mazel.

Branch, C. H. Hardin, and Linda J. Eurman. 1980. "Social attitudes toward patients with anorexia nervosa." *American Journal of Psychiatry* 137: 631–32.

Bruch, Hilde. 1981. "Developmental considerations of anorexia nervosa and obesity." *Canadian Journal of Psychiatry* 26: 212–16.

Chernin, Kim. 1981. *The Obsession: Reflections on the Tyranny of Slendemess*. New York: Harper & Row.

Crisp, A. H. 1977. "The prevalence of anorexia nervosa and some of its associations in the general population." *Advances in Psychosomatic Medicine* 9: 38–17.

Crisp, A. H., R. L. Palmer, and R. S. Kalucy. 1976. "How common is anorexia nervosa? A prevalence study." *British Journal of Psychiatry* 128: 549–54.

Dejong, William. 1980. "The stigma of obesity: The consequences of naive assumptions concerning the causes of physical deviance." *Journal of Health and Social Behavior* 21: 75–87.

Fox, K. C, and N. Mel. James. 1976. "Anorexia nervosa: A study of 44 strictly defined cases." *New Zealand Medical Journal* 84: 309–12.

Garner, David M., Paul E. Garfinkel, Donald Schwartz, and Michael Thompson. 1980. "Cultural expectations of thinness in women." *Psychological Reports* 47: 483–91.

Goffman, Erving. 1963. *Stigma*. Englewood Cliffs, NJ: Prentice Hall.

Halmi, Katherine A., James R. Falk, and Estelle Schwartz. 1981. "Binge-eating and vomiting: A survey of a college population." *Psychological Medicine* 11: 697–706.

Herzog, David B. 1982. "Bulimia: The secretive syndrome." *Psychosomatics* 23: 481–83.

Hughes, Everett C. 1958. *Men and Their Work*. New York: Free Press.

Humphries, Laurie L., Sylvia Wrobel, and H. Thomas Wiegert. 1982. "Anorexia nervosa." *American Family Physician* 26: 199–204.

Johnson, Craig L., Marilyn K. Stuckey, Linda D. Lewis, and Donald M. Schwartz. 1982. "Bulimia: A descriptive survey of 316 cases." *International Journal of Eating Disorders* 2(1): 3–16.

Kalucy, R. S., A. H. Crisp, and Britta Harding. 1977. "A study of 56 families with anorexia nervosa." *British Journal of Medical Psychology* 50: 381–95.

Lacey, Hubert J., Sian Coker, and S. A. Birtchnell. 1986. "Bulimia: Factors associated with its etiology and maintenance." *International Journal of Eating Disorders* 5: 475–87.

Lemert, Edwin M. 1951. *Social Pathology*. New York: McGraw-Hill.

———. 1967. *Human Deviance, Social Problems and Social Control*. Englewood Cliffs, NJ: Prentice Hall.

Minuchin, Salvador, Bernice L. Rosman, and Lester Baker. 1978. *Psychosomatic Families: Anorexia Nervosa in Context.* Cambridge, MA: Harvard University Press.

Orbach, Susie. 1979. *Fat Is a Feminist Issue.* New York: Berkeley.

————. 1985. "Visibility/invisibility: Social considerations in anorexia nervosa—a feminist perspective." In S. W. Emmett (ed.), *Theory and Treatment of Anorexia Nervosa and Bulimia: Biomédical, Socio cultural, and Psychological Perspective,* pp. 127–38. New York: Brunner/Mazel.

Ritenbaugh, Cheryl. 1982. "Obesity as a culture-bound syndrome." *Culture, Medicine and Psychiatry* 6: 347–61.

Russell, Gerald. 1979. "Bulimia nervosa: An ominous variant of anorexia nervosa." *Psychological Medicine* 9: 429–48.

Schlesier-Stropp, Barbara. 1984. "Bulimia: A review of the literature." *Psychological Bulletin* 95: 247–57.

Schur, Edwin M. 1971. *Labeling Deviant Behavior.* New York: Harper & Row.

————. 1979. *Interpreting Deviance: A Sociological Introduction.* New York: Harper & Row.

————. 1984. *Labeling Women Deviant: Gender, Stigma, and Social Control.* New York: Random House.

Schwartz, Donald M., and Michael G. Thompson. 1981. "Do anorectics get well? Current research and future needs." *American Journal of Psychiatry* 138: 319–23.

Schwartz, Donald M., Michael G. Thompson, and Craig L. Johnson. 1982. "Anorexia nervosa and bulimia: The socio-cultural context." *International Journal of Eating Disorders* 1(3): 20–36.

Selvini-Palazzoli, Mara. 1978. *Self-Starvation: From Individual to Family Therapy in the Treatment of Anorexia Nervosa.* New York: Jason Aronson.

Stangler, Ronnie S., and Adolph M. Printz. 1980. "DSM-III: Psychiatric diagnosis in a university population." *American Journal of Psychiatry* 137: 937–10.

Theander, Sten. 1970. "Anorexia nervosa." *Acta Psychiatrica Scandinavica Supplement* 214: 24–31.

Thompson, Michael G., and Donald M. Schwartz. 1982. "Life adjustment of women with anorexia nervosa and anorexic-like behavior." *International Journal of Eating Disorders* 1(2): 47–60.

Willi, Jurg, and Samuel Grossmann. 1983. "Epidemiology of anorexia nervosa in a defined region of Switzerland." *American Journal of Psychiatry* 140: 564–67.

26

Convicted Rapists'
Vocabulary of Motive

DIANA SCULLY AND JOSEPH MAROLLA

Scully and Marolla's study of the way rapists rationalize their behavior offers a fascinating glimpse into the accounts offered by criminals. They interview the most hard-core segment of the rapist population, those sentenced to prison time. In analyzing these men's rationalizations, Scully and Marolla draw on Scott and Lyman's (1968) classic typology of accounts: excuses and justifications. In using excuses, men acknowledge the wrongfulness of the act but deny full responsibility. These, they find, are primarily used by those who admit to their deviant acts. Men who deny having committed rape (over 80% of the population), are more prone to use justifications, where they accept responsibility for their act but provide reasons that legitimate their behavior as not wrong. Scully and Marolla examine the various disavowal techniques, shed light on the repertoire of culturally available neutralizing accounts, and analyze the connection between types of accounts used and the way offenders locate blame.

Which types of accounts do you find more compelling, excuses or justifications? How does this article make you feel about the effectiveness of accounts in neutralizing people's views of themselves as deviant? How effective do you think they are in neutralizing others' views of them?

Psychiatry has dominated the literature on rapists since "irresistible impulse" (Glueck, 1925: 243) and "disease of the mind" (Glueck, 1925: 243) were introduced as the causes of rape. Research has been based on small samples of men, frequently the clinicians' own patient population. Not surprisingly, the medical model has predominated: rape is viewed as an individualistic, idiosyncratic symptom of a disordered personality. That is, rape is assumed to be a

From Diana Scully and Joseph Marolla, "Convicted Rapists Vocabulary of Motive: Excuses and Justifications." *Social Problems*, Vol. 31, No. 5, 1984. Copyright © 1984 Society for the Study of Social Problems. All rights reserved. Reprinted by permission of University of California Press Journals and Diana Scully.

psycho-pathologic problem and individual rapists are assumed to be "sick." However, advocates of this model have been unable to isolate a typical or even predictable pattern of symptoms that are causally linked to rape. Additionally, research has demonstrated that fewer than 5 percent of rapists were psychotic at the time of their rape (Abel et al. 1980).

We view rape as behavior learned socially through interaction with others; convicted rapists have learned the attitudes and actions consistent with sexual aggression against women. Learning also includes the acquisition of culturally derived vocabularies of motive, which can be used to diminish responsibility and to negotiate a nondeviant identity.

Sociologists have long noted that people can, and do, commit acts they define as wrong and, having done so, engage various techniques to disavow deviance and present themselves as normal. Through the concept of "vocabulary of motive," Mills (1940: 904) was among the first to shed light on this seemingly perplexing contradiction. Wrongdoers attempt to reinterpret their actions through the use of a linguistic device by which norm-breaking conduct is socially interpreted. That is, anticipating the negative consequences of their behavior, wrongdoers attempt to present the act in terms that are both culturally appropriate and acceptable.

Following Mills, a number of sociologists have focused on the types of techniques employed by actors in problematic situations (Hall and Hewitt, 1970; Hewitt and Hall, 1973; Hewitt and Stokes, 1975; Sykes and Matza, 1957). Scott and Lyman (1968) describe excuses and justifications, linguistic "accounts" that explain and remove culpability for an untoward act after it has been committed. *Excuses* admit the act was bad or inappropriate but deny full responsibility, often through appeals to accident, or biological drive, or through scapegoating. In contrast, *justifications* accept responsibility for the act but deny that it was wrong—that is, they show in this situation the act was appropriate. *Accounts* are socially approved vocabularies that neutralize an act or its consequences and are always a manifestation of an underlying negotiation of identity.

Stokes and Hewitt (1976: 837) use the term "aligning actions" to refer to those tactics and techniques used by actors when some feature of a situation is problematic. Stated simply, the concept refers to an actor's attempt, through various means, to bring his or her conduct into alignment with culture. Culture in this sense is conceptualized as a "set of cognitive constraints—objects—to which people must relate as they form lines of conduct" (1976: 837), and includes physical constraints, expectations and definitions of others, and personal biography. Carrying out aligning actions implies both awareness of those elements of normative culture that are applicable to the deviant act and, in addition, an actual effort to bring the act into line with this awareness. The result is that deviant behavior is legitimized.

This paper presents an analysis of interviews we conducted with a sample of 114 convicted, incarcerated rapists. We use the concept of accounts (Scott and Lyman, 1968) as a tool to organize and analyze the vocabularies of motive which this group of rapists used to explain themselves and their actions. An analysis of their accounts demonstrates how it was possible for 83 percent (n = 114)[1] of these convicted rapists to view themselves as nonrapists.

When rapists' accounts are examined, a typology emerges that consists of admitters and deniers. Admitters (n = 47) acknowledged that they had forced sexual acts on their victims and defined the behavior as rape. In contrast, deniers[2] either eschewed sexual contact or all association with the victim (n = 35),[3] or admitted to sexual acts but did not define their behavior as rape (n = 32).... By and large, the deniers used justifications while the admitters used excuses. In some cases, both groups relied on the same themes, stereotypes, and images: some admitters, like most deniers, claimed that women enjoyed being raped. Some deniers excused their behavior by referring to alcohol or drug use, although they did so quite differently than admitters. Through these narrative accounts, we explore convicted rapists' own perceptions of their crimes....

JUSTIFYING RAPE

Deniers attempted to justify their behavior by presenting the victim in a light that made her appear culpable, regardless of their own actions. Five themes run through rapists' attempts to justify their rapes: (1) women as seductresses; (2) women mean "yes" when they say "no"; (3) most women eventually relax and enjoy it; (4) nice girls don't get raped; and (5) guilty of a minor wrongdoing.

(1) Women as Seductresses

Men who rape need not search far for cultural language which supports the premise that women provoke or are responsible for rape. In addition to common cultural stereotypes, the fields of psychiatry and criminology (particularly the subfield of victimology) have traditionally provided justifications for rape, often by portraying raped women as the victims of their own seduction (Albin, 1977; Marolla and Scully, 1979). For example, Hollander (1924: 130) argues:

> Considering the amount of illicit intercourse, rape of women is very rare indeed. Flirtation and provocative conduct, i.e. tacit (if not actual) consent is generally the prelude to intercourse.

Since women are supposed to be coy about their sexual availability, refusal to comply with a man's sexual demands lacks meaning and rape appears normal. The fact that violence and, often, a weapon are used to accomplish the rape is not considered. As an example, Abrahamsen (1960: 61) writes:

> The conscious or unconscious biological or psychological attraction between man and woman does not exist only on the part of the offender toward the woman but, also, on her part toward him, which in many instances may, to some extent, be the impetus for his sexual attack. Often a women [sic] unconsciously wishes to be taken by force—consider the theft of the bride in Peer Gynt.

Like Peer Gynt, the deniers we interviewed tried to demonstrate that their victims were willing and, in some cases, enthusiastic participants. In these accounts, the rape became more dependent upon the victim's behavior than upon their own actions.

Thirty-one percent (n = 10) of the deniers presented an extreme view of the victim. Not only willing, she was the aggressor, a seductress who lured them, unsuspecting, into sexual action. Typical was a denier convicted of his first rape and accompanying crimes of burglary, sodomy, and abduction. According to the presentence reports, he had broken into the victim's house and raped her at knife point. While he admitted to the breaking and entry, which he claimed was for altruistic purposes ("to pay for the prenatal care of a friend's girlfriend"), he also argued that when the victim discovered him, he had tried to leave but she had asked him to stay. Telling him that she cheated on her husband, she had voluntarily removed her clothes and seduced him. She was, according to him, an exemplary sex partner who "enjoyed it very much and asked for oral sex.[4] Can I have it now?" he reported her as saying. He claimed they had spent hours in bed, after which the victim had told him he was good looking and asked to see him again. "Who would believe I'd meet a fellow like this?" he reported her as saying.

In addition to this extreme group, 25 percent (n = 8) of the deniers said the victim was willing and had made some sexual advances. An additional 9 percent (n = 3) said the victim was willing to have sex for money or drugs. In two of these three cases, the victim had been either an acquaintance or picked up, which the rapists said led them to expect sex.

(2) Women Mean "Yes" When They Say "No"

Thirty-four percent (n = 11) of the deniers described their victim as unwilling, at least initially, indicating either that she had resisted or that she had said no. Despite this, and even though (according to presentence reports) a weapon had been present in 64 percent (n = 7) of these 11 cases, the rapists justified their behavior by arguing that either the victim had not resisted enough or that her "no" had really meant "yes." For example, one denier who was serving time for a previous rape was subsequently convicted of attempting to rape a prison hospital nurse. He insisted he had actually completed the second rape, and said of his victim: "She semistruggled but deep down inside I think she felt it was a fantasy come true." The nurse, according to him, had asked a question about his conviction for rape, which he interpreted as teasing. "It was like she was saying, 'rape me.'" Further, he stated that she had helped him along with oral sex and "from her actions, she was enjoying it." In another case, a 34-year-old man convicted of abducting and raping a 15-year-old teenager at knife point as she walked on the beach, claimed it was a pickup. This rapist said women like to be overpowered before sex, but to dominate after it begins.

> A man's body is like a Coke bottle, shake it up, put your thumb over the opening and feel the tension. When you take a woman out, woo her, then she says "no, I'm a nice girl," you have to use force. All men do this. She said "no" but it was a societal no, she wanted to be coaxed. All women say "no" when they mean "yes" but it's a societal no, so they won't have to feel responsible later.

Claims that the victim didn't resist or, if she did, didn't resist enough, were also used by 24 percent (n = 11) of admitters to explain why, during the incident, they believed the victim was willing and that they were not raping. These rapists didn't redefine their acts until some time after the crime. For example, an admitter who used a bayonet to threaten his victim, an employee of the store he had been robbing, stated:

> At the time I didn't think it was rape. I just asked her nicely and she didn't resist. I never considered prison. I just felt like I had met a friend. It took about five years of reading and going to school to change my mind about whether it was rape. I became familiar with the subtlety of violence. But at the time, I believed that as long as I didn't hurt anyone it wasn't wrong. At the time, I didn't think I would go to prison, I thought I would beat it.

Another typical case involved a gang rape in which the victim was abducted at knife point as she walked home about midnight. According to two of the rapists, both of whom were interviewed, at the time they had thought the victim had willingly accepted a ride from the third rapist (who was not interviewed). They claimed the victim didn't resist and one reported her as saying she would do anything if they would take her home. In this rapist's view, "She acted like she enjoyed it, but maybe she was just acting. She wasn't crying, she was engaging in it." He reported that she had been friendly to the rapist who abducted her and, claiming not to have a home phone, she gave him her office number—a tactic eventually used to catch the three. In retrospect, this young man had decided, "She was scared and just relaxed and enjoyed it to avoid getting hurt." Note, however, that while he had redefined the act as rape, he continued to believe she enjoyed it.

Men who claimed to have been unaware that they were raping viewed sexual aggression as a man's prerogative at the time of the rape. Thus they regarded their act as little more than a minor wrongdoing even though most possessed or used a weapon. As long as the victim survived without major physical injury, from their perspective, a rape had not taken place. Indeed, even U.S. courts have often taken the position that physical injury is a necessary ingredient for a rape conviction.

(3) Most Women Eventually Relax and Enjoy It

Many of the rapists expected us to accept the image, drawn from cultural stereotype, that once the rape began, the victim relaxed and enjoyed it.[5] Indeed, 69 percent (n = 22) of deniers justified their behavior by claiming not only that the victim was willing, but also that she enjoyed herself, in some cases to an immense degree. Several men suggested that they had fulfilled their victims' dreams. Additionally, while most admitters used adjectives such as "dirty," "humiliated," and "disgusted" to describe how they thought rape made women feel, 20 percent (n = 9) believed that their victim enjoyed herself. For example, one denier had posed as a salesman to gain entry to his victim's house. But he claimed he had

had a previous sexual relationship with the victim, that she agreed to have sex for drugs, and that the opportunity to have sex with him produced "a glow, because she was really into oral stuff and fascinated by the idea of sex with a black man. She felt satisfied, fulfilled, wanted me to stay, but I didn't want her." In another case, a denier who had broken into his victim's house but who insisted the victim was his lover and let him in voluntarily, declared "She felt good, kept kissing me and wanted me to stay the night. She felt proud after sex with me." And another denier, who had hid in his victim's closet and later attacked her while she slept, argued that while she was scared at first, "once we got into it, she was OK." He continued to believe he hadn't committed rape because "she enjoyed it and it was like she consented."

(4) Nice Girls Don't Get Raped

The belief that "nice girls don't get raped" affects perception of fault. The victim's reputation, as well as characteristics or behavior which violate normative sex role expectations, are perceived as contributing to the commission of the crime. For example, Nelson and Amir Menachem (1975) defined hitchhike rape as a victim-precipitated offense.

In our study, 69 percent (n = 22) of deniers and 22 percent (n = 10) of admitters referred to their victims' sexual reputation, thereby evoking the stereotype that "nice girls don't get raped." They claimed that the victim was known to have been a prostitute, or a "loose" woman, or to have had a lot of affairs, or to have given birth to a child out of wedlock. For example, a denier who claimed he had picked up his victim while she was hitchhiking stated, "To be honest, we [his family] knew she was a damn whore and whether she screwed one or 50 guys didn't matter." According to presentence reports this victim didn't know her attacker and he abducted her at knife point from the street. In another case, a denier who claimed to have known his victim by reputation stated:

> If you wanted drugs or a quick piece of ass, she would do it. In court
> she said she was a virgin, but I could tell during sex [rape] that she was
> very experienced.

When other types of discrediting biographical information were added to these sexual slurs, a total of 78 percent (n = 25) of the deniers used the victim's reputation to substantiate their accounts. Most frequently, they referred to the victim's emotional state or drug use. For example, one denier claimed his victim had been known to be loose and, additionally, had turned state's evidence against her husband to put him in prison and save herself from a burglary conviction. Further, he asserted that she had met her current boyfriend, who was himself in and out of prison, in a drug rehabilitation center where they were both clients.

Evoking the stereotype that women provoke rape by the way they dress, a description of the victim as seductively attired appeared in the accounts of 22 percent (n = 7) of deniers and 17 percent (n = 8) of admitters. Typically, these descriptions were used to substantiate their claims about the victim's reputation. Some men went to extremes to paint a tarnished picture of the victim, describing her as dressed in tight black clothes and without a bra; in one case, the victim was portrayed as sexually provocative in dress and carriage. Not only did she wear short skirts, but she was observed to "spread her legs while getting out of cars." Not all of the men attempted to assassinate their victim's reputation with equal vengeance. Numerous times they made subtle and offhand remarks like, "She was a waitress and you know how they are."

The intent of these discrediting statements is clear. Deniers argued that the woman was a "legitimate" victim who got what she deserved. For example, one denier stated that all of his victims had been prostitutes; presentence reports indicated they were not. Several times during his interview, he referred to them as "dirty sluts," and argued "anything I did to them was justified." Deniers also claimed their victim had wrongly accused them and was the type of woman who would perjure herself in court.

(5) Only a Minor Wrongdoing

The majority of deniers did not claim to be completely innocent and they also accepted some accountability for their actions. Only 16 percent (n = 5) of deniers argued that they were totally free of blame. Instead, the majority of deniers pleaded guilty to a lesser charge. That is, they obfuscated the rape by pleading guilty to a less serious, more acceptable charge. They accepted being oversexed, accused of poor judgment or trickery, even some violence, or guilty of adultery or contributing to the delinquency of a minor, charges that are hardly the equivalent of rape.

Typical of this reasoning is a denier who met his victim in a bar when the bartender asked him if he would try to repair her stalled car. After attempting unsuccessfully, he claimed the victim drank with him and later accepted a ride. Out riding, he pulled into a deserted area "to see how my luck would go." When the victim resisted his advances, he beat her and he stated:

> I did something stupid. I pulled a knife on her and I hit her as hard as I would hit a man. But I shouldn't be in prison for what I did. I shouldn't have all this time [sentence] for going to bed with a broad.

This rapist continued to believe that while the knife was wrong, his sexual behavior was justified.

In another case, the denier claimed he picked up his under-age victim at a party and that she voluntarily went with him to a motel. According to presentence reports, the victim had been abducted at knife point from a party. He explained:

> After I paid for a motel, she would have to have sex but I wouldn't use a weapon. I would have explained. I spent money and, if she still said no, I would have forced her. If it had happened that way, it would have been rape to some people but not to my way of thinking. I've done that kind of thing before. I'm guilty of sex and contributing to the delinquency of a minor, but not rape.

In sum, deniers argued that, while their behavior may not have been completely proper, it should not have been considered rape. To accomplish this, they attempted to discredit and blame the victim while presenting their own actions as justified in the context. Not surprisingly, none of the deniers thought of himself as a rapist. A minority of the admitters attempted to lessen the impact of their crime by claiming the victim enjoyed being raped. But despite this similarity, the nature and tone of admitters' and deniers' accounts were essentially different.

EXCUSING RAPE

In stark contrast to deniers, admitters regarded their behavior as morally wrong and beyond justification. They blamed themselves rather than the victim, although some continued to cling to the belief that the victim had contributed to the crime somewhat, for example, by not resisting enough.

Several of the admitters expressed the view that rape was an act of such moral outrage that it was unforgivable. Several admitters broke into tears at intervals during their interviews. A typical sentiment was,

> I equate rape with someone throwing you up against a wall and tearing your liver and guts out of you.... Rape is worse than murder ... and I'm disgusting.

Another young admitter frequently referred to himself as repulsive and confided:

> I'm in here for rape and in my own mind, it's the most disgusting crime, sickening. When people see me and know, I get sick.

Admitters tried to explain their crime in a way that allowed them to retain a semblance of moral integrity. Thus, in contrast to deniers' justifications, admitters used excuses to explain how they were compelled to rape. These excuses appealed to the existence of forces outside of the rapists' control. Through the use of excuses, they attempted to demonstrate that either intent was absent or responsibility was diminished. This allowed them to admit rape while reducing the threat to their identity as a moral person. Excuses also permitted them to view their behavior as idiosyncratic rather than typical and, thus, to believe they were not "really" rapists. Three themes run through these accounts: (1) the use of alcohol and drugs; (2) emotional problems; and (3) nice guy image.

(1) The Use of Alcohol and Drugs

A number of studies have noted a high incidence of alcohol and drug consumption by convicted rapists prior to their crime (Groth, 1979; Queen's Bench Foundation, 1976). However, more recent research has tentatively concluded that the connection between substance use and crime is not as direct as previously thought (Ladouceur, 1983). Another facet of alcohol and drug use mentioned in the literature is its utility in disavowing deviance. McCaghy (1968) found that child molesters used alcohol as a technique for neutralizing their deviant identity. Marolla and Scully (1979), in a review of psychiatric literature, demonstrated how alcohol consumption is applied differently as a vocabulary of motive. Rapists can use alcohol both as an excuse for their behavior and to discredit the victim and make her more responsible. We found the former common among admitters and the latter common among deniers.

Alcohol and/or drugs were mentioned in the accounts of 77 percent (n = 30) of admitters and 84 percent (n = 21) of deniers and both groups were equally likely to have acknowledged consuming a substance—admitters, 77 percent (n = 30); deniers, 72 percent (n = 18). However, admitters said they had been affected by the substance; if not the cause of their behavior, it was at least a contributing factor. For example, an admitter who estimated his consumption to have been eight beers and four "hits of acid" reported:

Rapists' Accounts of Own and Victims' Alcohol and/or Drug (A/D) Use and Effect

	Admitters n = 39%	Deniers n = 25%
Neither self nor victim used A/D	23	16
Self used A/D	77	72
Of self used, no victim use	51	12
Self affected by A/D	69	40
Of self affected, no victim use or effect	54	24
Self A/D users who were affected	90	56
Victim used A/D	26	72
Of victim used, no self use	0	0
Victim affected by A/D	15	56
Of victim affected, no self use or effect	0	40
Victim A/D users who were affected	60	78
Both self and victim used and affected by A/D	15	16

Straight, I don't have the guts to rape. I could fight a man but not that. To say, "I'm going to do it to a woman," knowing it will scare and hurt her, takes guts or you have to be sick.

Another admitter believed that his alcohol and drug use,

… brought out what was already there but in such intensity it was uncontrollable. Feelings of being dominant, powerful, using someone for my own gratification, all rose to the surface.

In contrast, deniers' justifications required that they not be substantially impaired. To say that they had been drunk or high would cast doubt on their ability to control themselves or to remember events as they actually happened. Consistent with this, when we asked if the alcohol and/or drugs had had an effect on their behavior, 69 percent (n = 27) of admitters, but only 40 percent (n = 10) of deniers, said they had been affected.

Even more interesting were references to the victim's alcohol and/or drug use. Since admitters had already relieved themselves of responsibility through claims of being drunk or high, they had nothing to gain from the assertion that the victim had used or been affected by alcohol and/or drugs. On the other hand, it was very much in the interest of deniers to declare that their victim had been intoxicated or high: that fact lessened her credibility and made her more responsible for the act. Reflecting these observations, 72 percent (n = 18) of deniers and 26 percent (n = 10) of admitters maintained that alcohol or drugs had been consumed by the victim. Further, while 56 percent (n = 14) of deniers declared she had been affected by this use, only 15 percent (n = 6) of admitters made a similar claim. Typically deniers argued that the alcohol and drugs had sexually aroused their victim or rendered her out of control. For example, one denier insisted that his victim had become hysterical from drugs, not from being raped, and it was because of the drugs that she had reported him to the police. In addition, 40 percent (n = 10) of deniers argued that while the victim had been drunk or high, they themselves either hadn't ingested or weren't affected by alcohol and/or drugs. None of the admitters made this claim. In fact, in all of the 15 percent (n = 6) of cases where an admitter said the victim was drunk or high, he also admitted to being similarly affected.

These data strongly suggest that whatever role alcohol and drugs play in sexual and other types of violent crime, rapists have learned the advantage to be gained from using alcohol and drugs as an account. Our sample were aware that their victim would be discredited and their own behavior excused or justified by referring to alcohol and/or drugs.

(2) Emotional Problems

Admitters frequently attributed their acts to emotional problems. Forty percent (n = 19) of admitters said they believed an emotional problem had been at the root of their rape behavior, and 33 percent (n = 15) specifically related the problem to an unhappy, unstable childhood or a marital-domestic situation. Still others claimed to have been in a general state of unease. For example, one admitter said that at the time of the rape he had been depressed, feeling he couldn't do anything right, and that something had been missing from his life. But he also added, "being a rapist is not part of my personality." Even admitters who could locate no source for an emotional problem evoked the popular image of rapists as the product of disordered personalities to argue they also must have problems:

> The fact that I'm a rapist makes me different. Rapists aren't all there.
> They have problems. It was wrong so there must be a reason why I did
> it. I must have a problem.

Our data do indicate that a precipitating event, involving an upsetting problem of everyday living, appeared in the accounts of 80 percent (n = 38) of admitters and 25 percent (n = 8) of deniers. Ofthose experiencing a precipitating event, including deniers, 76 percent (n = 35) involved a wife or girlfriend. Over and over, these men described themselves as having been in a rage because of an incident involving a woman with whom they believed they were in love.

Frequently, the upsetting event was related to a rigid and unrealistic double standard for sexual conduct and virtue which they applied to "their" woman but which they didn't expect from men, didn't apply to themselves, and, obviously, didn't honor in other women. To discover that the "pedestal" didn't apply to their wife or girlfriend sent them into a fury. One especially articulate and typical admitter described his feeling as follows. After serving a short prison term for auto theft, he married his "childhood sweetheart" and secured a well-paying job. Between his job and the volunteer work he was doing with an ex-offender group, he was spending long hours away from home, a situation that had bothered his wife. In response to her request, he gave up his volunteer work, though it was clearly meaningful to him. Then, one day, he discovered his wife with her former boyfriend "and my life fell apart." During the next several days, he said his anger had made him withdraw into himself and, after three days of drinking in a motel room, he abducted and raped a stranger. He stated:

> My parents have been married for many years and I had high expecta-
> tions about marriage. I put my wife on a pedestal. When I walked in on
> her, I felt like my life had been destroyed, it was such a shock. I was
> bitter and angry about the fact that I hadn't done anything to my
> wife for cheating. I didn't want to hurt her [victim], only to scare and
> degrade her.

It is clear that many admitters, and a minority of deniers, were under stress at the time of their rapes. However, their problems were ordinary—the types of upsetting events that everyone experiences at some point in life. The overwhelming majority of the men were not clinically defined as mentally ill in court-ordered psychiatric examinations prior to their trials. Indeed, our sample is consistent with Abel et al. (1980) who found fewer than 5 percent of rapists were psychotic at the time of their offense.

As with alcohol and drug intoxication, a claim of emotional problems works differently depending upon whether the behavior in question is being justified or excused. It would have been counter-productive for deniers to have claimed to have had emotional problems at the time of the rape. Admitters used psychological explanations to portray themselves as having been temporarily "sick" at the time of the rape. Sick people are usually blamed for neither the cause of their illness nor for acts committed while in that state of diminished capacity. Thus, adopting the sick role removed responsibility by excusing the behavior as having been beyond the ability of the individual to control. Since the rapists were not "themselves," the rape was idiosyncratic rather than typical behavior. Admitters asserted a non-deviant identity despite their self-proclaimed disgust with what they had done. Although admitters were willing to assume the sick role, they did not view their problem as a chronic condition, nor did they believe themselves to be insane or permanently impaired. Said one admitter, who believed that he needed psychological counseling: "I have a mental disorder, but I'm not crazy." Instead, admitters viewed their "problem" as mild, transient, and curable. Indeed, part of the appeal of this excuse was that not only did it relieve responsibility, but, as with alcohol and drug addiction, it allowed the rapist to "recover." Thus, at the time of their interviews, only 31 percent (n = 14) of admitters indicated that "being a rapist" was part of their self-concept. Twenty-eight percent (n = 13) of admitters stated they had never thought of themselves as rapists, 8 percent (n = 4) said they were unsure, and 33 percent (n = 16) asserted they had been a rapist at one time but now were recovered. A multiple "ex-rapist," who believed his "problem" was due to "something buried in my subconscious" that was triggered when his girlfriend broke up with him, expressed a typical opinion:

> I was a rapist, but not now. I've grown up, had to live with it. I've hit the bottom of the well and it can't get worse. I feel born again to deal with my problems.

(3) Nice Guy Image

Admitters attempted to further neutralize their crime and negotiate a non-rapist identity by painting an image of themselves as a "nice guy." Admitters projected the image of someone who had made a serious mistake but, in every other respect, was a decent person. Fifty-seven percent (n = 27) expressed regret and sorrow for their victim indicating that they wished there were a way to apologize for or amend their behavior. For example, a participant in a rape-murder, who insisted his partner did the murder, confided, "I wish there was something I could do besides saying 'I'm sorry, I'm sorry.' I live with it 24 hours a day and, sometimes, I wake up crying in the middle of the night because of it."

Schlenker and Darby (1981) explain the significance of apologies beyond the obvious expression of regret. An apology allows a person to admit guilt while at the same time seeking a pardon by signaling that the event should not be considered a fair representation of what the person is really like. An apology separates the bad self from the good self, and promises more acceptable behavior in the future. When apologizing, an individual is attempting to say: "I have repented and should be forgiven," thus making it appear that no further rehabilitation is required.

The "nice guy" statements of the admitters reflected an attempt to communicate a message consistent with Schlenker's and Darby's analysis of apologies. It was an attempt to convey that rape was not a representation of their "true" self. For example,

> It's different from anything else I've ever done. I feel more guilt about this. It's not consistent with me. When I talk about it, it's like being

assaulted myself. I don't know why I did it, but once I started, I got into it. Armed robbery was a way of life for me, but not rape. I feel like I wasn't being myself.

Admitters also used "nice guy" statements to register their moral opposition to violence and harming women, even though, in some cases, they had seriously injured their victims. Such was the case of an admitter convicted of gang rape:

> I'm against hurting women. She should have resisted. None of us were the type of person that would use force on a woman. I never positioned myself on a woman unless she showed an interest in me. They would play to me, not me to them. My weakness is to follow. I never would have stopped, let alone pick her up without the others. I never would have let anyone beat her. I never bothered women who didn't want sex; never had a problem with sex or getting it. I loved her—like all women.

Finally, a number of admitters attempted to improve their self-image by demonstrating that, while they had raped, it could have been worse if they had not been a "nice guy." For example, one admitter professed to being especially gentle with his victim after she told him she had just had a baby. Others claimed to have given the victim money to get home or make a phone call, or to have made sure the victim's children were not in the room. A multiple rapist, whose pattern was to break in and attack sleeping victims in their homes, stated:

> I never beat any of my victims and I told them I wouldn't hurt them if they cooperated. I'm a professional thief. But I never robbed the women I raped because I felt so bad about what I had already done to them.

Even a young man, who raped his five victims at gun point and then stabbed them to death, attempted to improve his image by stating:

> Physically they enjoyed the sex [rape]. Once they got involved, it would be difficult to resist. I was always gentle and kind until I started to kill them. And the killing was always sudden, so they wouldn't know it was coming.

SUMMARY AND CONCLUSIONS

Convicted rapists' accounts of their crimes include both excuses and justifications. Those who deny what they did was rape justify their actions; those who admit it was rape attempt to excuse it or themselves. This study does not address why some men admit while others deny, but future research might address this question. This paper does provide insight on how men who are sexually aggressive or violent construct reality, describing the different strategies of admitters and deniers.

Admitters expressed the belief that rape was morally reprehensible. But they explained themselves and their acts by appealing to forces beyond their control, forces which reduced their capacity to act rationally and thus compelled them to rape. Two types of excuses predominated: alcohol/drug intoxication and emotional problems. Admitters used these excuses to negotiate a moral identity for themselves by viewing rape as idiosyncratic rather than typical behavior. This allowed them to reconceptualize themselves as recovered or "ex-rapists," someone who had made a serious mistake which did not represent their "true" self.

In contrast, deniers' accounts indicate that these men raped because their value system provided no compelling reason not to do so. When sex is viewed as a male entitlement, rape is no longer seen as criminal. However, the deniers had been convicted of rape, and like the admitters, they attempted to negotiate an identity. Through justifications, they constructed a "controversial" rape and attempted to demonstrate how their behavior, even if not quite right, was appropriate in the situation. Their denials, drawn from common cultural rape stereotypes, took two forms, both of which ultimately denied the existence of a victim.

The first form of denial was buttressed by the cultural view of men as sexually masterful and women as coy but seductive. Injury was denied by portraying the victim as willing, even enthusiastic, or as politely resistant at first but eventually yielding to "relax and enjoy it." In these accounts, force appeared merely as a seductive technique. Rape was disclaimed: rather than harm the woman, the rapist had fulfilled her dreams. In the second form of denial, the victim was portrayed as the type of woman who "got what she deserved." Through attacks on the victim's sexual reputation and, to a lesser degree, her emotional state, deniers attempted to demonstrate that since the victim wasn't a "nice girl," they were not rapists. Consistent with both forms of denial was the self-interested use of alcohol and drugs as a justification. Thus, in contrast to admitters, who accentuated their own use as an excuse, deniers emphasized the victim's consumption in an effort to both discredit her and make her appear more responsible for the rape. It is important to remember that deniers did not invent these justifications. Rather, they reflect a belief system that has historically victimized women by promulgating the myth that women both enjoy and are responsible for their own rape.

While admitters and deniers present an essentially contrasting view of men who rape, there were some shared characteristics. Justifications particularly, but also excuses, are buttressed by the cultural view of women as sexual commodities, dehumanized and devoid of autonomy and dignity. In this sense, the sexual objectification of women must be understood as an important factor contributing to an environment that trivializes, neutralizes, and, perhaps, facilitates rape.

Finally, we must comment on the consequences of allowing one perspective to dominate thought on a social problem. Rape, like any complex continuum of behavior, has multiple causes and is influenced by a number of social factors. Yet, dominated by psychiatry and the medical model, the underlying assumption that rapists are "sick" has pervaded research. Although methodologically unsound, conclusions have been based almost exclusively on small clinical populations of rapists—that extreme group of rapists who seek counseling in prison and are the most likely to exhibit psychopathology. From this small, atypical group of men, psychiatric findings have been generalized to all men who rape. Our research, however, based on volunteers from the entire prison population, indicates that some rapists, like deniers, viewed and understood their behavior from a popular cultural perspective. This strongly suggests that cultural perspectives, and not an idiosyncratic illness, motivated their behavior. Indeed, we can argue that the psychiatric perspective has contributed to the vocabulary of motive that rapists use to excuse and justify their behavior (Scully and Marolla, 1984).

Efforts to arrive at a general explanation for rape have been retarded by the narrow focus of the medical model and the preoccupation with clinical populations. The continued reduction of such complex behavior to a singular cause hinders, rather than enhances, our understanding of rape.

NOTES

1. These numbers include pretest interviews. When the analysis involves either questions that were not asked in the pretest or that were changed, they are excluded and thus the number changes.

2. There is, of course, the possibility that some of these men really were innocent of rape. However, while the U.S. criminal justice system is not without flaw, we assume that it is highly unlikely that this many men could have been unjustly convicted of rape, especially since rape is a crime with traditionally low conviction rates. Instead, for purposes of this research, we assume that these men were guilty as charged and that their attempt to maintain an image of nonrapist springs from some psychologically or sociologically interpretable mechanism.

3. Because of their outright denial, interviews with this group of rapists did not contain the data being analyzed here and, consequently, they are not included in this paper.

4. It is worth noting that a number of deniers specifically mentioned the victim's alleged interest in oral sex. Since our interview questions about sexual history indicated that the rapists themselves found oral sex marginally acceptable, the frequent mention is probably another attempt to discredit the victim. However, since a tape recorder could not be used for the interviews and the importance of these claims didn't emerge until the data was being coded and analyzed, it is possible that it was mentioned even more frequently but not recorded.

5. Research shows clearly that women do not enjoy rape. Holmstrom and Burgess (1978) asked 93 adult rape victims, "How did it feel sexually?" Not one said they enjoyed it. Further, the trauma of rape is so great that it disrupts sexual functioning (both frequency and satisfaction) for the overwhelming majority of victims, at least during the period immediately following the rape and, in fewer cases, for an extended period of time (Burgess and Holmstrom, 1979; Feldman-Summers et al., 1979). In addition, a number of studies have shown that rape victims experience adverse consequences prompting some to move, change jobs, or drop out of school (Burgess and Holmstrom, 1974; Kilpatrick et al., 1979; Ruch et al., 1980; Shore, 1979).

REFERENCES

Abel, Gene, Judith Becker, and
Linda Skinner. 1980. "Aggressive
behavior and sex." *Psychiatric Clinics of
North America* 3(2): 133–151.

Abrahamsen, David. 1960. *The Psychology of
Crime.* New York: John Wiley.

Albin, Rochelle. 1977. "Psychological
studies of rape." *Signs* 3(2): 423–435.

Burgess, Ann Wolbert, and Lynda
Lytle Holmstrom. 1974. *Rape: Victims
of Crisis.* Bowie: Robert J. Brady.

———. 1979. "Rape: Sexual disruption
and recovery." *American Journal of
Orthopsychiatry* 49(4): 648–657.

Feldman-Summers, Shirley, Patricia
E. Gordon, and Jeanette R. Meagher.
1979. "The impact of rape on sexual
satisfaction." *Journal of Abnormal
Psychology* 88(1): 101–105.

Glueck, Sheldon. 1925. *Mental Disorders
and the Criminal Law.* New York:
Little, Brown.

Groth, Nicholas A. 1979. *Men Who Rape.*
New York: Plenum Press.

Hall, Peter M., and John P. Hewitt. 1970.
"The quasi-theory of communication
and the management of dissent." *Social
Problems* 18(1): 17–27.

Hewitt, John P., and Peter M. Hall. 1973.
"Social problems, problematic situa-
tions, and quasi-theories." *American
Journal of Sociology* 38(3): 367–374.

Hewitt, John P., and Randall Stokes. 1975.
"Disclaimers." *American Sociological
Review* 40(1): 1–11.

Hollander, Bernard. 1924. *The Psychology of
Misconduct, Vice and Crime.* New York:
Macmillan.

Holmstrom, Lynda Lytle, and Ann
Wolbert Burgess. 1978. "Sexual
behavior of assailant and victim during
rape." Paper presented at the annual
meetings of the American Sociological
Association, San Francisco,
September 2–8.

Kilpatrick, Dean G., Lois Veronen, and
Patricia A. Resnick. 1979. "The
aftermath of rape: Recent empirical
findings." *American Journal of
Orthopsychiatry* 49(4): 658–669.

Ladouceur, Patricia. 1983. "The relative
impact of drugs and alcohol on serious
felons." Paper presented at the annual
meetings of the American Society of
Criminology, Denver, November
9–12.

Marolla, Joseph, and Diana Scully. 1979.
"Rape and psychiatric vocabularies of
motive." In Edith S. Gomberg and
Violet Franks (eds.), *Gender and
Disordered Behavior: Sex Differences in
Psychopathology* (pp. 301–318). New
York: Brunner/Mazel.

McCaghy, Charles. 1968. "Drinking and
deviance disavowal: The case of child
molesters." *Social Problems* 16(1):
43–49.

Mills, C. Wright. 1940. "Situated actions
and vocabularies of motive." *American
Sociological Review* 5(6): 904–913.

Nelson, Steve, and Amir Menachem. 1975.
"The hitchhike victim of rape: A
research report." In Israel Drapkin and
Emilio Viano (eds.), *Victimology:
A New Focus* (pp. 47–65). Lexington,
KY: Lexington Books.

Queen's Bench Foundation. 1976. *Rape:
Prevention and Resistance.* San Francisco:
Queen's Bench Foundation.

Ruch, Libby O., Susan Meyers Chandler,
and Richard A. Harter. 1980. "Life
change and rape impact." *Journal of
Health and Social Behavior* 21(3):
248–260.

Schlenker, Barry R., and Bruce W. Darby.
1981. "The use of apologies in social
predicaments." *Social Psychology
Quarterly* 44(3): 271–278.

Scott, Marvin, and Stanford Lyman. 1968.
"Accounts." *American Sociological
Review* 33(1): 46–62.

Scully, Diana, and Joseph Marolla. 1984. "Rape and psychiatric vocabularies of motive: Alternative perspectives." In Ann Wolbert Burgess (ed.), *Handbook on Rape and Sexual Assault*. New York: Garland Publishing.

Shore, Barbara K. 1979. "An examination of critical process and outcome factors in rape." Rockville, MD: National Institute of Mental Health

Stokes, Randall, and John P. Hewitt. 1976. "Aligning actions." *American Sociological Review* 41(5): 837–849.

Sykes, Gresham M., and David Matza. 1957. "Techniques of neutralization." *American Sociological Review* 22(6): 664–670.

27

The Devil Made Me Do It: Use of Neutralizations by Shoplifters

PAUL CROMWELL AND QUINT THURMAN

Cromwell and Thurman offer a discussion of shoplifters' rationalizations that many people will find familiar. Stealing from stores has long been widespread among American youth, and practitioners have found it convenient and easy to rationalize pilfering from large companies that do not have a visible or identifiable local owner. This chapter compliments the Scully and Marolla analysis by drawing on Sykes and Matza's (1957) techniques of neutralizations, a conceptualization of accounts that predates the distinction between excuses and justifications. Cromwell and Thurman show how shoplifters make ample use of these existing categories and invent a few new ones of their own. These accounts, like all others, help individuals deflect the labeling process and the deviant identity.

How would you divide the techniques of neutralization in this chapter into the category of excuses or justifications laid out in Scully and Marolla's chapter? Which ones of these do you find offer the most compelling argument, and why?

"**Y**ou know that cartoon where the guy has a little devil sitting on one shoulder and a little angel on the other? And one is telling him 'Go ahead on, do it,' and the angel is saying 'No, don't do it.' You know?... Sometimes when I'm thinking about boosting something, my angel don't show up." (30-year-old male shoplifter)

Nearly five decades ago Gresham Sykes and David Matza (1957) introduced neutralization theory as an explanation for juvenile delinquency. Sykes and Matza's (1957) theory is an elaboration of Edwin Sutherland's (1947) proposition that individuals can learn criminal techniques, and the "motives, drives, rationalizations, and attitudes favorable to violations of the law." Sykes and Matza argued that these justifications or rationalizations protect the individual from self-blame and the blame of others. Thus, the individual may remain committed to the value system of the dominant culture while committing criminal acts without experiencing the cognitive dissonance that might be otherwise expected. He or she deflects or "neutralizes" guilt in advance, clearing the way to blame-free crime. These neutralizations also protect the individual from any residual guilt following the crime. It is this ability to use neutralizations that differentiates delinquents from non-delinquents (Thurman 1984).

While Sykes and Matza (1957) do not specifically maintain that only offenders who are committed to the dominant value system make use of these techniques of neutralizations, they appear to contend that delinquents maintain a commitment to the moral order and are able to drift into delinquency through the use of techniques of neutralization. This approach assumes that should delinquents fail to internalize conventional morality, neutralization would be unnecessary since there would be no guilt to neutralize.

One issue that has not been satisfactorily settled is when neutralization occurs. Sykes and Matza (1957) contend that deviants must neutralize moral prescriptions prior to committing a crime. However, most research is incapable of determining whether the stated neutralization is a before-the-fact neutralization or an after-the-fact rationalization.

TECHNIQUES OF NEUTRALIZATION

Sykes and Matza (1957) identified five techniques of neutralization commonly offered to justify deviant behavior—denial of responsibility, denial of injury, denial of the victim, condemning the condemners, and appeal to higher loyalties.

Five additional neutralization techniques have since been identified. These include defense of necessity (Klockars 1974), metaphor of the ledger (Minor 1981), denial of the necessity of the law, the claim that everybody else is doing it, and the claim of entitlement (Coleman 1994).

This article examines neutralization theory as it might apply to a specific form of criminal activity that is highly prevalent across a wide range of the population. The purpose of this study is to determine the extent to which adult shoplifters use techniques of neutralizations and to analyze the various neutralizations available to them. We examine offenders who shoplift and explore the justifications that they say they rely upon to excuse behavior they also acknowledge as morally wrong.

STATEMENT OF THE PROBLEM

Shoplifting may be the most serious crime with which the most people have some personal familiarity. Research has shown that one in every 10–15 persons who shops has shoplifted at one time or another. Further, losses attributable to shoplifting are considerable, with estimates ranging from 12 to 30 billion dollars lost annually. Shoplifting also represents one of the most prevalent forms of larceny, accounting for approximately 15 percent of all larcenies according to data maintained by the Federal Bureau of Investigation (1996).

Unlike many other forms of crime, people who shoplift do not ordinarily require any special expertise or tools to engage in this crime. Consequently, those persons who shoplift do not necessarily conform to most people's perception of what a criminal offender is like. Instead, shoplifters tend to be demographically similar to the "average person." In a large study of non-delinquents, Klemke (1982) reported that as many of 63 percent of those persons he interviewed had shoplifted at some point in their lives. Students, housewives, business and professional persons, as well as professional thieves constitute the population of shoplifters. Loss prevention experts routinely counsel retail merchants that there is no particular profile of a potential shoplifter. Turner and Cashdan (1988) conclude, "While clearly a criminal activity, shoplifting borders on what might be considered a 'folkcrime.' " In her classic study, Mary Cameron (1964 xi) wrote:

> Most people have been tempted to steal from stores, and many have been guilty (at least as children) of "snitching" an item or two from counter tops. With merchandise so attractively displayed in department stores and supermarkets, and much of it apparently there for the taking, one may ask why everyone isn't a thief.

Neutralization theory argues that ordinary individuals who engage in deviant or criminal behavior may use techniques that permit them to recognize extenuating circumstances that enable them to explain away delinquent behavior. Without worrying about guilty feelings that would stand in their way of committing a criminal act, the theory asserts that those persons are free to participate in delinquent acts that they would otherwise believe to be wrong.

METHOD

The data presented here were obtained in 1997 and 1998 in Wichita, Kansas. We obtained access to a court-ordered diversion program for adult "first-offenders" charged with theft. Of these, the majority of offenders were charged with misdemeanor shoplifting and required to attend an eight-hour therapeutic/education program as a condition of having their record expunged. A new group met each Saturday. The average group size was 18–20 participants. Participants were encouraged by the program facilitator to discuss with the group the offense that brought them to the diversion program, why they did what they did, and how they felt about it. We obtained interviews with 137 subjects from approximately 350 subjects who were approached. Ethnicity and gender of the sample are shown in Table 27.1. The mean age of the sample was 26. The age range was 18 to 66 years of age. Although the diversion program was designed for first offenders, over one-half of the participants had been apprehended for shoplifting in the past.

T A B L E 27.1   **Neutralizations by Shoplifter Respondents by Gender and Ethnicity (N = 137)**

	White	Hispanic	Black	Total
Male	48	11	29	88
Female	30	6	13	49
Total	78	17	42	137

FINDINGS

The informants appeared to readily use neutralization techniques. We identified nine categories of neutralizations; the **five Sykes and Matza (1957) categories,** the **Defense of Necessity** and **Everybody Does It,** identified by Coleman (1994) and two additional, which we labeled **Justification by Comparison** and **Postponement.** Only 5 of the 137 informants failed to express a rationalization or neutralization when asked how they felt about their illegal behavior. Three of these subjects responded by admitting their guilt and expressing remorse. Two others simply stated that they had nothing to say on that issue. In many cases, the respondents offered more than one neutralization for the same offense. For example, one female respondent stated, "I don't know what comes over me. It's like, you know, is somebody else doing it, not me" (Denial of Responsibility). "I'm really a good person. I wouldn't ever do something like that, stealing, you know, but I have to take things sometimes for my kids. They need stuff and I don't have any money to get it" (Defense of Necessity). They frequently responded with a motivation ("I wanted the item and could not afford it") followed by a neutralization ("Stores charge too much for stuff. They could sell things for half what they do and still make a profit. They're just too greedy"). Thus, in many cases, the motivation was linked to excuse in such a way as to make the excuse a part of the motivation. The subjects were in effect explaining the reason the deviant act occurred and justifying it at the same time. The following section illustrates the neutralizations we discovered in use by the informants.

Denial of Responsibility ("I Didn't Mean It")

Denial of responsibility frees the subject from experiencing culpability for deviance by allowing him or her to perceive themselves as victims of their environment. The offender views him- or herself as being acted upon rather than acting. Thus, attributing behavior to poor parenting, bad companions, or internal forces (the devil made me do it) allows the offender to avoid disapproval of self or others, which in turn, diminishes those influences as mechanisms of social control. Sykes and Matza (1957: 666) describe the individual resorting to this neutralization as having a "billiard ball conception of himself in which he see himself as helplessly propelled into new situations."

> I admit that I lift. I do. But, you know, it's not really me—I mean, I don't believe in stealing. I'm a church-going person. It's just that sometimes something takes over me and I can't seem to not do it. Its like those TV shows where the person is dying and he goes out of his body and watches them trying to save him. That's sorta how I feel sometimes when I'm lifting. (26-year-old female)
>
> I wasn't raised right. You know what I mean? Wasn't nobody to teach me right from wrong. I just ran with a bad group and my mamma didn't ever say nothin' about it. That's how I turned out this way—stealin' and stuff. (22-year-old female) If it wasn't for the bunch I ran

with at school I never would have started taking things. We used to go the mall after school and everybody would have to steal something. If you didn't get anything, everybody called you names—chicken-shit and stuff like that. (20-year-old male)

Many of the shoplifter informants neutralized their activities citing loss of self-control due to alcohol or drug use. This is a common form of denial of responsibility. If not for the loss of inhibition due to drug or alcohol use, they argue, they would not commit criminal acts.

I was drinking with my buddies and we decided to go across the street to the [convenience store] and steal some beer. I was pretty wasted or I wouldn't done it. (19-year-old white male)

I never boost when I'm straight. It's the pills, you know? (30-year-old white female)

Denial of Injury ("I Didn't Really Hurt Anybody")

Denial of injury allows the offender to perceive of his or her behavior as having no direct harmful consequences to the victim. The victim may be seen as easily able to afford the loss (big store, insurance company, wealthy person) or the crime may be semantically recast, as when auto theft is referred to as joyriding, or vandalism as a prank.

They [stores] big. Make lotsa money. They don't even miss the little bit I get. (19-year-old male)

They write it off their taxes. Probably make a profit off it. So, nobody gets hurt. I get what I need and they come out O.K. too. (28-year-old male)

Them stores make billions. Did you ever hear of Sears going out of business from boosters? (34-year-old female)

Denial of the Victim ("They Had It Coming")

Denial of the victim facilitates deviance when it can be justified as retaliation upon a deserving victim. In the present study, informants frequently reported that the large stores from which they stole were deserving victims because of high prices and the perception that they made excessive profits at the expense of ordinary people. The shoplifters frequently asserted that the business establishments from which they stole overcharged consumers and thus deserved the pay back from shoplifting losses.

Stores deserve it. It don't matter if I boost $10,000 from one, they've made 10,000 times that much ripping off people. You could never steal enough to get even...I don't really think I'm doing anything wrong. Just getting my share. (48-year-old female)

Dillons [food store chain] are totally bogus. A little plastic bag of groceries is $30, $25. Probably cost them $5....Whatta they care about me? Why should I care about them? I take what I want. Don't feel guilty a bit. No sir. Not a bit. (29-year-old female)

I have a lot of anger about stores and the way they rip people off. Sometimes I think the consumer has to take things into their own hands. (49-year-old female)

Condemning the Condemners ("The System Is Corrupt")

Condemning the condemners projects blame on law-makers and law-enforcers. It shifts the focus from the offender to those who disapprove of his or her acts. This neutralization views the "system" as crooked and thus unable to justify making and enforcing rules it does not itself live by. Those who condemn their behavior are viewed as hypocritical since many of them engage in deviant behavior themselves.

I've heard of cops and lawyers and judges and all kind of rich dudes boosting. They no better than me. You know what I'm saying. (18-year-old male)

Big stores like J.C. Penneys—when they catch me with something— like two pairs of pants, they tell the police you had like 5 pairs of pants and 2 shirts or something like that. You know what I'm saying? What they do with the other 3 pairs of pants and shirts? Insurance company pays them off and they get richer—they's bigger crooks than me. (35-year-old female)

They thieves too. Just take it a different way. They may be smarter than me—use a computer or something like that—but they just as much a thief as me. Fuck'em. Cops too. They all thieves. Least, I'm honest about it. (22 year-old male)

Appeal to Higher Loyalties ("I Didn't Do It For Myself")

Appeal to higher loyalties functions to legitimize deviant behavior when a non-conventional social bond creates more immediate and pressing demands than one consistent with conventional society. The most common use of this technique among the shoplifters was pressure from delinquent peers to shoplift and the perceived needs of one's family for items that the informant could not afford to buy. This was especially common with mothers shoplifting for items for their children.

I never do it 'cept when I'm with my friends. Everybody be taking stuff and so I do too. You know—to be part of the group. Not to seem like I'm too good for 'em. (17-year-old female)

I like to get nice stuff for my kids, you know. I know it's not O.K., you know what I mean? But, I want my kids to dress nice and stuff. (28-year-old female)

The Defense of Necessity ("I Had No Other Choice")

The defense of necessity (Coleman 1998) serves to reduce guilt through the argument that the offender had no choice under the circumstances but to engage in a criminal act. In the case of shoplifting, the defense of necessity is most often used when the offender states that the crime was necessary to help one's family.

> I had to take care of three children without help. I'd be willing to steal to give them what they wanted. (32-year-old female)
>
> I got laid off at Boeing last year and got behind on all my bills and couldn't get credit anywhere. My kids needed school clothes and money for supplies and stuff. We didn't have anything and I don't believe in going on welfare, you know. The first time I took some lunch meat at Dillons (grocery chain) so we'd have supper one night. After that I just started to take whatever we needed that day. I knew it was wrong, but I just didn't have any other choice. My family comes first. (42-year-old male)

Everybody Does It

Here the individual attempts to reduce his or her guilt feelings or to justify his or her behavior by arguing that the behavior in question is common (Coleman 1998). A better label for this neutralization might be "diffusion of guilt." The behavior is justified or the guilt is diffused because of widespread similar acts.

> Everybody I know do it. All my friends. My mother and her boyfriend are boosters and my sister is a big-time booster. (19-year-old female)
>
> All my friends do it. When I'm with them it seems crazy not to take something too. (17-year-old male) I bet you done did it too... when you was coming up. Like 12–13 years old. Everybody boosts. (35-year-old female)

Justification by Comparison ("If I Wasn't Shoplifting I Would Be Doing Something More Serious")

This newly identified neutralization involves offenders justifying their actions by comparing their crimes to more serious offenses. While it might be argued that Justification by Comparison is not a neutralization in the strict Sykes and Matza (1957) sense in that these offenders are not committed to conventional norms, they are nonetheless attempting to maintain their sense of self-worth by arguing that they could be worse or are not as bad as some others. Even persons with deviant lifestyles may experience guilt over their behavior and/or feel the necessity to justify their actions to others. The gist of the argument is that "I may be bad, but I could be worse."

> I gotta have $200 every day—day in and day out. I gotta boost a thousand, fifteen-hundred dollars worth to get it. I just do what I gotta do....Do I feel bad about what I do? Not really. If I wasn't boosting, I'd be robbing people and maybe somebody would get hurt or killed. (40-year-old male)

Looka here. Shoplifting be a little thing. Not a crime really. I do it 'stead of robbing folks or breaking in they house. [Society] oughta be glad I boost, stead of them other things. (37-year-old male)

It's no thing. Not like its "jacking" people or something. It's just a little lifting. (19-year-old male)

Postponement ("I Just Don't Think About It")

In a previous study one of the present authors (Thurman 1984) suggested that further research should consider the excuse strategy of Postponement, by which the offender suppresses his or her guilt feelings—momentarily putting them out of mind to be dealt with at a later time. We found this strategy to be a common occurrence among our informants. They made frequent statements that indicated that they simply put the incident out of their mind. Some stated that they would deal with it later when they were not under so much stress.

I just don't think about it. I mean, if you think about it, it seems wrong, but you can ignore that feeling sometimes. Put it aside and go on about what you gotta do. (18-year old male)

Dude, I just don't deal with those kinda things when I'm boosting. I might feel bad about it later, you know, but by then it's already over and I can't do anything about it then, you know? (18-year-old male)

I worry about things like that later. (30-year-old female)

DISCUSSION AND CONCLUSION

We found widespread use of neutralizations among the shoplifters in our study. We identified two new neutralizations: *Justification by Comparison* and *Postponement*. Even those who did not appear to be committed to the conventional moral order used neutralizations to justify or excuse their behavior. Their use of neutralizations was not so much to assuage guilt but to provide them with the necessary justifications for their acts to others. Simply because one is not committed to conventional norms does not preclude their understanding that most members of society do accept those values and expect others to do so as well. They may also use neutralizations and rationalizations to provide them with a convincing defense for their crimes that they can tell to more conventionally oriented others if the need arises.

As stated earlier, our research approach could not determine whether the informants neutralized before committing the crime or rationalized afterwards. Pogrebin, Poole, and Martinez (1992: 233) suggest that post-event reasons given for deviant behavior are not neutralizations but accounts, or "socially approved vocabularies that serve as explanatory mechanisms for deviance." No one, however, has yet been able to empirically verify the existence of pre-event neutralizations. In fact, neutralization theory depends upon analysis of post-event accounts by the offender. We suggest that accounts, neutralizations, and rationalizations are essentially the same behavior at different stages in the criminal event. We argue that Hirschi (1969) was correct in stating that a post-crime rationalization may serve as a pre-crime neutralization the next time a crime is contemplated. Whether neutralization allows the offender to mitigate guilt feelings before the crime is committed or afterward, the process still occurs. Once an actor has reduced his or her guilt feelings through the use of techniques of neutralization, he or she can continue to offend, assuaging guilt feelings and cognitive dissonance both before and after each offense. It would follow that continued utilization of neutralization and rationalization habitually over time might serve to weaken the social bond, reducing the need to neutralize at all.

Our exploratory study of shoplifters' use of neutralization techniques also suggests that neutralization (theory) may not be a theory of crime but rather a description of a process that represents an adaptation to morality that leads to criminal persistence. Neutralization focuses on how crime is possible, rather than why people might choose to engage in it in the first place. In a sense, neutralization serves as a form of situational morality. While the offender knows an act is morally wrong (either in his or her eyes or in the eyes of society), he or she makes an adaptation to convention that permits deviation under certain circumstances (the various neutralizations discussed). Whether the adaptation is truly neutralizing (before the act) or rationalizing (after the act) the result is same—crime without guilt.

REFERENCES

Cameron, Mary. 1964. *The Booster and the Snitch*. New York: Free Press.

Coleman, James W. 1994. "Neutralization Theory: An Empirical Application and Assessment." Ph.D. Dissertation, Oklahoma State University, Department of Sociology, Stillwater.

Coleman, James W. 1998. *Criminal Elite: Understanding White Collar Crime*. New York: St. Martin's Press.

Federal Bureau of Investigation 1996. *Crime in the United States—1995*. Washington, DC: U.S. Department of Justice.

Hirschi, Travis. 1969. *Causes of Delinquency*. Berkeley, CA: University of California Press.

Klemke, Lloyd. 1982. "Exploring Juvenile Shoplifting." *Sociology and Social Research* 67: 59–75.

Klockars, Carl B. 1974. *The Professional Fence*. New York: Free Press.

Minor, William W. 1981. "Techniques of Neutralization: A Reconceptualization and Empirical Examination." *Journal of Research in Crime and Delinquency* (July): 295–318.

Pogrebrin, M., E. Poole, and A. Martinez. 1992. "Accounts of Professional Misdeeds: The Sexual Exploitation of Clients by Psychotherapists." *Deviant Behavior* 13: 229–52.

Sutherland, Edwin H. 1947. *Principles of Criminology*. Philadelphia: Lippincott.

Sykes, Gresham M., and David Matza. 1957. "Techniques of Neutralization: A Theory of Delinquency." *American Sociological Review* 22(6): 664–70.

Thurman, Quint C. 1984. "Deviance and Neutralization of Moral Commitment: An Empirical Analysis." *Deviant Behavior* 5: 291–304.

Turner, C. T., and S. Cashdan. 1988. "Perceptions of College Students' Motivations for Shoplifting." *Psychological Reports* 62: 855–62.

28

Men Who Cheer

MICHELLE BEMILLER

Just as the lesbian athletes discussed by Blinde and Taub violated gender roles in being intercollegiate athletes, Bemiller's male cheerleaders encounter gender stigma from venturing into a female-dominated activity. Female labels of lesbian in sport correspond to male labels of homosexuality in cheerleading. The men Bemiller studied know that their descent into a girls' realm will lead to masculinity challenges of various sorts from the people they encounter, and they take a variety of measures intended to forestall their deviant labeling. Their face-saving strategies are fairly aggressive, as they attempt to invoke hypermasculine demeanors to counter their taint of female association. This chapter, like many in the book, reveals the hierarchy of gender stratification that positions hypermasculine men at the top, soft/gentle/androgynous men in a lower position, gay men below them, and all women at the bottom. In attempting to elevate themselves on this ladder, the male cheerleaders demean the role of their female squadmates to distance themselves and to enhance their position. We earlier noted this behavior in Tuggle and Holmes' article on the anti-smoking campaign, where nonsmokers gained status and power by stigmatizing and diminishing smokers. Male cheerleaders also draw on other high-status attributes of their gender role by emphasizing hypermasculine features such as toughness and the sexual objectification of women. Demeaning women is revealed as more than an innocuous form of male jocularity; it is a powerful strategy for maintaining differential access to status, opportunity, and power in society.

How would you compare the stigma faced by the women athletes to that of the male cheerleaders? How would you compare their adaptations? To what do you attribute these differences?

The institution of sports has long been associated with the construction and maintenance of masculinity among boys and men (Anderson 1999; Connell 1995; Koivula 2001; Lantz and Schroeder 1999; Messner 2002). As an institution, sports reinforce the patriarchal superstructure where masculinity is valued over femininity. The devaluation of femininity is reflected in the subordination

From Michelle Bemiller, "Men Who Cheer." *Sociological Focus, the Journal of the North Central Sociological Association*, Vol. 38, No. 3, August 2005. Reprinted by permission of the North Central Sociological Association.

of women, as well as men who participate in non-masculine activities or exhibit non-masculine characteristics or mannerisms. Participation in competitive sports that emphasize physical size, strength, and power reinforces and reaffirms the masculinity of men who participate as viewers or players (Connell 2002; Messner 1992; Suitor and Reavis 1995). Thus, sports such as football, basketball, ice hockey, and baseball that emphasize mental toughness, competitiveness, and domination are viewed as the domain of men (Griffin 1995).

Athletics provide young men with status among their peers, increasing their popularity and acceptance (Griffin 1995), assuming, of course, that these men are participating in appropriate "male" sports. Men who do not participate in masculine sports are stigmatized, leading to negative appraisals regarding their gender and sexuality (Suitor and Reavis 1995).

Despite the possibility of negative appraisals, men have become more visible within female-dominated sports such as cheerleading, leading to a unique opportunity for research on gender presentation, relations, and identity. Yet this area has not received a lot of attention to date. In contrast, notable work has been done on men's entry into female-dominated occupations. Williams (1989, 1995), for example, indicates that when men do women's work, gender differences are reproduced. Men are viewed as highly competent at their work and rise quickly through the ranks. The same is not true for women in male-identified occupations.

Men in female-dominated occupations do encounter questions regarding their sexuality. This questioning, however, does little to impede their progress in the organization. To reaffirm their masculinity, these men seek out male-identified specialties, emphasize masculine aspects of the job, and pursue administrative positions (Williams 1989, 1995). Similarly, in her work on men working in "safe" and "embattled" organizations, Dellinger (2004) found that when men work in an organization that is dominated by feminist ideals, they construct their masculinity by separating themselves from women in the work context and aligning with other males. In contrast, when men work in an environment that is supportive of masculinity, they have better relationships with their female co-workers.

While these findings are useful in helping us understand men who do women's work, we still know little about men who do women's sports. Do these same patterns and outcomes emerge when men participate in women's sports? To further our understanding of men in female-dominated arenas, this paper will use cheerleaders at one northeastern Ohio university to examine the maintenance of gender and sexuality in a female-dominated sport....

METHODS

Sample and Procedures

Participants for this study were selected from a cheerleading squad at a northeastern Ohio public university. To recruit participants, I attended a cheerleading practice and asked for volunteers to participate in a study about men who cheer. I was introduced by the cheerleading coach as a sociologist interested in doing research on cheerleaders. The coach's introduction provided me with status as a legitimate researcher, which may have influenced the cheerleaders' decision to participate in the study. Upon introduction, I simply told the cheerleaders that I was interested in learning about men's participation as cheerleaders and that I would appreciate their assistance in learning more about the men who cheer. At the time of recruitment, the men and women had just finished practice and were talking among themselves about their plans after practice. Most of them were planning on going out to the local bars. A few men and women agreed to participate. Once these individuals agreed, their friends decided to participate as well. My assumption was that they agreed to participate together, because they were all going out after the practice.

Convenience sampling—sampling cases that were available at the time of the study—was used (Singleton, Straits, and Straits 1993). Out of 25 possible partici- pants, 17 volunteered: 8 men and 9 women between the ages of 18 and 25. Four men and four women declined to participate. Because both men and women were equally willing to participate, there does not seem to be anything unique about the individuals who chose to participate. The individuals who chose not to participate did not provide me with a reason for declining. Of the 17 participants in the study, no racial minorities were present. Had any minorities participated, some of the information provided by the respondents might have been different, since experi- ences may have differed not only based on gender, but also based on race.

The data provided are meant to present a glimpse into the lives of men who cheer at one university, not to be generalized to all cheerleaders at all universi- ties. University and regional culture may certainly play a role in an individual's experiences, with the size of the university and region and the cultural diversity of the campus and community affecting individual attitudes regarding men's and women's participation in gendered sports. The community where the university is located is a large urban area with over 200,000 residents. The residents of the city are predominantly white, middle class individuals with high school educa- tions. The university is a large, urban campus with roughly 20,000 undergradu- ate students; roughly 11,000 are women and 9,000 are men. Non-whites make up roughly 20% of the overall student population.

Data collection consisted of two stages. Focus group discussions were held in the summer of 1999. Reviews of earlier versions of the focus group research in- dicated that men may not be willing to discuss issues related to sexuality in focus group settings so in-depth; one-on-one interviews were conducted in 2001 to probe for a deeper understanding of issues related to sexuality and stigmatization. One-on-one interviews were conducted with both new participants (n = 7) as well as participants from the 1999 focus groups (n = 4)....

FINDINGS

Two main themes emerged from the cheerleaders' narratives. The first was the stigma that coincides with being a male cheerleader. Stigmatization included the negative experiences men had because they are cheerleaders as well as accusations regarding their sexuality. The second theme analyzes face-saving strategies that men use to protect their masculinity in a female-dominated sport. These strategies include emphasizing the masculine qualities of cheerleading (e.g., injury and risk) and acting in hyperheterosexual ways (e.g., claiming ownership over the sport and objectifying the female cheerleaders).

Stigma

Goffman (1963) argued that an individual is stigmatized when they possess an undesired differentness from what is anticipated. In the present study, the differentness under investigation is men participating in cheerleading. Goffman (1963) pointed to the need to determine if one's stigma is evident (e.g., race) or less visible and difficult to discern. Men who cheer possess a potentially discreditable identity due to their deviation from gendered proscriptions regarding participation in sports. This identity is "discreditable" because it is not a status that everyone necessarily knows about, yet if known or found out, it can be stigmatizing.

Participation in a Feminine Sport   Throughout the focus group discussions and one-on-one interviews, the male and female cheerleaders talked about the stigmatization and resulting undesirable outcomes associated with being a male cheerleader. This is consistent with prior research showing that men are stigmatized because of their participation in what is considered a feminine sport (Connell 1987, 1992; Goffman 1963; Griffin 1995, Kimmel 1996; Messner 1992; Messner and Sabo 1996; Suitor and Reavis 1995). Thus, male cheerleaders are labeled as non-masculine and homosexual for "crossing over" into a female domain. The following quotes capture some of these comments. According to Betty in her one-on-one interview:

> Cheerleading is known more as a girl's sport than a guy's sport, so the guys get a lot of teasing. I give them a lot of credit for putting up with people talking about them. The comments bother them, but they really like doing it, so they put up with them.

Annie elucidates this point further, "I think it is more acceptable to be a girl cheerleader than a guy cheerleader on campus. It is hard for people to adjust to the idea that men are cheerleaders too." In the all-male focus group discussion, one participant asserted that his fraternity brothers give him a hard time about being a cheerleader, teasing and taunting him about participation in a female-dominated sport. Another stated that he works in construction and that the guys at work "rib him pretty good" about being a male cheerleader.

The stigma of participation is further magnified because cheerleading is in a category of activities that many people would not define as a sport at all. John discusses other men's views of cheerleading as a sport by specifically focusing on the teasing that goes along with cheerleading. He claims that, "men from other sports say 'you can't participate in a real sport.'" The suggestion that cheerleading is not a "real" sport implies that men should be playing football or some other contact sport that demonstrates their manliness and that the majority of society labels as a sport (Suitor and Reavis 1995).

Brett provides an interesting look at the importance of playing a "real" sport as opposed to a feminine sport. While Brett participates in cheerleading practices, he has not yet performed at a football or basketball game. In other words, he has not made a "public" appearance as a male cheerleader. Brett tells me that he does not intend to cheer at the games. Although he enjoys cheerleading, he fully understands and attempts to avoid the stigma that he faces as a male cheerleader. "I'd rather be playing football than cheering for the football team. It would hurt my self-esteem, because guys don't cheer. I mean what percentage of the male population cheers? I mean, I like cheerleading, but it's a girl's sport." By participating in the cheerleading practices but not the public events, Brett attempts to have his cake and eat it too. In other words, Brett enjoys participating in the practices, but has avoided being publicly labeled as "a man who cheers." Thus, he has attempted to avoid the stigma associated with participation in a female activity. The emphasis on "real" sports not only stigmatizes the males who choose to be cheerleaders but also marginalizes cheerleading as a sport altogether.

Sexuality   Besides the stigma that occurs with participation in a female-dominated sport, men's participation in cheerleading calls into question their sexual identity, interpreted through the lens of gender. Men who cheer are perceived and labeled as homosexual. As a case in point, prior to becoming a male cheerleader, Adam assumed that men who cheered were homosexual. "I was hesitant to become a cheerleader because of the idea that you have to be gay to be a cheerleader." After discussing this issue with several of the men and women who cheer, Adam decided to participate in the sport despite these stereotypes. Even after discussing this issue with his teammates, however, Adam still faces stereotyping regarding his and his teammate's sexuality. "A lot of people think that the men are gay and ask me if they are. People make fun of them. People say they're all a bunch of fags." Similarly, Brett is teased by his close friends. "People definitely perceive that the male cheerleaders are fags. All of my friends give me a hard time about being a cheerleader." Brett's words demonstrate that not only do strangers react to male cheerleaders, but also the people who know them. Since significant others (e.g., family and friends) often have a strong impact, Brett's friends' reactions affected how he saw himself as a cheerleader. Thus, Brett's friends' reactions probably had a stronger impact on how he saw himself as a cheerleader than strangers' comments would.

Perceptions about male cheerleaders' sexuality, however, do not just come from external forces. As in the cases of Adam and Brett, men who cheer bring internalized stereotypes with them into the sport. Specifically, many of the respondents claimed that they thought that male cheerleaders were gay prior to their own participation in the sport, and some current participants indicated that some of the men on the squad might be gay. Brett provides an example of that belief:

> The men here have more feminine characteristics. I would assume that they are gay. I would say they seem to be gay because they are

cheerleaders but then I put myself in that group. I think that I perceive them as gay because they gossip a lot and have more girl friends than guy friends. Something is weird about a guy who can have all girls for friends.

By claiming that men who exhibit these qualities are gay, Brett buys into the stereotypes associated with nonmasculine men or men who participate in non-masculine activities. Brett acknowledges that he is a male cheerleader, but he does not belong "in that group" (i.e., gay cheerleaders). Both Adam and Brett distance themselves from the homosexual stereotype of male cheerleaders by re-ferring to other male cheerleaders as "the men" and "they." By using the third person, they verbally and mentally remove themselves from an association with men whom they perceive as gay. In other words, they might be cheerleaders, but they are certainly not gay.

Brett and Adam articulate the gendered belief system that limits men and women to certain activities and claims that deviation must relate to sexuality and a departure from heterosexual normativeness (Connell 1987; Lorber 1994; Pharr 1997), For example, Brett's comment regarding the strangeness of males with female friends coincides with perceptions that all male-female relationships are inherently sexual. In other words, if a male has a female friend, he must have a sexual interest in her, and if he does not, he must be gay. Brett's comments reaffirm what is normatively assumed and accepted, that women and men cannot be friends unless a sexual relationship exists. Brett's assumptions regarding cross-gender friendships are not necessarily supported by research on this topic. While some research on cross-gender friendships does indicate that male-female friends may experience sexual feelings toward one another (Egland, Spitzberg, and Zormeier 1996), other research finds the opposite to be true. It is possible for men and women to be friends without a sexual interest or dynamic (Monsour 2002).

In Annie's discussion of male cheerleaders, she draws attention to the male cheerleaders' tendency to believe in the stereotypical image of men who cheer:

We had a guy come in the last week of tryouts and he fit the media's image of a gay person and the guys made fun of him behind his back. It's almost like the guy cheerleaders believe the perception that male cheer-leaders are gay. So, they participate but they still believe the stereotype.

This adherence to stereotypical images of male cheerleaders, however, does not rest solely with men who cheer. The female cheerleaders also indicated that they had thought all male cheerleaders were gay until they participated in college cheerleading. In her one-on-one interview, Cindy asserted:

Before I started cheering, I thought it was different for guys to cheer be-cause when I was in high school we only had girls on the squad. People think the guys are gay and they say they wouldn't want to cheer. They say 'they're gay' and I tell them that I know all of them and they're not gay.

Cindy's views are not far from the other women's perceptions. In the focus group discussions, one woman said, "I thought they were gay" and another woman stated, "Yeah, I thought they were freaky."

Throughout both the focus group discussions and the one-on-one interviews, the male and female cheerleaders acknowledged that it is more acceptable
for females to cheer based on perceptions about sexuality. One woman explains
why participation is less acceptable for the men. "The people that don't know
the men still have the idea that the guys are gay and the girls are okay." This
response was followed by nods of agreement by the rest of the females in the
focus group. In his one-on-one interview, Adam states, "I've been made fun of
by people, they've said like, 'What are you doing? You're in a girl's sport, you're
gay, blah, blah, blah.'" These responses capture a central issue: if the image of
male cheerleading can be heterosexually validated, then any man should be
able to cheer without the assumption that he is homosexual. Unfortunately, the
link that was established by the female participants between being gay and being
"freaky" reflects the power of the labeling and stigmatization process of people
believed to be sexually deviant (Connell 1987; Lorber 1994; Pharr 1997; Schur
1984). Homophobia limits choices by labeling anyone who deviates from
gender-appropriate norms as sexually deviant or gay (Johnson 1997).

SAVING FACE

In response to stigma and stereotyping, the male cheerleaders participate in strategies to help them save face as they participate in a female-dominated activity.
According to Goffman (1959), face-saving behavior involves attempts to salvage
an interactional performance that hasn't gone as planned. By participating in a
female-dominated sport, men who cheer fail to "do gender" appropriately because of their failure to participate in masculine sports. They, therefore, must use
face-saving techniques to be viewed as acceptable in interactions. The men in
this study saved face by acting in hypermasculine ways. According to Connell
(1992) hypermasculinity becomes manifest when hostility exists toward homosexual men, and heterosexual men attempt to create social distance from homosexuality by emphasizing their heterosexuality. For the men who cheer this
hypermasculinity was demonstrated as the men claimed territoriality over the
sport, stressed the masculine nature of the sport, and sexually objectified the female cheerleaders. Through these actions, the men attempted to deflect accusations of homosexuality.

Territoriality   Both the male and female cheerleaders discussed the fact that
cheerleading is viewed as a female-dominated sport. However, many of the
male cheerleaders insisted that cheerleading is becoming a male-dominated sport
and that the female cheerleaders would not be able to participate in this sport
without the help of the men. Female cheerleaders have been cheering without
men at the high school and professional level for quite some time (Hanson
1995). Yet, these statements coincide with attitudes of entitlement, superiority,
and solidarity that exist in male athletics, which encourage homophobia and
sexism (Griffin 1995).

This sense of entitlement, superiority, and solidarity was apparent during the focus group discussions. The men were adamant about the importance of men in cheerleading, marginalizing female participation. The tenor of the conversation became tense and defensive as the men proclaimed their dominance in the sport. One male stated, "Males started the sport of cheerleading in the first place." This comment was followed by agreement from other respondents, "Yeah, they wouldn't let women do it. So, we started it, we're just coming back." Males' reclaiming the sport requires marginalizing the women's status. Women's importance in the sport has been relegated to the margins because "men started the sport." Once this territoriality was established, the atmosphere became much more comfortable. They had asserted their authority and defended their masculinity (McGuffey and Rich 1999).

In the all-female focus group, the female cheerleaders acknowledged that cheerleading started as a male-dominated sport. One female said, "Cheerleading started with men. I think the media has turned it into a sexualized female sport. That's what people like to see." In so saying, the women recognize the secondary, sexualized status of women in cheering. At the same time, the women are invested in helping the men to protect and maintain their masculine guise. The women's willingness to elevate men into a superior position within the sport demonstrates that gender maintenance occurs in social interactions with both men and women cooperating. By subordinating their role as cheerleaders, the women "do femininity" as they demonstrate submissiveness to the men who cheer (West and Zimmerman 1987). The women also help the males to "do masculinity" by assisting in the construction of cheerleading as a masculine sport through the emphasis placed on aggression and injury.

Masculine Aspects of the Sport: Toughness and Aggression   The male cheerleaders used imagery and examples from their cheerleading lives to demonstrate their heterosexuality and establish their masculinity. Through these masculine examples, the men saved face, or protected their masculine identities. Specifically, some of the men referred to fighting, or the possibility of fighting, with individuals who made derogatory comments to them about participation in cheerleading. These men said that no one would have the nerve to say anything offensive for fear of being injured for their remarks. One male stated, "I don't think that anyone's ever had the balls to say anything negative to me," implying that there would be consequences for anyone who voiced negative comments. Another respondent demonstrated his masculinity by stating, "Me and Bob fought the football team one year. I don't think that had anything to do with cheerleading though. We kicked their asses." Demonstrating physical prowess and the ability to defeat the most masculine of sports teams, the two cheerleaders not only saved face, but also were elevated in status. Adam, in a one-on-one interview, alluded to this incident with the football team, saying: "I've heard of cheerleaders taking on the football team and winning before. I wasn't a part of that but I did hear about it." Again, he uses this incident to demonstrate that male cheerleaders should not be messed with and that they are able to protect themselves through violence if necessary. Since he had heard of this incident, it is apparent that the story had been talked about within the cheerleading group, serving to reinforce the idea that the men who cheer can take care of themselves physically. This storytelling demonstrates how the men collectively maintain their masculinity in a female-dominated activity.

During the female focus group discussion, this masculine facade was also discussed. One female commented that, "They always say, 'They won't mess with me, I'm a cheerleader.'" This comment and the comments stated above illustrate how the men are creating and exuding a collective identity in which male cheerleaders are defined as dominant and aggressive. These statements demonstrate how the male cheerleaders maintain their masculinity by emphasizing their ability to defend themselves in physical altercations with other men. The use of violence and aggression are common characteristics utilized in maintaining masculinity for men (Connell 1995, 2002; Griffin 1995; Messner 2005).

The emphasis on toughness and aggression is also apparent when the male and female cheerleaders discuss the men's role as cheerleaders. Male-dominated sports such as football, wrestling, and hockey are often labeled as "real" sports because they contain elements of violence and an increased likelihood of injury. In order to equate cheerleading with these "real" sports, Leeann talks about the men's injuries and the need for strength to masculinize cheerleading, showing that cheerleading is not just a "girl's sport."

> You're always going to have people that think it's just a girl's sport. But, as people start to see more men doing it and once people see what they do and see all of these bloody noses and broken mouths, then they realize that it's not a girl's sport. It's tough for them. They do a lot of lifting and stuff that requires a lot of strength.

Similarly, Mary states, "I think guys like cheerleading because they get the satisfaction of knowing that they can lift two girls at once. It takes a lot of strength." Cindy also acknowledges the difficulty of the sport, "It's a lot more physical than you would think." Adam agrees with the women as he states, "I don't think that people realize how hard it is." Brett also emphasizes the difficulty of cheerleading for guys. He says, "It's physical. I'm tired [when I cheer]."

The male and female cheerleaders define cheerleading as a sport because it requires strength, manual labor, physical exertion, and involves competition, much like sports defined as masculine (e.g., football, wrestling). The male cheerleaders act tough and aggressive to prove their masculinity, which then confirms their heterosexuality. The link between toughness, masculinity, and heterosexuality for these men is woven throughout their face-saving strategies.

Sexual Objectification of Women   Connell (1992) asserts that hypermasculinity becomes manifest when hostility exists toward homosexual men, and heterosexual men attempt to create social distance. In cheerleading, the men do this in large part by sexualizing the female cheerleaders. The women indicated this sexual objectification in both the focus group discussions and in the one-on-one interviews. One participant stated, "People say the guys are girly. Not at all ... they are probably more manly than guys who don't participate in the sport. They're perverted and sexual sometimes." In agreement with this female, another participant stated, "The male cheerleaders are the most heterosexual males I have ever met, so people have the wrong perception when they say they are gay. It makes me laugh. They are the most perverted guys that I have ever met." By "perverted," the women mean that the men talk about the women's bodies among themselves and to the women. For example, one female focus group respondent stated, "They say, like, 'Oh people think I'm gay but I get to grab your butt.' They're perverts." Another cheerleader in the female focus group said that, "They always think all the girls want them. They'll say, 'She wants me.' "

The female focus group participants agreed that when a group of men and women work closely, sexual innuendos occur, and sexual tensions build. Cindy provides an explanation why the male cheerleaders sexualize the females:

> When the guys are accused of being gay, I think they try to over-compensate for these accusations by being all about the girls. They act very sexual toward girls. I think that the guys look at us as sex objects, but all guys would have that attraction to the women. But they've never made me or any of the other girls feel uncomfortable. I'm sure they find us attractive, but it's kind of more like a sisterly-brotherly thing.

Cindy's statement is contradictory as she asserts that the men are sexually attracted to the women, but that the relationship is sisterly-brotherly. This confusion continues as another participant also comments on the attraction between the men and women as well as the family-like relationship between the male and female cheerleaders:

> At first, I think that the girls and guys are attracted to each other. It's only natural when you have guys and girls together in a sport. You are constantly touching and it is sexual at first, but you get over that. It becomes like kissing your grandma.

The contradiction between sexual and familial relationships demonstrated by the females reveals the limited frame of reference available for mixed gender settings. The women construct the men as both "brotherly" and "perverted." Both instances provide defenses for the men's sexualization of the women. In the first instance, the women argue that the men's comments are often misconstrued as perverted when in actuality they are simply jokes and that their touching is more like that of a brother than a boyfriend. By claiming this, the women become accepting of the men's antics. In the second instance, the women do claim that the men are perverted. However, the women defend the men's comments and actions as "boys being boys." In essence, the women normalize the perverse comments and actions by inadvertently stating that this sexual banter is part of the men's attempts to demonstrate their masculinity. By defending the men's actions, the women allow the men to display their gender (Lorber 1994; Lucal

1999; West and Zimmerman 1987), which serves to negate perceptions that male cheerleaders are gay.

Both the men and the women see the objectification of the women as a component of being a man or being masculine within society (Connell 1987; Johnson 1997; Pharr 1997). While the women demonstrate contradictions regarding their relationships with the male cheerleaders, the men emphasize a sexualized relationship with the women as opposed to a familial relationship. When asked why they chose to cheer, many of the men asserted that it was because of the presence of the beautiful girls and because they get to have intimate physical contact with the women. Brett said,

> I participate in cheerleading because of the girls. Most of the cheerleaders are hot all around the board. I would love to go to a cheerleading competition. There are tons of girls there. That's the only reason that I'm a cheerleader.

George sees the female cheerleaders as sex objects because all of the women are in good physical shape. George states, "If they were ugly cheerleaders, I probably wouldn't cheer."

In the male focus group discussion the men continuously talked about the fact that they get to touch the female cheerleaders. The males asserted that one of the best perks of being a male cheerleader is the closeness to the females' bodies. The "hot chicks" that stand beside them are seen as prizes and a major reason for participating in the sport of cheerleading. One male even stated that people who might make allegations of homosexuality do not realize that they get to "touch the girls' butts and stuff." Another respondent stated, "I worked at a trucking company for three years and all the guys loved it (that I was a male cheerleader). They would come over and ask me stories and stuff. Like, what do you do with these girls?"

The construction of masculinity through the objectification of women is applied when men are in the minority, engaged in a female-dominated activity. The route to power in this situation is the use of sex and sexuality to realize gender relations. By talking about these women as sex objects, they are subordinating women within the sport. The men were so excited about touching the women that they even suggested that more men might be interested in cheering if they were aware of how beautiful the women are and how much time they would get to spend with them, talking to them, and touching them. One male specifically suggested that the athletic department needs to "sell the female cheerleaders" in order to recruit more men.

The objectification of women provides the male cheerleaders with a mechanism for asserting their heterosexuality and masculinity in the context of cheering to the non-cheering world. In so doing, the male cheerleaders are maintaining a socially constructed ideal of manliness through the objectification of women, which confirms their heterosexuality and masculinity to themselves, while also reinforcing hegemonic, dominating, sexualized, masculinity for public consumption.

CONCLUSION: CROSSING THE GREAT
GENDER DIVIDE

The aim of this research was to explore male participation in a female-dominated sport by focusing on men who cheer. The findings highlight the methods used by both male and female cheerleaders to redefine men's roles and activities within cheerleading in ways that stabilize and reassert hegemonic masculinity. Both the male and female cheerleaders articulated the stigma that goes hand in hand with participation as a male cheerleader.

In an attempt to masculinize cheerleading, the male and female cheerleaders focused attention on the men's strength and toughness. The male cheerleaders asserted their dominance through claims that cheerleading started as a male sport and that the women "need" the men in order to perform stunts. In addition, the males used objectification of the women to pronounce their heterosexuality and counter the stigma attached to men engaged in "women's" activities.

Claiming territoriality over a female-domain happens in other female-dominated areas besides sports, because in a patriarchal society maleness is valued over femaleness, allowing men to take over organizations that were previously female-identified. For example, Williams (1989, 1995) found that men in female-dominated occupations were paid better and promoted more quickly than females in the organizations. Some of these men, however, were perceived as homosexuals when outsiders observed their participation in a female-dominated occupation. Because of these perceptions, the men adhered to a macho image and distanced themselves from the women in the organization by participating in male-identified specialties, emphasizing the masculine nature of their jobs, and pursuing higher administration jobs. Similar to Williams' findings, men who cheer also experience accusations of homosexuality because of their participation in a female-dominated sport. Contrary to Williams' findings, however, the men who cheer did not distance themselves from their female counterparts. Instead, to prove their masculinity, these men physically objectified the female cheerleaders. This sexual objectification may be unique to the sport of cheerleading because of the close physical contact that is essential within the sport. Men and women are expected to perform stunts that require physical contact, and this physical contact is used by the men to demonstrate their heterosexuality.

These findings demonstrate that both male and female cheerleaders redefine cheerleading to emphasize masculinity and subordinate femininity. The tactics used to re-create and maintain masculinity for the male cheerleaders demonstrate the importance of maintaining male dominance over women and gay men. While the negotiation of masculinities is discussed in the masculinity literature (Anderson 1999; Bordo 1993; Connell 1987), the cheerleaders' adherence to male dominance and male power within cheerleading reinforces the maintenance of a masculinity that emphasizes strength, skill, aggression, and competition (Anderson 1999), as well as heterosexuality.

REFERENCES

Anderson, Kristin. 1999. "Snowboarding: The Construction of Gender in an Emerging Sport." *Journal of Sport and Social Issues* 23: 55–79.

Bordo, Susan. 1993. *Unbearable Weight*. Berkeley: University of California Press.

Connell, Robert W. 2002. *Gender*. Cambridge: Black-well Publishers.

———. 1995. *Masculinities*. Berkeley: University of California Press.

———. 1992. "A Very Straight Gay: Masculinity, Homosexual Experience, and the Dynamics of Gender." *American Sociological Review* 57: 735–751.

———. 1987. *Gender and Power: Society, the Person, and Sexual Politics*. Stanford, CA: Stanford University Press.

Dellinger, Kirsten. 2004. "Masculinities in 'Safe' and 'Embattled' Organizations: Accounting for Pornographic and Feminist Magazines." *Gender & Society* 18: 545–566.

Egland, Kori, Brian H. Spitzberg, and Michelle M. Zormeier. 1996. "Flirtation and Conversational Competence in Cross-Sex Platonic and Romantic Relationships." *Communication Reports* 9: 105–117.

Goffman, Erving. 1963. *Stigma: Notes on the Management of Spoiled Identity*. Englewood Cliffs, NJ: Prentice Hall.

———. 1959. *The Presentation of Self in Everyday Life*. Garden City: Doubleday.

Griffin, Pat. 1995. "Homophobia in Sport: Addressing the Needs of Lesbian and Gay High School Athletes." Pp. 53–65 in *The Gay Teen: Educational Practice and Theory for Lesbian, Gay, and Bisexual Adolescents*. G. Unks, ed New York: Routledge.

Hanson, Mary E. 1995. *Go, Fight, Win! Cheerleading in American Culture*.

Bowling Green, Ohio: Bowling Green State University Popular Press.

Johnson, Allan G. 1997. *The Gender Knot: Unraveling our Patriarchal Legacy*. Philadelphia: Temple University Press.

Kimmel, Michael. 1996. *Manhood in America*. New York: The Free Press.

Koivula, Nathalie. 2001. "Perceived Characteristics of Sports Categorized as Gender-Neutral, Feminine, and Masculine." *Journal of Sport Behavior* 24: 377–393.

Lantz, Christopher D., and Peter J. Schroeder. 1999. "Endorsement of Masculine and Feminine Gender Roles: Differences between Participation in and Identification with the Athletic Role." *Journal of Sport Behavior* 22: 545–557.

Lorber, Judith. 1994. *Paradoxes of Gender*. New Haven: Yale University Press.

Lucal, Betsy. 1999. "What It Means to Be Gendered Me: Life on the Boundaries of a Dichotomous Gender System." *Gender and Society* 13. 781–797.

McGuffey, C. Shawn, and B. Lindsay Rich. 1999. "Playing in the Gender Transgression Zone: Race, Class and Hegemonic Masculinity in Middle Childhood." *Gender & Society* 13: 608–627.

Messner, Michael. 2005. "Still a Man's World?" Pp. 313–326 in *Handbook of Studies of Men & Masculinities*. M.S. Kimmel, J. Hearn, and R.W. Connell, eds. Thousand Oaks, CA: Sage.

———. 2002. *Taking the Field*. Minneapolis: University of Minnesota Press.

———. 1992. *Power at Play: Sports and the Problem of Masculinity*. Boston: Beacon Press.

Messner, Michael and Donald Sabo. 1996. *Sex, Violence and Power in Sports: Rethinking Masculinity*. Thousand Oaks, CA: Sage Publications.

Monsour, Michael. 2002. *Women and Men as Friends: Relationships across the Life Span in the 21st Century*. Mahwah, NJ: Laurence Erlbaum Associates, Inc.

Pharr, Suzanne. 1997: *Homophobia: A Weapon of Sexism*. Berkeley, CA: Chardon Press.

Schur, E. 1984. *Labeling Women Deviant: Gender, Stigma, and Social Control*. New York: Random House.

Singleton, Royce A., Bruce C. Straits, and Margaret Miller Straits. 1993. *Approaches to Social Research*. New York: Oxford University Press.

Suitor, Jill J., and Rebel Reavis. 1995. "Football, Fast Cars, and Cheerleading: Adolescent Gender Norms, 1978–1989." *Adolescence* 30: 265–270.

West, Candance, and Don Zimmerman. 1987. "Doing Gender." *Gender & Society* 1–2: 125–151.

Williams, Christine. 1995. *Still a Man's World: Men Who Do 'Women's Work.'"* Berkeley, CA: University of California Press.

———. 1989. *Gender Differences at Work: Women and Men in Nontraditional Occupations*. Berkeley, CA: University of California Press.

29

Negotiating White Power
Activist Stigma

PETE SIMI AND ROBERT FUTRELL

White power activists occupy an interesting position in society: they belong to a dominant group, yet their attitudes and beliefs stigmatize them. Simi and Futrell describe a range of strategies they use to reconcile their inner feelings and outward displays. They contrast their experiences and adaptations differently according to their audience: intimate friends and family, coworkers and fellow students, strangers in public. In each of these settings, Aryan activists pursued a range of behaviors that ranged from concealment to disclosure.

How would you apply Heckert and Heckert's typologies to this group of people? How would you describe their reaction to society's definition of their deviance compared to the groups described in previous chapters?

Despite claims that we have become a "movement society,"... explicit and outspoken activism remains a relatively uncommon deviant act.... This article discusses how members of one of the most radical, deviant, and stigmatized social movements—the U.S. white power movement (WPM)—manage the intersectional tensions they face in everyday nonmovement contexts. We describe a process that pivots on strategies of calculated concealment and revelation of their Aryan activist identity. On the one hand, embracing an Aryan identity obliges one to challenge openly those who do not see the world, its problems, and the solutions in the same way. On the other hand, their radically racist attitudes contrast sharply with contemporary integrationist attitudes and multicultural ethics held by many they interact with on a daily basis. The "strong codes [that now exist] against the direct expression of racist views" (Billig 2001: 270; see also Van Dijk 1992) mean that Aryans face the constant prospect of ire and indignation from others if they reveal their beliefs. To reduce the chance for unwanted conflicts, Aryan activists often cover their identity to "get along" with others. Yet, covering such a salient identity creates dissonance. They manage this dissonance by devising techniques to accomplish a degree of expressive balance between who they are and how they portray themselves. The techniques are survival strategies that help them avoid many of the everyday conflicts their identity may bring. But, Aryans experience these concealment strategies as resistance rather then acquiescence to anti-Aryan culture. Concealment is a form of activism because it is integral to how they sustain themselves as activists....

ARYAN STIGMA, DISSONANCE, AND EXPRESSIVE BALANCE

Popular images present white power movement activists as strident, hostile fanatics that stand out from the crowd. But as with all stereotypes, the reality is more complicated. In many everyday settings it is difficult to determine who is an Aryan and who is not. Committed white power adherents are not typically "out" about their Aryan leanings. Instead, they are covert about who they are. Their "calculated conformity" (Scott 1985) to mainstream expectations masks their activist identity, which helps them avoid extreme Aryan stigma.

Their identity is built around a radically racist and anti-Semitic worldview[1]. White power members embrace a sense of exceptionalism. They feel they have special insight into the "true" nature of the world that allows them to "see through" and reject attempts by nonwhites to destroy Aryan culture and eliminate the "white race." They see themselves defending the white race from genocide by Jews and their "nonwhite pawns." Their utopian vision is of a racially exclusive world dominated by Aryans, where "nonwhites" are eliminated, separated, or at least subordinated to Aryan authority. This world is imagined in the popular mantra among WPM members known as the "14 Worlds" statement—"We must secure the existence of our people and a future for white children." Many support the vision of Aryan militarist nationalism that requires the creation and defense of an all-white, non-Jewish homeland. They also abhor homosexuality, interracial sex, marriage, and procreation, and tend to idealize conservative traditional patriarchal family forms and community relations dominated by Aryan kinship.

Aryan stigma flows from the many sources that oppose their beliefs and practices....

Aryan activists are clearly aware of the stigma others attach to their beliefs and most perceive great personal risk in publicly communicating their ideas. These tensions create discomfort and influence when and how they reveal who they are. WPM members describe how openly expressing their beliefs disrupts their personal relationships with non-WPM members (e.g., neighbors shun and even picket their residence when they are exposed) and is a factor in job loss. Most of the Aryans we interviewed report fears of being shunned, or even surveilled and arrested, if their activism became known to non-Aryans.

Consequently, a major concern of many in the movement is how and when to conceal or reveal their identity as Aryans. On both organizational and interpersonal levels, identity concealment is particularly vexing because a central part of being an Aryan is openly advocating for one's beliefs.... They negotiate these contexts by strategically deploying their identity in ways that enable them to avoid the full contempt of others. They do not, however, rely solely on complete concealment, but instead probe the situational constraints to see how much they can also reveal of their Aryan selves. We describe their efforts as a strategic search for "expressive balance." This "balance" is struck, on one side, by revealing aspects of their extreme racism, which helps them sustain a sense of resistance, efficacy, and authenticity as true Aryans; on the other side, they simultaneously conceal many aspects of their activist selves to avoid the constant grind of conflict that they anticipate from others. To be clear, this "balance" is seldom weighted evenly. Across the settings we discuss, Aryans always conceal much more than they reveal about their racist ideas.... We assess the type of contexts in which Aryans strategically avoid or diminish interactional conflicts over their deviance, what their strategies are, why they select them, and how their efforts help them carry on their resistance.

METHOD AND DATA

We draw primarily from ethnographic data collected on various white power activists and groups between 1996 and 2005. Our multimethod approach includes interviews, participant observation, and content analysis of WPM Web sites other literature. Interviews included one-to-three-hour, face-to-face, and telephone interviews with 89 Aryan activists. Seventeen respondents were group leaders and 72 were rank-and-file members. Ninety-four follow-up interviews with primary contacts led to 183 total interviews. Snowball and purposive sampling strategies produced contacts with a wide range of white power networks active in 24 states. Specific organizations represented in the sample include: White Aryan Resistance, Aryan Nations and local branches of Aryan Nations, Hammerskins, National Alliance, and branches of the KKK.

Of the 89 interviewees, 65 were male and 24 were female. Their ages ranged from 15 to 25 years ($n = 12$), 26 to 35 years ($n = 35$), 36 to 45 years ($n = 16$), 46 to 55 years ($n = 16$), and 55 and over ($n = 10$). Our informants represent a broad cross section of socioeconomic status found in the movement (see also Aho 1990; Blee 2002). The majority ($n = 61$) of subjects described either their current or childhood socioeconomic status as "middle class." We confirmed that a sizable minority ($n = 21$) were working in mid-to-upper-level professional occupations (e.g., attorney, college instructor, x-ray technician, etc.). Most of the subjects' educational level included a high school diploma or equivalency and a quarter ($n = 23$) of the interviewees attended some college or higher.

Participant observation was done with Christian Identity adherents in Arizona and Utah, Aryan Nations members in Idaho, and a variety of Aryans in Southern California. The events observed in Utah and Arizona included 23 house visits lasting from one to three days and a variety of social gatherings (e.g., parties, Bible study sessions, hikes, etc.). Additionally, there were four three-to-five-day visits to the Aryan Nations' former headquarter in Hayden Lake, Idaho to observe activities and interview participants at Aryan Nations World Congresses and other more informal gatherings. Fieldwork in Southern

California included observations of various social gatherings and 22 stints in activists' homes ranging from two days to five weeks. Involvement in these settings allowed for, among other things, insight into how Aryans talk and feel about who they are. These insights are not available through sole reliance on secondary sources and movement propaganda that many studies rely on (see Blee 2002 for an eloquent elaboration of this point). We analyzed secondary sources in an attempt to verify data we collected through primary interview and observational means....

NEGOTIATING ACTIVIST STIGMA
IN EVERYDAY SETTINGS

Aryans face complicated choices about what to conceal and reveal about their political commitments and they manage their stigma with situationally contingent responses that involve varying the degree to which they conceal and disclose their activist identity. In some instances, activists completely cover their Aryan identity in order to "get along" as "normals" and avoid attacks to self. But our observations suggest that full concealment is rare....

Responses to Conformity Pressures of Family and Friends

While WPM members' parents, siblings, relatives, and even nonmovement friends are typically aware of their white power leanings, they do not necessarily share those views. These differences are a significant source of tension when they are together and Aryans commonly talk of their parent's disapproval and concern as a strain they seek to avoid. Cal, a veteran Southern California skinhead, described how his activism influences his relationship with his father:

> He didn't like it at all. He still doesn't like it. Till this day he doesn't view the skinhead movement as a good thing. He thinks that no skinhead can possibly make anything of himself. He thinks I should be more focused on a career and not so much on the white race and making sure the white race survived, that I should be focused on the here and now. I wish he could accept me for who I am and what I am ... (interview 8/10/02).

Indeed, many of our informants can describe in vivid detail their family's reaction when they first revealed their Aryan leanings to them. Samuel, a White Aryan Resistance devotee, describes an experience that is typical of young recruits we spoke to who still lived with their parents when they joined the movement:

> When I was about 16 my parents found out about my views. They blew a serious gasket. Couldn't believe I thought that way. They wanted me out [of the movement] 'cause they thought I was going to get killed or end up in prison. They tried everything they could to get me out; forced me to go to counselors and all that ... (interview 3/12/02).

Committing to WPM beliefs severely strains friendships as well. Many members talk of losing close companions because of their racist commitments.

> After I started getting racially aware and talking to my friends about my new views they started drifting away [and] it was hard you know. I'd been hanging out with some of these guys my whole life and even my best friend thought I was going crazy or something. When you have to deal with these issues it really creates an inner struggle ... (Hank, Southwest Aryan, 2/10/99).

Leading a Double Life Activists respond to this inner struggle in several ways. Some disengage from those who disapprove. Eddie, a SoCal Aryan, claimed to live a completely "dual life" (interview 6/26/04) in which friends and family know nothing of his racist activism. As James Downton and Paul Wehr (1997) have shown, avoiding family and friends who oppose one's activism is a strategy used by activists in other movements as well. Some Aryans voluntarily separate themselves by simply not visiting relatives, attending family gatherings, or befriending non-Aryans.

Most activists we spoke with, however, are very reluctant to completely cut ties because of the emotional, relational, and the financial costs involved. For these members, family is not an "either or" question. It is neither necessary nor desirable to completely sacrifice family relations for their political beliefs. They want to both "be Aryans" and sustain their connections to parents, siblings, and other kin. Especially among younger activists, this reluctance to sever relationships with parents stems, in part, from their financial dependence on them. Recruits living at home literally cannot afford it. There is also a desire for approval and other forms of social support from parents and friends that many are not willing to give up. But, while family ties are felt to transcend their activist commitments, they are also unwilling to drop their movement loyalties.

Strategic Silence Instead, they devise strategies for simultaneously sustaining family bonds and their Aryan devotion. Most often this is accomplished with strategic silence on topics that would draw attention to their extreme racism.

> Even after I left my parent's house they would still give me trouble about my personal beliefs. I just try to respect them as best I can and the best way for me to do that is not discussing my beliefs in front of them. That's the only way I can be around them. Otherwise it gets really brutal; we've had some pretty big fights over the years about this stuff (Samuel, 2/10/99).
>
> I can be in the same room with them [relatives who do not share his views] as long as they don't want to get into a political discussion and I just try to avoid any topics that will cause problems (Tom, Aryan Resistance, 3/12/01).
>
> My philosophy on the family front is to just keep the preaching down to a minimum. I hide my white pride stuff, do the typical suck up crap ... (Mack, Aryan Front, 6/25/04).

Hiding the "white pride stuff" involves more than just avoiding the topic in conversation. It also means hiding visual evidence of their commitments, particularly tattoos and other adornments. Aryan tattoos are extremely popular among activists and as permanent symbols they convey a deep commitment to the messages they signify. But, as Melanie, a Southwest Aryan Separatist, observes, they are often an "open invitation" to conflict when people see them (interview 1/17/97). Consequently, some activists who may desire tattoos decide to totally avoid them and those who get tattoos often place them in inconspicuous places on the body and cover them around nonmovement others.

> I got my first tattoo when I was 14 and I had to get it covered by another so that I could get a job. For most racial tattoos they're best kept where they can't be seen unless you're willing to handle the opposition that having visible racial tattoos come with (Grant, Texas Hammerskin, interview 7/13/02).

For young activists living with parents, their status as resource-poor and parentally dependent minors means the costs of exposing their Aryan leanings can be high. Consequently, even the privacy of one's bedroom is so limited that open displays of Aryanism are quashed. For instance, as Charlie, a Southern California Aryan, became increasingly unguarded in his displays, conflict with his parents escalated, and they eventually prohibited such display. To quell family tensions, Charlie hid the offensive materials.

> When I first started getting racial I tried to be somewhat subtle. I hung a Vinland flag then I purchased a Celtic cross flag ... Then I finally said screw it and ordered a basic swastika flag and they (parents) hated it. So I just keep the flags in my room in a box with some other stuff I collect and that way it doesn't cause any problems (interview 1/16/01).

But hiding the flags did not signal the end of his resistance. Short of throwing out his collection, hiding was the only option and it came with some risk of more conflict if his parents found it. Charlie's calculated conformity disguised the actual defiance of his parent's demands for him to reject Aryanism. For him, keeping the flags was a form of struggle amidst the overt compliance that helped him deflect more pressures to conform. Now in his mid-30s, Charlie has remained a committed Aryan for almost twenty years.

Selective Disclosure   Most WPM members report strong desires to find ways they can enact their Aryan self. The interpersonal loyalties felt among family members both constrained and enabled self-expression....

> I just stayed quiet about it unless they would ask my opinion about something, and then I just always made sure to throw in my two cents. That's what I still do [with family]. I just show my side little by little ... (Charlie, Southern California skinhead, interview 6/27/04).

Others actively explain their politics, albeit with caution to not totally alienate family. They talk about these efforts as a calculated risk that is well worth it because these expressions help them feel they are authenticating their Aryan self and decreases the dissonance between who they are and how they act. James (American Front) explained that "by working like this I think I feel less isolated from who I really am ..." (interview 6/13/01). Similarly, Cindy, a SWAS member, explained that these limited expressions of Aryan commitment help her feel more "in tune with being true to myself. It's very difficult, but it's also absolutely essential" (interview 1/20/99).

There is consistent reference among our informants to seeking a balance between deception and disclosure among family. Randy (SoCal Skin) describes the situation as a "compromise."

> I'm pretty selective in revealing all of my views. The best I can explain is like a compromise that helps me sustain my personal beliefs without compromising my relationships. I show some of who I am and hide other parts (interview 6/29/04).

Managing Expressive Constraints at Work and School

...The workplace is filled with sources of tension for Aryans. It is a context where activists directly confront a culturally diverse world that is the antithesis of what they desire. They perceive a clear (and in their view, extremely biased) expectation to adapt to non-Aryan cultures. For instance, many jobs encourage employees to learn at least some foreign language (e.g., Spanish to serve Hispanic clientele). Aryans see such demands as capitulation to multicultural ethics, which they define as a major problem with contemporary life. The culturally diverse context severely limits opportunities for openly expressing their white power identity. Aryans feel obliged to adhere to workplace norms that prohibit displays of racial hatred and they expect to be fired if their extremism is revealed to employers and coworkers. Indeed, more than half the participants we interviewed attribute their loss of a job to an employer's opposition to their white power beliefs. So keeping their job means outwardly conforming to an "oppressive" cultural diversity.

Avoiding Others   Activists speak of a sense of realism and practicality about voicing extremist attitudes at work and the internal fortitude required to play one's work roles in ways that are not disruptive. But they are quick to stress that they do this without the inner identification to multicultural values they see dominating their work environment.

> [I'm] practical about things. We can't all move to a compound in Idaho. A pure white homeland is not going to happen in a big shoot-out tomorrow afternoon. We've got to deal with what we have in front of us. For many white nationalists that means blacks at work, Jew bosses, you name it ... If you're going to be a racialist you have know who you are, in your mind, and what you believe but that doesn't mean you can't at the same time live in the world and deal with it (William, Southern California activist, interview 6/9/00).

Some deal with the workplace oppressions they perceive by avoiding others to reduce the time they must cover their beliefs.

> One coping strategy I use is ... I try to limit the time I have to personally interact with these types (i.e., non-Aryans) for my health and sanity. But it is unavoidable, especially at work, and in that situation I just act professionally ... (Angie, Southern California activist, interview 6/9/00).

False Fronts   Others play at being a multiculturalist. They describe an ironic pleasure in "getting over" or "fooling" non-Aryans such as coworkers, schoolmates, teachers, and coworkers, but also deep frustrations about having to deny their most salient role. Yet, they experience their role playing as a form of resistance that amplifies and reinforces their Aryan self.

> I try to think about work like [White Aryan Resistance leader] Tom Metzger said. I may swallow my words all day so I don't get fired, but it's kind of fun after a while to act like a lefty wing scum bag and spout off a bunch of liberal crap just to keep them fooled ... It keeps me strong (Lance, Southern California skinhead, interview 6/27/04).

That Aryans are circumspect about revealing their beliefs at work should not be surprising. Most employees consider the impressions they give off and how these may affect coworkers, bosses, and opportunities for promotion. But, WPM activists are not totally silent about their beliefs at work. Our respondents search for expressive balance through opportunities to communicate their racial consciousness without disrupting the workplace or completely discrediting themselves....

> When I have to deal with this liberal shit at work I just usually bite my tongue unless they insult me directly... unless someone attacks me first, then I'll say something. I don't raise a big fuss, I usually just let the niggers cry about how they're oppressed ... (Cal, Southern California, 7/19/04).

Others are more stealthy about how they convey Aryan principles in their work.

> I can't reveal my beliefs at work because [it] is so intolerant of racism. I know that I'd be unemployable in my field if colleagues learned about me being white power ... but it is galling to have to concede even that much to the racial enemy. I've found that life involves trade-offs, and it takes time to discover how fully open you can be about your views while still maintaining a life for yourself in the world as we find it... (Richard, Aryan Nationalist, interview 6/28/04).

Strategic Silence   Aryans do not need to provoke nonwhite coworkers or outwardly express the contempt they feel toward minorities in order to sustain their activist self. They often secretly read racist literature, listen to Aryan music, and surf white power Web sites as a way to link into Aryanism and reinforce their most salient identity in a context where they are constrained to keep their racism quiet. They also talk of an ongoing internal dialogue that helps justify their decisions to restrain themselves and hold back their white power affinities.

> "You can't always speak your mind. I tell myself that sometimes it's better to just keep it down and save it for the right place. [I will listen to] a Final War or Brutal Attack CD [white power music bands] ... to get my head cleared ..." (Ralph, Aryan Nations, interview 7/30/99).

That the expression remains internal does not weaken or lessen its significance to them. Rather, their strategic silence is an active part of resisting the repression they must endure to keep their job.

The education system is the institution that Aryans typically blame most for creating and perpetuating the multiculturalism they despise. They feel they are under constant surveillance at school by peers and authorities on the lookout for deviance of any type, particularly racism, which prompts intense social control. Activists typically talk of high school and college as a necessary evil—a context dominated by the oppressive multiculturalist values they despise, but one that holds the promise of a degree that is necessary to find the kind of work they need to support themselves and the movement. Trent (Southern California Aryan) explained:

> You can't improve your race without first improving yourself. The movement is changing, we're adapting to the world and there's a new game plan these days. It's all about being low key while you're in school so that if you decide to go into Special Forces or run for office or be an attorney (interview 6/17/04).

Many of our interviewees committed to the movement during their high school years and recall in detail the tensions they felt as an Aryan outsider and how they dealt with it. As with work, most talked of "going along to get along."

> In high school I didn't go around my school preaching and I tried to keep my beliefs to myself, but some of my enemies were aware of my beliefs ... At one point I started getting all of this crap from teachers when I started to read Turner Diaries. One teacher said I was too young and not developed to understand. My counselor said it was politically incorrect so I had to say that I was researching white power groups and didn't believe in them ... (Bradley, SWAS, interview 3/19/99).
>
> It's (school) like a game. I listen to what they say, but don't buy into it. I just remember who I am and what I believe. As long as they think I'm conforming to their ideal student, then they don't ride you ... (Schmidt, Southern California activist, interview 9/14/02).

The Aryans we interviewed felt that relations with others at school were bound by tight codes of conduct with excessive monitoring and little opportunity for open self-expression. In these contexts, covering their identity is less about loyalty to significant others and interest in sustaining relations with them, as in the family, and more about avoiding retribution (e.g., job loss, expulsion, etc.) for their beliefs. Nevertheless, most activists we interviewed found ways to deploy their white power identity to achieve some self-esteem and consistency with their Aryan self within the constraints of these tightly bound contexts. Some expressed themselves privately.

> In school I was very circumspect about my beliefs. I kept a journal of all my thoughts and feelings. No matter what it was, I wrote it down and I still do this. It really helps out when you're swimming in emotion and you just want to scream at the top of your lungs. Let everything flow from your head to your pen. When I was in school the journal was pretty much my only outlet to vent (Jane, Northern Hammerskin, interview 7/28/00).

… Aryans experience work and school as the primary institutional settings that perpetuate their categorization as social outcasts. But, they cannot easily avoid these contexts. Inside the movement, members place a great deal of emphasis on the notion that being a good Aryan requires that they get a degree and a good job to support themselves and the movement. Thus, they must tolerate work and school by outwardly complying to multicultural norms. They constantly guard their expressions, while exploiting the limited opportunities to minimally display their Aryanism. They acknowledge that these displays are risky and hold little potential for changing their status in these contexts, but nevertheless experience these displays as meaningful challenges to the status quo that accentuate feelings of efficacy and persistence in the face of ideological opposition.

Active and Passive Identity Displays in Public

Aryans must also decide how much to reveal of themselves in everyday public spaces such as restaurants, stores, banks, and other service settings. These places are routinely populated by a diverse array of people who are relatively unknown to one another. For most people, the limited interaction with strangers in public settings is routine and not overtly political in meaning, but for committed Aryans these culturally diverse spaces are yet another context where they see multiculturalism supported and they must interact with blacks, Jews, gays, and others whom they despise. Brian describes a sense of alienation in public that is common among our interviewees.

> You can't go anywhere without scum. The malls are shoulder to shoulder with people, dirty, smelly, ugly people that have nothing to do with my people, my culture. I get sick of looking at my people acting like disgusting heathens, listening to nigger music, trying to be gang members, the drugs, I can't relate to any of it. I'm surrounded by sludge. The only escape I have was when I get together with racialists…
> (Idaho Aryan, interview 71/21/00).

Likewise Jimmy explained: "When I go out I'm disgusted by what I see: wiggers, niggers, and all these other muds. I feel completely alone in this cesspool of diversity" (Washington skin-head, interview 4/28/97).

Kathleen Blee (2002) has noted that many Aryan activists take great care to suppress their racialist leanings in public: "those who use overtly racist symbols in public or who adopt an exaggerated racist style [are seen] as movement novices" (p. 167). Only the most inexperienced or maverick racists openly display their Aryan identity to others in public settings. Veterans tend to operate with a great deal of circumspection around non-Aryans. This can mean completely covering their identity so as to not draw attention and just "get along" in these settings.

Passive Displays   Without an attitude of restraint, white power activists antici-pate that they would be constantly retaliating against the evils they perceive as surrounding them in everyday public settings. If they reveal their identity in overt and disruptive ways, they expect hostility from non-Aryans that will dis-rupt the mundane tasks they are trying to complete and even threaten their safety. Most of our respondents talk about the aggressive looks and comments they get from those who suspect them of racial extremism. Some talked of in-cidents in which they were asked to leave restaurants, grocery stores, and being denied other services when owners and patrons identified them as Aryans. Most of our interviewees talked about working to restrain themselves and using cov-ering strategies to mask their real attitude as an important accomplishment that helps them sustain their Aryan selves....

A range of people and activities are often tolerated in public settings as long as they do not disrupt the activities or services of others in the setting. Aryans often respond by passively displaying Aryan symbols (e.g., tattoos, clothing insignia, etc.) while simultaneously suppressing more active expressions of their Aryanism (e.g., loud racist talk, overt confrontations with "racial enemies" etc.). Of course, the ex-tent to which they openly deploy their identity is a matter of degree. While they may feel less constrained in public, they are still quite attuned to the need to shield themselves from attacks against self. Thus, in the diner, the group openly displayed their movement insignia, but otherwise remained reserved. Talk included virulent racist themes, but the comments were made "under the breath" to be heard only by other activists at the table around them. We saw this pattern repeated across restaurants, bars, groceries, sporting events, court houses, and doctor's offices.

Passive displays of movement symbols is a tactic Aryans use to balance ex-pressions of their activist self and achieve some sense of self-esteem, efficacy, and authenticity while simultaneously attending to others' resentment of them by limiting full demonstrations of their radicalism. Their displays are not so much for others, but to communicate and reinforce who they are to themselves. Our informants describe feelings of honor and pride when challenging normative conventions through symbolic displays.

> We know they're looking at us and talking about us. That's fine. That doesn't change how we feel when we're wearing these [symbols]. It's not about the stares or name calling, it's about honor and displaying honor by wearing your uniform and honoring your heritage and race even if most of our own people are blind (Mick, Aryan Nations, interview 4/8/97).

Active Displays   Other WPMers feel that open displays of white power symbolism are acts of courage, a trait highly esteemed among Aryans. Nathan, a Colorado skinhead, strikes a balance between concealment and disclosure by not "getting in people's faces" about his white power beliefs, but not completely masking his leanings either.

> With my head shaved and all the tats I've got, when I'm out in public people get a pretty good idea of who I am. I guess I look the part so a lot of the time I figure I'll go ahead and wear a white power t-shirt and that feels pretty good being that open about it and not really hiding much (interview 7/16/02).

Feeling "pretty good" about expressing his most salient sense of self is a significant accomplishment for someone hearing such a highly stigmatized status. These small-scale expressions of their Aryan self are a primary strategy for outwardly expressing their activism and provide them a palpable sense of resistance that contrasts with their conformity across many everyday contexts.

Public Legitimation   Aryans perceive the unambiguous expression of racism and the creation of a white dominated world as ideal, but what they actually do in covering or guarding token expressions of their ideology is a reflection of different situational constraints. This is why WPMers sometimes express the exact opposite of what might commonly be expected from them. For instance, one of the authors and an Aryan skinhead played doubles pool for more than an hour against a team of one white and one African American. Afterward, Nathan, the white power skinhead, walked over to the two, shook hands with both, and began small talk with the African American. He later explained:

> I'm not going to be a dick to him just cause he's black as long as he's cool and that and we're just playing a game of pool. I'll be respectful, but then that doesn't mean that if I could make things the way I want he'd be around either. You know what I mean? (interview 8/21/02).

Stan, a veteran OC skinhead, explained that his public interactions with racial enemies are punctuated by impression management that stresses a sense of cultured civility.

> Now me, as a skinhead, I go to a restaurant and they [a minority] bring me my food and I say, "thanks," and I leave them a tip if they're worth it. They bring out my food on time, they don't make a mistake, I give them a tip and say, "Thanks a lot" and "Have a good night." I might be a white power skinhead but I'm not rude and I'm not an illiterate low class (interview 6/12/01).

These types of individual displays resemble an organizational strategy Mitch Berbrier (1998, 1999, 2000, 2002) has identified among some WPM groups who attempt to neutralize the stigma of racism with public legitimation efforts. Specifically, they try to combat stereo types of Aryans as boorish, irrational, and violent racists with claims that they are thoughtful, respectable, mainstream people who are simply interested in their cultural heritage. In short, they are reframing their public message to change how people perceive them. At the individual level, the displays of civility toward enemies that we observed also disguise the extent of their racism. These WPMers are part of the most radical and extreme groups in the movement, but they navigate many everyday situations with great flexibility in how they display their Aryanism to others, even those they detest....

CONCLUSION

We have explained that, by using various ploys of concealment and revelation, Aryans project an image of themselves that hides much about their extremism. They do so primarily to avoid the strong interactional tensions that flow from their stigmatization by others. Downplaying and concealing their Aryanism in everyday situations such as family interactions, work, school, and public settings moderates the social psychological demands of an identity that draws strong ire and contempt from others. But, it is never a straightforward issue about how much to conceal or reveal who they are. Covering their identity is complicated by the role expectations that oblige Aryan activists to be open to others about their beliefs. If they are open to others about their beliefs then they risk repression, but completely concealing who they are produces discomforting inconsistencies with their most salient identity. How they manage this dissonance is crucial to sustaining their activist identity. Working this out requires expressing some degree of their activist beliefs. Aryans are not simply trying to "pass as normal," but to find an expressive balance between revealing a degree of their "Aryan self" while covering some of the more extreme features. Their disclosures are a form of individual everyday activism to resist social controls that subjugate them to others' values and identity expectations. These displays are meaningful to activists as a form of resistance to the constraints they perceive. They feel they are fulfilling the obligations of their activist role.

Mundane everyday struggles demonstrate the creative capacities for persistence and inventiveness that occur under social constraints. Concealing some of the most salient aspects of their activist identity is not a sign of Aryan weakness, passivity, and acquiescence to non-Aryans' normative expectations. They do not play down their identity because they are ashamed of their stigmatized qualities or accept normalized assumptions of moral worth. As Kanuha (1999) observes:

> If passing is constructed and subsequently employed to mitigate the effects of social discrimination due primarily if not solely to stigma [then] *passing is not an act of assimilation*, but *an act of resistance to social oppression* ... Passing becomes an act of resistance because [the] passer never really assimilates (pp. 39–40; emphasis in original).

Their disguised struggles amidst overt compliance are part of a calculated survival strategy they accomplish daily across numerous contexts. As we have argued elsewhere, Aryans have constructed a rich, albeit hidden, infrastructure of "free spaces" where they openly express their Aryanism to one another in ways that sustain WPM collective identity (Futrell and Simi 2004). But, for most Aryans, these safe havens are relatively few and far between, while everyday life is constant. They find some esteem and authenticity as an Aryan activist in the nominal displays of self that they manage in everyday settings.

To be sure, this form of resistance leaves a lot to be desired for Aryans....

NOTES

1. The white power movement in the United States is made up of groups such as the Ku Klux Klan (KKK), Christian Identity sects, neo-Nazis, and white power skinheads. The oldest and, historically, the most influential organization in the WPM is the Klan whose roots date to late-nineteenth-century Reconstruction. Christian Identity groups trace their roots back to nineteenth-century British Israelism, which claimed that Anglo-Saxons are the "true" Israelites and Anglo Christians are God's chosen race. The U.S. neo-Nazi branch of the WPM is rooted in the American Nazi Party and organized around Adolf Hitler's racial purity ideals. Umbrella groups such as the Aryan Nations (AN) have led the trend of Klan members, skinheads, and others to increasingly embrace Nazi symbols and ideology, along with Christian Identity theology. White power skinheads are the fourth, and newest, major wing of the WPM. The members are linked together by such cultural symbols and practices as shaven heads, white power music, racist politics, and a propensity for racial violence.

REFERENCES

Billig, Michael. 2001. "Humour and Hatred: The Racist Jokes of the Ku Klux Klan." *Discourse and Society* 12: 267–88.

Blee, Kathleen. 2002. *Inside Organized Racism: Women in the Hate Movement.* Berkeley: University of California Press.

Downton, James and Paul Wehr. 1997. *The Persistent Activist: How Peace Commitment Develops and Survives.* Boulder, CO: Westview Press.

Kanuha, Valli Kalei. 1999. "The Social Process of 'Passing' to Manage Stigma: Acts of Internalized Oppression or Acts of Resistance?" *Journal of Sociology and Social Welfare* 26: 27–46.

Van Dijk, Teun A. 1992. "Discourse and the Denial of Racism." *Discourse and Society* 3: 87–118.

30

Fitting In and Fighting Back: Homeless Kids' Stigma Management Strategies

ANNE R. ROSCHELLE AND PETER KAUFMAN

The homeless occupy a particularly stigmatized position in society, serving as general pariahs. People go out of their way to avoid seeing them or interacting with them, and as Reinarman notes, the American "vocabulary of attribution" assigns blame to them based on their individual failures rather than to the unequal opportunity structure of society. Nowhere is this blame less worthy than it is for homeless kids, who have inherited their homeless status from parents unable to house them. Based on research conducted in moderate-term housing shelters for (usually) single mothers with children, Roschelle and Kaufman articulate some of the strategies these youngsters use to disguise or manage their deviant status.

They divide their techniques into strategies of inclusion and exclusion. In the former, children attempt to fit into society and attain the appearance, friendships, and acceptance they see among their "homed" peers. Their attempts to pass, cover, and forge relationships are poignant, revealing their pain and insecurity. When these fail, however, and they cannot escape their stigma, they muster a bravado designed to achieve a tough and intimidating persona. Like the cheerleaders and the bankrupt, they seek to raise their status by comparing themselves to others whom they deem lower than themselves, although in so doing they denigrate others in similarly unfortunate situations whom they can construct as more socially and morally abject than themselves.

Why do you think these homeless kids pursue such different approaches in dealing with in-groups and out-groups? How effective do you think these two approaches are at protecting them from stigma?

Beginning in the 1980s the gap between the rich and the poor widened significantly, and there was a concomitant increase in homelessness. Social scientists responded to this crisis by studying the rates and causes of homelessness. However, with the exception of a few notable studies (Liebow 1993; Snow and Anderson 1993), there has been little ethnographic research on the daily struggles

From Anne R. Roschelle and Peter Kauffman, "Fitting In and Fighting Back: Homeless Kids' Stigma Management Strategies." *Symbolic Integration*, Vol. 27, No. 1, 2004. All rights reserved. Reprinted by permission of the University of California Press Journals.

this population encounters. Moreover, research has been slow to address the growing feminization of the homeless. The proportion of women and children constituting the urban homeless population increased from 9 percent in 1987 to 34 percent in 1997 to a staggering 40 percent in 2001. Although there has been some recent work on familial homelessness, most accounts have disproportionately examined street homelessness among single men. More research is needed on women and children who are homeless and, in particular, on the strategies they use to construct meaning, participate in social interactions, and negotiate the boundaries with the nonhomeless world....

In our analysis, stigma and homelessness are both construed as structural locations. Like stigma, homelessness must be recognized as a structural component characterizing the individual's relationship to the social world. Individuals may find themselves delegitimized socially, politically, or economically if they cannot accumulate normative resources, are unable to receive positive appraisals, and are incapable of following expected rules of behavior. Such is the case with homeless individuals and other stigmatized populations. In daily life, these populations often find themselves disadvantaged because they do not have the means to engage in successful social interactions. Implicitly then, stigma, like homelessness, is about power—or the lack thereof. As Link and Phelan (2001, p. 367) argue, "[S]tigmatization is entirely contingent on access to social, economic, and political power that allows the identification of differentness, the construction of stereotypes, the separation of labeled persons into distinct categories, and the full execution of disapproval, rejection, exclusion, and discrimination."

Recognizing stigma as a condition deriving from macro-level forces does not negate the micro-level processes that characterize an individual's stigma management. Although stigma should be understood as a consequence of structural relationships, the ways in which individuals manage their stigma is micro-interactional. Acknowledging the macro-origins of stigma forces researchers to incorporate an analysis of the structural while studying the ways in which individuals manage their stigma interpersonally. Because stigmatized individuals lack power, their ability to protect their sense of self may be severely compromised. As a result, their actions may unintentionally augment their stigmatization and perpetuate the structural relationships that generate their stigmatized status (Link and Phelan 2001). Much like impoverished individuals, therefore, acquiring the capital (social, cultural, economic, political, etc.) that is needed to overcome stigma may be difficult because of the spoiled identity. In short, stigma may be a chronic status until the individual accumulates the resources necessary to break the cycle.

Much of the existing literature concentrates on strategies that presumably lessen stigma and neglects to consider the extent to which stigma management strategies may perpetuate the individual's stigmatized status. Since Goffman's 1963 work, the assumption that stigma management strategies result in positive outcomes has prevailed. Researchers generally explore the ways in which stigmatized individuals protect their sense of self and attempt to gain social acceptance. The underlying assumption is that through these strategies, deviant individuals will achieve some degree of normalcy. Clearly, some actions benefit the individual's social standing. However, more attention should be given to the process through which stigma management strategies might result in the acquisition of characteristics that further spoil one's identity. Recognizing stigma management strategies as micro-level reactions to macro-level conditions elucidates how such strategies may lead to unintended and potentially negative consequences.

In the case of kids who are homeless, the structural disadvantages are significant. They come from poor families and are also marginalized because of their age, race, ethnicity, and gender. Unlike some of their privileged peers who may go to great lengths to distinguish themselves through dress, taste, and behavior, kids who are homeless experience what Goffman (1963, p. 5) calls "undesired differentness." Homeless kids are social outcasts because of the situation into which they were born or because of their parents' current predicament. Consequently, when we attempt to understand the homeless kids' strategies to manage their stigma, we must examine how structural disparities influence these strategies and how the nonhomeless interpret them. As we illustrate, although some of their stigma management strategies produced positive results with regard to their identities and social standing, others led to unanticipated and negative consequences. In effect, it is through the use of these strategies that kids who are homeless, like some stigmatized populations, unwittingly reproduce their stigmatization and cement their status loss.

RESEARCH SITE

The research site is an organization in San Francisco called A Home Away From Homelessness. Home Away serves homeless families living in shelters, residential motels, foster homes, halfway houses, transitional housing facilities, and low-income housing. The program operates a house in Marin County (called the Beach House), provides shelter support services, a crisis hotline, a family drop-in center (the Club House), a mentorship program, and, in conjunction with the San Francisco Unified School District, an afterschool educational program (the School House). Home Away is neither a typical homeless service agency nor a shelter.

Home Away serves a population of approximately one hundred five- to eighteen-year-old children annually. Fifty percent of the participants are boys and 50 percent are girls. The racial-ethnic breakdown of homeless families participating in Home Away programs is 40 percent African American, 30 percent white, 20 percent Latino, and 10 percent multiracial. All the kids participating in Home Away programs lived with at least one parent (none are runaways or homeless youth living independently), although some were essentially on their own as a result of parental neglect. Many of the kids suffered from a variety of physical, emotional, and developmental deficits, which is not surprising given the harsh conditions under which they live (see, e.g., Bassuk and Gallagher 1990; Rafferty 1991).

A majority of Home Away's families come from northern California; some families are from southern California and the Pacific Northwest. These families, often mother-only, typically come from chronically poor communities and usually become homeless after losing a job or stable housing. When extended kinship networks deteriorate as a result of poverty (Menjivar 2000; Roschelle 1997) and violence, these transient families are forced to rely on institutional forms of social support. There are primarily two types of families using the services of Home Away: short-term participants who experience brief spells of homelessness and the chronically homeless who use programs over several years....

Chronically homeless families who cycled in and out of Home Away were the most frequent users of Home Away programs. Because of the severe housing shortage and exorbitant rents in San Francisco, many homeless families had their shelter stays extended past the three-month deadline. Some families eventually moved to motels, others doubled up with family members, and some shuffled between substandard apartments in violent neighborhoods. Many of the chronically homeless kids went to the Beach House on a weekly basis over the course of several years. As they got older, some of the teenagers who no longer wanted to go to the Beach House went to the Club House a few times a week. Some of these kids attended the afterschool educational program several times a week, but their transience made it difficult for many to stay in the program. During the past six years, nearly one thousand children and their parents have participated in various programs provided by Home Away.

METHODS AND DATA

The ethnographic component of our research included participant observation at the Beach House, the School House, and the family drop-in center where Anne collected the data and did volunteer work for four years (1995–99). During this time, she also attended meetings of relevant social service agencies at which she took copious notes and conducted observational research at residential motels, transitional housing facilities, and homeless shelters throughout the San Francisco Bay area. In addition, she conducted thousands of hours of informal interviews, sometimes asking leading questions (Gubrium and Holstein 1997) and sometimes just listening. Many of the informal interviews were taped and transcribed. In addition, she conducted and transcribed verbatim formal taped interviews with ninety-seven kids and parents who were currently or previously homeless. While in the field, when something that seemed profound about the homeless experience was uttered or occurred, Anne would go to the bathroom and quickly record it. This strategy was necessary because sitting in a room full of kids and simultaneously taking notes creates an artificial atmosphere that inspires skepticism and mistrust among kids who may already be wary of adults. Anne typically spoke her field notes and critical interpretations of the days' happenings into a tape recorder immediately after working with the kids. These tapes were eventually transcribed....

Gathering ethnographic data among kids who are homeless presents a number of methodological challenges. The first is the difficulty of gaining entry, although this proved easier than expected. Anne developed rapport with the kids by spending considerable time with them at a variety of locations. Entry was further facilitated by the House Mother (a formerly homeless woman) who regularly conveyed to the kids her support for and fondness of Anne. This legitimacy was crucial because it allowed kids to be interviewed and observed in the context of their social group interactions....

The second, related challenge is being attentive to their devalued social position. This awareness is particularly necessary because of our interest in how homeless kids manage their stigma. As noted, because these kids are poor, young, and predominantly racial-ethnic minorities, their behavior is often interpreted pejoratively even when it mirrors that of their nonhomeless peers. For this reason, it is important to record and respect the ways in which kids construct meanings and to not assume "the existence of a unidimensional external reality" (Charmaz 2000, p. 522)....

The third strategy, and challenge, was participating in impromptu conversations, which captured the ways kids managed their devalued social status. These gatherings, which Anne tape recorded and later transcribed verbatim, were not focus groups because they had neither an identifiable agenda nor a formal mediator. Rather, these were freewheeling conversations that allowed Anne to "remain as close as possible to accounts of everyday life while trying to minimize the distance between [herself] and [the] research participants" (Madriz 2000, p. 838). These conversations were particularly appropriate because they allowed for the expression of ideas in a forum where individuals felt comfortable speaking up. Furthermore, talking with kids in relaxed group settings in which the kids outnumber the adults, minimizes the inherent power differential between the adult researcher and the respondents, and gives voice to those who have been subjugated.

STIGMA MANAGEMENT STRATEGIES

Goffman (1963, p. 3) suggests that stigma should be understood as "a language of relationships" as opposed to the attributes a person possesses. Moreover, he notes that "the stigmatized are not persons but rather perspectives" (p. 138). These ideas are particularly relevant for understanding the stigmatization of kids who are homeless. While these kids do not necessarily exhibit physical manifestations of their stigma, they are stigmatized because of their marginalized status in society. The discourse surrounding poverty and homelessness has a long history of blaming individuals for their predicament. Kids who may have been defined in the past as deserving of societal sympathy have more recently been recast as part of the legions of the undeserving poor.

Home Away kids were aware of their relationship to normative society and understood that others generally saw them as undesirable. Because of the large numbers of homeless in San Francisco and the visibility of the street homeless, there were numerous negative public discussions about the issue. The local newspapers constantly featured articles that were contemptuous of the homeless, and mayoral races often focused on ridding the city of its unsightly homeless population. The kids in the sample were attuned to the negative discourse surrounding homelessness and often expressed their anxiety about being demonized by the public. In fact, the kids spent many hours sitting in front of the fireplace discussing how hard it was for them to be routinely disparaged. As Dominic, an articulate sixteen-year-old, said, "Everyone hates the homeless because we represent what sucks in society. If this country was really so great there wouldn't be kids like us."...

Kids who are homeless manage their stigma in a variety of ways. One common typology of stigma management strategies assumes an in-group/out-group dichotomy (Anderson, Snow, and Cress 1994; Blum 1991). Although this typology is useful for understanding some stigmatized populations, the stigma management strategies of Home Away kids were more fluid and could not be so neatly categorized. As kids who are homeless make their way through the world, they transgress—yet simultaneously create—boundaries and often use similar stigma management strategies with both peers and strangers.

Although the in-group/out-group dichotomy did not fit our data, we developed an alternative schema that enabled us to better categorize the stigma management strategies Home Away kids use. We observed that the kids displayed two sets of strategies. The first set conformed to societal norms of appropriate behavior and aimed at creating a harmonious environment with both peers and strangers. In other words, these strategies represented attempts at establishing self-legitimation in both hostile and supportive environments. We refer to these as *strategies of inclusion* because they reflected the kids' desire to eradicate the boundary between a homeless and a nonhomeless identity. Through these inclusive strategies, Home Away kids hoped to be recognized simply as kids—without the stigmatizing label and discredited status of being homeless. The most common strategies of inclusion among Home Away kids were forging friendships, passing, and covering.

The second set of strategies were also attempts at gaining social acceptance but were not necessarily aimed at creating a harmonious atmosphere. We refer to these as *strategies of exclusion* because Home Away kids use them to distinguish themselves from both peers and strangers. With these strategies, kids who are homeless attempted to redress their spoiled identity by declaring themselves tougher, more mature, and better than others. These exclusive stigma management strategies included verbal denigration and physical and sexual posturing. Unlike strategies of inclusion in which kids used conciliatory tactics to be accepted, strategies of exclusion were aggressive and forceful attempts by the kids to blend in. These strategies largely reflected the kids' interpretations of socially acceptable behavior. However, given their disenfranchised social position, these behaviors were often perceived as maladaptive and threatening. As a result, when kids engaged in strategies of exclusion, they provided members of the dominant culture with a seemingly legitimate justification to further disqualify and disparage them....

STRATEGIES OF INCLUSION

Forging Friendships

The language of relationships that identifies kids who are homeless as a stigmatized group is so embedded in society that it is implicit in all their social relations. Even when these kids are in situations in which their homelessness is unknown or unimportant, they still feel the need to manage their spoiled identities. For example, one would expect that in the consonant social environment of the Beach House they would not have to engage in stigma management strategies. However, because their stigmatization is defined by their relationship to mainstream society, their stigma is always part of their identity....

At the Beach House, the kids attempted to construct a positive identity. Children were treated with dignity and respect by volunteers and were included in important decision-making processes. The services provided by Home Away gave kids an opportunity to experience childhood in a way most individuals take for granted. In addition to providing a break from the difficulties of living in shelters, transitional housing, residential motels, and so on, Home Away gave the kids a place to forge friendships with caring adults. Many of these relationships offered the only opportunity for homeless kids to obtain positive self-appraisals from nondisenfranchised adults. This supportive environment allowed for greater self-legitimation, gave the kids a respite from their stigmatization, and provided them with a sense of belonging (Brooks 1994). As a result of this inclusive strategy, many of the kids developed more favorable self-images. Silvia's discussion of her friendship with Tami, a volunteer, illustrates the importance of forging friendships as a way to manage stigma.

SILVIA: I call her whenever I feel really bad. She is so nice. She makes me feel better when I'm depressed and she never makes me feel like a freak because I'm homeless.

ANNE: Is that important to you?

SILVIA: Yeah. Most of the time I feel pretty bad about my life. I mean my mom has a new boyfriend every few weeks, we live in this nasty ass hotel, and I feel like everyone knows I'm a loser. Tami is always trying to make me feel better about my life. She tells me how smart and pretty I am and that I should feel good about being such a great older sister. Tami really cares about me and makes me feel better about myself. I don't know what I'd do without her.

Home Away also provided these kids with the opportunity to befriend other impoverished youths. By embracing other disenfranchised children, Home Away kids created a safe space where they could construct a positive identity and manage their stigmatized status. For example, when new kids were incorporated into Beach House activities, instead of rejecting them, the "old-timers" served as mentors and attempted to create a harmonious climate. Old-timers initiated the new kids into the program by teaching them the rules, showing them around, and introducing them to secret hiding places. Much like the traditional African

American role of "old heads" and "other mothers," this mentor relationship allowed the old-timers to gain self-esteem. By initiating newcomers, they became experts at something and shared their wisdom with other impoverished kids. In addition, as the following conversation suggests, old-timers took great pride in their knowledge of the surrounding environment.

CARLOS: Hey, Hernán, don't go in the water without your life jacket.

HERNÁN: *No hay problema*—I'm a great swimmer.

CARLOS: It doesn't matter, man, the undertow is really strong and you can get swept under really easily.

HERNÁN: Don't be such a pussy.

CARLOS: Seriously man, people drown here all the time. Last week some kid almost died.

HERNÁN: Really?

CARLOS: Yeah, man. Listen I been coming here for two years and I've seen a lot of shit—you gotta believe me.

HERNÁN: *Gracias*, Carlos—thanks for watching my back. You really are a cool dude. I guess I better to stick close to you so I don't get into any trouble.

CARLOS: Hey after we finish swimming Marcus and I can show you the secret hiding place.

HERNÁN: Cool.

Forging friendships with newcomers is an important stigma management strategy because it enables kids who are homeless an opportunity to transcend their discredited status and assume a role invested with interactional legitimacy. Through forging friendships, Carlos is able to negate feelings of worthlessness bestowed on him by society and feel like a valuable member of the kids' community. Similarly, Hernán's stigma is mitigated because he now feels like a legitimate member of Home Away. This strategy of inclusion anchors kids in a particular social group and subsequently provides them with a desired social identity that is conferred by significant others.

Passing

Goffman (1963) suggests that visibility is a crucial factor in attempts at passing. To pass successfully, an individual must make his or her stigma invisible so that it is known only to himself or herself and to other similarly situated individuals. Unlike their nonhomeless peers who have legitimate access to the public domain, kids who are homeless must often pass as nonhomeless as a means of appropriating heretofore unavailable and legitimate public space. One "passing" strategy kids in our study used entailed adopting the dress and demeanor of non-homeless kids. Whenever clothing was donated to Home Away, the kids selected outfits based on style rather than function. It was extremely important that clothing and shoes looked new and were "hip." On numerous occasions, kids refused to take donated coats during the winter because they were ugly and out of style. The importance of fitting in is evidenced by the following conversation between Anne, Jamie, and Cynthia (Jamie's mom) while they were hanging out at Stonestown Mall.

JAMIE: Hey, do you think these people can tell we are homeless?

ANNE: No, how could they possibly know?

JAMIE: I don't know. I always feel like people are looking at me because they know I am poor and they think I am a loser.

CYNTHIA: I feel like that a lot too—it makes me feel so bad—like I'm a bad mother and somehow being homeless is my fault. I feel so ashamed

JAMIE: Me too.

ANNE: Jamie, what are some of the ways you keep people from knowing you are homeless?

JAMIE: I try and dress like the other kids in my school. When we get clothes from Home Away, I always pick stuff that is stylin' and keep it clean so kids won't know I'm poor. Sometimes it's hard though because all the kids try and get the cool stuff and there isn't always enough for every one. I really like it when we get donations from people who shop at the Gap and Old Navy. I got one of those cool vests and it made me feel really great.

ANNE: Is it important for you to keep your homelessness a secret?

JAMIE: Yeah, I would die if the kids at school knew.

Home Away kids also attempt to pass by using code words. Their use of code words illustrates the importance of language as a symbolic indicator of membership in a social group. As Herman (1993) argues, individuals selectively withhold or disclose information as a way to maintain secrecy about their negative attributes. Knowing the rules of social interaction and the symbolic importance of words, Home Away kids resist language that reveals their homelessness to others. They purposefully choose words they associate with middle-class life to articulate their social reality and simultaneously conceal their marginalized social existence. The following impromptu conversation illustrates this point.

ROSINA: I hate that kid Jamal that lives with us in Hamilton [Family Shelter], you know his cot is three over from mine.

SHELLEY: Sssh, be quiet, someone will hear you and then people will know we are homeless.

ROSINA: I don't care.

SHELLEY: I do.

LINDA: So do I. You should say that you don't like Jamal who lives three houses down—that way people will think you are talking about a kid in your neighborhood.

ANNE: Is that how you guys talk in school?

SHELLEY: Yeah, we say things like that and we make up other stuff so people don't know we live in the shelter.

LINDA: Or in the motels.

SHELLEY: When we talk about our caseworkers we say our aunts and when we talk about shelter staff we call them our friends.

ANNE: That is a really clever way of keeping people from knowing you're homeless.

ROSINA: It totally is, but then you can't invite friends over after school because they think you live in a house.

LINDA: We can't hang out with kids who are not poor. There is no way I would invite a kid from school over to my room in that skanky motel we live in, I'd be so embarrassed.

SHELLEY: Yeah, we can't make friends with a lot of kids because how can we bring them to the shelter after school?

This example illustrates how homeless kids use words to construct a positive identity, protect their sense of self, and feel integrated with the larger society. Moreover, it shows that language reflects and reproduces power relations in society. Interestingly, although these kids use code words to mask their stigmatized status and construct a positive identity, their language choices disqualify them from participating in normative social interactions. These verbal gestures reflect the extent to which homeless kids are in danger of having their homelessness revealed. When they do not use code words, their stigmatized identity will be evident, and they will be unlikely to befriend middle-class children. Alternatively, when they do use code words, they reduce their chances of befriending nonhomeless kids because they risk exposing their stigma. In managing stigma through passing, the threat of discovery is ever present. Although the kids desire acceptance in mainstream society, the threat of discovery leads them to monitor and curtail their social involvement.

Covering

Individuals engage in covering when they attempt to minimize the prominence of their spoiled identity. Covering allows individuals to participate in more normative social interactions by reducing the effects their stigma elicits (Goffman 1963). Unlike passing, the point of covering is not to deny one's stigma but rather to make it less obtrusive and thereby reduce social tension (Anderson, Snow, and Cress 1994). Home Away kids often engaged in this stigma management strategy when they became friends with nonhomeless kids who knew about their predicament. Home Away kids would especially use this strategy around the parents of their non-homeless friends, and they would often ask the staff to advise them on appropriate dress or behavior when they were going out with non-homeless kids and their families.

One Home Away kid, Ellie, became a close friend of an affluent schoolmate, Carol, who lived in the Marina district of San Francisco. Ellie was honest with Carol and her family about where she lived. Still, when Ellie went to Carol's house for dinner, she wore the least tattered, cleanest clothes she owned and would eliminate her ghetto swagger and jargon. As she said to Anne, "They know I'm homeless and all, but I don't want to act like I'm homeless. I don't want to embarrass them. You know my clothes aren't that fancy and I'm used to eating at the shelter where everyone is talking really loud and eating with their hands and being kinda sloppy." To fit in and be "normal," Ellie decided to minimize the obvious manifestations of her homelessness.... For the most part, these strategies had the intended effect of protecting the kids' identities by offering them a degree of social legitimacy and by aligning them with nonhomeless individuals. In spite of the chaotic nature of their lives and their awareness of their stigmatization, it is noteworthy that these kids attempt to conform to society through socially acceptable means. In this sense, Home Away kids do not fit the traditional conception of the homeless as disaffiliated and socially isolated individuals. They seem surprisingly resilient in their attempts to develop relationships with nonhomeless people in spite of being denigrated by them....

STRATEGIES OF EXCLUSION

Verbal Denigration

When individuals face a social world that labels them deviant, they are likely to fight back by maligning others as a way to augment their self-esteem. Termed "defensive othering" by Schwalbe et al. (2000), this type of stigma management strategy was common among Home Away kids. Many kids in the sample protected their sense of self by verbally denigrating other stigmatized groups such as homosexuals and homeless street people. This was a form of identity work that allowed homeless kids to distance themselves from the stigmatized "other" (Snow and Anderson 1987) and proclaim their superiority over these similarly disparaged groups. Because homeless kids recognize that they are problematic in the eyes of society, their denigration of other stigmatized groups is a "largely verbal effor[t] to restore or assure meaningful interaction" and align themselves with the dominant culture (Stokes and Hewitt 1976, p. 838).

Along these lines, many of the kids were homophobic and freely expressed their disgust for homosexuality. This attitude can be attributed to the kids' (arguably accurate) interpretation of societal norms and values with regard to homosexuality. By portraying gays and lesbians as "freakin' faggots" and "child molesters," the kids were placing others lower than themselves in the social hierarchy. The kids' stigmatized status was deflected onto others, thereby bolstering their own sense of self. This exclusionary strategy was especially interesting in the context of San Francisco—a city in which there is a large population of gay and lesbian activists and citizens, many of whom have achieved positions of power and prestige and who themselves often denigrate the homeless. The following conversation illustrates the pejorative discourse Home Away kids often used when talking about gays and lesbians.

ANTOINE: Look at those homos, they make me sick.

FRED: Yeah, they be all trying to grab your ass when you walk by.

ANTOINE: I know man, they'd love a piece of us but I'd make 'em suck on a bullet before I'd let 'em suck on my thang.

FRED: People think we are nasty because we live at the Franciscan, but at least we don't do little boys. I mean those guys are freaks.

ANTOINE: I hear ya, I'd rather be a dope fiend livin' in the Tenderloin than a fuckin' faggot! [Loud laughter]

FRED: I'd rather be a dope fiend, livin' in the Tenderloin, selling crack to ho's than be a fuckin' faggot! [Louder laughter]

Homeless kids also spoke disparagingly about homeless street people. Homeless kids in our sample lived in shelters, residential motels, transitional housing, foster homes, and other institutional settings. Though many of them have spent a night or two sleeping in parked cars, in a park, or on the street with their parents, their homeless experience has taken place primarily in some type of sheltered environment. The main reason they have not spent the majority of their lives on the streets is because there are many more programs for homeless families in San Francisco than there are for childless homeless adults. Essentially, the only factor preventing their parents from becoming part of the homeless street population is them. Despite this, Home Away kids often made fun of homeless street people.

ROSITA: Man look at those smelly street people, they are so disgusting, why don't they take a shower.

JALESA: Yeah, I'm glad they don't let them into Hamilton with us.

ROSITA: Really, they would steal our stuff and stink up the place! [Laughter]

JALESA: Probably be drunk all the time too.

ROSITA: Yeah, and smokin' crack all night long!

Ironically, the mothers of both these girls have struggled with drug and alcohol addiction and have had several episodes of homelessness. By distancing themselves from the "true" social pariahs of San Francisco, Jalesa and Rosita mitigate their own stigmatized status and maintain some semblance of a positive self. Further, identifying a group as more discredited than themselves allows the girls to feel superior to "those losers on the street."…

Physical Posturing

Physical posturing is another form of identity work that grants homeless and non-homeless kids a momentary degree of empowerment. Kids who are homeless use physical posturing to feel powerful in their interaction with nondisenfranchised kids, a feeling that is rarely available to them. It has long been recognized that many adolescents are filled with insecurity as they attempt to establish their identities. However, middle- and upper-class kids have more socially acceptable means than low-income ones to demonstrate to others (and to themselves) that they are important. As Anderson (1999, p. 68) notes, privileged kids "tend to be more verbal in a way unlike those of more limited resources.

In poor inner-city neighborhoods verbal prowess is important for establishing identity, but physicality is a fairly common way of asserting oneself. Physical assertiveness is also unambiguous." In this sense, Home Away kids' use of physical demeanor is a stigma management technique that emerges from their social structural location and protects them from a hostile world.

One common manifestation of this physical posturing was the use of body language. When encountering nonhomeless children, kids in our study often adopted threatening postures by altering their walk, speech, and clothing to mimic "gangsta" bravado. In short, these kids adopted what Majors (1986) refers to as the "cool pose." For example, to get from the parking lot to the beach, we had to walk over a very small, narrow wooden bridge. As we crossed the bridge, we often passed kids coming from the opposite direction. As soon as the Beach House kids spotted other kids coming toward them, they would immediately change their demeanor. They metamorphosed from sweet cuddly kids to ghetto gangstas. The kids grabbed their pants and pulled them down several inches to mimic the large baggy low-riding pants of the gangbanger. They turned their baseball caps around so that the brim was in the back and swaggered in exaggerated ways. Their speech became filled with ghetto jargon, and they spoke louder than usual. When encountering other kids, the topic of conversation on the bridge would also suddenly shift from how much fun we just had to the fate of a gang member they knew who had just been arrested.

These self-presentations mirror what Anderson (1990, p. 175) calls "going for bad." Anderson argues that this intimidation tactic is clearly intended to "keep other youths at bay" and allow disempowered kids to feel tougher, stronger, and superior. Like verbal denigration, this strategy of exclusion also helped Home Away kids to lessen their stigma. Interestingly, these behaviors clearly imitate images of adolescence that pervade popular culture. In music videos, movies, television shows, video games, and so on, images of baggy pants, baseball caps, and swaggering walks abound. Although this strategy had the intended effect of empowering Home Away kids by intimidating their nonhomeless peers, it also reinforced their stigmatization. As Nonn (1998, p. 322) notes, "While the coping mechanism of cool pose weakens the stigma of failure, it undermines identity … and contribute[s] to their own alienation from other groups in society." Though some kids recognized that their behavior may stigmatize them further, they still engaged in such posturing because it was one of the few areas in their lives over which they had some control....

Sexual Posturing

Some Home Away kids used sexuality to validate themselves. Although nonhomeless youth also engage in sexual posturing to establish a sense of self in their social groups, Home Away kids engage in it more explicitly and overtly than their nonhomeless peers. For Home Away kids, sexual posturing and promiscuity articulate the sexual exploitation and violence they experienced both within and outside the family. As researchers have documented, victims of child sexual abuse often resort to promiscuity in adolescence and adulthood.

Molestation by older men was not uncommon, and many of these kids learned at an early age to use their sexuality to gain status among their peers. For example, several young women in the sample dressed and behaved in overtly sexualized ways that surpassed what we expect from the budding sexuality of "normal" adolescents. In one poignant incident, a fourteen-year-old girl was teaching a younger girl how to perform oral sex on an eleven-year-old boy. By bragging to his friends about his newfound sexual prowess and achieving prominence among his peers, this boy exhibited an exaggerated masculine alternative commonly found among lower-income racial-ethnic males (Oliver 1984). The girls involved increased their status by demonstrating a level of sexual maturity that is typically associated with older women.

In another example, Patti, a thirteen-year-old, discussed the self-esteem she gained through her sexual posturing.

> I mean not everyone is pretty enough to get a man to pay for a room for the night. At least I know that I can get anything I need from a man because I am totally hot. I get lots of attention and some of my friends are jealous of me because they know I got it going on. Some girls are so butt ugly no man would ever even want to fuck them anyway—but not me— they think I'm a hotty—you know what they say—if you got it flaunt it!

As these examples illustrate, sexual posturing is an exclusionary tactic kids use to distinguish themselves from their peers and to lessen their stigmatization. Research has shown that some poor racial-ethnic girls invoke a discourse of sexuality in order to negotiate and construct a more empowering identity (Emihovich 1998), and others may attempt to achieve similar results through motherhood (Luker 1996). In a society bombarded with images of hyper-sexuality, it is not surprising that Home Away kids imitate these sexual scripts in an attempt to strengthen their social standing....

CONCLUSION

In this article, we examine the stigma management strategies of kids who are homeless. Although researchers of stigma management have studied a variety of populations, our work contributes to existing knowledge by including this previously neglected group. By examining the stigma management strategies homeless kids use, we address a number of gaps in the literature. First, our work emphasizes the need to acknowledge stigma and homelessness as structural locations. Much like homelessness, we must posit stigma not as an individual attribute but as a relationship to the social structure (Goffman 1963; Link and Phelan 2001). This perspective is noteworthy because it attends to how individuals' behaviors are both informed by and interpreted through their social structural location. This insight is particularly true of homeless kids who are oppressed socially because of their age, race, ethnicity, and social class. Kids who are homeless encounter and interpret a world that is characterized by hunger, uncertainty, chaos, pain, drug abuse, violence, sexual abuse, degradation, and social rejection, among other things. This social reality epitomizes the violence of poverty and ultimately results in a lack of consistency, stability, and safety in their lives. Furthermore, these kids exist in a constrained public domain and are forced to carve out their own space in a limited urban environment that is generally hostile to them. It is in this environment that kids who are homeless engage in social interactions that aim to construct positive identities and overcome their discredited status.

By positing stigma and homelessness as social structural phenomena, our work also illustrates the processes whereby stigma may become a chronic status. In contrast to much of the literature on stigma management, we found that the tactics used by Home Away kids sometimes had the unintended effect of perpetuating their spoiled identities. Although their actions were attempts at protecting their sense of self and gaining a degree of social acceptance, strategies such as sexual posturing and verbal denigration substantiated societal stereotypes of kids who are homeless as violent, disrespectful, and dangerous delinquents to be avoided. Obviously, it is not these kids' intention to engage in behaviors that perpetuate their stigmatized identities and their disenfranchised positions. Rather, it is their social structural location that offers them limited opportunities to exert their agency in a socially acceptable way.

In attempting to negate their stigmatization, Home Away kids engaged in strategies that often imitated the behaviors of mainstream youth. By interpreting popular culture and the social interactions of their nonhomeless peers, homeless kids behaved in ways that are often exhibited, condoned, and even rewarded when enacted by their more privileged peers. In mimicking this behavior, Home Away kids naively expected to obtain a modicum of social acceptance. Unfortunately, they failed to understand that the parameters of acceptable and unacceptable behavior are mediated by one's social location. In other words, the deviant behaviors middle-class and affluent peers engage in have different consequences than when they are perpetrated by homeless kids (Chambliss 1973).

REFERENCES

Anderson, Elijah. 1990. *Streetwise: Race, Class, and Change in an Urban Community.* Chicago: Chicago University Press.

———. 1999. *Code of the Street: Decency, Violence and the Moral Life of the Inner City.* New York: Norton.

Anderson, Leon, David A. Snow, and Daniel Cress. 1994. "Negotiating the Public Realm: Stigma Management and Collective Action among the Homeless." *Research in Community Sociology* (Supplement 1): 121–43.

Bassuk, Ellen L., and Ellen M. Gallagher. 1990. "The Impact of Homelessness on Children." *Child and Youth Services* 14(1): 19–33.

Blum, Nancy. 1991. "The Management of Stigma by Alzheimer Family Caregivers." *Journal of Contemporary Ethnography* 20(3): 263–84.

Brooks, Robert B. 1994. "Children at Risk: Fostering Resilience and Hope." *American Journal of Ortho-psychiatry* 64(4): 545–53.

Chambliss, William J. 1973. "The Saints and the Roughnecks." *Society* 2(1): 24–31.

Charmaz, Kathy. 2000. "Grounded Theory: Objectivist and Constructivist Methods." Pp. 509–35 in *Handbook of Qualitative Research*. N. K. Denzin and Y. S. Lincoln, eds. Thousand Oaks, CA: Sage.

Emihovich, Catherine. 1998. "BodyTalk: Discourses of Sexuality among Adolescent African American Girls." Pp. 113–33 in *Kids Talk: Strategic Language Use in Later Childhood*. S. M. Hoyle and C. Temple Adger, eds. Oxford: Oxford University Press.

Goffman, Erving. 1963. *Stigma: Notes on the Management of Spoiled Identity*. New York: Simon and Schuster.

Gubrium, Jaber F., and James A. Holstein. 1997. *The New Language of Qualitative Method*. New York: Oxford University Press.

Herman, Nancy J. 1993. "Return to Sender: Reintegrative Stigma-Management Strategies of Ex-Psychiatric Patients." *Journal of Contemporary Ethnography* 22(3): 295–330.

Liebow, Elliot. 1993. *Tell Them Who I Am: The Lives of Homeless Women*. New York: Penguin.

Link, Bruce G., and Jo C. Phelan. 2001. "Conceptualizing Stigma." *Annual Review of Sociology* 27: 363–85.

Luker, Kristine. 1996. *Dubious Conceptions: The Politics of Teenage Pregnancy*. Cambridge, MA: Harvard University Press.

Madriz, Esther. 2000. "Focus Groups in Feminist Research." Pp. 835–50 in *Handbook of Qualitative Research*. N. K. Denzin and Y. S. Lincoln, eds. Thousand Oaks, CA: Sage.

Majors, Richard. 1986. "Cool Pose: The Proud Signature of Black Survival." *Changing Men: Issues in Gender, Sex and Politics* 17: 5–6.

Menjivar, Cecilia. 2000. *Fragmented Ties: Salvadoran Immigrant Networks in America*. Berkeley: University of California Press.

Nonn, Timothy. 1998. "Hitting Bottom: Homelessness, Poverty, and Masculinity." Pp. 318–27 in *Men's Lives*, edited by M. S. Kimmel and M. S. Messner. Boston: Allyn and Bacon.

Oliver, W. 1984. "Black Males and the Tough Guy Image: A Dysfunctional Compensatory Adaptation." *Western Journal of Black Studies* 8: 201–2.

Rafferty, Yvonne. 1991. "Developmental and Educational Consequences of Homelessness on Children and Youth." Pp. 105–39 in *Homeless Children and Youth*. J. H. Kryder-Coe, L. M. Salamon, and J. M. Molnar, eds. New Brunswick, NJ: Transaction Publishers.

Roschelle, Anne R. 1997. *No More Kin: Exploring Race, Class, and Gender in Family Networks*. Thousand Oaks, CA: Sage.

Schwalbe, Michael, Sandra Godwin, Daphne Holden, Douglas Schrock, Shealy Thompson, and Michele Wolkomir. 2000. "Generic Processes in the Reproduction of Inequality: An Interactionist Analysis." *Social Forces* 79(2): 419–52.

Snow, David A., and Leon Anderson. 1987. "Identity Work among the Homeless: The Verbal Construction and Avowal of Personal Identities." *American Journal of Sociology* 92: 1336–71.

———. 1993. *Down on Their Luck: A Study of Homeless Street People*. Berkeley: University of California Press.

Stokes, Randall, and John R. Hewitt. 1976. "Aligning Actions." *American Sociological Review* 41: 838–49.

31

Collective Stigma Management and Shame: Avowal, Management, and Contestation

DANIEL D. MARTIN

The way organizations help people collectively manage their stigma is the focus of Martin's study of three stigma management groups associated with obesity: Overeaters Anonymous (OA), Weight Watchers (WW), and the National Association to Advance Fat Acceptance (NAAFA). Martin compares the way these groups frame their purpose and set their goals. While OA and WW help members navigate their way through the world and conform to the prevailing body norms, NAAFA fights these norms and seeks to re-define them. Martin ties the characteristics of these organizations to the way they deal with shame, avowing it, managing it, and contesting it. The selection offers an excellent comparative view of the varied rationales and strategies associated with differently structured collec tive stigma management groups.

Looking at the breakdown of participants into each of these groups by gen der, why do you think certain groups attract higher rates of men versus women? Which of these types of strategies are more effective in combating stigma?

■ ■ ■ ■ **B**oth cross-cultural research and feminist studies have observed the connection between shame and gender identity, demonstrating that, while women are more susceptible to body shame, for men the emotion is associated with failure to live up to culturally prescribed norms of masculinity (Gilmore 1987; Horowitz 1983).

Feminist scholars investigating the U.S. beauty culture have observed its emergence in the 1870s (Banner 1983; Schwartz 1986) as new appearance norms were created and distributed by industries such as cinema (Featherstone 1982), advertising (Ewen 1976), and scale and corset companies (Schwartz 1986). As a result, the social formation that exists at the end of the twentieth century is a "cult of thinness" (Hesse–Biber 1996) that promotes and normalizes slenderness

From Daniel D. Martin, "Organizational Approaches to Shame: Avowal, Management, and Contestation." *The Sociological Quarterly*, Vol. 41, No.1, 2000. Copyright © 2000 by Blackwell Publishers. Reprinted by permission of the publisher.

and its attendant anxieties (Bordo 1993). This cult has far-reaching effects. Barrie Thorne and Zella Luria's (1986) research on children's games involving cross-sex interaction reveal that girls' bodies are more sexually defined and accrue more penalties for an overweight appearance than do boys'. This pattern is consistent with findings of cross-cultural research on mate selection that demonstrate that men evaluate the social value of women more heavily in terms of appearance and that women evaluate the social value of men in terms of their occupational status and earning potential (Buss 1989). In the United States, where fat is stigmatizing (Allon 1982; Cahnman 1968), feelings of shame may result in debilitating eating disorders. Research on adolescent girls has demonstrated that the internalization of beauty norms is responsible for producing high degrees of body dissatisfaction and a profound sense of body shame (McFarland and Baker-Baumann 1990) leading to bulimia and anorexia nervosa (Rodin, Striegel-Moore, and Silberstein 1990, p. 362). Of course, the fat content of bodies, along with the degree to which it might be stigmatized and accompanied by body shame, is variable. A slightly overweight body may be experienced as an object of great shame and the focus of disordered eating, or it may be experienced as only a "minor bodily stigma" (Ellis 1998).

However, ... the research on ... feminist studies of body shame or sociological studies on shaming as a form of "strategic interaction" (Goffman 1969) have [not] addressed how organizations attempt to assist their members in managing shame....

Drawing upon Erving Goffman's (1986) frame analysis, I assess how shame is managed within three different "appearance organizations" through the discursive and bodily strategies that they supply their members. By appearance organizations, I mean organizations for whom the physical appearance of members is a primary concern. These organizations include Overeaters Anonymous (OA), Weight Watchers, Inc. (WW), and the National Association to Advance Fat Acceptance (NAAFA). The theoretical and substantive questions concerning these organizations are twofold. First, what kinds of organizational frames do these organizations offer their members to make sense of shame? Second, what strategies are used within the organizations in managing or contesting experiences of shame?

THE ORGANIZATIONS

Given the sex ratio of the organizations, all three of the appearance organizations I studied might properly be recognized as "women's organizations." Therefore, the present analysis of shame is an analysis of women's shame. During interviews and participant observation, I found that men rarely talked about shame or embarrassment over the body while women seemed to be continually, acutely aware of it. Based upon information reported by the organizations, participation rates reveal significant sex differences in membership (Table 31.1). These differences were also revealed in the accounts that women and men constructed about joining and participating in the organizations and about the gender relations that were negotiated within them—a topic beyond the scope of the present article (Martin 1995).

T A B L E   31.1   Organizational Membership

	Sex Differences in Participation		
	WW	**NAAFA**	**OA**
Women	95%	78%	86%
Men	5%	22%	14%
Total*	100%	100%	100%

*These figures represent national membership rather than participation rates in local chapters.

At the beginning of data collection, Weight Watchers Inc. (WW) was the leading national weight loss organization in the United States, with annual revenues of approximately $1.3 billion (Weber 1990, p. 86). Of its 15 million members worldwide, approximately 14.3 million are women. In contrast, the exact size and composition of Overeaters Anonymous (OA), a program for compulsive overeaters, remains undetermined, even though the organization estimates that 86 percent of its U.S. members are female (OA 1992, p. 1). Because anonymity in the twelve-step program is strictly enforced, there is no comprehensive roster of OA members. Currently, the number of OA groups is estimated at over seven thousand worldwide (OA 1987, p. 10), but group size varies from five to twenty-five people, making estimates of total membership difficult.

The National Association to Advance Fat Acceptance (NAAFA) describes itself as a civil rights organization in the "size rights movement." It also defines itself as a social support organization and as a self-help group (NAAFA 1990, pp. 1–6). Unlike members of OA and WW, the NAAFA members in the local chapter I studied engaged in a variety of social and political activities. These ranged from informal parties and organized dances, to speaking at community conferences, to holding protests and conducting write-in campaigns. The national organization, founded in 1969, has headquarters in Sacramento, California, and a membership of 2,500 to 3,000 members. NAAFA consists of a loosely federated set of local chapters and special interest groups, including gay and lesbian groups, fat admirers groups, couples groups, singles, teen and youth groups, groups for super-sized and mid-sized individuals, and feminist groups.

METHODS

Over the course of approximately two years, I conducted participant observation and in-depth interviews at Weight Watchers and NAAFA. In attempting to gain access to OA, I sought out an acquaintance and long-standing group leader in OA who was centrally located in local OA networks. She was helpful in providing me with extensive information about the organization, its program, and its local chapters. Believing that her interest in my project, her sensitivity to research needs, and the fact that we had worked together indicated an openness to facilitating entree, I directly broached the topic. My request for an introduction into

TABLE 31.2 **Interviews**

	Women	Men
WW	20	5
NAAFA*	8	4
OA**	41	8
Total	69	17

*Defines the entire population of active chapter members during the period of my observation.

**Includes recorded personal stories of members from the OA audiotape library.

the closed meetings and access to OA members was met, instead, by recalcitrance motivated by her desire to ensure the anonymity of local members. I was frozen out of the local chapters and was unable to conduct participant observation in groups other than the publicly available "open meetings." A couple of months later, I learned of a local OA audiotape library. I selectively sampled personal stories and presentations that had been taped at national and local conferences and then were produced for OA members as well as members of Alcoholics Anonymous. I utilized the strategy of "theoretical saturation" recommended by Barney G. Glaser and Anselm L. Strauss (1967), selecting audiotapes for analysis until the additional data yielded few additional insights. I was assisted by the proprietor of the service, who was instrumental in locating tapes containing life stories that were as complete as possible.[1] I conducted interviews with all of the active members of NAAFA after I had established myself with the group and had been conducting participant observation and with members of Weight Watchers who responded to ads that I had run in local newspapers. The total number of interviews for all three organizations is in Table 31.2. Because the organizations themselves constituted the sampling frames, little variation in race, class, or ethnicity was provided within the samples. All of the informants in this study were white and most were middle income.

DATA COLLECTION, EMBARRASSMENT, AND SHAME

Because my own bodily appearance serves as a "dis-identifier" (Goffman 1967), a symbol belying a legitimate, potential, future claim for group membership in WW, OA, and NAAFA, I intentionally gained about twenty-five pounds before participation. I hoped to learn as much as I could about members' own meanings and feelings of the body and participation as well as how the organizational "frames" that were established shaped emotional experience and participation. Having gained my undergraduate degree on a wrestling scholarship attuned me to the issues of extreme dieting, binge-eating, and weigh-ins, which could similarly be found in the lived experience of Weight Watchers, NAAFA, and OA members. While my own weight gain facilitated somatic insight into the lives and meanings of members of OA and Weight Watchers, my burgeoning body size was clearly not comparable to the experience of members of NAAFA. Because I was not subjected to the stigmatization or public inconvenience suffered daily by NAAFA members (some of whom weighed in excess of three hundred pounds) my own "fat identity" never fully crystallized. Indeed, if anything, I was considered a novelty among friends, peers, and colleagues who issued positive sanctions for my "sociological commitment."

At Weight Watchers, I regularly attended weekly meetings, which entailed a logical stream of activities once members entered the meeting place. These included paying weekly dues, being weighed on physician's scales by WW personnel, receiving organizational literature concerning meal plans along with myriad other promotional materials distributed by the organization (such as the monthly newspaper), and finally selecting a seat in the meeting area. As a participating observer, I experienced the anxiety that members later recounted in interviews about "facing the scale," that is, weigh-ins. Because weigh-ins take place in semipublic space, it is possible that queuing members will learn of one's weight, increasing the anxiety that is already present for some members. Having failed weigh-in several times by gaining weight, I was struck by the capacity for the ritual to evoke, simultaneously, feelings of dependency and embarrassment. WW personnel are aware of these feelings, and they commonly query deviating members about the possible causes of weight gain. They also join in the construction of accounts and remedial work directed at either exonerating deviating members or diminishing their presumed culpability.

ORGANIZATIONAL FRAMES

Experiences of shame, humiliation, and embarrassment can be found in the life stories of members of all three appearance organizations. What establishes the meaning of these experiences is the organizational "frame" (Goffman 1986) within which the experiences of members are socially and discursively organized Table 31.3. A "frame," according to Goffman (1986, pp. 10–11), is a set of "definitions of situations" that are "built up in accordance with the principles of organization which govern events—at least social ones—and our subjective involvement in them." *Organizational* frames are those definitions constructed and maintained by organizational actors within which experience, interaction, and communication are structured and rendered both personally and organizationally meaningful. For the programs of organizations to be subjectively meaningful, they must facilitate a linkage of individual interpretations to organizational meanings and definitions, that is, "frame alignment" (Snow, Rochford, Worden, and Benford 1986).

In the case of these appearance organizations, the meanings, as well as the strategies that are dispensed to members for dealing with shame, reflect the structure, agenda, and ideology of the organization, its "frame." The organizational frames of Weight Watchers, OA, and NAAFA represent three unique sets of

T A B L E 31.3   Shame Work: A Comparison of Organizational Frames

	Overeaters Anonymous	Weight Watchers	NAAFA
Type of Organization	Twelve-step program	Multinational corporation	Civil rights organization
Organizational Frame	Redemption	Rationality	Activism sociality
Organizational Goal	Support members in abstinence from overeating	Help clients lose weight/profit	Organize against "size discrimination"
Source of Shame	Compulsive overeating/fat body	Fat body/body image	Societal definitions of beauty, cultural appearance norms
Consequence of Shame	Inhibits recovery	Leads clients to exit program	Inhibits activism
Shame Strategy	Shame avowal/ expiation	Shame management	Contestation of shame
Approach to Shame	Self-transformation	Bodily transformation	Societal transformation
Ritual for Shame Removal	Shame avowal	Dieting	Identity announcement/ public confrontation
Meaning of the Body	Body as symptomatic display of spiritual deficit; thinner body as a symbol of regaining control over personal, spiritual, and emotional life	Body as a site of contestation over appetite: locus of self-control and self-indulgence	Body as symbol of self-acceptance; political transformation
Body as Medium of Communication	"Body announcement" used as evidence of program efficiency; thin bodies as part of personal testimonies	"Body announce-ment" via fashion shows; display and glorification of thin bodies	"Body announcement" via fashion shows; display and glorification of fat bodies
Vocabulary of Motive	Overeating as disease	Overeating due to irrational management and lack of education; program as a skilling process for a total lifestyle change	Genetic accounts: large body a product of nature; program for empowerment; stories as "Oppression Tales"

social and discursive practices developed in accordance with different historical circumstances and audiences. Thus, while the autobiographical content of participants' shame experiences seemed to bear great similarity across the organizations, the "organizational" meaning of these experiences and the strategies employed to manage or alleviate them differed vastly.

The Organizational Frame of OA: Redemption

The Overeaters Anonymous program is a redemptive model of treatment directed at developing a spiritual consciousness though a therapeutic group process. OA meetings, whether open to the public ("open meetings") or open to OA members only ("closed meeting"), are typically held in public facilities, often churches. Meetings begin with a recitation of OA's preamble and the evening's speaker testifying to the effectiveness of the OA program in her or his life. Most meetings end with members joining in the "serenity prayer."[2] OA explicitly acknowledges its reliance upon the Alcoholics Anonymous program of recovery, including the Twelve Steps and the Twelve Traditions developed by Bill W. and other AA founders. Reproduced in most literature published by the organization, the twelve-step program serves as a blueprint for achieving abstinence from compulsive overeating (OA 1990, p. 114).

The Twelve Steps of Overeaters Anonymous

1. We admitted we were powerless over food—that our lives had become unmanageable.

2. Came to believe that a power higher than ourselves could restore us to sanity.

3. Made a decision to turn our will and our lives over to the care of God *as we understood Him.*

4. Made a searching and fearless moral inventory of ourselves.

5. Admitted to God, to ourselves and to another human being the exact nature of our wrongs.

6. Were entirely ready to have God remove all these defects of character.

7. Humbly ask Him to remove our shortcomings.

8. Made a list of all persons we had harmed, and became willing to make amends to them all.

9. Made direct amends to such people wherever possible, except when to do so would injure them or others.

10. Continued to take personal inventory and when we were wrong, promptly admitted it.

11. Sought through prayer and meditation to improve our conscious contact with God *as we understood Him,* praying only for knowledge of his will for us and the power to carry that out.

12. Having had a spiritual awakening as the result of these steps, we tried to carry this message to compulsive overeaters and to practice these principles in all our affairs.

Essentially the organization prescribes a spiritual program of recovery for what it considers to be an "incurable disease"—compulsive overeating. The concept of disease represents OA's primary "vocabulary of motive" (Mills 1940) that alleviates members of responsibility for their unhealthy overeating: "OA believes that compulsive overeating is an illness—a progressive illness—which cannot be cured but which, like many other illnesses, can be arrested.... Once compulsive overeating as an illness has taken hold will power is no longer involved because the suffering overeater has lost the power of choice over food" (OA 1988, p. 2). In defining "compulsive overeating," OA tells the prospective member that "in OA, compulsive overeaters are described as people whose eating habits have caused growing and continuing problems in their lives. It must be emphasized that only the individuals involved can say whether food has become an unmanageable problem" (OA 1988, p. 2).

The redemptive aspect of OA's program is both ideological and structural, as well as observable in relationships that members have with their sponsors. The alignment of personal with collective definitions of compulsive overeating is accomplished, in part, with the assistance of an OA sponsor, a person with substantial "program experience" who serves as the member's confessor, friend, advocate, and spiritual leader as well as a purveyor and mediator of organizational ideology. Sponsors, along with other OA members, are part of the emotion management team that members may use in expressing and policing emotions and securing social support. Redemption from compulsive overeating and an obsessive-compulsive self, according to OA members, is facilitated by sponsors and fellow group members as one "works through denial"—that is, gives up one's idiopathic justifications for compulsive overeating and the avoidance of unpleasant emotions in favor of collective definitions and meanings found in OA's twelve steps and twelve traditions.

The Organizational Frame of NAAFA: Activism

Throughout its history, NAAFA has mobilized lobbying efforts for antidiscrimination bills with state legislatures,[3] held rallies, conducted protests,[4] and brought cases of discrimination to the attention of the mass media. The objective of such action is the creation and enforcement of human rights provisions under which fat people might be identified as a protected group. Yet a bifurcation of NAAFA's primary objectives can be found in the orientation literature for new members: NAAFA refers to itself as both a "human rights organization" (NAAFA 1990, p. ii) and "a self-help group" (NAAFA 1990, p. 2). For NAAFA members both intensive involvement in social activities and activist participation constitute the dominant frame of meaning or, in the words of NAAFA members, "a way of life." Activism, as defined by the organization, includes a broad array of personal and political activities that are marked by a displayed willingness to engage in confrontation. Such activism, as described by the organization (NAAFA 1990, p. 3–4), may include:

> *Personal Activism:* Educating people around you, not letting negative comments about your weight or preference go unchallenged, and your life as a "role model" are all forms of personal activism.

> *Legislative Activism:* is specific activist work that leads to changes in the law. Considering the amount of time, effort, and expertise required in such undertakings, it deserves a category all its own.

Advocacy Activism: includes letter writing and other forms of communication with the "powers that be" regarding your opinions. Did you like how the fat person was portrayed on the TV show? Are you happy with the article in the magazine? Did the salesperson treat you with disrespect because of your fat? Writing letters of praise or protest to the station, the magazine, or the store owner are examples of advocacy activism.

The organizational frame of activism in NAAFA represents a way in which participants situate themselves, emotionally and practically,[5] within the ideological contours of the organization. It is a "relevance structure" through which not only social or political events but also interpersonal lines of action are defined, evaluated, and constructed.

The Organizational Frame of WW: Rationality

The weekly Weight Watchers meetings were held in weight loss centers located in shopping malls, high-rise business complexes, and basements leased from other companies. In contrast to OA, where developing a meal plan and taking inventory of daily consumption is strongly encouraged though largely voluntary, these activities are preestablished, compulsory features of WW's program. The official purpose of the program is to help clients achieve bodily reduction. Hence, emotional and spiritual "recovery" is not pertinent to WW clients as it is for OA members, and bodily reduction for clients of WW is largely a matter of technocratic administration or "technique,"[6] not spiritual practice.

The materials distributed to new clients during the first week of WW membership include a basic program guidebook (containing a multi-item questionnaire assessing eating patterns, levels of desire to succeed in Weight Watchers, and the degree of stress in one's life), a "food diary" that includes daily menus, and a list of items from various food groups. In each subsequent week, members are given additional diaries to keep along with new daily menus and comprehensive guides on various topics including exercise, eating out, socializing, tips for better eating, and dealing with obstacles to weight loss. "Portion control" (the allotment of measured meals items for which WW markets food scales, frozen entrees, and cookbooks) is the fundamental principle underlying its program.

While the topic of compulsive overeating may receive a modicum of attention within meetings, the term cannot be found within WW's literature. Instead, the term "volume eating" is used, and what is emphasized is the type rather than the amount of food consumed. "Portion control" is to be applied within those food groups that are seen as leading to the creation of fat bodies but can be ignored within food groups whose caloric content is negligible. Thus, according to WW, there are no good or bad foods, only those necessitating more or less portion control....

SHAME WORK

In *The Managed Heart*, Arlie Russell Hochschild (1983, p. 7) described "emotion work" as labor that "requires one to induce or suppress feeling in order to sustain

the outward countenance that produces the proper state of mind in others."
Hochschild's definition pertains to the self-monitoring, management, and modeling of emotion as a strategy used by service personnel to evoke certain feelings.
But other activities in which people engage (to elicit, constrain, and manage the
emotions of others or encourage their self-management) might also be classified as
emotion work, given a less restrictive definition of the term.[7] For example, confronting other people about the discrepancy between their verbal actions and non-
verbal cues, such as the tone in their voice, or pointing out apparent discrepancies
between seemingly frustrating situations and a lack of emotional response (as family
therapists can attest) are very much work and can be emotionally exhausting.
Hence, evoking emotional expression within WW's men's meetings might be
considered emotion work, while displacing or channeling such expression constitutes work within women's meetings. Within OA, "working through" denial is a
form of emotional labor, while for members of NAAFA, emotion work includes
attempting to impassion members over issues of weight-based discrimination.

Within all three organizations, a common form of emotion work is "shame
work," that is, emotional labor aimed at evoking, removing, or managing
shame—though in the contemporary contexts of OA, WW, and NAAFA only
the latter two objectives are sought. Within OA and WW, shame work involves
activities directed at mitigating the internalized experience of shame that ema-
nated from the personal and social practices of consuming food. Within NAAFA
shame work was directed at removing shame that had been acquired through the
stigmatization of a "fat identity." Like other forms of emotional labor, shame
work includes communicative and expressive action that may take both discursive and bodily forms. In the following sections, I discuss the use of shame
avowal (OA), shame management (WW), and shame contestation (NAAFA)
and how these are accompanied by use of "body announcements" in managing
and systematizing members' shame.

Shame Work in Overeaters Anonymous

For members of OA, patterns of compulsive overeating and resultant body size are
seen as a source of shame. Yet this is "only secondary shame" insofar as these patterns have developed as a result of some earlier "primary shame" experience invoked by others. Both female and male members commonly located the
development of primary shame experiences in early childhood, citing failures at living up to adult expectations as the reason for their present "shame-based" state.

Primary sources of shame, as OA members define them, are profoundly social,
most often residing in interaction episodes with significant others who have knowingly or unintentionally evoked it. One strategy used by OA members engaged in
shame work might best be termed "shame avowal," an open acknowledgement of
past and present shame experiences that serves to expiate the shame experience.
Such avowals are commonly woven into the public testimony of OA members:

> Jason (open OA meeting): I also need to say I've never had one perfect
> day of abstinence, there is no such thing for me. You know there is no
> perfect abstinence. I've lost weight in this program. I've gained weight

in this program. But I have had enough shame over my food and my weight to last me the rest of my life. I don't need to put more on me. You know my goal weight … somebody asked me at a convention what my goal weight was. And I said, "My goal weight, if I'm abstinent, it's exactly what I weigh today."

The acknowledgment of shame is cited by OA members as problematic because it is premised on a self-awareness that, if not already present, must be organizationally manufactured. As indicated by one member:

Rob (OA conference workshop): The second part [of dealing with shame] is to recognize it. To even find out that we have it. And as far as I'm concerned that is the most difficult part of it. To recognize that we have it is, is the thing that's so easy to cover up with denial. I've been in the OA program for about five years and AA about six years. And it took a long time for me to discover that I had any shame at all.

Determining whether the self exists in a deep shame-based state is a subjective evaluation, but the evaluation is also linked to a collective assessment as OA sponsors and other group members attempt to facilitate the awareness of shame-based actions on the part of nascent members. While such an awareness involves the acquisition and application of an organizational vocabulary of motive that is acquired through socialization in OA, it also necessitates the presence of viable experiences and circumstances to which it can be applied. As in other twelve-step programs (Denzin 1987; Rudy 1986), shame experiences are recognized and formulated as members of Overeaters Anonymous pragmatically invoke the organizational vocabulary for understanding and overcoming patterns of compulsive overeating. As it is applied to shame, the motive of denial is used in retrospectively interpreting compulsive overeating as behavior connected to a shame-based state. Working through denial is facilitated by "hitting bottom." Incidences of binging, stealing food, or lying about consumption, which lead to acute intrapersonal states of shame, degradation, and humiliation, may all be defined subjectively as "hitting bottom," that is, reaching the lowest possible point in one's life spiritually, emotionally, and socially.[8] According to the redemptive frame of the OA, salvation from a shame-based state of compulsive overeating is only possible after one acknowledges both to self and others the causes and consequences of compulsive overeating and then turns one's life over to a "higher power." As in Alcoholics Anonymous, the concept of a "higher power" is one that is idiosyncratically constructed,[9] yet members are encouraged to let it intervene in their lives and assist them in working through their denial of compulsive overeating.…

Shame Work in Weight Watchers

Within Weight Watchers, NAAFA, and OA, body shame is commonly discussed by women. Female members in OA also cite shame experiences in episodes of emotional, physical, or sexual abuse. By contrast, most male members of Weight Watchers and NAAFA appear to be exempt from experiences of body shame:

neither did male members in OA seem to share experiences of body shame though they mentioned shame experiences rooted in a general failure to live up to a multiplicity of social expectations. Weight Watchers group leaders claim body shame as exclusive to the experience of female members:

> Robin: Men are not as shameful about their bodies. They don't care if they are thirty pounds overweight, they go ahead and take off their shirts at the beach anyway. Women just aren't able to do that—we're ashamed to wear bathing suits and show off our cellulite or flabby legs or varicose veins at the beach. We are overwhelmingly told we can't do that, that we must be slim.

As a former longtime member of Weight Watchers and now group leader, Robin claims that body shame is not only central to the experience of women vis-à-vis men but that being female makes one susceptible to body shame in ways that men are not. Some men in WW, however, did discuss similar experiences:

> Carl: For phys-ed class we had to go swimming. And I always got the largest swim suit. And people would just laugh at me and call me "fatso" and, you know, names. And then if I went to lunch no one would sit with me.

Carl does not specifically identify a personal sense of shame as a residual of this experience but he cites feelings of profound differences induced by episodes of stigmatization. While it seems reasonable to expect the presence of shame in episodes such as the one above, it remained liminal in the experiences of the men I interviewed. In contrast to the OA strategy of shame avowal, the work of WW personnel consisted of shame management that is, attempts to neither deny, contest, or specifically avow the experience but to contain it in hopes of a future, natural dissipation through dieting and weight loss. The management of shame represents a change in WW's treatment ideology over the course of its thirty-year history. Until the 1970s the organization had relied heavily upon the "shame-aversion" strategy (Serber 1970) of "card calling" in modifying the eating behaviors of clients.[10] Card calling involved placing a client's name along with the number of pounds that the client had either gained or lost during the week on an index card. The cards of all clients would then be read publicly at the beginning of each meeting. Similar instances of shaming appear to have been used in other weight loss organizations during this same period. Marcia Millman's *Such a Pretty Face* (1980) reveals that the shaming ritual used to discipline candy-sneaking "kids at fat camp" (children at summer weight loss camps) was to extract public confessions from these children on stage, humiliating them in front of their peers. Earlier research on the organization Take Off Pounds Sensibly (TOPS) reported the use of an equally drastic strategy for motivating clients to lose weight:

> There is a public announcement of each member's success or failure during the previous week. When a client has lost weight, there is applause and much vocal behavior; if she has gained weight, there is obvious disapproval with booing and derision.... In some groups the

member who has gained the most weight is given the title of "Pig of the Week" and may be made to wear a bib with a picture of a pig on it or may have to sit in a specified area called the "pig pen." (Wagonfeld and Wolowitz 1968)

The loss of Weight Watchers revenues, which resulted when clients terminated their membership after such experiences, proved to be a compelling reason for abandoning shame aversion strategies in favor of strategies directed at its containment. One former client and now group leader of Weight Watchers recounted the outcome: "Those were the old days. Jeez, can you imagine how uncomfortable everyone was? We found that half the group had left before we even got seated." However, the absence of shame talk in WW meetings also reflects corporate concerns for liability. The training provided group leaders does not equip them to conduct psychotherapy or deal intensively with revelation of traumatic events such as sexual, emotional, or physical abuse that might produce shame. In light of episodes where women may make such disclosures, WW developed a strategy that allows organizational personnel to maneuver efficiently through the most troublesome situations. When I asked a group leader what happens if people divulge very personal or very traumatic information that is related to weight loss, she replied:

> The line is drawn that you never touch anything that is not directly affecting the members' weight. If they can't verbalize it you move on.... You don't touch it, you let them tell you. And they'll take care of it. It's just amazing. I've never been as scared as when that woman remembered in the meeting having been raped. Because I didn't know what to do with her. And the question that we tell leaders and that we practice in any group—men, women, any kind of group that we're doing—is, "And how does that affect your weight control?" That's your appropriate follow up, no matter what they say, if you think you're into something that you're not qualified for, you let them answer and then you let the group take care of that person.... You know, there's always someone that's gonna say, "Well, gee, you really need counseling for rape." So that's the point, once you've thrown it back to them, to back off.... [Y]ou don't have anything to offer them. You're not qualified. If we could just know what we're doing we could do so much more. And we do have an awful lot of psychology background given to us by the company but we can't use it; we're not really qualified.

Here, the emotion work of leaders must strike a precarious balance between the emotional resolution of members' personal problems and corporate exposure, which writes large for group leaders as "uncertified" professionals. This is accomplished by displacing the responsibility for resolving emotionally charged situations onto members themselves. Thus, group leaders do shame work as well as other kinds of emotion work but always within limits rationally guided by concerns for organizational liability.

The emotion work now done by WW personnel in women's meetings consists of assisting in the management of client's shame experiences. Shame management in WW largely included remedial work done during weight loss meetings as well as teaching clients intrapersonal strategies for minimizing body shame. Remedial work within the social context of group meetings primarily involved supplying clients with viable disclaimers of excuses (Hewitt and Stokes 1975; Lyman and Scott 1970) for program violation. An example of the latter is demonstrated in the following interaction:

LEADER: How did everyone's week go this week?

CLIENT 2: [female, approximately age twenty-four]: I almost didn't come in to-night because I was afraid to face the scale.

LEADER: Ohhhh … what happened?

CLIENT 2: I was really stressed this week and I ate everything in sight. I went off the plan, I'm afraid. I kept saying to myself [laughs] I wonder if they take your ribbon back [a red ribbon is given to clients after they lose their first ten pounds].

LEADER: Okay … but the positive thing is that you came back this week, see … you could have done a lot of other unhealthy things to yourself than just eat. Does anyone have anything to say to [name]?

CLIENT 3: (Woman looks at client 2) Well, tell her why you were so stressed.

CLIENT 2: Well, I went to visit my mother and there was food everywhere. My future brother-in-law made it to the finals at the state wrestling tournament, and a cousin who I was very close to died this last week.

CLIENT 3: I think you need to give yourself a break.

CLIENT 4: I think you are being way too hard on yourself, you shouldn't worry about the program [WW] with all that you're going through.

LEADER: Like I said, I think it's very positive that you *did* decide to come back this week, knowing that you may have not stuck with the program. I think that's just positive in itself. [To other clients] Don't you agree? [Everyone nods their heads yes.]

Here, the group leader enlists the support of other group members in ratifying the excuse. Because bodily monitoring means heightened awareness of body size, it evokes body shame for some members. In such cases, group leaders also recommended nondiscursive strategies for dealing with shame:

> Margaret [group leader]: I had one woman who was ashamed to find out how many inches she had lost every week and so instead of using a measuring tape would use different colored yarns to measure her bust, hips, waist, thighs, calves, and upper arms. Each week, this member would cut the tails off these pieces of yarn according to how many inches she had reduced and therein came to amass a pile of different colored yarn. She could then hold and feel the cut off yarn which re-presented her weight loss.

In suggesting that clients objectify their weight loss, the group leader offers a technique by which clients might manage shame and gain a sense of control over body size and weight. The tactile strategy offered above is designed to contain or manage rather than avow shame....

Shame Work in NAAFA

In contrast to avowing or managing shame, NAAFA members contest it. The objective of activism as presented in NAAFA's national newsletter is to "Change the World, Not Your Body" (Wolfe 1992, p. 5). Such contestation can readily be seen in the communicative but nondiscursive practice of making a "body announcement," where the fat body is displayed as shameless. NAAFA members make a public avowal of a "fat identity" not only through these displays but also through forms of public and private confrontation. Letter-writing campaigns and confrontations with public officials, as well as proprietors of businesses and services who engage in size discrimination, comprise part of the protest activities of NAAFA members. No social context is considered exempt from "fat activism." What is formulated in these activities, according to NAAFA members, is a way of life, an organized set of attitudes, and a mode of responding to myriad situations that members face daily.

> Beth: Like one time they were making cracks in the lounge about eating, well it was at lunchtime and, oh God, this one woman said, who's always dieting, "If we eat this we'll all have to shop at Women's World [clothing store for large women]." And everybody laughed. And I said, "Oh pardon me." I said, "Don't make fun of the places where I buy my clothes." I just said it in a nice, lighthearted tone. There was just dead silence. God, everybody at the table was embarrassed to death. I thought, "Hey Beth, good for you for saying that."
>
> Deborah: So I was shopping and all of a sudden I found myself in front of this huge section of Slimfast products. And all of a sudden the idea came to me, [shouts] gee, I don't have to use the entire card [NAAFA business card]. So I just tore the bottom half of the card off, the part that had the NAAFA address and left the part that said, "Do something about your weight, accept it." And I just stuck it on the shelf, sort of like behind one of those little plastic place cards and said, "There."

Contestation emanates from the lived experiences of members who organize their lives around their organizational "fat"—identity. The identity is viewed as relevant in all of the daily activities of NAAFA members, whether confronting fellow employees like Beth or grocery shopping like Deborah. According to NAAFA members, shame militates against the active initiation of individual and, hence, collective, political practice. NAAFA sees social stigmas as directly linked to the internalized oppression of shame. Shame contestation is thus a requisite component of identity politics where the aggrieved attempts to transform themselves by transforming both societal definitions of beauty and human value and the feeling rules that govern fat bodies....

CONCLUSION

Sociologists studying formal organizations contend that organizations are boundary-maintaining social units where society and culture are both experienced by individuals and reproduced in various sets of social practices (Perrow 1986). Society, it is argued, is now absorbed by organizations that mediate culture and cultural themes for the individuals who participate within them. Rudolph Bell's (1985) analysis of "Holy Anorexia" has delineated the historic role of the Catholic church in the creation and social reproduction of themes of shame and obesity, purity and thinness, as they came to be interwoven with the phenomenon anorexia from the thirteenth century on. Feminist scholars (Bordo 1993: Hesse-Biber 1996; Schwartz 1986; Wolf 1991) have argued that the increasing commercialization of the body and bodily needs for the sake of expanding markets has ensured that themes of shame, slothfulness, loss of control, and embarrassment will continue to be associated with fat bodies, particularly fat female bodies. The present study indicates that the cultural meanings of shame associated with the body are not simply residues that exist as historical abstractions.[11] Rather, it is in interaction that takes into consideration the organizational frames that a shame experience is formulated as a social object and given meaning. Organizational frames may be quite variable depending upon the nature, objectives, and ideology within which the organizations attempts to align members' experiences, yet they provide the template in which shame experiences may be systematized in organizational routines.

NOTES

1. Many of the tapes were truncated or contained several short testimonies by members of how OA had helped restore their lives. Yet the tapes yielded little information about the lived experience of the person or how she or he came to OA.

2. The serenity prayer of OA: "God grant me the serenity to accept the things I cannot change; the courage to change the things I can; and the wisdom to know the difference."

3. One of the more recent efforts was bill A 3484 New York State, sponsored by assemblyman Daniel Feldman. The bill was not supported by Governor Mario Cuomo. The event was reported in NAAFA's national newsletter, which commented, "Asked by his interviewer whether questions on the bill had him skating on thin ice with voters who are fat, Cuomo quipped, 'If you are overweight, you shouldn't do that—you're liable to fall through the ice'" (NAAFA 1993, p. 1).

4. On May 23, 1992, NAAFA chapters in five cities launched demonstrations against Southwest Airlines for ejecting a very large man from a half-full flight and for disallowing another large passenger to board after she had already completed one leg of her flight. (NAAFA, 1992, p. 1)

5. I use the term "practically" in reference to the "investment model" of participation, discussed by Rudy and Greil (1987), observing that all organizational members mobilize personal

resources to be used in and by the organizations. This is clear in the case of WW where both time and money represent "sunken costs." Yet it is also the case in OA and NAAFA where members invest time, money, and intellectual and emotional labor to keep the organization operating.

6. The collection of all shame management strategies may be labeled "technique." I have in mind Jacques Ellul's (1964, p. vi) meaning: a "complex of standardized means for attaining a predetermined result. Thus it converts spontaneous and unreflective behavior into behavior that is deliberate and rationalized." Here, the emphasis must be on the idea of a "complex," that is, not only the measurement of food and calories but the restructuring of social relations and development of adaptive strategies for dealing with unexpected situations.

7. Goffman's notion of "cooling the mark out" (1952) would appear to be a rather pervasive form of emotion management found among all types of service personnel. Yet, curiously, in light of a rather extensive citation of Goffman's works, Hochschild (1983) does not mention it. Beyond the management of emotion, the concept of emotion work suggests a range of interactional strategies that might be used in managing the emotions of others. Lying, for example, might be used to "cool out" airline passengers who might otherwise become disruptive.

8. Rudy (1986), in his analysis of Alcoholics Anonymous, observes that "hitting bottom" is ultimately a subjective perception.

9. While some OA members refer to their higher power as "God," others adopt a Durkheimian (Durjheimian 1965) conception of this power, defining it as the social force that exists outside of themselves and abides in the group.

10. Shaming appears to have been a treatment modality that was gaining limited popularity within quite diverse fields. Serber (1970), in his research on behavioral modification among transvestites, referred to the treatment as "shame aversion therapy." Braithwaite (1989) revisited the idea in the concept of "reintegrative shaming" within the context of criminal justice.

11. Pareto observed that "residues" (nonscientific belief systems) rarely mobilize people into action even though they may historically express deep collective sentiments (Coser 1977). My point is that cultural themes such as shame are socially reproduced within concrete episodes of interaction.

REFERENCES

Allon, Natalie. 1982. "The Stigma of Overweight in Everyday Life." Pp. 130–174 in *Aspects of Obesity*. Benjamin B. Wolman, ed. New York: Van Nostrand Reinhold.

Banner, Lois W. 1983. *American Beauty*. New York: Knopf.

Bell, Rudolph. 1985. *Holy Anorexia*. Chicago: University of Chicago Press.

Bordo, Susan. 1993. *Unbearable Weight*. Berkeley: University of California Press.

Braithwaite, John. 1989. *Crime Shame and Reintegration*. New York: Cambridge University Press.

Buss, David M. 1989. "Sex Differences in Human Mate Preferences: Evolutionary Hypotheses Tested in 37 Cultures." *Behavioral and Brain Sciences* 12: 1–49.

Cahnman, Werner. 1968. "The Stigma of Obesity," *The Sociological Quarterly* 9: 283–299.

Coser, Lewis A. 1911. *Masters of Sociological Thought: Ideas in Historical and Social Content.* 2nd ed. New York: Harcourt, Brace, Jovanovich.

Denzin, Norman K. 1987. *The Recovering Alcoholic.* Beverly Hills, CA: Sage.

Durkheim, Emile. 1965. *The Elementary Forms of Religious Life.* New York: The Free Press.

Ellis, Carolyn. 1998. "'I Hate My Voice': Coming to Terms with Minor Bodily Stigmas." *The Sociological Quarterly* 39: 517–538.

Ellul, Jacques. 1964. *The Technological Society.* New York: Vintage.

Ewen, Stuart. 1976. *Captains of Consciousness: Advertising and the Roots of the Consumer Culture.* New York: McGraw-Hill.

Featherstone, Mike. 1982. "The Body in Consumer Culture." *Theory Culture & Society* 1: 18–33.

Gilmore, David B. 1987. *Honor and Shame and the Unity of the Mediterranean.* Washington, DC: American Anthropological Association.

Glaser, Barney G., and Anselm L. Strauss. 1967. *The Discovery of Grounded Theory.* Chicago: Aldine de Gruyter.

Goffman, Erving. 1952. "On Cooling the Mark Out: Some Aspects of Adaptation to Failure." *Psychiatry* 15: 451–163.

———. 1967. *Interaction Ritual.* Garden City, NY: Anchor.

———. 1969. *Strategic Interaction.* Philadelphia: University of Pennsylvania Press.

———. 1986. *Frame Analysis.* Boston, MA: Northeastern University Press.

Hesse-Biber, Sharlene. 1996. *Am I Thin Enough Yet? The Cult of Thinness and the Commercialization of Beauty.* New York: Oxford University Press.

Hewitt, John P., and Randall Stokes. 1975. "Disclaimers." *American Sociological Review,* 60: 1–11.

Hochschild, Arlie Russell. 1983. *The Managed Heart: Commercialization of Human Feeling.* Berkeley: University of California Press.

Horowitz, Ruth. 1983. *Honor and the American Dream: Culture and Identity in a Chicano Community.* New Brunswick,NJ: Rutgers University Press.

Lyman, Stanford, and Marvin B. Scott. 1970. *A Sociology of the Absurd.* Pacific Palisades, CA: Goodyear.

Martin, Daniel D. 1995. "The Politics of Appearance: Managing Meanings of the Body, Organizationally." Ph.D. dissertation, University of Minnesota.

McFarland, Barbara, and Tyeis L. Baker-Baumann. 1990. *Shame and the Body: Culture and the Compulsive Eater.* Deerfield Beach, FL: Health Communications.

Millman, Marcia. 1980. *Such a Pretty Face: Being Fat in America.* New York: W. W. Norton.

Mills, C. Wright. 1940. "Situated Actions and Vocabularies of Motive." *American Sociological Review* 5: 904–913.

National Association to Advance Fat Acceptance (NAAFA). 1990. *NAAFA Workbook: A Complete Study Guide.* Sacramento, CA: NAAFA.

———. 1992. "Southwest Protest: NAAFAns Demonstrate in Five Cities." *NAAFA Newsletter* XXII: 1.

———. 1993. "Cuomo: One Law Too Many!" *NAAFA Newsletter* XXIII: 6 (May): 1.

Overeaters Anonymous (OA). 1987. *To the Newcomer: You're Not Alone Anymore.* Torrance, CA: OA.

———. 1988. *Questions & Answers About Compulsive Overeating and the OA Program.* Torrance, CA: OA.

————. 1990. *The Twelve Steps of Overeaters Anonymous*. Torrance, CA: OA.

————. 1992. *Overeaters Anonymous: Membership Survey Summary*. Torrance, CA: OA.

Perrow, Charles. 1986. *Complex Organizations*. 3rd ed. New York: McGraw-Hill.

Rudy, David R. 1986. *Becoming Alcoholic: Alcoholics Anonymous and the Reality of Alcoholism*. Carbon-dale: Southern Illinois University Press.

Rudy, David R., and Arthur L. Greil. 1987. "Taking the Pledge: The Commitment Process in Alcoholics Anonymous." *Sociological Focus* 20: 45–59.

Schwartz, Hillel. 1986. *Never Satisfied: A Cultural History of Diets, Fantasies and Fat*. New York: Free Press.

Serber, Michael. 1970. "Shame Aversion Therapy." *Experimental Psychiatry* 1: 213–215.

Snow, David A., E. Burke Rochford, Jr., Steven K. Worden, and Robert D. Benford. 1986. "Frame Alignment Processes, Micromobilization, and Movement Participation." *American Sociological Review* 51: 461–481.

Thorne, Barrie, and Zella Luria. 1986. "Sexuality and Gender in Children's Daily Worlds." *Social Problems* 33: 176–190.

Wagonfeld Samuel, and Howard M. Wollowitz. 1968. "Obesity and the SelfHelp Group: A Look at TOPS." *American Journal of Psychiatry* 125: 249–252.

Weber, Joseph. 1990. "The Diet Business Takes It on the Chin." *Business Week*, April 16, pp. 86–88.

Wolf, Naomi. 1991. *The Beauty Myth: How Images of Beauty Are Used against Women*. New York: William Morrow.

Wolfe, Louise. 1992. "Boston 'Free' Party: The Revolution Within; the Revolution Without." *NAAFA Newsletter* 23: 5.

The Social Organization
of Deviance

In Part VI we turn to a closer examination of the lives and activities of deviants. Once they get past dealing with outsiders, they must deal with other members of their deviant communities and with the specifics of accomplishing their deviance. There are several ways of looking at how deviants organize their lives. We start by looking at the relationships among groups of deviants, focusing on the character, structure, and consequences of different types of organizations. These encompass the structure or patterns of relationships in which individuals engage when they enter the pursuit of deviance.

As Best and Luckenbill (1980) have noted in their analysis of the social organization of deviants, relationships among deviants can follow many models. These vary along a dimension of sophistication, involving complexity, coordination, and purpose. Deviant associations vary in their numbers of members, the task specialization among members, the stratification within the group, and the amount of authority concentrated in the hands of a leader or leaders. Some groups of deviants are loose and flexible, with members entering or leaving at their own will, uncounted or monitored by anybody. Others maintain more rigid boundaries, with access granted only by the consent of one or more insiders. Membership rituals may vary from none to highly specific acts that must be performed by prospective inductees, thereby granting them not only membership but also a place in the pecking order once they are inside. In some ways, rigidity inside deviant groups is related to its insulation from conventional society: the more its members withdraw into a social and economic world of their own, the more they will develop norms and rules to guide them, replacing those of the outside order.

Groups of deviants also vary in their organizational sophistication, with the more organized groups capable of more complex activities. Such organized groups provide greater resources and services to their members; they pass on the norms, values, and lore of their deviant subculture; they teach novices specific skills and techniques where necessary; and they help one another out when they get in trouble. As a result, individuals who join more tightly knit deviant scenes tend to be better protected from the efforts of social control agents and more deeply committed to a deviant identity.

Best and Luckenbill outlined a range of ways by which deviants may socially organize. **Loners** are the most solitary, interacting with people, but keeping their deviant attitudes, behaviors, or conditions secret. They lack the company of other, similar deviants with whom they can share their interests, troubles, and strategies. Serial rapists or murderers and embezzlers commit their acts without the benefit of the camaraderie of like others. Many individuals who hold themselves as loner deviants in the real world, however, have been able to find that they are not alone due to the rise of Internet communities. Without jeopardizing their identities and social relations with conventional people, they have found ways to connect anonymously with people who share their deviance, seeking their company and advice. People involved in deviance such as sexual asphyxiates, self-injurers, anorectics and bulimics, computer hackers, depressives, pedophiles, and others, now have the opportunity to go online and find international cyber-communities populated 24/7 by a host of like others. These Web sites offer chat rooms, Usenet groups, e-mail discussion lists, and bulletin/message boards for individuals to post where they can seek the advice and cyber-company of others. Some, such as the "proana" (anorexia) and "promia" (bulimia) sites explicitly state that they reinforce and support the deviant behavior, regarding this as a lifestyle choice (Force 2005). Others, such as many self-injury sites, purport to help users desist from their deviance, but may actually end up reinforcing it by providing a supportive and accepting community where individuals can go when they feel misunderstood and rejected by the outside world, as we note in our own chapter 33 on the cyber-communities of self-injury.

Whether the sites aim to reinforce or discourage the deviance, nearly all tend to serve several unintended functions that have significant consequences for participants. First, they transmit knowledge of a practical and ideological sort among people, enabling them to more effectively engage in and legitimate the behavior. This helps people learn new variants of their activities, how to carry them out, how to obtain medical or legal services, and how to deal with outsiders. Second, they tend to be leveling, bringing people together into a common discourse regardless of their age, gender, marital status, ethnicity, or socioeconomic status (although users do need a computer, and most have high-speed Internet access). Third, they bridge huge spans of geographic distance, putting Americans in contact with English-speaking people from the UK, Australia, New Zealand, Canada, and all over the world.

These interactions, regularly conducted among a range of regular and moderate users as well as periodic posters and "lurkers" (those who read but do not post), forge deviant communities. Participants develop ties to them by virtue of the support and acceptance they offer, especially to individuals who are lonely or semi-isolated. People unable to find "real" friends "FTF" (face-to-face) may come to rely on these cyber-communities and cyber relationships, interacting with members for years and even traveling large distances to meet each other. They may, then, take the place of core friendships. In this way, if in no other, they reinforce continuing participation in the deviance as a way of maintaining membership. The stronger and more frequent these bonds, the greater effect they have on strengthening members' deviant identities. Deviant cyber-communities thus provide a space and mechanism for deviance to grow and thrive in a way that it has not previously had.

Colleagues represent the next most organizationally sophisticated associational form. Participants have face-to-face relationships with other deviants like themselves but do not need the cooperation of fellow deviants to perform their deviant acts. The jump from loners to colleagues is the greatest leap in the spectrum of deviant social organization, as mutual association brings the possibilities of membership in a deviant subculture or counterculture from which people can learn specific norms, values, rationalizations, helpful information, specialized terms or vocabulary, and gossip about people like them. From others they can gain social support, as we see with the expressive groups discussed earlier, and a sense of their position in the status hierarchy of their kind. Deviants organizing as colleagues include the homeless, recreational drug users, and con artists. Colleagues may interact and perform their deviance with non-deviants, such as the lowest-level drug dealers and their customers.

Deviants socially organized as **peers** engage in their deviance with others like themselves, but have no more than a minimal division of labor. Neighborhood gangs who congregate with their friends generally engage in all of the same types of activities, and only see role specialization when it comes to the leader versus the followers. Most peers traffic in a black market of illegal goods and services such as drugs, guns, endangered species, stolen art, and exotic forms of sex.

Especially fascinating to the media and the public is the **crew** form, where groups of anywhere from three to a dozen individuals band together to engage in more sophisticated deviant capers than less organized deviants can accomplish.

Crews fascinate observers because their more sophisticated division of labor usually requires specialized training and socialization, giving them a more professional edge. Bound by their lack of affiliation with other crews, they are dependent on a leader who organizes and recruits them, sets and enforces the group rules, plans their activities, and organizes travel and lodging if they go on the road. Crews usually commit intricate forms of theft, but they may also engage in smuggling and hustling at cards and dice.

The top of this continuum is deviant **formal organizations**, which are much larger than crews and extend over time and space. They may stand alone or be connected to other, similar, organizations domestically or even internationally, as we see with the Cosa Nostra Mafia families and the Colombian drug cartels. Their affiliations may take the form of what Godson and Olson (1995) call "transnational links," where they have regular connections to do business or exchange services with other criminal organizations, or they may have a "global scope," where they conduct extensive operations in various continents through franchised branches of their own organization located in different places, akin to multinational corporations. Much larger in size than crews, deviant formal organizations may have 100 members or more so that when their leaders are killed the group endures. Ethnically homogeneous, these organizations trade in a currency of violence, are vertically and horizontally stratified, and have the resources to corrupt law enforcement. They are the most organizationally sophisticated of the deviant associations formed for purely deviant purposes.

Legitimate individuals and organizations also engage in deviant activities, although these may be their side rather than primary purpose. It is worth noting that while most studies of crime and deviance focus primarily on crime in the streets, a more socially injurious amount of deviance occurs at the top, in the suites, through **white-collar crime**. But the FBI's Uniform Crime Reports means "street crime in the United States." So in this document you will read about burglary, robbery, and theft. There is nothing in it about price-fixing, corporate fraud, pollution, or public corruption.

In the Introduction to Part III, we noted Cloward and Ohlin's belief, advanced in their differential opportunity theory, that access to illegitimate opportunity is unequal. They talked about people from distinct neighborhoods, ethnic groups, and criminal ladders having better criminal opportunities, but their concept of differential opportunity can apply to the privileged as well. White-collar crime is directly related to opportunities to abuse positions of financial, organizational, and political power. We often tend to associate white-collar crimes with strictly financial activities, but they extend to bodily injury and death as well. The FBI estimates that 19,000 Americans are murdered every year.

Compare this to the 56,000 Americans who die every year on the job or from occupational diseases such as black lung and asbestosis and the tens of thousands of other Americans who fall victim to the silent violence of pollution, contaminated foods, hazardous consumer products, and hospital malpractice. These deaths are often the result of criminal recklessness. They are sometimes prosecuted as homicides or as criminal violations of federal laws. And environmental crimes often result in death, disease, and injury. In 1998, for example, a Tampa, Florida, company and the company"s plant manager were found guilty of violating a federal hazardous waste law. Those illegal acts resulted in the deaths of two nine-year-old boys who were playing in a dumpster at the company's facility.

Perhaps the most telling statistic in this field is that the cost of white-collar deviance to the average citizen of the U.S. is much greater than that of so-called street crime. The FBI estimates the U.S. loses $3.8 billion a year due to burglary and robbery versus the loss of $300 to $500 billion a year for health care fraud alone. Yet the perception of many is that we are at a greater risk because of street crimes than those that emanate from executive suites. This is reflected in the justice system: the average sentence for bank robbery is 7.8 years; 2.4 years for embezzling money from the same institution.

White-collar crime can be divided into two main sub-sections: occupational and organizational crime. **Occupational crime** is pursued by individuals acting on their own behalf. Employees at all levels of organizations may steal from their companies, and we have also seen the rise of embezzlement (recently, from the Red Cross) and computer crime. Corporate executives at such firms as Enron, Tyco, and WorldCom looted their companies, shareholders, and employee retirement plans of millions through fraudulent accounting, offshore and dummy corporations, and the manipulation of information to live in high style. Individuals in charge of purchasing for their firms also frequently accept bribes to give business to sales vendors. Ponzi schemes, such as the ones run by Bernard L. Madoff, Allen Stanford, Michael Kelly, the Villalobos brothers, and others defrauded investors by allegedly generating high rates of returns on investments that were secretly generated only by the influx of funds from new subscribers. These are named after Charles Ponzi, the "king of get rich quick," who became a millionaire in six months by promising investors a 50 percent return in 45 days on international postal coupon investments.

In the government sector we see people evading taxes through offshore companies and fraudulent tax shelters, often sold to them by top accounting and brokerage firms who charged millions for these services. Politicians have been caught selling power, especially those in charge of awarding government contracts, such as jailed U.S. Republican Congressman Randy "Duke"

Cunningham, the former Air Force flying ace (who Tom Cruise portrayed in the film *Top Gun*), who had a price list in the tens of thousands for military appropriations. Politicians also sell business to companies (sometimes in no-bid contracts) whose products and services are inferior or if they have a financial stake in their operations, such as we saw with Vice-President Dick Cheney, former CEO of Halliburton, who continued to receive "deferred compensation" from the firm throughout his term in the White House (see the discussion of this in chapter 37), and U.S. Democratic Congressman William Jefferson, who accepted $100,000 to steer contracts to a broadband telecommunications company in Nigeria and hid it in his freezer. Politicians and police officers may also receive individual remuneration for selling immunity from prosecution to criminals and companies, either in direct cash payments or campaign contributions. People connected to the government may also sell their influence, such as we saw in the scandals surrounding former U.S. Republican Congressman Tom DeLay and lobbyist Jack Abramoff, who collected millions from Indian tribes to secure their gambling interests.

Professionals are not above collecting money for their individual benefit, as we see with doctors who accept gifts from pharmaceutical companies to steer their patients towards certain drugs, who overcharge and over-service their patients, and who commit Medicare and Medicaid fraud. Top stockbrokers and their clients make money through insider trading, such as we saw in the Martha Stewart scandal.

Organizational crime, committed with the support and encouragement of a legitimate formal organization, is intended to advance the goals of the firm or agency. Looking at the corporate world, environmental crimes top the list, doubling the next closest offenders. We also see many instances of false advertising, where products are misleadingly alleged to do one thing and either fail to do so or have the reverse effect (air and water purifiers, fire retardants) and fraud, where companies misrepresent themselves to investors and the general public. Antitrust violations are the second most common types of corporate offenses, where companies engage in monopolistic practices to control the market (Microsoft), artificially subsidizing or cheapening their products or services to drive competitors out of business (microchips, airlines), or conspiring with other companies to set minimum threshold prices for consumers (Samsung, General Electric). Corruption among companies with government service contracts is rife, with $5 to $7 billion lost annually during the Iraq war alone. Because of their immense political power, big corporations have the resources to defend themselves in courts of law and in the court of public opinion.

Injury and loss of life may result from unsafe working conditions, such as we saw in the numerous mining deaths of 2005, where governmental regulators let enforcement slide among several drilling organizations to strengthen their business. Widespread illness and fatalities have also arisen due to the working conditions found in nuclear power plants, oil and chemical companies, and pesticide manufacturers. But few Americans realize that when they buy Exxon stock, or when they fill up at an Exxon gas station, they are in fact supporting a criminal recidivist corporation. For every company convicted of polluting the nation's waterways, there are many others who are not prosecuted because their corporate defense lawyers are able to offer up a low-level employee to go to jail in exchange for a promise from prosecutors not to touch the company or high-level executives. Unsafe products represent another area where companies put their balance sheet above the lives of consumers, figuring that it is cheaper to settle lawsuits against them than to fix their goods. Notable offenders are the pharmaceutical companies, the automobile and tire industry, and medical manufacturers. This system continues to thrive because corporations define the laws under which they live. For example, the automobile industry over the past 30 years has worked its will on Congress to block legislation that would impose criminal sanctions on knowing and willful violations of the federal auto safety laws. Now, if an auto company is caught violating the law, and if the cops are not asleep at the wheel, only a civil fine is imposed.

A disturbing amount of government activity also falls into this category, with politicians abusing the public trust, manipulating information, and breaking laws to advance their administrations. In fact, campaign finance represents the third most common area of corporate crime. Yet for every corporation convicted of bribery or of giving money directly to a public official in violation of federal law, there are thousands who give money legally through political action committees to candidates and political parties. They profit from a system that effectively has legalized bribery. American international policy is often clearly tied to the interests of the corporate sector, most notably recently with the oil industry in Middle-Eastern diplomatic and military activities. The K Street project was designed by Republican strategist Karl Rove to engineer a Republican takeover of the lobbying industry, bringing corporate and governmental interests and financial obligations closer together to enrich politicians and favor their contributors. Numerous domestic governmental scandals have erupted in violation of the law such as the Watergate break-in, the Iran-Contra scandal, and the NSA warrantless surveillance controversy. The intervention of the CIA, the military, the FBI, and private burglars into the telephone records, bank accounts, Internet logs, library records, and credit card transactions of alleged terrorists may be acceptable to the American public, but when these things are done in violation of law or directed for political parties against reporters, political opponents, chaplains or lawyers counseling political prisoners, or antiwar activists, they are regarded as very grave indeed. International violations have also been common, with the secret CIA "black site" torture prisons in unknown Eastern European countries, Iraq's Abu Ghraib prisoner abuse violations, and the numerous political dirty tricks and secret assassination attempts. All of these white-collar crimes have led to greater cost, loss of life, forfeit of international prestige, and violation of conventional norms and values than the sum total of conventionally recognized crime and deviance. Yet big companies that are criminally prosecuted represent only the tip of a very large iceberg of corporate wrongdoing.

32

Drug Use and Disordered Eating Among College Women

KATHERINE ANN SIRLES

The intersection between eating disorders and drug use represents a growing form of contemporary deviance. Sirles examines this hidden and highly stigmatized behavior, drawing stark contrasts between her two dimensions: priority (which came first, eating disorder or drug use) and the legality of the substances used (pharmaceuticals versus street drugs). Her resulting four-fold table illuminates several pathways that college women take in adapting to the enormous pressures found in contemporary society, especially among her population, to conform to feminine standards of beauty. You may be alternately drawn to the easy solutions her subjects offer and repulsed by them, but they will not be easily forgotten. This behavior compares to other loner forms of deviance including sexual asphyxia, anorexia and bulimia, embezzling, rape, and physician and pharmacist drug addiction.

How would you assess the relative stigma of each of her four types? How would you assess these in terms of Heckert and Heckert's categories? How do they make you feel about these categories?

When I was an undergraduate sociology student, I read the story of a young woman's long-time struggles with disordered eating. Her narrative had an impact on me, particularly because of her descriptions of street amphetamine use for appetite control. While I was certainly familiar with eating disorders generally, I was awestruck that this young woman reported using powerful, potentially dependence-producing substances in order to control her weight. Entering graduate school, I turned to this topic avidly, and was not surprised to find that sociological research had not previously been used to analyze the relationship between drug use and eating disorders, most prior studies coming from the medical establishment. Sociological scholarship on substance use seemed to focus on

From Katerine Anne Sirles, *Drug Use and Disorderly Eating Among College Women.* Reprinted by permission of the author.

either recreational or medicinal manifestations, of which this specific type was neither. Instead, the use of drugs for weight control struck me as utilitarian, purposeful, and extreme. In addition, the use of substances in this manner was largely the pursuit of women, a population that I was most suited to research. This research reports original research on college women who used licit pharmaceutical drugs or illicit street drugs in an ongoing effort to manage their body weight. My goal was to analyze women's use of these substances as a tool in their attempts to modify their bodies.

Extreme weight control practices, which I term eating disorders or disordered eating, are a serious problem. Although there is evidence that eating disorders have existed since ancient times, before the late 1960s they were virtually unknown to the general public. Diagnosis of anorexia nervosa, bulimia nervosa, and other eating related medical syndromes skyrocketed during the 1970s. As rates of disordered eating increased among young women, the public took notice. Mass media fueled interest in the subject as women began starving themselves, or bingeing and purging. This increased interest led to not only popular reporting of the phenomenon, but also academic scholarship in the field. Since the 1980s, researchers have analyzed problematic eating behaviors from numerous different perspectives.

The majority of research focusing on women's efforts to control and manage their weight has failed to recognize the potentially extreme measures that young women may take in an effort to conform to an American ideal of feminine beauty. Increasingly, women who are or wish to be a part of the "cult of thinness" are turning to street drugs and illegally or unethically obtained prescription drugs in an effort to be ultra-slim. Despite the substantial amount of research in the area of risky weight management, this drug use, both licit and illicit, has not been documented (although see Sirles, forthcoming). Existing literature on the relationship between substance use and weight loss has understood drug use (such as alcohol, depressants, or anti-depressants) mainly as a coping mechanism for the trials and tribulations associated with extreme weight-controlling behaviors. While the exact extent of drug use and abuse is not known, the lack of scholarly inquiry into the relationship between substance use and intentional weight management has left the impression that they were two completely distinct behavioral patterns.

METHODS

In this paper I draw on in-depth life-history interviews I conducted with 57 college age women at a large, public university. This was an appropriate place to study drug use and eating disorders because body image distortions and disturbances in eating were common among college women, and illicit drug use was widespread at university campuses. As women transitioned from high school to college, changes occurred socially, psychologically, and academically. Women's eating patterns, usually set by family in the past, were subject to change, and the pressures at college of academics, dating, and peer expectations were precursors to developing eating disorders. Finding subjects for this study was difficult, as this behavior is hidden by people, even from their closest friends. I gathered a convenience sample of anyone I could find to interview, culling research participants through the posters with which I blanketed the campus and from visits I conducted to many classes (upper and lower division), where I announced my intentions for this project. Participants contacted me via e-mail or phone after my research solicitations, whether they heard about it directly or through others on campus. I pre-screened research candidates before scheduling an interview to insure that individuals currently or historically used drugs, either licit or illicit, for the primary purpose of weight management.

Class rank among participants ranged from freshman to seniors, and also included three recent college graduates who remained engaged in the college environment. Women lived both on and off campus. All participants were between the ages of 18–25, with most identifying as white. As college students, women in this sample represented a relatively privileged, well-educated group, predominantly reporting growing up in either middle or upper-middle class homes. As such, participants fell squarely within the population that has already been identified by researchers as most prevalent among women with disordered eating. I conducted semi-structured interviews that were very open and conversational in the privacy of a campus faculty office or empty classroom, and these usually lasted between one and two hours. After assuring my participants of complete confidentiality, they were more than willing to talk to me about their drug use and histories of disordered eating.

TYPOLOGY OF INSTRUMENTAL DRUG USERS

Participants reported using two distinct types of substances: licit (pharmaceutical) and illicit (street) drugs, all falling into the category of stimulants. The packaging and distribution of these substances varied, but they all shared the side effect of appetite control. Women's goal-orientation (as opposed to recreation or experimentation) in their drug use defined them as *instrumental* users, motivated by the substances' specific effects. Not unlike bodybuilders who used steroids instrumentally, women in this research conceived of their drug use as essentially performance enhancing.

At the same time, instrumental drug using women varied according to the *temporal* nature of their disturbed eating and drug use. Some women reported disordered eating behaviors *before* the onset of their instrumental substance use. For these women, the discovery that there were drugs that could assist them in achieving their body and weight-control goals followed months or years of experience with significant and deliberate weight management. Other participants reported the development of non–normative weight managing behaviors *after* a period of drug use. Generally, these women transformed their personal drug usage patterns from recreational or medicinal into instrumental use. This usually followed positive social reinforcement and personal satisfaction about changes in their bodily appearance. Women who then identified drug use as a

T A B L E   32.1

	Licit Drug Users	**Illicit Drug Users**
Disordered Eating Foundation	Conventional Over-Conformist	Scroungers
Drug Use Foundation	Journeyers	Opportunists

desirable means to maintain or continue weight loss, and perceived the results of their efforts as positive, were compelled to further develop their behaviors. To be clear, I termed the behavior women engaged in first, whether it was drug use or problematic eating, as women's instrumental drug using *foundation*. Table 32.1 introduces the four types of instrumental drug users analyzed in this research:

The first category of women consisted of the "conventional over-conformists." These women reported a history (foundation) of disordered eating prior to their instrumental prescription drug use for weight loss. They were conventional in their choice to use the more socially accepted prescription drugs instead of street drugs. Although they used drugs instrumentally, their overall motivation centered on achieving the cultural ideal of thinness; their goal was conformist. Most of these women's weight management goals evolved from conforming to over-conforming, with an acute fixation on weight that tended to exceed average social expectations for personal body modification. Participants' excessive adherence to ideals of beauty, along with their non-normative means used to accomplish this ideal, distinguished them as deviants (although their deviant means were largely unknown to others in everyday life). Most conventional over-conformists presented as thin, but not too thin, and constituted the largest category in my typology of users ($n = 24$).

The second largest category of instrumental drug users ($n = 13$) were the "scroungers." This group consisted of women who reported a foundation of disordered eating, only later (after the onset of problematic weight control) turning to street drugs for weight control. I call them scroungers because their choice of street drugs represented a much less socially accepted form of substance use. Many of the women conceived of these drugs as "dirty," "unacceptable," or "inappropriate," highlighting their conception of illicit drugs. Their access to illicit substances was customarily not as consistent or reliable as it was for those using pharmaceuticals, leaving them, at times, forced to forage or scrounge for their supply. Generally speaking, however, women reported scarcely more difficulty in obtaining street drugs than was typically expected for illicit substances.

Third, women who used prescription drugs recreationally or medicinally prior to their instrumental use for weight control made up the category of "journeyers" ($n = 11$). This term depicts the journey, or evolution, through which their drug use patterns evolved. While some women in this category reported using pharmaceuticals instrumentally for academic purposes, intentionally gearing their drug use towards weight management shifted aspects of their deviant career in ways that were specific to their body modification goals. For example, journeyers tended to ration their supply of pharmaceuticals in a different manner once weight management became a priority.

The last, and smallest, category was the "opportunists" ($n = 9$). Opportunists were women who initially used street drugs recreationally, and later transformed their drug use into instrumental patterns for weight control purposes. I call them opportunists for the way they recognized the positive social feedback about their drug-assisted weight loss and defined it as an opportunity for the transformation of self. Like journeyers, opportunists engaged in substance use before they turned into instrumental drug users. Opportunists, like journeyers, shifted a wide array of behavioral practices in order to accommodate their instrumental drug use. Opportunists did not necessarily stop using drugs recreationally during their periods of instrumental use; in fact, many participants (not just journeyers or opportunists) reported recreational drug use, some on a fairly regular basis.

SOLITARY DEVIANCE

Some deviance is practiced by individuals alone, away from the company of others. Scholars have conceptualized forms of solitary deviance in a number of ways. Best and Luckenbill (1980) described individuals engaged in deviance alone as "loners." These people did not associate with others "for the purpose of sociability, the performance of deviant activities, or the exchange of supplies and information" (p.15). Prus and Grills (2003) further elaborated categories of individual deviance through their work on "solitary operators" and "subcultural participants." Solitary operators, like loners, acted alone, and did not associate with deviant others. Subcultural participants also acted alone, but their deviant behaviors were heavily influenced by particular group memberships. Other examples of loner deviants include sexual asphyxiates, self-injurers, substance abusing pharmacists, embezzlers, and anorectics and bulimics. While loners deviants lack contact with the company of fellow similar deviants but may victimize others, as is the case with obscene phone callers or violent individuals, the women in this research were completely solo actors.

In Adler and Adler's study of self-injurers (2005: 352), they described loners as "on their own," noting that they "must find the deviance, decide to engage in it, and figure out how to do it themselves." Unlike other forms of deviant associations, where individuals learn from and support each other, loners evolve from conforming behavior to non-conforming behavior without any aid. Such an evolution demanded that individuals singularly create the means and rationalizations for any given behavior. This, in a large way, differentiated loners from other varieties of deviants. They lacked others to introduce them to specific behavior and guide them through the learning process, to offer support and guidance throughout their deviant careers, and to provide them with alternative values and ideals, helping them define and rationalize their behavior. They also lacked help dealing with the practical hurdles or problems of the deviant lifestyle. Instrumental users were unable or unwilling to seek out deviant others, and thus lived without the support that potentially accompanied deviant associations.

Generally, loners subscribed to normative social values, ideas, and behaviors. They were "entrenched" in the dominant culture and "likely, then, to view their deviant acts through the value system of conventionality" (Adler and Adler 2005: 347). This contradiction of normative values and deviant actions was ever-present for women in this research, causing a strain that many felt forced them to keep non-normative behaviors private.

Loners and Secrecy

For the most part, women in this research reported employing lies and secrecy during the course of their deviant behaviors. They were fully capable of engaging in, or at least sharing information about, their deviance with trusted others, yet they consistently chose to keep these behaviors hidden. In an effort to lessen the potential negative consequences (such as labeling) that might result from others knowing, individuals chose the loner lifestyle. Their fear of stigmatization was not the only motivation for keeping behaviors private; many women feared that if others knew about their instrumental drug use, they would be forced to stop.

Women who were motivated to adopt extreme weight control practices needed to look no further than an Internet search on "pro-anorexia" or "pro-bulimia" to find other like-minded individuals gathered in an online community. They could have thus easily sought out the company of like others. Online, in-dividuals were willing to trade tips and tricks for weight loss, explaining and neu-tralizing their behaviors as a "lifestyle choice." However, outside of the anonymous support and camaraderie an Internet community might have offered, women practicing extreme weight control were often embarrassed about their methods. As a result, they went to great lengths to maintain secrecy. This consis-tent drive to conceal their chosen weight control method highlights the extreme deviance of these behaviors.

In addition to drug use, the specific weight controlling behaviors my subjects practiced at one time or another included severe caloric restriction, episodes of bingeing and purging, laxative abuse, cigarette smoking, dishonesty in the course of medical care, and obsessive thoughts about weight and body management. Most of these behaviors were likely to be viewed as non-normative by the women themselves. Although their means were deviant, these behaviors were specifically aimed at achieving an appearance that would be praised and admired by others. Thus women's secrecy did not surround the results of their drug use (i.e., their thinner bodies); rather it centered on their pathways.

Generally, my research participants were high achievers or perfectionists, ful-filling or exceeding societal expectations in a variety of arenas. These privileged and socially accepted individuals included honors students, college athletes, social leaders, award winners, and future professionals. Through their pro-social bonds, ideals, and entrenchment, these women had high levels of attachment, and thus a high "stake" in conventional society. With much to lose, many perceived the con-sequences of being caught and labeled as deviant to be severe, even unacceptable.

Secrecy among Licit Substance Users   Women who engaged in pharmaceu-tical substance use displayed differences from those using illicit substances in their level and intensity of secrecy about their weight control methods. Many college campuses reported high rates of prescription stimulant use, but such behaviors were more socially acceptable when aimed at academic performance (McCabe et al. 2005; McCabe, Teter, and Boyd 2005). Women in this study feared that their instrumental drug use would be too readily associated with disordered eating, which was generally negatively stigmatized by others. For example, Corina, a twenty-two-year-old college senior studying sociology, reported that:

> Um, I don't think anyone knows. I never said anything and um.... I don't really want to. I've definitely, uh, thought about it, like who knows? Who knows? ... But I think mostly I'm being paranoid 'cause I don't know why they would.... Sometimes I talk about using Adderall to study, um, but that's, you know, different. No one cares about that; they'll just ask you if they can have some.

Given that it was relatively easy to hide both pharmaceutical drugs and their ingestion, many licit substance users suspected that no one knew about their use at all.

Pharmaceutical users employed a variety of means for hiding their behavior. Women often employed secrets and lies to obtain their medications. Getting their drugs required them to construct "covers" for their frequent visits to the doctor. Students, who routinely had to visit doctors on campus, did so during the weekdays, spending an hour at the campus health center instead of eating lunch with friends. They created a host of alibis for these visits. Cynthia, a twenty-one-year-old young woman studying biology, spoke directly to this point:

> What would I tell people? Oh I dunno. Ha, I mean it's not that much of a stretch.... Once a month.... I say something like uh, um, say, "I have to get my teeth cleaned." Or "I have a group project meeting in [the dorms]." ... No one, no one thinks, you know, no one thinks too much of it.

Secrecy among Illicit Substance Users When compared to licit substance users, women using illicit drugs reported a different kind of secrecy. The use of street drugs was not only illegal, but it was largely frowned upon socially. Regardless, subcultures surrounding black market drugs have existed throughout history, populated by individuals who, despite dominant cultural proscriptions, engaged in deviant drug use. As a result, illicit drug users had access to others who valued and used, to one degree or another, psychoactive substances. For example, Opal, twenty-year-old college sophomore and cocaine user, told me:

> A lot it's by myself but, uh, you know, I always do, when my dealer is around, uh, not too much, you know, but always some.... I have friends who I sniffed up with but, uh, also people who did not by any means, you know, blow coke, like ever.

Study participants were generally discrete about using illicit drugs in casual everyday conversations with their peers, but were able to let loose in the company of others using substances. Their secrecy surrounded their motivations for using drugs and the regularity of their consumption. Sasha, a twenty-one-year-old college senior, reported extreme reluctance to talk with friends or family who did not use illegal drugs, noting that her family was particularly unfamiliar with drugs:

> Absolutely not, no way, uh-uh.... They would shit. I mean, look, let me tell you that my family is completely against drugs so I don't know why they even let me come to [this school].... Really they just have no clue about anything. They'd be like that woman who thought that a bong was, um, a horn.... If they knew about any of this, well I bet my dad'd say that I was going to end up jumping out of a window.

SOCIAL ISOLATION

As a result of keeping their deviance hidden from others, loners kept an important dimension of their lives secret. Unlike the self-injurers described by Adler and Adler (2005) who wanted to concentrate fully on themselves during the act, these instrumental drug users preferred to be alone primarily so others would not find out what they were doing. Some women reported that they had rituals surrounding drug use which they enjoyed, but isolating themselves during episodes of drug use was a choice. Ophelia, a 21 year-old junior, told me:

> I did coke and stuff at parties; it's not like I have a problem with drugs at all. I mean, I don't really care what people do, whatever. I'd do stuff with my friends and drink. But mostly since I was using all the time, I ended up keeping it to myself because, uh, I don't know. I was embarrassed how much I cared about being skinny.

Many instrumental users feared that if others found out how they were controlling their weight, the benefits others associated with their weight control would be diminished. Women enjoyed the idea that others thought they were "naturally thin." In order to maintain that appearance, they had to keep secrets from their friends and sneak around, creating a wall between others and themselves.

PRACTICAL HURDLES

To manage the impressions others developed about them, the women in my study were forced to navigate the practical problems they encountered in maintaining their deviance alone. Many women identified with the common narratives of eating disorders, but a piece of the puzzle was missing. They lacked access to information regarding substance use for weight control.

Health Consequences of Instrumental Drug Use Very little was known or discussed about the behaviors described in this research. Consequentially, women were left to create their own drug-using systems. These included assessing their health risks, such as how much drug use was physiologically safe. They were forced to rely on self-created systems of interpreting signs and signals regarding changes in their bodies. This began, but did not end, with rapid or excessive weight loss. Carla, a twenty-year-old college junior, discussed some of the other symptoms she noticed:

> Sometimes I can, uh, feel like, my heart beating a little bit faster. Like a little bit.... It definitely raced sometimes, but not a lot.... And it sometimes gives you this taste, um, "metally," in your mouth. That happens when you really don't eat.

When physical signs like these presented, women dealt with them on their own.

While pharmaceutical drug users could mention any physical symptoms to their doctors, many of my subjects felt constrained, often withholding negative information from their doctors in order to protect their prescriptions. Cheyenne, a twenty-year-old junior and former cross-country runner, said:

> These appointments are short, ya know? So I just kinda, um, say things are good, you know, whatever. It's working.... Sometimes in the beginning he would ask me how, uh, or why I thought it was working and I'd give some bullshit story... But it's not like a physical exam or anything.... He doesn't ask too much about my health besides asking about how it's going with my dose.

Since many women went to psychiatrists for their medications, appointments did not generally include any physical exams. As such, any health problems that arose from women's drug use often went undocumented and untreated by the medical establishment.

Illicit substance users, like licit users, most often dealt with health-related concerns that resulted from drugs, on their own. The types of health questions or problems often varied according to the amount of drugs they were consuming. Higher doses or prolonged use often led to greater health consequences. Sammy, a college sophomore, recalled an incident that was related to her drug use and health:

> Well, I passed out once, full on.... I was standing by my closet folding some laundry and I sort of, uh, fell into the clothes that were hanging there. I hit the wall with my head.... Everything went totally black.... But it only lasted like, um, five seconds. It was weird, but it didn't, like, scare me or anything.

Like Sammy, a few participants reported dizzy spells, which were sometimes blamed on caloric restriction instead of drug use. In addition, many women explained that consistent low calorie diets caused feelings of weakness or disconnection.

All participants reported that using drugs had effects on their moods and energy levels. For many, this aspect of drug use was a two-sided coin. First, stimulants gave an initial boost, a general feeling of well-being for a period of time following consumption. However, after time, many women reported that these substances made them irritable or cranky. Savannah, a college senior, told me:

> I'd be gritting my teeth, just so irritated with the world.... You know, especially in the morning, I'd sometimes just feel like shit.... You'd want to stay away from me, trust me on that one.

Reports of mood swings were quite common, and were generally regarded as an annoyance by participants. Stimulants also interfered with normal sleeping and eating patterns.

Financing Drug Use   Another practical problem these women encountered involved financing their drug use. The associated costs varied according to the regularity and dosages of drug use, varying also by specific substances. For example, illicit drug users, who tended to prefer cocaine, faced relatively high street costs for their supplies. On average, women using cocaine reported spending between fifty and one hundred dollars per gram. Pharmaceutical users reported variations in cost as well, but these were generally reported as a per-month estimation, whereas illicit users reported their costs by weight. Prescriptions tended to cost women between forty and two hundred dollars a month.

Supporting a cocaine habit placed different levels of strain on women's finances depending on how much and how often they used, as well as their general financial situations. For some women, money flowed from their families, endowed with hefty enough allowances to support drug use. I asked Odessa, a twenty-one-year-old college student who received such an allowance, if she told her parents what she spent money on. She said:

> They don't really know. I mean, I think clothes and going out or whatever, they don't really ask.... Once my dad found shit in my bathroom though, and he asked me about it. Not money, I mean; he asked about if I was using drugs.... I don't think they know.

Some women, on the other hand, did not have parents willing or able to support them while they were in school. Even those who received moderate support were sometimes forced to finance drugs on their own.

Specific means for securing monies ranged greatly among participants. Many women held jobs while they went to school. Outside employment was not generally full-time, but for many, it was enough to supplement their income. Sally, a junior studying biology, reported a scheme she used throughout college:

> I sign up for eighteen credits, then my parents pay my tuition.... Then I wait 'til school starts and drop classes, so I've got like, uh, twelve credits.... I have it set up so that the refund from that tuition, you know, goes into my bank.... I've done it a few times.... I get a chunk of money.

Contrary to my expectations, participants did not report engaging in illicit drug sales in order to fund their drug use. While a few women had acted at one point or another, as middle-men, "hooking" friends up with drugs, regular systematic dealing was not reported.

Although women did not become sellers themselves, many reported that the more time they spent immersed in drug subcultures, hanging out with dealers or fellow users, the less money their drugs cost them. However, because most illicit users were relatively secretive about the regularity of their use, their dealers were privy to more information than were their fellow drug users. Close relationships with dealers were useful for some women, but price structures for cocaine were still set by the local black market. Accordingly, even though frequent contact with the drug world may have sometimes yielded lower prices, drugs ended up being a major financial cost in illicit users' lives.

Pharmaceutical users' reports of financial strain were very different from street drug users' experiences. Since women did not obtain their substances from the black market, their costs remained relatively stable, depending on how many prescriptions they were filling and what types of pills they received. In addition, many women were able to at least partially, if not wholly, cover the costs of their medications with health insurance. A thirty-day supply of Adderall cost one woman roughly forty dollars. That same supply, same brand, same dose, cost another participant around one hundred dollars. The former had health insurance; the latter paid out-of-pocket.

Financing drug use certainly put constraints on many women. At times, use patterns would be affected by individuals' pocketbooks. Times of plenty enabled more frequent or heavier use. When money was scarce, many women were forced to use less. Plenty of participants reported a regular system for funding drug use. Women used certain amounts regularly and figured out how to pay for their supplies. While some women reported shifts in their use patterns, many participants maintained fairly stable habits for significant chunks of time. The relative privilege of women who participated in this research may have accounted for their ability to continue using. In addition, these types of weight managing behaviors may have been largely self-selected by those who were able to support consistent drug use. For example, there could have been women who employed extreme weight control techniques who would have adopted drug use as well, if not for the cost. Instrumental users' reports of financial strain were common during interviews. However, most did not report money as the cause of significant concern. While one might think that, especially for illicit drug users, finances would eventually force them out of their deviant career, this was generally not the case.

CONCLUSION

The deviant associations reported by the women discussed in this study varied by the legal status of their drug of choice. Although a few pharmaceutical users obtained their pills on the black market, most purchased these drugs through conventional medical routes. As a result, licit drug users were not forced to interact with other drug users. Street drug users were more likely, however, to interact with other drug users, and reported many non-normative associations. While they were not comfortable talking with these people about their drug use for weight control, illicit drug users were at least likely to engage in sociability with other drug users. Yet all of the women discussed in this study hid their instrumental drug use and its relation to their feelings about their bodies and weight. The goals of their drug use, the regularity of their drug use, and the combination of their drug use with their eating disorders shamed them into maintaining a degree of secrecy that kept them from opening up to even their closest friends and family members about this behavior. As such, they were alone with their deviance.

REFERENCES

Adler, Patricia, and Peter Adler. 2005. "Self-Injurers as Loners: the Social Organization of Solitary Deviance." *Deviant Behavior* 26: 345–378.

Best, Joel and David F. Luckenbill. 1980. "The Social Organization of Deviants." *Social Problems* 28: 14–31.

McCabe, Sean E., John R. Knight, Christian J. Teter, and Henry Wechsler. 2005. "Non-Medical Use of Stimulants among U.S. College Students: Prevalence and Correlates from a National Survey." *Addictive Behaviors* 30: 789–805.

McCabe, Sean E., Christian J. Teter, and Carol J. Boyd. 2005. "Illicit Use of Prescription Pain Medication among College Students." *Drug and Alcohol Dependence* 77: 34–47.

Prus, Robert, and Scott Grills. 2003. *The Deviant Mystique: Involvements, Realities, and Regulation.* Westport, CN: Praeger.

33

Cyber Communities of Self-Injury

PATRICIA A. ADLER AND PETER ADLER

Self-injurers, those who cut, burn, brand, pick at, or otherwise injure themselves in a deliberate but non-suicidal attempt to achieve relief by harming themselves, grew from a relatively small and unknown population into a burgeoning but largely secretive group in the late 1990s. Although these people are no longer regarded through the mental illness or suicidal lens to the degree that they were, a strong stigma remains attached to the behavior. As such, they remain, for the strongest part, loners in the solid (or real life) world, hiding or giving legitimate accounts for their scars. Yet the early 2000s saw the rise of online communities of self-injurers, first just as places where individuals could find each other and gain non-judgmental acceptance, but later as support groups composed of like-minded others. Self-injurers thus represent a hybrid associational form, behaving as loners in the solid world and colleagues in the cyber world. Based on extensive online research and 81 in-depth, life-history interviews, the Adlers give us a rich portrayal of these deviant communities and the relationships that form within them.

What do you think this means for the vast numbers of other, formerly loner deviants? Which types of loner deviants are most likely to see the support of others online? Which are less likely? How do you think online support groups might affect their identity and stigma?

Research in the sociology of deviance has characterized different types of deviant acts by the social organization of participants. Best and Luckenbill (1982) have suggested that some deviants organize and commit their acts as loners, without the support of fellow deviants. According to this definition, loners such as sexual asphyxiates (O'Halloran and Dietz 1993; Lowery and Wetli 1982), anorectics and bulimics (Gordon 1990; McLorg and Taub 1987; Way 1995), embezzlers (Cressey 1971), rapists (Scully and Marolla 1984; Stevens 1999), and physician (Winick 1964) and pharmacist drug addicts (Dabney and Hollinger 1999) do not know other individuals who participate in their form of deviance, or if they do, they generally do not congregate with these people and do not discuss their deviance together. This relative isolation requires loner deviants to move into their norm violations on their own, without the help and support of others. They must decide to do their deviance themselves and figure out on their own how to do it. Without the company of others, they lack the benefits of a deviant subculture from which to draw rationalizations and justifications that might help them neutralize their acts. Of all forms of deviants, loners are characterized as those most entrenched in the normative subculture and are most likely, then, to view their deviant acts through a conventional value system.

In this paper we examine people who self-injure, either by cutting, burning, or branding, the majority in the former category. The research draws on 25 in-depth interviews with self-injurers conducted between 2001 and 2004. Participants ranged in age from 16 to 35 and had mostly, but not entirely, given up the behavior. Most self-injury occurred when people were in middle and high school, with only a smattering of individuals continuing past that age. Nearly three-quarters of the people we interviewed were women, and all were white. Subjects were gathered through a convenience sample of individuals who heard, usually on one of our campuses, that we were interested in talking with people about their self-injury. Those who were interested came forward and contacted us by e-mail, asking for an interview. All of the interviews were conducted on campus in our faculty offices, many with college students, friends of students, university employees, or local high school students. If there is a bias in this self-selected sample, it may be that these people do not represent the most severe segment of self-injurers. Conversations with friends and acquaintances who worked in hospital emergency rooms as well as articles and books about self-injury (Conterio and Lader 1998; Favazza 1996; Favazza and Conterio 1989; Harris 2000; Strong 1998) indicate that some people perform more damaging acts of mutilation on themselves than the people with whom we spoke. Our sample, however, likely represents the majority of self-injurers.

Not all of the self-injurers we interviewed were loners. Some cut, branded, burned, or electroshocked themselves in the company of others. The social dynamics and meanings of this kind of self-injury were dramatically different from those in the loner group. In this paper we focus only on the loners, who comprised nearly 80 percent of our sample. We outline the characteristics of loners and describe the way our self-injurers correspond to or differ from Best and Luckenbill's (1982) ideal typical model.

THE SOCIAL ORGANIZATION OF SOLITARY DEVIANCE

People became involved in self-injury as loners for a variety of reasons, including depression, malaise, alienation, and rebellion. For these young people, self-injury provided a form of comfort that assisted them during a stressful period of their lives.

Formulating Deviant Ideology

As loners, people who self-injure were on their own in formulating the mean-ings and set of rationalizations legitimating their deviance. They often drew on their respectable training and experiences, not only to develop their techniques but to develop their rationales as well. We see this in the rationalizations of con-victed rapists (Stevens 1999; Scully and Marolla 1984), for instance, where the men commonly denied the violent and forced nature of their acts and suggested instead that their victims precipitated or desired the incidents. Rapists drew on cultural myths, learned-hypermasculinity, and their sense of righteous entitle-ment to justify their behavior. Self-injurers had a much more difficult time giving social meanings and legitimacy to their acts, which were often, especially initially, unclear and undefined. Natalie, a 19-year-old college sophomore, discussed how she viewed her self-injury:

> I guess at first I didn't think much about it. I knew that it was a source of relief for me, and that was all that mattered to me. And, of course, over time when it becomes more of an issue, and people start noticing it, and other people maybe start commenting on it. And then I had to start thinking more about it and what I was really doing and the con-sequences and what it meant. And I guess just the way that I thought about it was, at first, I was glad that I was able to do it because it made me feel better.

After some time they developed personally acceptable views of their devi-ance. Some people focused on their neatness, that they were able to do it with-out making a mess. For others, control was the issue: they could control where their hurt would be. A common feature that many self-injurers shared was their relationship to the pain. Dana, a 19-year-old college sophomore, talked about her pain:

> The thing with emotional pain—you can't see it! It's all inside. I keep it bottled up inside 90 percent of the time, and people can never, like, quantify emotional pain because it's all inside. And so I try to put a picture to that. That's how much I hurt; I did that to myself. Those cuts, that pain, came from inside here. It's kind of a representation of … I mean, no cut on my body will ever embody what I feel inside, but it's a start.

Kyle, a 20-year-old junior, described how he would say to himself when he was ready to begin an episode of branding, "It's time for some pain."

Social Isolation

For loners, self-injury deviance was personal. Part of the reason they stayed to themselves was that they viewed their behavior as private, not to be shared with others. Unlike people such as embezzlers or pharmacist drug addicts, who had no special feeling of personal intensity about committing their deviant self-injurers, like many sexual asphyxiates (O'Halloran and Dietz 1993), the focus and concentration of being alone while they were engaged in their deviance. It was all about them, and they were focused so completely on themselves while in the act that it would detract from what they could get out of the experience if they did it in the company of others. Dana discussed the feeling she had about her inner-directedness:

> When I hurt like that, I get really self-involved. I get my blinders on. I'm all about me, and don't disturb me ... so that if someone was cutting themselves in my house, even though I do it, I'd be uncomfortable. It's my thing, you know? I'm in control.

When presented with the opportunity to meet or interact with other people who self-injured, many cutters withdrew from or avoided the interactions. While some knew others who self-injured or were introduced to the idea by knowing others who did it, they generally did not want to form a subculture of self-injurers and did not want to know or be responsible for others. When approached in high school by a classmate who tried to bond with her over their cutting, Mandy, an 18-year-old college freshman, rejected these overtures:

> It scared me, I think, more than anything, because I didn't want to be the person she depended on because I didn't feel ready for that. I still wouldn't, even if she came to me today and said that she needed something. I would be like, "I'm sorry."

One of the primary reasons people self-injured was that they were lonely and depressed. Episodes of self-injury tended to occur when people were away from the company of friends and family, often in the afternoons after school or at night. They had time to sit around and reflect, and they felt bad. In thinking back on high school, many people noted this as a period in their lives where they spent a lot of time alone. It is ironic that while people self-injured to avert their feelings of loneliness and depression, their self-injury could exacerbate this condition. This often occurred when they held themselves back from being with people in situations where their scars would be noticeable. Janice flunked physical education, and endured the ignorant jeers of her classmates for it, because she did not want to let the scars on her legs show. Alice described a negative consequence she incurred as a result of her cutting:

> Sometimes I would just, I would not go with my friends to a hot tub at a hotel or something. We were all having a good time, but I would stay up in the room by myself. And then I'd end up in tears up there because I was so frustrated with myself and with the fact that I have to live with that.

Practical Problems

Lacking a deviant subculture, self-injurers often found themselves on their own in coping with the practical problems posed by their deviance. Many of them worried about how to deal with these issues. Dana recalled a conversation she had with a therapist who pointed out some of the auxiliary issues she might have to deal with in the future if she continued with her cutting:

> The practical side to it—how am I going to explain these cuts all over myself in the summer, to my friends? Am I going to go to a job interview with a big scar or a cut on my arm? And that really freaked me out—I don't want anyone to know; no one can know, no!

Many were unable to anticipate what people might say to them or ask them, and they had no ready response when confronted by others. Prior to 1996 questions about scars were not as great a problem, because people could easily explain them away with almost any ridiculous answer, and nobody questioned them. Alice talked about the kind of carte blanche she had as a 12- and 13-year-old to cut without being challenged:

> You know, sometimes stuff that didn't even need to appear very realistic, but people believed it because why wouldn't they? I don't think that many people thought about it when they saw cuts, what if that's self-inflicted?

This all changed, however, when self-injury began to be more widely recognized and people became more suspicious. Longer-term cutters, whose parents had become aware of their behavior, were watched very carefully and often quizzed about their scars. This led them to move their cutting away from their hands and arms to less visible bodily locations such as their stomachs and the inside of their thighs.

In contrast to other forms of loner behavior such as sexual asphyxia (Lowery and Wetli 1982), where participants often shared their knowledge with a nonparticipant who assisted them in their deviance and also helped them keep it secret, self-injurers lacked this type of support. Cutters and burners sometimes told their closest friends or boyfriends about their behavior, but these others usually tried to get them to desist, rather than aiding them. Amy, a 19-year-old young woman working part-time in a hospital while attending community college, recalled that as a burner during high school, she had a boyfriend who cut himself and twice did it when he called her on the phone. Trying to convince him to stop, she said that she would burn herself if he cut himself. Although he denied cutting during the conversations, she felt she could tell from the quivering tone of his voice and the lags in their talk that he was incurring pain. Following through on her threat, she burned herself with a lighter (her preferred method), but this proved ineffective in restraining him. This dual self-injury happened once again, when they both were interrupted by a girlfriend of Amy's who came in, figured out what was going on, grabbed the phone, somehow got in the middle, and stopped them both. Maggie, a 19-year-old college sophomore, described the way a friend of hers who self-injured relied on her for help in restraining herself:

> She'd call me once in a while and be like, "I'm gonna." I told her not to do it, I told her to call me or do something, so she'd call me

sometimes and be like, "I'm in the bath," and I'd be like, "I'm coming to get you," or we'd talk for a long time if I wasn't in a position where I could leave.

Normative Socialization

Another ironic juxtaposition about loners is that according to Best and Luckenbill (1982), they are socialized by society, not by fellow deviants, yet they choose deviance. They choose deviance not because they want to contradict their socialization but because they face situations where respectable courses of action are unattractive or unsatisfactory. Dana described the nature of her inner ambivalence:

> It's not, and I'm not, like, and I never really argue with myself, like, I really want to cut myself but I shouldn't, you know? If I really want to, I do, because it's not all the time, so when it does, I just do it because I'm desperate to feel better, so it's never like, I never, I'm never at war with how I should deal with it, like "Oh, I really want to do it, where's the knife," and my other side being like, "Dana, don't do that." It's always like, one or the other. If I have the urge, I will.

As a result, people who self-injured often condemned their behavior and felt ashamed of themselves. Lisa, a 20-year-old college sophomore, talked about how she viewed her deviance:

> Oh yeah. I was ashamed of myself because it's disgusting and it's not normal, which is OK, but it's just bad to do, I think, to yourself, especially if it's because someone else is hurting you or some other reason. People that do it because someone else is doing it and get a high from it, I think that's sick, too.

Strain

Without the support of fellow deviants, loners are unstable in their deviance, as Best and Luckenbill (1982) have suggested, and they have more difficulty sustaining their deviance over extended periods of time. Ellen compared the isolation of her cutting with other forms of individual deviance such as eating disorders:

> Women hear it all the time. Not so much with cutting, but with bulimia—you hear about it all the time happening, and percentages, and how many women are bulimic and how many women are anorexic. So therefore you, you not necessarily find a common bond with other people, but more like, you know, you know that other people do it. You know that you're not weird doing it. It's not like that with cutters.

For people who self-injured, there was often a structural strain between their normative expectations and their deviant behavior. Some wanted to rebel, yet they did not want to rebel too far. One young woman found an intermediate point for balancing this strain where she could burn herself occasionally but never so much that it endangered her access to the benefits of conventional society. Like many self-injurers, she "drifted" (Matza, 1964) in deviance, keeping one foot firmly anchored in legitimacy while she dabbled in deviance, able to return to a normative lifestyle without unduly damaging her identity.

Another form of strain experienced by loners arose from their lack of fellow deviants who might share their perspectives and reaffirm the meaning of their deviance. A few people we met did have contact with other self-injurers. None cut together, but they had some limited contact. Maggie described the sense of contact she got from two other cutters she knew, one whom she described as a leader and the other as a copycat:

> I don't think they ever sat down and said, "Let's cut together," but I know they discussed it, and they were like, "Oh, I use a razor; what do you use?" you know? And I know they had conversations—while I was never, you know, directly involved in the conversations, I know they happened because of what they said. If I was with one or the other, they would say something that would make me think that they discuss this with each other.

When self-injurers moved away from these relationships, no matter how superficial, they noted how strongly they felt their absence. Lilly, a 21-year-old college senior, traced the demise of her high school cutting to moving to another school where she was away from the presence of a cutting acquaintance. By her own admission, they had not talked about it much. At most they occasionally said things to each other such as, "Had a bad night last night," and this would signify a cutting incident. But in the new environment, she really noted the absence of this support:

> It wasn't that we relied on each other so much. Not at all. But somehow when I was at the new school and she wasn't there, I suddenly felt her absence a lot. It was like it had been propping me up more than I realized. Without her there, I moved away from those thoughts and those feelings and got into a new life easier.

Most loners, then, lacking this kind of support, had difficulty sustaining their behavior over extended periods of time.

DISCUSSION

As loners, self-injurers represent the least organizationally sophisticated form of deviant association. They are on their own without the benefits of fellow deviants to either assist them in their deviant acts or to keep them company in their private backstage moments when they are not engaged in deviance. They thus lack not only the human resources to mount intricate deviant capers characterized by multiple members and differential role specialization but also the basic rudiments of deviant camaraderie to provide social support; a guide to core deviant norms and values; an ideology that offers rationalizations and neutralizations legitimating their deviant acts; information diffusal providing practical, legal, and medical advice; subcultural jargon and stories to enrich the deviant experience; and a system of status stratification to help them measure participants against each other. Although they become absorbed in their deviance, they often find themselves lonely.

REFERENCES

Best, Joel, and David F. Luckenbill. 1982. *Organizing Deviance.* Englewood Cliffs, NJ: Prentice Hall.

Conterio, Karen, and Wendy Lader. 1998. *Bodily Harm: The Breakthrough Treatment Program for Self-Injurers.* New York: Hyperion.

Cressey, Donald R. 1971. *Other People's Money: A Study in the Social Psychology of Embezzlement.* Belmont, CA: Wadsworth.

Dabney, Dean A., and Richard C. Hollinger. 1999. "Illicit Prescription Drug Use Among Pharmacists: Evidence of a Paradox of Familiarity." *Work and Occupations* 26(1): 77–107.

Favazza, Armand R. 1996. *Bodies Under Siege: Self-Mutilation and Body Modification in Culture and Psychiatry,* 2nd ed. Baltimore: Johns Hopkins University Press.

Favazza, Armand R., and Karen Conterio. 1989. "Female Habitual Self-Mutilators." *Acta Psychiatrica Scandinavica* 79(3): 283–89.

Gordon, Richard. 1990. *Anorexia and Bulimia: Anatomy of a Social Epidemic.* Cambridge, MA: Basil Blackwell.

Harris, Jennifer. 2000. "Self Harm: Cutting the Bad Out of Me." *Qualitative Health Research.* March 10(2): 164–73.

Lowery, Shearon A., and Charles V. Wetli. 1982. "Sexual Asphyxia: A Neglected Area of Study." *Deviant Behavior* 4: 19–39.

Matza, David. 1964. *Delinquency and Drift.* New York: Wiley.

McLorg, Penelope A., and Diane E. Taub. 1987. "Anorexia and Bulimia: The Development of Deviant Identities." *Deviant Behavior* (8): 177–89.

O'Halloran, Ronald L., and Park Elliott-Dietz. 1993. "Autoerotic Fatalities with Power Hydraulics." *Journal of Forensic Sciences,* JFSCA 38(2): 359–64.

Scully, Diana, and Joseph Marolla. 1984. "Convicted Rapists' Vocabulary of Motive: Excuses and Justifications." *Social Problems* 31(5): 530–44.

Stevens, Dennis J. 1999. *Inside the Mind of a Serial Rapist.* San Francisco: Austin & Winfield.

Strong, Marilee. 1998. *A Bright Red Scream: Self-Mutilation and the Language of Pain.* New York: Penguin Putnam.

Way, Karen. 1995. "Never Too Rich ... or Too Thin: The Role of Stigma in the Social Construction of Anorexia Nervosa." Pp. 91–113 in Donna Maurer and Jeffrey Sobal, eds., *Eating Agendas: Food and Nutrition as Social Problems.* Hawthorne, NY: Aldine de Gruyter.

Winick, Charles. 1964. "Physician Narcotic Addicts." Pp. 261–80 in Howard S. Becker, ed., *The Other Side: Perspectives on Deviance.* New York: Free Press.

34

Cooks Are Like Gods: Hierarchies in Methamphetamine-Producing Groups

ROBERT JENKOT

With methamphetamine replacing crack cocaine as one of the fastest-growing and most dangerous drugs, national attention has increasingly been drawn to it. Yet meth has not attracted the same demographic of drug users. Coming initially from the West Coast, it became as popular among white, rural populations as inner-city minority groups. Unlike crack, meth can be manufactured using simple (although controlled) chemical substances that do not need to be imported from South America. As such, it represents a more homegrown drug. Jenkot gives us a rare, rich portrait of the social organization and status hierarchies in methamphetamine groups, discussing the various roles in the operation, how some people are brought into them, and how they view their lives.

Why do you think these subcultural groups have such a stronger vertical hierarchy than the support groups from the last chapter? Why do you think methamphetamine is more widely dispersed in the population?

In 1965 members of the Hell's Angels Motorcycle Club found that they could produce the synthetic drug methamphetamine; their efforts provide the first documented clandestine methamphetamine production. The "discovery" of clandestine methamphetamine production roughly coincided with legislation to control its illicit use. Since the 1970s, we have seen an increase in the domestic clandestine production of methamphetamine and a proportionate rise in known methamphetamine use through the 1990s. Little is known about the social relations within the groups that produce methamphetamine. Even less is known about women's social position within these groups.

The present study, part of a larger study of women involved with methamphetamine use, sales, and production, seeks to inform our understanding of the social relations within these groups. This study in particular uncovers the types of hierarchies present within methamphetamine-producing groups. Understanding the types of hierarchies that exist within these groups can shed light on how members of a methamphetamine-producing group function over time as new members arrive, members leave, or new groups are formed. Further, because the sample is exclusively female, some findings will also illuminate how gendered relations are affected by the hierarchies present in methamphetamine-producing groups.

METHODS

This project was approved by the Human Subjects Committee at Southern Illinois University. The data for this study were obtained through in-depth surveys with 31 women incarcerated in county jails in Missouri and Arkansas. Using current lists provided by each facility, every female inmate charged with drug-related offenses (i.e., possession, intent to deliver, maintaining a drug premises) was contacted personally and requested to take part in the study. Two women refused to take part in the study. Each participant selected a pseudonym to allow for confidentiality. Each interview lasted at least one hour, to a maximum of three hours. Most of the interviews were recorded on audiotape; several participants did not want to be recorded.

The average age of the sample was 36 years old, with a range of 18 to 48 years old. One woman was 18 years old. Seven women were between 21 and 29 years old, 12 women were between 30 and 39 years old, and 11 women were between 40 and 49 years old. The sample consisted of 28 white women, 1 African-American woman, and 2 Hispanic women. The majority of the sample, 19 women, were single at the time of their interview; 4 women were married, 4 women were separated, and 4 women were divorced. Of the 31 women involved in this study, 18 stated that they had "cooked" methamphetamine; the same 18 reported that they had sold or traded methamphetamine for money or other items of value. All 31 women reported that they had used methamphetamine at least one time.

Every woman interviewed was employed prior to incarceration; however, their employment status varied considerably. Fifteen women had regular legitimate occupations (e.g., restaurant mangers, retail clerks, and fast food cooks), 11 women were employed in seasonal or family-operated businesses (e.g., drywall installers, roofing companies, and house painters), and the remaining 5 women drifted between low-level minimum wage jobs and/or maintained illegitimate occupations (e.g., methamphetamine production, prostitution).

With regard to educational attainment, 26 women had a high school diploma or a GED and the remaining 5 women possessed an Associate's degree, Bachelor's degree, or some form of post-secondary education (e.g., Med-Tech training, Paramedic training).

The combination of educational attainment and occupation can be considered hallmarks of class standing. The women in this sample can be considered largely lower- to working-class individuals. Many, if not most, had illegitimate income in addition to income derived from their occupations (e.g., illicit drug sales and/or prostitution).

THE STATUS HIERARCHY

The hierarchy within methamphetamine-producing groups focuses on maintaining a supply of the drug. From the participant's comments, every action is connected with the production process or used to rank the people present. Of the 18 participants who had experience as a cook, they all related that a similar hierarchy was present in their group. The responses from these women varied in detail. Annie relates the hierarchy present in her group in great detail from highest status to lowest: Cook, Gas Man/Juicer, Shopper, Dope Ho, and lastly the "simple user." Because Annie's experiences with a methamphetamine-producing group were related in the greatest detail, her comments comprise the bulk of the narrative regarding statuses within these groups.

The Methamphetamine Cook

Annie (a 32-year-old white woman) is 5'2" tall, blonde, currently separated from her second husband, and she has 3 children. She appears to be in good health and claims that the jail food has "bulked" her up. Annie has a long sentence yet appears in good humor. Her good humor was evidenced by the pseudonym she chose. She said that Annie was short for anhydrous ammonia, a key ingredient to the production of methamphetamine. She has earned a college degree and worked as a Registered Nurse and has had paramedic training. Her second husband began sexually molesting her oldest child from her first marriage; she subsequently separated from him. She stated that the stress of the abuse of her child combined with being alone caused her to gain weight. Her weight ballooned to 285 pounds. Annie stated that her existing stress was compounded by her own self-image as being "fat." It is at this point that she contacted an old friend from high school. The old friend and Annie used to use drugs together during high school. It was this old friend who first offered Annie methamphetamine as a means to control her weight and feel better. She initially began to use methamphetamine to escape from her feelings of powerlessness regarding her second husband's sexual abuse of her oldest daughter. As she said, "I had to just [long pause] get my mind off that shit; meth'll do that for ya for sure." A bounty hunter captured Annie; she had multiple outstanding warrants for drugs. Upon her arrival at the jail, she was in possession of both methamphetamine and marijuana.

All 18 women stated that the cook holds the highest position of privilege and prestige within the group. Annie explains:

> If you are a cook you are all set. I mean, like, you could have anything you wanted. You want other drugs? You got 'em. You want a stereo?

You got it. It might be hot, but you got it. Everyone in every group I saw was like tuned-in to the cook. [What do you mean, "tuned-in"?] Well, like the cook is the top dog. Without the cook you'd have to go buy meth on your own—or schmooze [persuade] it outa somebody else.

Reinforcing her experience with methamphetamine-producing groups, Annie clarifies the position of cooks:

Anyway, at the top of the group was the cook. There might be like two or three cooks in a group-like mine, we had, wait, let's see, 5 people who could cook decent dope. Cooks are like gods. I mean everyone does whatever they can to keep the cook happy. Food, stereos, supplies, sex, whatever they want they got.

Annie's recollection of methamphetamine cooks as "top dog" constructs the position of methamphetamine cook as a goal for non-cooks. Attaining this position includes a constant supply of methamphetamine, deference from others, and the ability to have anything you want. This power can be considered economic in nature, with methamphetamine being the currency.

Group members had to learn that the cook was the most valued member of the group. Although learning this may appear to be simple, learning who holds the greatest power within the group aids in the neophyte understanding the entire structure of the group. As Annie's comments continue, we see how members of the group relegate value and status to its members relative to their behavior within the group.

The Gas Man/Juicer

Annie also provides another position in the hierarchy of methamphetamine-producing groups:

Above the Shoppers were the Gas Men or Juicers. [What is a Juicer or Gas Man?] These are the guys—usually guys—that would go get the anhydrous ammonia. It was a real ordeal trying to get anhydrous, if ya fucked up you'd blow up or get burned by the anhydrous. A couple of weeks back I was driving on 55 [Interstate 55] and I saw this car burning on the side of the road and you could smell the, well, it smells special, that smell of anhydrous. They fucked up.

Second only to the cook, whose behavior is very risky and highly valued by the group, being a Gas Man is much more risky. A Shopper (discussed later) can succeed in her or his role by legitimately buying the necessary items while a Gas Man can not. Gas Men run the risk of arrest but also run the risk of injury and death.

The increased risk Gas Men face is due to the need for anhydrous ammonia. Anhydrous ammonia (a key precursor chemical in the production of some forms of methamphetamine) is a "dry" form of household ammonia that is in a gaseous state and when it comes into contact with air, it chemically tries to bond with the water molecules present in the air. If it comes into contact with human skin, it leaches out the water in the skin, resulting in a chemical burn. If inhaled, the anhydrous ammonia will leach out the water in the mouth, sinuses, throat, and lungs, resulting in internal chemical burns. Additionally, anhydrous ammonia is explosive. With this in mind, Gas Men are at substantially higher risk than any other group member who does not handle the substance. The higher risk accords them more status and privilege within the group.

Whereas 17 women noted the status of Gas Man or Juicer from their experiences, 1 woman was involved with a group that did not use anhydrous ammonia. Elizabeth detailed her assistance in the production process: "They needed red phosphorus to cook with, so I would get it for 'em" Elizabeth, (a 45-year-old white woman) is 5'7" tall, blonde, divorced, and she has 2 children. She stated that she was bi-polar and had only received one of her two daily injections to control her condition. As a result she was pacing in the small interview/visitor's room. Although she was very pleasant and talkative, she was apparently agitated, or on edge. She had a high school diploma and worked (until recently) at her husband's restaurant. Elizabeth claimed that her husband was the son of the local mafia boss. As her marriage began to dissolve, largely due to her husband's use of crack cocaine, she stated that her husband had hired a "hit-man" to kill her and that her husband had tried to kill her with a kitchen knife as well. She began using methamphetamine when friends offered it to her husband, as she said, "When in Rome." She was arrested after a traffic stop resulted in the police finding methamphetamine in her purse. She is unable to pay her bond because none of her friends will accept a collect call from jail, and she is too afraid of her husband to call him. As a result, she is just waiting for her case to come to court.

Regardless of the method of producing methamphetamine used, the person who supplied the integral ingredient held a higher status. Again, status in the group is connected with the risk taken by the group member. With regard to the hierarchy Annie detailed, Elizabeth would hold a status about equal with a Shopper and below a Gas Man. Elizabeth explains:

INTERVIEWER: Did you buy it [red phosphorus], or what?

ELIZABETH: Well, I used to think that you bought like a can of it but all you gotta do is scrape off the striker part of book of matches. [You mean the match heads? The top end that you light with?] Oh no! On the actual book, the little strip that you use to light the match. That is where the red phosphorus is. All you gotta do is scrape it away. Takes forever, but you gotta do it just so. I mean if you dig too deep you get paper, but you want all the red phosphorus. So ya gotta do it just so and I was good at it. So I'd lend a hand doing it. I'd sit there for hours scraping away with a knife. We'd have piles of matchbooks but no way to light them! [laughs] [So, you'd watch them cook and just scrape away huh?] Yeah, separating those pills takes a while. So we'd bullshit as I would scrape and then by the time they were ready for the red phosphorus I'd be about done. Course if I wasn't done they'd have to wait for me. Shit I remember once I showed up and there was this asshole scraping matchbooks, I was kinda pissed cuz he was like taking my job ya know? Then Joe [a pseudonym] told him to stop and for me to take over.

Elizabeth's status was reaffirmed when the "temp scraper" was pushed aside by the cook so that she could resume her "job." In order for Elizabeth to perform her task within the production process, she had to learn the techniques specific to the task. How did she come to know that the red phosphorus was contained in the striker of the matchbook and not the match head? She learned this from an existing "scraper."

The Shopper

There are other levels of power and status within these groups, as Annie explains:

Now above the users and Dope Ho's were the people that would actually help out. First ya got the Shoppers. [What did the Shoppers do?] They would go get anything. I mean anything. They'd get the supplies to cook with: pills, buckets, lithium, tubing, whatever. Shit, I remember this one cook's car broke down and she asked for a Thunderbird. So this Shopper I know goes out and steals one—bingo! The cook is happy again. The best Shoppers were the ones who would really put their ass on the line. The ones that used like real money to buy pills were still good and all, but the ones that would hold up a store and take all their pills—now that was great. You still had your cash, and the pills. So I guess there is levels within the levels of power there.

The establishment of a specialized role in the methamphetamine-producing group to obtain the goods requested by the cook reaffirms the formal social structure within the group. In their quest to obtain the requested goods any means were acceptable, even theft. In fact, Annie states that the more risk the Shopper takes, the greater she or he is valued. What is important to note is that Shoppers are integral to the production process within the group.

Brandy (a 42-year-old white woman) is 5'5" tall with dark brown hair; her skin appears to be blotchy, red, and irritated. She is single and has a 19-year-old son. She considers herself to be a functioning addict. She will use a class of drugs (e.g., stimulants or depressants) for a time, then switch to another class of drugs. Much of her drug use parallels what she can obtain via theft and fraud. She has an off-putting personality and is not very talkative. When she responds to a question it is usually a one-word response. Further probing gains little additional information. She is currently in jail for cooking methamphetamine in her house.

Brandy could produce methamphetamine on her own, but often chose to be an assistant. As she stated, "I would shop a lot, you know go get the pills. Truck stops are great for that, plus you get to go on a nice drive!" Additionally, she would, "... just lend a hand here or there."

Each of the 18 women spoke of their group having at least 1 Shopper; some groups had up to 4 Shoppers. As they described the behaviors of these group members, they echoed Annie's comments. If members of the group wanted anything, especially the cook, the shopper was the person slated to obtain it.

The Dope Ho

Although "simple users" may be at the bottom of the methamphetamine group hierarchy, another status, Dope Ho, is only slightly above them. Most of the participants knew Dope Ho's (15 of the 18 participants); the remaining 3 had heard of men and women trading sex for drugs but had never personally experienced the phenomena. Annie explains the in-group social position of Dope Ho's:

> Along with users are Dope Ho's. Now Dope Ho's are not a problem really. They are around just to trade a blow or a lay for some meth. They are ALWAYS there. Like I said, they are not a problem like the users but they really don't do anything to help out. Dope Ho's are like baggage, they are there taking up space. Now some guy cooking meth would like to have 'em. [Why would guy cooks like them?] OH! Well, the Dope Ho's take care of the cook, with sex. They are not there for everyone to fuck, just the cook. So, like guys are right, they always wanna get laid so the Dope Ho's handle that. You know, there might be a few Dope Ho's at a time. It's funny, it's like the cook has a choice who he's gonna bang, "No, not her, not her, yeah I'll bang her today!" That sort of thing.

Positions similar to that of a Dope Ho are not unique among drug-using groups. We know about people trading sex for crack cocaine, even for a hit of that drug. However, with regard to crack cocaine, many of these women are prostitutes who trade sex with "Johns" for the drug that they hold. As Annie reports, Dope Ho's are accepted members of the group unlike the "simple users." Dope Ho's function to keep the cook happy (sexually), which aids in the production process. The fascinating thing about the presence of Dope Ho's is how this (usually) heterosexual relationship interacts with other heterosexual relationships.

INTERVIEWER: What about a wife or girlfriend? Wouldn't they get mad? Or were the wives and girlfriends of these guys the Dope Ho's?

ANNIE: Nah, they were nobody's girlfriend or wife, just Ho's. Nobody really cared about them either, they were just always there. They were cool and all, just kinda looked down at, I mean, shit, you know, they were tradin' a blowjob for a buzz—not a bag of Dope, just a buzz. Kinda sad now that I think of it.

INTERVIEWER: Were there guys as Dope Ho's too?

ANNIE: Yeah, I saw a few and heard of more. But, you know how girls are, they can get laid anytime they want and they don't have to give meth away to get laid! Guys will jump on anything, anytime—"sex? I'll do it!"—so why have the burden of carrying someone else's habit just to get laid. Still, some chicks would have some around but it was not like normal to see Guy-Ho's.

Annie's comments regarding the relationship between Dope Ho's and men are important. As Annie said, "nobody really cared about them," indicating that Dope Ho's hold a certain status within the group. They occupy a low status position in which they are marginalized to such a degree that wives and girl-friends apparently do not consider them threats to their monogamous relationship with the male cooks.

To hear Annie talk about Dope Ho's, her inflection is important; these people are looked down on. However, the status of Dope Ho can be considered slightly higher than that of the "pain in the ass" user.

The User of Methamphetamine

Every women involved in this project agreed that the position that lacks any prestige is that of the simple user. Annie provides a very clear image of the user:

> At the bottom were the users. These were the people that just wanted to buy meth if ya think of the most strung out, tweeked freaks, that is the user. They are not really in the group. I mean, we all know them, but they are more of a pain in the ass. They always show up at the worst times. They show up when the batch [of methamphetamine] ain't done yet. They show up when you wanna sleep. They show up, well just like a pain in the ass, there is no good time.

The presence of users in a group creates the issue of risk and trust as being at odds with each other. Members of the group know the users or else they would not be allowed to socialize with the group. However, these people also pose a risk if they are undercover police officers or user-informers. Users are a burden to the group.

Users Versus Simple Users

It is important to differentiate between the types of methamphetamine users: users and "simple users." All of the participants in this study had used methamphetamine at some point in their lives. Most of the methamphetamine cooks (16 of the 18 cooks) were also current methamphetamine users. However, those women who took part, in whatever way, in the production process held a status above the "simple user." The "simple user" only uses the drug. The methamphetamine user is part of the group; the "simple user" is a "pain in the ass," meaning not part of the group.

As Annie (and others) relate, there is a distinct hierarchy within methamphetamine-using groups. Status within these groups is related to the activity regarding the methamphetamine production process. The greater the involvement and/or risk with the production process, the higher the status. Other participants in this study provided information on the process of upward mobility in the group as well as some variations of the statuses in these groups.

In-Group Mobility and Status Variations

There is a process involved in the production of methamphetamine. This process includes multiple people performing specific tasks. The performance of these tasks relates to the performance of social roles in the group. Brandy stated that she was able to cook, purchase the pills used as the base for the drug, and help out where needed. Other tasks that need to be completed in order for the meth-amphetamine production to be successful include: obtaining key precursor chemicals (P2P, red phosphorus, or anhydrous ammonia), obtaining the other items and compounds used in the production process (containers, lithium, hydrochloric acid, and hot plates), and the actual production of methamphetamine. These associations form a peer group for Brandy where she would, "… shop a lot." Her performance at this task was positive for the group and she was not stopped from doing it. Because she was able to cook methamphetamine as well, she was able—and allowed—to perform other functions.

The key point to understand is that these groups grow and splinter into networks that maintain some degree of association with each other. In these groups, gender differences fade as the actor rises in status within the group. Once the status of cook has been achieved, the drive for quality drugs equalizes the gender disparity evident at lower levels of these methamphetamine production groups.

Annie knew how to cook and did so frequently. However, she would also take part in schemes to obtain anhydrous ammonia, illustrating her mobility within her group. She has earned the highest status, but was able to choose to work at a lower status. For example, Annie stated:

> Me and another girl would get all dolled up and go to farmers' houses. We'd knock on the door, wiggle, wink, giggle and shit. Then just ask if we could have some anhydrous. That always worked. [So would you be treated as a Juicer when you did that?] Fuck no! [laughs] Shit once you can cook you are golden, you know. I was just helpin' out. Now the guy we was with, he was the Juicer. [What about the woman you went with?] Well, actually she was a Dope Ho. But she was cool.

Status can be earned by working with other members of the group and learning by their example. However, a formal learning process also takes place within methamphetamine-using groups. Cammy (a 42-year-old white woman) is 5'3" tall with brown hair and lives in a suburban area. She is fairly thin, but not as thin as some of the women in this study. Cammy appeared to be depressed and sad about her current situation. She was willing to take part in the interview, yet would often reply with one-word answers and little more when prodded. She did not want to say if she had any children, but she was separated from her husband. Her arrest occurred at a methamphetamine lab raided by the police. She possessed marijuana. Cammy illustrates how she learned to cook within the structure of the methamphetamine-producing group when she states:

> I was livin' with this cook, right? We was jus' like in the same house, not fuckin' or nothin'. OK, so I know how to cook but not real good. I asks this guy, don't wanna say his name, if he can teach my boyfriend to cook, right? So he's like, "cool," right? OK, so he's showin' my man how to cook and I am learnin' too, right? OK, so like now we both are cooks and we get our own thing goin' and we cook like crazy! It was cool.

Cammy, due to her status with her house-mate and as a cook, was able to bring her non-cooking boyfriend up in status. Once she and her boyfriend were both cooks, their position within their group was solidified; however, shortly afterward they left this group to form their own group. In their new group they were able to complete all of the functions necessary to produce methamphetamine. Cammy's experiences provide us with a way that methamphetamine groups spread. As the unique knowledge is disseminated so too do the groups that hold this knowledge spread. It should be clear that these groups will be connected in a network of multiple cells of methamphetamine production.

The goal for these groups is the production of methamphetamine, not its sale. The various members of the group operate within a hierarchy where a neophyte can be upwardly mobile within the group, roles are defined, and power and prestige are linked to the status one holds. Interestingly, because the goal is paramount, in these groups they are more willing to dispose of social constructs valid in the dominant culture in order to further their goal. As a result, women who move up in the hierarchy of the production process are not stigmatized for the roles they play. Instead, women appear to become, or perceive themselves to be, the equals of their male counterparts.

35

Gender and Victimization Risk among Young Women in Gangs

JODY MILLER

Miller offers a glimpse into the contemporary urban world of street gangs in this analysis of the role and dangers faced by female gang members. Gang members not only associate together, they need each others' participation in the deviant act to function (no man or woman is a gang unto him or herself). Once nearly faded to obscurity, gangs made a rebound in American society in the late 1980s, fueled by the drug economy and the increasing economic plight of urban areas. Since that time they have evolved considerably, adding sophisticated nuances and female members. Miller finds that while women gain status, social life, and some protection from the hazards of street life in joining gangs, they exchange this for a new set of dangers. By entering the gang world, they are exposing themselves to violence, both from rival gang members as well as their own homeboys. Miller discusses the particularly gendered status dilemmas and risks for these young women, and how these vary depending on their activities, stance, and associations within the group.

How do the gender relations in these gangs compare with those in the meth-producing groups? What factors do you think give women greater power and status in the last chapter but so little in this one?

An underdeveloped area in the gang literature is the relationship between gang participation and victimization risk. There are notable reasons to consider the issue significant. We now have strong evidence that delinquent lifestyles are associated with increased risk of victimization (Lauritsen, Sampson, and Laub 1991). Gangs are social groups that are organized around delinquency (see Klein 1995), and participation in gangs has been shown to escalate youth's involvement

From Jody Miller, "Gender and Victimization Risk Among Young Women in Gangs."
Journal of Research in Crime & Delinquency (Vol. 35, Issue 4). Copyright © 1998. Reprinted by permission of Sage Publications, Inc.

in crime, including violent crime (Esbensen and Huizinga 1993; Esbensen, Huizinga, and Weiher 1993; Fagan 1989, 1990; Thornberry et al. 1993). Moreover,
research on gang violence indicates that the primary targets of this violence are
other gang members (Block and Block 1993; Decker 1996; Klein and Maxson
1989; Sanders 1993). As such, gang participation can be recognized as a delinquent lifestyle that is likely to involve high risks of victimization (see Huff
1996: 97). Although research on female gang involvement has expanded in
recent years and includes the examination of issues such as violence and victimization, the oversight regarding the relationship between gang participation and
violent victimization extends to this work as well.

The coalescence of attention to the proliferation of gangs and gang violence
(Block and Block 1993; Curry, Ball, and Decker 1996; Decker 1996; Klein 1995;
Klein and Maxson 1989; Sanders 1993), and a possible disproportionate rise in
female participation in violent crimes more generally (Baskin, Sommers, and
Fagan 1993; but see Chesney-Lind, Shelden, and Joe 1996), has led to a specific
concern with examining female gang members' violent activities. As a result,
some recent research on girls in gangs has examined these young women's participation in violence and other crimes as offenders (Bjerregaard and Smith 1993;
Brotherton 1996; Fagan 1990; Lauderback, Hansen, and Waldorf 1992; Taylor,
1993). However, an additional question worth investigation is what relationships
exist between young women's gang involvement and their experiences and risk of
victimization. Based on in-depth interviews with female gang members, this article
examines the ways in which gender shapes victimization risk within street gangs....

METHODOLOGY

Data presented in this article come from survey and semistructured in-depth interviews with 20 female members of mixed-gender gangs in Columbus, Ohio.
The interviewees ranged in age from 12 to 17; just over three-quarters were
African American or multiracial (16 of 20), and the rest (4 of 20) were White.
The sample was drawn primarily from several local agencies in Columbus working with at-risk youths, including the county juvenile detention center, a shelter
care facility for adolescent girls, a day school within the same institution, and a
local community agency.[1] The project was structured as a gang/nongang comparison, and I interviewed a total of 46 girls. Gang membership was determined
during the survey interview by self-definition: About one-quarter of the way
through the 50+ page interview, young women were asked a series of questions
about the friends they spent time with. They then were asked whether these
friends were gang involved and whether they themselves were gang members.
Of the 46 girls interviewed, 21 reported that they were gang members[2] and an
additional 3 reported being gang involved (hanging out primarily with gangs or
gang members) but not gang members. The rest reported no gang involvement.

The survey interview was a variation of several instruments currently being
used in research in a number of cities across the United States and included a

broad range of questions and scales measuring factors that may be related to gang membership.[3] On issues related to violence, it included questions about peer activities and delinquency, individual delinquent involvement, family violence and abuse, and victimization. When young women responded affirmatively to being gang members, I followed with a series of questions about the nature of their gang, including its size, leadership, activities, symbols, and so on. Girls who admitted gang involvement during the survey participated in a follow-up interview to talk in more depth about their gangs and gang activities. The goal of the in-depth interview was to gain a greater understanding of the nature and meanings of gang life from the point of view of its female members. A strength of qualitative interviewing is its ability to shed light on this aspect of the social world, highlighting the meanings individuals attribute to their experiences (Adler and Adler 1987; Glassner and Loughlin 1987; Miller and Glassner 1997). In addition, using multiple methods, including follow-up interviews, provided me with a means of detecting inconsistencies in young women's accounts of their experiences. Fortunately, no serious contradictions arose. However, a limitation of the data is that only young women were interviewed. Thus, I make inferences about gender dynamics, and young men's behavior, based only on young women's perspectives.

GENDER, GANGS, AND VIOLENCE

Gangs as Protection and Risk

An irony of gang involvement is that although many members suggest one thing they get out of the gang is a sense of protection (see also Decker 1996; Joe and Chesney-Lind 1995; Lauderback et al. 1992), gang membership itself means exposure to victimization risk and even a willingness to be victimized. These contradictions are apparent when girls talk about what they get out of the gang, and what being in the gang means in terms of other members' expectations of their behavior. In general, a number of girls suggested that being a gang member is a source of protection around the neighborhood. Erica,[4] a 17-year-old African American, explained, "It's like people look at us and that's exactly what they think, there's a gang, and they respect us for that. They won't bother us.... It's like you put that intimidation in somebody." Likewise, Lisa, a 14-year-old White girl, described being in the gang as empowering: "You just feel like, oh my God, you know, they got my back. I don't need to worry about it." Given the violence endemic in many inner-city communities, these beliefs are understandable, and to a certain extent, accurate.

In addition, some young women articulated a specifically gendered sense of protection that they felt as a result of being a member of a group that was predominantly male. Gangs operate within larger social milieus that are characterized by gender inequality and sexual exploitation. Being in a gang with young men means at least the semblance of protection from, and retaliation against, predatory men in the social environment. Heather, a 15-year-old White girl, noted, "You feel more secure when, you know, a guy's around protectin' you, you know, than you would a girl." She explained that as a gang member, because "you get protected by guys ... not as many people mess with you." Other young women concurred and also described that male gang members could retaliate against specific acts of violence against girls in the gang. Nikkie, a 13-year-old African American girl, had a friend who was raped by a rival gang member, and she said, "It was a Crab [Crip] that raped my girl in Miller Ales, and, um, they was ready to kill him." Keisha, an African American 14-year-old, explained, "If I got beat up by a guy, all I gotta do is go tell one of the niggers, you know what I'm sayin'? Or one of the guys, they'd take care of it."

At the same time, members recognized that they may be targets of rival gang members and were expected to "be down" for their gang at those times even when it meant being physically hurt. In addition, initiation rites and internal rules were structured in ways that required individuals to submit to, and be exposed to, violence. For example, young women's descriptions of the qualities they valued in members revealed the extent to which exposure to violence was an expected element of gang involvement. Potential members, they explained, should be tough, able to fight and to engage in criminal activities, and also should be loyal to the group and willing to put themselves at risk for it. Erica explained that they didn't want "punks" in her gang: "When you join something like that, you might as well expect that there's gonna be fights.... And, if you're a punk, or if you're scared of stuff like that, then don't join." Likewise, the following dialogue with Cathy, a white 16-year-old, reveals similar themes. I asked her what her gang expected out of members and she responded, "to be true to our gang and to have our backs." When I asked her to elaborate, she explained,

CATHY: Like, uh, if you say you're a Blood, you be a Blood. You wear your rag even when you're by yourself. You know, don't let anybody intimidate you and be like, "Take that rag off." You know, "You better get with our set." Or something like that.

JM: OK. Anything else that being true to the set means?

CATHY: Um. Yeah, I mean, just, just, you know, I mean it's, you got a whole bunch of people comin' up in your face and if you're by yourself they ask you what's your claimin', you tell 'em. Don't say, "Nothin'."

JM: Even if it means getting beat up or something?

CATHY: Mmhmm.

One measure of these qualities came through the initiation process, which involved the individual submitting to victimization at the hands of the gang's members. Typically this entailed either taking a fixed number of "blows" to the head and/or chest or being "beat in" by members for a given duration (e.g., 60 seconds). Heather described the initiation as an important event for determining whether someone would make a good member:

When you get beat in if you don't fight back and if you just like stop and you start cryin' or somethin' or beggin' 'em to stop and stuff like that, then, they ain't gonna, they'll just stop and they'll say that you're not gang material because you gotta be hard, gotta be able to fight, take punches.

In addition to the initiation, and threats from rival gangs, members were expected to adhere to the gang's internal rules (which included such things as not fighting with one another, being "true" to the gang, respecting the leader, not spreading gang business outside the gang, and not dating members of rival gangs). Breaking the rules was grounds for physical punishment, either in the form of a spontaneous assault or a formal "violation," which involved taking a specified number of blows to the head. For example, Keisha reported that she talked back to the leader of her set and "got slapped pretty hard" for doing so. Likewise, Veronica, an African American 15-year-old, described her leader as "crazy, but we gotta listen to 'im. He's just the type that if you don't listen to 'im, he gonna blow your head off. He's just crazy."

It is clear that regardless of members' perceptions of the gang as a form of "protection," being a gang member also involves a willingness to open oneself up to the possibility of victimization. Gang victimization is governed by rules and expectations, however, and thus does not involve the random vulnerability that being out on the streets without a gang might entail in high-crime neighborhoods. Because of its structured nature, this victimization risk may be perceived as more palatable by gang members. For young women in particular, the gendered nature of the streets may make the empowerment available through gang involvement an appealing alternative to the individualized vulnerability they otherwise would face. However, as the next sections highlight, girls' victimization risks continue to be shaped by gender, even within their gangs, because these groups are structured around gender hierarchies as well.

Gender and Status, Crime and Victimization

Status hierarchies within Columbus gangs, like elsewhere, were male dominated (Bowker, Gross, and Klein 1980; Campbell 1990). Again, it is important to highlight that the structure of the gangs these young women belonged to—that is, male-dominated, integrated mixed-gender gangs—likely shaped the particular ways in which gender dynamics played themselves out. Autonomous female gangs, as well as gangs in which girls are in auxiliary subgroups, may be shaped by different gender relations, as well as differences in orientations toward status, and criminal involvement.

All the young women reported having established leaders in their gang, and this leadership was almost exclusively male. While LaShawna, a 17-year-old African American, reported being the leader of her set (which had a membership that is two-thirds girls, many of whom resided in the same residential facility as her), all the other girls in mixed-gender gangs reported that their Original Gangster was male. In fact, a number of young women stated explicitly that only male gang members could be leaders. Leadership qualities, and qualities attributed to high-status members of the gang—being tough, able to fight, and willing to "do dirt" (e.g., commit crime, engage in violence) for the gang—were perceived as characteristically masculine. Keisha noted, "The guys, they just harder." She explained, "Guys is more rougher. We have our G's back but, it ain't gonna be like the guys, they just don't give a fuck. They gonna shoot you in a minute." For the most part, status in the gang was related to traits such as the willingness to use serious violence and commit dangerous crimes and, though not exclusively, these traits were viewed primarily as qualities more likely and more intensely located among male gang members.

Because these respected traits were characterized specifically as masculine, young women actually may have had greater flexibility in their gang involvement than young men. Young women had fewer expectations placed on them—by both their male and female peers—in regard to involvement in criminal activities such as fighting, using weapons, and committing other crimes. This tended to decrease girls' exposure to victimization risk comparable to male members, because they were able to avoid activities likely to place them in danger. Girls *could* gain status in the gang by being particularly hard and true to the set. Heather, for example, described the most influential girl in her set as "the hardest girl, the one that don't take no crap, will stand up to anybody." Likewise, Diane, a white 15-year-old, described a highly respected female member in her set as follows:

> People look up to Janeen just 'cause she's so crazy. People just look up to her 'cause she don't care about nothin'. She don't even care about makin' money. Her, her thing is, "Oh, you're a Slob [Blood]? You're a Slob? You talkin' to me? You talkin' shit to me?" Pow, pow! And that's it. That's it.

However, young women also had a second route to status that was less available to young men. This came via their connections—as sisters, girlfriends, cousins—to influential, high-status young men.[5] In Veronica's set, for example, the girl with the most power was the OG's "sister or his cousin, one of 'em." His girlfriend also had status, although Veronica noted that "most of us just look up to our OG." Monica, a 16-year-old African American, and Tamika, a 15-year-old African American, both had older brothers in their gangs, and both reported getting respect, recognition, and protection because of this connection. This route to status and the masculinization of high-status traits functioned to maintain gender inequality within gangs, but they also could put young women at less risk of victimization than young men. This was both because young women were perceived as less threatening and thus were less likely to be targeted by rivals, and because they were not expected to prove themselves in the ways that young men were, thus decreasing their participation in those delinquent activities likely to increase exposure to violence. Thus, gender inequality could have a protective edge for young women.

Young men's perceptions of girls as lesser members typically functioned to keep girls from being targets of serious violence at the hands of rival young men, who instead left routine confrontations with rival female gang members to the girls in their own gang. Diane said that young men in her gang "don't wanna waste their time hittin' on some little girls. They're gonna go get their little cats [females] to go get 'em." Lisa remarked,

> Girls don't face much violence as [guys]. They see a girl, they say, "we'll just smack her and send her on." They see a guy—'cause guys are like a lot more into it than girls are, I've noticed that—and they like, well, "we'll shoot him."

In addition, the girls I interviewed suggested that, in comparison with young men, young women were less likely to resort to serious violence, such as that involving a weapon, when confronting rivals. Thus, when girls' routine confrontations were more likely to be female on female than male on female, girls' risk of serious victimization was lessened further.

Also, because participation in serious and violent crime was defined primarily as a masculine endeavor, young women could use gender as a means of avoiding participation in those aspects of gang life they found risky, threatening, or morally troubling. Of the young women I interviewed, about one-fifth were involved in serious gang violence: A few had been involved in aggravated assaults on rival gang members, and one admitted to having killed a rival gang member, but they were by far the exception. Most girls tended not to be involved in serious gang crime, and some reported that they chose to exclude themselves because they felt ambivalent about this aspect of gang life. Angie, an African American 15-year-old, explained,

> I don't get involved like that, be out there goin' and just beat up people like that or go stealin', things like that. That's not me. The boys, mostly the boys do all that, the girls we just sit back and chill, you know.

Likewise, Diane noted,

> For maybe a drive-by they might wanna have a bunch of dudes. They might not put the females in that. Maybe the females might be weak inside, not strong enough to do something like that, just on the insides.... If a female wants to go forward and doin' that, and she wants to risk her whole life for doin' that, then she can. But the majority of the time, that job is given to a man.

Diane was not just alluding to the idea that young men were stronger than young women. She also inferred that young women were able to get out of committing serious crime, more so than young men, because a girl shouldn't have to "risk her whole life" for the gang. In accepting that young men were more central members of the gang, young women could more easily participate in gangs without putting themselves in jeopardy—they could engage in the more routine, everyday activities of the gang, like hanging out, listening to music, and smoking bud (marijuana). These male-dominated mixed-gender gangs thus appeared to provide young women with flexibility in their involvement in gang activities. As a result, it is likely that their risk of victimization at the hands of rivals was less than that of young men in gangs who were engaged in greater amounts of crime.

Girls' Devaluation and Victimization

In addition to girls choosing not to participate in serious gang crimes, they also faced exclusion at the hands of young men or the gang as a whole (see also Bowker et al. 1980). In particular, the two types of crime mentioned most frequently as "off-limits" for girls were drug sales and drive-by shootings. LaShawna explained, "We don't really let our females [sell drugs] unless they really wanna and they know how to do it and not to get caught and every thing." Veronica described a drive-by that her gang participated in and said, "They wouldn't let us [females] go. But we wanted to go, but they wouldn't let us." Often, the exclusion was couched in terms of protection. When I asked Veronica why the girls couldn't go, she said, "so we won't go to jail if they was to get caught. Or if one of 'em was to get shot, they wouldn't want it to happen to us." Likewise, Sonita, a 13-year-old African American, noted, "If they gonna do somethin' bad and they think one of the females gonna get hurt they don't let 'em do it with them…. Like if they involved with shooting or whatever, [girls] can't go."

Although girls' exclusion from some gang crime may be framed as protective (and may reduce their victimization risk vis-à-vis rival gangs), it also served to perpetuate the devaluation of female members as less significant to the gang—not as tough, true, or "down" for the gang as male members. When LaShawna said her gang blocked girls' involvement in serious crime, I pointed out that she was actively involved herself. She explained, "Yeah, I do a lot of stuff 'cause I'm tough. I likes, I likes messin' with boys. I fight boys. Girls ain't nothin' to me." Similarly, Tamika said, "girls, they little peons."

Some young women found the perception of them as weak a frustrating one. Brandi, an African American 13-year-old, explained, "Sometimes I dislike that the boys, sometimes, always gotta take charge and they think, sometimes, that the girls don't know how to take charge 'cause we're like girls, we're females, and like that." And Chantell, an African American 14-year-old, noted that rival gang members "think that you're more of a punk." Beliefs that girls were weaker than boys meant that young women had a harder time proving that they were serious about their commitment to the gang. Diane explained,

> A female has to show that she's tough. A guy can just, you can just look at him. But a female, she's gotta show. She's gotta go out and do some dirt. She's gotta go whip some girl's ass, shoot somebody, rob somebody or something. To show that she is tough.

In terms of gender-specific victimization risk, the devaluation of young women suggests several things. It could lead to the mistreatment and victimization of girls by members of their own gang when they didn't have specific male protection (i.e., a brother, boyfriend) in the gang or when they weren't able to stand up for themselves to male members. This was exacerbated by activities that led young women to be viewed as sexually available. In addition, because young women typically were not seen as a threat by young men, when they did pose one, they could be punished even more harshly than young men, not only for having challenged a rival gang or gang member but also for having overstepped "appropriate" gender boundaries.

Monica had status and respect in her gang, both because she had proven herself through fights and criminal activities, and because her older brothers were members of her set. She contrasted her own treatment with that of other young women in the gang:

> They just be puttin' the other girls off. Like Andrea, man. Oh my God, they dog Andrea so bad. They like, "Bitch, go to the store." She like, "All right, I be right back." She will go to the store and go and get them whatever they want and come back with it. If she don't get it right, they be like, "Why you do that bitch?" I mean, and one dude even smacked her. And, I mean, and, I don't, I told my brother once. I was like, "Man, it ain't even like that. If you ever see someone tryin' to disrespect me like that or hit me, if you do not hit them or at least say somethin' to them...." So my brothers, they kinda watch out for me.

However, Monica put the responsibility for Andrea's treatment squarely on the young woman: "I put that on her. They ain't gotta do her like that, but she don't gotta let them do her like that either." Andrea was seen as "weak" because she did not stand up to the male members in the gang; thus, her mistreatment was framed as partially deserved because she did not exhibit the valued traits of toughness and willingness to fight that would allow her to defend herself.

An additional but related problem was when the devaluation of young women within gangs was sexual in nature. Girls, but not boys, could be initiated into the gang by being "sexed in"—having sexual relations with multiple male members of the gang. Other members viewed the young women initiated in this way as sexually available and promiscuous, thus increasing their subsequent mistreatment. In addition, the stigma could extend to female members in general, creating a sexual devaluation that all girls had to contend with.

The dynamics of "sexing in" as a form of gang initiation placed young women in a position that increased their risk of ongoing mistreatment at the hands of their gang peers. According to Keisha, "If you get sexed in, you have no respect. That means you gotta go ho'in' for 'em; when they say you give 'em the pussy, you gotta give it to 'em. If you don't, you gonna get your ass beat. I ain't down for that." One girl in her set was sexed in and Keisha said the girl "just do everything they tell her to do, like a dummy." Nikkie reported that two girls who were sexed into her set eventually quit hanging around with the gang because they were harassed so much. In fact, Veronica said the young men in her set purposely tricked girls into believing they were being sexed into the gang and targeted girls they did not like:

> If some girls wanted to get in, if they don't like the girl they have sex with 'em. They run trains on 'em or either have the girl suck their thang. And then they used to, the girls used to think they was in. So, then the girls used to just come try to hang around us and all this little bull, just 'cause, 'cause they thinkin' they in.

Young women who were sexed into the gang were viewed as sexually promiscuous, weak, and not "true" members. They were subject to revictimization and mistreatment, and were viewed as deserving of abuse by other members, both male and female. Veronica continued, "They [girls who are sexed in] gotta do whatever, whatever the boys tell 'em to do when they want 'em to do it, right then and there, in front of whoever. And, I think, that's just sick. That's nasty, that's dumb." Keisha concurred, "She brought that on herself, by bein' the fact, bein' sexed in." There was evidence, however, that girls could overcome the stigma of having been sexed in through their subsequent behavior, by challenging members that disrespect them and being willing to fight. Tamika described a girl in her set who was sexed in, and stigmatized as a result, but successfully fought to rebuild her reputation:

> Some people, at first, they call her "little ho" and all that. But then, now she startin' to get bold.... Like, they be like, "Ooh, look at the little ho. She fucked me and my boy." She be like, "Man, forget y'all. Man, what? What?" She be ready to squat [fight] with 'em. I be like, "Ah, look at her!" Uh huh.... At first we looked at her like, "Ooh, man, she a ho, man." But now we look at her like she just our kickin'-it partner. You know, however she got in that's her business.

The fact that there was such an option as "sexing in" served to keep girls disempowered, because they always faced the question of how they got in and of whether they were "true" members. In addition, it contributed to a milieu in which young women's sexuality was seen as exploitable. This may help explain why young women were so harshly judgmental of those girls who were sexed in. Young women who were privy to male gang members' conversations reported that male members routinely disrespect girls in the gang by disparaging them sexually. Monica explained,

> I mean the guys, they have their little comments about 'em [girls in the gang] because, I hear more because my brothers are all up there with the guys and everything and I hear more just sittin' around, just listenin'. And they'll have their little jokes about "Well, ha I had her," and then and everybody else will jump in and say, "Well, I had her, too." And then they'll laugh about it.

In general, because gender constructions defined young women as weaker than young men, young women were often seen as lesser members of the gang. In addition to the mistreatment these perceptions entailed, young women also faced particularly harsh sanctions for crossing gender boundaries—causing harm to rival male members when they had been viewed as nonthreatening. One young woman[6] participated in the assault of a rival female gang member, who had set up a member of the girl's gang. She explained, "The female was supposingly goin' out with one of ours, went back and told a bunch of [rivals] what was goin' on and got the [rivals] to jump my boy. And he ended up in the hospital." The story she told was unique but nonetheless significant for what it indicates about the gendered nature of gang violence and victimization. Several young men in her set saw the girl walking down the street, kidnapped her, then brought her to a member's house. The young woman I interviewed, along with several other girls in her set, viciously beat the girl, then to their surprise the young men took over the beating, ripped off the girl's clothes, brutally gang-raped her, then dumped her in a park. The interviewee noted, "I don't know what happened to her. Maybe she died. Maybe, maybe someone came and helped her. I mean, I don't know." The experience scared the young woman who told me about it. She explained,

> I don't never want anythin' like that to happen to me. And I pray to God that it doesn't. 'Cause God said that whatever you sow you're gonna reap. And like, you know, beatin' a girl up and then sittin' there watchin' somethin' like that happen, well, Jesus that could come back on me. I mean, I felt, I really did feel sorry for her even though my boy was in the hospital and was really hurt. I mean, we coulda just shot her. You know, and it coulda been just over. We coulda just taken her life. But they went farther than that.

This young woman described the gang rape she witnessed as "the most brutal thing I've ever seen in my life." While the gang rape itself was an unusual event, it remained a specifically gendered act that could take place precisely because young women were not perceived as equals. Had the victim been an "equal," the attack would have remained a physical one. As the interviewee herself noted, "we coulda just shot her." Instead, the young men who gang-raped the girl were not just enacting revenge on a rival but on a *young woman* who had dared to treat a young man in this way. The issue is not the question of which is worse—to be shot and killed, or gang-raped and left for dead. Rather, this particular act sheds light on how gender may function to structure victimization risk within gangs.

DISCUSSION

Gender dynamics in mixed-gender gangs are complex and thus may have multiple and contradictory effects on young women's risk of victimization and repeat victimization. My findings suggest that participation in the delinquent lifestyles associated with gangs clearly places young women at risk for victimization. The act of joining a gang involves the initiate's submission to victimization at the hands of her gang peers. In addition, the rules governing gang members' activities place them in situations in which they are vulnerable to assaults that are specifically gang related. Many acts of violence that girls described would not have occurred had they not been in gangs.

It seems, though, that young women in gangs believed they have traded unknown risks for known ones—that victimization at the hands of friends, or at least under specified conditions, was an alternative preferable to the potential of random, unknown victimization by strangers. Moreover, the gang offered both a semblance of protection from others on the streets, especially young men, and a means of achieving retaliation when victimization did occur....

Girls' gender, as an individual attribute, can function to lessen their exposure to victimization risk by defining them as inappropriate targets of rival male gang members' assaults. The young women I interviewed repeatedly commented that young men were typically not as violent in their routine confrontations with rival young women as with rival young men. On the other hand, when young women are targets of serious assault, they may face brutality that is particularly harsh and sexual in nature because they are female—thus, particular types of assault, such as rape, are deemed more appropriate when young women are the victims.

Gender can also function as a state-dependent factor, because constructions of gender and the enactment of gender identities are fluid. On the one hand, young women can call upon gender as a means of avoiding exposure to activities they find risky, threatening, or morally troubling. Doing so does not expose them to the sanctions likely faced by male gang members who attempt to avoid participation in violence. Although these choices may insulate young women from the risk of assault at the hands of rival gang members, perceptions of female gang members—and of women in general—as weak may contribute to more routinized victimization at the hands of the male members of their gangs. Moreover, sexual exploitation in the form of "sexing in" as an initiation ritual may define young women as sexually available, contributing to a likelihood of repeat victimization unless the young woman can stand up for herself and fight to gain other members' respect.

Finally, given constructions of gender that define young women as non-threatening, when young women do pose a threat to male gang members, the sanctions they face may be particularly harsh because they not only have caused harm to rival gang members but also have crossed appropriate gender boundaries in doing so. In sum, my findings suggest that gender may function to insulate young women from some types of physical assault and lessen their exposure to risks from rival gang members, but also to make them vulnerable to particular types of violence, including routine victimization by their male peers, sexual exploitation, and sexual assault.

NOTES

1. I contacted numerous additional agency personnel in an effort to draw the sample from a larger population base, but many efforts remained unsuccessful despite repeated attempts and promises of assistance. These included persons at the probation department, a shelter and outreach agency for runaways, police personnel, a private residential facility for juveniles, and three additional community agencies. None of the agencies I contacted openly denied me permission to interview young women; they simply chose not to follow up. I do not believe that much bias resulted from the nonparticipation of these agencies. Each has a client base of "at-risk" youths, and the young women I interviewed report overlap with some of these same agencies. For example, a number had been or

were on probation, and several reported staying at the shelter for runaways.

2. One young woman was a member of an all-female gang. Because the focus of this article is gender dynamics in mixed-gender gangs, her interview is not included in the analysis.

3. These include the Gang Membership Resistance Surveys in Long Beach and San Diego, the Denver Youth Survey, and the Rochester Youth Development Study.

4. All names are fictitious.

5. This is not to suggest that male members cannot gain status via their connections to high-status men, but that to maintain status, they will have to successfully exhibit masculine traits such as toughness. Young women appear to be held to more flexible standards.

6. Because this excerpt provides a detailed description of a specific serious crime, and because demographic information on respondents is available, I have chosen to conceal both the pseudonym and gang affiliation of the young woman who told me the story.

REFERENCES

Adler, Patricia A. and Peter Adler. 1987. *Membership Roles in Field Research.* Newbury Park, CA: Sage.

Baskin, Deborah, Ira Sommers, and Jeffrey Fagan. 1993. "The Political Economy of Violent Female Street Crime." *Fordham Urban Law Journal* 20: 401–17.

Bjerregaard, Beth and Carolyn Smith. 1993. "Gender Differences in Gang Participation, Delinquency, and Substance Use." *Journal of Quantitative Criminology* 4: 329–55.

Block, Carolyn Rebecca and Richard Block. 1993. "Street Gang Crime in Chicago." *Research in Brief,* Washington, DC: National Institute of Justice.

Bowker, Lee H., Helen Shimota Gross, and Malcolm W. Klein. 1980. "Female Participation in Delinquent Gang Activities." *Adolescence* 15(59): 509–19.

Brotherton, David C. 1996. "'Smartness,' 'Toughness,' and 'Autonomy': Drug Use in the Context of Gang Female Deliquency." *Journal of Drug Issues* 26(1): 261–77.

Campbell, Anne. 1990. "Female Participation in Gangs." Pp. 163–82 in *Gangs in America.* G. Ronald Huff, ed. Beverly Hills, CA: Sage.

Chesney-Lind, Meda, Randall G. Shelden, and Karen A. Joe. 1996. "Girls, Delinquency, and Gang Membership." Pp. 185–204 in *Gangs in America,* 2nd ed. C. Ronald Huff, ed. Thousand Oaks, CA: Sage.

Curry, G. David, Richard A. Ball, and Scott H. Decker. 1996. Estimating the National Scope of Gang Crime from Law Enforcement Data Research in Brief. Washington, DC: National Institute of Justice.

Decker, Scott H. 1996. "Collective and Normative Features of Gang Violence." *Justice Quarterly* 13(2): 243–64.

Decker, Scott H. and Barrik Van Winkle. 1996. *Life in the Gang.* Cambridge, UK: Cambridge University Press.

Esbensen, Finn-Aage and David Huizinga. 1993. "Gangs, Drugs, and Delinquency in a Survey of Urban Youth." *Criminology* 31(4): 565–89.

Esbensen, Finn-Aage, David Huizinga, and Anne W. Weiher. 1993. "Gang and Non-Gang Youth: Differences in Explanatory Factors." *Journal of Contemporary Criminal Justice* 9(2): 94–116.

Fagan, Jeffrey. 1989. "The Social Organization of Drug Use and Drug Dealing among Urban Gangs." *Criminology* 27(4): 633–67.

———. 1990. "Social Processes of Delinquency and Drug Use among Urban Gangs." Pp. 183–219 in *Gangs in America*. C. Ronald Huff, ed. Newbury Park, CA: Sage.

Glassner, Barry and Julia Loughlin. 1987. *Drugs in Adolescent Worlds: Burnouts to Straights*. New York: St. Martin's.

Huff, C. Ronald. 1996. "The Criminal Behavior of Gang Members and Nongang At-Risk Youth." Pp. 75–102 in *Gangs in America*, 2d ed., edited by C. Ronald Huff Thousand Oaks, CA: Sage.

Joe, Karen A. and Meda Chesney-Lind. 1995. "Just Every Mother's Angel: An Analysis of Gender and Ethnic Variations in Youth Gang Membership." *Gender & Society* 9(4): 408–30.

Klein, Malcolm W. 1995. *The American Street Gang: Its Nature, Prevalence and Control*. New York: Oxford University Press.

Klein, Malcolm W. and Cheryl L. Maxson. 1989. "Street Gang Violence." Pp. 198–231 in *Violent Crime, Violent Criminals*. Neil Weiner and Marvin

Wolfgang, eds. Newbury Park, CA: Sage.

Lauderback, David, Joy Hansen, and Dan Waldorf. 1992. "'Sisters Are Doin' It for Themselves': A Black Female Gang in San Francisco." *The Gang Journal* 1(1): 57–70.

Lauritsen, Janet L., Robert J. Sampson, and John H. Laub. 1991. "The Link between Offending and Victimization among Adolescents." *Criminology* 29(2): 265–92.

Miller, Jody and Barry Glassner. 1997. "The 'Inside' and the 'Outside': Finding Realities in Interviews." Pp. 99–112 in *Qualitative Research*, edited by David Silverman. London: Sage.

Sanders, William. 1993. *Drive-Bys and Gang Bangs: Gangs and Grounded Culture*. Chicago: Aldine.

Taylor, Carl. 1993. *Girls, Gangs, Women and Drugs*. East Lansing: Michigan State University Press.

Thornberry, Terence P., Marvin D. Krohn, Alan J. Lizotie, and Deborah Chard-Wierschem. 1993. "The Role of Juvenile Gangs in Facilitating Delinquent Behavior." *Journal of Research in Crime and Delinquency* 30(1): 75–85.

36

International Organized Crime

ROY GODSON AND WILLIAM J. OLSON

If subcultural participants have loose relationships characterized by socializing together and gang participants have tighter relationships based on living, partying, and fighting together, individuals who belong to deviant formal organizations share the bond of membership in large-scale, highly-structured deviant associations that extend over time and space. Deviant formal organizations entail more highly sophisticated relationships than the less-structured or committed crews, or rings, where we first see an emerging division of labor, so that individual members learn specific skills and pursue these specialized tasks within the group. Members of deviant formal organizations work together in enterprises that may be specialized or diverse, tightly connected from top to bottom or portioned out in authority to separate subspheres, ethnically and/or familially homogeneous, and capable of earning vast amounts of money. Godson and Olson offer a rare depiction of the modern breed of international cartels that contains a description and analysis of the nature, scope, type of organization, history, and international consequences for crime, law enforcement, and the erosion of legitimate control over this most sophisticated form of deviant group. In so doing they contrast this level of deviant relationships to the less organizationally sophisticated gangs that operate domestically in our major urban areas.

What features of the ICOs described by Godson and Olson apply to the situation in Afghanistan, Pakistan, and other parts of the Middle East? How well do they fit the South American criminal organizations? What are the structural characteristics that differ between these regions of the world and how might they affect their criminal organizations?

On August 18, 1989, in the middle of an adoring crowd, a gunman murdered Luis Carlos Galan, the leading candidate for the presidency of Colombia. The act shocked the nation. Political murder was not a new phenomenon in Colombia. What was new were the perpetrators. The assassin was not an individual acting alone, nor was he a member of a guerrilla group, of which Colombia has several violent examples. Instead, the assassin was a hireling, a *sicario*, acting on the orders of the Medellín Cartel, one of the world's major international criminal organizations. The murder was only the beginning. The Medellín Cartel launched a full-scale terrorist assault on the country. Public facilities and newspaper offices were bombed. Members of leading families were kidnapped. Hundreds of policemen were murdered. A national airline flight was blown up in mid-flight. The cartel waged war against the Colombian state. Its aim was to force the government to come to terms with the cartels, in effect, to share power with the drug traffickers.

The Colombian government, which had been trying to control not only Medellín groups but also the less prominent Cali group, now faced a far more violent and direct threat to its institutions. It called for help. The United States, which was already trying to support Colombian efforts, came forward with an emergency aid package and promises of more aid to follow. The United States provided upwards of $400 million in police, military, and advisory assistance over five years. These funds were intended to eliminate the major drug trafficking organizations in Colombia, and many millions more were spent to help attack the overseas operations responsible for producing and transshipping almost all the cocaine in the world.

The level of support and cooperation was unprecedented. And the threat? A drug-trafficking organization with the wealth and power to challenge the internal stability of one country while it defied the power and authority of the world's remaining superpower. Hubris? Perhaps, but the nature of the confrontation and the fact that it is not over says something fundamental about the modern world, about the nature of state power, international relations, and the stability of governments. And the situation in Colombia is far from the whole picture.

In 1991 and 1992 the disruptive influence of organized criminal activity rocked the foundations of political stability in Italy. Since World War II organized crime has carried out a wide range of domestic activities, using violence, extortion, bribery, and murder to advance its interests. More recently the Sicilian Mafia specifically has been locked in a murderous struggle with the government, assassinating judges, policemen, and those seen as interfering in its operations, and, more ominously, using its economic power to try to corrupt the political process itself. The scandals surrounding official corruption linked to the Sicilian, Neapolitan, and Calabrian Mafias have touched the very heart of the Italian government, undermining its credibility and effectiveness.

In Burma, large parts of the country are under the control of separatist movements who finance their activities by selling opium on the international market. The government itself engages in or countenances the production and trafficking of opium to help finance its operations. All over Asia, organized criminal groups, Pakistani, Thai, Chinese, or Japanese, operate vast international organizations trafficking in drugs or engaging in a wide variety of other criminal activities, in many cases with the complicity of local government and military officials.

In the former Soviet Union and in the struggling states of Eastern Europe, criminal organizations, long held in check, are beginning to grow. They have developed international links to improve their own organizational abilities and marketing contacts. Of more concern, these criminal groups are penetrating local governments (which are often struggling for cohesion and lacking resources) by using bribery and violence to win protection for their expanding operations. Governmental resources, strained to cope with a wide range of social and economic problems, are completely inadequate to respond; in fact, governments are unable to assess the extent of the problem accurately. Political paralysis and economic hardship have combined to give various criminal organizations considerable freedom to operate, even when local governments are not cooperating with criminal elements. Governments, however, are not the only institutions vulnerable to criminal penetration.

In a New York courtroom in 1992, Clark Clifford, an adviser to presidents and one of the most respected men in the United States, was called as a defendant in a case involving a vast illegal international financial enterprise, the Bank of Credit and Commerce International (BCCI). So far, BCCI is the biggest such case, but it illustrates only too graphically the extent to which banking and financial systems are vulnerable to penetration, manipulation, and fraud by criminal groups. The mechanisms whereby incredible sums of illegal proceeds—perhaps $300 billion in drug money alone—are laundered and massive frauds are perpetrated through the world's financial markets are still only dimly understood, but the realities of the process underscore the permeability of the system. This permeability of governments and private business and the growth of major international organized crime raise concerns for the future.

Whether in the developed or in the developing world, criminal organizations' scope of action and range of capabilities are undergoing a profound change. Decline in political order, deteriorating economic circumstances, a growing underground economy that habituates people to working outside the legal framework, easy access to arms, the massive flow of emigrants and refugees, and the normal difficulties involved in engendering meaningful state-to-state cooperation are working to the advantage of criminal organizations. The rise of better-organized, internationally based criminal groups with vast financial resources is creating a new threat to the stability and security of the international system. As Senator John Kerry noted, "this is new. This is something that none of us has ever experienced before. It is not ideological. It has nothing to do with right or left, but it is money-oriented, greed-based criminal enterprise that has decided to take on the lawful institutions and civilized society." The growth of these organizations presents a major challenge to the quality of life in the United States and to U.S. interests.

ORGANIZED CRIME AND BUSINESS

Although major criminal organizations pose a new and compelling challenge to national and international interests, the extent of the threat should not be exaggerated. It is clear that the wealth and power of individual organizations has grown and there are increasing signs of international links between various criminal organizations. This does not mean, however, that there is an integrated, centrally directed criminal conspiracy. The first business of criminal organizations is usually business, its promotion and protection. In this sense criminal organizations are similar to legitimate enterprises. Like the activities of their legal twins, the activities of separate "corporations" can be cooperative or competitive by turns. The long-term threat from these organizations is subtle and more insidious than images of criminal masterminds seeking to dominate the globe in some vast, shared, and centrally coordinated enterprise. It is important and difficult to measure and to understand the true nature and composition of the threat.

Criminal organizations, of course, are not new. Oliver Twist's Fagin is only one of the many memorials to the possibilities of an organized criminal underground. Nor is there anything particularly new about the ethnic composition of such organizations; the Sicilian Mafia and the Chinese Triads, in particular, are of venerable lineage, and many have had international dimensions. Yet there is something fundamentally different in the threat that such organizations now pose to organized society that must be understood so that the United States and its friends and allies around the world can undertake a reasonable, timely, and effective response. First, however, it is useful to define the nature and contours of the emerging problem.

It is essential to come to terms with what is meant by criminal organization. What distinguishes it from regular criminal activity, from a legitimate business enterprise, or from economic activity in underground or informal economies?

In many parts of the world, there are forms of entrepreneurial activity that are classified as illegitimate if they do not meet the state's test for permits, licenses, and so on. These informal economic activities now account for a significant proportion of all meaningful economic activity in many parts of the Third World. In Peru, for example, upwards of 50 percent of the economically active population are engaged in the informal economy, generating as much as 40 percent of the gross domestic product (GDP), all of it illegal under existing law. (This does not include illegal coca cultivation and cocaine processing.) There is considerable organization in this effort. This does not mean, however, that this activity is indicative of organized crime, although there are some important parallels. It is important to keep this distinction in mind. It was not that long ago, for instance, that all nonstate economic activity was illegal in the former Soviet Union. As the economy of Russia struggles to make the transition from statist control to free market and many of the people formerly engaged in illegal activities begin to emerge into the new economy, it will be important to understand and to be able to draw the distinction between true criminals and those who were criminals by definition. What is involved? There are a variety of definitions and definitional approaches, but several elements are essential.

First, the activities involved must be criminal. They must violate laws for which there is a punishment prescribed by a legal authority capable of enforcing the laws. This raises a problem, as the trouble with informal economies indicates. Clearly, many societies, including our own, make the informal economy illegal and provide punishment. By definition, then, these activities are criminal, and when they become a major component of the GDP outside the formal economy and the tax base these activities can adversely affect the growth of the formal economy. However, the informal economy can also make a major contribution to the quality of life, as in the Soviet case, where the average citizen would have been far worse off far sooner if it had not been for private entrepreneurs providing a wide range of goods and services. The dividing line is blurred. Nevertheless, most societies, past and present, have defined a number of behaviors—such as murder, drug trafficking, prostitution, extortion, kidnapping, and theft—as not only outside the law but fundamentally wrong. By contrast, the informal economy essentially encompasses "normal" economic activity that is legitimate in the formal sector. But the primary concern here is not just with crime, per se, but with major crime, and there are additional features to help sharpen the picture.

A second central characteristic of the crime, which does present a significant threat to established societies, is that the criminals engaged in particular activities must be organized. While trite, it is important to understand that the individuals involved are not acting alone, and the activities in which they are engaged are not random. Further, the economic behavior in mature criminal organizations, unlike that of groups in an illegal, informal economy in which groups may loosely cooperate, is intentional. The activities are usually directed by identifiable leaders. Mature criminal organizations operate with varying organizational structures for a common purpose, which is outside the law.

Organization is key, yet there is no standardized organizational chart for a developed criminal organization. There are varying types of organizational patterns. Like a legitimate business enterprise, a criminal organization may employ various features best designed to carry out its purposes. Thus it can be vertically organized and fairly tightly controlled, as are the Colombian cocaine cartels; or it may be regionally organized, often around functions, as is the American Mafia; or it may be even more loosely organized, as are the Jamaican Yardies in England. It may have a quasi-religious character, as do the Chinese Triads, or a semi-political/military organization, as does the Shan United Army in Burma. The organizational nature, then, while a key component, is not the sole defining feature.

The purposes to which the organization is dedicated ultimately define its legality or criminality. The activities of criminal organizations are equivalent to many of the efforts of legitimate business: export-import, trade in various articles, wholesale and retail sales, services. The members of criminal organizations, however, seek to operate in areas outside legal guidelines and generally trade in items also defined as illegal—such as drugs. However, as in the case of the Chinese Triads, they may use their organization for both legal and illegal activities.

Interestingly, there are indications that many of the present major criminal organizations began not as deliberately criminal groups but as protective-benevolent or secret societies for the welfare of persecuted ethnic or political groups. The Chinese Triads and the Sicilian Mafia began not as bodies to carry out illegal economic activities but as organizations to provide a type of community for their members. They provided aid and comfort to members in tough times. They shielded them against turmoil, anarchy, and arbitrary government. They served as resistance movements. Robin Hood and Jesse James of legend and the movies were the leaders of such groups. In the government's eyes they were thugs. In legend they were heroes. This shadowy area between heroic resistance to injustice and criminal activity will continue to pose difficulties in sorting out criminals from patriots.

Over time, however, these groups, acting outside the law and in opposition to existing authority, typically began to focus increasingly on illegal (and legal) acts for profit rather than for a cause. As the profit motive took precedence, resistance took a back seat. Not all criminal organizations, however, began as failed resistance efforts. Many evolved from groups of thieves or gangs that always sought profit outside the law. Some of these groups claimed political motives. But a gang, while organized, is generally a very small and localized affair with very limited means. In general, major criminal organizations of the type that are of greatest concern here have grown into substantial enterprises, often with transnational connections, involve hundreds if not thousands of "employees," and are no longer confined to localized areas. The third point to note about criminal organizations, then, is that their underlying purpose is to make a profit from illegal acts and that they employ a large number of people whose activities are coordinated over time. The organization usually is neither ephemeral nor temporary.

A fourth characteristic of major criminal organizations is their willingness to use violence to promote and protect their interests. Violence and crime often go together. But criminal organizations use violence deliberately. They control its use and direct it in specific cases to achieve defined goals. Violence is a "business" tool and not a random or individual act. There is sometimes a lack of discipline or acts of individual cruelty inside organized crime, but generally violence is used for business purposes. It is directed outward to intimidate or eliminate rivals and threats, and it is directed inward to enforce discipline within the organization. The level of violence may vary—the Medellín Cartel, for example, is far more prone to resort to violence than is the Cali Cartel—but it remains a consciously controlled instrument.

A corollary to the use of violence is the purposeful use of bribery. It should be clear that criminal organizations are in direct conflict with police and other governmental agencies. In some cases, the criminal organization may have more firepower than the state—as with the Shan United Army—but generally they cannot sustain direct violence against official bodies. Instead, they use bribery in order to corrupt the legal system and evade prosecution. The availability of large amounts of ready cash allow the criminal organizations considerable flexibility in using the power of money to suborn government officials on a large scale, sometimes including government ministers. In many parts of the world bribery and corruption are endemic. In these cases, organized crime is just another business group that uses bribery to go about pursuing its business.

FAMILY TIES

Finally, although it is not true in every case, most major criminal organizations have a family or ethnic base. They operate out of a small, tight-knit community. Family ties, especially in circumstances where a member's family can be held accountable for the member's disloyalty, present a practical solution to the problem of ensuring fidelity and obedience. Codes of allegiance, rituals, ethnic bonds, and quasi-religious ceremonies, whether linked to familial ties or not, also help to engage the compliance and loyalty of individuals within organizations. In addition, they create distinguishing codes of recognition that reduced the chances of hostile penetration. The fact that involvement in such an organization places an individual outside the law and subject to arrest also helps to reinforce the ties that bind, and when all else fails, murder is the final sanction to ensure loyal silence.

This is not hard to understand. Members of criminal organizations need to trust each other. The illegal and dangerous nature of the work plus the fact that law enforcement will seek to penetrate and disrupt the organization make some form of security discrimination vital to survival. It is easier to enforce operations security within a group known to one another and bound by ties of kinship or race. It is also easier to control membership and to spot outsiders. One of the advantages that ethnic-based criminal organizations have when they operate outside of their place of origin is that language and culture offer added barriers to fend off or identify outsiders. It is essential for such organizations to protect themselves from a hostile environment, to guard access to information, to ensure the success of operations, to minimize losses, and to guarantee loyalty.

Characteristically, then, organized crime is defined by a more or less formal structure that endures over time, is directed toward a common purpose by a recognizable leadership operating outside the law, is quite often based on family or ethnic identity, and is prepared to use violence or other means to promote and protect common interests and objectives. As noted at the outset, however, there is nothing particularly new about such organizations; they have existed for centuries. A number of factors are now at work that argue that the nature and role of these organizations are raising to a new level the threat that they pose to social order and the stability of nations.

There are three major new characteristics of organized crime at the end of the twentieth century. First is the broader, global canvas of the traditional criminal activity. Second is the growth of transnational links between criminal organizations and between criminal organizations and other groups. Third is the growing ability and power of international criminal organizations (ICOs) to threaten the stability of states, to undermine democratic institutions, to hinder economic development, to undermine alliance relationships, and to challenge even a superpower.

There are a number of factors that aid the ICOs' growing ability to challenge individual states. These factors are not so much characteristics of ICOs as of the environment in which they exist. They benefit, for example, from weak governments without the will or the resources to cope with rich and powerful ICOs. They enjoy fantastic sums of money generated by illegal activities, especially drug production, which gives them maximum flexibility to employ bribery or violence to achieve their ends. They are able to take advantage of the movement of large numbers of people internationally, which gives various organizations a recruitment base around the world. They are also able to capitalize on a decline in economic and political order, especially thriving on the growth of parallel or informal economies that subvert loyalty from the nation–state and government and habituate people to operating outside the legal framework. The ready availability of sophisticated arms and other technologies gives ICOs better means to protect and promote their interests. And systemic limits on the ability of individual states and international organizations to coordinate effective transnational anticriminal programs provide ICOs with maneuvering room to adjust to enforcement threats.

These features, taken separately or together, mean that today's international criminal syndicates are powerful enough to challenge, sometimes to destabilize, and so far, rarely, to control small, weak states. As a recent U.S. Senate report noted, these "new international criminals" represent a threat to international security that no single state can control alone.

These three major features, global operations, transnational links, and the ability to challenge national authorities, will be considered in turn.

THE NEW INTERNATIONAL CRIMINAL

The major ICOs have all the same characteristics and features of more traditional, nationally based criminal organizations. What distinguishes their ability to conduct global operations on the order of a major multinational corporation is their transnational scale and their ability to challenge national and international authority. Disposing of large quantities of ready cash, diversified into a wide range of activities, and employing a workforce spread around the globe, the ICOs represent a different order of magnitude in criminal operations.

The ICOs differ from traditional criminal organizations in the *global scope of their operations*. Traditional organized crime groups have their roots within individual countries, and although they may have overseas connections they do not operate on an international scale. Their organizations and operations are confined to nations or regions, and cities within nations. The America Mafia, also commonly known as La Cosa Nostra (LCN), is a well-known example of this older type. LCN emerged in the 1930s from conflict among gangs of Sicilian immigrants in U.S. cities. Although its members drew on the traditions of their Sicilian origins, LCN was never a subsidiary or arm of the Sicilian Mafia; it is a distinctly American organization. While LCN has had international connections, these have been largely related to being buyers of alcohol and heroin from foreign groups, not as being part of those groups. LCN's organization and operations are essentially domestic and regional.

Many other organized crime groups operating in the United States are primarily of this type. Black and Hispanic groups, for example, are generally localized gangs. They often dominate criminal activity in their respective ethnic neighborhoods. Typically, they control much street-level drug dealing and some distribution activity above the street level. They often interface with international traffickers who control wholesaling and regional distribution. Motorcycle gangs, such as the Hell's Angels, have also become well organized and engage in a wide variety of criminal activity, sometimes developing international suppliers.

The new international criminal groups differ sharply from these domestic groups. They are organized for and engage in large-scale criminal activity across international boundaries. Perhaps the greatest such organizations are Colombian. The Colombian cartels are vertically integrated global businesses. They have tens of thousands of specialized employees and associated individuals or businesses worldwide. Similarly, the Chinese Triads, although more loosely structured, have also developed extensive overseas operations, often in the wake of Chinese emigration. Such global networks provide mobility, an effective communications infrastructure, and international connections for criminal enterprise and sometimes for noncriminal groups who want to use their services. These structures also enhance the criminal groups' ability to create whole new markets for goods and services. This can be done either by creating new products, like "crack," which revolutionized the U.S. cocaine market in the mid-1980s, or by opening up new market areas, as the cocaine cartels have attempted to do in Europe, establishing links to the Mafia or other European criminal organizations.

International networks also provide flexibility to adapt quickly and creatively to enforcement efforts. For example, after U.S. enforcement efforts shut off the flow of heroin originating from Turkey, new sources developed in Southeast and Southwest Asia and Mexico. U.S. law enforcement agencies noted in 1991 the "inherent flexibility" of traffickers in shifting routes and modes of transport in response to enforcement efforts. When enforcement was stepped up in Florida and the Caribbean, cocaine was routed increasingly through Central America and Mexico. There is another aspect to this flexibility: by operating in the international arena, crossing national boundaries at will, the ICOs are often able to thwart localized law enforcement efforts. Diversification of operations and locale and diffusion of risk greatly enhance the ICOs' ability to recover from losses. They are also better able to adjust to changing situations in one country and exploit gaps in international law enforcement cooperation.

One of the emerging characteristics of the major ICOs is the extent of their *transnational links:* their growing interconnectivity with other transnational, nonstate actors. Although traditional criminal organizations have links to similar groups outside their own countries, they generally do not conduct extensive overseas operations and have only limited contact with other criminal groups. The major ICOs, however, have an international focus and operate vast transnational business empires. Their activities go beyond establishing subsidiaries. In addition to operating across international boundaries, the new ICOs have also begun to establish links to other nonstate groups, such as insurgents and terrorists, and similar criminal organizations. These linkages are diverse and in some cases tenuous and tense, but the trend that is emerging is toward closer cooperative relationships. The nature of the relationship can be quite complex.

Traditional, nationally based criminal organizations pose a variety of threats to public order and legitimate business. The U.S. experience with LCN is typical: corruption of officials, penetration of unions, money laundering, prostitution, street crime, gambling, violent internecine power struggles, drug trafficking; in short, the whole range of criminal activity that can be organized for profit. As rich and powerful as these organizations have been, however, they are generally in no position to challenge political order directly. Indeed, in the case of the LCN, recent law enforcement successes have decimated its ranks and may have dealt it a crippling blow. The major ICOs, however, pose a more dangerous threat, one that is again defined by its scope and sheer audacity: a *challenge to authority*.

The Medellín Cartel felt powerful enough to challenge the sovereignty and integrity of the Colombian state, and along with it the United States. The last five years of struggle have damaged the Medellín Cartel, at considerable loss of life and capital, but the Colombian cocaine entrepreneurs remain in business, not only evading annihilation but continuing to prosper and diversify their operations. Alone or in conjunction with various guerrilla groups in Colombia and Peru, they are able to control large areas of the Andes in defiance of government authority. They are also able to transship immense quantities of drugs through the Caribbean, Central America, and Mexico to the United States. In many cases, even in totalitarian Cuba, the Medellín Cartel has been able to corrupt officials throughout the hierarchy, including ranking military officers and ministers of state. Their ability to penetrate governments has even led to major disruptions in the relations between nations, as the Enrique Camarena case in Mexico showed only too clearly.

There is also mounting evidence to indicate that the major ICOs can have a profound effect on local economies. In the Andes, for example, the diversion of labor into illegal activities, the destruction of land and its use for nonproductive crops, and the generation of inflationary pressures all work to undermine the viability of local economies, already none too strong in Bolivia and Peru. Added to this is the penetration of financial markets and the international banking system. Corruption of financial institutions is now a major and growing concern, as the ICOs use international financial networks to launder money and in some cases to provide cover to further illegal activities. Even major developed countries are not immune. The French government, for example, has become concerned with the penetration of the Italian Mafia in southern France. This is also one of the major reasons the British government established the National Criminal Intelligence Service.

The major ICOs enjoy a number of advantages denied to smaller groups. The scale of their operations, their growing international connectivity, and the power and influence that they have garnered at the expense of governments make them a formidable challenge. They enjoy the advantages of economy of scale in their operations. Their enormous financial resources and diversification operations give them maneuvering room in responding to law enforcement encroachments. Their ability to operate across many legal jurisdictions reinforces this inherent flexibility. Moreover, their contacts with other nonstate actors, such as insurgent groups and terrorists, means that they can call increasingly upon allies to help distract the government or even challenge its authority.

The cumulative effect of these advantages puts them in a position of great strength.

THE FUTURE

International criminal groups in the United States and worldwide are likely to expand. A number of factors are likely to aid their growth.

Economics of Production

For small farmers in many countries, choosing to grow drug-related crops makes the most sense economically. Markets for other commodities are less profitable and less stable. In many cases, even where the necessary marketing infrastructure and expertise exist, government controls make entry into those markets difficult or impossible for peasants. At the same time, drug entrepreneurs are expanding into markets where drugs have not been a major problem in the past. Without dramatic and unlikely changes, raw materials for drug production will continue to be readily available.

Furthermore, the United States is one of the world's most lucrative markets for illegal as well as legal enterprise. It will continue to attract trade in illegal products. Europe, too, is a large market, and the creation of the Common Market has significantly reduced the extent of border controls that might have helped to restrain drug trafficking and other transnational criminal activities.

International Ungovernability

The growth of international crime parallels a global trend toward ungovernability, that is, the declining ability of governments to govern, to manage a modern state, and to provide adequate or effective services. In some cases criminal organizations have been able to capitalize on the fact that large areas, such as the Andes and the Amazon regions of Latin America, were never under much central government control. They have moved into these remote regions and have begun to provide the major form of authority in much of the region. In other cases, they have begun to contest local control of areas with the government, as have groups in Burma. There are dozens of places, such as Peru and Burma, where state authority has lapsed in whole or in part. It is not limited to small states, either. There are indications that areas of some of the Central Asian Republics have been given over to drug cultivation. Similarly, areas in Mexico, Pakistan, and southern China appear to be largely beyond government control. This situation provides favorable conditions for criminal groups and bases of operations and safe havens in areas key to drug trafficking and alien smuggling. Experts in political geography predict continuing global fragmentation. Criminal organizations thrive where governments are weak.

IMMIGRATION STREAMS

Ethnic criminal organizations are likely to follow immigration patterns. They do not always do so, but there has often been a strong correlation between the two. In the 1990s economic pressures and widespread ethnic turmoil are likely to generate refugees and immigrants from regions where international criminal groups are based. Between 1980 and 1990 the Asian population in the United States alone grew by 108 percent, from 3.5 million to 7.3 million. The Chinese population grew by 104 percent, from 806,000 to 1.6 million. While the vast majority of immigrants are law-abiding, criminal organizations tend to exploit immigrant communities in a variety of ways. They provide cover and concealment. Immigrant pools also provide a pool of recruits. In addition, the immigrants are usually fearful of law enforcement. Their recent experience in their country of origin makes them reluctant to cooperate with the police in their new countries. The police, moreover, historically do not provide the same degree of service to immigrants. The immigrants do not have important political connections, and the police find it difficult to cooperate with them because of their strange cultures and languages. Hence many experts anticipate increased international organized criminal activity accompanying the immigration of Russians, East Europeans, Asians, Middle Easterners, Kurds, and others.

Border Porosity

The United States' long open borders with Mexico and Canada provide ready access for criminals and illegal goods, and tens of thousands of miles of U.S. coastline are virtually uncontrollable. The opening of free-trade areas, such as the North American Free Trade Agreement and the EC, will lower many existing safeguards and customs inspections as well.

Trends in Technology

Continued advances in technology and international transportation will facilitate growth in international organized crime. The ease of modern communications makes contact among international criminal organizations easy, fast, and more secure. For example, new digital technologies make it more difficult for law enforcement bodies to intercept their communications. The movement of trillions of dollars in wire transfers each day makes it possible for many actors to evade state monitoring.

Relative Disorganization of Law Enforcement

Preventing, disrupting, and successfully prosecuting organized crime in most parts of the world is difficult enough in the best of times. Many traditional organized criminal organizations have survived the onslaught of law enforcement organizations for decades.

Now, however, the U.S. and other states are faced with international criminal groups. As was described earlier, they are bigger and more powerful than most of their predecessors. They operate globally, making it impossible for law enforcement in any one jurisdiction to neutralize major parts of their activities. While some degree of cooperation exists among law enforcement agencies, and new initiatives are getting under way, many observers believe that it is inadequate to the task. In 1992, for example, a U.S. Senate report noted that there is little evidence to suggest that either U.S. or foreign law enforcement entities are currently equipped to meet the challenge of this new breed of international criminal.

37

War Profiteering: Iraq and Halliburton

DAWN ROTHE

The complimentary interplay between governmental and corporate interests has given rise, especially during the Bush years, to a rash of state-sponsored and supported crime. During these years we have seen the ascendance of the neoconservative philosophy that governmental functions are best contracted out to private industry. At the same time, government agencies have lost funding and employees, with an associated weakening in their regulatory and oversight capacities. The original rationale underpinning this transfer was that private industry would operate more efficiently and profitably than government bureaucracy, as it is driven by competitive market forces. But what has happened, instead, is that corporate and governmental interests have become incestuously joined so that favoritism and no-bid contracts have replaced the free market economy. This climate has fostered one of the greatest environments for the growth of white-collar crime ever seen. The oil industry, the tobacco industry, and the pharmaceutical industry are three that notably come to mind as enmeshed in governmental connections and decision-making.

The twenty-first century has seen one company after another taken down, their employees' pension funds and shareholders' investments robbed by the corporate fraud of top executives. Yet an even higher price has been less visibly paid by members of the ordinary public through state-supported corporate crime. Politicians have fostered this practice by decreasing business regulation and creating a revolving door between business, lobbying, and government.

One of the most dramatic case examples lies in the connection between the Bush administration, through former Vice-President Dick Cheney, and Halliburton. In this chapter, Rothe gives us some background on the rise and proliferation of Halliburton and its subsidiaries, charting their history of international, flagrant corporate malfeasance and ethical violations. We see how controls imposed to prevent crony-fueled corporate crime by the Clinton administration were

From Michalowski, Raymond J., and Ronald C. Kamer, eds., *State-Corporate Crime: Wrongdoing at the Intersection of Business and Government.* Copyright © Rutgers, the State University. Reprinted by permission of Rutgers University Press.

dismantled by the Bush regime, paving the way for Halliburton to gain an ever-greater share of governmental contracts. Rothe shows us the movement back and forth between top political position and corporate power, with an elite inner circle of those with the right connections amassing great wealth while critical domestic re-construction and international warfare are shabbily underfunded. At the same time, today's taxpayers and their children will be left facing the burden of financing these state-corporate white-collar crimes.

To what extent do you think things have changed or stayed the same since this chapter was first written in 2006? What other kinds of organizations do you think might be operating under these kinds of collusions?

The intersection of state and corporate interests during times of war is a fundamental part of the war-making process. Every capitalist country must rely on private-sector production to produce the weapons of war. In the United States, for example, major auto manufacturers such as Chrysler, Ford, and Chevrolet retooled to produce tanks, guns, and missiles instead of cars during World War II, while many other companies refocused some or all of their production to serve the war effort. With the introduction of a permanent wartime economy after the end of World War II, amid concerns that the United States was coming to be dominated by a military-industrial complex, major providers of weapons and logistical support such as General Electric, Boeing, Bechtel Group, and Lockheed Martin became regular recipients of government contracts. They were also repeatedly at the center of controversies concerning cost overruns and questionable charges.

The close alignment of corporate and government interests in the production and procurement of the weapons of war is a vivid example of the "revolving door" effect as described by C. Wright Mills (1956) in *The Power Elite*. As executives from major military contractors fill elected or appointed government positions, the interests of the state become increasingly entangled with prior corporate loyalties.

In recent years the integration of state interests with those of the private corporation has intensified. This integration began with efforts to adapt to a downsized military through increased reliance on just on time privatized logistic contracts. The move to an active war footing following the attacks of 9/11, including the wars in Afghanistan and Iraq and the permanent "war on terror," further cemented the private-public strategy for war making in the United States.

The controversy surrounding links between Vice President Dick Cheney and Halliburton, the company he formerly headed, provides a demonstration of the potential for state-corporate crime embedded in this new policy of war by subcontract. There have been claims that the association between Cheney and Halliburton resulted in no-bid, cost-plus contractual work without competitive pricing or oversight. According to some, the affiliation between Cheney and Halliburton has established war profiteering as an acceptable and systematic practice within the Bush administration by rewarding "corporations for who they know rather than what they know, and a system in which cronyism is more important than competence" (W. Hartung 2004: 26).

This chapter examines the relationship between Halliburton, the current Bush administration, the "war on terrorism," and war profiteering. In doing so, I incorporate themes from previous state-corporate crime literature, particularly the concepts of state-facilitated and state-initiated forms of state-corporate crime in delineating the relationships between Halliburton and the U.S. government. On the one hand, I suggest that war profiteering in the form of overcharges is state-facilitated crime insofar as the government was aggressive in its refusal to take appropriate and available regulatory action. On the other hand, the Bush administration's repeal of the Clinton administration ruling regulating state contracts can be analyzed as state-initiated crime to the extent that these repeals allowed Halliburton to attain state contracts for which it would have not qualified previously....

BRIEF HISTORY OF HALLIBURTON

Halliburton was first established in 1919. Since that time the company has purchased several subsidiaries that include Brown and Root (including the consortium of Devonport Management Ltd.), Dresser Industries (known as KBR after the purchase of M. W. Kellogg by Dresser), Landmark Graphics Corporation, Wellstream, Well Dynamics, Eventure, and Subsea 7. The success of the Halliburton Corporation is the consequence of a range of strategic practices. Since the mid-1990s, however, many of Halliburton's corporate actions have come under the scrutiny of several U.S. governmental oversight organizations (such as the Securities and Exchange Commission, U.S. General Accounting Office, and congressional leaders), criminologists, and international critics. More specifically, the GAO charged Halliburton with improper billing for questionable expenses associated with its logistical work in the Balkans and the Defense Department charged fraudulent claims were submitted for work at Fort Ord, California. Among these corporate actions are a series of Halliburton's practices that can be classified as corporate crime. Halliburton's actions of systematically overcharging the U.S. government for contracted work, utilizing bribes to attain foreign contracts, and using subsidiaries and foreign joint ventures to bypass U.S. law restricting trade embargos have a long history.

Foreign Trade Barred under International Sanctions

Halliburton's participation in the practices of overcharging, bribing, and utilizing "loopholes" in general to bypass U.S. trade law or international sanctions cannot be traced solely to the 2003 invasion and subsequent occupation of Iraq. The company's business practices of corruption and corporate crime were evident during the 1990s when Dick Cheney was chief executive officer. For example, in 2001 the Treasury Department opened an inquiry into whether Halliburton had used transnational trade loopholes that allowed the company to circumvent sanctions on Iran by doing business with that country through foreign subsidiaries. In another instance, Halliburton's subsidiary, Dresser Inc., did substantial business with Iraq from 1997 through the summer of 2000, closing $73 million in deals with Saddam Hussein at a time when such dealings were prohibited by international trade sanctions. Many of these contracts occurred under the United Nation's oil-for-food program through joint ventures with the Ingersoll-Rand Company via subsidiaries known as the Dresser-Rand and Ingersoll Dresser Pump companies. Although Cheney claimed that Halliburton divested itself of the subsidiaries in 1998 as soon as it learned of the trading in violation of U.S. legislation prohibiting business ventures while Iraq was under sanctions by the United States and the United Nations, the firms continued trading with Baghdad for over a year past the time of Cheney's initial "awareness." Cheney signed nearly $30 million in contracts before he sold Halliburton's 49 percent stake in Ingersoll Dresser Pump Company in December 1999 and the 51 percent stake in Dresser-Rand in February 2000.

International Bribery Charges

In 2004 Halliburton came under investigation by the French government, the United States Department of justice, and the Securities and Exchange Commission for international bribery. The U.S. Department of justice conducted a criminal investigation into an alleged $180 million bribe paid by Halliburton and three other companies to the government of Nigeria. The alleged bribe was paid in exchange for awarding a contract to the companies to build a $4 billion natural gas plant in Nigeria's southern delta region. France is also investigating a former Halliburton executive for his role in the scheme. Investigators said $5 million of the bribes intended for Nigeria were deposited into the Swiss bank account of former KBR chairman Jack Stanley, who retired from the company on December 31, 2003. In 2002, the U.S. Securities and Exchange Commission investigated a second bribery case involving Nigeria. Halliburton admitted that its employees paid a $2.4 million bribe to a government official of Nigeria in order to receive favorable tax treatment, in violation of the U.S. Foreign Corrupt Practices Act and the convention adopted by the Organization for Economic Cooperation and Development prohibiting making bribes in the course of commercial transactions. At this writing the cases remain ongoing.

History of Fraud and Overcharges

In 1997 the U.S. General Accounting Office charged Halliburton with billing the U.S. Army for questionable expenses associated with its logistical work in the Balkans. These charges included billing $85.98 per sheet of plywood that cost Halliburton $14.06 and "cleaning" offices up to four times a day. A 2000 follow-up report by the GAO regarding Halliburton's contract in the Balkans found continuous systematic overcharges via inflated costs submitted in its billing to the army. Halliburton paid $2 million in fines to resolve the fraudulent overcharges.

In a separate inquiry, the Defense Department inspector general and a federal grand jury had investigated allegations that a subsidiary of Halliburton, KBR, defrauded the government of millions of dollars through inflated prices for repairs and maintenance for work at Fort Ord in California. In February

2002 Halliburton paid an additional $2 million in fines to resolve the fraud claims.

As these examples show, Halliburton has a history of corporate criminality and questionable organizational practices. However, it is the recent intermingling of Halliburton and Vice President Cheney that makes its corporate practices a case of state-initiated and/or state-facilitated corporate crime.

HALLIBURTON-CHENEY CONNECTIONS

The connections between Halliburton and Cheney date back to the early 1990s. Dick Cheney, as Ronald Reagan's secretary of defense, assigned Halliburton subsidiary Brown & Root the task of conducting a classified survey detailing how private corporations such as itself could provide logistical support for U.S. military forces scattered around the world. At that time Halliburton prepared a report to implement the privatization of everyday military activities and logistical planning, for which it earned $3.9 million. During the latter part of 1992, Halliburton received an additional $5 million for a follow-up study to outline how private firms could supply the logistical needs of several contingency plans at the same time. This led to "a five-year contract to be the U.S. Army's on-call private logistics arm," what was known as the Logistics Civil Augmentation Program (LOGCAP). Halliburton held this contract until 1997, when Dyncorp, another private firm specializing in providing military logistical support, beat Halliburton's competitive bid.

When Cheney's term as secretary of defense ended in 1993, he and his deputy secretary of defense, David Gribbin, were hired by Halliburton: Cheney as acting CEO and Gribbin as the official go-between to obtain contracts from the U.S. government. Cheney gave Halliburton "a level of access that no one else in the oil sector could duplicate" (Dean 2004: 43). Between 1995 and 2000 intense lobbying efforts paid off with a doubling of the value of Halliburton's government contracts. During 1999 and 2000, Halliburton reported spending $1.2 million on lobbying efforts while obtaining approximately $1 billion in defense contracts. The pattern of paying lobbyists to represent and to obtain future contracts quickly diminished once Cheney took office as vice president. As will be seen, the ratio of money spent on lobbying declined significantly while the value of contracts awarded to Halliburton increased notably. The Cheney-Halliburton marriage, as with all marriages, incorporated distant family members that include some members of the Bush family tree. William H. (Bucky) Bush, the uncle of George W., is a trustee on the board of Lord and Abbott, one of Halliburton's top shareholders. Indeed, this relationship may have played a role in prime contracts recently awarded to Lord Abbott in Iraq. The purchase of Dresser Inc. (1998) by Halliburton further enhanced the family tree of the Halliburton-Cheney marriage. Prescott Bush, father of George H. W. Bush, was the bank representative who financed Dresser and a member of the company's board for several years. The former president of Dresser Industries, Neil Mallon, was a close family friend and mentor to George H. W. Bush, and it was Mallon who was responsible for getting Bush into the oil industry.

Republican Party presidential nominee George W. Bush hired Cheney to oversee the selection process for a vice-presidential candidate. Just as Cheney was finding the right candidate (May–June 2000) to run on Bush's ticket, he sold 100,000 shares of Halliburton stock for 50.97 dollars a share for an approximate value of $5.1 million. The first week of July 2000 the news was official: it would be a Bush-Cheney ticket. Cheney resigned from Halliburton in August 2000 with a retirement package on a future contract worth $45 to $62.2 million, which included stocks, options, and deferred income payments. Shortly after his role as CEO of Halliburton ended and he announced he was running for vice president, Cheney sold another 660,000 shares of stock (worth approximately $36 million). However, he continued to hold 433,000 stock options....

Normally politicians put their stock assets into a blind trust after being elected to high office, so that someone else manages their stock portfolio. However, Cheney continued to hold 140,000 shares of unvested stock that is worth $7.6 million at 2005 stock prices. This stock could not be managed or sold by anyone until 2002, because it was unvested; thus it could not be put into a blind trust. Therefore Cheney had a direct financial interest in the value of Halliburton's stock and the financial profitability of Halliburton the first two years of his vice presidency. Cheney also owns great amounts of Halliburton stock that are safely tucked away in a blind trust for post-vice presidency personal use....

The Cheney-Halliburton relationship had indeed proved to be mutually beneficial while Cheney acted as CEO. Halliburton's revenue from state defense contracts such as LOGCAP nearly doubled (from $1.1 to $2.3 billion) under Cheney's five-year tenure as CEO compared with the five prior years. For example, in 1995 Halliburton jumped from seventy-third to eighteenth on the Pentagon's list of top contractors, benefiting from at least $3.8 billion in federal contracts and taxpayer-insured loans, according to the Center for Public Integrity.

HALLIBURTON AND
CHENEY-POST-"RETIREMENT"

Although it may appear to many that the Cheney-Halliburton marriage ended with the selling of stocks and options, the relationship continued. During his tenure as vice president, Cheney drew income both from U.S. taxpayers and from Halliburton. As Bivens (2004: 1) stated, "billions are slyly, secretively and controversially showered on the entity [Halliburton] that paid Dick Cheney 178,437 dollars this year, by the entity [the federal government] that paid him 198,600 dollars." For the previous year, 2002, Cheney received $162,392 from Halliburton and $190,134 as vice-presidential pay.

A Halliburton financial statement of January 2, 2001, showed that $147,579 was paid to Cheney that day as payout of salary from the company's Elective

Deferral Plan. This amount was a part of the salary Cheney earned in 1999 but had chosen to receive in five installments spread over five years. Another financial statement, of January 18, 2001, showed an additional $1,451,398 was paid under the company's "Incentive Plan C" for senior executives. This sum was Cheney's incentive compensation (yearly bonus based on the company's performance in 2000). Cheney's personal financial disclosure forms show that Cheney received $398,548 in deferred salary from Halliburton as vice president. Moreover, Cheney received another payment in 2004, and a final payment was made in 2005. As previously mentioned, Halliburton drastically reduced its lobbying for governmental contracts once Cheney took office. In the two years prior to Cheney's election as vice president, Halliburton spent $1.2 million lobbying and attained contracts worth approximately $900 million a year. During 2001–2002, Halliburton spent $600,000 dollars lobbying for contracts. In 2003 Halliburton lobbyist Charles Dominy (a retired general with the Army Corps of Engineers, which oversees contracts awarded in Iraq) spent only $300,000 lobbying Congress on behalf of Halliburton. Overall, from 2001 through 2003 Halliburton and its subsidiaries earned $6 billion in U.S. government contracts while spending only $900,000 lobbying, less than they would have spent in one year before their former CEO became vice president. As Thurber (2004: 1) observed, "They are already in; they don't need to lobby any more."

Although the relationship between Cheney and Halliburton appeared to be a major factor in awarding contracts to Halliburton, Cheney denied any involvement in the contracting process. On "Meet the Press" he said: "As Vice President, I have absolutely no influence of, involvement of, knowledge of in any way, shape or form of contracts let by the Army Corps of Engineers or anybody else in the Federal Government." Private memos, however, proved otherwise. An internal Pentagon e-mail (March 5, 2003) sent by an Army Corps of Engineer official claimed that Douglas Feith, the Defense Department's undersecretary for policy, approved arrangements for a multibillion dollar contract for Halliburton "contingent on informing the WH tomorrow. We anticipate no issues since action has been coordinated w/VP office" (Time 2004: 1). Within three days Halliburton received one of the first State Department contracts for Iraq worth as much as $7 billion, according to information on the Army Corps of Engineers Web site. Thus state-initiated actions put Halliburton in a favorable position to attain future multibillion-dollar contracts.

Halliburton Contracts

Immediately after September 11, 2001, the neoconservatives and many corporations seized the moment for personal, political, and economic gain. The "war on terrorism" was announced, the long-sought plans to attack Iraq were jump-started, and Halliburton was ready to cash in on its relationship with its past CEO. In November 2001, Halliburton subsidiary Brown & Root received a contract worth $2 million to reinforce the U.S. embassy in Tashkent, Uzbekistan. By December 2001, Halliburton had won back the cost-plus LOGCAP contract to provide facilities, logistic support, and provisions for U.S. troops in places such as Afghanistan, Qatar, Kuwait, Georgia, Jordan, Djibouti, and Uzbekistan. The contract was originally won back through a competitive bid. However, additional no-bid contracts were awarded as the holder of the quick-response LOG-CAP contract was already providing logistical help for the U.S. military and thus was ready at hand. "Halliburton was the obvious choice," said Army Corps of Engineers commander Lt. Gen. Robert Flowers. "To invite other contractors to complete to perform a highly classified requirement that KBR [Halliburton] was already under a competitively awarded contract to perform would have been a wasteful duplication of effort" (Flowers 2003). Unlike the previous LOG-CAP contract, the new contract extended over a ten-year period with an estimated value of $830 million to over $1 billion.

Halliburton (KBR) also received contracts worth $110 million to build prison cells and other facilities at Guantanamo Bay. With the recent addition of Camp 5 (a permanent addition also built by KBR), the prison capacity grew to 1,100 detainees....

During September 2002, 1,800 Halliburton employees were present in Kuwait and Turkey (under a contract for nearly $1 billion) to provide temporary housing (tents) and logistical support for the invasion into Iraq....

Under the competitively bid contract, KBR provides for the support of the Reception, Staging, Onward Movement, and Integration (RSOI) process of U.S. forces as they enter or depart their theater of operation by sea, air, or rail. The post for the Halliburton employees, Camp Arifjan, includes a gymnasium and fast food outlets, including, Burger King, Baskin-Robbins, and Subway, all paid for by U.S. taxpayers. While Halliburton employees are eating fast food, U.S. troops are served mess hall food and live in tents. Excessive U.S. taxpayer money is spent on cost-plus contracts allowing posh conditions for private contractors such as the one in Camp Arifjan while troops are left without the necessary equipment such as bullet-proof vests and armored vehicles. Moreover, Camp Arifjan is the same base in which a Saudi subcontractor hired by KBR billed for 42,042 meals a day on average but served only 14,053 meals a day....

Not only has Halliburton received billions of dollars from the state through competitive and noncompetitive contracts, but most of these were cost-plus contracts. Cost-plus contracts are essentially blank checks that ensure that Halliburton is reimbursed for whatever it bills for its services as well as an additional percentage (between 2 percent and 7 percent) for the company's profits (fees). These types of open-ended contracts are incentives to maximize expenditures to attain an increase in the total value of the contract and profits. Moreover, the larger the contract, the more valuable becomes Halliburton's stock. In October 2002, for example, Halliburton's stock was $12.62 a share. When the KBR Iraq restructure contract was awarded, its stock rose to $23.90 a share (see Halliburton stock portfolios 2001–2004). According to Henry Bunting's testimony to the Democratic Policy Committee, the Halliburton motto in Iraq is "don't worry about it, it's cost plus" (Bunting 2004). In essence, no one questioned pricing. "The comment by both Halliburton buyers and management was 'it's cost plus,' don't waste time finding another supplier."...

Under the Bush-Cheney administration, the profit from the war on terror benefited those corporations that were part of the "family."[1] Few other United States, foreign, or most significantly, Iraqi contractors benefited from U.S. government contracts resulting from the Iraq war. In May 2004, a Pentagon program management office in Baghdad reported that only 24,179 Iraqis were employed in the postwar rebuilding efforts (less than 1 percent of Iraq's total work force of seven million). Meanwhile, just 25 percent of Halliburton's employees in Iraq—6,000 out of 24,000 total—were Iraqis.

The close relationship between the administration and Halliburton constitutes a form of state-initiated war profiteering. While Halliburton may be guilty of inflating total contract values through overcharges and/or charges for services not provided, the opportunities for profiteering were the products of the cozy relationship between the company and a sitting administration whose vice president was Halliburton's former CEO.

STATE FACILITATION OF CORPORATE CRIME

Halliburton and its subsidiaries have engaged in systematic and significant overcharging for services for contracts awarded in Iraq. This is not new behavior for the company. Thus it is not surprising that Halliburton would use "war on terrorism" cost-plus contracts as an opportunity for overcharging. Previously, systemic overcharging by corporations potentially could have resulted in periods of ineligibility for new federal contracts. Specifically, some of the added language required a satisfactory record of integrity and business ethics, including satisfactory compliance with the relevant labor and employment, environmental, antitrust, and consumer protection laws.

The burden of enforcement was on the contracting officers to consider all relevant credible information, with the greatest weight given to offenses adjudicated within the past three years. Thus it relied on the compliance of contracting officers for enforcement.

During the Clinton administration, requirements for contractors bidding on federal contracts were strengthened. New "blacklisting" regulations would have barred contractors from future contracts if they had committed past labor, environmental, or violations of federal trade laws. On April 1, 2001, however, the Bush administration revoked this regulation (no. 65 FR 80255) with no. 66 FR 17754, thus undoing the tightening of regulations put forth by the Clinton administration. This change made it possible for Halliburton and other corporate criminals to obtain contracts regardless of previous or current allegations of illegal practices. Moreover, although payments to corporations under investigation by a federal agency are supposed to be deferred, Halliburton continued to receive its pay as investigations were being carried out, thereby facilitating Halliburton's alleged illegal activities. For example, Halliburton was under investigation by the SEC for accounting fraud that was alleged to have occurred from 1999 to 2001, and the Justice Department was conducting an investigation on charges of bribery connected with the Nigerian official to attain an oil contract in Nigeria. After contracts were awarded to Halliburton in Iraq, the company continued to come under investigations by the Congressional Oversight Committee and the Department of Defense for overcharges, as we shall see.

In 2003 a Pentagon audit found that Halliburton (KBR) had overcharged the U.S. government for approximately fifty-seven million gallons of gasoline delivered to Iraqi citizens under a no-bid contract. These overcharges totaled nearly $61 million from May through September 2003. KBR was charging from $2.27 to $3.09 a gallon to import gasoline from Kuwait, while a different contractor delivered gas from Turkey to Iraq for $1.18 a gallon. Iraq's state oil company (SOMA) was charging 96 cents a gallon for gasoline delivered to the same depots in Iraq, utilizing the same military escorts.

Further exacerbating the problem, part of the money for the KBR gas service contract came from the United Nation's oil-for-food program (now the Development Fund for Iraq). Under the terms of UN Security Resolution 1483, an independent board called the International Advisory and Monitoring Board was to be created to ensure that UN oil-for-food funds were spent for the benefit of Iraqi citizens. The purpose of this agency was to be "the primary vehicle for guaranteeing the transparency of the DFI and for ensuring the DFI funds are used properly" (U.S. House 2003: 6). As of the end of 2003, this body had not been created. Thus the use of these funds to pay inflated prices to Halliburton ($600 million out of $1 billion in funds was transferred to Halliburton) by the U.S. Coalition Provisional Authority went uncontested. In this case the government's failure to provide the necessary oversight agency constitutes a case of state-facilitated wrongdoing.

After it won a ten-year contract worth $3.8 billion to provide food, wash clothes, deliver mail, and other basic services, Halliburton continued to systematically overcharge the government for services rendered (and unrendered). In one case Halliburton charged the government $67 million more for military dining services than the corporation had paid to the actual subcontractors who provided the service. The *Wall Street Journal* reported that Pentagon auditors believed the corporation overcharged $16 million for meals served at Camp Arifjan (subcontracted to Tamimi Global Company). Moreover, the military was already paying Halliburton $28 a day per soldier. In December 2003, Halliburton had estimated it served twenty-one million meals to 110,000 soldiers at forty-five sites in Iraq. Early in 2004 military auditors suspected the corporation was cooking the numbers and overcharging the government millions of dollars. The fact that these overcharges occurred in at least five of Halliburton's facilities suggests they were part of a systematic effort to increase profit margin.

Not only did Halliburton overcharge the government (nearly three times the number of meals than were actually provided to soldiers in Kuwait over a nine-month period), it had been repeatedly warned and audited for its dining service conditions by the Coalition Provisional Authority's inspector general Bowen. The claims were that the food was dirty, blood was consistently found on the kitchen floors, the utensils were dirty, and meats were rotting in four of the military messes the company operates in Iraq. Moreover, Halliburton's promises of improvement in these messes were empty as they "have not been followed through" (NBC News 2003). Regardless of the Pentagon report warning of "serious repercussions," no actions to date have been taken. The government has thus facilitated illegal and unethical profiteering by allowing charges for meals never provided and unsafe food handling and preparations (NBC News 2003)....

Beyond overcharging and purchasing unnecessary and/or excessive products, Halliburton systematically billed for labor never performed. For example, Representative Henry Waxman posted whistleblower testimony on *his* Web site revealing systematic practices of overpaying employees for hours of labor never performed and billed to the U.S. government. One of the testimonials, from Mike West, stated he was hired as a labor foreman at a salary of $130,000. Moreover, he stated he was paid despite the fact that he had no work; "I only worked one day out of six in Kuwait." During his tenure at Al Asad he claimed to have worked one of every five days, although he was told by his supervisor to bill for twelve hours of labor every day.

The failure of the House of Representatives Government Reform Committee to hear whistleblower testimony suggests that Halliburton's actions clearly fall in the category of state-facilitated corporate crime.

Halliburton's practice of billing for delivering supplies has amounted to systematic overcharges. The U.S. taxpayer has been billed nearly $327 million as of mid-2004 for these runs, and Halliburton was expecting to charge an additional $230 million more. Yet many of these runs have been unnecessary, because at least one in three trucks makes the three-hundred-mile trip empty, while others may carry only one pallet of supplies. Moreover, of the fleet of trucks (Mercedes and Volvos), dozens have not been used. Trailers are left along the roadside when the slightest mechanical problem or flat tire occurs, or when the convoy lacks necessary maintenance items. It was also reported that one Halliburton employee took a video in January 2004 of fifteen empty trailers on the road and stated, "This is just a sample of the empty trailers we're handling called sustainers. And there's more behind me.... his is fraud and abuse."

As controversy continues to shroud the Bush-Cheney administration, little to no public outcry has occurred over the blatant misuse of a political office. In part this is due to the ideology of unquestioning patriotism during times of war, and also due to the lack of attention by news media to these issues. This has led to state-facilitated profiteering by Halliburton as an agent of the state. After all, Halliburton is the "biggest contractor to the U.S. government in Iraq earning three times as much as Bechtel, its nearest competitor... earning $3.9 billion dollars from the military in 2003, a dizzying 680% increase from 2002 when it earned $483 million" (Chatterjee 2004: 39).

The Bush-Cheney team has achieved a level of secrecy and symbolic power unlike that of any other administration. Criminologists and the public must delve into understanding how and why the Cheney-Halliburton marriage has been able to remain and prosper in the White House. Not doing so increases the probability of future abuses of power, corrupt relationships, and war profiteering....

CONCLUSION

The atrocity of September 11, 2001, clearly was a factor in enabling the Bush administration to gain public support for the war on Iraq. Moreover, the timing of the attacks coincided with the "right" administration being placed in the White House. Halliburton was perfectly positioned to seize the moment to attain additional state contracts. Moreover, the direct connection to Cheney provided further opportunities for Halliburton that would not have been present without the aforementioned conditions.

While war profiteering by Halliburton has been characterized by defense officials as stupid mistakes that can be made right by *nole contendere* payments, the systematic practice of over-costs, overcharges, failure to provide services charged for, and kickback profits are actually a result of the incestuous relationship between Halliburton, Cheney, and Bush. Beyond their existing empowered roles within the state, their political agendas have paved the way for further privatizing areas of the world deemed U.S. interests. More specifically, the Bush administration's imperial agenda, coupled with its private interest in fostering economic expansion through privatization for its "family" companies, has created an environment conducive to war profiteering. Thus the motive for economic gain is both personal and political, serving both administration members' individual financial situations and their neoconservative political agenda. Moreover, Cheney's ties with Halliburton "represent a continuing financial interest in those employers which makes them potential conflicts of interests" (Congressional Research Service, quoted in Chatterjee 2004: 44). Hence the Supreme Court rulings appointing Bush and Cheney into the White House, coupled with the September 11, 2001, attacks, brought an explosion of opportunities for the administration, Halliburton, and war profiteering.... efforts to control these forms of state-corporate crimes must address all levels of the model: actors; the organizational, structural, and economic culture of hypercapitalism; and the international arena. As state and state-corporate crime literature suggests, there must be internal and external controls. Until measures are taken to provide international regulations for transnational corporations and accountability measures for states utilizing privatization of defense work, no external controls will exist. Currently there are little to no incentive or enforcement mechanisms for the state to adhere to any international laws. Therefore an empowered universal criminal court that is empowered to address states and corporations must be allowed to exist within the international arena.

As long as the current administration's use of secrecy and flagrant violations of checks and balances remains unchallenged by Congress, the public, and the press, little will be done to stop the practices of granting unregulated defense contracts. Internal regulations must be established to separate state from corporate interests. These must include an end to the practice of lobbying and campaign contributions. The revolving door between public and private must be closed. Without these internal and external controls, war profiteering will continue.

NOTE

1. The Bush-Cheney family includes the Carlyle Group (Where the senior Bush was a board member and holds significant stock shares); Lockhead Martin (Lynne Cheney was a broad member from 1994 to January 2001, as well as a director); Engineered Support System (William Bush is on the board of directors); and lord and Abbott (William Bush is acting trustee).

REFERENCES

Bivens, M. 2004. "Vice President Halliburton." *The Nation*, April 14.

Bunting, H. 2004. In *Testisitony Given to Senate Democratic Policy Committee.* Session 12: Democratic Policy Committee on Iraq Contact Abuses. Washington, DC, February 13.

Chatterjee, P. 2004. *Iraq Inc.: A Profitable Occupation.* New York: Seven Stories Press.

Dean, J. 2004. *Worse than Watergate: The Secret Presidency of George W. Bush.* New York: Little, Brown and Company.

Flowers, General Robert, 2003. Memo Response to House of Representative Waxman. http://www.house.gov/ Waxman/. Also available in testimony of Senate Democratic Policy Committee Hearing, http://democrats. senate.gov/dpc/hearings/hearings24/ transcript.pdf.

Hartung, W. 2004. *How Much Are You Making on the War Daddy? A Quick and Dirty Guide to War Profiteering in the Bush Administration.* New York: Nation Books.

Mills, C. W. 1956. *The Power Elite.* New York: Oxford University Press.

NBC News. 2003. Pentagon Report News Coverage. September 14. Archived Transcripts. http://www.nbc.com.

Time. 2004. "The Paper Trail: Did Cheney Okay a Deal?" May 30, 1.

Thurber, J. 2004. The *Progress Report* Archive. *American Progress Report.* http://www.americanprogress.org/ site/pp.asp?c=biJRJ8OVF&b=9328 (accessed November 17, 2004).

U.S. House of Representatives. 2003. See Flowers (2003).

Structure of the Deviant Act

Although the structure of deviant associations is revealing, in Part VII we investigate the characteristics of the acts of deviance themselves. Deviant associations involve the social organization of the deviants as people; it depicts the types of relationships they have with other deviants. Deviant acts focus on the particular instance of deviance, not the relationships surrounding them. When we look at the structure of deviant acts, we look at the nature of the transaction: its length, its goals, its stability, the degree of cooperation or conflict involved, the number of parties involved, and the way the participants interact (or do not interact) with one another.

Deviant acts involve one or more people aiming to accomplish a particular deviant goal. These vary widely in character from those enduring over a period of months to the more fleeting encounters that last only a few minutes, from those conducted alone to those requiring the participation of several or many people, and from those where the participants are face-to-face to those where they are physically separated. At the same time, acts of deviance can be looked at in terms of what they have in common. All deviant acts consist of purposeful behavior intended to accomplish a gratifying end, require the coordination of participants (if there are more than one), and depend on individuals reacting flexibly to unexpected events that may arise in this relatively unstructured and unregulated arena. Like the relations among deviants, deviant acts fall along a continuum of sophistication and organizational complexity. Following Best and Luckenbill's (1981) typology, we arrange them here according to the minimum number of their participants and the intricacy of the relations among these participants, moving again from the least to the most organizationally sophisticated.

Some deviant acts can be accomplished by a lone **individual**, without recourse to the assistance or presence of other people. This does not mean that others cannot accompany the deviant, either before or during the deviant act, or even that two deviants cannot commit acts of individual deviance together. Rather, the defining characteristic of individual deviance is that it can be committed by one person, to that person, on that person, for that person. A teenager's suicide, a drug addiction, a skid row transient's alcoholism, and a self-induced abortion are all examples of individual behavioral deviance. Non-behavioral forms of individual deviance include obesity, minority group status, a physical disability, and a deviant belief system (such as alternative religious or political beliefs). Individual deviance has areas of overlap with loner deviance, discussed in Part VI, but there are also ways in which they diverge. Sexual asphyxia, eating disorders, and suicide all fall within both categories, able to be accomplished alone and usually done without the benefit of associations with other like deviants. But individual deviants, unlike loners, can hang around and participate in subcultures and countercultures with other fellow deviants as long as they can accomplish their deviant act alone. Individual deviants, such as illicit drug users, stutterers, transvestites, the depressed, the obese, and the homeless, are colleagues. On the other hand, loners, unlike individual deviants, need not rely exclusively on themselves to accomplish their acts of deviance; they may have victims. Rapists, murderers, embezzlers, physician drug addicts, and obscene telephone callers are loners, but not individual deviants. Turvey's chapter 38 on sexual asphyxia discusses such a solitary deviant practice, where people diminish the flow of oxygen to their brains during autoeroticism in order to enhance their sexual climaxes.

A second type of deviant act involves the **cooperation** of at least two voluntary participants. This cooperation usually involves the transfer of illicit goods, such as pornography, arms, or drugs, or the provision of deviant services, such as those in the sexual or medical realm. Cooperative deviant acts may involve the exchange of money. Where this is absent, participants usually trade reciprocal acts. They both come to the interaction wanting to give and get something. In deviant sales, one participant supplies an illicit good or service in exchange for money. One or more of the participants in such acts may be earning a living through this means.

Draus and Carlson's chapter on crack whores illustrates the way prostitutes exchange sex for drugs, where both parties gain something in the transaction. Durkin's chapter on cybershrews shows how men are willing to humiliate, degrade, and impoverish themselves in online interactions with dominatrixes. Again, in this illustration, both sides agree to participate in the exchange consensually.

The final type of deviant act is one of **conflict** between the involved parties. One or more perpetrators force the interaction on the unwilling other(s), or an act seemingly entered into through cooperation turns out with one party setting up the other. In either case, the core relationship between the interactants is one of hostility, with one person getting the more favorable outcome. Conflictual acts may be carried out through secrecy, trickery, or physical force, but they end up with one person giving up goods or services to the other, involuntarily and without adequate compensation. Conflictual acts may be highly volatile in character, as victims may complain to the authorities or enlist the aid of outside parties if they have the chance. To be successful, therefore, perpetrators must control not only their victims' activities, but also victims' perception of what is going on. Such acts can range from kidnapping and blackmail to theft, fraud, arson, pickpocketing, trespassing, and assault.

Various types of conflictual and exploitive deviance abound and are thriving, both domestically and internationally. We have witnessed the repopularization of kidnapping abroad for political, military, and financial purposes. Domestic rates of rape, committed by strangers, friends, and family members have never been higher. The prevalence of fraud is also rising precipitously, aided by the Internet, through fake stock tips, travel scams, identity theft, "phishing" (where victims disclose account passwords and other data online in response to e-mails that seem to come from legitimate business), "pharming" (where experienced hackers are able to redirect people from a legitimate site to a bogus site without users even knowing it), mail-order bride schemes, and "advance fee" 419 scams (where you are contacted by a solicitor from abroad offering fabulous riches if you will help them recover some lost fortune). Identity theft is also prevalent, and apparently popular among methamphetamine addicts, since the skill set of meth users facilitates this kind of fraud. In this Part, you will find examples of deviant acts full of conflict, such as Armstrong, Hamilton, and Sweeney's example of sexual assaults on college campuses and Engdahl's propositions for opportunities for white-collar crime. In both these articles, the parties involved, unlike in the case of cooperative acts, do not agree to be part of the act, and only one side acts as the perpetrator and the other side are the victims.

38

Autoerotic Sexual Asphyxia

BRENT TURVEY

Turvey debunks previous images of sexual asphyxia, otherwise known as the "ultimate orgasm," offering rare insights into this highly secretive and hidden form of deviance. Primarily a solitary, loner practice, sexual asphyxia is pursued by individuals who desire to raise their level of orgasmic pleasure through self-strangulation. So deviant that practitioners rarely reveal their interest in this act even to friends and lovers, it is accomplished outside of any deviant support group or subculture. Turvey outlines some of the features of this highly secretive form of individual deviance, the characteristics of individuals who engage in it, and the driving force behind their involvement with an emphasis on the myths, criteria, and issues faced by a medical examiner or Coroner dealing with autoerotic fatalities.

Although Turvey attempts to debunk certain stereotypes, which of them do you still believe have some validity? Why do you think so many of those who die are young? What are some of the methodological problems in a study like this?

Autosexuality, the same thing as autoeroticism, is defined as "perversions performed on oneself, including masturbation" (Holmes[6]). It must be assumed that shared sexuality, by inference, would be defined by Holmes as perversions performed on others. Holmes, and others who engage in the autoerotic debate, often suffer from such failures to resolve conflicts between public and private views on sexuality. This tendency often brings poorly defined morality to the debate, and detracts from the purposes of the Forensic Sciences. Autoeroticism may be defined as masturbation and other forms of self-gratification. Auto-erotic fatality may be defined as any death that occurs as a result of behavior that is performed as a form of self-gratification.

Example: "The victim, a twenty-six-year-old white male, died while suspended by leather wrist restraints from a hook in the ceiling. When found, he was wearing a commercially produced 'discipline Mask' and had a bit in his mouth. A length of rope was attached to each end of the bit and ran over his shoulders, going through an eyelet at the back of a specially designed belt he was wearing. The pieces of rope ran to eyelets on both sides of his body and were connected to wooden dowels that extended the length of his legs. The ropes were attached to two plastic water bottles, one on each ankle. The bottles were filled with water and each weighed 7 pounds. The victim's ankles had leather restraints about them. A clothespin was affixed to each of the victim's nipples. The victim's belt had a leather device that ran between his buttocks and was attached to the rear in front of his belt. This belt device included a dildo that was inserted in his anus and an aperture through which his penis protruded. His penis was encased in a piece of pantyhose and a toilet-paper cylinder. A small red ribbon was tied in a bow at the base of his penis." (Hazelwood, Burgess, & Dietz[5])

This case demonstrates a blatant, undeniable autoerotic fatality that is complete with props. But not every case will look like it, or even be as overt. Each autoerotic fatality is as different or as similar in its engagement as the personality of the individual who orchestrates it. Every autoerotic death has its own personal script. That is due in part to the fact that masturbation is a deeply personal, sexual act. This is a critical notion that is often dismissed by even the most seasoned death investigators. Failure to accept this notion will assist in the pathologist's failure to recognize autoerotic fatalities when they are so *confronted*. Again, autoerotic behavior is a kind of masturbation, and masturbation is a personal and dynamic behavior.

Specific circumstantial elements that can help a forensic pathologist distinguish an autoerotic fatality will be discussed later on.

WHY?

The general appeal of autoerotic behavior is fairly straightforward: sexual gratification.

There are dangerous autoerotic behaviors that individuals find similarly appealing. Of these, perhaps the most prevalent is autoerotic asphyxia.

An important question surrounding autoerotic asphyxia, for those who are not familiar with the term, is why. Why is engagement in autoerotic asphyxia pleasurable? Where does the pleasure come from?

The pleasure can be generally understood as arriving from two distinct sources (distinct but not exclusive). The first source of pleasure is physical, and the second is psychological. Both are equally potent pleasure sources on their own. Put them together and the combination can easily provide the foundation for a dangerous habit.

The physical pleasure from autoerotic asphyxia comes with the reduction of oxygen to the brain, or Hypoxia, which just means partial oxygen deprivation (DiMaio & DiMaio[3]). This is simple euphoric asphyxia. Less oxygen to the brain equals a semi-hallucinogenic, lucid state. It is pleasurable enough on its own to be engaged in without bondage or genital manipulation. It can be performed while entirely clothed.

Dietz[2] gives us an example of a death by sexual asphyxia (classified as an autoerotic fatality), with all of the classic earmarks, yet little sexual obviousness at the scene:

> A 42-year-old Asian man was found hanging by the neck, suspended by a rope attached to the raised shovel of a John Deere Model JD410, diesel powered, backhoe tractor.... The decedent was suspended in a semi-sitting position by a cloth safety harness strap wrapped around his neck and clipped to a rope that was hooked to the raised shovel of the backhoe tractor. A towel was between the loose fitting strap and the victim's neck. A long piece of plastic pipe was connected on one end by conduit tape to the hydraulic control lever of the shovel in the operator's compartment of the tractor. A broom stick was taped to the other end of the pipe and was partially under the decedent's buttocks. The hydraulic shovel could be easily raised or lowered by slight pressure applied to the broomstick. The decedent was fully clothed, and his genitals were not exposed. No pornographic materials, women's clothing items, or mirrors were at the scene.... He had no known psychiatric illness.

Determination of autoerotic death was made from decedent history and circumstantial indicators. The victim kept a journal of love poetry dedicated to his tractor that he had named "Stone," outlining his desire for them to "soar high" together. The victim was unmarried and lived with his parents on their farm. He also had a reasonable expectation of privacy for an extended period, as he engaged in this behavior in the late evening down by the barn. Cause of death was determined to be accidental autoerotic asphyxiation with carbon monoxide intoxication as a contributor.

The psychological source of pleasure from autoerotic asphyxia is personal, and therefore difficult to generalize. The pleasure is best understood as residing in the fantasy. It is widely accepted that the fantasy is fueled by the masochistic/cordophilic aspect of the behavior. The sexual pleasure associated with binding oneself up in a restrictive and/or complex fashion can have a twofold effect: (1) Self-restriction, and (2) Pain/pleasure. The psychological pleasure derived from either of those fantasy behaviors is sufficient reason for many individuals to engage in that form of sexual activity. Bondage and masochism are widely practiced without the element of hypoxia.

An individual involved in dangerous autoerotic behavior of any kind generally has a rich and intense fantasy life. The most accurate way to understand that form of fantasy and pleasure, on an individual basis, is to have the individual explain it to you themselves, in their own words, or to read about it in a journal of love poetry they wrote in honor of their backhoe tractor.

What can be seen and understood of the fantasy, by the pathologist, is the object. Every fantasy requires an object to fulfill it. In the above case it was the backhoe tractor. In other cases it may be complex ligature, pornographic paraphernalia, women's undergarments, or perhaps some other masochistic element. All of these objects assist the fantasy and accelerate sexual arousal. If the pathologist or death investigator can identify the object of the decedent's fantasy, the autoerotic behavior will begin to explain itself.

Additional explanations include masochistic sensations when approaching death and backing off at the last possible second. Prevailing over that brush with mortality is often perceived as empowering. On that note, many individuals who engage in autoerotic asphyxia may do so in concert with genital masturbation and insertion of objects into their body's orifices for further sexual stimulation, although not necessarily.

Combining all of these elements together, it becomes clearer as to why some extreme types of autoerotic behavior (including autoerotic asphyxia), although dangerous, are a behavior of choice for certain individuals. Individuals of all ages and social strata find behaviors akin to autoerotic asphyxia pleasurable. This is not disputed.

MYTHS

There are many common myths surrounding autoerotic fatalities. This is largely the product of social fear and social ignorance which girdles the issue. It is widely documented that parents or loved ones alter the scene of victims in such cases[5] in order to mislead investigators. They wish to avoid embarrassment. They wish to hide the truth of their loved one's demise and put it away where no one can see it. In addition, investigators and pathologists have their own problems with the issue. Some have problems because they consider the behavior perverse, others because they simply do not recognize it for what it is.

Autoerotic asphyxia is, as discussed earlier, a form of masturbation. Masturbation is one of the few cultural taboos that older society pretends to hold on to. There is also a great deal of cultural evidence to suggest that we are still very publicly ashamed of our sexuality. It is therefore no great wonder that bad and often judgmental information can lead the way to investigating or even discussing autoerotic fatalities.

In discussions on this topic with colleagues, the author has noted that several individuals labor under the impression that the deceased in these cases should be regarded as criminal. Holmes[6] lists Erotic Asphyxiation under the heading "Dangerous Sex Crimes," along with others including Lust Killers, Pyromaniacs, and Necromaniacs. That classification is an egregious error for too many reasons to list here.

It is important to express that individuals who die while engaging in autoeroticism are not guilty of a crime, unless perhaps they live in Missouri or Mississippi. There is nothing criminal about exercising careless masturbation unless someone else is killed or property is damaged. In autoerotic asphyxia and other types of autoerotic fatalities, this is rarely the case. Once a death is ruled to be an autoerotic fatality, law enforcement is generally out of the picture.

Moreover, the author perceives four principal myths surrounding autoerotic fatalities. To effectively engage in the death investigation of a possible autoerotic fatality, the pathologist or death investigator must reconcile these myths with the documented facts. They are as follows:

Myth # 1—Age

"Decedents tend to be young boys."

Adelson[1], in his book, *The Pathology of Homicide*, published in 1973, was a proponent of this theory. He stated, in reference to autoerotic deaths, that they were "a unique group of accidental hangings usually involving young boys ages nine and fourteen or fifteen." And he described it as the termination of a dangerous game played by boys. He was later cited by Geberth[4] and Holmes[6] concerning this specific issue

This statement is a myth because it is only partly accurate. According to the study of autoerotic asphyxial deaths published by Hazelwood, Burgess, and Dietz[5], operating with the largest subject population of any study to date (N = 132), 37 of the subjects were white teenage males. However, 42 of the subjects were white males (plus one black) between the ages of 20 and 29. An additional 28 subjects were white males (plus one Hispanic and two black) between the ages of 30 and 39. This clearly shows that each of those three age clusters are strongly represented by the data. In light of this sampling, the age generalization cannot practically be applied to the occurrence of autoerotic fatalities. When applied to a death investigation, the need for reconciliation of this myth is compounded.

> *Example* [5]: "A 47-year-old divorced dentist was found on the floor of his office by the janitor. He was lying face down on the floor with an anesthesia mask held in place over his mouth and nose by the weight of his head. His shirt was open and his trousers unzipped. He was alleged to have taken sexual advantage of his patients while they were under anesthesia in his office."

Failure to terminate inhalation of the anesthetic agent, nitrous oxide, resulted in the death of this individual. He was an older man; a professional with an education. A man with some intimate understanding of anatomy, physiology, and the potency of the hypoxia caused by nitrous oxide. He was not ignorant to the potential danger of his activities and he was not a teenager engaging in sexual self, discovery–type behavior. His age group is not to be ignored for the possibility of autoerotic fatalities.

Myth # 2—Gender

"Autoerotic fatalities occur only in men."

This is by far the most concerning myth. It harkens back to a misguided male mind set that females do not have the same sexual desires as males, and therefore do not masturbate. Not only is it supported by Adelson[1], but Geberth[4].

Similarly, DiMaio and DiMaio[3] minimize female occurrences by saying of sexual asphyxia: "Such deaths are rare, with the victim virtually always a male. Only a few cases involving a females have been reported:"

The inferences made by the above authors are entirely misleading. Although female occurrences are not as frequent as male occurrences, they do exist in the data. If the Pathologist or death investigator does not think to look at female cases with the possibility of autoerotic fatality in mind, then something may be overlooked in the examination of the body, the scene, or the history.

In a lecture that the author attended in the winter of this year given by S.A. Max Thiel (ret.)[8] of the FBI on the subject of autoerotic fatalities, there was a marked show of public embarrassment and disbelief in the audience. One female attendee asked how any female could possibly perform an autoerotic act. She seemed unbelieving of the answer that she received. Female data are presented by Hazelwood, Burgess, and Dietz[5], Sass[7], and Holmes[6].

Example [5]: "A thirty-year-old single woman was found dead in her locked apartment. She was nude and lying supine on a blanket on the bedroom floor. A pillow beneath her buttocks elevated them. Her legs were slightly spread, and her arms were by her sides. A blouse was lodged in her mouth and covered her face. Next to the body was a dental plate belonging to the victim. Near her left foot were an empty beer can, an ashtray, and a drinking glass. Neither the body nor the scene exhibited signs of a struggle. The victim's clothes and purse (containing her keys) were on her bed. A vibrator and leather bondage materials were found in her closet. The door was locked with a spring bolt. The autopsy report indicated that she had choked to death."

Example [5]: "A black woman in her early twenties was discovered in a severely decomposed condition. She was found on a bed in her locked apartment where she had resided alone. She was nude and lay face down with a pillow under her abdomen and her buttocks in the air. Her right hand was beneath her, near her vagina. Her face was turned to one side, and a knife was beneath her cheek. On the bed immediately below her vagina lay a long sausage, which in all probability, fell from her vagina after death. On the kitchen counter a package of similar sausages, once frozen, had since thawed. The apartment door had been locked from within, and no other persons were known to possess a key."

Hazelwood, Burgess, and Dietz[5] note that the cause of death in this second example remained undetermined due to severe decomposition, but included it because of a similar Japanese case that presented a woman who died while masturbating with a carrot (Tomita & Uchida[9]). The cause of death was determined, in that case, to have been a subarachnoid hemorrhage, which is a form of stroke.

Example [7]: "This case occurred in a midwestern city … and involved a woman 35 years of age, a divorcee with a nine-year-old daughter.

The mother was found deceased by the daughter *in* the morning after the child arose from a night's sleep in an adjoining room.

The child had gone to bed at 10:00 p.m. ... upon awakening noticed a strange humming noise coming from her mother's room. After entering the room, she found her mother hanging deceased in a small closet off the bedroom.

The victim was found completely nude lying on a small shelved space at the rear of the closet. Her feet were against the wall and her body was extended in a prone position, head downward ... There was a folded quilt placed on the front portion of the shelf that was immediately under her abdomen and upper thighs....

... She died of strangulation. An electric vibrator connected to an extension cord was found running. The vibrator was positioned between her thighs and the hard rubber massage head in contact with the victim's vulva. There was a string-type clothespin on the nipple of her right breast, compressing the nipple, and another clothespin of the same type was found immediately below her left breast....

... Over the place where the body was lying on this shelved area was a small narrow shelf 66 in. above the floor. This was attached to the wall by two steel brackets and the one closest to the shelved area had a nylon hose tied around it which formed a long loop. The victim has placed her head in the loop and placed a hand towel between her neck and the nylon hose. Her face was turned toward the wall and laying against it."

Women masturbate. Women engage in autoerotic behavior. Women who engage in dangerous forms of autoerotic behavior can die from it. Asphyxia and trauma are not sexually discriminate in their effects on human anatomy. If that tenet of autoerotic fatalities is ignored by a death investigator, or a pathologist, then autoerotic fatalities among women may be overlooked. The belief that it doesn't happen among women may create classification errors in future reporting despite any previous documentation to the contrary.

Myth # 3—Nudity

"Nudity, or partial nudity, is always a feature in autoerotic death scenes."

As Thiel[8] reminds us, nudity must be explained at any death scene. Nudity can be a feature of an autoerotic fatality. However, nudity is not a necessary feature of an autoerotic death, as was demonstrated by the example in the section entitled. "Why"... Many serious researchers make the statement that nudity or partial nudity is an element of an autoerotic fatality (DiMaio & DiMaio[3], Holmes[6], and Thiel[8]). This is misleading, again, because it is only mostly true.

Nudity or partial nudity can help with a pathologist's determination as to whether or not the decedent was engaged in autoerotic behavior. However there are many documented cases of autoerotic fatalities that do not have a feature of nudity ([2]; [5]). If cases that do not have a feature of nudity are excluded as possible autoerotic fatalities on that basis alone, a classification error may occur.

Myth # 4—Transvestitism

"Most autoerotic deaths are characterized by transvestitism."

Transvestitism [5]: Recurrent and persistent cross-dressing by a heterosexual male for whom there is no explanation other than sexual excitement for the cross-dressing behavior.

There are widespread anecdotal reports of male decedents being discovered wearing female undergarments or clothing. A sampling of the literature yields these results: Holmes[6] notes cross-dressing as a typical element in an autoerotic hanging; DiMaio and DiMaio[3], on the other hand, note a less common tendency in decedents to wear female articles of clothing. Adelson[1] takes his conjecture further, saying, " … one aspect of sexual psychopathy is observed occasionally in … fatal hangings involving boys and men who are transvestites…. When discovered dead by hanging, they are wearing female undergarments and occasionally, female outer clothing." This demonstrates the diversity of thought on the matter among an array of published experts. This also likely demonstrates that what is typical to these experts is probably a function of personal experience, and not necessarily typical for the entire population of autoerotic asphyxial decedents.

Hazelwood, Burgess, and Dietz[5] and Thiel[8] are more careful in their reporting of the data. They note that sometimes the decedent is attired in one or more articles of female clothing. 20.5% of their sample population were cross-dressed at death. But Hazelwood, Burgess, and Dietz[5] also note that this is probably not transvestitism. They hypothesize that individuals found cross-dressed are probably utilizing the female articles for their masochistic value. They diagnosed only 3.9% of their sample population as transvestites.

Geberth[4] includes their comments in his chapter on the phenomenon of autoerotic fatalities. Not surprisingly, his criterion for making a determination of autoerotic death does not include transvestitism or cross-dressing. Geberth[4] also cites DiMaio and DiMaio[3].

The best data does not support the claim that most autoerotic deaths are characterized by transvestitism. Transvestitism occurs in only a slight portion of autoerotic death cases. Cross-dressing is a little more common, but only one-fifth of the time. In either case, the idea that tranvestitism is prevalent in either form is untrue.

The trained pathologist or death investigator has an obligation to the decedent to resolve these myths and conduct an objective investigation. The failure to resolve any one of these myths is enough to mislead even the most seasoned death investigator. The importance of reconciling personal experience with overall data is equally important.

THE OBJECTIVE CRITERIA

There are many laundry lists available that characterize typical elements of an autoerotic death. Unfortunately, they are generalizations. While they are good compasses for a bewildered investigation, they do **not** apply to every case.

The following is a list of the objective criteria that should be used to assist the pathologist or death investigator to determine autoerotic death. Recall the definition:

> **Autoerotic fatality:** Any death that occurs as a result of behavior that is performed as a form of self-gratification.

Criteria[4]

1. Evidence of a physiological mechanism for obtaining or enhancing sexual arousal that provides a self-rescue mechanism or allows the victim to voluntarily discontinue its effect
2. Reasonable expectation of privacy
3. Evidence of solo sexual activity
4. Evidence of sexual fantasy aids
5. Evidence of prior dangerous autoerotic practice
6. No apparent suicidal intent

> *Example* [5]: "A twenty-two year old single woman was discovered dead by her sister, who had been staying with the victim temporarily. The sister had been away for two days and returned on Sunday at 9:00 p.m.... She went directly to her bedroom and did not discover the victim until the following morning.
>
> The deceased was found in an arched position with an electrical cord attached to her neck by a slip knot, passing over a doorknob, and wrapped around her ankles. Her abdomen, thighs, and forearms rested on the floor, and her feet were pulled back toward her head. The right side of her head was against the door's edge, and her hair was entangled in the slip knot. She was clothed in a blouse that she normally wore for sleeping. Commercial lubrication cream was found in the victim's vagina, and a battery-operated vibrator was found 4 feet from her body. The only trauma was a 1 1/2-inch contusion above and behind her right ear. The scene was not disturbed, and there was no sign of a struggle. On her bed were a series of drafted letters she had written in response to an advertisement seeking a possible sexual liaison.
>
> Autopsy revealed no evidence of recent intercourse, and no alcohol or other drugs were detected in the body. The cause of death was determined to be asphyxia due to laryngeal compression.
>
> The victim had been in excellent physical condition, had made plans for a canoe trip on the day following her death, and had recently been in good spirits. She was sexually active but was reportedly disappointed in her sexual relationships as she had difficulty attaining orgasm. She used contraceptive cream and a diaphragm to prevent pregnancy, and these items were located in her car."

This case demonstrates all of the above mentioned criteria. Her hands were free to push herself up at any time and interrupt the laryngeal compression, but she clearly passed out before she could do so. She was dating, and concerned about pregnancy, but those items associated with blocking potential pregnancy during sexual intercourse were located in her vehicle. If she were not alone while engaging in her sexual behavior, it would stand to reason that those articles would have been found to be in use at the scene of her death.

The presence of the vibrator and the letters on her bed demonstrate the presence of the sexual fantasy aids. The complexity of the bondage involved demonstrates complex fantasy behavior, and is indicative of prior fantasy and therefore represents an escalation of fantasy behavior. Rarely will an individual hog-tie themselves to a doorknob with a slip knot on their first time out. The planning of the canoe trip and the reports of her being in good spirits indicate that she was not suicidal. Also, there was no suicide note. By itself that fact has little meaning as suicide notes are not always left by those who commit suicide. Circumstantially, however, the absence of a suicide note does contribute to the picture of an autoerotic death. If there had been a note present, it would have been helpful in dismissing the possibility of an autoerotic death.

> *Example* [5]: "An eighteen-year-old white male was discovered by his mother in what she believed to be an unconscious state. She drove him to a local hospital where he was pronounced dead. Upon arrival at the hospital, he wore only a pair of red women's panties. Markings around his chest led to further questioning of his mother who then stated that when she found her son, there had been a plastic bag around his head that was secured around his neck with a rubber band, and he had been wearing a brassiere and a slip. She had removed all of these things before taking him to the hospital. A search of his room at home disclosed an extensive collection of women's clothing and several other plastic bags. The plastic bag he had used during the fatal episode had holes in it that had been repaired with masking tape."

This case is a good example of suffocation to induce euphoric hypoxia, rather than the more common compression/hanging techniques. His hands were not bound, so he could have punctured the bag at any time to discontinue its effect (as he had obviously done in the past). From all indications, he was alone at the time of death. The female clothing represents a significant fantasy aid. Holes in the one bag, the presence of other bags, and the presence of a collection of women's clothing suggests a great deal of previous engagement in this dangerous autoerotic behavior. The existence of prior incidents using the same repaired bag, in tandem with sexual fantasy material, would suggest that his intention was pleasure, not death.

The above criteria for determining autoerotic fatalities are fairly objective. They do not exclude on the basis of gender, skin color, age, or lifestyle. They also depend heavily on victim history. Adherence to these criteria could assist greatly in keeping each of the four main myths previously mentioned from misleading a death investigation. It would also assist in barricading against other classic personal and political considerations that are prone to interfere with investigations of a private, sexual, and potentially socially embarrassing nature.

MANNER OF DEATH

Determining the manner of death is sometimes very problematic for a medical examiner or coroner. A definition is in order.

> **Manner of Death** [3]: The manner of death explains how the cause of death came about. Manners of death are generally considered to be natural, homicide, suicide, accident, and undetermined.... The manner of death as determined by the forensic pathologist is an opinion based on the known facts concerning the circumstances leading up to and surrounding the death in conjunction with the autopsy findings and the laboratory tests.

Autoerotic fatalities are, by definition, accidental deaths. They are not suicides. Suicide is the intentional taking of one's own life. Accidents are unforeseen and unintentional.

Last month, a colleague wrote the author of this work and stated that he "would consider it [autoerotic death] (assuming that the pathologist has identified the death as autoerotic asphyxia) as suicide, simply because the action is as voluntary as suicide." This is not an uncommon argument. However, the argument is only sustainable on a superficial level. By that same reasoning, traffic fatalities would be determined as suicides, because everyone knows that being in a car or walking along the side of the road can kill you with more frequency than any dangerous autoerotic behavior.

DiMaio and DiMaio[3] opine on the case of a 21-year-old white male in their discussion of autoerotic asphyxiation and end their section on the subject with the following:

> The danger of this[transitory anoxia] is that a few seconds miscalculation can cause loss of consciousness and the individual will hang himself. The key to the diagnosis of this entity is the presence of a towel or some other article of clothing between the noose and the neck.... The intention is not to die, but to produce sexual gratification.

Those who engage in autoerotic behavior are doing so for pleasure. They have no expectation or intention of death. They have made provisions for their future and for future autoerotic behavior. Failure to surmise the intent of sexual arousal in autoerotic fatalities should be avoided in determining manner of death. There is little disagreement among the experts ([1], [2], [3], [4], [5], [6], [7], and [8]) on this issue.

CONCLUSION

Dr. Park Dietz[5] begins the second chapter of his work with a statement as to the nature of autoerotic asphyxia that pathologists and other death investigators cannot afford to ignore:

> For certain individuals, the preferred or exclusive mode of producing sexual excitement is to be mechanically or chemically asphyxiated to or beyond the point at which consciousness or perception is altered by cerebral Hypoxia (diminished availability of oxygen to the brain).

There is a diverse population of individuals that find autoerotic asphyxia and other dangerous autoerotic behavior sexually gratifying. Their autoerotic behavior is not criminal. It is a dangerous form of masturbation. Their subsequent death is accidental. For whatever social or personal reasons, death investigators and pathologists can fall into the ignorance of some alluring myths surrounding autoerotic death. This is a failing that cannot be afforded in light of the pathologist's responsibility to the decedent. There is a great deal of literature that works against reconciling popular myths in favor of good data. That literature must be reconciled with objective data, and objective criteria for determining autoerotic fatalities. If death investigators and pathologists are to maintain any scientific credibility at all in this area, the need for the more universal, more objective criteria must not be ignored.

BIBLIOGRAPHY

AdeIson, Lester. *The Pathology of Homicide.* Springfield, III: Charles C. Thomas, Pub., 1973), pp. 552–553.

Dietz, P. E., and O'Halloran, Ronald. "Autoerotic Fatalities with Power Hydraulics," *Journal of Forensic Sciences, Sciences,* No. 2, March 1993, pp. 359–364.

DiMaio, D., and DiMaio, V. *Forensic Pathology,* Boca Raton: CRC Press, 1993, pp. 246–247.

Geberth, Vernon. *Piactical Homicide Investigation,* 2nd ed., Boca Raton: CRC Press, 1993.

Hazelwood, Roy, Burgess, Ann, and Dietz, Park. *Autoerotic Fatalities.*

Lexington, Mass: D.C. Heath & Co., 1983.

Holmes, Ronald. *Sex Crimes,* London: Sage Publications, 1991, pp. 62–65.

Sass, F.A., "Sexual Asphyxia in the Female." *Journal of Forensic Sciences,* No. 20, 1973, pp. 181–185.

Thiel, Max, S. A. (ret.). Lecture: "Autoerotic Death," University of New Haven, Feb. 2, 1995.

Tomita, K., & Uchida, M. "On a Case of Sudden Death While Masturbating." *Japanese Journal of Legal Medicine,* Vol. 26, 1972, pp. 42–45.

39

Trading Sex for Crack:
Gender and Power

PAUL J. DRAUS AND ROBERT G. CARLSON

Draus and Carlson take us into the dynamics of women drugs users in this chapter, illustrating the way crack-using women try to obtain their drugs. We see an age-old order reproduced here, where men engage in dealing networks to obtain drugs, and women use their sexuality to barter their services for it. Money transaction is bypassed by a direct trade of goods for services. Yet how do the participants in this scene set a value for these goods and services? A variety of interesting roles are sketched out in this mixed-race community, from prostitutes to dope boys to sugar daddies. The desperation of the powerlessness of drug-addicted street women is portrayed poignantly, as well as their abandonment of caring about conventional mores. We also see their vulnerability to exploitation in a variety of ways. Yet they continue to negotiate for their needs, often falling short of their goals.

How does the portrayal of this subculture compare with the methamphetamine groups from chapter 34? What gives the men in this chapter so much more power than in that one? How do the relative status and power of the men and women in this chapter compare to the gangs?

The advent of "crack" or "rock" cocaine as a drug-use trend had a broad impact on American society in the late twentieth century. Although originally reported in coastal urban centers such as New York City, Los Angeles, and Miami, by the late 1980s, crack cocaine markets were well established throughout the United States. Because its most destructive effects were concentrated in poor urban communities, threatening images associated with crack cocaine soon became embedded in popular depictions of "inner-city" life. Some especially disturbing trends related to sexual violence, such as rape and physical attack, were committed

From Paul J. Draus and Robert G. Carlson, "Trading Sex for Crack: Gender and Power."
Journal of Contemporary Ethnography. Copyright © 2009. Reprinted by permission
of Sage Publications.

largely by men on women, and "unsafe" sex acts were committed by both men and women, largely in situations of male domination and female exploitation.

As these associations became widely publicized, several myths about crack also gained quick currency. One belief was that crack's physical effects were so powerful that initiates were "hooked" immediately on first use and quickly descended into a ceaseless cycle of crack seeking. Another myth associated crack's effects with a desire for (and openness to) unprecedented levels of sexual activity. This is sometimes referred to as the "hypersexuality" myth. These two powerful myths, in turn, reinforced the prevalent image of "crack whores"—sometimes known as "skeezers" or "strawberries"—women who were willing to perform any debasing sexual act in exchange for even a very small amount of crack cocaine.

The sexual behavior of women crack users became a major concern of researchers as well. As Maher (1996) critically noted, "women crack users who engage in sexual practices are readily positioned as vectors of AIDS, drug use, and moral contamination" (p. 144). Much of the public health literature on the "crack–sex nexus" was indeed focused on the potential for increased transmission of the HIV/AIDS virus due to unprotected and frequent sexual activity among crack users. These investigations often linked crack cocaine use to increased impulsivity or relaxed attitudes toward condom use. Other researchers examined predisposing factors within crack-abusing women, such as individual psychosocial characteristics or histories of sexual abuse and violence in the home.

Some scholars viewed the crack epidemic and the sexual behavior that accompanied it as either an effect or a reflection of broader structural conditions. For these authors, the harsh environment of the inner-city streets, the lack of other sources of income aside from crack selling and prostitution, and the objectification and degradation of women in general shaped and intensified the effects of crack with destructive and often tragic results. As stated by Bourgois and Dunlap (1993), "Crack is merely the latest medium through which the already desperate are expressing publicly their suffering and hopelessness" (p. 98). Carlson (1996) argued that exchanging sex for crack was a means for those without resources to participate in capitalist society in structural and symbolic terms, while Bourgois (2003) viewed crack–sex exchanges as a perverse by-product of the "structural violence" inflicted on marginalized groups by oppressive social forces.

The focus of this research, however, was rarely women's *agency* but rather their *domination*—by the powers of an addictive substance, by society at large, or by males within their immediate milieu. In fact, Anderson (2005) has identified an undue emphasis on the "pathology and powerlessness" of women in the drug research literature. Ironically, perhaps, studies of sex workers were more likely to portray women as active agents who sought to negotiate and reduce risk, although their ability to do so was also highly contingent on other factors, such as degree of substance dependency and the circumstances of exchange. Studies that focused on the role of women in the underground drug economy —as sellers or intermediaries, for example—also tended to grant them more agency, although this was within a realm that was highly dominated by men.

This article adds to the scholarly literature concerning the interrelationship of crack cocaine use, sexual behavior, and social context through an examination of beliefs and experiences surrounding sexual behavior among recent crack cocaine users living in small towns in central Ohio....

SETTING AND METHOD

This study results from three years of ethnographic field research, conducted in conjunction with a five-year epidemiological study investigating patterns of illicit stimulant use in central Ohio. The epidemiological study employed respondent-driven sampling, to recruit 249 recent (last thirty days) users of illicit stimulants (cocaine, crack cocaine, or methamphetamine) in three adjacent counties with populations ranging from approximately 47,000 to 55,000 persons in areas that are probably best described as the "rural–urban fringe ..."

As we found in our recruitment efforts, it is difficult to talk openly about illicit drug use and sexual behavior, much less actually witness them, in "natural" settings, such as the bars or front porches where researchers were engaging in participant observation activity. Ideals of ethnographic immersion aside, the goal of inserting oneself into such personal and sensitive realms is often impractical and quite possibly unethical (Vanderstaay 2005). For this reason, in-depth qualitative interviews and focus groups were also conducted with ninety-seven different individuals. The interviews were semistructured, covering various "domains" of experience, from individual social history and community involvement to drug use practices, health issues, and sexual behavior.

Most participants were active and former drug users, though some were family members or substance abuse counselors. They were contacted directly through fieldwork or were referred by other study participants or community members. Some were interviewed as many as five times, and fourteen of them returned for one or more follow-up interviews at different stages of the project. Of the qualitative interviews conducted, forty-three involved recent crack cocaine users, and seven involved recovering crack cocaine users. All participants were over age eighteen, all were legal residents of the target counties, and all had signed an informed consent approved by the Wright State University Institutional Review Board. Interviews were conducted in private, secure locations, and most lasted between one and two hours. Participants were compensated $20, regardless of the amount of time they spent. All interviews were audio recorded and transcribed verbatim and later coded and analyzed by the first author using the software package NVivo, which is designed for in-depth examination of rich qualitative data....

CRACK AND SEX: DRUG EFFECTS AND GENDER

Most of the accounts provided by participants belied the myth that the use of crack cocaine itself causes people to become more sexually active. As articulated by Danny, a forty-one-year-old white man, extensive crack use was just as likely to have the opposite effect:

> You're just exhausted from smoking dope and you're gonna go lay
> down and set there and stare at the ceiling for about six hours, ya know?
> You can't sleep, you can't eat, you can't have sex, a lot of people say
> that they do, but they're lying.

When asked if his crack use affected his sexual behavior, a forty-three-year-old African American man named Calvin responded, "Oh hell yeah. You don't get none. You're not interested. You don't feel like having sex and your dick won't get hard." Renee, a forty-one-year-old white woman, also stated that when she was using crack,

> I have no desire whatsoever. None. I'm not sexually promiscuous, never have been, and I just, I don't want it. I don't wanna nothin' to do with it. I don't want no one to touch me or anything. I just wanna keep gettin' high.

In fact, she specifically avoided using with men for this reason. Lana also stated that she preferred to smoke crack with other women because,

> I don't like getting high with males because they always want somethin', and they either want to suck their dick or they want some pussy and I'm not into that when I'm getting high.

Alexis, a twenty-nine-year-old white woman, began smoking crack while working as a prostitute in a larger nearby city. As for the effects of the crack itself, however, she simply said, "If I just smoke crack, then I don't want to have sex, I don't want anybody to look at me or touch me." Rory, a twenty-one-year-old woman of white and African American parentage, likewise stated, "I was never horny, and I never got horny off of it. I didn't even wanna have sex. The only reason why I did was so I could get high. That's how it affected me."

Aside from Alexis, no other participants admitted to engaging in formal prostitution. Three participants, however, made reference to "tricking." Rory stated, "I wasn't a prostitute, I mean go out on the street, and do stuff like that, but there was a couple dope boys, ya know, that I did things with, to get crack. I don't know if that's considered a prostitute or not, but I don't consider it that." When asked if she used a condom during these episodes, she replied, "I didn't even think about that, I just thought about getting high … and then too paranoid to go out and get money so I would just do some-thin' with them because they were already there."

Others made reference to the more informal practice of "hooking up." Felicia, a thirty-three-year-old African American woman, stated that she had exchanged sex for money about "four or five times" in the previous six months. She said that it usually occurred when "we'd be at a friend's house or I run into the person and we normally exchange like that and they'll be like, 'hey let's hook up'." She emphasized that these were people she already knew, not people she met on the street.

Men tended to view sex-for-crack exchange in a matter-of-fact manner. In a focus group consisting entirely of men who had recently smoked crack, Isaac stated that women would be less likely to participate in paid research interviews because it would be "easier" for them to simply have sex with a crack dealer:

> Instead of coming down and here and being seen, they can just go straight to the dope man's house and lay it with dope man, do it with the dope man, get high all they want to. That's what I'm saying see cause I watched it happen last night.

Elmer, a twenty-three-year-old white man, agreed, saying, "Any female who's a crack head ain't gonna care."

CRACK—SEX NEGOTIATIONS

Crack—sex exchanges, as described by women participants, often involved intense bargaining and implicit or explicit coercion, including threats of physical violence. Nadine, a forty-one-year-old African American woman, said, "If I don't have no feelings for them I'm just gonna go ahead and do what they want me to do to them." However, she would try other means of avoiding sex when possible. She described one situation where she was in a hotel bathroom with a man who kept buying more crack for her while trying to convince her to have sex:

> I would tell [him] well I'm getting ready to go and he'd say I'll go get some more, don't go no where.... I was more or less playing him, trying to buy him before I have to do anything.

This started at around eleven o'clock at night, and they went through four "twenty-rocks," while she tried to "talk my way out of having sex with him." However, he made her stay in the bathroom "until he got what he wanted" sometime early the next morning.

A similar situation to that described by Nadine, albeit with a different result, was recounted by Lana:

> Well, he did want sex until he started smoking.... I guess when he smokes he can't do nothing ... but when they come down that's a different story, that's when either you're gone, party's over and you ain't giving up nothing.

Another situation that was described by study participants involved two women, who were themselves sexually involved with each other, visiting local bars to attract the interest of men who were looking for crack but also expected sex. One of the women was African American, the other was racially "mixed," and the men whom they sought to attract were mostly white. The women had ready access to crack suppliers but no money to purchase the drug, while the situation of the "target" male was exactly the reverse. Such a situation was preferable because it involved less isolation with a man, thus reducing sexual risk.

For women, as noted above, the relationship between sexual behavior and crack cocaine had little to do with sexual excitement. From the women's standpoint, the ideal situation involved no sexual exchange at all. Mary, who was openly a lesbian, also had to face the expectation of exchanging sex with men when she purchased crack cocaine. She declared,

> I don't give 'em sex. I said, I got money, and I said, I'll give you a little bit if you go get it for me, a little bit a rock, okay and they don't touch me, because see when I was younger, when I was twenty-one, I could

lift three hundred and fifty pounds on my back and press three hundred and fifty pounds on my legs. I could kick more than one man's ass at a time. But I'm old now, and I can't fight like I could, but they still remember that reputation and therefore they're still scared of me.

CRACK, SEX, AND VIOLENCE

Some crack-related sexual encounters also involved either threats or actual violence. As mentioned above, Nadine was threatened with physical violence during her extended encounter in the hotel bathroom. Others had much worse outcomes. On one occasion, Felicia was attacked by a man she met in a bar:

> He invited me and my cousin to come over and drink, and, it just got crazy. Like I said, I was getting ready to go home and, I never gave him no indication that I was gonna lay down with him, and he said let's go lay down and I said I didn't wanna lay down, and he got violent.

In that case, she fought back with a kitchen knife. The police were called, and the man ended up in the hospital.

However, Felicia also described another incident that occurred in a larger nearby city, where she sometimes traveled to smoke crack:

> I told him "no" and he, first ripped my panties off through my pants and I just kept telling him "no," well course it was someone that I knew, so I didn't make a police report or nothing like that, but he was just like "no you gonna, ya know have sex with me" and I'm like "no I don't want to" and he just kinda strong-armed me....

Even more disturbing was an episode recounted by Rory after going to the same city to buy and smoke a "twenty-piece" of crack. She said, "I was kidnapped, raped, and assaulted for three days, beat for three days, the guy held me in a room and raped me and, [pause] raped me and like messed up my face where I looked like I was in a car accident." She was hospitalized as a result of the incident but never filed charges or sought professional counseling, saying, "I just been dealing with it on my own, it's driving me crazy, though. I just don't believe in asking anybody for help."

This is the most extreme episode of violence recounted in this study. Notably, it occurred outside the town itself. However, the same dynamic of gender domination was present in most other accounts of sex-for-crack exchanges. Perhaps unsurprisingly, women did not have to go outside their own intimate relationships to encounter threats of violence related to sex and crack use. As Nadine reported concerning her fiancé,

> we use crack [and] drink and he would accuse me of tricking for crack, after he got high, he would accuse me of being with different guys and then it turned into where he'd be beating me with his fist or with objects.

In this case, it is the man's assumption of the woman's sexual behavior related to crack that serves as the basis for anger and violent domination.

DOPE BOYS AND SUGAR DADDIES

When asked about the assumption, among men, that women could get crack whenever they wanted simply by exchanging sex for it, Lana provided a complicated response. On one hand, she affirmed this, saying, "I tried to hang around females because I know females can get money quicker than a male." However, she also stated that this was something she expressly tried to avoid through engaging men in other ways, offering them conversation, attention, or companionship instead of sex in return for sharing drugs:

> That's what I usually try to do, because if you know how to use your mouth-piece then you don't have to lay down with nobody to get no money for no drugs. A dope boy you have to, though.

As Lana's statement implies, "dope boys" or crack dealers were one category of men who were in a powerful position over women who could not afford to buy crack outright. Some women also admitted regularly having sex with "sugar daddies," men who provided them with money that they then used to buy crack. Rory, who had several such relationships, explained how one of them came about:

> I just found out about one of 'em because I found out other girls were going there and then he just ended up just liking me, ya know, didn't mess with other girls no more, so I could go there and just ask him for money without doing anything and he would give it to me. There were some times when I would do something so I could get extra.

All of her sugar daddies were older white men, and though she did have sex with them, this was something she actively tried to avoid:

> [I would] tell 'em a lame excuse sometimes when I was already high, try to come up with something and lie about it, or sometimes I would start up and then he, he'd just give it to me, I wouldn't have to do a favor for the money anymore, 'cause he was actually starting to care about me, ya know.

THE LURE OF SEX, THE LURE OF THE DRUG

Jerome, one of our key informants, stated straightforwardly that "when a guy gets high he wants to have sex, when women get high it turns them off from sex, so women will use sex in order to continue on getting the money in order to get high." He offered some useful insights into the crack–sex dynamic as it related to both men and women:

> Okay when I take a hit, first thing come to my mind is sex. Now a woman, they don't feel that way … but they also know that men feel that way … but if he take more than one hit then she knows that she can sit there and smoke with him all night and he won't be able to do anything … because he can think sex but his genitals won't work, so girls use, the lure of sex in order to get high, guys use the lure of the drug in order to get sex, you follow me?

According to Jerome, a significant shift in power sometimes took place when a woman was able to exert her own influence in a skillful way:

> After she's been there for a while and she's gotten high, and she's been used or been abused, there a point where she, she won't do that, she'll say listen, give me mine up front and I'll do it but if you can't I'm only gonna do it for three, four minutes, if you don't get off by then I'm quitting … so now it's so much that he has the power, ya know the power has been shifted, see, cause now she knows what he can do and can't do … she didn't know what he can do and what he can't do, then he has the power, but once she realizes, now she has the power … now she has the power … I've seen guys do it, she can't do him but he just wants to see her naked and long as he can get to look at her, he can fantasize but he can't really do anything.…

When asked about the relationship between crack cocaine and the abuse of women, Jerome responded,

> Related to crack, yea, it's a lot a abuse, and not so much … physical as it is mental … feeling the need that you wanna get high real bad, and the only way you can get high is you have to be, be able to degrade yourself to do certain acts, ya know, sexually.

On the male side, Jerome agreed that power over women was definitely a part of the drug's appeal, especially among those who sold it:

> That's why everybody wants to be a dope boy.… 'Cause these guys don't smoke and they need possession, and they'll make her go suck their dick or they'll make her fuck everybody in the room.… That's pretty common, that's why everybody wants to be a dope boy. The lure, it's not so much … for the money they're making, as it is the power, or the lure of sex that you can get, because if you find a girl out there, if she's smoking dope, you can, you can have her one way or another, you eventually, if you don't get her right away but you will eventually have her, but she'll come down, she won't have enough money … and she'll trade herself for it, so that's why most … [a] lot of these guys wouldn't even have sex if it wasn't for dope.

THE GAME TURNS ON YOU

Lana concurred with Jerome's statements that for dealers in particular, sex-for-crack exchanges are more about power than about any kind of sexual attraction or desire:

> With a dope boy it's a power thing, because as long as he has the dope in his hand, he knows he got power, he could probably get five girls at one time suck his dick, that's how powerful that shit is, I think it is.

With other men, however, relations of power were much more malleable, although they might aspire to the same level of domination that dope boys exercised. Lana stated straightforwardly that men who smoke crack with women "always want something." The paradox of this phenomenon was that many men, in accordance with findings cited above, were unable to achieve sexual climax when they were using crack. However, Lana claimed, "they still wanna try."

> They'll sit there and know that they can't do nuthin'—I ran into one last night—I've been doing him for a while and stuff just got carried away and, he was smoking and stuff and like I said they always want head [oral sex] … and I'm doing that and it's not doing nuthin', I'm like then why, why bother?

This very fact, however, could sometimes be used by a woman as a means of limiting her involvement with a man, while simultaneously maximizing her "return." In describing her "negotiations" with men, Lana explained,

> Sometimes you can use your mouth piece and talk where you don't have to do nuthin'; sometime they're like no, no, no cause they're tired a getting used and then you have to say well I'll do this and they'll say well okay and then you end up having to do something before you get the money, to go get it, but after that you're cool, ain't nuttin' but a couple minutes cause you know what I mean, well come on, I wanna go, let's just get this over…

In such cases—in most cases—Lana stated, "It's not about sex. It's just about giving him what he wants so you can get what you want." This statement characterizes the crack-for-sex exchange as a kind of sexual barter, with each party seeking to get the better of the deal but both getting something that they want. Also significant is her use of the term *getting used,* implying acknowledgment that the man is being manipulated sexually. However, Lana's later experiences, which involved providing regular sexual favors to sugar daddies for money that she could use to buy crack, revealed the downside of relying on one's bodily "capital" as the primary source of leverage in such deals.

> It used to be somethin' I didn't do, but the longer you're in the game, [it]turns on you. Sometimes you gotta do something you don't wanna do to get what you want, and that's what I've been doing.…

CONCLUSION

These findings suggest that issues of gender and power are central to risk reduction among crack cocaine users in rural as well as urban areas and that gender-based approaches to violence and sexual risk are necessary. However, such programs must be adapted to the particular social context. Such "tailored interventions" might operate on a variety of levels. Ethnographic understandings of crack–sex relations may contribute to peer education that allows women to share experience, to "coach" each other in the techniques of risk reduction: not just how to use a condom but how to negotiate interaction, how to offer men the opportunity to fantasize rather than engaging in actual sexual acts, how to select interaction sites and contexts that are demonstrably safer, how to screen out potentially violent partners, and so on. Building peer networks among women in locally specific drug scenes may also yield unanticipated benefits in other areas as well by enhancing the power and agency of women generally. The possibility of underlying issues of trauma and depression, especially in women, should inform these intervention efforts. In the case of drug-using couples, interpersonal dynamics must also be considered as a factor that may contribute to continued risk exposure. By the same token, men might also be more systematically educated on issues of gender domination...

One common theme in our accounts was the assumption on the part of men that women are willing participants in sex-for-crack exchanges or that such exchanges are obligatory if a man is supplying money or crack. From the perspectives of women, these exchanges were viewed as neither desirable nor obligatory but were sometimes accepted as unavoidable in particular situations. Much as Wesely (2003) found in her ethnographic interviews of exotic dancers, women in crack cocaine scenes actively confront symbolic violence and seek to counter it as individuals, but by and large, they do not challenge its legitimacy, much less that of the larger social structure that enables it...

REFERENCES

Anderson, Tammy L. 2005. Dimensions of women's power in the illicit drug economy. *Theoretical Criminology* 9 (4): 371–400.

Bourgois, Philippe, and Eloise Dunlap. 1993. Exorcising sex-for-crack: An ethnographic perspective from Harlem. In *Crack Pipe as Pimp: An Ethnographic Investigation of Sex-for-crack Exchanges.* Mitchell S. Ratner ed. 197–132. New York: Lexington Books.

Carlson, Robert G. 1996. The political economy of AIDS among drug users in the United States: Beyond blaming the victim or powerful others. *American Anthropologist* 98 (2): 266–78.

Maher, Lisa. 1996. Hidden in the light: Occupational norms among crack-using street-level sex workers. *Journal of Drug Use* 26 (1): 143–74.

Wesely, Jennifer K. 2003. Exotic dancing and the negotiation of identity: The multiple uses of body technologies. *Journal of Contemporary Ethnography* 32 (6): 643–69.

40

Show Me the Money: Cybershrews and On-line Money Masochists

KEITH F. DURKIN

A long-time sex researcher, Durkin turns his gaze to the fascinating but little-known cyber relationship between money mistresses and the slaves who worship them. Another deviant world and subculture that has been facilitated by the medium of the Internet, financial slavery offers a compelling service to men with this particular inclination. The complementary need of individuals on both sides of these financial transactions sheds insight into an unusual dimension of deviant reciprocity. At the same time, the potential for fraud in these Internet relationships is great. Willing slaves go to great lengths to establish the authenticity of their mistress, even though she is someone they will likely never meet in the solid (real) world.

How would you assess the likelihood and potential for fraud and abuse in the cyber subcultures described here compared to the support communities of self-injurers? What factors are likely to make them different? How do the needs of self-injurers compare and contrast with those of money slaves?

The Internet has created a fertile opportunity structure for deviant behavior. Accordingly, there has been a vast array of deviant practices surrounding this technological innovation. Hacking, or the unauthorized intrusion into a computer system or network, is an excellent example. Fraud and other deceptive practices are commonplace on the Internet. Some examples include stock manipulation, the misappropriation of credit card information, investment swindles, and on-line auction fraud. White supremacist groups are using the Internet for the dissemination of propaganda as well as the recruitment of new members. Evidence suggests that cyberstalking, sending harassing or threatening electronic communications to other computer users, is becoming a frequent occurrence. Internet gambling is a rapidly growing phenomenon. Also, the illegal sale of prescription drugs, guns, and alcoholic beverages transpires over the Internet....

In terms of sexual deviance, one of the most sociologically significant aspects of the Internet is that it serves as a social consolidation mechanism, bringing

From Durkin, Keith F, "Show Me the Money: Cybershrews and On-Line Money Masochists." *Deviant Behavior.* 28.4. Copyright © 2007. Reprinted by permission of the publisher, Taylor and Francis Ltd. www.informaworld.com.

together people with similar sexual interests. On the Internet, one finds "a community of like-minded enthusiasts willing to discuss their enthusiasm in length and in detail" (Leiblum 1997:25). For instance, Walton (2001:21) noted that the emerging Internet culture has afforded "a forum for bestiality enthusiasts and practitioners to share their interests or fantasies thorough a variety of chat rooms and web sites." Moreover, Davis (2001) documented a loosely organized subculture of individuals interested in "cyber flashing," which involves posting photos of themselves in various stages of undress or engaging in sex acts. Additionally, pedophiles frequently use the Internet to communicate with each other, share information, and provide mutual support and validation for their deviant sexual identity. The purpose of this article is to report on a group of Internet users involved in a practice called money slavery.

METHODOLOGY

The analysis of Websites and other forms of computer-mediated communication has been used in a number of recent studies of deviant behavior ... The data for this research were gathered over a period of approximately four years. They were collected from home-pages, message forums, Yahoo groups, user profiles, and blogs. Hundreds of hours were spent examining these materials on-line, and approximately 500 printed pages were printed out for analysis. This topic was discovered accidentally by the author in the course of his ongoing investigation of deviance on the Internet. Specifically, the author found an advertisement from a woman who described herself as a "money mistress" and claimed she was seeking "money slaves." The initial advertisement provided a brief description of the "services" she provided. Popular search engines such as Google and Yahoo were used to search for key words such as "money slavery" and "money mistress." The subsequent data collection strategy resembled a snowball sample, except it used Internet sites for information referrals, rather than individuals. In their research on Internet rape sites, Gossett and Byrne (2002) found that one site often gave links to several others sites with a similar theme. Likewise, the examination of a particular money slavery site often yielded links to several others. The current study was completely unobtrusive. At no point in time did they author ever interact with or correspond with any of the participants in the Internet money slavery subculture.

Obviously, the sample is in no way representative of all Internet money slavery sites. Also, many of these Websites, discussion forums, and profiles were ephemeral in nature. During the course of this research, many simply disappeared, while others were created. Despite the fluid nature of the Internet, these type of data "can be useful in providing a snapshot of a given subject at a particular point in time" (Hegland and Nelson 2002:142). Rather than setting particular parameters for their analysis, researchers who have used this type of data examined their data for recurrent themes. The data in the current study were examined in order to identify common themes, characteristics, and tendencies.

MONEY SLAVERY

The phenomenon called "money slavery" involves males giving money or gifts to women they meet on-line in exchange for being degraded, humiliated, or blackmailed. According to one columnist in an on-line S&M magazine, "surely it is the deepest way to mix real-everyday life to a condition of slavery … the ultimate depiction of economic dehumanization" (Skorpio 2001:2). Regarding this practice, one blogger noted:

> There's often a financial component to any aspect of consensual BDSM play (just browse through the sex ads in your local alt weekly), but in the world of money mistresses, pay pigs, and human ATMs, the exchange of cold hard cash for the privilege of being abused, domi-nated, humiliated, and/or ignored is the whole point of the action. (Financial Slavery 2006)

A variety of other terms are sometimes used to describe the practice, including financial servitude, financial rape, wallet rapping, extreme spoiling, and financial domination.

The initial contact between participants can be made via the money mistresses' Web pages. Alternately, interested parties can be located through the scores of discussion groups dedicated to this practice, such as "The Real Money Slaves," "Money Slaves 101," "Cash Fetish," and "Money Slaves Fellowship Forum." The females, or money mistresses, frequently place advertisements on the Internet to recruit men. The following are some examples:

> I am a beautiful 23-year-old college student who loves to humiliate men as they worship me and drain their bank accounts in my honor. I have expensive tastes, and there is no limit to the amount of money I might demand. Whether you are a millionaire, or a regular Joe, rest assured that I can reduce you to poverty. So if you have the balls, which I doubt you do, you can apply to be my money slave simply by making a tribute. When I receive your tribute I will E-mail with my demands.
>
> I am now accepting cash cows that need to be milked. You must submit your mind, soul, body and wallet to me. Arrangements will be made to drain every cent you have. Do you like pain? Humiliation? Are you a sissy maid? I promise I will bring you to your knees and ruin you forever.
>
> Mature Money Domme Helga will wickedly lead you to your own financial ruination, bankruptcy as you become her cash cow, human ATM, pay pig, money slaves. Domme Helga is your financial dom for financial domination, so drain your credit cards now & give Goddess your cash!!!
>
> I wish to fuck your rock hard credit card dry! Take me for a ride on the streets of CA$H & PLEA$URE$ NOW! I will take from you NOW! You will submit to my every desire, & demand! I am stunning, & in control! I hit you like the last drink at the bar, the one that makes you feel warm & fuzzy & at the same time a bit out of control & dizzy!

I seduce your wallet away, as you fall into my lair! Welcum to my world, you will never leave! Contact me NOW!

Although advertisements from male participants do not appear to be as prevalent, nonetheless some money slaves place ads in hopes of establishing contact with an appropriate money mistress:

I'm looking for a superior female who wants to control my entire life, including total control over my finances. I'm earning about $35,000 a year and I'm willing to give it to a real Goddess. The only thing I want is that she treats me like the shit I am. She should be willing to degrade and destroy me completely.

Money pig, 55, white, seeks spoiled PRINCESS between 18 & 25, to e-mail me every Friday (payday), and demand all extra money from my pay check. When SHE receives the money, SHE will e-mail me to remind me what a stupid pig I am and that I am getting absolutely nothing for my money. I prefer a PRINCESS that I can mail cash or money order to. I must see a picture of the PRINCESS, posing wearing high heels. Prefer a PRINCESS with a web site, but not necessary. PRINCESS may also demand that I get a second job, so SHE can have more money.

The money mistresses request various forms of remuneration from the men to maintain ongoing contact. They commonly require the money slaves to send tributes (normally $25 or $50) to them electronically by credit card or Pay Pal, or to a P.O. Box via cash, check, or money order. Many money mistresses request an "initiation fee" or "introductory tribute" before they will take the men on as money slaves or even respond to an e-mail. Some money mistresses also require their money slaves to pay off a bill of theirs each month, such as rent, car, electric, phone, or gym membership. The women also may request that the men buy items from a computerized "wish list," which links to on-line stores such as Saks Fifth Avenue, Bloomingdales, Neiman Marcus, and Victoria Secret. A few of the money mistresses claim to be college students and request the men buy their textbooks at Amazon.Com or the Barnes and Noble on-line store. In exchange, the women may send e-mail or pictures to the money slaves, or allow the men to view their Web cam or speak with them on the phone or via instant messenger. Evidently some men actually give exorbitant amounts of money to these women. For instance, one woman's Website has a copy of a $50,000 wire transfer allegedly from a money slave, as well as copies of credit card receipts totaling $17,000 (all from the same account), which were supposedly for "services" another incurred on her behalf. However, there is little, if any, evidence that any physical meetings ever occur between the money slaves and the money mistresses.

However, some of the money mistresses provide more elaborate services. For instance, some offer a "blackmail service." The man fills out an on-line application with his name, address, and telephone number of his girlfriend, wife, or employer as well as some discrediting personal information about him. The money slave is then required to pay money to avoid having this information revealed to his significant other or employer by the money mistress. Also, some money mistresses claim to provide a "chastity belt" program in which the money slave buys the device and sends her the key. In turn, he is required to pay a fee to have the key returned to him. Furthermore, some women offer outrageously priced goods and services. For example, one money mistress was selling her used panties ($75), locks of her hair ($100), and worn socks ($45) on her Website. Another offers phone sex calls for $9.99 a minute. One money slave reported paying $330 for a conversation. Some of the money mistresses also utilize a commercial e-mail service that charges a fee (e.g., $50) when the recipient opens the e-mail.

While the money mistresses appear to be motivated by financial considerations, sexual interests seem to motivate the money slaves. Although psychological pain can play an important role in masochism, psychology pain is also important to many masochists. This pain "encompasses feelings of helplessness, subservience, humiliation, and degradation" (Moser and Levitt 1987:332). Many money slaves reported being sexually aroused by making payments. In a posting, one money slave stated:

> I have found the act of paying so amazing that I actually masturbate when get the credit card bill. I jerk off.

Another remarked:

> The act of paying can be a very stimulating experience, at the time I do it, but there is usually some means of manipulative pressure [on the part of the money mistress] by the way of pushing my submissive button. Going on that makes the act of transferring cash feel like a turn on.

In turn, the money mistresses are obviously aware of the sexual arousal associated with the act of making a payment. Accordingly, they readily acknowledge this in the information they post. The following statements from various money mistresses illustrate this strategy:

> Feel the excitement build in your pants as your brain tries to resist your uncontrollable urge to give me every cent that you have.
> Your back at home surfing the web, reading my site and stroking that pathetic cock of yours. Why not kill all of the pretenses of dating and come visit me weekly, or daily and just pay your damn masturbation tax.
> You learn to crave bleeding from me, you start to actively seek me out financially—to burn you, fuck with your mind, make you incapable of enjoying normal-nice relationships. You not only enjoy being humiliated by me, but the emotional turmoil you experience after the fact. You start loving the scars.

SOCIAL CONTROL AND MONEY SLAVERY

As Evans (2001) noted, sanctions can have an important role in Internet culture. Social control plays an important part in the phenomenon of money slavery. By its very nature, this practice is ripe with opportunities for fraud, deception, and deceit. For instance, the money mistresses may receive money or gifts from men and not reciprocate by providing them with e-mail responses, chat time, or other services. Additionally, the money mistresses can deceive men by using photos of other women in their profiles or Websites. Moreover, it is possible to disguise one's gender on the Internet. Regarding this deceptive practice, one money slave argued:

> To be misled by a 45-year-old male posing as a bitchy, cocky, arrogant, beautiful 19-year-old girl in order to fool me out of my money because he knows that I wouldn't offer it to him otherwise is FRAUD.

There is evidence that at least some of these so-called money mistresses and "financial domination" sites are nothing more than an elaborate hoax. For instance, the same exact photo was used on the profiles of at least a half-dozen money mistresses. Also, a professional dominatrix conveyed the following information in a discussion forum dedicate to sadomasochism enthusiasts:

> (A friend) knew a few guys who had this great idea to hire some models to take a bunch of pictures of them and then create financial slavery sites of these "Dommes". Most of the models had no idea what their pictures were being used for other than an adult site. They were paid their standard fee and sent home.

A similar statement appeared in a discussion about money slavery on a forum dedicated to webmasters who host adult sites. One male user stated:

> A couple of years ago when I was in university, I was surfing through Yahoo chat rooms and found a money slaves forum. I sat in there for about an hour and realized what was going on. Then I set up a fake account as a Mistress (using a fake pic) to see if I could get one of the slaves in the channel to send me money. Within about 10 minutes I had a guy sending me $50.... This is when the channel was new and I made about $2000 doing it ... but the slaves started to get wise and ask for proof and such.

In an attempt to legitimate their identities, some money mistress hold up a piece of paper with their name on it, or simply the words "real deal" to "prove" that they are the individual pictured in the photo. One money mistress, who is an advocate of this approach, stated on her Website:

> The idea was born because of the rampant amount of fake dommes that troll the web using borrowed or stolen photographs, many of them being men behind the computer screen and not even women. I offered the idea up to several dommes (on line) ... unfortunately there wasn't much interest. I wonder why.

In an effort to protect their interests, money slaves have collectively formed discussion groups such as the "Money Slaves Fellowship Forum" and

"Find Fake Money Slaves" to share information on detecting and avoiding frauds. One poster to a forum shared tips on how to make sure a money mistress is "legitimate," including asking for two or three photos and a Web cam view of the woman before sending any money. Another money slave warned his peers:

> I have seen several posts and ads by someone calling themselves Asha, and the photo that they were using is actually that poor woman, that ex-porno actress, that has AIDS.

One group even contains a picture of the "Fake of the Month." Recently, there was a picture of a Madame Jennifer prominently posted. The group's moderator noted "we all appreciate calling out trailer park tricks like this uneducated fake."

On the other hand, the money mistresses utilize their own social control strategies. Apparently, some of the male participants engage in deceptive practices of their own. For example, some money slaves lie about forthcoming payments in order to obtain services such as Web cam views and chat time. Others may agree to pay a particular bill for a specified period of time and fail to fulfill their part of the arrangement. Some money mistresses publicly post the online identities of these men. For instance, one posted a "loser-list" that, by her description, contained "all of the e-mail addresses and Yahoo usernames of all of the men who pay once and are never heard from again." On one discussion forum, the money mistresses have created a "fakers list" consisting of men who have been deceptive about payment. These men, in turn, are banned from accessing certain forums. In a rather extreme form of social control, one money mistress posts chat transcripts, along with the name and e-mail addresses, of non-paying money slaves in a public forum. In one such transcript, the male was engaged in an interactive erotic discussion about his fantasies about his mother and his desire to perform oral sex on another man. Other women have gone as far as posting the names and telephone numbers of non-paying men.

However, social control can also consist of rewarding desirable behaviors. The money mistresses frequently give public acknowledgment to those money slaves who make substantial contributions. On her Website, one thanks by name all of the men who pay her bills. On another Website, a money mistress announced:

> Slipjockey is the big donation winner (read: loser) of the day. He spent about $185 on the phone and another $200 on Pay Pal.

Another money mistress created a special feature on her Website called the "Money Slave Wall of Fame" to recognize the top contributor of the month. She noted, for the month of July, the slave of the month was

> Perky Pee Pee in a landslide!! This pathetic Pee Pee has contributed over $2600 to his adorable Mistress. Way to go! Let's see if we can make it two months in a row. As for the rest of you slackers, you have a lot of work to do....

DISCUSSION

New forms of sexual behavior frequently develop as an adaptive response to technological innovations. Although the practice of paying for sexual fantasy is not new, the phenomenon of money slavery appears to be a novel manifestation of this type of deviance that is predicated on the existence of the Internet. Traditionally, certain commercial establishments and prostitutes have provided services to submissive men. However, the services provided included actual physical interactions. The primary contacts between the money mistresses and money slaves transpire over the Internet. Although subsequent contacts may occur over the telephone or through the mail, there is no evidence of actual physical contact between any of the participants involved in the practice of money slavery....

Money slavery involves the presentation and consumption of images—images of a shrewish and dominant woman being driven by financial concerns are being consumed by a male with masochist traits. The money mistress is not a "real" person in the traditional sense. It is a character who exists in cyberspace—whose creator may not even be a female! Nonetheless the money slaves appear to react to this character as if it is a real person.

Money slavery appears to be a novel form of sexual deviance, and this phenomenon manifests some decidedly postmodern characteristics. However, money slavery exhibits some characteristics of more traditional forms of deviant behavior. For example, the participants, both money slaves and money mistresses, offer accounts for their deviance. The use of accounts is a type of stigma management technique. Also, there is some self-regulation of deviant activity by participants. They engage in social control strategies (e.g., fake lists and loser lists). This is likely an adaptive response to the opportunities for fraud that are inherent in this type of computer mediated interaction.

Social learning theory (see Akers 2000) may be useful for understanding this phenomenon. Durkin, Forsyth, and Quinn (2006:601) posited that the Internet allows for "interaction with others holding similar interests that reinforce their deviant interests, teach methods of achieving deviant goals and support rationales for the abrogation of basic norms." Other members of this Internet subculture can serve as differential associations, teaching both the techniques for, and mind the set involved in, participating in the practice of money slavery. What may be even more important in understanding this phenomenon however is the concept of differential reinforcement. This consists of "the balance of anticipated and actual rewards and punishments that follow or are consequences of a behavior" (Akers 2000:78). On the one hand, the "money slaves" receive reinforcement through sexual gratification. On the other hand, the "money mistresses" receive financial remuneration that is reinforcing to them. The participants may also learn definitions that are conducive to this behavior on line. For instance, the accounts found in this research as considered neutralizing definitions under social learning theory (Akers 2000).

There are plenty of reasons to suspect that at least some of these money slaves are experiencing negative consequences in their daily lives because of their on-line activities. Some of these men are spending hundreds, if not thousands, of dollars on these money mistresses. They may be forsaking financial obligations, including those to their own family. In on-line discussion forums, some of these men admitted to neglecting to pay personal bills to give money to these women, whereas others indicated they have "maxed out" their credit cards or taking "payday" loans to get money for the money mistresses. Given the increasing number of people seeking counseling for Internet-related issues, therapists are likely to being encountering male clients who are dealing with the ramifications of "money slavery."

Future research on this topic should examine the personal ramifications of these "money slaves" activities. It would also be useful to try to determine if the "money mistresses" are solely motivated by financial consideration. Also, it would be particularly helpful to ascertain to what degree these "money mistresses" use deception in their Internet self-presentation. For instance, how many of them are men falsely presenting themselves as women? More generally, researchers must recognize that the Internet appears to have spawned a vast array of deviant subcultures involving individuals with the most esoteric sexual predilections. It offers a seemingly endless inventory of people who have deviant ideologies or engage in deviant activities. At the same time, the Internet offers seemingly endless opportunities for behavioral scientists to conduct investigations of a wide variety of deviants and deviance.

REFERENCES

Akers, Ronald L. 2000. *Criminological Theories: Introduction, Evaluation, and Application.* 3rd ed. Los Angeles: Roxbury.

Davis, Phillip W. 2001. "Exhibitionism." Pp. 84–89. In *Encyclopedia of Criminology and Deviant Behavior, Volume III: Sexual Deviance,* edited by C. D. Bryant. Philadelphia: Brunner-Routledge.

Durkin, Keith F., Craig J. Forsyth, and James F. Quinn. 2006. "Pathological Internet Communities: A New Direction for Sexual Deviance Research in the Postmodern Era." *Sociological Spectrum* 26(6):595–606.

Evans, Rhonda. 2001. "Examining the Informal Sanctioning of Deviance in a Chat Room Culture." *Deviant Behavior* 22:195–210.

Financial Slavery. 2006, January 4. Appeared on www.gasgrassass.com. (retrieved February 21, 2006).

Gossett, Jennifer Lynn, and Sarah Byrne. 2002. "Click Here: A Content Analysis of Internet Rape Sites." *Gender & Society* 16:689–709.

Hegland, Jane E., and Nancy J. Nelson. 2002. "Cross-Dressers in Cyberspace: Exploring the Internet as a Tool for Expressing Gender Identity." *International Journal of Sexuality and Gender Studies* 7:139–161.

Leiblum, Sandra G. 1997. "Sex and the Net: Clinical Implications." *Journal of Sex Education and Therapy* 22:21–27.

Moser, Charles, and Eugene E. Levitt. 1987. "An Exploratory-Descriptive Study of a Sadomasochistically Orientated Sample." *Journal of Sex Research* 22:322–337.

Skorpio. 2001. "The Sting: High Heeled Business." www.bssmrealm.net (posted July 13 2001).

Walton, Charles E. 2001. "Bestiality." Pp. 19–22. In *Encyclopedia of Criminology and Deviant Behavior. Volume III: Sexual Deviance.* C. D. Bryant, ed. Philadelphia: Brunner-Routledge.

41

Sexual Assault on Campus

ELIZABETH A. ARMSTRONG, LAURA HAMILTON,
AND BRIAN SWEENEY

In the twenty-first century American college and universities have been rocked by alcohol-related scandals leading to rape and death. School administrators have tried to clamp down on students with punitive measures such as "strikes," probations, and expulsions. Students living in university housing have been particularly vulnerable, as they are under the watchful eye of resident advisors. These restrictions have pushed student partying—what Armstrong, Hamilton, and Sweeney call most prevalent among white, middle-class populations— increasingly into the fraternity scene. There, they find that women with these demographics are most at risk of rape.

We have known for more than a decade that college women's risk of sexual assault by people they knew far outweighed that of stranger rape. Armstrong, Hamilton, and Sweeney explore some of the popular explanations for the pervasiveness of fraternity rape, from individual bad boys, to fraternity culture, to dangerous environments, and integrate these all by going beyond them. They locate the problem for women in a structural situation where they are forced out of their dorms to party by harsh sanctions against alcohol in the residence halls. The party scene they find is located in private environments where men control access to alcohol, transportation, and, more importantly, social status through their attentions to women. Here, traditional gender roles end up contributing to the victimization of women as men and women voluntarily engage in a dance where women seek flirtation to gain status and men offer flirtation and status to gain sex. Most women, being disempowered in these male-dominated settings, put themselves into situation where they are at high risk of victimization. When this occurs, they are likely to attribute blame to their girlfriends individually (remember Reinarman's comments

From Elizabeth A. Armstrong, Laura Hamilton, and Brian Sweeney, "Sexual Assault on Campus: A Multilevel, Integrative Approach to Party Rape." *Social Problems*, Vol. 53, No. 4, 2006. All rights reserved. Reprinted by permission of University of California Press Journals.

about the vocabulary of attribution being individualistic rather than structural?) rather than banding together to fight the unequal power structure in which men have the control and advantage. Older and higher-statused women look down on their less fortunate female schoolmates as "stupid," or "asking for it," despite the likelihood that they may have experienced these same troubles themselves at an earlier age.

Armstrong, Hamilton, and Sweeney offer disturbing insight into how women fight to protect their access to the party scene despite its risk for them of being taken advantage of and disempowered. We are reminded that fraternity culture, despite its deviant aspects, represents an enclave of the dominant culture where women are complicit in their own victimization and men use their gender advantage to callously foster their own ends.

How would you compare the social power of women in this scene to those in the sex-for-crack scene, the women gang members, and the meth cooks? What factors influence the relative status and opportunity? What are the repercussions of this scene's location in the dominant majority culture for the position of women and men?

A 1997 National Institute of Justice study estimated that between one-fifth and one-quarter of women are the victims of completed or attempted rape while *in* college (Fisher, Cullen, and Turner 2000). College women "are at greater risk for rape and other forms of sexual assault than women in the general population or in a comparable age group" (Fisher et al. 2000: iii).[2] At least half and perhaps as many as three-quarters of the sexual assaults that occur on college campuses involve alcohol consumption on the part of the victim, the perpetrator, or both (Abbey et al. 1996; Sampson 2002). The tight link between alcohol and sexual assault suggests that many sexual assaults that occur on college campuses are "party rapes." A recent report by the U.S. Department of Justice defines party rape as a distinct form of rape, one that "occurs at an off-campus house or on—or off—campus fraternity and involves ... plying a woman with alcohol or targeting an intoxicated woman" (Sampson 2002: 6).[1] While party rape is classified as a form of acquaintance rape, it is not uncommon for the woman to have had no prior interaction with the assailant, that is, for the assailant to be an in-network stranger (Abbey et al. 1996).

Colleges and universities have been aware of the problem of sexual assault for at least 20 years, directing resources toward prevention and providing services to students who have been sexually assaulted. Programming has included education of various kinds, support for *Take Back the Night* events, distribution of rape whistles, development and staffing of hotlines, training of police and administrators, and other efforts. Rates of sexual assault, however, have not declined over the last five decades (Adams-Curtis and Forbes 2004: 95; Bachar and Koss 2001; Marine 2004; Sampson 2002: 1).

Why do colleges and universities remain dangerous places for women in spite of active efforts to prevent sexual assault? While some argue that "we know what the problems are and we know how to change them" (Adams-Curtis and Forbes 2004: 115), it is our contention that we do not have a complete explanation of the problem. To address this issue we use data from a study of college life at a large midwestern university and draw on theoretical developments in the sociology of

gender. Continued high rates of sexual assault can be viewed as a case of the reproduction of gender inequality—a phenomenon of central concern in gender theory.

We demonstrate that sexual assault is a predictable outcome of a synergistic
intersection of both gendered and seemingly gender neutral processes operating
at individual, organizational, and interactional levels. The concentration of homog-
enous students with expectations of partying fosters the development of sexualized
peer cultures organized around status. Residential arrangements intensify students'
desires to party in male-controlled fraternities. Cultural expectations that partygoers
drink heavily and trust party-mates become problematic when combined with expectations that women be nice and defer to men. Fulfilling the role of the partier
produces vulnerability on the part of women, which some men exploit to extract
non-consensual sex. The party scene also produces fun, generating student investment in it. Rather than criticizing the party scene or men's behavior, students
blame victims. By revealing mechanisms that lead to the persistence of sexual
assault and outlining implications for policy, we hope to encourage colleges and
universities to develop fresh approaches to sexual assault prevention.

APPROACHES TO COLLEGE SEXUAL ASSAULT

Explanations of high rates of sexual assault on college campuses fall into three
broad categories. The first tradition, a psychological approach that we label the
"individual determinants" approach, views college sexual assault as primarily a
consequence of perpetrator or victim characteristics such as gender role attitudes,
personality, family background, or sexual history. While "situational variables" are
considered, the focus is on individual characteristics. For example, Antonia Abbey
and associates (2001) find that hostility toward women, acceptance of verbal pressure as a way to obtain sex, and having many consensual sexual partners distinguish men who sexually assault from men who do not. Research suggests that
victims appear quite similar to other college women (Kalof 2000), except that
white women, prior victims, first-year college students, and more sexually active
women are more vulnerable to sexual assault (Adams-Curtis and Forbes 2004;
Humphrey and White 2000).

The second perspective, the "rape culture" approach, grew out of second
wave feminism. In this perspective, sexual assault is seen as a consequence of widespread belief in "rape myths," or ideas about the nature of men, women, sexuality,
and consent that create an environment conducive to rape. For example, men's
disrespectful treatment of women is normalized by the idea that men are naturally
sexually aggressive. Similarly, the belief that women "ask for it" shifts responsibility
from predators to victims. This perspective initiated an important shift away from
individual beliefs toward the broader context. However, rape supportive beliefs
alone cannot explain the prevalence of sexual assault, which requires not only an
inclination on the part of assailants but also physical proximity to victims.

A third approach moves beyond rape culture by identifying particular contexts—fraternities and bars—as sexually dangerous. Ayres Boswell and Joan

CHAPTER 41 SEXUAL ASSAULT ON CAMPUS   **497**

Spade (1996) suggest that sexual assault is supported not only by "a generic culture surrounding and promoting rape," but also by characteristics of the "specific settings" in which men and women interact (p. 133). Mindy Stombler and Patricia Yancey Martin (1994) illustrate that gender inequality is institutionalized on campus by "formal structure" that supports and intensifies an already "high-pressure heterosexual peer group" (p. 180). This perspective grounds sexual assault in organizations that provide opportunities and resources.

We extend this third approach by linking it to recent theoretical scholarship in the sociology of gender. Martin (2004), Barbara Risman (1998; 2004), Judith Lorber (1994), and others argue that gender is not only embedded in individual selves, but also in cultural rules, social interaction, and organizational arrangements. This integrative perspective identifies mechanisms at each level that contribute to the reproduction of gender inequality (Risman 2004). Socialization processes influence gendered selves, while cultural expectations reproduce gender inequality in interaction. At the institutional level, organizational practices, rules, resource distributions, and ideologies reproduce gender inequality. Applying this integrative perspective enabled us to identify gendered processes at individual, interactional, and organizational levels that contribute to college sexual assault....

METHOD

Data are from group and individual interviews, ethnographic observation, and publicly available information collected at a large midwestern research university. Located in a small city, the school has strong academic and sports programs, a large Greek system, and is sought after by students seeking a quintessential college experience. Like other schools, this school has had legal problems as a result of deaths associated with drinking. In the last few years, students have attended a sexual assault workshop during first-year orientation. Health and sexuality educators conduct frequent workshops, student volunteers conduct rape awareness programs, and *Take Back the Night* marches occur annually.

The bulk of the data presented in this paper were collected as part of ethnographic observation during the 2004–05 academic year in a residence hall identified by students and residence hall staff as a "party dorm." While little partying actually occurs in the hall, many students view this residence hall as one of several places to live in order to participate in the party scene on campus. This made it a good place to study the social worlds of students at high risk of sexual assault—women attending fraternity parties in their first year of college. The authors and a research team were assigned to a room on a floor occupied by 55 women students (51 first-year, 2 second-year, 1 senior, and 1 resident assistant [RA]). We observed on evenings and weekends throughout the entire academic school year. We collected in-depth background information via a detailed nine-page survey that 23 women completed and conducted interviews with 42 of the women (ranging from 1¼ to 2½ hours). All but seven of the women on the floor completed either a survey or an interview.

With at least one-third of first-year students on campus residing in "party dorms" and one-quarter of all undergraduates belonging to fraternities or sororities, this social world is the most visible on campus. As the most visible scene on campus, it also attracts students living in other residence halls and those not in the Greek system. Dense pre-college ties among the many in-state students, class and race homogeneity, and a small city location also contribute to the dominance of this scene. Of course, not all students on this floor or at this university participate in the party scene. To participate, one must typically be heterosexual, at least middle class, white, American-born, unmarried, childless, traditional college age, politically and socially mainstream, and interested in drinking. Over three-quarters of the women on the floor we observed fit this description.

There were no non-white students among the first and second year students on the floor we studied. This is a result of the homogeneity of this campus and racial segregation in social and residential life. African Americans (who make up 3% to 5% of undergraduates) generally live in living-learning communities in other residence halls and typically do not participate in the white Greek party scene. We argue that the party scene's homogeneity contributes to sexual risk for white women. We lack the space and the data to compare white and African American party scenes on this campus, but in the discussion we offer ideas about what such a comparison might reveal....

Selves and Peer Culture in the Transition
from High School to College

Student characteristics shape not only individual participation in dangerous party scenes and sexual risk within them but the development of these party scenes. We identify individual characteristics (other than gender) that generate interest in college partying and discuss the ways in which gendered sexual agendas generate a peer culture characterized by high-stakes competition over erotic status.

Non-Gendered Characteristics Motivate Participation in Party Scenes   Without individuals available for partying, the party scene would not exist. All the women on our floor were single and childless, as are the vast majority of undergraduates at this university; many, being upper-middle class, had few responsibilities other than their schoolwork. Abundant leisure time, however, is not enough to fuel the party scene. Media, siblings, peers, and parents all serve as sources of anticipatory socialization (Merton 1957). Both partiers and non-partiers agreed that one was "supposed" to party in college. This orientation was reflected in the popularity of a poster titled "What I Really Learned in School" that pictured mixed drinks with names associated with academic disciplines. As one focus group participant explained:

> You see these images of college that you're supposed to go out and
> have fun and drink, drink lots, party and meet guys. [You are] supposed
> to hook up with guys, and both men and women try to live up to that.

I think a lot of it is girls want to be accepted into their groups and guys want to be accepted into their groups.

Partying is seen as a way to feel a part of college life. Many of the women we observed participated in middle and high school peer cultures organized around status, belonging, and popularity (Eder 1985; Eder, Evans, and Parker 1995; Milner 2004). Assuming that college would be similar, they told us that they wanted to fit in, be popular, and have friends. Even on move-in day, they were supposed to already have friends. When we asked one of the outsiders, Ruth, about her first impression of her roommate, she replied that she found her:

> Extremely intimidating. Bethany already knew hundreds of people here. Her cell phone was going off from day one, like all the time. And I was too shy to ask anyone to go to dinner with me or lunch with me or anything. I ate while I did homework.

Peer Culture as Gendered and Sexualized   Partying was also the primary way to meet men on campus. The floor was locked to non-residents, and even men living in the same residence hall had to be escorted on the floor. The women found it difficult to get to know men in their classes, which were mostly mass lectures. They explained to us that people "don't talk" in class. Some complained they lacked casual friendly contact with men, particularly compared to the mixed-gender friendship groups they reported experiencing in high school.

Meeting men at parties was important to most of the women on our floor. The women found men's sexual interest at parties to be a source of self-esteem and status. They enjoyed dancing and kissing at parties, explaining to us that it proved men "liked" them. This attention was not automatic, but required the skillful deployment of physical and cultural assets. Most of the party-oriented women on the floor arrived with appropriate gender presentations and the money and know-how to preserve and refine them. While some more closely resembled the "ideal" college party girl (white, even features, thin but busty, tan, long straight hair, skillfully made-up, and well-dressed in the latest youth styles), most worked hard to attain this presentation. They regularly straightened their hair, tanned, exercised, dieted, and purchased new clothes.

Women found that achieving high erotic status in the party scene required looking "hot" but not "slutty," a difficult and ongoing challenge. Mastering these distinctions allowed them to establish themselves as "classy" in contrast to other women. Although women judged other women's appearance, men were the most important audience. A "hot" outfit could earn attention from desirable men in the party scene. A failed outfit, as some of our women learned, could earn scorn from men. One woman reported showing up to a party dressed in a knee-length skirt and blouse only to find that she needed to show more skin. A male guest sarcastically told her "nice outfit," accompanied by a thumbs-up gesture....

Men also sought proof of their erotic appeal. As a woman complained, "Every man I have met here has wanted to have sex with me!" Another interviewee reported that: this guy that I was talking to for like ten/fifteen minutes says,

"Could you, um, come to the bathroom with me and jerk me off?" And I'm like, "What!" I'm like, "Okay, like, I've known you for like, fifteen minutes, but no." The women found that men were more interested than they were in having sex. These clashes in sexual expectations are not surprising: men derived status from securing sex (from high-status women), while women derived status from getting attention (from high-status men). These agendas are both complementary and adversarial: men give attention to women en route to getting sex, and women are unlikely to become interested in sex without getting attention first.

University and Greek Rules, Resources, and Procedures

Simply by congregating similar individuals, universities make possible heterosexual peer cultures. The university, the Greek system, and other related organizations structure student life through rules, distribution of resources, and procedures.

Sexual danger is an unintended consequence of many university practices intended to be gender neutral. The clustering of homogeneous students intensifies the dynamics of student peer cultures and heightens motivations to party. Characteristics of residence halls and how they are regulated push student partying into bars, off-campus residences, and fraternities. While factors that increase the risk of party rape are present in varying degrees in all party venues (Boswell and Spade 1996), we focus on fraternity parties because they were the typical party venue for the women we observed and have been identified as particularly unsafe (see also Martin and Hummer 1989; Sanday 1990). Fraternities offer the most reliable and private source of alcohol for first-year students excluded from bars and house parties because of age and social networks.

University Practices as Push Factors The university has latitude in how it enforces state drinking laws. Enforcement is particularly rigorous in residence halls. We observed RAs and police officers (including gun-carrying peer police) patrolling the halls for alcohol violations. Women on our floor were "documented" within the first week of school for infractions they felt were minor. Sanctions are severe—a $300 fine, an 8-hour alcohol class, and probation for a year. As a consequence, students engaged in only minimal, clandestine alcohol consumption in their rooms. In comparison, alcohol flows freely at fraternities.

The lack of comfortable public space for informal socializing in the residence hall also serves as a push factor. A large central bathroom divided our floor. A sterile lounge was rarely used for socializing. There was no cafeteria, only a convenience store and a snack bar in a cavernous room furnished with big-screen televisions. Residence life sponsored alternatives to the party scene such as "movie night" and special dinners, but these typically occurred early in the evening. Students defined the few activities sponsored during party hours (e.g., a midnight trip to Wal-Mart) as uncool....

Male Control of Fraternity Parties The campus Greek system cannot operate without university consent. The university lists Greek organizations as student clubs, devotes professional staff to Greek-oriented programming, and disbands fraternities that violate university policy. Nonetheless, the university lacks full authority over fraternities; Greek houses are privately owned and chapters answer to national organizations and the Interfraternity Council (IFC) (i.e., a body governing the more than 20 predominantly white fraternities).

Fraternities control every aspect of parties at their houses: themes, music, transportation, admission, access to alcohol, and movement of guests. Party themes usually require women to wear scant, sexy clothing and place women in subordinate positions to men. During our observation period, women attended parties such as "Pimps and Hos," "Victoria's Secret," and "Playboy Mansion"— the last of which required fraternity members to escort two scantily clad dates. Other recent themes included: "CEO Secretary Ho," "School Teacher Sexy Student," and "Golf Pro/Tennis Ho."

Some fraternities require pledges to transport first-year students, primarily women, from the residence halls to the fraternity houses. From about 9 to 11 P.M. on weekend nights early in the year, the drive in front of the residence hall resembled a rowdy taxi-stand, as dressed-to-impress women waited to be carpooled to parties in expensive late-model vehicles. By allowing party-oriented first-year women to cluster in particular residence halls, the university made them easy to find. One fraternity member told us this practice was referred to as "dorm-storming."

Transportation home was an uncertainty. Women sometimes called cabs, caught the "drunk bus," or trudged home in stilettos. Two women indignantly described a situation where fraternity men "wouldn't give us a ride home." The women said, "Well, let us call a cab." The men discouraged them from calling the cab and eventually found a designated driver. The women described the men as "just dicks" and as "rude."

Fraternities police the door of their parties, allowing in desirable guests (first-year women) and turning away others (unaffiliated men). Women told us of abandoning parties when male friends were not admitted. They explained that fraternity men also controlled the quality and quantity of alcohol. Brothers served themselves first, then personal guests, and then other women. Non-affiliated and unfamiliar men were served last, and generally had access to only the least desirable beverages. The promise of more or better alcohol was often used to lure women into private spaces of the fraternities.

Fraternities are constrained, though, by the necessity of attracting women to their parties. Fraternities with reputations for sexual disrespect have more success recruiting women to parties early in the year. One visit was enough for some of the women. A roommate duo told of a house they "liked at first" until they discovered that the men there were "really not nice."

The Production of Fun and Sexual Assault in Interaction

Peer culture and organizational arrangements set up risky partying conditions, but do not explain *how* student interactions at parties generate sexual assault. At the interactional level we see the mechanisms through which sexual assault is produced. As interactions necessarily involve individuals with particular characteristics and occur in specific organizational settings, all three levels meet when interactions take place. Here, gendered and gender neutral expectations and routines are intricately woven together to create party rape. Party rape is the result of fun situations that shift—either gradually or quite suddenly—into coercive situations. Demonstrating how the production of fun is connected with sexual assault requires describing the interactional routines and expectations that enable men to employ coercive sexual strategies with little risk of consequence.

College partying involves predictable activities in a predictable order (e.g., getting ready, pre-gaming, getting to the party, getting drunk, flirtation or sexual interaction, getting home, and sharing stories). It is characterized by "shared assumptions about what constitutes good or adequate participation"—what Nina Eliasoph and Paul Lichterman (2003) call "group style" (p. 737). A fun partier throws him or herself into the event, drinks, displays an upbeat mood, and evokes revelry in others. Partiers are expected to like and trust party-mates. Norms of civil interaction curtail displays of unhappiness or tension among party-goers. Michael Schwalbe and associates (2000) observed that groups engage in scripted events of this sort "to bring about an intended emotional result" (p. 438). Drinking assists people in transitioning from everyday life to a state of euphoria.

Cultural expectations of partying are gendered. Women are supposed to wear revealing outfits, while men typically are not. As guests, women cede control of turf, transportation, and liquor. Women are also expected to be grateful for men's hospitality, and as others have noted, to generally be "nice" in ways that men are not. The pressure to be deferential and gracious may be intensified by men's older age and fraternity membership. The quandary for women, however, is that fulfilling the gendered role of partier makes them vulnerable to sexual assault.

Women's vulnerability produces sexual assault only if men exploit it. Too many men are willing to do so. Many college men attend parties looking for casual sex. A student in one of our classes explained that "guys are willing to do damn near anything to get a piece of ass." A male student wrote the following description of parties at his (non-fraternity) house:

> Girls are continually fed drinks of alcohol. It's mainly to party but my roomies are also aware of the inhibition-lowering effects. I've seen an old roomie block doors when girls want to leave his room; and other times I've driven women home who can't remember much of an evening yet sex did occur. Rarely if ever has a night of drinking for my roommate ended without sex. I know it isn't necessarily and assuredly sexual assault, but with the amount of liquor in the house I question the amount of consent a lot.

Another student—after deactivating—wrote about a fraternity brother "telling us all at the chapter meeting about how he took this girl home and she was obviously too drunk to function and he took her inside and had sex with her." Getting women drunk, blocking doors, and controlling transportation are common ways men try to prevent women from leaving sexual situations. Rape culture beliefs, such as the belief that men are "naturally" sexually aggressive, normalize these coercive strategies. Assigning women the role of sexual "gate-keeper" relieves men from responsibility for obtaining authentic consent, and enables them to view sex obtained by undermining women's ability to resist it as "consensual" (e.g., by getting women so drunk that they pass out).[2]

In a focus group with her sorority sisters, a junior sorority woman provided an example of a partying situation that devolved into a likely sexual assault.

ANNA: It kind of happened to me freshman year. I'm not positive about what happened, that's the worst part about it. I drank too much at a frat one night, I blacked out and I woke up the next morning with nothing on in their cold dorms, so I don't really know what happened and the guy wasn't in the bed anymore, I don't even think I could tell you who the hell he was, no I couldn't.

SARAH: Did you go to the hospital?

ANNA: No, I didn't know what happened. I was scared and wanted to get the hell out of there. I didn't know who it was, so how am I supposed to go to the hospital and say someone might've raped me? It could have been any one of the hundred guys that lived in the house.

SARAH: It happens to so many people, it would shock you. Three of my best friends in the whole world, people that you like would think it would never happen to, it happened to. It's just so hard because you don't know how to deal with it because you don't want to turn in a frat because all hundred of those brothers ...

ANNA: I was also thinking like, you know, I just got to school, I don't want to start off on a bad note with anyone, and now it happened so long ago, it's just one of those things that I kind of have to live with.

This woman's confusion demonstrates the usefulness of alcohol as a weapon: her intoxication undermined her ability to resist sex, her clarity about what happened, and her feelings of entitlement to report it. We collected other narratives in which sexual assault or probable sexual assault occurred when the woman was asleep, comatose, drugged, or otherwise incapacitated.

Amanda, a woman on our hall, provides insight into how men take advantage of women's niceness, gender deference, and unequal control of party resources. Amanda reported meeting a "cute" older guy, Mike, also a student, at a local student bar. She explained that, "At the bar we were kind of making out a little bit and I told him just cause I'm sitting here making out doesn't mean that I want to go home with you, you know?" After Amanda found herself stranded by friends with no cell phone or cab fare, Mike promised that a sober friend of his would drive her home. Once they got in the car Mike's friend refused to take her home and instead dropped her at Mike's place. Amanda's concerns were heightened by the driver's disrespect. "He was like, so are you into ménage à trois?" Amanda reported staying awake all night. She woke Mike early in the morning to take her home. Despite her ordeal, she argued that Mike was "a really nice guy" and exchanged telephone numbers with him. These men took advantage of Amanda's unwillingness to make a scene. Amanda was one of the most assertive women on our floor. Indeed, her refusal to participate fully in the culture of feminine niceness led her to suffer in the social hierarchy of the floor and on campus. It is unlikely that other women we observed could have been more assertive in this situation. That she was nice to her captor in the morning suggests how much she wanted him to like her and what she was willing to tolerate in order to keep his interest.[3] This case also shows that it is not only fraternity parties that are dangerous; men can control party resources and work together to constrain women's behavior while partying in bars and at house parties. What distinguishes fraternity parties is that male dominance of partying there is organized, resourced, and implicitly endorsed by the university. Other party venues are also organized in ways that advantage men.

We heard many stories of negative experiences in the party scene, including at least one account of a sexual assault in every focus group that included heterosexual women. Most women who partied complained about men's efforts to control their movements or pressure them to drink. Two of the women on our floor were sexually assaulted at a fraternity party in the first week of school—one was raped. Later in the semester, another woman on the floor was raped by a friend. A fourth woman on the floor suspects she was drugged; she became disoriented at a fraternity party and was very ill for the next week.

Party rape is accomplished without the use of guns, knives, or fists. It is carried out through the combination of low level forms of coercion—a lot of liquor and persuasion, manipulation of situations so that women cannot leave, and sometimes force (e.g., by blocking a door, or using body weight to make it difficult for a woman to get up). These forms of coercion are made more effective by organizational arrangements that provide men with control over how partying happens and by expectations that women let loose and trust their partymates. This systematic and effective method of extracting non-consensual sex is largely invisible, which makes it difficult for victims to convince anyone—even themselves—that a crime occurred. Men engage in this behavior with little risk of consequences.

Student Responses and the Resiliency of the Party Scene

The frequency of women's negative experiences in the party scene poses a problem for those students most invested in it. Finding fault with the party scene potentially threatens meaningful identities and lifestyles. The vast majority of heterosexual encounters at parties are fun and consensual. Partying provides a chance to meet new people, experience and display belonging, and to enhance social position. Women on our floor told us that they loved to flirt and be admired, and they displayed pictures on walls, doors, and websites commemorating their fun nights out.

The most common way that students—both women and men—account for the harm that befalls women in the party scene is by blaming victims. By attributing bad experiences to women's "mistakes," students avoid criticizing the party scene or men's behavior within it. Such victim-blaming also allows women to feel that they can control what happens to them. The logic of victim-blaming suggests that sophisticated, smart, careful women are safe from sexual assault. Only "immature," "naïve," or "stupid" women get in trouble. When discussing the sexual assault of a friend, a floor resident explained that:

> She somehow got like sexually assaulted ... by one of our friends' old roommates. All I know is that kid was like bad news to start off with. So, I feel sorry for her but it wasn't much of a surprise for us. He's a shady character.

Another floor resident relayed a sympathetic account of a woman raped at knife point by a stranger in the bushes, but later dismissed party rape as nothing to worry about "'cause I'm not stupid when I'm drunk." Even a feminist focus group participant explained that her friend who was raped "made every single mistake and almost all of them had to with alcohol.... She got ridiculed when she came out and said she was raped." These women contrast "true victims" who are deserving of support with "stupid" women who forfeit sympathy (Phillips 2000). Not only is this response devoid of empathy for other women, but it also leads women to blame themselves when they are victimized (Phillips 2000).

Sexual assault prevention strategies can perpetuate victim-blaming. Instructing women to watch their drinks, stay with friends, and limit alcohol consumption implies that it is women's responsibility to avoid "mistakes" and their fault if they fail. Emphasis on the precautions women should take—particularly if not accompanied by education about how men should change their behavior—may also suggest that it is natural for men to drug women and take advantage of them. Additionally, suggesting that women should watch what they drink, trust partymates, or spend time alone with men asks them to forgo full engagement in the pleasures of the college party scene.

Victim-blaming also serves as a way for women to construct a sense of status within campus erotic hierarchies. As discussed earlier, women and men acquire erotic status based on how "hot" they are perceived to be. Another aspect of erotic status concerns the amount of sexual respect one receives from men. Women can tell themselves that they are safe from sexual assault not only because they are savvy, but because men will recognize that they, unlike other women, are worthy of sexual respect. For example, a focus group of senior women explained that at a small fraternity gathering their friend Amy came out of the bathroom. She was crying and said that a guy "had her by her neck, holding her up, feeling her up from her crotch up to her neck and saying that I should rape you, you are a fucking whore." The woman's friends were appalled, saying, "no one deserves that." On other hand, they explained that: "Amy flaunts herself. She is a whore so, I mean ..." They implied that if one is a whore, one gets treated like one.[4]

Men accord women varying levels of sexual respect, with lower status women seen as "fair game." On campus the youngest and most anonymous women are most vulnerable. High-status women (i.e., girlfriends of fraternity members) may be less likely victims of party rape.[5] Sorority women explained that fraternities discourage members from approaching the girlfriends (and ex-girlfriends) of other men in the house. Partiers on our floor learned that it was safer to party with men they knew as boyfriends, friends, or brothers of friends. One roommate pair partied exclusively at a fraternity where one of the women knew many men from high school. She explained that "we usually don't party with people we don't know that well." Over the course of the year, women on the floor winnowed their party venues to those fraternity houses where they "knew the guys" and could expect to be treated respectfully.

Opting Out   While many students find the party scene fun, others are more ambivalent. Some attend a few fraternity parties to feel like they have participated in this college tradition. Others opt out of it altogether. On our floor, 44 out of the 51 first-year students (almost 90%) participated in the party scene. Those on the floor who opted out worried about sexual safety and the consequences of engaging in illegal behavior. For example, an interviewee who did not drink was appalled by the fraternity party transport system. She explained that:

> All those girls would stand out there and just like, no joke, get into these big black Suburbans driven by frat guys, wearing like seriously no clothes, piled on top of each other. This could be some kidnapper taking you all away to the woods and chopping you up and leaving you there. How dumb can you be?

In her view, drinking around fraternity men was "scary" rather than "fun."

Her position was unpopular. She, like others who did not party, was an outsider on the floor. Partiers came home loudly in the middle of the night, threw up in the bathrooms, and rollerbladed around the floor. Socially, the others simply did not exist. A few of our "misfits" successfully created social lives outside the floor. The most assertive of the "misfits" figured out the dynamics of the floor in the first weeks and transferred to other residence halls.

However, most students on our floor lacked the identities or network connections necessary for entry into alternative worlds. Life on a large university campus can be overwhelming for first-year students. Those who most needed an alternative to the social world of the party dorm were often ill-equipped to actively seek it out. They either integrated themselves into partying or found themselves alone in their rooms, microwaving frozen dinners and watching television. A Christian focus group participant described life in this residence hall: "When everyone is going out on a Thursday and you are in the room by yourself and there are only two or three other people on the floor, that's not fun, it's not the college life that you want."…

DISCUSSION AND IMPLICATIONS

Individual characteristics and institutional practices provide the actors and contexts in which interactional processes occur. We have to turn to the interactional level, however, to understand *how* sexual assault is generated. Gender neutral expectations to "have fun," lose control, and trust one's party-mates become problematic when combined with gendered interactional expectations. Women are expected to be "nice" and to defer to men in interaction. This expectation is intensified by men's position as hosts and women's as grateful guests. The heterosexual script, which directs men to pursue sex and women to play the role of gatekeeper, further disadvantages women, particularly when virtually *all* men's methods of extracting sex are defined as legitimate.

The mechanisms identified should help explain intra-campus, cross-campus, and overtime variation in the prevalence of sexual assault. Campuses with similar students and social organization are predicted to have similar rates of sexual assault. We would expect to see lower rates of sexual assault on campuses characterized by more aesthetically appealing public space, lower alcohol use, and the absence of a gender-adversarial party scene. Campuses with more racial diversity and more racial integration would also be expected to have lower rates of sexual assault because of the dilution of upper-middle class white peer groups. Researchers are beginning to conduct comparative research on the impact of university organization on aggregate rates of sexual assault. For example, Meichun Mohler-Kuo and associates (2004) found that women who attended schools with medium or high levels of heavy episodic drinking were more at risk of being raped while intoxicated than women attending other schools, even while controlling for individual-level characteristics. More comparative research is needed.

This perspective may also help explain why white college women are at higher risk of sexual assault than other racial groups. Existing research suggests that African American college social scenes are more gender egalitarian (Stombler and Padavic 1997), African American fraternities typically do not have houses, depriving men of a party resource. The missions, goals, and recruitment practices of African American fraternities and sororities discourage joining for exclusively social reasons (Berkowitz and Padavic 1999), and rates of alcohol consumption are lower among African American students (Journal of Blacks in Higher Education 2000; Weschsler and Kuo 2003). The role of party rape in the lives of white college women is substantiated by recent research that found that "white women were more likely [than non-white women] to have experienced rape while intoxicated and less likely to experience other rape" (Mohler-Kuo et al. 2004: 41). White women's overall higher rates of rape are accounted for by their high rates of rape while intoxicated. Studies of racial differences in the culture and organization of college partying and its consequences for sexual assault are needed.

Our analysis also provides a framework for analyzing the sources of sexual risk in non-university partying situations. Situations where men have a home turf advantage, know each other better than the women present know each other, see the women as anonymous, and control desired resources (such as alcohol or drugs) are likely to be particularly dangerous. Social pressures to "have fun," prove one's social competency, or adhere to traditional gender expectations are also predicted to increase rates of sexual assault within a social scene.

This research has implications for policy. The interdependence of levels means that it is difficult to enact change at one level when the other levels remain unchanged. Programs to combat sexual assault currently focus primarily or even exclusively on education. But as Ann Swidler (2001) argued, culture develops in response to institutional arrangements. Without change in institutional arrangements, efforts to change cultural beliefs are undermined by the cultural commonsense generated by encounters with institutions. Efforts to educate about sexual assault will not succeed if the university continues to support organizational arrangements that facilitate and even legitimate men's coercive sexual strategies. Thus, our research implies that efforts to combat sexual assault on campus should target all levels, constituencies, and processes simultaneously. Efforts to educate both men and women should indeed be intensified, but they should be reinforced by changes in the social organization of student life.

Researchers focused on problem drinking on campus have found that reduction efforts focused on the social environment are successful (Berkowitz 2003: 21). Student body diversity has been found to decrease binge drinking on campus (Weschsler and Kuo 2003); it might also reduce rates of sexual assault. Existing student heterogeneity can be exploited by eliminating self-selection into age-segregated, white, upper-middle class, heterosexual enclaves and by working to make residence halls more appealing to upper-division students. Building more aesthetically appealing housing might allow students to interact outside of alcohol-fueled party scenes. Less expensive plans might involve creating more living-learning communities, coffee shops, and other student-run community spaces.

While heavy alcohol use is associated with sexual assault, not all efforts to regulate student alcohol use contribute to sexual safety. Punitive approaches sometimes heighten the symbolic significance of drinking, lead students to drink more hard liquor, and push alcohol consumption to more private and thus more dangerous spaces. Regulation inconsistently applied—e.g., heavy policing of residence halls and light policing of fraternities—increases the power of those who can secure alcohol and host parties. More consistent regulation could decrease the value of alcohol as a commodity by equalizing access to it.

Sexual assault education should shift in emphasis from educating women on preventative measures to educating both men and women about the coercive behavior of men and the sources of victim-blaming. Mohler-Kuo and associates (2004) suggest, and we endorse, a focus on the role of alcohol in sexual assault. Education should begin before students arrive on campus and continue throughout college. It may also be most effective if high-status peers are involved in disseminating knowledge and experience to younger college students....

NOTES

1. On party rape as a distinct type of sexual assault, see also Ward and associates (1991). Ehrhart and Sandler (1987) use the term to refer to group rape. We use the term to refer to one-on-one assaults. We encountered no reports of group sexual assault.

2. In ongoing research on college men and sexuality, Sweeney (2004) and Rosow and Ray (2006) have found wide variation in beliefs about acceptable ways to obtain sex even among men who belong to the same fraternities. Rosow and Ray found that

fraternity men in the most elite houses view sex with intoxicated women as low status and claim to avoid it.

3. Holland and Eisenhart (1990) and Stombler (1994) found that male attention is of such high value to some women that they are willing to suffer indignities to receive it.

4. Schwalbe and associates (2000) suggest that there are several psychological mechanisms that explain this behavior. Trading power for patronage occurs when a subordinate group accepts their status in exchange for compensatory benefits from the dominant group. Defensive othering is a process by which some members of a subordinated group seek to maintain status by deflecting stigma to others. Maneuvering to protect or improve

individual position within hierarchical classification systems is common; however, these responses support the subordination that makes them necessary.

5. While "knowing" one's male partymates may offer some protection, this protection is not comprehensive. Sorority women, who typically have the closest ties with fraternity men, experience more sexual assault than other college women (Mohler-Kuo et al. 2004). Not only do sorority women typically spend more time in high-risk social situations than other women, but arriving at a high-status position on campus may require one to begin their college social career as one of the anonymous young women who are frequently victimized.

REFERENCES

Abbey, Antonia, Pam McAuslan, Tina Zawacki, A. Monique Clinton, and Philip Buck. 2001. "Attitudinal, Experiential, and Situational Predictors of Sexual Assault Perpetration." *Journal of Interpersonal Violence* 16: 784–807.

Abbey, Antonia, Lisa Thomson Ross, Donna McDuffie, and Pam McAuslan. 1996. "Alcohol and Dating Risk Factors for Sexual Assault among College Women." *Psychology of Women Quarterly* 20: 147–69.

Adams-Curtis, Leah, and Gordon Forbes. 2004. "College Women's Experiences of Sexual Coercion: A Review of Cultural, Perpetrator, Victim, and Situational Variables." *Trauma, Violence, and Abuse: A Review Journal* 5: 91–122.

Bachar, Karen and Mary Koss. 2001. "From Prevalence to Prevention: Closing the Gap between What We Know about Rape and What We Do." Pp. 117–42 in *Sourcebook on*

Violence against Women, edited by C. Renzetti, J. Edleson, and R. K. Bergen. Thousand Oaks, CA: Sage.

Berkowitz, Alan. 2003. "How Should We Talk about Student Drinking—And What Should We Do about It?" *About Campus* May/June: 16–22.

Berkowitz, Alexandra, and Irene Padavic. 1999. "Getting a Man or Getting Ahead: A Comparison of White and Black Sororities." *Journal of Contemporary Ethnography* 27: 530–57.

Boswell, A. Ayres, and Joan Z. Spade. 1996. "Fraternities and Collegiate Rape Culture: Why Are Some Fraternities More Dangerous Places for Women?" *Gender & Society* 10: 133–47.

Eder, Donna. 1985. "The Cycle of Popularity: Inter-personal Relations among Female Adolescents." *Sociology of Education* 58: 154–65.

Eder, Donna, Catherine Evans, and Stephen Parker. 1995. *School Talk: Gender and Adolescent Culture.* New

Brunswick, NJ: Rutgers University Press.

Ehrhart, Julie, and Bernice Sandler. 1987. "Party Rape." *Response* 9: 205.

Eliasoph, Nina, and Paul Lichterman. 2003. "Culture in Interaction." *American Journal of Sociology* 108: 735–94.

Fisher, Bonnie, Francis Cullen, and Michael Turner.2000. "The Sexual Victimization of College Women." Washington, DC: National Institute of Justice and the Bureau of Justice Statistics.

Holland, Dorothy and Margaret Eisenhart. 1990. *Educated in Romance: Women, Achievement, and College Culture.* Chicago: University of Chicago Press.

Humphrey, John, and Jacquelyn White. 2000. "Women's Vulnerability to Sexual Assault from Adolescence to Young Adulthood." *Journal of Adolescent Health* 27: 419–24.

Journal of Blacks in Higher Education. 2000. "News and Views: Alcohol Abuse Remains High on College Campus, but Black Students Drink to Excess Far Less Often Than Whites." *The Journal of Blacks in Higher Education.* 28: 19–20.

Kalof Linda. 2000. "Vulnerability to Sexual Coercion among College Women: A Longitudinal Study." *Gender Issues* 18: 47–58.

Lorber, Judith. 1994. *Paradoxes of Gender.* New Haven, CT: Yale University Press.

Marine, Susan. 2004. "Waking Up from the Nightmare of Rape." *The Chronicle of Higher Education.* November 26, p. B5.

Martin, Patricia Yancey. 2004. "Gender as a Social Institution." *Social Forces* 82: 1249–73.

Martin, Patricia Yancey, and Robert A. Hummer. 1989. "Fraternities and Rape on Campus." *Gender & Society* 3: 457–73.

Merton, Robert. 1957. *Social Theory and Social Structure.* New York: Free Press.

Milner, Murray. 2004. *Freaks, Geeks, and Cool Kids: American Teenagers, Schools, and the Culture of Consumption.* New York: Routledge.

Mohler-Kuo, Meichun, George W. Dowdall, Mary P. Koss, and Henry Weschler. 2004. "Correlates of Rape While Intoxicated in a National Sample of College Women." *Journal of Studies on Alcohol* 65: 37–45.

Phillips, Lynn. 2000. *Flirting with Danger: Young Women's Reflections on Sexuality and Domination.* New York: New York University.

Risman, Barbara. 1998. *Gender Vertigo: American Families in Transition.* New Haven, CT: Yale University Press.

———. 2004. "Gender as a Social Structure: Theory Wrestling with Activism." *Gender & Society* 18:429–50.

Rosow, Jason and Rashawn Ray. 2006. "Getting Off and Showing Off: The Romantic and Sexual Lives of High Status Black and White Status Men." Department of Sociology, Indiana University, Bloomington, IN. Unpublished manuscript.

Sampson, Rana. 2002. "Acquaintance Rape of College Students." Problem-Oriented Guides for Police Series, No. 17. Washington, DC: U.S. Department of Justice, Office of Community Oriented Policing Services.

Sanday, Peggy. 1990. *Fraternity Gang Rape: Sex, Brother-hood, and Privilege on Campus.* New York: New York University Press.

Schwalbe, Michael, Sandra Godwin, Daphne Holden, Douglas Schrock, Shealy Thompson, and Michele Wolkomir. 2000. "Generic Processes in the Reproduction of Inequality: An Interactionist Analysis." *Social Forces* 79: 419–52.

Stombler, Mindy. 1994. "'Buddies' or Slutties': The Collective Reputation of Fraternity Little Sisters." *Gender & Society* 8: 297–323.

Stombler, Mindy, and Patricia Yancey Martin. 1994. "Bringing Women In, Keeping Women Down: Fraternity Little Sister' Organizations." *Journal of Contemporary Ethnography* 23: 150–84.

Stombler, Mindy, and Irene Padavic. 1997. "Sister Acts: Resisting Men's Domination in Black and White Fraternity Little Sister Programs." *Social Problems* 44: 257–75.

Sweeney, Brian. 2004. "Good Guy on Campus: Gender, Peer Groups, and Sexuality among College Men." Presented at the American Sociological Association Annual Meetings, August 17, Philadelphia, PA.

Swidler, Ann. 2001. *Talk of Love: How Culture Matters*. Chicago: University of Chicago Press.

Ward, Sally, Kathy Chapman, Ellen Cohn, Susan White, and Kirk Williams. 1991. "Acquantance Rape and The College Social Scene." *Family Relations* 40: 65–71.

Weschsler, Henry, and Meichun Kuo. 2003. "Watering Down the Drinks: The Moderating Effect of College Demographics on Alcohol Use of High-Risk Groups." *American Journal of Public Health*. 93: 1929–33.

42

Opportunity Structures for White-Collar Crime

OSKAR ENGDAHL

Returning once again to the crimes of the powerful, we see a smaller scale example of fraud and its relation to American culture than the Halliburton fiasco. Our society has been rocked over the last decade by the unraveling of large numbers of white-collar crimes. New instances of fraud are revealed every month, with devastating financial consequences for millions. Not just the domain of the rich and well-connected, fraud is alive and flourishing in our capitalist system from top to bottom.

Engdahl illustrates his analysis with the fraud of a stock broker who flew beyond the reach of regulators, buoyed beyond suspicion by a history of high financial returns. He shows the way individuals with little expertise in the inner workings of the complex system of derivates and other financial instruments put their trust in people to manage their hard-earned money. Firms with the responsibility for overseeing brokers' fiduciary responsibility gave these individuals enormous flexibility as long as they generated profits for their organization. Regulators were likewise blinded by their close ties to the financial industry and their political belief in the capitalist system. All parties to these transactions believed that the smart, well-connected segment of the population deserved to prosper at the expense of lesser folk. As a result, Engdahl depicts the loss of control that arose in the financial world.

How does this story compare to the events that led to the financial crash of 2008 and beyond? How does this compare to the giant Ponzi scheme perpetrated by Bernard Madoff, or to the real estate bubble that was buoyed by loose loans and their repackaging into complex packages of derivates? Whose responsibility is it, or should it be, to regulate such behavior? Why has such regulation weakened, and why has it proved so difficult to reinstate? Has the public become protected from these kinds of financial frauds to any extent, and how so? What are the structural causes and motivations of this type of crime, compared to street crime? How is it viewed as similar to or different from street crime? How is it viewed as similar to or different from infractions of social values, such as abortion or gay marriage?

Possibility or "opportunity" is a central component in many explanatory models for criminality. In research on white-collar crime, this emerges especially through an emphasis on the importance of social position for the possibility of carrying out crime. The emphasis has been a key aspect of economic-crime research since Sutherland, using the concept of white-collar crime, began to study criminality among upper social classes, which in his view was made possible by "positions in power" (Sutherland 1983: 7). By white-collar crime Sutherland meant primarily people who held positions in the sense that they were regarded as "respectable" and had "high social status." He connected such positions with the holders' "professional practice." Criminality then had to do with the fact that the position conveyed by the profession was misused in order to commit crime.

Sutherland's conceptualization has had great influence on how crime in the world of companies and businesses is understood and investigated in criminology and related disciplines. The discussion of which component is most central among those that Sutherland included in his concept has been extensive, as have attempts to refine the concept. Of the better-known notions that have defined the orientation of this research field, the most important are considered to be "corporate crime" and "occupational crime," which place the focus on crimes that occur through and on behalf of companies, or are committed by virtue of the position that accrues to a person in his or her professional role. Common to the diverse choices of concept is, however, a tendency to see it as essential to contextualize people and their activities by setting them in some form of social position with respect to each other. Equally often, the aim is seemingly to clarify that it is the *position* in the profession or company that create *opportunities* for crime. This is plainly expressed by Vaughan (1983: 85) when, in a study of corporate misconduct, she says that "[p]osition is a key variable for understanding the response of members to the tensions organizations experience when competing for scarce resources. The skills used to commit a violation are those associated with a particular position in the organization."

In sharp contrast to the relatively great efforts made with other aspects of white-collar crime research, much less attention than might be expected has been devoted to explaining *how* social positions create opportunities for committing crime.... My approach to these issues will maintain the following:

1. The more or less explicit ideas advanced by research in the area can be systematized and classified according to different types of resources with whose help a position makes crime possible. These resources are understood in terms of access to authority, social contact networks, and technical-administrative systems.

2. Goffman's concepts of "barriers" and "back regions" can be used to clarify what it is in a social position that creates opportunities for crime, because they have to do with how a concealed space for maneuvering is established by preventing others' insight....

BARRIERS AS OPPORTUNITY STRUCTURES FOR WHITE-COLLAR CRIME: AN EMPIRICAL EXAMPLE

Background

In order to clarify both the theoretical content and the empirical relevance of the barrier concept, the argument that follows is illustrated with a case of white-collar crime. It involves a broker in a well-reputed brokerage firm who was found guilty of breach of trust (SNECB 2000; SDC 2001, 2003; SAC 2002; SC 2003). The case is treated as a typical one for strategic reasons so as to demonstrate and stress essential characteristics. At the core of the case is a losing deal that the broker perpetrated after having worked in the firm for a couple of years. The broker conducted a large number of deals on behalf of clients, among them the firm's most important private client. Both the client and the broker enjoyed high status at the firm. On a certain occasion, one of the broker's deals for this client did not proceed as planned, resulting in a loss corresponding to one million USD. The broker tried to hide the bad deal from the client and employees at the firm. He did so temporarily by transferring the deal to one of the firm's accounts for ongoing and unfinished deals, and permanently by conducting other deals secretly—through accounts belonging to clients or the firm—in order to generate profits that could cover the loss. The broker succeeded in concealing the loss for four years, but his secret deals failed to create profits that covered the initial loss. The total loss grew to 21 million USD by the time the irregularities were brought to light.

During those four years, no suspicions of the irregularities arose. The fact that the broker could hide extensive losses and deals for so long without being suspected can be explained: his relations with the client and the firm's other employees, chiefs, and accounts were permeated with barriers that obstructed suspicion and detection of crime. These are referred to in the following analysis as financial self-interest, low priority of control, and interpretative primacy. The great importance of these barriers are central to understanding the broker's case; it was not until the broker turned himself in that his irregularities came into light. During the four years of irregularities he had—at least at a couple of occasions—made so many good deals that he had been close to erasing his initial loss. But he never succeeded fully in erasing the loss, and when he later—once again—started making big losses he, in his own words, "felt that I was on the verge of what I could endure" (SNECB 2000: 88). During the four years he had, for periods of time, suffered from psychological stress, and the day following his confession he was hospitalized for a heart condition.

Financial Self-Interest

The relations between the broker and the client involved informal and oral agreements in person; no agreements were codified in writing. At first, the broker and client met "over a cup of coffee" to examine the deals, but this did not lead to any special basic orders. Instead, the client gave the broker general instructions of the type "do the deals you think are good" (SNECB 2000: 60, 211, 243; SDC 2001: 13f.). The client felt sure that the broker and his way of work-ing were in line with reasonable business strategies. Moreover, the client believed that it was in his own interest to exploit the broker's knowledge, which he did by committing funds to the broker's care. The client not only regarded the bro-ker as knowledgeable quite generally, but spoke of him as the country's "deriva-tive king" (SNECB 2000: 62). It should be added that the client considered the broker to be very reliable. The client claimed to have wide experience of brokers who attempted to enrich themselves on others' deals, and according to him it was therefore normally necessary to constantly oversee brokers who were retained and to check their deals. However, he did not think such control nec-essary in the present case because he perceived this broker to be highly reliable. Hence the client handed over the entire responsibility for all deals on one of his accounts to the broker, and handled the related papers himself only sporadically. The papers went "straight into the notebook" with no thorough control. The client described the broker as "the most serious person you can imagine" and commented further that "It's like I can rely on my own father" (SNECB 2000: 62). The broker was well aware that the client did not interfere with what-ever positions were taken on the account and did not control it afterward: "The only thing he looks at now and then is when he gets an account statement once a month and sees that the balance is more or less okay" (SNECB 2000: 177).

Thus, the client considered himself to have good knowledge of and trust in the broker. The business relationship functioned "extremely well" according to him, and was gradually complemented by the fact that, according to them both, they "got close to each other" (SNECB 2000: 62). This was manifested by the broker being one of those who accompanied the client on trips, and by the cli-ent being best man at the broker's wedding. The client's perception of good knowledge about and trust in the broker contributed to his letting the broker manage his money. It should be noted, however, that good knowledge of how a broker functions can nonetheless include knowledge that leads one to refrain from committing assets to management by others. This knowledge, therefore, is not in itself decisive for the realization of an assignment of management. It is rather the perception that such commitment is in one's self-interest that is central for doing so. In the present case, the client judged the broker's skill, reliability, and loyalty to fulfill the requirements. His judgment was also confirmed in a manner clear to him: during the period of handling his deals, the broker was able to take out tens of million USD in profits.

From the broker's position, financial self-interest acted in two respects: be-sides the client's interest in letting the broker manage parts of his assets, the firm also showed this interest. The broker was known to be highly trusted among other employees in the firm, and quickly became operative chief of the options department. Initially this happened because he was one of the few who were acquainted with the business area of options, an area in which the firm wanted to expand its activities. The trust in him also increased when he conducted deals that satisfied clients, generated courtage for the firm, and built up the firm's stock trade with good results. Moreover, it was to him that other brokers in the firm left deals, clients, or problems of relatively complicated nature. Not least due to these aspects, it lay in the firm's interest that he should take care of the present client. This client was very wealthy and constituted by far the biggest private client of the firm. For him, the firm managed large assets and carried out numerous deals that yielded sizable courtage income for it. The client was regarded as a "pro," strongly interested in "generating profits," and "demanding" (SNECB 2000: 60, 22, 243). By virtue of his position, the client had good insight into the firm as a whole and socialized with several of its employees. He helped the firm in various ways when it got into difficulties, and was also a landlord and something of a "royal purveyor" of residences for a number of the firm's employees. Thus, he was a key client in diverse respects. At the firm it was well known, too, that the client had great trust in the broker concerned, who was regarded as "smart at handling demanding clients" (SNECB 2000: 243). It therefore lay in the firm's interest that he took care of this client.

Low Priority of Control (or Preoccupation with Other Matters)

Another aspect that is central for understanding the broker's opportunity structure has its basis in the fact that the client was continually involved in many extensive deals, which he had no possibility of conducting and controlling by himself. The client was also more interested in and preoccupied with business expansion, than with administration and control of his own assets. He thus left it to the broker to carry out deals in certain areas and, as mentioned earlier, he was sparing with examination of the account statements and other papers that were sent to him. Satisfied with checking whether the account balance was plus or minus, he limited his information to the latest daily telephone talk that he had with the broker, or when he visited the firm. The client's neglect to control the conduct and administration of the deals was due partly to his scarce time for controlling all the deals, but mainly to his giving priority to the planning and initiation of deals. He himself thought that he was "almost unhealthily interested in deals," yet also that he found it "nice to avoid the constant supervision of deals" (SNECB 2000: 61, 38f.).

Possibly one can understand the client's actions in terms of ignorance, lack of interest, or the often-used term "absence of capable guardians" (Felson and Clarke 1998). However, in cases that can be said to concern absence of capable guardians, there is a strong tendency to point out primarily what does *not* happen, at the same time as one overlooks the relational components that allow this lack of control to arise. In the present case, the reason for neglect of control was that the client prioritized other matters than administration and control—a prioritization that created a barrier. It should thus be most plausible to conceptualize this aspect in terms of low priority of control, or perhaps of preoccupation with other matters. Here lies an explanation for why the control is deficient and creates opportunities for crime. In short, my view is that the problem does not essentially involve an "absence" of anything, but an activity's orientation toward something else so strongly that the control function is given low priority. It is the strength of this orientation that creates barriers that ultimately protect criminality, because people do not see what is happening "alongside" what they are preoccupied with. In the present brokerage firm, this barrier included a large number of people around the broker.

Just as the client was busy with other projects and therefore did not control his deals to any great extent, the firm was busy expanding in the years when the broker worked there. No great interest existed in administration and control. The firm made clear to the broker that he was employed to make deals and be income-generating. For this purpose he received responsibility and leeway for action as large as the concern was small in administration and control of him. He never got training or an introduction to relevant regulations in the area. The firm's attitude was expressed perhaps most plainly when he worked on new blank forms for options trade and one of his chiefs remarked, "Don't worry about the administrative stuff, you're employed to make deals" (SDC 2001: 25). As a result, the broker was able to create possibilities of concealing the bad deal. The clearest example was when he used the firm's "question-mark account." The broker knew that control of this account was deficient. Considering also that the firm had limited control over the security requirements when issuing new options, the broker began systematically to use the question-mark account for re-booking the loss so that nobody would notice it. He also used the account for conducting secret deals. Normally, options issued and bought by the firm were supposed to undergo an assessment so that the firm knew the parties could fulfill their promises when the options expired. But this was not done systematically and automatically—it required an agreement to be written. Only when this had been done were deals examined by the firm's lawyers. Therefore, the broker began to construct options by himself. These might be worthless, but because the broker wrote no agreement that he gave to the legal department, he avoided control. The constructed options were purchased by him for a small sum and placed on the client's account. Shortly afterward, he saw to it that the options were bought by the firm's question-mark account for a much higher price. The loss hole in the client's account was thereby covered. Obviously the firm's account had paid an over-price that would later be realized at a loss—but as long as the option had not expired, the loss was only potential and did not appear in the book-keeping as such for the uninitiated. The broker bought and sold options in such a way that the time it took for a loss to be realized was constantly "rolled" into the future. Worthless options passed to the firm, which neither had control over its accounts nor could judge the options' value. This brings us to another type of barrier.

Interpretative Primacy

That the type of deals that the broker conducted were notoriously complicated, and that his own knowledge in the area was matched by ignorance from clients, colleagues, chiefs, and other people related to his work, were further aspects that created opportunities for the broker to commit crime without being detected. Here it is less important that he was indisputably adept in the area, or that the deals he made were regarded as extremely complicated. It is not mainly in environments with such conditions that one should look to find opportunities for crime. Instead one should look in environments where the differences in knowledge give certain actors an *interpretative primacy* over others. In the broker's case, the knowledge gap meant that in practice he acquired an interpretative primacy regarding the content determination and evaluation of various transactions, accounts, and transfers. The broker also realized that the deals he made were hard to understand and check the contents of. This applied to his colleagues at the firm as well as to accounts and clients. Besides being aware that the client did not always check his deals very carefully, the broker thought that many of the deals were so complex that the client in question "never really understood what it was about" (SNECB 2000: 5) when he executed transactions on the client's account. The client knew this too, and thought that when it came to option deals a lot was "so complicated that I had no idea what was going in and out, shifting here and there...." (SNECB 2000: 62). Further, the broker had this advantage in relation to the firm's accountants:

> It's some women who have audited ... they have often sat and asked me about things they don't understand and then I've answered them about it. Certainly they haven't asked about [the account I myself managed for the client] ... as to whether this account is unbalanced or whether it has an actual loss. That has also been very hard to detect. I don't think their competence is up to seeing it. (SNECB 2000: 179)

SUMMARY

What have been designated here as financial self-interest, low priority of control, and interpretative primacy are three examples of barriers that obstruct other people (such as clients, colleagues, chiefs, etc.) from suspecting and discovering criminal events. Concretely they meant that the broker's relations with these other people were characterized *by* his being considered so able in the area that it was in their self-interest that he handled their deals; *by* them being more preoccupied with completing deals and expanding than with administration and control; and *by* the broker having an interpretative primacy in the area that led them to rely on his statements. These conditions functioned as barriers and allowed opportunities to accrue for his commission of acts whose real content was concealed, explaining why he could perform his hidden rolling program and keep it going for four years.

CONCLUSIONS

In this article, Goffman's concepts of "barriers" and "back regions" have been used to show more precisely how social positions strengthen the possibility of carrying out economic crime. The fundamental idea is that opportunities for crime arise in social situations where individuals, by virtue of their positions, build up barriers that hinder others from controlling a course of events. This can happen firstly through their obstructing suspicion and detection, secondly through their impeding investigation and—once suspicion is established—assessment of an event as a crime, and thirdly through their preventing legal action and implementation of sanctions. With an empirical case study, the reasoning has been deepened as regards the type of barrier that creates opportunities for crime by hindering suspicion and detection. Here it was shown how three variants of this type of barrier—termed financial self-interest, low priority of control, and interpretative primacy—enabled a broker, by virtue of his position, to gather opportunities for operating without insight in back regions and committing crime.

The barrier concept offers, I think, a more viable explanation for how opportunities of white-collar crime are created than what has previously been proposed in the field. It is undoubtedly true that the resources emphasized earlier, which in summary are access to authority, social contact networks, and technical-administrative systems, create possibilities for committing crime. As regards the previous explanatory models, however, the issue is rather of resources that improve the opportunity for realizing actions *in general,* not the opportunity of committing *criminal* acts. Through the concepts of barriers and back regions, the possibility of crime becomes clearer. These concepts should therefore, in my opinion, be incorporated and refined in the research on white-collar crime. They have good prospects of serving as an analytical apparatus that heightens the sensitivity to what occurs, or can occur, in certain environments and contributes to knowledge of decisive factors....

REFERENCES

Felson, M. and R. V. Clarke. 1998. *"Opportunity Makes the Thief"—Crime Detection and Prevention Series.* London, UK: Home Office.

Sutherland, E. 1983. *White Collar Crime: The Uncut Version.* New Haven: Yale University Press.

Vaughan, D. 1983. *Controlling Unlawful Organizational Behavior: Social Structure and Corporate Misconduct.* Chicago: The University of Chicago Press.

CASE MATERIAL CONSULTED

SAC (Svea Appeals Court). 2002. Decision of Svea Appeals Court 26 April 2002 in case B 5803-01.

SDC (Stockholm District Court). 2001. Decision of Stockholm District Court 12 July 2001 in case B 10030-94.

SC (Supreme Court). 2003. Decision of Supreme Court 14 October 2003 in case B 2100 02.

SNECB (Swedish National Economic Crime Bureau). 2000. Preliminary Investigative protocol in case B 10030-94. Stockholm: Swedish National Economic Crime Bureau, East Department.

PART VIII

Deviant Careers

One of the fascinating things about people's involvement in deviance is that it evolves, yielding a shifting and changing experience. Doing something for the first time is very different from doing it for the hundredth time. It is fruitful, then, to consider involvement in deviance from a career perspective, to see what the nature of deviance is and how it develops over the course of people's involvement with it. Sociologists have documented various stages of people's participation in such things as drug use, drug dealing, fencing, carrying out a professional hit, engaging in prostitution, and shoplifting. Although these activities are very different in character, they have structural similarities in the way people experience them according to the stage of people's involvement. In fact, the career analogy has been applied fruitfully to the study of deviance because people go through many of the same cycles of entry, upward mobility, achieving career peaks, aging in the career, burning out, and getting out of deviance as they do in legitimate work.

Six themes tend to be most commonly addressed in the literature on deviant careers. **Entering deviance** attracts the greatest bulk of scholarly attention for two reasons: policy makers have great interest in finding out how and why people enter deviance so that they can prevent it, and it represents fairly easy data for most scholars to gather since every individual or group of deviants can tell their story of how they got into the scene. Over the last couple of decades sociologists have worked to discover and disseminate information that has been adopted by the public in making decisions aimed at influencing and deterring potential deviants. First, they have developed the concept of "at risk" populations and articulated a range of risk factors associated with various forms of deviance such as gang membership, dropping out of school, unwed pregnancy, suicide, depression, eating disorders, detainment, arrest, incarceration, etc. (Loeber and Farrington 1998; Werner and Smith 1992). Complementing these, they have identified protective factors that, in the face of exposure to multiple risks, help prevent individuals from becoming involved in these forms of deviance (Werner and Smith 1982).

Although some people venture into deviance on their own, the vast majority do it with the encouragement and assistance of others, often joining cooperative deviant enterprises. The turning points that mark significant phases in their transitions have been explored, as well as their changing self-identities. Most commonly, people who become involved in deviance do so through a process of shifting their circle of friends. They drift into new peer groups as they are drifting into deviance, or their whole peer group drifts into deviance together as the members enter a new phase of the life cycle.

Second, the career perspective incorporates an interest with the **training and socialization** of new deviants. Relatively little has been written about this area for several reasons. First, most deviants, although they might be socialized to the norms and values of their activity through their contacts with fellow deviants, get relatively little explicit training in how to perform their deviance, how to avoid detection, how to deal with the police, and other important concerns. Second, real training generally occurs when deviants are working together, side-by-side, as a team in their enterprise. That leaves only crews and deviant formal organizations as the likely places where training is apt to occur, and these forms of deviance organization are relatively rare. In their analysis of the career of a professional burglar and fence, Steffensmeier and Ulmer (2005) have suggested that the kind of professional criminals engaged in crew operations has declined.

Third, focusing on careers in deviance enables people to study how individuals' involvement in their deviant worlds and with their deviant associates and activities **changes over time**. This type of processual analysis represents a highly nuanced understanding of deviance that cannot easily be captured by the frozen-in-time snapshot of most survey research. Longitudinal studies of deviant careers are rare but valuable assets in this literature, as they distinguish for us some of the different motivations, rewards, conflicts, and problems that deviants encounter over the course of their participation in deviance. These are enormously helpful to both people who struggle to understand and to help themselves, friends, and family members caught in the lure of deviance as well as policy makers, as they illuminate motivations and deterrents that are more or less effective at different career stages.

Over the course of their deviant careers, participants must face the various challenges involved in managing their deviance. They must navigate the changing dimensions of available opportunities to commit their deviance, evolving technologies that can enable and catch them, their relationships within deviant communities, their safety from agents of social control, and must evolve a personal style for their deviance. They must balance their deviance with the non-deviant aspects of their lives, such as their relationships with family members, people in the community, and those on whom they rely to meet their legitimate needs. Yip's (1997) work on gay male Christian couples (chapter 44), for example, illustrates some of the creative ways that homosexuals find to maintain their relational commitment in a social environment where their union is sanctioned by neither church nor state.

Wanting out or **exiting deviance** represents the fourth major area in this literature. Like entering deviance there is a high political interest in this topic, as policy makers are looking for ways to induce people to quit their deviance. Information on longer-term deviants and their attitudes toward the scene, the people in them, their satisfactions and dissatisfactions, and their hopes or dreams for the future is somewhat hard to get. People tend to feel most comfortable talking to others like themselves, and the most active researchers are young. Yet there are valuable studies of aging deviants.

A variety of factors "push" people out of the deviant life and "pull" them back into the conventional world. People are pushed out by factors intrinsic to the deviant experience and lifestyle. They may burn out from the hours, the stress, the transience, and the drug use. Friends or associates who get arrested, jailed, injured, or killed may make them rethink their continuing involvement with deviance. Moreover, each time they get arrested, they face an increasing likelihood of doing longer jail sentences. People who have spent some years in prison know that their next arrest is likely to lead to a more serious stint or incarceration. Loathe to return, they may look for other things they can do to make a living. The longer people stay in deviance, the greater the likelihood is that there will be a change in the nature of the experience. What initially seemed daring and glamorous eventually becomes mundane, and the excitement turns to paranoia. People change during their involvement with deviance as well.

Pull factors are located outside of the deviant arena and entice people to leave that world behind and return to conventionality. Individuals such as friends, girlfriends, spouses, children, or other family members may encourage or intervene with deviants to entice or pressure them to quit their deviant ways. Legitimate recreational and occupational interests are key in helping to facilitate individuals' transition out of deviance. Yet returning to legitimate jobs where their earning potential is reduced may involve restricting their spending patterns, something that people find difficult. They also become accustomed to the free-wheeling lifestyle and open value system associated with a deviant community, where conventional norms are disdained.

Reentering the straight world with its morality may chafe. Finding legitimate work may be difficult, especially if they were involved in occupational deviance, where they were making money through illicit means. Former deviants often have difficulty putting together a resume that accounts for their gap in legitimate employment and finding someone who will hire them. They may find adhering to the structure of the 9-to-5 straight world overly constraining. Yet most people do not want to spend their whole lives engaged in deviance.

Very little information is available on the **post-deviant** features of individuals' lives. These are the hardest data to get because just as developing a deviant identity, as we described in Part V, moves people out of their conventional friendships and social worlds into those populated by deviants, quitting deviance usually requires exiting from these same relationships and scenes. Once people decide to get out and actually make that move, they disperse and leave no forwarding address.

Finally, there is a literature in this field on crime and deviance as work, which compares occupational deviance with legitimate jobs and examines **deviant versus legitimate careers**. Working in deviant fields holds many similarities to the skills, professionalism, connections, and attitudes needed for conventional jobs (Letkemann 1973). Goods and services may be bought and sold, credit arranged and extended, costs and profits calculated, and business associates, suppliers, and customers assessed. Contracts cannot be legally enforced in deviant occupations, however, nor are associates as reliable or durable. Due to the high turnover of personnel and the greater likelihood of drug use involved in all facets of deviant work people are less likely to have expertise in their trade or to deliver on promises made.

There are also limitations to the career analogy, since while legitimate work may have several structures (the compressed career, the bureaucratic career, the entrepreneurial career), the patterns for deviant careers are more generally entrepreneurial. Entry may take many shapes and lengths of time. Behavioral shifts once in deviance may be lateral and downward as well as upward, precipitous as well as gradual and controlled, repetitive as well as dissimilar, and involve continuity or complete shift into other venues (Luckenbill and Best 1981). Exits are problematic, varying in their degree of self- or other-directed degree of initiation, being temporary or lasting, and involve anything from going out on top to slinking away in debt and disgrace. Perhaps the biggest contrast between deviant and legitimate careers (taking the bureaucratic, organizational form for the latter) lies in the legitimate career's slower ascent at the beginning and the greater stability and security towards the end, compared to the deviant career's rapid upward mobility and earlier burnout (as we see in chapter 45 on the pimp-controlled prostitute's career).

43

Deciding to Commit a Burglary

RICHARD T. WRIGHT AND SCOTT H. DECKER

In this classical occupational study of deviance, Wright and Decker share with us their insights into the motivations and behavior of residential burglars. Simply written and filled with rich quotes, this chapter affirms the view that most burglaries are committed spontaneously by semiskilled criminals. Crimes of opportunity, these burglaries are fueled by perpetrators' desire for money. Although most attempt to diminish the stigma of their crimes by rationalizing that they steal to support their basic living expenses, Wright and Decker undercut these accounts as impression management, citing subjects' behavior and alternative explanations that they steal to gain money for drugs, partying, impressing women, and to sustain an overall high lifestyle with the trappings of material success. Enmeshed in the world of instant gratification, these burglars give lip service to their desire for legitimate jobs, but have neither the patience nor the interest in developing the skills of legitimate work or working their way up the ladder of legitimate career success. For most of Wright and Decker's subjects, burglary is their "main line," although not the only line of deviant income. In addition to the financial yield, they are attracted to residential burglary by the excitement, the freedom, the adventure, the spontaneity, the identity, and the instant gratification. These people enact a criminal lifestyle that is reinforced by the norms and values of the deviant subculture in which they are ensconced.

The demographic characteristics of residential burglars have been well documented. As Shover (1991) has observed, such offenders are, among other things, disproportionately young, male, and poor. These characteristics serve to identify a segment of the population more prone than others to resort to breaking in to dwellings, but they offer little insight into the actual causes of residential burglary. Many poor, young males, after all, never commit any sort of serious offense, let alone a burglary. And even those who carry out such crimes are not offending most of the time. This is not, by and large, a continually motivated group of criminals; the motivation for them to offend is closely tied to their assessment of current circumstances and prospects. The direct cause of residential burglary is a perceptual process through which the offense comes to be seen as a means of meeting an immediate need, that is, through which a motive for the crime is formed. Walker (1984: viii) has pointed out that, in order to develop a convincing explanation for criminal behavior, we must begin by "distinguishing the states of mind in which offenders commit, or contemplate the commission of, their offenses." Similarly, Katz (1988: 4), arguing for increased research into what he calls the foreground of criminality, has noted that all of the demographic information on criminals in the world cannot answer the following questions: "Why are people who were not determined to commit a crime one moment determined to do so the next?" This is the question to which the present chapter is addressed. The aim is to explore the extent to which the decision to commit a residential burglary is the result of a process of careful calculation and deliberation.

In the overwhelming majority of cases, the decision to commit a residential burglary arises in the face of what offenders perceive to be a pressing need for cash. Previous research consistently has shown this to be so and the results of the present study bear out this point. More than nine out of ten of the offenders in our sample—95 of 102—reported that they broke into dwellings primarily when they needed money.

> Well, it's like, the way it clicks into your head is like, you'll be thinking about something and, you know, it's a problem. Then it, like, all relates. "Hey, I need some money! Then how am I going to get money? Well, how do you know how to get money quick and easy?" Then there it is. Next thing you know, you are watching [a house] or calling to see if [the occupants] are home. (Wild Will—No. 010) …

These offenders were not motivated by a desire for money for its own sake. By and large, they were not accumulating the capital needed to achieve a long-range goal. Rather, they regarded money as providing them with the means to solve an immediate problem. In their view, burglary was matter of day-to-day survival.

> I didn't have the luxury of laying back in on damn pinstriped [suit]. I'm poor and I'm raggedy and I need some food and I need some shoes … So I got to have some money some kind of way. If it's got to be the wrong way, then so be it. (Mark Smith—No. 030) …

Given this view, it is unsurprising that the frequency with which the offenders committed burglaries was governed largely by the amount of money in their pockets. Many of them would not offend so long as they had sufficient cash to meet current expenses.

> Usually what I'll do is a burglary, maybe two or three if I have to, and then this will help me get over the rough spot until I can get my shit straightened out. Once I get it straightened out, I just go with the flow until I hit that rough spot where I need the money again. And then I hit

it ... the only time I would go and commit a burglary is if I needed the money at that point in time. That would be strictly to pay light bill, gas bill, rent. (Dan Whiting—No. 102)

Long as I got some money, I'm cool. If I ain't got no money and I want to get high, then I go for it. (Janet Wilson—No. 060)

You know how they say stretch a dollar? I'll stretch it from here to the parking lot. But I can only stretch it so far and then it breaks. Then I say, "Well, I guess I got to go put on my black clothes. Go on out there like a thief in the night." (Ralph Jones—No. 018)

A few of the offenders sometimes committed a burglary even though they had sufficient cash for their immediate needs. These subjects were not purposely saving money, but they were unwilling to pass up opportunities to make more. They attributed their behavior to having become "greedy" or "addicted" to money.

I have done it out of greed, per se. Just to be doing it and to have more money, you know? Say, for instance, I have two hundred dollars in my pocket now. If I had two more hundreds, then that's four hundred dollars. Go out there and do a burglary. Then I say, "If I have four hundred dollars, then I can have a thousand." Go out there and do a burglary. (No. 018) ...

Typically, the offenders did not save the money that they derived through burglary. Instead, they spent it for one or more of the following purposes: (1) to "keep the party going"; (2) to keep up appearances; or (3) to keep themselves and their families fed, clothed, and sheltered.

KEEPING THE PARTY GOING

Although the offenders often stated that they committed residential burglaries to "survive," there is a danger in taking this claim at face value. When asked how they spent the proceeds of their burglaries, nearly three-quarters of them—68 of 95—said they used the money for various forms of (for want of a better term) high-living. Most commonly, this involved the use of illicit drugs. Fifty-nine of the 68 offenders who spent the money obtained from burglary on pleasure-seeking pursuits specifically mentioned the purchase of drugs. For many of these respondents, the decision to break into a dwelling often arose as a result of a heavy session of drug use. The objective was to get the money to keep the party going.

The drug most frequently implicated in these situation was "crack" cocaine.

[Y]ou ever had an urge before? Maybe a cigarette urge or a food urge, where you eat that and you got to have more and more? That's how that

> crack is. You smoke it and it hits you [in the back of the throat] and you
> got to have more. I'll smoke that sixteenth up and get through, it's like I
> never had none. I got to have more. Therefore, I gots to go do another
> burglary and gets some more money. (Richard Jackson— No. 009) ...

Lemert (1953:304) has labelled situations like these "dialectical, self-enclosed
systems of behavior" in that they have an internal logic or "false structure,"
which calls for more of the same. Once locked into such events, he asserts,
participants experience considerable pressure to continue, even if this involves
breaking the law.

> A man away from home who falls in with a group of persons who have
> embarked upon a two or three-day or even a week's period of drinking
> and carousing ... tends to have the impetus to continue the pattern
> which gets mutually reinforced by [the] interaction of the participants,
> and [the pattern] tends to have an accelerated beginning, a climax and a
> terminus. If midway through a spree a participant runs out of money,
> the pressures immediately become critical to take such measures as
> are necessary to preserve the behavior sequence. A similar behavior
> sequence is [evident] in that of the alcoholic who reaches a "high point"
> in his drinking and runs out of money. He might go home and get
> clothes to pawn or go and borrow money from a friend or even apply
> for public relief, but these alternatives become irrelevant because of the
> immediacy of his need for alcohol. (Lemert, 1953: 303)

Implicit in this explanation is an image of actors who become involved in
offending without significant calculation; having embarked voluntarily on one
course of action (e.g., crack smoking), they suddenly find themselves being
drawn into an unanticipated activity (e.g., residential burglary) as a means of sustaining that action. Their offending is not the result of a thoughtful, carefully
reasoned process. Instead, it emerges as part of the natural flow of events, seemingly coming out of nowhere. In other words, it is not so much that these actors
consciously choose to commit crimes as that they elect to get involved in situations that drive them toward lawbreaking.

Beyond the purchase of illicit drugs and, to a lesser extent, alcohol, 10 of the
68 offenders—15 percent—also used the proceeds from their residential burglaries
to pursue sexual conquests. All of these offenders were male. Some liked to flash
money about, believing that this was the way to attract women....

> [I commit burglaries to] splurge money with the women, you know,
> that's they kick, that's what they like to do. (Jon Monroe—No. 011) ...

Like getting high, sexual conquest was a much-prized symbol of hipness through
which the male subjects in our sample could accrue status among their peers on
the street. The greatest prestige was accorded to those who were granted sexual
favors solely on the basis of smooth talk and careful impression management.
Nevertheless, a few of the offenders took a more direct approach to obtaining
sex by paying a streetcorner prostitute (sometimes referred to as a "duck") for

it. While this was regarded as less hip than the more subtle approach described above, it had the advantage of being easy and uncomplicated. As such, it appealed to offenders who were wrapped up in partying and therefore reluctant to devote more effort than was necessary to satisfy their immediate sexual desires.

> I spend [the money] on something to drink, ... then get me some [marijuana]. Then I'm gonna find me a duck. (Ricky Davis—No. 015)

It would be misleading to suggest that any of the offenders we spoke to committed burglaries *specifically* to get money for sex, but a number of them often directed a portion of their earnings toward this goal.

In short, among the major purposes for which the offenders used the money derived from burglary was the maintenance of a lifestyle centered on illicit drugs, but frequently incorporating alcohol and sexual conquests as well. This lifestyle reflects the values of the street culture, a culture characterized by an openness to "illicit action" (Katz, 1988: 209–15), to which most of our subjects were strongly committed. Viewed from the perspective of the offenders, then, the oft-heard claim that they broke into dwellings to survive does not seem quite so farfetched. The majority of them saw their fate as inextricably linked to an ability to fulfill the imperatives of life on the street.

KEEPING UP APPEARANCES

Of the 95 offenders who committed residential burglaries primarily for financial reasons, 43 reported that they used the cash to purchase various "status" items. The most popular item was clothing; 39 of the 43 said that they bought clothes with the proceeds of their crimes. At one level, of course, clothing must be regarded as necessary for survival. The responses of most of the offenders, however, left little doubt that they were not buying clothes to protect themselves from the elements, but rather to project a certain image; they were drawn to styles and brand names regarded as chic on the streets.

> See, I go steal money and go buy me some clothes. See, I likes to look good. I likes to dress. All I wear is Stacy Adams, that's all I wear. [I own] only one pair of blue jeans cause I likes to dress. (No. 011) ...

After clothes, cars and car accessories were the next most popular status items bought by the offenders. Seven of the 43 reported spending at least some of the money they got from burglaries on their cars.

> I spent [the money] on stuff for my car. Like I said, I put a lot of money into my car... I had a '79 Grand Prix, you know, a nice car. (Matt Detteman—No. 072)

The attributes of a high-status vehicle varied. Not all of these offenders, for example, would have regarded a 1979 Grand Prix as conferring much prestige on its owner. Nevertheless, they were agreed that driving a fancy or customized car, like wearing fashionable clothing, was an effective way of enhancing one's street status....

> I don't know if you've ever thought about it, but I think every crook likes the life of thieving and then going and being somebody better. Really, you are deceiving people; letting them think that you are well off ... You've got a nice car, you can go about and do this and do that. It takes money to buy that kind of life.

Shover and Honaker (1990: 11) have suggested that the concern of offenders with outward appearances, as with their notorious high-living, grows out of what is typically a strong attachment to the values of street culture; values that place great emphasis on the "ostentatious enjoyment and display of luxury items." In a related vein, Katz (1988) has argued that for those who are committed to streetlife, the reckless spending of cash on luxury goods is an end in itself, demonstrating their disdain for the ordinary citizen's pursuit of financial security. Seen through the eyes of the offenders, therefore, money spent on such goods has not been "blown," but rather represents a cost of raising or maintaining one's status on the street.

KEEPING THINGS TOGETHER

While most of the offenders spent much of the money they earned through residential burglary on drugs and clothes, a substantial number also used some of it for daily living expenses. Of the 95 who committed burglaries to raise money, 50 claimed that they needed the cash for subsistence.

> I do [burglaries] to keep myself together, keep myself up.
> (Games Brown—No. 025) ...

Quite a few of the offenders—13 of 50—said that they paid bills with the money derived from burglary. Here again, however, there is a danger of being misled by such claims. To be sure, these offenders did use some of their burglary money to take care of bills. Often, though, the bills were badly delinquent because the offenders avoided paying them for as long as possible-even when they had the cash–in favor of buying, most typically, drugs. It was not until the threat of serious repercussions created unbearable pressure for the offenders that they relented and settled their accounts.

> [Sometimes I commit burglaries when] things pressuring me, you know? I got to do somethin' about these bills. Bills. I might let it pass that mornin'. Then I start trippin' on it at night and, next thing you know, it's wakin' me up. Yeah, that's when I got to get out and go do a burglary. I *got* to pay this electric bill off, this gas bill, you know?
> (No. 009) ...

Spontaneity is a prominent feature of street culture (Shover and Honaker, 1992); it is not surprising that many of the offenders displayed a marked tendency to live for the moment. Often they would give every indication of intending to take care of their obligations, financial or otherwise, only to be distracted by more immediate temptations. For instance, a woman in our sample, after being paid for an interview, asked us to drive her to a place where she could buy a pizza for her children's lunch. On the way to the restaurant, however, she changed her mind and asked to be dropped off at a crack house instead....

Katz (1988: 216) has suggested that, through irresponsible spending, persistent offenders seek to construct "an environment of pressures that guide[s] them back toward crime." Whether offenders spend money in a conscious attempt to create such pressures is arguable; the subjects in our sample gave no indication of doing so, appearing simply to be financially irresponsible. One offender, for example, told us that he never hesitated to spend money, adding, "Why should I? I can always get some more." However, the inclination of offenders to free-spending leaves them with few alternatives but to continue committing crimes. Their next financial crisis is never far around the corner.

The high-living of the offenders, thus, calls into question the extent to which they are driven to crime by genuine financial hardship. At the same time, though, their spendthrift ways ensure that the crimes they commit will be economically motivated (Katz, 1988). The offenders perceive themselves as needing money, and their offenses typically are a response to this perception. Objectively, however, few are doing burglaries to escape impoverishment.

WHY BURGLARY?

The decision to commit a residential burglary, then, is usually prompted by a perceived need for cash. Burglary, however, is not the only means by which offenders could get some money. Why do they choose burglary over legitimate work? Why do they elect to carry out a burglary rather than borrow the money from a friend or relative? Additionally, why do they select burglary rather than some other crime?

Given the streetcorner context in which most burglary decisions were made, legitimate work did not represent a viable solution for most of the offenders in our sample. These subjects, with few exceptions, wanted money there and then and, in such circumstances, even day labor was irrelevant because it did not respond to the immediacy of their desire for cash (Lemert, 1953). Moreover, the jobs available to most of the offenders were poorly paid and could not sustain their desired lifestyles. It is notable that 17 of the 95 offenders who did burglaries primarily to raise money *were* legitimately employed.

> [I have a job, but] I got tired of waiting on that money. I can get money like that. I got talent, I can do me a burg, man, and get me five or six hundred dollars in less than a hour. Working eight hours a day and waiting for a whole week for a check and it ain't even about shit. (No. 022)....

Beyond this, a few of the offenders expressed a strong aversion to legitimate employment, saying that a job would impinge upon their way of life.

> I ain't workin' and too lazy to work and just all that. I like it to where I can just run around. I don't got to get up at no certain time, just whenever I wake up. I ain't gotta go to bed a certain time to get up at a certain time. Go to bed around one o'clock or when I want, get up when I want. Ain't got to go to work and work eight hours. Just go in and do a five minute job, get that money, that's just basically it.
> (Tony Scott—No. 085) …

Nevertheless, a majority of the offenders reported that they wanted lawful employment; 43 of the 78 unemployed subjects who said that they did burglaries mostly for the money claimed they would stop committing offenses if someone gave them a "good" job.

> I'm definitely going to give it up as soon as I get me a good job. I don't mean making fifteen dollars an hour. Give me a job making five-fifty and I'm happy with it. I don't got to burglarize no more. I'm not doing it because I like doing it, I'm doing it because I need some [drugs]. (No. 079) …

When faced with an immediate need for cash, then, the offenders in our sample perceived themselves as having little hope of getting money both quickly *and* legally. Many of the most efficient solutions to financial troubles are against the law (Lofland, 1969). However, this does not explain why the subjects decided specifically on the crime of residential burglary. After all, most of them admitted committing other sorts of offenses in the past, and some still were doing so. Why should they choose burglary?

For some subjects, this question held little relevance because they regarded residential burglary as their "main line" and alternative offenses were seldom considered when the need for money arose.…

> [I do burglary] because it's easy and because I know it. It's kind of getting a speciality or a career. If you're in one line, or one field, and you know it real well, then you don't have any qualms about doing it. But if you try something new, you could really mess up … At this point, I've gotten away with so much [that] I just don't want to risk it—it's too much to risk at this point. I feel like I have a good pattern, clean; go in the house, come back out, under two minutes every time.
> (Darlene White—No. 100) …

When these subjects did commit another kind of offense, it typically was triggered by the chance discovery of a vulnerable target … most of the burglars we interviewed identified themselves as hustlers, people who were always looking to "get over" by making some fast cash; it would have been out of character for them to pass up any kind of presented opportunity to do so.

> If I see another hustle, then I'll do it, but burglary is my pet.
> (Larry Smith—No. 065) …

THE SEDUCTIONS OF RESIDENTIAL BURGLARY

For some offenders, the perceived benefits of residential burglary may transcend the amelioration of financial need. A few of the subjects we interviewed—7 of 102—said that they did not typically commit burglaries as much for the money as for the psychic rewards. These offenders reported breaking into dwellings primarily because they enjoyed doing so. Most of them did not enjoy burglary per se, but rather the risks and challenges inherent in the crime.

> [I]t's really because I like [burglaries]. I know that if I get caught I'm a do more time than the average person, but still, it's the risk. I like doin' them. (No. 013)

> I think [burglary is] fun. It's a challenge. You don't know whether you're getting caught or not and I like challenges. If I can get a challenging [burglary, I] like that. It's more of the risk that you got to take, you know, to see how good you can really be. (No. 103)

These subjects seemingly viewed the successful completion of an offense as "a thrilling demonstration of personal competence" (Katz, 1988: 9). Given this, it is not surprising that the catalyst for their crimes often was a mixture of boredom and an acute sense of frustration born of failure at legitimate activities such as work or school.

> [Burglary] just be something to do. I might not be workin' or not going to school—not doing anything. So I just decide to do a burglary. (No. 017)

The offense provided these offenders with more than something exciting to do, it also offered them the chance to "be somebody" by successfully completing a dangerous act. Similarly, Shover and Honaker (1992: 288) have noted that, through crime, offenders seek to demonstrate a sense of control or mastery over their lives and thereby to gain "a measure of respect, if not from others, at least from [themselves]." ...

While only a small number of the subjects in our sample said that they were motivated *primarily* by the psychic rewards of burglary, many of them perceived such rewards as a secondary benefit of the offense. Sixteen of the 95 offenders who did burglaries to raise cash also said that they found the crime to be "exciting" or "thrilling." ...

> [Beyond money], it's the thrill. If you get out [of the house], you smile and stand on it, breathe out. (No. 045)
>   It's just a thrill going in undetected and walking out with all they shit. Man, that shit fucks me up. (No. 022) ...

Finally, one of the offenders who did burglaries chiefly for monetary reasons alluded to the fact that the crime also provided him with a valued identity....

SUMMARY

Offenders typically decided to commit a residential burglary in response to a perceived need. In most cases, this need was financial, calling for the immediate acquisition of money. However, it sometimes involved what was interpreted as a need to repel an attack on the status, *identity*, or self-esteem of the offenders.

Whatever its character, the need almost invariably was regarded by the offenders as pressing, that is, as something that had to be dealt with immediately. Lofland (1969: 50) has observed that most people, when under pressure, have a tendency to become fixated on removing the perceived cause of that pressure "as quickly as possible." Those in our sample were no exception. In such a state, the offenders were not predisposed to consider unfamiliar, complicated, or long-term solutions (see Lofland, 1969: 50–54) and instead fell back on residential burglary, which they knew well. This often seemed to happen almost automatically, the crime occurring with minimal calculation as part of a more general path of action (e.g., partying). To the extent that the offense ameliorated their distress, it nurtured a tendency for them to view burglary as a reliable means of dealing with similar pressures in the future. In this way, a foundation was laid for the continuation of their present lifestyle which, by and large, revolved around the street culture. The self-indulgent activities supported by this culture, in turn, precipitated new pressures; and thus a vicious cycle developed.

That the offenders, at the time of actually contemplating offenses, typically perceived themselves to be in a situation of immediate need has at least two important implications. First, it suggests a mindset in which they were seeking less to maximize their gains than to deal with a present crisis. Second, it indicates an element of desperation which might have weakened the influence of threatened sanctions and neutralized any misgivings about the morality of breaking into dwellings....

REFERENCES

Katz, J. 1988. *Seductions of Crime: Moral and Sensual Attractions in Doing Evil.* New York: Basic Books.

Lemert, E. 1953. "An Isolation and Closure Theory of Naive Check Forgery." *Journal of Criminal Law, Criminology, and Police Science* 44: 296–307.

Lofland, J. 1969. *Deviance and Identity.* Englewood Cliffs, NJ: Prentice Hall.

Shover, N. 1991. "Burglary." In Tonry, M., *Crime and Justice: A Review of Research.* vol. 14. pp. 73–113. Chicago: University of Chicago Press.

Shover, N., and Honaker, D. 1990. "The Criminal Calculus of Persistent Property Offenders: A Review of Evidence." Paper presented at the Forty-second Annual Meeting of the American Society of Criminology, Baltimore, November.

_____. 1992. "The Socially Bounded Decision Making of Persistent Property Offenders." *Howard Journal of Criminal Justice* 31. no. 4: 276–93.

Walker, N. 1984. "Foreword." In Bennett, T., and Wright, R. *Burglars on Burglary: Prevention and the Offender.* pp. viii–ix. Aldershot: Gower.

44

Gay Male Christian Couples and Sexual Exclusivity

ANDREW K. T. YIP

Yip offers a fascinating look into another end of the homosexual spectrum from the cruising scene in his study of the sexual exclusivity of Christian gay men. While many portrayals of homosexuals sensationalize their behavior and emphasize promiscuity, disease, and stigma, this selection discusses the feelings of satisfaction gay couples have with each other. It sensitively contrasts the commitment and expectations that parallel and contrast homosexual and heterosexual relationships. Without the institutional reinforcement of the church and the state sanctioning their liaisons, Yip finds, gay men's commitments lack the "side bets" available to heterosexual marriages. The gay culture also accepts promiscuity to a greater degree than is found in the straight community, partly because of the unavailability of marriage. Yet, many gay men maintain their deviant relationships for years, despite the cultural and structural obstacles that beset them. The way they deal with sexual non-exclusivity is certainly relevant beyond the confines of homosexuality, as the larger heterosexual population engages in considerable extra-marital sexuality, and divorce rates are high. Yip describes how some couples maintain commitment in the face of sexual non-exclusivity by being discreet in their affairs, while others stay together for precisely the opposite reason: they have a searing commitment to honesty. A range of ground rules and strategies are discussed that help participants navigate these difficult and unconventional relationships and encounters over the course of their lifetimes, keeping them together despite the obstacles challenging them from the gay and straight worlds.

How do the relationships described for these gay couples and the regulations that hold them compare and contrast to heterosexual relationships? What are the implications of this chapter for the issue of gay marriage?

From Andrew K. T. Yip, *Sociology*, 31(2), pp. 289–306. Copyright © 1997 by Cambridge University Press. Reprinted by permission of SAGE.

The issue of sexual exclusivity constitutes one of the most researched areas in the studies on gay male couples. My review on the empirical literature in this field revealed that it is one of the five most prominent themes (Yip 1995). In a gay male partnership itself, sexual exclusivity is one of the major issues with which the partners have to grapple (Silverstein 1981). In his study on the factors leading to the dissolution of gay and lesbian partnerships, Kurdek (1991: 269) reported that sexual non-exclusivity is ranked third, closely behind "partner's non-responsiveness" and "partner's personal problems."

Research evidence tends to suggest that the majority of gay male partnerships are sexually non-exclusive in nature. Many researchers argued that sexual exclusivity in gay male partnerships is the exception rather than the rule (Saghir and Robins 1973; Bell and Weinberg 1978; Mendola 1980; Peplau and Cochran 1981; Blumstein and Schwartz 1983; Peplau and Gordon 1983; McWhirter and Mattison 1984; Blasband and Peplau 1985; Buunk and Van Driel 1989; Davies et al. 1993).

Nevertheless, there exists more than one way of defining sexual exclusivity. Most researchers define sexual exclusivity in terms of the *behaviour* of the partners. A partnership is defined as sexually exclusive if both partners do not have sexual encounters outside the framework of the partnership throughout a particular period of time prior to the research. Researchers use different time periods in this connection, for instance, six months (Peplau 1981), a year (Harry and DeVall 1978), or the entire length of the partnership (Saghir and Robins 1973; Mendola 1980; Peplau and Cochran 1981; Blumstein and Schwartz 1983; McWhirter and Mattison 1984).

However, Hickson (1991) argued that there should be two classificatory systems in this respect—in terms of behaviour, as discussed, but also in terms of the partners' *expectation*. Based on the second criterion, a sexually exclusive partnership is defined as one in which sexual exclusivity is acknowledged by both partners. This acknowledgment can take the form of an explicit agreement or an implicit assumption either at the beginning of the partnership or it may be negotiated as the partnership develops. Therefore, a partnership with an expectation of sexual exclusivity but which is behaviourally otherwise over a stipulated period of time cannot be satisfactorily defined as sexually non-exclusive in general terms. In this case, the partnership is expectationally exclusive but behaviourally non-exclusive.

I support Hickson's (1991) argument. Unlike heterosexual couples who in general share the cultural ideal of sexual exclusivity and therefore the disapproval of non-exclusivity (Reiss et al. 1980; Lawson and Samson 1988; Greeley 1991), gay male couples do not have such a cultural assumption. They therefore have to resort to actively negotiating the constitutional arrangement of their partnership in this respect. Most gay male couples use a trial-and-error approach to construct relationship rules due to the lack of structural and cultural guidelines (Harry and DeVall 1978). Thus, the negotiation process that forms the expectation of their partnership must be taken into consideration alongside their actual behaviour when the issue of sexual exclusivity is examined.

The analysis of the different attitudes adopted by the couples in the area of sexual exclusivity also throws light on the complexity in the organisation of personal identity in postmodern society. All the respondents are currently in an advanced stage of their "moral career." They have already undergone what Humphreys (1972: 148) called "stigma redemption," a process through which gay Christians justify the acceptability of their sexuality—their discrediting attribute—with religious and moral rhetoric. Instead of succumbing to shame and guilt or attempting to rectify their discrediting attribute in the face of stigmatisation (Goffman 1963), they manage the stigma of being gay Christians by developing "accounts" (Lyman and Scott 1970) or "vocabularies of motives" (Mills 1940). This is done not only to defend their personal identity and the continuation of their social actions, but also to discredit and challenge the stigmatiser, namely the Church (for more details on this issue, see Yip 1997a; 1997b; 1997c).

Nevertheless, in spite of locating themselves within the social category of gay male Christians, the respondents do not speak with one voice with regards to the appropriate Christian moral framework within which their sexuality should be practised. As I will demonstrate later, the respondents hold differing perceptions of conventional Christian sexual ethics on intimate relationships which emphasise monogamy and "fidelity." Having justified the acceptability of their sexuality, they still need to negotiate a sexual lifestyle that incorporates harmoniously the religious and sexual aspects of their identity. This is but one of the primary issues that gay Christians have to negotiate in the construction of self identities and satisfactory partnerships. Their experiences illustrate the complexity of the organisation of personal identity in postmodern society.

This paper, therefore, aims to contribute to the acutely under-researched area of same-sex partnerships. It first demonstrates the necessity to define sexual exclusivity in terms of expectation and behaviour in the case of gay male couples. It then presents a typology comprising three categories of gay male Christian couples. Their justifications for their different sexual lifestyles are examined, particularly in relation to conventional Christian sexual ethics. It concludes that there is no significant difference between these couples in terms of their level of relationship satisfaction and commitment.

THE STUDY

Data collected through semi-structured interviews with thirty gay male Christian couples in Britain is presented here. The respondents were primarily recruited through personal contacts and three national gay Christian organisations. The organisations are: the Lesbian and Gay Christian Movement (LGCM), the organisation for lesbian and gay Catholics known as QUEST, and the Anglican Clergy Consultation (ACC). The ACC is a support group for Church of England priests and their partners.

For every couple, each partner was interviewed separately for approximately 70 minutes, followed by a couple interview of about 30 minutes. In view of the sensitive nature of the information pertaining to sexual exclusivity, I elicited all the data concerned in the individual rather than the couple interviews. Almost all the interviews took place in the respondents' homes. Fieldwork was carried out between June and September 1993.

The respondents' ages ranged from early 20s to late 70s, with an average of 42.9. They have been in partnerships between one and 33 years. The mean duration of the partnerships is 12 years and 3 months. Of these respondents, 63.3 percent and 21.7 percent respectively were affiliated to the Church of England and the Roman Catholic Church. The remaining respondents were affiliated to other denominations such as the Baptist, the Methodist and the United Reformed Church.

Except one Anglo-Chinese, one Japanese, and one Afro-American, all the respondents were white, with the majority living in Greater London and the South-East. In the main, the respondents were highly educated. Half of the sample held a first degree, with another 14 (23.3 percent) possessing a postgraduate qualification. In addition, 38 respondents (63.3 percent) had some form of professional qualifications. In terms of occupation, 15 of the 52 respondents in employment (28.2 percent) were priests, followed by teachers/lecturers (8, 15.4 percent) and managers (5, 9.6 percent).

TYPOLOGY OF GAY MALE CHRISTIAN COUPLES

Employing both classificatory systems, I constructed a typology which takes into consideration both expectation and behaviour throughout the entire duration of the partnership:

Category A: Couples who expect the partnership to be sexually exclusive, and are behaviourally so ($N = 9$)

Category B: Couples who expect the partnership to be sexually exclusive, but are behaviourally non-exclusive ($N = 8$)

Category C: Couples who expect the partnership to be sexually non-exclusive, and are behaviourally so ($N = 13$)

Category D: Couples who expect the partnership to be sexually non-exclusive but are so far behaviourally exclusive ($N = 0$)

The typology above shows four categories of couples. At the point of interview, no couples studied were in Category D. In terms of behaviour, 9 (30 percent) of the 30 couples are sexually exclusive (Category A). On the other hand, 21 couples (70 percent) are sexually non-exclusive in terms of behaviour, with 8 in Category B and 13 in Category C. On the whole, 20 couples (66.7 percent) have had an explicit agreement about sexual (non-)exclusivity since the beginning of their partnerships. The other 10 couples (33.3 percent) have an explicit assumption about it.

This typology reveals a scenario contradictory to Blasband and Peplau's (1985) argument that there is a consistency between partners' agreements about sexual exclusivity and their actual behaviour. All the thirteen couples in Category C who are sexually non-exclusive in terms of expectation are behaviourally so. However, only nine (52.9 percent) of the seventeen couples in Category A and Category B who are sexually exclusive in terms of expectation are behaviourally so. The consistency between agreement and behaviour is found only in the former. Understandably, couples in Category C can achieve this consistency substantially more easily compared to couples in Category A and Category B.

Category A: Couples Who Are Expectationally and Behaviourally Exclusive

Research evidence suggests that gay male couples tend to demonstrate a trend towards sexual non-exclusivity over time. McWhirter and Mattison (1984), for instance, reported that all the 156 couples they studied whose partnerships had persisted for over five years adopted sexual non-exclusivity. Davies et al. (1993) also reported that 72.6 percent of the partnerships that had lasted over five years which they studied were sexually non-exclusive. Harry and DeVall (1978) also found that most partnerships lasting longer than two years were non-exclusive.

These findings, however, are not confirmed by the nine couples in this category. Six of the partnerships are longer than five years. The shortest length is one year, and the longest 27 years. The mean length of partnership is nine years and five months.

Reasons for Sexual Exclusivity   Three major reasons can be identified for these couples' adherence to the ideal of sexual exclusivity. First, they considered sexual exclusivity a symbol of *total* commitment between partners. Sexual non-exclusivity is therefore perceived to be a threat to this total commitment. Respondent No. 10B who has been in a partnership for eight years and two months expresses this point:

> If there is a second or third person in the sharing of sex, I am not necessarily getting all the attention.... There are also the second or the third person's feelings and thoughts to take account of as well. So it then means that you could end up with a less-than-100-percent relationship because part of the relationship belongs to somebody else. It's detrimental to the relationship.

This personal commitment, clearly illustrated in the above comment, is also reported to be the main reason for sexual exclusivity in Blasband and Peplau's (1985) study. Seventy-nine percent of the couples in sexually exclusive partnerships they studied cited this reason.

Sexual exclusivity is also perceived as a symbol of *complete* mutual satisfaction the partners provide for each other. Therefore, the inclusion of a third party into the sexual dimension of their partnership would be an indication of their failure in mutually providing satisfaction. Respondent No. 12B who is in a one-year-old partnership expresses this sentiment:

> I think it [sexual exclusivity] is really important.... I think that if [his partner] or I felt the need to look elsewhere for sexual gratification, it wouldn't be just pure sex. I think that is dangerous. I think that is the sign that there are cracks in our relationship or our way of communicating or our emotional relationship, that we need to look elsewhere for gratification. I do think it is very important.

Finally, some respondents explicitly attributed their belief in sexual exclusivity to their commitment to the conventional Christian sexual ethics for intimate relationships. They argued that the Christian ideal of faithfulness, monogamy, and fidelity should apply to both same-sex and cross-sex partnerships. While rejecting the Church's conventional interpretation of the Bible on the issue of homosexuality (see Yip 1997a; 1997c), they nevertheless refer to the Bible for moral guidelines for their sexual behavioural patterns. Respondent No. 56A argues this point:

> Christians … really should stick with one partner. And I believe that quite strongly. Because I don't think there is any other theological model for sexual relationship that works in Christian terms. You can't make it fit what I think as the inside of scripture and tradition about what a sexual relationship is…. I think faithfulness to one person actually is quite a profound thing. I don't think it is just a social convention. It's something that affects who we are and the people we grow into. It has something to do with the fact that we are made in God's image and that we are capable of faithfulness.

This view upholds the "ethic of sexual monogamy" which argues that conventional Christian sexual ethics apply to both same-sex and cross-sex partnerships (John 1993:2). This is further elaborated below:

> Christianity has something to do with this [his commitment to sexual exclusivity]. It has to do with valuing the other person. There is an element of self-sacrifice for the other person … of saying that there is every aspect of our relationship, it is not just about personal satisfaction. It is about what we can give to one another. That's what love is about. It's about putting another person first. Regarding sex as just about having fun and enjoying yourself actually removes the possibility of sex being about something that you give. It makes it something you take.
> *(Resp. No. 47B)*

These views stand in stark contrast to that of many respondents who considered the Bible inadequate in providing moral guidelines for same-sex partnerships, since it remains silent on this topic. To them, the behavioural script for intimate relationships propounded by the Bible is meant solely for heterosexual relationships. The ethic of sexual monogamy should therefore be rejected in the case of same-sex partnerships. This point will be developed later.

Category B: Couples Who Are Expectationally Exclusive but Behaviourally Non-Exclusive

This category comprises eight couples who began their partnerships with the expectation that it should be exclusive, but either one or both partners violated that expectation at a certain point of their partnerships. All but one of the respondents in this category have had outside sexual encounters, albeit with differing degrees of activeness and regularity.

What brings about the change in the constitutional arrangement in the sexual dimension of their partnerships? Non-exclusivity became a feature of these partnerships within six months to two years of their inception. Three major factors lead to sexual non-exclusivity, despite the initial expectation of exclusivity: natural progression; dissatisfaction with certain aspects of the partnership; and desire for sexual experimentation.

To most couples, the first outside sexual encounter took place unexpectedly. Having experienced it and realised that it did not necessarily lead to relationship breakdown, they were encouraged to continue. This precipitated a process of reevaluation and renegotiation of their initial expectation. In certain cases, the boundary of the sexual dimension of their partnerships was redefined.

On the whole, no respondents reported that they are compelled to sexual non-exclusivity because of their dissatisfaction with the frequency and quality of love-making within the partnership. This contradicts research findings that the decline of love-making between partners encourages outside sexual activity (e.g. Saghir and Robins 1973; Blumstein and Schwartz 1983).

Regulatory Mechanisms   Most couples developed several regulatory mechanisms to manage their non-exclusive lifestyles. The chief objective of the employment of these mechanisms is to reap the benefits of both worlds—being able to experience the security of a primary partnership and having the opportunity to seek sexual gratification outside it.

Four mechanisms have been developed in this connection: (a) the establishment of explicit ground rules; (b) the concealment of information about outside sexual encounters; (c) the disclosure of information about outside sexual encounters; and (d) the prevention of casual sexual encounters from developing into ongoing affairs. The mechanisms are generally employed in tandem with each other to achieve the maximum effect.

> a. The establishment of ground rules clearly draws out the framework within which outside sexual encounters are considered acceptable to each partner. Two examples of ground rules are discussed:

> > I am sure he still has flings outside. <Are you upset about that?> No, not really. I would feel upset if he were with somebody in the house when I came home. He sees others outside or when I am away. That I don't mind. We have a sort of house rule. People don't come back if the other one is here because it is not very nice. *(Resp. No. 9A)*

The account above illustrates the ground rule for this couple—casual sex partners can only be brought home in the *absence* of the other partner. This is for the obvious reason of minimising embarrassment and jealousy. For another couple, the ground rule is just the opposite. Casual sex partners can only be brought home in the *presence* of the other partner:

> We had an arrangement … that we would not bring someone back here as individuals. But if we saw someone that we thought might be attracted to the other one, then we will have a threesome here…. That

was the arrangement. No one was going to be brought back here without the other person being here…. So it wouldn't be done until it was discussed or arranged between the two of us. *(Resp. No. 50A)*

For this couple, the primary reason for this ground rule of engaging in threesomes is the maximisation of participation of both partners as a couple, and in return the minimisation of a sense of exclusion and jealousy.

Ground rules perform two functions—manifest and latent. They stipulate various terms and conditions such as the regularity of outside sexual activity, with whom, the type of sexual activity, and the inclusion or exclusion of partner. This performs the manifest function of ensuring the smooth operation of such an activity. However, it also performs its latent function in reinforcing the *specialness* of the primary partner and the partnership. The compliance to the mutually agreed ground rule is a *sign of trust* between partners. The violation of the ground rule, not the actual sexual encounter, is perceived as the betrayal of that trust.

> b. Concealment of information about outside sexual encounters is used when a respondent realises that such information would prove distressing to his partner. The concealment aims to minimise his partner's jealousy and a sense of insecurity. Information about outside sexual encounters can lead to three types of jealousy: possessive jealousy—one's property rights are violated; exclusive jealousy—being left out of partner's experience; and fearful jealousy—fear of losing partner (Mazur 1977; Silverstein 1981).

This is especially true for a couple in which one partner regularly seeks outside sexual encounters while his partner does not, although the latter is generally accepting of it:

> I don't think it [sexual non-exclusivity] would bother me because I know that there is no way that [his partner] would leave me for anybody else. If sex happens, it's sex. It's not a threat to me…. If he should have a sexual relationship with somebody else, it wouldn't bother me. Although I am not sure I necessarily want to hear the details of it. *(Resp. No. 55B)*

Realising his partner's position in this respect, as shown in the data above, respondent No. 55A resorts to concealing all the information about his outside sexual encounters.

> c. In stark contrast to the mechanism above, some couples had mutually agreed to freely disclose information about outside sexual encounters between themselves. This policy of honesty is to minimise a sense of exclusion a partner might feel in response to the encounter of his partner. Mutually disclosing information about outside sexual encounters also indicates the equality they uphold in their partnership. In this connection, respondent No. 51A explains:
>
> Because he has done something similar [having outside sexual encounters] and told me, so I must tell him too. In this way it balances each other and so it doesn't create a problem for us.

It is clear from this account that the respondents perceived fidelity as a form of mutual honesty rather than sexual exclusivity itself. Therefore, sexual non-exclusivity only proves problematic to the partnership if information is deliberately concealed.

> d. The prevention of the possible development of a casual sexual encounter or "fling" into an ongoing affair is greatly emphasized. This attitude is prevalent in respondents who strongly believed in the difference between *making love* and *having sex*. One makes love to one's primary partner with unreserved emotional attachment. But one has sex with a casual sex partner for mutual sexual gratification without or with little emotional attachment (Harry 1977; Silverstein 1981). Respondent No. 7B explains the distinction:
>
> A fling is purely lust. I can tolerate that. But I probably couldn't tolerate if it were lust and emotional. I think a relationship is about two things, sexuality and the emotional side.

This distinction is firmly held in order that one does not compromise the primacy of one's partnership with casual sexual encounters. This is to prevent the sexual gratification obtained outside the partnership from eclipsing the ultimate significance of the primary partnership.

It can be concluded that sexual non-exclusivity that sets in at a particular point of the partnership with the knowledge of both partners leads to a process of deconstruction of the initial arrangement and the subsequent reconstruction of the new. In the process the establishment of several regulatory mechanisms for the maintenance of the new arrangement emerge. Most couples who have undergone the negotiation process reported that they were handling the situation successfully. This is mainly due to the fact that they have developed different regulatory mechanisms to manage the constitutional change in order to minimise the negative impact such change might exert on the partnership. One of the most widely-used mechanisms is the establishment of ground rules. It appears that it is the *violation* of such ground rules that threatens the stability of the partnership and not the actual outside sexual encounter itself.

Category C: Couples Who Are Expectationally and Behaviourally Non-Exclusive

The thirteen couples in this category began their partnerships with the expectation of non-exclusivity and have been so behaviourally. Three reasons were cited in support of this arrangement. The majority of respondents drew a clear line of demarcation between sex within and outside of the primary partnership (Silverstein 1981). With their primary partners, they make love. With casual sex partners, they have sex. Outside sexual encounters of this nature, or "flings," are perceived to be purely for the purpose of sexual variety and excitement:

> It [sexual non-exclusivity] didn't detract us from the fact that I love [his partner]. It wasn't a case that I stopped loving him for somebody else.

I think that is an important difference. I think being unfaithful is when you sort of want to love somebody else. I think that's what unfaithful means. I think having sex with somebody else isn't quite the same as being unfaithful. *(Resp. No. 11A)*

The search for sexual variety and excitement appears to be the main reason for sexual non-exclusivity, also reported by other researchers (e.g. McWhirter and Mattison 1984; Blasband and Peplau 1985). This search for sexual excitement is facilitated by the male sex-role socialisation process which encourages men, both gay and heterosexual, to place great importance on frequent and varied sexual activity (Berzon 1979) and the high degree of availability of casual and anonymous sex in the gay scene (Jay and Young 1977; Harry and DeVall 1978; Spada 1979; Peplau 1981). Having sexual encounters outside the partnership is not perceived to be unfaithfulness or infidelity, since both partners have either explicitly agreed or implicitly assumed that the partnership is of this nature. This attitude is pervasive among the respondents in this category.

The second reason for sexual non-exclusivity is closely related to the absence of normative guidelines for same-sex partnerships. Certain respondents considered this one of the advantages of being in a gay partnership. The flip side of the absence of a social script is the abundance of freedom and flexibility to negotiate the constitutional arrangement of the sexual dimension of their partnership. Therefore, the partnership would be non-exclusive if both partners agree that this should be the arrangement. This sentiment is clearly articulated in the following comment:

The reason for sexual non-exclusivity is that we don't conform to marriage where men and women generally [do] ... well they have sex with other people but it is more difficult because they have got children, social conventions and so on. Whereas with us the Church, for instance, has never recognised the relationship. So what the hell? And so, on the whole, sexuality seems much more liberal for us. *(Resp. No. 3A)*

The third reason in support of sexual non-exclusivity pertains to the issue of egalitarianism. It is argued that if a gay partnership should maximise the in-built freedom and flexibility, the partners themselves should empower each other to utilise such freedom. It also helps prevent interpartner possessiveness (Silverstein 1981; Peplau and Gordon 1983; McWhirter and Mattison 1984; Blasband and Peplau 1985). This sentiment is strongly shared:

It's part of trust. It's so important not to cling on to someone in a relationship. Not trying to control their thoughts nor their body. If I feel anyone is trying to cling on to me, my immediate reaction is to pull myself away. So, I think in a relationship you give the person the freedom to go away or to come towards you. And that's the sort of freedom which I hope I am giving [his partner]. And this is the sort of freedom I expect from him. I don't want to be hung on to. *(Resp. No. 48B)*

The account above illustrates the argument that giving the partner the freedom to sexually experiment if he so wishes is a sign of trust and love for him.

Partners should liberate each other at the outset before they can fully experience the freedom of being in a gay partnership. In this connection, McWhirter and Mattison (1984: 256) reported that, "the single most important factor that keeps couples together past the 10-year mark is the lack of possessiveness they feel. Many couples learn very early in their relationship that ownership of each other sexually can become the greater internal threat to their staying together [compared to non-exclusivity]." It follows that sexual non-exclusivity actually facilitates the development of a long-term partnership in this case (Warren 1974; Harry and DeVall 1978; Blasband and Peplau 1985).

Rejection of Conventional Christian Sexual Ethics   Unlike some respondents in Category A who upheld the ethic of sexual monogamy, the majority of the respondents in this category firmly rejected the conventional Christian sexual ethics as the basis on which they should organise their sexual lifestyles. This rejection stems from their perception of the lack of recognition from the institutionalised Church and its silence on the sexual ethics for gay Christian partnerships:

> I think one of the things that I constantly reevaluate is, is our relationship just aping a heterosexual married couple? Because I think the Church has kind of excluded us on paper. There is no official marriage ceremony or anything like that. I think therefore we've got a license to do whatever we feel. I think we should make our own rule. I think what we actually do is what we are happy with, what we want to do. It's what we consider to be appropriate, or certainly what I consider to be appropriate. *(Resp. No. 1A)*

The lack of recognition and acceptance from the Church results in the distancing of many respondents from the Church and its official stance on homosexuality. It is therefore not surprising to observe that many respondents were more inclined to organise their sexual lifestyles on the basis of their own sense of morality which is broadly derived from what Ellison (1994: 236–441) called "the ethic of common decency," with its emphasis on Christian principles such as love, justice and responsibility. However, the specific emphasis of the conventional sexual ethics on, for instance, exclusivity and monogamy, is rejected. This appears to be a manifestation of their rejection of the Church which discredits their gay identity and the individualised spirituality they have developed which is broadly based on Christian principles rather than specifically dependent on the Church. The following respondent offers a glimpse of such an attitude:

> I suppose Paul talked about the body being a temple of God and actually treating your body like that in that sort of way really. But I don't think that necessarily means that you are exclusive. I guess it has to do with what *is* going on between that kind of encounter and how *it* relates to others and whether there is abuse.... I can't see what the Church can say...because it doesn't say anything, does it? But I think it does in the sense that I follow it from the point of view of

responsibility.... I respect even people I meet in the cottage [public toilet], you know, that they are human beings. It [the Church] has got nothing to say. The relationship is something that it doesn't support. *(Resp. No. 3A)*

In rejecting the ethic of sexual monogamy, many respondents shared an affinity with the "theology of friendship" which encourages, *inter alia,* "inclusiveness" (Stuart 1992: 2; see also Stuart 1995; Rudy 1996). However, their sexual attitudes still reflected the broad Christian norms of justice and love, although their rejection of the Church as their moral arbiter is indisputably strong.

Compared to couples in Category B, couples in this category relied less heavily on ground rules to manage their non-exclusive lifestyle. This is because both partners shared the expectation of a non-exclusive partnership. However, this does not preclude the existence of certain regulatory mechanisms to minimise the possible emergence of conflict. These mechanisms share great similarity with what I have discussed in the preceding section. I therefore will not repeat them here.

SEXUAL EXCLUSIVITY, RELATIONSHIP SATISFACTION, AND COMMITMENT

Much research evidence suggests that there is no significant difference between sexually exclusive and non-exclusive couples in terms of relationship satisfaction, adjustment and commitment (e.g. Peplau 1981; Blumstein and Schwartz 1983; Blasband and Peplau 1985; Kurdek and Schmitt 1986; Kurdek 1988). This section assesses this claim by comparing all three categories of couples. Each respondent was asked to rate, on a scale of one to ten, his level of satisfaction with his sex life within the partnership and with the partnership in general.

Table 1 indicates that Category A has the *highest* mean rating for sex life within partnership and the partnership in general—7.6 and 9.0 respectively. Taking Category B and Category C together as behaviourally non-exclusive couples, the mean ratings for sex life within partnership and the partnership in general are 6.9 and 8.7, which are lower than those of Category A.

It can therefore be concluded that couples in Category A who are expectationally and behaviourally exclusive have a *higher* level of satisfaction with their sex life within partnership and the partnership in general, compared to their counterparts in Category B who are expectationally exclusive but behaviourally non-exclusive and those in Category C who are expectationally and behaviorally non-exclusive.

However, it must be emphasised that the difference in mean ratings in these cases is not significantly great. This seems to lend credence to the research evidence cited above. In terms of the partner's commitment to the longevity of the partnership, two couples were facing the prospect of dissolution due to non-sexual problems. The other 28 couples (93.3 percent), regardless of their current

T A B L E 44.1   Level of Satisfaction with Sex Life Within Partnership and Partnership in General

Category	Average rating for sex life with partnership	Average rating for partnership in general
A (N = 9)	7.6	9.0
B (N = 8)	7.2	8.4
C (N = 13)	6.7	8.8
B + (N – 21)	6.9	8.7

sexual arrangements, reported that they were committed to a lifelong partnership. Below is a typical demonstration of this commitment:

> Yes, that [to be together till death] is the intention and we have made wills with the intention. We have talked about the fact that we are totally committed to each other for the length of our shared life.... That is in a sense a duty on each other because it is a costly thing to promise to your partner that you will be faithful with the understanding that the other is doing the same thing.... So it is till death do us part. That is definitely our commitment. I mean we have formalised that in a ceremony. *(Resp. No. 52A)*

Thus, it can be concluded that sexual non-exclusivity need not be problematic to a gay partnership. Its impacts tend to depend on the current constitutional arrangement of the partnership and its ability to adapt to change. Sexually non-exclusive partnerships in terms of behaviour should not be misconstrued as being less committed, loving and stable than exclusive ones (Isay 1989).

REFERENCES

Bell, A. P., and M. S. Weinberg. 1978. *Homosexualities: A Study of Diversity Among Men and Women*. New York: Simon and Schuster.

Berzon, B. 1979. "Achieving Success as a Gay Couple." In B. Berzon and R. Leighton, eds., *Positively Gay*. Berkeley, CA: Celestial Arts.

Blasband, D., and L. A. Peplau. 1985. "Sexual Exclusivity Versus Openness in Gay Male Couples." *Archives of Sexual Behaviour* 14 (5): 395–412.

Blumstein, P., and P. Schwartz. 1983. *American Couples: Money, Work, Sex*. New York: Simon and Schuster.

Buunk, B. P., and B. Van Driel. 1989. *Variant Lifestyles and Relationships*. Newbury Park, CA: Sage.

Davies, P. M., F. C. I. Hickson, P. Weatherburn, and A. J. Hunt. 1993 *Sex, Gay Men and AIDS*. London: Falmer Press.

Ellison, M. M. 1994. "Common Decency: A New Christian Sexual Ethics." In J. B. Nelson and S. P. Longfellow, eds., *Sexuality and the Sacred: Sources for Theological*

Reflection. Lexington, KY: Westminster John Knox Press.

Goffman, E. 1963. *Stigma: Notes on the Management of Spoiled Identity*. Englewood Cliffs, NJ: Prentice Hall.

Greeley, A. M. 1991. *Faithful Attraction: Discovering Intimacy, Love, and Fidelity in American Marriage*. New York: Doherty.

Harry, J. 1977. "Marriage Among Gay Males: The Separation of Intimacy and Sex." In S. G. McNall, ed., *The Sociological Perspective: Introductory Readings*, 4th ed. Boston: Little, Brown.

Harry, J., and W. B. DeVall. 1978. *The Social Organization of Gay Males*. New York: Praeger.

Hickson, F. C. I. 1991. "Sexual Exclusivity, Non-Exclusivity and HIV." London: Project SIGMA Working Paper No. 13.

Humphreys, R. A. L. 1972. *Out of the Closet: The Sociology of Homosexual Liberation*. Englewood Cliffs, NJ: Prentice Hall.

Isay, R. A. 1989. *Being Homosexual: Gay Men and Their Development*. Harmondsworth, England: Penguin.

Jay, K., and A. Young. 1977. *The Gay Report: Lesbian and Gay Men Speak Out About Sexual Experiences and Lifestyles*. New York: Summit Books.

John, J. 1993. *Permanent, Faithful, Stable: Christian Same-Sex Partnerships*. London: Affirming Catholicism.

Kurdek, L. A. 1988. "Relationship Quality of Gay Men in Closed or Open Relationships." *Journal of Homosexuality* 15: 93–118.

Kurdek, L. A. 1991. "The Dissolution of Gay and Lesbian Couples." *Journal of Social and Personal Relationships* 8 (2): 265–78.

Kurdek, L. A., and J. P. Schmitt. 1986. "Relationship Quality of Gay Men in Closed or Open Relationships." *Journal of Homosexuality* 12 (2): 85–99.

Lawson, A., and L. Samson. 1988. "Age, Gender and Adultery." *British Journal of Sociology* 39: 409–40.

Lyman, S. M., and M. B. Scott. 1970. *A Sociology of the Absurd*. Pacific Palisades, CA: Goodyear.

Mazur, R. 1977. "Beyond Jealousy and Possessiveness." In G. Clanton and L. Smith, eds., *Jealousy*. Englewood Cliffs, NJ: Prentice Hall.

McWhirter, D. P., and A. M. Mattison. 1984. *The Male Couple: How Relationships Develop*. Englewood Cliffs, NJ: Prentice Hall.

Mendola, M. 1980. *The Mendola Report: A New Look at Gay Couples*. New York: Crown.

Mills, C. W. 1940. "Situated Actions and Vocabularies of Motives." *American Sociological Review* 5: 904–13.

Peplau, L. A. 1981. "What Homosexuals Want in Relationships." *Psychology Today 15,* March: 28–38.

Peplau, L. A., and S. D. Cochran. 1981. "Value Orientations in the Intimate Relationships of Gay Men." *Journal of Homosexuality* 6 (3): 1–19.

Peplau, L. A., and S. L. Gordon. 1983. "The Intimate Relationships of Lesbians and Gay Men." In E. R. Allegeier and N. B. McCormick, eds., *Changing Boundaries: Gender Roles and Sexual Behavior*. Palo Alto, CA: Mayfield.

Reiss, I. L., Anderson, R. E., and G. C. Sponaugle. 1980. "A Multivariate Model of Determinants of Extramarital Permissiveness." *Journal of Marriage and the Family* 42: 395–411.

Rudy, K. 1996. "Where Two or Three Are Gathered: Using Gay Communities as a Model for Christian Sexual Ethics." *Theology and Sexuality* 4: 81–99.

Saghir, M., and E. Robins. 1973. *Male and Female Homosexuality: A Comprehensive Investigation*. Baltimore: Williams and Wilkins.

Silverstein, C. 1981. *Man to Man: Gay Couples in America*. New York: William Morrow.

Spada, K. J. 1979. *The* Spada *Report: The Newest Survey of Gay Male Sexuality*. New York: Signet.

Stuart, E. 1992. *Daring to Speak Love's Name: A Gay and Lesbian Prayer Book*. London: Hamish Hamilton.

Stuart, E. 1995. *Just Good Friends: Towards a Lesbian and Gay Theology of Relationships*. London: Mowbray.

Warren, C. A. B. 1974. *Identity and Community in the Gay World*. New York: Wiley.

Yip, A. K. T. 1995. "Gay Christian Partnerships." Unpublished doctoral dissertation, University of Surrey.

Yip, A. K. T. 1997a. "Attacking the Attacker: Gay Christians Talk Back." *British Journal of Sociology* 48 (1): 113–27.

Yip, A. K. T. 1997b. "Gay Christians' Perceptions of the Christian Community in Relation to Their Sexuality." *Theology and Sexuality*.

Yip, A. K. T. 1997c. "The Politics of Counter–Rejection: Gay Christians and the Church." *Journal of Homosexualit*.

45

Pimp-Controlled Prostitution

CELIA WILLIAMSON AND TERRY CLUSE-TOLAR

*Although underrepresented in the sociological literature on prostitution, the rela-
tionship between pimps and prostitutes is legendary, yet often misunderstood, in
popular culture. Based on qualitative interviews, Williamson and Cluse-Tolar's
study offers an insightful analysis of pimp-controlled prostitutes' careers. Pimps
often "turn prostitutes out," introducing them to the sex work industry. But
while these women are seduced into accepting a pimp as their manager by the
impression he gives that he is romantically interested in them, this behavior often
turns out to be part of his "game," where he does whatever it takes to lure them
into an obligatory relationship that supports him in flashy style. The authors
show how the power relationship between these prostitutes and their pimps shifts
dramatically in a predictable fashion over the course of their deviant careers. At the
beginning the women have the greatest cachet, as the men must woo them into
their service by "gaming" them with their charm and enticements of money and
control over the customers. For a brief "honeymoon" period the women have the
freedom to move around from one pimp to another, but even here the men dominate these exchanges ("bros before ho's"). The further they get into the relationship, the less the pimps need to woo them or treat them well, and they
eventually become subjected to severe forms of emotional and physical manipulation that is often violent in nature. Their careers in pimp-controlled prostitution
peak early and go through a gradual but early decline, landing them worse off
than before they entered the relationship. Only once they have hit bottom do they
get the courage to exit, often fleeing with nothing more than their lives.*

*In what ways do the relationships here compare and contrast to those of
married couples? How do they compare and contrast to the drug dealers and the
crack-addicted women? To the male and female gang members? Can you think of
any other deviant careers that follow a similar trajectory?*

From Celia Williamson and Terry Cluse-Tolar, "Pimp-Controlled Prostitution," *Violence
Against Women*, Vol. 8, No. 9. Copyright © 2002. Reprinted by permission of Sage
Publications.

A pimp is one who controls the actions and lives off the proceeds of one or more women who work the streets. Pimps call themselves "players" and call their profession "the game." The context in which this subculture exists is called "the life" (Milner & Milner, 1972). Social scientists of the 1960s and 1970s devoted a significant amount of research energies toward exposing and understanding pimp-controlled prostitution within street-level prostitution (Goines, 1972; Heard, 1968; Milner & Milner, 1972; Slim, 1967, 1969). Street-level prostitution entails sexual acts for money or for barter that occur on and off the streets and include sexual activities in cars and motels, as dancers in gentlemen's clubs, massage parlor work, truck stops, and crack house work (Williamson, 2000). It represents that segment of the prostitution industry where there is the most violence.

... This study aims to examine pimp-related violence toward women involved in street level prostitution within the context of pimp-controlled prostitution. To understand contemporary pimp controlled prostitution and, more specifically, pimp-related violence, it is necessary to examine the type of relationships between pimps and prostitutes, the roles that each play in the business, and the social rules that accompany the lifestyle.

METHOD

... Information regarding the traditional pimp-prostitute phenomenon was obtained from a larger study that included both independent and pimp-controlled women. Criteria for inclusion in the study were women 18 years of age and older who were no longer involved in prostitution activities. Participants were selected through a process of purposive, or snowball, sampling by word of mouth. In total, 21 former street prostitutes from the Midwest were interviewed. Respondents ranged in age from 18 to 35. Of the total sample, 13 were Appalachian white women, 7 were African American women, and one was a Hispanic woman. The time spent in prostitution ranged from 3 months to 13 years. From this total sample, 6 of the women had pimps and 13 women worked independently. The small number of women found by the researcher who worked for pimps and were willing to be interviewed may underscore the limited access researchers have to this population and hence the importance of research in this area.

Of the six women who are the focus for this report, five were Appalachian white and one was Hispanic. They ranged in age from 18 to 28. For this subgroup, the time spent in prostitution ranged from four to eight years.

The researcher spent six months on the streets, three days per week, learning the culture, language, and geographic layout of the streets. The researcher learned where the dope houses were, who the pimps were, and how to identify a customer from a typical passerby.

Subsequently, in-depth, face-to-face interviews were conducted with six participants who were involved in pimp-controlled prostitution, and one interview was conducted with a pimp. Each interview lasted approximately two hours. Data were analyzed line by line. Codes were developed from the raw data. Codes were collapsed into larger themes. By connecting relevant themes, the researcher was able to develop the theoretical propositions that supported the subsequent theory of the lived experience of pimp-controlled prostitution.

In addition to these interviews, added interviews were conducted with some of the participants for the purpose of member checking, a process of clarification for qualitative methods, and to gather any additional missing data. Interviews were taped and transcribed verbatim. In addition to the member-checking techniques, the researcher engaged a group of social work experts in the area of street prostitution to critique the methodology and to provide guidance toward accurate interpretation of the data. This gathering is known as peer debriefing for the purpose of challenging the researcher's interpretations to increase the accuracy of the study findings. Both member checks and peer debriefing were used to enhance the credibility of the study.

FINDINGS

Pimping: Rules of the Game

Pimps involved in prostitution activities refer to this sector of the underground economy as "the game." Players, pimps, and macks are those at the top of the pimping game. To these men in power, it is a game in which they control and manipulate the actions of others subordinate to them. Monica, a prostituted woman for three years, explains,

> It's all about the game. Nothing in the game changes, but the name. It's all about getting that money. Some women have pimps that they give the money to, some are just out there on their own. (Monica)

A player or pimp has a particular manner or style of playing the game. The pimping game requires strict adherence to the rules. The idea of a game parallels the formal economy in that one can be said to be in a game; for example, he is in the real estate game. Pimps are also said to "have" game. To have game is to possess a certain amount of charisma and smooth-talking, persuasive conversation toward women.

There are several rules that one must be willing to follow to be a successful and professional pimp. Massi, a "bottom bitch"[1] to a pimp who boasts having six women in his stable,[2] outlines the rules for pimping. The most paramount rule in the pimping game is "the pimp must get paid" (Massi). This means there cannot be any "shame in your game" (Massi); one must require and, if necessary, demand the money without shame. Second, any successful pimp will remember that the game is "sold and not told." This means that pimps are expected to sell it to a prospective prostitute that he wants to occupy his stable without revealing his entire game plan. To do this, he has to develop his game or "his rap." These consist of a series of persuasive conversations similar to poetic and rhythmic scats that are philosophical in nature and ideological about life and making money. For Sonya, it was the combination of his rap and her need to feel loved by someone.

> For me, it was wanting to be loved and liked the words that was said. And you know, the nice things you got. I have two beautiful children that I wanted to take care of, and I guess that's the kind of hold they have on you. (Sonya)

… The third and final ingredient for successful pimping is that a pimp must have a woman or women that want to see him on top. He is looking for dedication. He is looking for someone who wants to see her man in fine clothes and driving fine cars. His success or lack of success is a reflection on her. If her man is not looking his best, then she is not a very successful ho, and this will make for an embarrassing impression. As a prostituted woman, she must work very hard to earn his respect and his love and to keep him achieving the best in material possessions. He in return invites her into his underground social network with the sense of belonging it brings and the promise of material possessions it provides.

> You just, you just take control of the tricks. You know what you gotta do to make your man happy…. Some prostitutes are out there for a man, for a pimp. We're out there bustin' our ass to get our money for a man. (Sonya)

> I worked for months to get my man into a new Cadillac. (Sandra)

The most well-respected pimps are called "macks." They are at the top of their game and employ many hardworking and successful prostitutes. Dominating the pimp scene are "players" who have an average stable of women, are well respected, and make a good living. Lowest in the hierarchy of pimping are tennis shoe pimps. These pimps may have one or possibly two prostitutes on the street. They are seen as least successful in the game, and unlike more successful pimps, they may do drugs and allow their women to do drugs. In this study, six of the women previously had pimps ranging from tennis shoe pimps to players.

Turning a Woman Out

A pimp's chance at gaining a woman's attention is by looking good, smelling good, flashing his possessions, and presenting himself as someone who can counter boredom with both adventure and excitement. This is rarely enough, however, to get a woman to prostitute herself. A pimp must be skilled at assessing a woman's needs and vulnerabilities. Understanding how to exploit those vulnerabilities and fulfill those unmet needs will enable him to prostitute her. Reese, a player in Toledo, Ohio, explains how he appeals to what women need:

> I tell her "Now, you need to leave them drugs alone" and I get her cleaned up. She may come here, on drugs or not on drugs, with nothing.

> I mean nothing. Dirty, strung out. Some of them don't even have a
> social security card or state ID, nothing. I ask 'em if they want some-
> thing better, you know, you can make some money. I'll set you up
> right. Let you have a few things in your life. You wanna have nice
> clothes, some good jewelry, be able to have your own place, maybe a
> little car to drive around in? (Reese)

A pimp offers hope for the future, and women see this as an opportunity to
be financially successful. During the time a prostitute is entering the profession of
street-level prostitution, the pimp is said to be "turning her out" or has "turned
her out" on the streets to make a profit.

> I knew this guy, and he brought me here and turned me out on the
> streets. He was a pimp…. The first day, I was scared, but I got the
> money. And once I seen the money, I mean, my first day I made $600
> in a three-hour period. (Sonya)

Women involved with a pimp in this study were typically not engaged in
drug abuse. Pimps realize that crack is the competition and frown upon any drug
abuse in their stable. However, two women involved with tennis shoe pimps
indulged in drug use along with their pimp.

Pimp-controlled women in the study were told they were beautiful and that
men wanted them—that they desired them so much, they would pay hard-
earned money for them. In the words of Massi, the message is conveyed early
in the relationship that women are literally "sitting on a gold mine. If they could
work the game good enough, the game would work for them."

Although pimps never guaranteed emotional or financial security, the potential for success inspired women to test the waters in this new life. There was a
sense of belonging that women longed for, a sense of exciting hope for the future,
an adventure that would take them from their meager existence into a life with a
man who told them they had special skills, intelligence, and beauty. In return for
his attention, protection, and love, she would be required to work to bring their
dream into reality. Reese speaks in terms of "goals" as he works his women:

> I have them set little goals for themselves. Say they want to buy some-
> thing they want; well, we would set a little goal. Say you make this
> certain amount of money: Keep working and I'll set aside a little at a
> time and you'll have what you want. Say if she wants a little piece a car,
> she can work and I'll make sure that she gets that car. So I try to have
> them set goals for themselves, something they're working for.

…Over time, as women learn the game and have become proficient in playing, they are known as thoroughbreds. Thoroughbreds are professionals in the
prostitution industry and are responsible for maintaining the market rates in the
profession. A thoroughbred is able to handle customers, command money, and
conduct business effectively and efficiently to maximize profits.

> When you're turned out, you're just out there. You don't know what
> you're doing. You're just being turned out for a new job. You're being

trained for it. And then once you get down the steps, you know, you become a thoroughbred. You don't let the guy take control of you, you take control of it. (Sonya)

Free Enterprise and Choosing Up

Pimps understand the meaning of business over personal ventures, that is, marketing a product and investing in your product first so your product can return profits. Thus, there is a honeymoon period or courting time between pimps and prostitutes. This is the time in which the pimp "runs his game." This may last one day or several months.

> He progressively led up to the fact that that's what he wanted. You know, he didn't come out that night when I met him and tell me, "This is what I am. This is what you need to do."... I think they really feel like they have to gain your trust before they can dump something like that on you. We spent a lot of time together. I mean ... we would go out to eat, go to the movies, and we did, you know, normal couple things. But ... in my head I'm just thinking it's just normal couple things, but he's thinking that he's winning ... that he's gonna win and I'm gonna end up doing what he wanted. And he was right. (Tracey)

Pimps understand the meaning of capitalism in that it is a pimp's prerogative to entice any woman away from another pimp. It is viewed as a component of free enterprise. Therefore, other pimps are free to attempt to seduce a woman away from her current pimp and into his stable for his financial gain. He may do this without retaliation from the current pimp, as the street rule is "bros before hoes" (Massi). The woman being approached is instructed not to respond to the seducing pimp's advances. She is never to make eye contact with another pimp. If she does, then she is "out of pockets," a term referring to a woman who puts a pimp's money at risk, and she is subject to "being broke," meaning physically reprimanded. On the other hand, the seducing pimp may also choose to "break her" and take all her money. These rules vary in situations where a woman is prohibited from making eye contact with a pimp to situations in which she is not allowed to make eye contact with any African American male.

> I mean, most of the time, if they're a true pimp, they're not gonna play like that. You know, they'll harass you and you mainly just turn away and look in the other direction or whatever and try not to come in contact with them, because if you do, then they do what you call "break you," they take your money.... He's allowed to harass you as much as he wants. But if I don't talk back to him, then I'm cool. But if I'm "out of pockets" that means you're doing something that you ain't suppose to be doing. You know, some pimps will beat you or you go through a lot of stuff.... They're in control. You do what they say. (Sonya)

In the event that a woman is dissatisfied with her current pimp, the appropriate way to switch pimps is to make a definite decision and "choose up."

You choose up. And if you're with a pimp and you want to go with another pimp, you have to put the money in the other pimp's hand and let your man know, you know, you're leaving and going with somebody else.... I've been with three. (Elsie)

Reese explains the transaction between pimps when a woman chooses up:

If he comes to me like a man and tells me "That's my ho now," and she done gave him the money, then that's cool. Leave your ho clothes here and go. You can take your regular clothes, the clothes I bought you to go see your family now and then, but you leave the ho clothes. But if she leaves here and is gone and then don't come back with my money and she been out there making money and giving it to him, "Nigga, that's *my* money you got."

Pimp and Prostitute Relationships in the Game

Each woman in the study had a pimp who set the rules, controlled her actions, and took her earnings. Most reported they were infatuated with their pimp, but not always. Women involved with a tennis shoe pimp, a man who had only one or two women, were more likely to consider themselves in love and defined the involvement with their pimp as a relationship. The more corporate the pimp, for instance, a player possessing three or more women, the less likely it was for women to describe their feelings as love or to define their interaction as a relationship. Women's feelings were instead described as ones of infatuation, admiration, and loyalty. The more women involved with a pimp, the less probable it became for each woman to achieve a status that allowed for the comforts of his affections, time, and attention. It was more likely that each became a part of his pimp family or stable that was made up of many women. This type of arrangement between women is known as a "wife-in-law" situation, in which each prostituted woman is a member of the family that works for the benefit of the same pimp. They are known as wife-in-laws to each other. However, some women did not tolerate such arrangements and moved on, whereas others welcomed the prestige of being with a successful pimp and willingly took on the challenge and responsibilities as a prostituted woman under his direction.

It's just like when a pimp goes out and gets another girl and she's in the family. She's whoring for him like you are. Like a wife-in-law is what they call it. Sometimes you just getting tired of it and you know cheating on me and you know the wife-in-law stuff where you know the wife-in-law is another girl that is working for him, and I just couldn't handle all that. (Tonya)

Wife-in-laws may be responsible for ongoing training of recent inductees. However, the availability of wife-in-law training depends on how large the stable and how corporate the pimp. A bottom bitch, or number one lady, may also be required to work but may only use her mouth or hands when working and to save intercourse for her pimp. She may live with her pimp and may be required to train the new women joining his stable. Women may even drop off money to her after work in the event that their pimp is otherwise occupied.

> I know about the game because I was [his] bottom bitch. I knew everything about hoeing, tricking, or whatever. I was with [him] for eight years. He had women out here working their asses off. Wouldn't even ask him for money or nothing, not even $5, thinking that's making him respect them more. (Massi)

The true talents of a pimp, however, are in his ability to keep his women happy, command money, and portray a deep mysterious and somewhat mean demeanor about him, one that conveys the message that he is not to be crossed. He is then said to be "cold-blooded" or "icy," able to turn off any warm feelings and loving affection in exchange for certain emotional cruelty and physical harm. Two famous and successful pimps, Iceberg Slim and Ice Tea, were said to be so cold blooded they called themselves "Ice" to let everyone know their capacity for heartlessness.

> He would just snap. Like his whole expression would change. One day, he came to my motel room to beat my ass. And made it clear that he came over to beat on me. He said he had some extra time on his hands, that he didn't have anything to do, so he wanted me to know that he knew I was thinking about doing something stupid. And I was too. I was thinking about leaving him again. The last time I left him, I ended up in Cleveland.... He beat me until I blacked out.... But he was like that. He could be so much fun one time, silly and playing around, and the next minute, he could be something else, somebody you don't want to fuck with. (Massi)

A pimp's approach is never to cow down to his woman at any time. He cannot let love cloud his judgments concerning business. If he lets these weaknesses show, he will be left vulnerable and runs the risk of being less successful. Although pimps appear to be in control, in a sense every pimp becomes a whore to his prostitutes. The pimp rule is "purse first, ass last" (Massi). He may treat his hoes in loving ways in return for the amount of money he requested she bring him. She must pay for his love with her sheer tenacity to work and bring him the money. She must in turn request little emotionally and financially. Because of his generosity, he gives her what he thinks she needs.

Pimp-Related Violence: Physical Control of Women

The extent to which women felt threatened by a pimp was, in part, a function of her evaluation of the likelihood that he will become violent. This threat had been realized by all of the women in the study. Pimp-related violence was sometimes unpredictable and took on many forms. However, the most revealing form of pimp-related violence was immediate attack following a violation of the rules. One such violation is leaving the "ho stroll" or designated work area early without making one's daily quota.

Different pimps have different rules. I mean some of 'em set quotas with the girls, you have to make a certain amount of money before you can go home.... When I first started, I was bringing in $1,000 a day. (Tonya)

After it was found out that Debbie was holding back some money from her pimp, without hesitation she was quickly and brutally assaulted.

He ended up getting mad at me one day and punched me in my chest and cracked my rib. That was cracked, and all I could remember is that I couldn't breathe. I mean, I passed out. I was knocked out all day. I was unconscious. (Debbie)

Some pimps use violence as a means of discouraging freelance work and coercing money from women who work within pimp territory but not for the benefit of any pimp.

There was this guy that kept beatin' me in my head, telling me I was gonna pay him, and every time he'd see me, if I didn't give him some money, he'd punch me in my forehead. (Cara)

In the instance that a woman is found to be "out of pockets," she is subject to being broke. Carol told of an incident when she took an unauthorized leave without the permission of her pimp.

When he caught me, he was like "I got you now," and he jumped out. We was in the projects. We were high as fuck off crack, me and Tony was. We were like "Oh, fuck." He was like "I got you now." He had a baseball bat, and Tony ran and left me. So, yes, I got the baseball bat, he beat me in my legs and told me "If you fall, bitch, I'm a hit you in your head and kill you." So I didn't fall, I just stood there and screamed and took it. The police came ... and they asked if I was going to press charges, and I said, "No." My face was swelling, I looked liked a cabbage patch, I was horrible. (Carol)

Pimp-Related Violence: Emotional Control of Women

A pimp's success is dependent on arousing love and fear in his women. By giving his attention to more than one woman at the same time, he heightens both the love each woman desires all to herself and the fear that she may lose any part of it. However, the negative consequences of such arrangements may be jealousy and rivalry for his affections.

He had got back with the girl that he had kids by, which she was already a seasoned hooker. She hated me from the jump start. Since they were in that life, he made her deal with me. When she found out that I wanted him for me, she wanted to fight me every time she would see me and we did.... She hit me in the head with a beer glass, and I had stitches in my head. (Chris)

Relationships require a level of trust and a degree of vulnerability, and pimp prostitute relationships are no different. Trust determines how vulnerable the person is willing to be. Without some degree of trust, interactions are limited to explicit contracts (Holmes, 1991), which is what prostitutes have with customers. "Trust involves coming to terms with the negative aspects of a partner, accepting or perhaps tolerating issues by buffering them in the broader context of the lifestyle" (Holmes, 1991, p. 79). Women take abuses from pimps in stride. They learn to cope with this relationship by not focusing on the abusive aspects for what they are but by instead encapsulating those aspects of their pimp that serve their needs for security and protection. Therefore, a pimp-prostitute relationship often lacks cognitive and behavioral consistency. What is believed and desired on the part of the prostitute and what actually happens in the relationship do not correspond and often require repeated leaps of faith on the part of the prostitute.

Leaving Pimp-Controlled Prostitution

Many factors prevent women from pursuing legal assistance. Often, women are fearful, intimidated by what may happen as a result of reporting, and may love their pimp despite his abuses. It is likely that she may buy into the rules of the pimping game and blame herself for violating them. Women who have previously experienced the reluctance of law enforcement to take their claims about customer-related violence seriously are reluctant to take such risks where pimps are concerned.

> I had this guy pull a gun on me, and he made me do things that I didn't want to do.... I ran to a gas station and called the police. The guy who worked at the gas station gave me his jacket to wear. All I had on was a shirt. I called the police and told them. They came. I described the guy to the police and showed them the spot. I told them what kind of car he had, what we was wearing, what he said, what he did, everything. They never even wrote anything down. They ran me for warrants, and when I didn't have any, they left. (Jerri)

Women who are fed up may choose to leave prostitution. The primary means for leaving pimp-controlled prostitution was escape.

> I had gotten like four calls that day. And I hadn't seen him, so I had all the money on me and I just took it. I mean, none of my clothes, none of my nothing. I just took a cab to the bus station, and I went in to Amtrak police and told them what was going on. He had his own driver, and he knew that when I didn't get in the driver's car, that something was up. I took a regular cab, and I went to Amtrak police and I knew that he was coming, so I told 'em what was going on.... And, um, then the Amtrak police... paid the cab driver to take me to the airport, and I caught a plane home. (Tracey)

DISCUSSION

Using the definition of pimping as controlling and living off the proceeds of one or more women, the findings suggest that pimp-controlled prostitution is still an integral part of street-level prostitution for some women and girls. Just how many is difficult to determine, because pimp-controlled women and girls would be those most unlikely to be able to respond to requests for interviews. Pimp-controlled women in the study were reportedly subject to following the rules of the game. The old adage that "nothing in the game changes but the name" may be truer than not when viewing the dynamics of pimp-controlled prostitution. It is clear that many of the themes identified in this study have appeared in varied form in earlier studies of the 1960s and 1970s (Goines, 1972; Heard, 1968; Milner & Milner, 1972; Slim, 1967, 1969). The important point is that although pimps and prostitutes may differ with the extent to which they apply and adhere to the rules, even allowing for the wide range of situational differences, this code of conduct, termed *pimpology,* is a common practice in this underground society and still exists today (Hughes, Hughes, & Messick, 1999; Milner & Milner, 1972; Owens & Shepard, 1998; Williamson, 2000).

On an interpersonal level, the power and control pimps maintain over women in their stable is akin to that used in abusive relationships. Just as pimps resemble batterers in intimate relationships (Giobbe, 1993), women working in pimp-controlled prostitution seem to be similar to those who are survivors of domestic violence. They often express feelings of love and admiration for the pimp, have their freedom and finances controlled, and may feel they somehow deserve the violence they are dealt. However, there are differences in terms of the cycle of violence. Domestic violence survivors will often express that they knew when the violence was about to occur as evidenced by the building up of tension in their mate before an explosive episode. Beatings and other forms of violence occurring among pimp-controlled women may not follow a familiar pattern and may instead occur by surprise.

NOTES

1. In a more corporate pimp family, the term *bottom bitch* refers to a woman who is the closest in rank to her pimp.

2. A *stable* is what a pimp calls a group of women that prostitute for him.

REFERENCES

Gobbe, E. 1993. A Comparison of Pimps and Batterers. *Michigan Journal of Gender and Law,* 1(1): 33–57.

Goines, D. 1972. *Whoreson: The Story of a Ghetto Pimp.* Los Angeles: Holloway House.

Heard, N. C. 1968. *Howard Street.* New York: Signet.

Holmes, J. C. 1991. Trust and the Appraisal Process in Close Relationships. In W. H. Jones and D. Perlman (eds.),

Advances in Personal Relationships (pp. 57–104). London: Jessica Kingsley.

Hughes, A., Hughes, A., and Messick, K. 1999. *American Pimp* [Film documentary]. United States: Metro Goldwyn Mayer Pictures.

Milner, C. A., and Milner, R. B. 1972. *Black Players*. Boston, MA: Little, Brown.

National Center for Missing and Exploited Children. 1992. *Female Juvenile Prostitution: Problem and Response*. Arlington, VA: Author.

Owens, B. (Producer/Director), and Shepard, B. (Coproducer). 1998. *Pimp Up Ho Down* [Film documentary]. United States: Home Box Office.

Slim, I. 1967. *Trick Baby*. Los Angeles: Holloway House.

Slim, I. 1969. *Pimp: The Story of My Life*. Los Angeles: Holloway House.

Williamson, C. 2000. Entrance, Maintenance, and Exit: The Socioeconomic Influences and Cumulative Burdens of Female Street Prostitution. *Dissertation Abstracts International*, 61(02). (UMI No. 9962789).

46

Shifts and Oscillations in Upper-Level Drug Traffickers' Careers

PATRICIA A. ADLER AND PETER ADLER

Adler and Adler discuss the process by which people burn out of deviance in this selection on exiting drug trafficking. After spending several years in the upper echelons of the drug trade, many marijuana dealers and smugglers, who were initially attracted to drug trafficking by the same lure of the excitement, high life, and spontaneity that drew Wright and Deckers' burglars to their deviance, eventually find that the drawbacks of the lifestyle exceed the rewards. Their initial challenges and thrills turn to paranoia, people whom they know get busted all around them, and their risk of arrest grows. Years of excessive drug use take its toll on them physically, and they come to reevaluate the straight life they formerly rejected as boring. Yet they cannot easily quit dealing; they have developed a high-spending lifestyle that they are loath to abandon. One thing that they do is to shift around in the drug world, making changes in their involvement. When this doesn't bring them satisfaction, or when the factors pushing them out continue to grow, they try to retire from trafficking. Commonly, however, they quickly spend all their money and are drawn back into the business. Their patterns of exiting, thus, often resemble a series of oscillations, or quittings and restartings, as they move out of deviance with great difficulty. It is interesting to note that this mode of oscillating in and out of deviance as a means of finally making an exit is often found in other forms of deviant careers such as quitting cigarette smoking and leaving an abusive relationship.

From Patricia A. Adler and Peter Adler, "Shifts and Oscillations in Deviant Careers: The Case of Upper-Level Drug Dealers and Smugglers." *Social Problems*, Vol. 31, No. 2, 1983. © 1983 Society for the Study of Social Problems. Reprinted by permission of University of California Press Journals.

The upper echelons of the marijuana and cocaine trade constitute a world that has never before been researched and analyzed by sociologists. Importing and distributing tons of marijuana and kilos of cocaine at a time, successful operators can earn upwards of a half million dollars per year. Their traffic in these so-called "soft"[1] drugs constitutes a potentially lucrative occupation, yet few participants manage to accumulate any substantial sums of money, and most people envision their involvement in drug trafficking as only temporary. In this study we focus on the career paths followed by members of one upper-level drug dealing and smuggling community. We discuss the various modes of entry into trafficking at these upper levels, contrasting these with entry into middle- and low-level trafficking. We then describe the pattern of shifts and oscillations these dealers and smugglers experience. Once they reach the top rungs of their occupation, they begin periodically quitting and reentering the field, often changing their degree and type of involvement upon their return. Their careers, therefore, offer insights into the problems involved in leaving deviance.

Previous research on soft drug trafficking has only addressed the low and middle levels of this occupation, portraying people who purchase no more than 100 kilos of marijuana or single ounces of cocaine at a time (Anonymous, 1969; Atkyns and Hanneman, 1974; Blum, 1972; Carey, 1968; Goode, 1970; Langer, 1977; Lieb and Olson, 1976; Mouledoux, 1972; Waldorf et al., 1977). Of these, only Lieb and Olson (1976) have examined dealing and/or smuggling as an occupation, investigating participants' career developments. But their work, like that of several of the others, focuses on a population of student dealers who may have been too young to strive for and attain the upper levels of drug trafficking. Our study fills this gap at the top by describing and analyzing an elite community of upper-level dealers and smugglers and their careers.

We begin by describing where our research took place, the people and activities we studied, and the methods we used. Second, we outline the process of becoming a drug trafficker, from initial recruitment through learning the trade. Third, we look at the different types of upward mobility displayed by dealers and smugglers. Fourth, we examine the career shifts and oscillations that veteran dealers and smugglers display, outlining the multiple, conflicting forces which lure them both into and out of drug trafficking. We conclude by suggesting a variety of paths which dealers and smugglers pursue out of drug trafficking and discuss the problems inherent in leaving this deviant world.

SETTING AND METHOD

We based our study in "Southwest County," one section of a large metropolitan area in southwestern California near the Mexican border. Southwest County consisted of a handful of beach towns dotting the Pacific Ocean, a location offering a strategic advantage for wholesale drug trafficking.

Southwest County smugglers obtained their marijuana in Mexico by the ton and their cocaine in Colombia, Bolivia, and Peru, purchasing between 10 and 40 kilos at a time. These drugs were imported into the United States along a variety of land, sea, and air routes by organized smuggling crews. Southwest County dealers then purchased these products and either "middled" them directly to another buyer for a small but immediate profit of approximately $2 to $5 per kilo of marijuana and $5,000 per kilo of cocaine, or engaged in "straight dealing." As opposed to middling, straight dealing usually entailed adulterating the cocaine with such "cuts" as manitol, procaine, or inositol, and then dividing the marijuana and cocaine into smaller quantities to sell them to the next-lower level of dealers. Although dealers frequently varied the amounts they bought and sold, a hierarchy of transacting levels could be roughly discerned. "Wholesale" marijuana dealers bought directly from the smugglers, purchasing anywhere from 300 to 1,000 "bricks" (averaging a kilo in weight) at a time and selling in lots of 100 to 300 bricks. "Multi-kilo" dealers, while not the smugglers' first connections, also engaged in upper-level trafficking, buying between 100 to 300 bricks and selling them in 25- to 100-brick quantities. These were then purchased by middle-level dealers who filtered the marijuana through low-level and "ounce" dealers before it reached the ultimate consumer. Each time the marijuana changed hands its price increase was dependent on a number of factors: purchase cost; the distance it was transported (including such transportation costs as packaging, transportation equipment, and payments to employees); the amount of risk assumed; the quality of the marijuana; and the prevailing prices in each local drug market. Prices in the cocaine trade were much more predictable. After purchasing kilos of cocaine in South America for $10,000 each, smugglers sold them to Southwest County "pound" dealers in quantities of one to 10 kilos for $60,000 per kilo. These pound dealers usually cut the cocaine and sold pounds ($30,000) and half-pounds ($15,000) to "ounce" dealers, who in turn cut it again and sold ounces for $2,000 each to middle-level cocaine dealers known as "cut-ounce" dealers. In this fashion the drug was middled, dealt, divided and cut— sometimes as many as five or six times—until it was finally purchased by consumers as grams or half-grams.

Unlike low-level operators, the upper-level dealers and smugglers we studied pursued drug trafficking as a full-time occupation. If they were involved in other businesses, these were usually maintained to provide them with a legitimate front for security purposes. The profits to be made at the upper levels depended on an individual's style of operation, reliability, security, and the amount of product he or she consumed. About half of the 65 smugglers and dealers we observed were successful, some earning up to three-quarters of a million dollars per year.[2] The other half continually struggled in the business, either breaking even or losing money.

Although dealers' and smugglers' business activities varied, they clustered together for business and social relations, forming a moderately well-integrated community whose members pursued a "fast" lifestyle, which emphasized intensive partying, casual sex, extensive travel, abundant drug consumption, and lavish spending on consumer goods. The exact size of Southwest County's upper-level dealing and smuggling community was impossible to estimate due to the secrecy of its members. At these levels, the drug world was quite homogeneous. Participants were predominantly white, came from middle-class backgrounds, and had little previous criminal involvement. While the dealers' and smugglers' social world contained both men and women, most of the serious business was conducted by the men, ranging in age from 25 to 40 years old.

We gained entry to Southwest County's upper-level drug community largely by accident. We had become friendly with a group of our neighbors who turned out be heavily involved in smuggling marijuana. Opportunistically (Riemer, 1977), we seized the chance to gather data on this unexplored activity. Using key informants who helped us gain the trust of other members of the community, we drew upon snowball sampling techniques (Biernacki and Waldorf, 1981) and a combination of overt and covert roles to widen our network of contacts. We supplemented intensive participant-observation, between 1974 and 1980,[3] with unstructured, taped interviews. Throughout, we employed extensive measures to cross-check the reliability of our data, whenever possible (Douglas, 1976). In all, we were able to closely observe 65 dealers and smugglers as well as numerous other drug world members, including dealers' "old ladies" (girlfriends or wives), friends, and family members....

SHIFTS AND OSCILLATIONS

... Despite the gratifications which dealers and smugglers originally derived from the easy money, material comfort, freedom, prestige, and power associated with their careers, 90 percent of those we observed decided, at some point, to quit the business. This stemmed, in part, from their initial perceptions of the career as temporary ("Hell, nobody wants to be a drug dealer all their life"). Adding to these early intentions was a process of rapid aging in the career: dealers and smugglers became increasingly aware of the restrictions and sacrifices their occupations required and tired of living the fugitive life. They thought about, talked about, and in many cases took steps toward getting out of the drug business. But as with entering, disengaging from drug trafficking was rarely an abrupt act (Lieb and Olson, 1976: 364). Instead, it more often resembled a series of transitions, or oscillations,[4] out of and back into the business. For once out of the drug world, dealers and smugglers were rarely successful in making it in the legitimate world because they failed to cut down on their extravagant lifestyle and drug consumption. Many abandoned their efforts to reform and returned to deviance, sometimes picking up where they left off and other times shifting to a new mode of operating. For example, some shifted from dealing cocaine to dealing marijuana, some dropped to a lower level of dealing, and others shifted their role within the same group of traffickers. This series of phase-outs and reentries, combined with career shifts, endured for years, dominating the pattern of their remaining involvement with the business. But it also represented the method by which many eventually broke away from drug trafficking, for each phase-out had the potential to be an individual's final departure.

Aging in the Career

Once recruited and established in the drug world, dealers and smugglers entered into a middle phase of aging in the career. This phase was characterized by a progressive loss of enchantment with their occupation. While novice dealers and smugglers found that participation in the drug world brought them thrills and status, the novelty gradually faded. Initial feelings of exhilaration and awe began to dull as individuals became increasingly jaded. This was the result of both an extended exposure to the mundane, everyday business aspects of drug trafficking and to an exorbitant consumption of drugs (especially cocaine). One smuggler described how he eventually came to feel:

> It was fun, those three or four years. I never worried about money or anything. But after awhile it got real boring. There was no feeling or emotion or anything about it. I wasn't even hardly relating to my old lady anymore. Everything was just one big rush.

This frenzy of overstimulation and resulting exhaustion hastened the process of "burnout" which nearly all individuals experienced. As dealers and smugglers aged in the career they became more sensitized to the extreme risks they faced. Cases of friends and associates who were arrested, imprisoned, or killed began to mount. Many individuals became convinced that continued drug trafficking would inevitably lead to arrest ("It's only a matter of time before you get caught"). While dealers and smugglers generally repressed their awareness of danger, treating it as a taken-for-granted part of their daily existence, periodic crises shattered their casual attitudes, evoking strong feelings of fear. They temporarily intensified security precautions and retreated into near-isolation until they felt the "heat" was off.

As a result of these accumulating "scares," dealers and smugglers increasingly integrated feelings of "paranoia"[5] into their everyday lives. One dealer talked about his feelings of paranoia:

> You're always on the line. You don't lead a normal life. You're always looking over your shoulder, wondering who's at the door, having to hide everything. You learn to look behind you so well you could probably bend over and look up your ass. That's paranoia. It's a really scary, hard feeling. That's what makes you get out.

Drug world members also grew progressively weary of their exclusion from the legitimate world and the deceptions they had to manage to sustain that separation. Initially, this separation was surrounded by an alluring mystique. But as they aged in the career, this mystique became replaced by the reality of everyday boundary maintenance and the feeling of being an "expatriated citizen within one's own country." One smuggler who was contemplating quitting described the effects of this separation:

> I'm so sick of looking over my shoulder, having to sit in my house and worry about one of my non–drug world friends stopping in when I'm doing business. Do you know how awful that is? It's like leading a

double life. It's ridiculous. That's what makes it not worth it. It'll be a lot less money [to quit], but a lot less pressure.

Thus, while the drug world was somewhat restricted, it was not an encapsulated community, and dealers' and smugglers' continuous involvement with the straight world made the temptation to adhere to normative standards and "go straight" omnipresent. With the occupation's novelty worn off and the "fast life" taken for granted, most dealers and smugglers felt that the occupation no longer resembled their early impressions of it. Once they reached the upper levels of the occupation, their experience began to change. Eventually, the rewards of trafficking no longer seemed to justify the strain and risk involved. It was at this point that the straight world's formerly dull ambiance became transformed (at least in theory) into a potential haven.

Phasing Out

Three factors inhibited dealers and smugglers from leaving the drug world. Primary among these factors were the hedonistic and materialistic satisfactions the drug world provided. Once accustomed to earning vast quantities of money quickly and easily, individuals found it exceedingly difficult to return to the income scale of the straight world. They also were reluctant to abandon the pleasure of the "fast life" and its accompanying drugs, casual sex, and power. Second, dealers and smugglers identified with, and developed a commitment to, the occupation of drug trafficking (Adler and Adler, 1982). Their self images were tied to that role and could not be easily disengaged. The years invested in their careers (learning the trade, forming connections, building reputations) strengthened their involvement with both the occupation and the drug community. And since their relationships were social as well as business, friendship ties bound individuals to dealing. As one dealer in the midst of struggling to phase-out explained:

> The biggest threat to me is to get caught up sitting around the house with friends that are into dealing. I'm trying to stay away from them, change my habits.

Third, dealers and smugglers hesitated to voluntarily quit the field because of the difficulty involved in finding another way to earn a living. Their years spent in illicit activity made it unlikely for any legitimate organizations to hire them. This narrowed their occupational choices considerably, leaving self-employment as one of the few remaining avenues open.

Dealers and smugglers who tried to leave the drug world generally fell into one of four patterns.[6] The first and most frequent pattern was to postpone quitting until after they could execute one last "big deal." While the intention was sincere, individuals who chose this route rarely succeeded; the "big deal" too often remained elusive. One marijuana smuggler offered a variation of this theme:

> My plan is to make a quarter of a million dollars in four months during the prime smuggling season and get the hell out of the business.

A second pattern we observed was individuals who planned to change immediately, but never did. They announced they were quitting, yet their outward actions never varied. One dealer described his involvement with this syndrome:

> When I wake up I'll say, "Hey, I'm going to quit this cycle and just run my other business." But when you're dealing you constantly have people dropping by ounces and asking, "Can you move this?" What's your first response? Always, "Sure, for a toot."

In the third pattern of phasing-out, individuals actually suspended their dealing and smuggling activities, but did not replace them with an alternative source of income. Such withdrawals were usually spontaneous and prompted by exhaustion, the influence of a person from outside the drug world, or problems with the police or other associates. These kinds of phase-outs usually lasted only until the individual's money ran out, as one dealer explained:

> I got into legal trouble with the FBI a while back and I was forced to quit dealing. Everybody just cut me off completely, and I saw the danger in continuing, myself. But my high-class tastes never dwindled. Before I knew it I was in hock over $30,000. Even though I was hot, I was forced to get back into dealing to relieve some of my debts.

In the fourth pattern of phasing out, dealers and smugglers tried to move into another line of work. Alternative occupations included: (1) those they had previously pursued; (2) front businesses maintained on the side while dealing or smuggling; and (3) new occupations altogether. While some people accomplished this transition successfully, there were problems inherent in all three alternatives.

1. Most people who tried resuming their former occupations found that these had changed too much while they were away. In addition, they themselves had changed: they enjoyed the self-directed freedom and spontaneity associated with dealing and smuggling, and were unwilling to relinquish it.

2. Those who turned to their legitimate front business often found that these businesses were unable to support them. Designed to launder rather than earn money, most of these ventures were retail outlets with a heavy cash flow (restaurants, movie theaters, automobile dealerships, small stores) that had become accustomed to operating under a continuous subsidy from illegal funds. Once their drug funding was cut off they could not survive for long.

3. Many dealers and smugglers utilized the skills and connections they had developed in the drug business to create a new occupation. They exchanged their illegal commodity for a legal one and went into import/export, manufacturing, wholesaling, or retailing other merchandise. For some, the decision to prepare a legitimate career for their future retirement from the drug world followed an unsuccessful attempt to phase-out into a

"front" business. One husband-and-wife dealing team explained how these legitimate side businesses differed from front businesses:

> We always had a little legitimate "scam" [scheme] going, like mail-order shirts, wallets, jewelry, and the kids were always involved in that. We made a little bit of money on them. Their main purpose was for a cover. But [this business] was different; right from the start this was going to be a legal thing to push us out of the drug business.

About 10 percent of the dealers and smugglers we observed began tapering off their drug world involvement gradually, transferring their time and money into a selected legitimate endeavor. They did not try to quit drug trafficking altogether until they felt confident that their legitimate business could support them. Like spontaneous phase-outs, many of these planned withdrawals into legitimate endeavors failed to generate enough money to keep individuals from being lured into the drug world.

In addition to voluntary phase-outs caused by burnout, about 40 percent of the Southwest County dealers and smugglers we observed experienced a "bust-out" at some point in their careers.[7] Forced withdrawals from dealing or smuggling were usually sudden and motivated by external factors, either financial, legal, or reputational. Financial bustouts generally occurred when dealers or smugglers were either "burned" or "ripped-off" by others, leaving them in too much debt to rebuild their base of operation. Legal bustouts followed arrest and possibly incarceration: arrested individuals were so "hot" that few of their former associates would deal with them. Reputational bustouts occurred when individuals "burned" or "ripped-off" others (regardless of whether they intended to do so) and were banned from business by their former circle of associates. One smuggler gave his opinion on the pervasive nature of forced phase-outs:

> Some people are smart enough to get out of it because they realize, physically, they have to. Others realize, monetarily, that they want to get out of this world before this world gets them. Those are the lucky ones. Then there are the ones who have to get out because they're hot or someone else close to them is so hot that they'd better get out. But in the end when you get out of it, nobody gets out of it out of free choice; you do it because you have to.

Death, of course, was the ultimate bustout. Some pilots met this fate because of the dangerous routes they navigated (hugging mountains, treetops, other aircrafts) and the sometimes ill-maintained and overloaded planes they flew. However, despite much talk of violence, few Southwest County drug traffickers died at the hands of fellow dealers.

Reentry

Phasing out of the drug world was more often than not temporary. For many dealers and smugglers, it represented but another stage of their drug careers (although this may not have been their original intention), to be followed by a period of reinvolvement. Depending on the individual's perspective, reentry into the drug world could be viewed as either a comeback (from a forced withdrawal) or a relapse (from a voluntary withdrawal).

Most people forced out of drug trafficking were anxious to return. The decision to phase out was never theirs, and the desire to get back into dealing or smuggling was based on many of the same reasons which drew them into the field originally. Coming back from financial, legal, and reputational bust-outs was possible but difficult and was not always successfully accomplished. They had to reestablish contacts, rebuild their organization and fronting arrangements, and raise the operating capital to resume dealing. More difficult was the problem of overcoming the circumstances surrounding their departure. Once smugglers and dealers resumed operating, they often found their former colleagues suspicious of them. One frustrated dealer described the effects of his prison experience:

> When I first got out of the joint [jail], none of my old friends would
> have anything to do with me. Finally, one guy who had been my
> partner told me it was because everyone was suspicious of my getting
> out early and thought I made a deal [with police to inform on his
> colleagues].

Dealers and smugglers who returned from bustouts were thus informally sub-jected to a trial period in which they had to reestablish their trustworthiness and reliability before they could once again move in the drug world with ease.

Reentry from voluntary withdrawal involved a more difficult decision–making process, but was easier to implement. The factors enticing individuals to reenter the drug world were not the same as those which motivated their original entry. As we noted above, experienced dealers and smugglers often privately weighed their reasons for wanting to quit and wanting to stay in. Once they left, their images of and hopes for the straight world failed to materialize. They could not make the shift to the norms, values, and lifestyle of the straight society and could not earn a living within it. Thus, dealers and smugglers decided to reenter the drug business for basic reasons: the material perquisites, the hedonistic gratifica-tions, the social ties, and the fact that they had nowhere else to go.

Once this decision was made, the actual process of reentry was relatively easy. One dealer described how the door back into dealing remained open for those who left voluntarily:

> I still see my dealer friends, I can still buy grams from them when I want
> to. It's the respect they have for me because I stepped out of it without
> being busted or burning someone. I'm coming out with a good repu-
> tation, and even though the scene is a whirlwind—people moving up,
> moving down, in, out—if I didn't see anybody for a year I could call
> them up and get right back in that day.

People who relapsed thus had little problem obtaining fronts, reestablishing their reputations, or readjusting to the scene.

Career Shifts

Dealers and smugglers who reentered the drug world, whether from a voluntary or forced phase-out, did not always return to the same level of transacting or commodity which characterized their previous style of operation. Many individuals underwent a "career shift" (Luckenbill and Best, 1981) and became involved in some new segment of the drug world. These shifts were sometimes lateral, as when a member of a smuggling crew took on a new specialization, switching from piloting to operating a stash house, for example. One dealer described how he utilized friendship networks upon his reentry to shift from cocaine to marijuana trafficking:

> Before, when I was dealing cocaine, I was too caught up in using the drug and people around me were starting to go under from getting into "base" [another form of cocaine]. That's why I got out. But now I think I've got myself together and even though I'm dealing again I'm staying away from coke. I've switched over to dealing grass. It's a whole different circle of people. I got into it through a close friend I used to know before, but I never did business with him because he did grass and I did coke.

Vertical shifts moved operators to different levels. For example, one former smuggler returned and began dealing; another top-level marijuana dealer came back to find that the smugglers he knew had disappeared and he was forced to buy in smaller quantities from other dealers.

Another type of shift relocated drug traffickers in different styles of operation. One dealer described how, after being arrested, he tightened his security measures:

> I just had to cut back after I went through those changes. Hell, I'm not getting any younger and the idea of going to prison bothers me a lot more than it did 10 years ago. The risks are no longer worth it when I can have a comfortable income with less risk. So I only sell to four people now. I don't care if they buy a pound or a gram.

A former smuggler who sold his operation and lost all his money during phase-out returned as a consultant to the industry, selling his expertise to those with new money and fresh manpower:

> What I've been doing lately is setting up deals for people. I've got foolproof plans for smuggling cocaine up here from Colombia; I tell them how to modify their airplanes to add on extra fuel tanks and to fit in more weed, coke, or whatever they bring up. Then I set them up with refueling points all up and down Central America, tell them how to bring it up here, what points to come in at, and what kind of receiving unit to use. Then they do it all and I get 10 percent of what they make.

Reentry did not always involve a shift to a new niche, however. Some dealers and smugglers returned to the same circle of associates, trafficking activity, and commodity they worked with prior to their departure. Thus, drug dealers' careers often peaked early and then displayed a variety of shifts, from lateral mobility, to decline, to holding fairly steady.

A final alternative involved neither completely leaving nor remaining within the deviant world. Many individuals straddled the deviant and respectable worlds forever by continuing to dabble in drug trafficking. As a result of their experiences in the drug world they developed a deviant self-identity and a deviant *modus operandi*. They might not have wanted to bear the social and legal burden of full-time deviant work but neither were they willing to assume the perceived confines and limitations of the straight world. They therefore moved into the entrepreneurial realm, where their daily activities involved some kind of hustling or "wheeling and dealing" in an assortment of legitimate, quasi-legitimate, and deviant ventures, and where they could be their own boss. This enabled them to retain certain elements of the deviant lifestyle, and to socialize on the fringes of the drug community. For these individuals, drug dealing shifted from a primary occupation to a sideline, though they never abandoned it altogether.

LEAVING DRUG TRAFFICKING

This career pattern of oscillation into and out of active drug trafficking makes it difficult to speak of leaving drug trafficking in the sense of final retirement. Clearly, some people succeeded in voluntarily retiring. Of these, a few managed to prepare a post-deviant career for themselves by transferring their drug money into a legitimate enterprise. A larger group was forced out of dealing and either didn't or couldn't return; the bustouts were sufficiently damaging that they never attempted reentry, or they abandoned efforts after a series of unsuccessful attempts. But there was no way of structurally determining in advance whether an exit from the business would be temporary or permanent. The vacillations in dealers' intentions were compounded by the complexity of operating successfully in the drug world. For many, then, no phase-out could ever be definitely assessed as permanent. As long as individuals had skills, knowledge, and connections to deal they retained the potential to reenter the occupation at any time. Leaving drug trafficking may thus be a relative phenomenon, characterized by a trailing–off process where spurts of involvement appear with decreasing frequency and intensity.

SUMMARY

Drug dealing and smuggling careers are temporary and fraught with multiple attempts at retirement. Veteran drug traffickers quit their occupation because of the ambivalent feelings they develop toward their deviant life. As they age in the career their experience changes, shifting from a work life that is exhilarating and free to one that becomes increasingly dangerous and confining. But just as their deviant careers are temporary, so too are their retirements. Potential recruits are lured into the drug business by materialism, hedonism, glamor, and excitement. Established dealers are lured away from the deviant life and back into the mainstream by the attractions of security and social ease. Retired dealers and smugglers are lured back in by their expertise, and by their ability to make money quickly and easily. People who have been exposed to the upper levels of drug trafficking therefore find it extremely difficult to quit their deviant occupation permanently. This stems, in part, from their difficulty in moving from the illegitimate to the legitimate business sector. Even more significant is the affinity they form for their deviant values and lifestyle. Thus few, if any, of our subjects were successful in leaving deviance entirely. What dealers and smugglers intend, at the time, to be a permanent withdrawal from drug trafficking can be seen in retrospect as a pervasive occupational pattern of mid-career shifts and oscillations. More research is needed into the complex process of how people get out of deviance and enter the world of legitimate work.

NOTES

1. The term "soft" drugs generally refers to marijuana, cocaine, and such psychedelics as LSD and mescaline (Carey, 1968). In this paper we do not address trafficking in psychedelics because, since they are manufactured in the United States, they are neither imported nor distributed by the group we studied.

2. This is an idealized figure representing the profit a dealer or smuggler could potentially earn and does not include deductions for such miscellaneous and hard-to-calculate costs: time or money spent in arranging deals (some of which never materialize); lost, stolen, or unrepaid money or drugs; and the personal drug consumption of a drug trafficker and his or her entourage. Of these, the single largest expense is the last one, accounting for the bulk of most Southwest County dealers' and smugglers' earnings.

3. We continued to conduct follow-up interviews with key informants through 1983.

4. While other studies of drug dealing have also noted that participants did not maintain an uninterrupted stream of career involvement (Blum, 1972; Carey, 1968; Lieb and Olson, 1976; Waldorf et al., 1977), none have isolated or described the oscillating nature of this pattern.

5. In the dealers' vernacular, this term is not used in the clinical sense of an individual psychopathology rooted in early childhood traumas. Instead, it resembles Lemert's (1962) more sociological definition that focuses on such behavioral dynamics as suspicion, hostility, aggressiveness, and even delusion. Not only Lemert, but also Waldorf et al. (1977) and Wedow (1979) assert that feelings of paranoia can have a sound basis in reality, and are therefore readily comprehended and even empathized with others.

6. At this point, a limitation to our data must be noted. Many of the dealers and smugglers we observed simply "disappeared" from the scene and were never heard from again. We therefore have no way of knowing if they phased-out (voluntarily or involuntarily), shifted to another scene, or

were killed in some remote place. We cannot, therefore, estimate the numbers of people who left the Southwest County drug scene via each of the routes discussed here.

7. It is impossible to determine the exact percentage of people falling into the different phase-out categories: due to oscillation, people could experience several types and thus appear in multiple categories.

REFERENCES

Adler, Patricia A., and Peter Adler. 1982. "Criminal Commitment among drug dealers." *Deviant Behavior* 3: 117–135.

Anonymous. 1969. "On selling marijuana." In Erich Goode ed., *Marijuana* (pp. 92–102). New York: Atherton.

Atkyns, Robert L., and Gerhard J. Hanneman. 1974. "Illicit drug distribution and dealer communication behavior." *Journal of Health and Social Behavior* 15(March): 36–43.

Biernacki, Patrick, and Dan Waldorf. 1981. "Snowball sampling." *Sociological Methods and Research* 10(2): 141–163.

Blum, Richard H. 1972. *The Dream Sellers.* San Francisco: Jossey-Bass.

Carey, James T. 1968. *The College Drug Scene.* Englewood Cliffs, NJ: Prentice Hall.

Douglas, Jack D. 1976. *Investigative Social Research.* Beverly Hills, CA: Sage.

Goode, Erich. 1970. *The Marijuana Smokers.* New York: Basic.

Langer, John. 1977. "Drug entrepreneurs and dealing culture." *Social Problems* 24(3): 377–385.

Lemert, Edwin. 1962. "Paranoia and the dynamics of exclusion." *Sociometry* 25(March): 2–20.

Lieb, John, and Sheldon Olson. 1976. "Prestige, paranoia, and profit: On becoming a dealer of illicit drugs in a university community." *Journal of Drug Issues* 6(Fall): 356–369.

Luckenbill, David F., and Joel Best. 1981. "Careers in deviance and respectability: The analogy's limitations." *Social Problems* 29(2): 197–206.

Mouledoux, James. 1972. "Ideological aspects of drug dealership." In Ken Westhues (ed.), *Society's Shadow: Studies in the Sociology of Countercultures* (pp. 110–122). Toronto: McGraw-Hill, Ryerson.

Riemer, Jeffrey W. 1977. "Varieties of opportunistic research." *Urban Life* 5(4): 467–477.

Waldorf, Dan, Sheila Murphy, Craig Reinarman, and Bridget Joyce. 1977. *Doing Coke: An Ethnography of Cocaine Users and Sellers.* Washington, DC: Drug Abuse Council.

Wedow, Suzanne. 1979. "Feeling paranoid: The organization of an ideology." *Urban Life* 8(1): 72–93.

47

Obstacles to Exiting Emotional Disorder Identities

JENNA HOWARD

Howard's chapter on how people with emotional disorders grow to challenge and become discontent with their diagnoses shows us the identity dimensions of exiting deviance. In reading about fat and bisexual identities earlier, we saw the kinds of processes people underwent to change and enter into deviant identities. But Howard shows how it is equally difficult to exit them, reinforced by the tendency of comfort and friendships to hold them to the status quo. The people with emotional disorders she describes have often bought into their psychological diagnoses with difficulty, suffering and in pain. Quitting them is likely to bring an equal amount of psychological trauma.

How does exiting emotional disorder identities compare to quitting drug trafficking? Are the stages of the process, the shifts around, or the oscillations in and out similar or different? What are factors pushing people out of each versus pulling them toward other activities or identities? How do Howard's existential, interactional, and cultural barriers to identity change compare to the active and passive status cues described by Degher and Hughes for the fat people?

Considering subjective identity career entrances and exits can be a rich source of social psychological insight into identity processes. At what point do particular self-definitions begin and at what point do they end? While some identity careers have "highly articulated" (Glaser and Strauss 1971) durations that are publicly marked by explicit symbols of entrance and exit (such as acquiring a uniform or receiving a diploma), the duration of other identity careers is more subjectively determined. One such identity career involves identities that are based on emotional disorder labels. Because the sensations and experiences that qualify as symptoms of these conditions tend to be internally located and lack visible boundaries, the determination of whether to consider oneself ill or not may be highly subjective. This study explores the subjective self-meanings of

From Jenna Howard. "Negotiating an Exit: Existential, Interactional, and Cultural Obstacles to Disorder Disidentification." *Social Psychology Quarterly* vol. 71(2). Copyright © 2008. Reprinted by permission of the American Psychological Association.

people who formerly identified with emotional disorder labels and no longer do (*delabelers*). My analysis of their narratives offers nuance to our understanding of identification and disidentification processes by highlighting the tension between the individual's decision to discard the disorder labels and the simultaneous reluctance to relinquish the associated identity. In particular. I focus on delabelers' descriptions of the difficulties involved in the disidentification process, classifying them as existential, inter actional, and cultural obstacles to disidentification ...

This study is based on in-depth interviews with 40 individuals who claim to have formerly identified with emotional disorder labels and no longer use the label as a source of subjective identification. I refer to these individuals as *delabelers*. These individuals formerly identified with a wide range of emotional disorder labels as diverse as "anorexic," "codependent," "bipolar," or "agoraphobic." Each of these individuals, by definition, have subjectively disidentified with their emotional disorder labels, and their narratives offer insight into the changing subjective meanings of their disorder identities over time as well as into the exiting process itself. One of the outstanding themes common to a majority of delabelers' narratives depicts the disidentification process as difficult ...

This focus on the challenges to exiting experienced by this underresearched population offers insight into the experiences of delabelers specifically and it provides a sensitizing framework for broadening our inquiry into the processes and con sequences of labeling within a mental health context.

DATA AND METHODS

The only criterion for being considered a delabeler is to have formerly identified oneself with a labeled emotional disorder. I do not distinguish between those who were professionally labeled or "self-labeled" (Thoits 1985), nor do I consider the current presence or absence of "symptoms" in my inclusion criterion. This means that being a delabeler is not necessarily synonymous with being "cured" (although in some cases it may be); it simply implies that one has chosen to no longer use the disorder label as a source of identity, for any reason. The scope of this work is limited to issues of self-identification; it does not address objective clinical outcomes ...

The unmarked nature of this population makes recruitment difficult because individuals who have disidentified from their labels generally cannot be found attending support group meetings or treatment centers. Therefore, to locate the forty delabelers that make up this sample, I depended on snowball sampling and advertising with flyers, including voluntary postings by two informants to online networks of therapists and social workers of which they are members. As a result, my informants came from ten different states, and all but four local respondents were interviewed in tape-recorded phone sessions.

It is a primarily female sample (thirty-one women and nine men), ranging in age from twenty to sixty-nine. More than a third are over 50, and half are in social service, mental health, or other health-related professions. The gender skew may be attributed to the increasing feminization of psychotherapy and other care-giving professions as well to the socialized gender differences in the level of comfort with speaking about emotional problems. The occupational concentration may be due in part to the recruitment from the two online postings that target professionals in these fields, as well as to the "professional-ex phenomenon" (Brown 1991), which acknowledges that former sufferers are often attracted to helping professions. One consequence is that I may have inadvertently selected an especially self-reflective sample, both because these qualities can be expected to increase with age and because social service and mental health professions encourage sophistication in psychological matters. The prevalence of these occupations in this sample may have additionally influenced my findings because these individuals likely had greater access to professional discourses on mental health than the average person. Exposure to these discourses could have provided them with interpretive resources that may have informed their disidentification experiences.

While the range of disorder labels represented in this sample is wide, the distribution leans heavily toward the conditions that would be classified in the DSM-IV-TR (2000) as anxiety, eating, substance, and mood disorders. There are only eight cases of identification with psychotic or dissociative disorders. Nearly one quarter of the sample identified/disidentified with more than one label. A majority identified with their labels for less than ten years, while eleven delabelers report having identified with the labels for more than ten years ...

OBSTACLES TO DISIDENTIFICATION

All delabelers, by definition, ultimately decide to discard their disorder labels. For most, however, this identity exit is fraught with intra- and interpersonal conflicts that make the process emotionally difficult, thus posing obstacles to the disidentification process. In what follows, I use excerpts from delabelers' narratives to illustrate these obstacles on existential, interactional, and cultural levels. While these three types of obstacles are experientially interrelated, I discuss them separately for analytic clarity.

EXISTENTIAL OBSTACLES

Delabelers' narratives suggest that exiting disorder identities can be an existentially uncomfortable experience. Several delabelers describe having gone through a period of questioning, "Who am I now?" after deciding to disidentify with their labels, and some talk about having anticipated the identity transition with a great deal of anxiety about a potential lack of self-meaning. These delabelers describe the existential uncertainty that can accompany the decision to discard the disorder label as a profound obstacle in the disidentification process.

One of the reasons that discarding disorder identities can be so existentially unsettling is that it involves a transition from a culturally "marked" category to an "unmarked" (Brekhus 1998) one. Many identity transitions involve a transition from one identity status to a subsequent "ex-role" (Ebaugh 1988), (i.e., employee to retiree; spouse to divorcee; native to immigrant); however, disidentifying from emotional disorder labels does not involve adopting a new, labeled status. Rather, the transition moves the exiting individual from a highly marked, culturally recognized status (with associated support groups, national organizations, media attention, and self-help literature directed toward that status) to a completely unmarked, unrecognized *non-identity*. Instead of replacing one identity with another (as when a transsexual trades one gender identity for a different one) this identity transition requires individuals to simply forfeit a source of identity …

In addition to letting go of a marked ientity in a cultural context that does not provide a marked ex-identity, delabelers face an additional existential challenge in their exiting processes due to their reason for discarding the disorder identity. Almost unanimously, delabelers explain their decision to discard the label as a result of becoming aware that the disorder identification had begun to have internally limiting consequences for their self-perceptions. More specifically, they commonly describe a realization that continuing to identify as "disordered" was narrowing the complexity of their self-concepts. In many cases, the disorder label had developed into a master status. As delabeler Gretchen remarks about her former "addict" identity, "I built who I was around it … My entire life was recovery!"

Many delabelers explain that this recognition of the limiting consequences of the disorder identity initiated a more general questioning of the nature and consequences of all individual identity. For this reason, many conclude that simply replacing their attachment to the disorder identity with another categorical entity would not help them to avoid the limitations that prompted them to discard the disorder identity in the first place. This creates an existential predicament for a number of delabelers after they decide to discard their disorder identities: they are faced with an *identity void*. Delabeler Eliza realized as she was discarding her disorder identity ("sex and love addict") that to replace it with another label would be "pointless": "It would be like sticking myself in another box that I would then have to climb out of!" From this perspective, the decision to discard the disorder labels is better characterized as walking into an identity void than as straddling two distinct identities.

For this reason many delabelers describe feeling a tremendous reluctance to turn in their illness identities. Anne's narrative offers some insight into the experience of the identity void. In her story about her exit from her identification as a "multiple" (multiple personality disorder) she explains why it can feel desirable to hold onto a label even after determining it has "out-served its usefulness." After having considered herself a "multiple" for many years she became aware that she "needed to be very cautious" about using the words "I am" in reference to her label. She ultimately came to believe, "By saying it over and over ('I am this; I am that') we start to define ourselves in a way that's hard to break because we really believe that's who we are, as opposed to being more than that." Despite this insight, however, the prospect of disidentifying with a label that had provided a way for her to understand her experience for so many years was unsettling. Articulating her reasoning for wanting to maintain her disorder identity, she poignantly explains, "It can be so comforting to know who you are, even if ifs a false self"...

Naomi's narrative offers a striking example of an extended experience of such ambivalence. She was diagnosed with multiple personality disorder and was hospitalized in an intensive "MPD unit," where she was assumed to be a "textbook" case of the disorder The staff's assessment, she recalls, was that "if I wasn't MPD, nobody was." There was, however, much more conflict in her ability to understand her own condition. She describes a dual relationship with her disorder identity: on the one hand, she claims that she always doubted whether the diagnosis was accurate, and at the same time, she was deeply attached to the label. She describes feeling great anxiety at the very thought of not having that label with which to identify. Describing these contradictory feelings she explains:

> I knew this diagnosis was wrong on a level that was not allowed to
> be discussed ... But at the same time I had become terrified that if any-
> one contradicted the idea that I was a 'multiple,' then what in the
> hell had my life been about? ... If I wasn't 'multiple' then what the hell
> was going on? I was very invested in, 'You better believe me! Don't
> you dare tell me I'm not 'multiple'. And, on another level I knew I
> wasn't.

Naomi struggled with this dual understanding of her identification for several years. So much of her self-understanding depended on her disorder label, and yet she was also eager to let it go because she was simultaneously convinced that "this was not [her] story." She had, however, "invested" so much of her sense of self into this label that the prospect of discarding it forced her to face a "terrifying" identity void ...

The anxiety of this existential uncertainty can present a serious obstacle to the disorder identity exiting process. Identity transitions of any kind can be difficult, but when they involve giving up an identity without the cultural support of a recognized ex-identity, there can be a disconcerting sense of existential loss. This challenge, delabelers' narratives suggest, is compounded when the exiting process is actually prompted by a questioning of the nature and consequences of personal identity itself.

International Obstacles

In addition to the existential anxieties about displaced identity, delabelers also describe international obstacles that make exiting disorder identities especially difficult and stressful. Issues of group solidarity are common in these narratives, particularly for individuals who participated in support groups or associated with other people who shared their disorder labels. Whereas the existential aspect of the exiting process tends to initiate feelings of anxiety, the international aspect of disassociating with the group identity can trigger feelings of guilt and fear. Both guilt and fear are closely associated with issues of loyalty to the group: one side includes individuals' feelings of indebtedness toward the group and the guilt that results from considering leaving (*the deserter complex*), whereas the other side involves the fear of being ostracized by the group for choosing to disidentify with the label (*reverse stigmatization*). Both are expressed in delabelers' narratives as consequences of considering the process of exiting the collective identity.

Deserter complex   Two similar examples of the deserter complex are expressed by Judy and Kasey who were participants in twelve-step recovery groups, Co-dependents Anonymous (CoDA) and Alcoholics Anonymous (AA), respectively. After several years, they both felt that they had "outgrown" these groups and the disorder labels associated with them. Despite this recognition, deciding to exit was not straightforward for either of them, as they both suffered from guilt for deserting the group that they felt had, at one time, been so helpful to them. Judy explains that even though she was "ready to move on," she remembers:

> I felt like I was abandoning them ... I thought I was supposed to stay.
> But, then I realized I can't rescue anyone. I had to do this for me.
> It's not that I didn't want to pay back what the group had done for
> me ... [but] I came to realize that I had been giving all along by partic-
> ipating in the group, even in my need. The hard part, though, is letting go.

Kasey describes a similar sentiment in her story about deciding to disidentify as an "alcoholic" and leave AA after nine years:

> I wasn't drinking anymore, and I wasn't having cravings. So, some-
> where in my ninth year I stopped feeling the need to go to meetings ...
> I didn't have as much time to spare to go to meetings since I started
> going to graduate school, but I was feeling guilty about not going.

Even after participation is no longer considered to be beneficial, loyalty to the group spawning the deserter complex can be understood by considering the group solidarity that is often generated in these small groups ...

Delabeler Reina describes having experienced feelings of solidarity guilt when she decided to minimize her involvement in the regional, telephone support network she had established for people suffering from anxiety and panic attacks. As the founder, Reina had developed a reputation within the network as being an especially supportive, sympathetic listener for "phobics" who called her in need. Similar to the twelve-step philosophy, her network was founded on the principle that identifying with fellow sufferers and sharing similar experiences is mutually beneficial for both participants' recovery processes. As her own "re-covery" progressed, however, she found herself less interested in talking about anxiety and decided to remove herself from the network she had built. She experienced a great deal of guilt when someone would call, and she would have to tell them that she did have the time to talk that she used to have. In her guilt, she would question herself; "Am I still a good person? I don't want to be an insensitive, uncaring person by not being there to talk to every phobic ... but I can't share that space with them anymore in the same way. I'm just not there."

This description of ambivalence and guilt for abandoning one's fellow sufferers parallels mobility experiences more generally because all mobility narratives, by definition, are formally similar in at least two ways: they involve both departure and progress. That is, one must not only leave (even if only symbolically) a former association but also surpass it for an association of a socially perceived higher status ...

Reverse Stigmatization   Delabelers narratives express both sides of the international coin: group loyalty not only has the capacity to trigger feelings guilt for "abandoning" the group but also fear of being ostracized by the group for choosing to leave. The prospect of losing close friends or being considered "in denial" is a difficult prospect for some individuals to face. This ostracism from the group (actual or anticipated) can be understood as a form of stigma for behaving as a deviant, from the perspective of the group of labeled individuals. I refer to this as reverse stigmatization because typical conceptions of stigma assume the culturally dominant "−normals" to be the "−reference" group" according to which the stigmatized deviants are defined. In this case, the reference groups are reversed. Delabelers' narratives suggest that this reverse stigma (or even the perceived potential for it) can be quite distressing and can discourage disidentification.

Gretchen's narrative illustrates this when she discusses her fear of stigmatization by her former recovery community for choosing to discard her "addict" identity. As a college student, she had lived in a special dorm for recovering students, regularly attended AA and NA meetings, and interacted only with friends who were "in recovery." When the semester ended she moved out of the recovery dorm and chose to stop going to meetings. Despite her conviction that she had made the right decision for herself; she finds herself "deathly afraid of the judgments" of her "recovery friends." Anticipating their reactions she admits, "I know I'll look like a failure to them. Even though I don't see it like that, to them I am. I dread that." Although this fear did not ultimately prevent her from exiting the disorder identity, she admits that even now (several months later) she has remained fearful of encountering friends from recovery and facing the anticipated criticism ...

Both the deserter complex and reverse stigmatization demonstrate a deep degree of attachment to the recovery community. This seems incongruous with delabelers' assertions about the disorder label having "outlived its purpose" or having already "gotten what [they] could" out of participation in the recovery group. Considering the expressed desire for disidentification from the disorder identity, it seems surprising that delabelers would care so much about what these former group members would think about their decision to I save. Why should the opinions of the group members matter if delabelers have already decided to extricate themselves from these groups? One answer reflects the crucial issue involved in collective disorder identification: the recovery group is not only a treatment resource but also a source of community. Thus, to dissociate with such a community involves both forfeiting a sense of belonging as well as rejecting the microculture of the local group. From this perspective, it is understandable that individuals would experience attachment to their recovery communities and care about the opinions of the other participants, even after deciding to discard their disorder labels.

Cultural Obstacles

In addition to the existential and international obstacles to disidentifying with their labels, delabelers also describe cultural pressure to remain identified as "disordered" ...

Delabelers' narratives reflect this cultural trend of assuming that a label is needed in order to understand and cope with life's difficulties. For example, delabelers Keith and Vicky suggest that this belief influenced their identification with their respective disorder labels. When Keith tells of how he came to see himself as "disordered," he explains that because he was unhappy and having problems in his marriage, he felt he "had to go somewhere," implying that he should participate in some kind of therapeutic setting. He says that because he did not know where else to go, he went to an Alanon meeting "because it was available" and he was familiar with the name. When he eventually concluded that he had "gotten all that [he] could" from Alanon, he continued to believe that he "had to go somewhere," and so he began identifying as a "codependent" and attending CoDA meetings, upon the advice of his mother.

Similarly, Vicky explains that after five years of AA membership, she concluded that she was not an "alcoholic" but found herself assuming, "I should be in something ..." She explains:

> I went around and around and could never figure out which group to
> go to: Should I go to AA again? No, that doesn't fit anymore.
> Should I go to an Adult Child meeting? Alanon? Nothing really ever
> fit right so I ended up never going back, but many times I thought
> maybe I should.

Like Keith, Vicky felt that because she continued to have some emotional difficulties, she assumed that she should find a new disorder label to classify her trouble.

The prevalent assumption that disorder labels are needed in order to understand and cope with difficult life experiences can be seen as symptomatic of the "triumph" of what Philip Rieff (1966) named the "therapeutic culture" in the 1960s ...

This increased psychologization of every day life has borne an explosion in the number of therapeutic practitioners and therapeutic self-help groups; the interplay between the expert domain of psychological professionals and popular self-help culture and media representations further reinforces a cultural preoccupation with therapeutics. As Dana Becker (2005-6) points out "[T]he ideas that emanate from both the popular and professional cultures ... are often combined, transformed, recycled, and used for purposes other than the therapeutic." The result is a culture that increasingly views normal human emotion in pathological terms.

This transformation in our understanding of emotional disorder is not only a matter of increasing diagnostic categorization, the very nature of emotional disturbance has also come to be seen more and more in biomedical terms. Karp

(2006-9) cautions, "With the increasing acceptance of the biomedical model, we begin to believe that more and more of our feelings are illegitimate and abnormal and require biological intervention to correct." He asserts that the consequence of this belief, which is "unrelentingly pushed by pharmaceutical companies and some doctors; poses a threat to "personal autonomy and responsibility" (208).

This potential is suggested in several delabelers' narratives that reveal an internalization of the disease concept of their emotional behavior made disidentifying with their disorder labels especially difficult. Eva, for example, was diagnosed as "clinically depressed" when she was in her early twenties. She explains:

> I was always told I had a "chemical imbalance" and that taking this pill everyday would make everything wonderful. I was given various pills over a period of twenty years.... The idea that "depression" is an illness is so pervasive on the TV., and I used to read articles in magazines and books, and these people like [William] Styron come out with these books and say they suffered all their lives, and they had a chemical imbalance and now they take this one pill everyday and everything is wonderful. I would read them, and I did kind of believe it was true ... I really wanted to believe because I was unhappy, and I wanted to believe that all we had to do was find the right pill and everything would be wonderful

And, I was like most people, wanting to put my trust and faith in somebody else, especially the medical profession and have them tell me what to do.

Eva's eventual inclination to disidentify with the disorder label posed a challenge for her because of her desire to trust the medical system, as well as the cultural encouragement to feel that she should trust it. In retrospect, she realizes that in the hands of the psychiatrists, she had become "very passive and dependent; dependent on somebody else to figure things out." She eventually began to internally question the psychiatric authorities, but she kept it a private struggle because she had "never heard of something that was not a biochemical analysis [of depression]." Deciding to discard the disorder label was, therefore, so difficult because it required her to take a stand against a cultural authority when she believed that she was alone in her views. She emphasizes, "I always thought it [doubting 'the system'] was just me." ...

DISCUSSION

Delabelers' narratives suggest that the decision to discard one's disorder identity is often just the beginning of a difficult process of disidentification, fraught with a variety of obstacles. It seems like, that the extent to which one is able to successfully negotiate the disorder identity exit would be related to the amount of "recovery capital" one possesses. Robert Granfield and William Cloud (1999) have coined this term to refer to the total number of one's resources that can be used to "promote and sustain a recovery experience" (179). They explain that such resources can include various forms of physical, social, and human capital such as one's financial status, friendship networks, and vocational skills ...

Individuals who have involvements in alternate jobs, relationships, and hobbies have a "far easier adjustment" than individuals who exited without such "bridges." As a general rule, Ebaugh(1998) suggests that "there seems to be a direct relationship between the number and quality of bridges and the degree of role adjustment and happiness after the exit."

In addition, delabeler Stacey suggests how financial resources may serve as a form of recovery capital. She started receiving Supplemental Security Income (SSI) after being diagnosed with Post-Traumatic Stress Disorder (PTSD) following what she describes as a traumatic loss. She explains that, until recently, her anxiety symptoms made holding a job impossible, and so she depended on the disability benefits for survival. She is now employed in her first part-time job since the diagnosis but does not feel quite ready for a full-time position. In the meantime, she continues to claim eligibility for half of her original benefits because her salary is only about $600 each month. She explains that although she no longer identifies with her diagnosis, using the disorder label to claim benefits makes a complete disidentification from the label difficult:

> One of the difficulties for me now is that, on the one hand, I don't want to be limited by a label or think I'm limited because of what I've gone through. But, at the same time, in terms of losing my benefits, sometimes I find myself having to argue for the limitations, and that's really frustrating for me. I don't want to be arguing it so convincingly that I start to convince myself!

Stacy's story suggests one way that financial resources can serve as recovery capital; if she had not been financially dependent on SSI, she likely would have felt free to disidentify from the label entirely.

To be clear, this discussion of disorder disidentification is not to suggest that every one who identifies with an emotional disorder label *should* eventually disidentify with it. In fact, as Estroff (1981) suggests, for many chronically ill psychiatric patients, the diagnostic label may provide a sense of identity and resources that they may be unlikely to receive otherwise. This analysis of delabelers is thus not *recommending* disidentification. It is, however, highlighting, the intra- and inter personal forces that may discourage disidentification, even in cases where it is desirable.

Several delabelers claim that their primary reason for participating in this study is to make it easier for others to discard their disorder labels than it was for them. Because the recovery discourse is so focused on acquiring disorder labels and coping with the symptoms of problematic emotional conditions, the possibility of exit is typically not emphasized. One important step in addressing the existential, international, and cultural obstacles to disidentification could be to incorporate a notion of "recovery from recovery" into the discourse so that disidentification can gain legitimacy as a possible course for some disorder identity careers.

REFERENCES

Becker, Dana. 2005. *The Myth of Empowerment: Women and the Therapeutic Culture in America*. New York and London: New York University Press.

Brekhus, Wayne. 1998. "A Sociology of the Unmarked: Redirecting Our Focus." *Sociological Theory* 16:34–49.

Brown, David J. 1991. "The Professional Ex: An Alternative for Exiting the Deviant Career." *Sociological Quarterly* 32(2):219–30.

Ebaugh, Helen Rose Fuchs. 1988. *Becoming an Ex: The Process of Role Exit*. Chicago and London: University of Chicago Press.

Estroff, Sue E. 1981. *Making It Crazy: An Ethnography of Psychiatric Clients in an American Community*. Berkeley and Los Angeles: University of California Press.

Glaser, Barney G, and Anselm L. Strauss. 1967. *The Discovery of Grounded Theory*. Chicago, IL: Aldine.

Granfield, Robert and William Cloud. 1999. *Coming Clean: Overcoming Addiction Without treatment*. New York: New York University Press.

Karp, David. 2006. *Is It Me or My Meds? Living with Antidepressants*. Cambridge, MA: Harvard University Press.

Rieff, Philip. 1966. *The Triumph of the Therapeutic: Uses of Faith After Freud*. Chicago, IL: University of Chicago Press.

Thoits, Peggy A. 1985. "Self-Labeling Processes in Mental Illness: The Role of Emotional Deviance." *American Journal of Sociology* 91:149–221.

References for the General and Part Introductions

Adler, Patricia A., and Peter Adler. 1987. *Membership Roles in Field Research*. Newbury Park, CA: Sage.

———. 1995. "The Demography of Ethnography." *Journal of Contemporary Ethnography* 24: 3–29.

———. 2007. "Deviant Identity." In George Ritzer, *Encyclopedia of Sociology*, Malden, MA: Blackwell.

Bandura, Albert. 1973. *Aggression: A Social Learning Approach*. Englewood Cliffs, NJ: Prentice-Hall.

Becker, Howard S. 1963. *Outsiders: Studies in the Sociology of Deviance*. New York: Free Press.

———. 1973. "Labeling Theory Reconsidered." Pp. 177–212 in *Outsiders*. New York: Free Press.

Best, Joel, and David F. Luckenbill. 1980. "The Social Organization of Deviants." *Social Problems* 28: 14–31.

———. 1981. "The Social Organization of Deviance." *Deviant Behavior* 2: 231–59.

Cloward, Richard, and Lloyd Ohlin. 1960. *Delinquency and Opportunity*. Glencoe, IL: Free Press.

Cohen, Albert. 1955. *Delinquent Boys*. Glencoe, IL: Free Press.

Cohen, Stanley. 1972. *Folk Devils and Moral Panics: The Creation of the Mods and the Rockers*. London: MacGibbon and Kee.

Conrad, Peter, and Joseph W. Schneider. 1980. *Deviance and Medicalization*. St. Louis: Mosby.

Davis, Fred. 1961. "Deviance Disavowal: The Management of Strained Interaction by the Visibly Handicapped." *Social Problems* 9:120–32.

Erikson, Kai T. 1966. *Wayward Puritans*. New York: Wiley.

Eysenck, Hans. 1977. *Crime and Personality*. 3rd ed. London: Routledge and Kegan Paul.

Force, William Ryan. 2005. "There are No Victims Here: Determination versus Disorder in Pro-Anorexia." Paper presented at the Couch-Stone Symposium of the Society for the Study of Symbolic Interaction. Boulder, CO, February.

Freud, Sigmund. 1925. *The Standard Edition of the Complete Psychological Works of Sigmund Freud*. London: Hogarth Press.

Galliher, John. 1995. "Chicago's Two Worlds of Deviance Research: Whose Side Are They On?" Pp. 164–187 in *A Second Chicago School?*, edited by Gary Alan Fine. Chicago: University of Chicago Press.

Goddard, Henry. 1979. *Feeblemindedness*. New York: Macmillan.

Goode, Erich, and Nachman Ben-Yehuda. 1994. *Moral Panics*. Cambridge, MA: Blackwell.

Goring, Charles. 1913. *The English Convict*. London: His Majesty's Stationary Office.

Goffman, Erving. 1961. *Asylums*. New York: Anchor.

———. 1963. *Stigma*. Englewood Cliffs, NJ: Prentice-Hall.

Gusfield, Joseph. 1967. "Moral Passage: The Symbolic Process in Public Designations of Deviance." *Social Problems* 15: 175–88.

Henry, Jules. 1964. *Jungle People*. New York: Vintage.

Hewitt, John P., and Randall Stokes. 1975. "Disclaimers." *American Sociological Review* 33: 46–62.

Hilgartner, Stephen, and Charles L. Bosk. 1988. "The Rise and Fall of Social Problems: A Public Arenas Model." *American Journal of Sociology* 94: 53–78.

Hooton, Earnest. 1939. *The American Criminal*. Westport, CT: Greenwood Press.

Hughes, Everett. 1945. "Dilemmas and Contradictions of Status." *American Journal of Sociology* 50: 353–59.

Kitsuse, John. 1962. "Societal Reactions to Deviant Behavior: Problems of Theory and Method." *Social Problems* 9: 247–56.

———. 1980. "Coming Out All Over: Deviants and the Politics of Social Problems." *Social Problems* 28: 1–13.

Krauthammer, Charles. 1993. "Defining Deviancy Up." November 22: 20–25.

Lemert, Edwin. 1951. *Social Pathology*. New York: McGraw-Hill.

Letkemann, Peter. 1973. *Crime as Work*. Englewood Cliffs, NJ: Prentice-Hall.

———. 1967. *Human Deviance, Social Problems, and Social Control*. New York: Prentice-Hall.

Loeber, Ron, and David P. Farrington, eds. 1998. *Serious and Violent Juvenile Offenders*. Thousand Oaks, CA: Sage.

Lombroso, Cesare. 1876. *On Criminal Man*. Milan, Italy: Hoepli.

———. 1920. *The Female Offender*. New York: Appleton.

Luckenbill, David F., and Joel Best. 1981. "Careers in Deviance and Respectability: The Analogy's Limitations." *Social Problems* 29: 197–206.

Lyman, Stanford M. 1970. *The Asian in the West*. Reno/Las Vegas, Nevada: Western Studies Center, Desert Research Institute.

Matza, David. 1964. *Delinquency and Drift*. New York: Wiley.

Merton, Robert. 1938. "Social Structure and Anomie." *American Sociological Review* 3: 672–82.

Miller, Walter. 1958. "Lower Class Culture as a Generating Milieu of Gang Delinquency." *Journal of Social Issues* 14: 5–19.

Moynihan, Daniel Patrick. 1993. "Defining Deviancy Down." *The American Scholar* 62: 17–30.

Polsky, Ned. 1967. *Hustlers, Beats, and Others*. Chicago: Aldine.

Quinney, Richard. 1970. *The Social Reality of Crime*. Boston: Little, Brown.

Schur, Edwin. 1979. *Interpreting Deviance*. New York: Harper and Row.

Scott, Marvin, and Stanford Lyman. 1968. "Accounts." *American Sociological Review* 33: 46–62.

Sellin, Thorsten. 1938. "Culture Conflict and Crime." A Report of the Subcommittee on Delinquency of the Committee on Personality and Culture, *Social Science Research Council Bulletin 41*. New York.

Sheldon, William. 1949. *Varieties of Delinquent Youth*. New York: Harper & Row.

Skinner, B. F. 1953. *Science and Human Behavior*. New York: Macmillan.

Spector, Malcolm, and John Kitsuse. 1977. *Constructing Social Problems*. Menlo Park, CA: Cummings.

Smith, Alexander B., and Harriet Pollack. 1976. "Deviance as a Method of Coping." *Crime and Delinquency* 22: 3–16.

Steffensmeier, Darrell J., and Jeffery T. Ulmer. 2005. *Confessions of a Dying Thief*. New Brunswick, NJ: Transaction.

Sumner, Colin. 1994. *The Sociology of Deviance: An Obituary*. New York: Continuum.

Sumner, William Graham. 1907. *Folkways*. New York: Vintage.

Sutherland, Edwin. 1934. *Principles of Criminology*. Philadelphia: J.B. Lippincott.

Sykes, Gresham, and David Matza. 1957. "Techniques of Neutralization: A Theory of Delinquency." *American Sociological Review* 22: 664–70.

Tannenbaum, Frank. 1938. *Crime and the Community*. Boston: Ginn.

Tittle, Charles, and Raymond Paternoster. 2000. *Social Deviance and Crime*. Los Angeles: Roxbury.

Turner, Ralph H. 1972. "Deviance Avowal as Neutralization of Commitment." *Social Problems* 19: 308–21.

Yochelson, Samuel, and Stanton Samenow. 1976. *The Criminal Personality*, vol. 1 and 2. New York: Jason Aronson.

Weatherford, Jack. 1986. *Porn Row*. New York: Arbor House.

Werner, Emmy E., and Ruth S. Smith. 1982. *Vulnerable but Invincible: A Study of Resilient Children*. New York: McGraw Hill.

———. 1992. *Overcoming the Odds: High Risk Children from Birth to Adulthood*. Ithaca, NY: Cornell University Press.

Whitt, Hugh P. 2006. "Where Did the Bodies Go?: The Social Construction of Suicide Data, New York City, 1976–1992." *Sociological Inquiry* 76: 166–87.

Yip, Andrew K.T. 1997. "Gay Male Christian Couples and Sexual Exclusivity." *Sociology* 31: 289–306.